SHIFTING THE CENTER

SHIFTING THE CENTER
Understanding Contemporary Families

Second Edition

Susan J. Ferguson
Grinnell College

Mayfield Publishing Company
Mountain View, California
London • Toronto

Library of Congress Cataloging-in-Publication Data

Shifting the center : understanding contemporary families / [compiled by] Susan J. Ferguson. — 2nd ed.
    p. cm.
  ISBN 0-7674-1642-2 (alk. paper)
   1. Family — United States. 2. Marriage — United States. 3. Kinship — United States. I. Ferguson, Susan J.

  HQ536.S488 2001
  306.8′0973 — dc21

                                   00-064732

Manufactured in the United States of America

10   9   8   7   6   5

Mayfield Publishing Company
1280 Villa Street
Mountain View, CA 94041

Sponsoring editor, Serina Beauparlant; production, Publishing Support Services; manuscript editor, Margaret Moore; design manager, Jean Mailander; text and cover designer, Linda M. Robertson; illustrator, Joan Carol, Lotus Art; manufacturing manager, Danielle Javier. The text was set in 10/12 Book Antiqua by ColorType, San Diego and printed on 45# Highland Plus by Malloy Lithographing, Inc.

Cover image: *Flower Drum Song*, Lesly-Claire Greenberg, Fairfax, VA. 31" x 25". Quilt hand stitched made of cotton fabric. From *Sewing on the Line* by Lesly-Claire Greenberg, © 1993, Martingale & Company, Woodinville, WA. Used by permission of the artist, author, and publisher.

With love to my parents, Jim and Janet Ferguson

Contents

PART V: PARENTS AND CHILDREN 209

PARENTS AND PARENTING

CHILDREN AND CHILDHOOD

PART VI: MOTHERHOOD AND FATHERHOOD 283

MOTHERHOOD

FATHERHOOD

Preface

This anthology originated in the classroom. Over the years, students have challenged me to bring in readings on the family that integrate material on race-ethnicity, social class, gender, and sexual orientation. The lack of fully integrated family texts has been frustrating and puzzling to me; most anthologies on the family "lump" family diversity into one section, which often appears at the end of the book. This placement is problematic because it still marginalizes those families that differ from the idealized traditional family of the dominant culture. Instead, the analysis and discussion of diverse family forms should occur throughout the selected topics of a family course. To achieve an integrated framework, I often have compiled large packets of material to bring diverse family experiences and a multicultural perspective into my classroom. After years of teaching family courses this way, I realized that a new anthology could *and* should be created to integrate the voices and experiences of diverse families. This book represents a collection of articles that meets four pedagogical goals: (1) to deconstruct the notion of a universal family over time and across cultures; (2) to reflect cutting-edge scholarship by well-known family scholars; (3) to integrate race-ethnicity, social class, gender, and sexuality in the analysis; and (4) to promote critical reading and thinking.

The title of this anthology, *Shifting the Center: Understanding Contemporary Families*, was inspired by Margaret Andersen and Patricia Hill Collins' essay "Shifting the Center and Reconstructing Knowledge" in *Race, Class, and Gender: An Anthology* (1995). In their essay, Andersen and Hill Collins argue for the need to shift the center of analysis away from the dominant culture to the experiences of all racial-ethnic and social class groups. In her book *Feminist Theory: From Margin to Center* (1984), bell hooks, too, argues that "much of feminist theory emerges from privileged women who live at the center, whose perspectives on reality rarely include knowledge and awareness of the lives of women and men who live in the margin" (p. x). Thus, hooks argues that in order for us to have an improved understanding of all human lives, we must place the experiences and knowledge of women of color at the center of feminist theorizing and activism. The same argument can be made for any area of scholarship, including the study of families.

In this anthology on families, "shifting the center" means that the research on families of color, gay and lesbian families, and working-class families is moved from the margins of analysis to the center of the analytical framework. In many texts, these family forms are treated as "alternative" or "deviant." By shifting our focus of inquiry away from family structures based only on traditional marriage, students can better understand that numerous family structures coexist. This anthology examines several family forms, including arranged marriages, cohabitation, heterosexual marriage, single-parent households, stepfamilies, and gay and lesbian families. "Shifting the center" encourages students to compare these diverse family forms to one another. This "shift" also enables the instructors to deconstruct the idealized, white, middle-class family and enables students to see how present conceptualizations of family have been socially constructed over time and across cultures.

In order to understand that the family is a social creation, students need to study the family both historically and comparatively. Historical and cross-cultural readings can help shatter the idea that one universal family form is constant across cultures and time. Thus, some of the articles I have selected show how current patterns of family formation and dissolution in the United States differ from those in our past and in other countries. The articles on various racial-ethnic families in the United States, including the selections on immigrant families, also demonstrate how families within a particular cultural group change over time. As family historian Stephanie Coontz argues in her book *The Way We Never Were* (1992), the study of family history enables students to dispel many myths about families in the United States. As students study family history, they more easily separate nostalgic misconceptions about the family from the realities of contemporary families.

In addition, the articles in this anthology use social science research to show how the institution of the family is related to other social institutions in society and how those institutions affect the intimate center of family lives. Thus, the readings encourage students to discern the relationships between families and society and among individuals within a family. For example, to help students see that family relations are inherently gendered, I have included selections that show how gender is constructed and maintained within the institution of the family and how gender affects power dynamics, communication, and intimacy among family members. Moreover, by reading articles on families, work, and poverty, students gain a better understanding of how socioeconomic class positions can affect family structure and relations. Reading articles that illuminate either the macrolevel of family structure in society or the microlevel of social interaction within families helps students perceive the multiple linkages between society, families, and individuals. Furthermore, when articles address the intersection of race-ethnicity, gender, social class, and sexual orientation at these two levels of study, students get a fuller picture of contemporary family diversity, including an understanding of how diverse families affect individual identities.

The articles in this anthology should enhance students' abilities to compare social science research findings with the assumptions underlying public debates about the family. Students will be better able to utilize research evidence in evaluating images of family life offered in the popular culture, especially in film, on television, and in music lyrics. If students learn to evaluate empirical evidence, they will be able to make better-informed decisions about public policy issues concerning families and perhaps, in the future, to shape better social policies for *all* families.

Ultimately, it is my hope that this anthology will instill a sociological imagination in students. By encouraging students to think critically about what they are reading, this anthology helps students understand the difference between family concerns that are "public issues" and those that are "private troubles." This anthology contains the most current, innovative work by family scholars — work that highlights the concepts, theories, and research methodologies currently used to study the family. I have tried to choose articles that are accessible, timely, and substantive and that will engage students and promote critical thinking. Thus, my assumption throughout has been not only that students are capable of understanding rigorous social science research on families, but that the research also can inspire students to think more critically about families and our social world.

Changes to the Second Edition

With this second edition, I have continued to select articles that either deconstruct the notion of a universal family or provide more coverage of family diversity by integrating race-ethnicity, social class, gender, or sexuality in their analysis. I also have strived to obtain the most recent innovative work by family scholars, which highlights the concepts, theories, and research methodologies currently used to study families. Recent scholarship includes work by authors such as Stephanie Coontz, Paul Amato, Sharon Hays, Rita Simon, Kathleen Bahr, Demie Kurz, Frances Goldscheider and Linda Waite, Stephen Sugarman, Colleen Fong and Judy Yung, among others. In particular, I have added twenty-one new selections that cover a wide range of family issues, including interracial relationships and marriage, courtship in Mexico, single parent families, infertility and reproductive technologies, children's adjustment to divorce, the "Mommy Wars" — conflicts between stay-at-home moms and mothers who work outside the home, gay men and fatherhood, divorce in a Jewish community, feminist research on domestic violence, research on elder abuse and child abuse, children's household chores, Anglo and Apache grandmothers, kinwork done by women in families, and transracial adoption. In addition, five of the new pieces provide more in-depth historical understanding of the family. These pieces include a work by Stephanie Coontz on historical perspectives of family diversity, Evelyn Nakano Glenn's analysis of Chinese American families, Martin King Whyte's history of courtship and dating, Maris A. Vinovskis' historical examination of parent-child relationships, and Andrew Cherlin and Frank Furstenberg's classic piece on the modernization of grandparenthood. Of course, for all of the readings, I have tried to choose selections that are interesting and accessible to students. Each reading has been carefully edited to provide the most comprehensible and accessible understanding without compromising the research. I also have written part introductions to help frame the readings and provide students with guidance in understanding why each selection was chosen and how it relates to other readings in the section. Please note that I welcome feedback from professors and students on this edition of *Shifting the Center: Understanding Contemporary Families.*

Printed Test Bank

I have written an accompanying test manual that contains many examination and discussion questions for each reading. As the editor of this anthology, I developed these items with the goal of helping instructors test students' understanding of key sociological concepts and themes.

Acknowledgments

Several people contributed to the research and development of this anthology on families. At Grinnell College, I am grateful for the ongoing support of my colleagues in the sociology department and for the labor provided by my student research assistants: Michelle Brunner and Carla Talarico. Michelle Brunner, Emily Kearney, Emily Larson, Natalia Ipatova, Julianna Serafini, and Jessica Halverston helped proofread page proofs. The Carnegie secretaries, Vicki Bunnell, Karen Groves, and Linda Price helped photocopy articles and type portions of the manuscript. Grinnell College also generously granted research support.

Off-campus, several sociologists and family scholars provided me with feedback on portions of the manuscript. I am especially indebted to Scott Coltrane and Gretchen Stiers for their helpful comments at various points in the project. My special thanks go to the reviewers: Sharon Abbott, Wittenberg University; Mary L. Ertel, Central Connecticut State University; Sally Gallagher, Oregon State University; Sharon Hays, University of Virginia; Pamela Jull, Western Washington University; Emily W. Kane, Bates College; Karen Kendrick, University of California, Irvine; Helen Mederer, University of Rhode Island; Chandra Muller, University of Texas, Austin; Sheryl Olson, University of Michigan; Beth Rushing, Georgia College and State University; Marsha Smith, Augustana College; Jerry Tyler, Stephen F. Austin State University; Celia Winkler, University of Montana; and Jiping Zuo, St. Cloud State University.

At Mayfield Publishing Company, I am appreciative of the good work done by Jay Bauer, Kate Schubert, Marty Granahan, Jean Mailander, April Wells-Hayes and Lynn Rabin Bauer. In addition, four other people on the production team need to be acknowledged: David Ellison and Erika Brant obtained the permissions in a timely fashion; Margaret Moore did a fine job copyediting the manuscript; and Vicki Moran kept the book on schedule. Last, but not least, I want to thank my editor, Serina Beauparlant, for her insight and support on this project.

The family is changing, not disappearing.
We have to broaden our understanding of it,
look for the new metaphors.

　　　　　　　　　—*Mary Catherine Bateson*

PART I

Introduction to the Study of Families

The sociological study of the institution of the family is a broad and ever-changing field. The family is one of the most private and pervasive social institutions in society: private in that many of the social problems related to families, such as child care, divorce, and family violence, are especially difficult to deal with; and pervasive in that it is the first institution in which we, as individuals, have contact with, and it tends to remain at the center of social life. Thus, all of us have had contact with at least one family, and many of us will be involved in several different families during our lifetimes. The family also is undergoing numerous transformations. To help us better understand these changes, recent social science research and data on the family are presented in this anthology.

Because your experience of the family is very personal and individual, what you read may not fit with your personal experience. That is to be expected, not only because of the vast diversity in family relationships and interaction on a microlevel, but also because you will be studying the institution of the family on a macrolevel as well. A family researcher named R. D. Laing (1971) once said, "The first family to interest me was my own. I still know less about it than I do about other families." Laing's quote makes sense because we are often too close, too emotionally involved, to study our own families objectively. Moreover, the experience of family varies considerably not only between unrelated persons, but also between related persons within the same family. The family you experience is very different from the one your siblings and parents experience. We each have a unique perception about our own families, and it is very difficult to be objective and unbiased about them.

To help us better understand the social institution of the family, this anthology has several themes: (1) to deconstruct idealized and stereotypical notions about the family, especially the idealized white, middle-class family, as the only family form; (2) to study the history of the family to understand contemporary families; (3) to examine diverse family forms, including diverse racial-ethnic, cultural, and gay and lesbian families; and (4) to understand that the family is shaped by other social institutions, including the economy, law, politics, and religion. Our analysis of the institution of the family will begin with a discussion about how to define family. All four articles in this section delineate different definitions of the family and address the themes listed above. In sum, all four selections argue that the institution of the family is socially constructed.

Social Construction of the Family

I often begin my first day of teaching the sociology of the family with a visualization exercise. I ask students to close their eyes and think about the family. I ask them, "When you hear the word *family*, what do you think of?

What images do you see when you hear the word *family*?" I repeat the word *family* several times before I have students open their eyes. I ask them to share the images or thoughts they had about family, and I write them on the blackboard. Students say over and over again that they see a husband and a wife, some children, maybe a family pet, often in front of a house with a station wagon or minivan, and so on. Next, as a class, we analyze the patterns in their images of family. Ultimately, the images are overwhelmingly positive, typically of biological mothers and fathers playing with children, or a family having Thanksgiving dinner or going on vacation. I then ask students, where are the other images of family life, such as sibling rivalry, divorce, or other types of family conflict? The students say that those images do not come to mind. As we investigate the images further, it becomes clear that most students have an idealized and even romanticized image of the family. Why is this problematic? To help students understand why these idealized and romanticized images are problematic, I ask my class to define what a family is based on using the list on the blackboard. I ask: "Which people are included, and which people are excluded? What activities define a family? Why do societies need families?" What becomes immediately clear to the students is that their idealized images of families are often based on white, middle-class assumptions about what a family should be. They quickly identify all the people missing from their images including unmarried heterosexual couples, cohabitors, same-sex couples, single parents, teen mothers, adopted and foster children, couples who are voluntarily or involuntarily childless, and so on. We talk about how families might vary on the basis of social class or race-ethnicity. In brief, I want them to deconstruct their stereotyped notions about family.

There are many different definitions of family. George Murdock, a prominent anthropologist, defines family as "a social group characterized by common residence, economic cooperation, and reproduction" (quoted in Morgan 1975:20). While this definition appears to suffice, many exceptions quickly arise. For example, many families do not share common residences, especially commuter families, families separated by divorce, or different generations living in different households. In some societies, the husbands and wives belong to different domestic groups. They may ritually see each other a couple of times a year, but live separately the rest of the time. We also can think of many families that are not based on economic cooperation (e.g., those involved in child-support disputes, those in which pre- or postnuptial agreements have been made) or on the sexual reproduction of children. Many couples are voluntarily or involuntarily childless. If a couple does *not* have children, are they disqualified from being a family?

The sociological definition of family also varies. Early sociological definitions are similar to those from anthropology as is evidenced in the work of Ernest Burgess, a family researcher in the early 20th century. Burgess defines family as "persons sharing a residence and a household who are related by biological ties, marriage, social customs, or adoption" (quoted in Sussman

1986). Burgess also argues that the family is "a unity of interacting person-alities existing chiefly for the development and gratification of its members . . . held together by internal cohesion rather than external pressure" (quoted in Sussman 1986). Similar to the blackboard exercise described earlier, Burgess is attempting to delineate who can be members of a family and what functions the institution of the family fulfills. Again, exceptions can be found utilizing his criteria. Thus, there is great difficulty in defining what a family is, and most of the anthropological and sociological definitions are problematic.

Still, to study the family, we need a working definition of the family that is broad enough to include diverse members and functions, but detailed enough to apply to the study of families across cultures. The working definition I often use in class is that the family is a social institution which (1) gives support to its members (emotional nurturing, physical caretaking, economic support, or some combination of the three); (2) binds the individual to a primary social group (it gives us our roots so to speak, a base to build from); and (3) socializes the person for participating in society outside the family. This definition of family is broad enough to include families of diverse domestic forms, whether married or unmarried, with or without children, and regardless of the sexual orientation of the members. The last two points of the working definition come from the work of Talcott Parsons and Robert Bales, who argued in 1955 that the only two remaining functions of the family are the stabilization of adults and the socialization of children. In Parsons' and Bales' eyes, over time, the multiple functions of the historic institution of the family had been reduced to two. However, these remaining two functions are important because they provide all individuals with the critical experience of childhood socialization and adults with a defining membership in a primary group.

The first reading in this section, "The Family in Question: What Is the Family? Is It Universal?" by a British anthropologist, Diana Gittins, examines how the family has been defined in both the anthropological and sociological research literature. She concludes that many of the "classic" definitions of family are too restrictive and that no one "universal" family form exists. Instead, Gittins argues, the family is socially constructed — that is, the meaning of family and the social functions fulfilled by the institution of the family vary across cultures and time periods. By defining the family as a social institution which performs certain functions in society, Gittins is arguing that the family is a *social construct*. The family is shaped by the social forces of the society in which it exists. In other words, the structure, content, and purpose of family vary by culture, historical context, race-ethnicity, gender, social class, and sexuality. To say the family is socially constructed means that each society defines the institution depending on its social and economic contexts. And, moreover, individuals within a given society also may define their experience of family different from one another. Thus, according to Gittins and other scholars, there is no one universal definition of family.

The Shaping of the Family by Race–Ethnicity, Social Class, Gender, and Sexual Orientation

The second reading in this section, "Feminist Rethinking from Racial-Ethnic Families," by Maxine Baca Zinn, builds on Gittins' arguments. Baca Zinn is a professor of sociology at Michigan State University where she is also a senior research associate in the Julian Samora Research Institute. Baca Zinn specializes in race relations, gender, and the sociology of the family, and the article that follows is representative of Baca Zinn's abilities to effectively combine these three research areas. Similar to Gittins, Baca Zinn argues that the family is socially constructed and linked to other social structures and institutions. In addition, according to Baca Zinn, social science scholarship on the family benefits from feminist and racial-ethnic perspectives on the family. In particular, family scholars need to examine race, social class, and gender simultaneously, in order to understand how these variables interact to shape both the structural and the relational dimensions of families.

One important theme in this book is that the family is a gendered institution. That is, the family is based on gender roles and the control of sexuality and reproduction. Baca Zinn looks at how productive and reproductive labor in the family vary not only by gender but by race-ethnicity as well. Other family scholars, including Scott Coltrane, also argue that gender is a critical lens in which to look through in order to understand the family. Coltrane, in his book *Gender and Families* (1998), states: "Gender relations and family life are so intertwined that it is impossible to understand one without paying attention to the other" (p. 1). In fact, we often take the gender dynamics in the family for granted or see them as natural, biologically determined roles that men and women fulfill. Or people argue that gender roles are the way they have always been, a part of tradition that mother always cooks the holiday dinners or father always does the yard work. In fact, these gender roles and the sexual division of labor are socially constructed. They are not biologically innate or unchangeable. Thus, to argue that the family is gendered also means recognizing that power dynamics often influence family relationships. Many of the readings in this volume address the relationship between gender and families, and whether these gender dynamics influence power differences within the family.

The third reading in this section, "Exiles from Kinship," is by Kath Weston, who is in the Department of Sociology at Brandeis University. This selection is taken from Weston's book *Families We Choose: Lesbians, Gays, Kinship* (1991). Like Gittins and Baca Zinn (see Readings 1 and 2), Weston challenges traditional definitions of family and demonstrates that the family is a social construction. Specifically, Weston argues that the conventional notion that family is based on biological or blood ties often assumed that gays and lesbians were antifamily and unable to establish families on their own. Weston explains how this monolithic and narrow definition of family has changed over time to become more inclusive of social relationships based on choice instead of on biology. Not only are many gays and lesbians accepted by their families of origin, but many also create their own families with friends, partners, and others in their communities. Moreover, gay and lesbian families are increasingly including children, via adoption, alternative insemination, and procreation.

Contemporary Debates about Families

The increasing numbers of gays and lesbians who are raising children is one of many contemporary debates about families in the United States. This debate usually revolves around the question "Is the institution of the family in decline or is it changing?" Some see the institution of the family as dying and in moral decay because of the high rates of divorce, teen pregnancy, domestic violence, and, of course, the lesbian baby boom. Others argue that this debate about the family reflects the larger "culture wars" going on in the United States (Hunter 1991), or that it reflects the stress existing in many other parts of society. Regardless, there can be no denying the ideological import of the family.

The last reading in this section, "The State of the American Family," is an excerpt from Arlene Skolnick's book *Embattled Paradise: The American Family in an Age of Uncertainty* (1991). In this selection, Skolnick addresses the public debate about American families. She deals with such questions as "Are families in crisis? Are families morally bankrupt and in decline? Is the institution of the family dying?" Instead of seeing the American family as in decline, Skolnick argues that the institution of the family is undergoing massive transformations, many of which reflect changes in the larger American culture. Specifically, the institution of the family is being affected by changes in the macrostructure of society, including shifts in the economic structure, changes in the demographics of the population, and an increase in the cultural emphasis on individual fulfillment and self-development.

REFERENCES

Coltrane, Scott. 1998. *Gender and Families.* Thousand Oaks, CA: Pine Forge Press.

Hunter, James Davison. 1991. *Culture Wars: The Struggle to Define America.* New York: Basic Books.

Laing, R. D. 1971. *The Politics of the Family and Other Essays.* New York: Pantheon Books.

Morgan, D. H. J. 1975. *Social Theory and the Family.* London: Routledge & Kegan Paul.

Parsons, Talcott and Robert F. Bales. 1955. *Family, Socialization and Interaction Process.* Glencoe, IL: The Free Press.

Skolnick, Arlene. 1991. *Embattled Paradise: The American Family in an Age of Uncertainty.* New York: Basic Books.

Sussman, Marvin B. 1986. *Handbook of Marriage and the Family.* New York: Plenum Press.

Weston, Kath. 1991. *Families We Choose: Gays, Lesbians, Kinship.* New York: Columbia University Press.

THE FAMILY IN QUESTION
What Is the Family? Is It Universal?

DIANA GITTINS

U ntil recently, most sociological studies of the family have been dominated by functionalist definitions of what the family is and what
"needs" it fulfills in society. Functionalists' theories of the family are
treated elsewhere at length (Gittins 1982; Morgan 1975), but it is worth examining some of their main assumptions briefly. Generally, functionalists
have argued that the family is a universal institution which performs certain
specific functions essential to society's survival. Murdock, for instance, defined the family as a "social group characterised by common residence, economic co-operation, and reproduction. It includes adults of both sexes, at
least two of whom maintain a socially approved sexual relationship, and one
or more children, own or adopted, of the sexually cohabiting adults."[1] The
four basic functions of the family, therefore, are seen as common residence;
economic co-operation, reproduction, sexuality. Let us examine each of these
in more detail.

Household is the term normally used to refer to co-residence. Murdock's
assumption is that it is also a defining characteristic of "the family," and vice
versa. It is generally assumed that a married couple, or parent and child(ren),
will form a household, and that family implies and presupposes "household." Yet this is by no means always so. Margaret Mead (1971) showed how
Samoan children chose the household where they wanted to reside, and often changed their residence again later. Sibling households—or frérèches—
were common in parts of Europe, and are a dominant form of household
among the Ashanti (Bender 1979:494).

There are numerous examples in contemporary society of families who
do not form households, or only form households for periods of time. Families where the husband is in the armed services, is a travelling salesman
or travels frequently abroad may only have the husband/father resident for
short periods of time. Families where partners have jobs some distance away
from one another may maintain a second household where one of them lives
during the week. Children who are sent to boarding school may spend little
more than a third of the year residing with their parent(s).

Gutman (1976) found that it was common among black slave families in
the USA for a husband and wife to live on different plantations and see one

---

Reprinted from *The Family in Question* 2nd ed. (1993) by Diana Gittins, with the permission of Macmillan Press, Ltd.

another for a few hours once or twice a week. Soliende de Gonzalez (1965) found this type of household very common in Black Carib society: "there are groupings which I have called 'dispersed families' in which the father, although absent for long periods of time, retains ultimate authority over a household for which he provides the only support, and where affective bonds continue to be important between him and his wife and children" (p. 1544). Obviously people can consider themselves "family" without actually co-residing, and can also co-reside without considering themselves to be "family."

On the other hand, households might be characterised by a shared set of activities such as sleeping, food preparation, eating, sexual relations, and caring for those who cannot care for themselves. Some have argued that a household can be defined to some extent in terms of a range of domestic activities. "Sharing the same pot" has traditionally been the boundary drawn by census enumerators for demarcating one household from another. Yet these activities need not necessarily, and often do not, occur within one household. Some members of a household may eat there all the time, while others only part of the time. Similarly, as mentioned before, some members may not always sleep in the household for a majority of the time. They may well consider themselves notwithstanding to be a family. Conversely, prisoners eat and sleep under the same roof, but do not consider themselves to be a family.

There is no hard and fast rule, much less a definition in universal terms, that can be applied to a household in terms of domestic activities. Whether in modern industrial society or in Africa or Asia "there is no basis for assuming that such activities as sleeping, eating, child-rearing and sexual relations must form a complex and must always occur under one roof" (Smith 1978:33). Household is thus in some ways just as nebulous a term as family, although it lacks the ideological implications that "family" carries.

Murdock further posits "economic co-operation" as a defining characteristic of all families. This is a very broad term and can encompass a wide range of activities from cooking to spinning to resources in terms of people and skills. Economic co-operation is something which can, and does, occur throughout all levels of society and is not specific to the family. Economic co-operation frequently occurs *between* households as well as between individuals within households. Undoubtedly households do entail an economic relationship in various ways; in particular, they entail the distribution, production and allocation of resources. Resources include food, drink, material goods, but also service, care, skills, time and space. The notion of "co-operation," moreover, implies an equal distribution of resources, yet this is seldom so. Allocating food, space, time and tasks necessitates some kind of a division of labour; different tasks need doing every day and may vary by week and by season. The number of people living together will be finite but also changeable — not just in terms of numbers, but also in terms of age, sex, marital status, physical capacity.

All resources are finite and some may be extremely scarce; some form of allocation therefore has to occur, and this presupposes power relationships. Food, work, and space are rarely distributed equally between co-residing individuals, just as they differ between households and social sectors. Most frequently, the allocation of resources and division of labour is based on differences according to sex and age. Rather than using Murdock's definition of "economic co-operation," it is thus more useful to understand families in terms of the ways in which gender and age define, and are defined by, the division of labour within, and beyond, households. These divisions also presuppose power relationships and inequality — in effect, patriarchy — rather than co-operation and equality.

Power relationships define and inform concepts of sexuality, Murdock's third defining category. His definition of sexuality is *hetero*sexuality, although this is only one of various forms of sexuality. Presumably this is because the final — and perhaps most important — "function" of families as seen by such theorists is reproduction, which necessitates heterosexual relations, at least at times. Sexuality is not something specific to families; rather, the assumption is that heterosexuality *should* be a defining characteristic of families. It also, according to Murdock, presupposes a "socially approved relationship" between two adults.

Social recognition of mating and of parenthood is obviously intimately bound up with social definitions and customs of marriage. It is often assumed that, in spite of a variety of marriage customs and laws, marriage as a binding relationship between a man and a woman is universal. Yet it has been estimated that only 10 per cent of all marriages in the world are actually monogamous; polyandry and polygyny are common in many societies, just as serial monogamy is becoming increasingly common in our own. Marriage is not always a heterosexual relationship; among the Nuer, older women marry younger women. The Nuer also practise a custom known as "ghost marriages," whereby when an unmarried or childless man dies, a relation of his then marries a woman "to his name" and the resulting children of this union are regarded as the dead man's children and bear his name (see Edholm 1982:172).

Marriage customs are not only variable between cultures and over time, but also vary between social classes. Moreover, Jessie Bernard (1973) has shown that the meanings which men and women attribute to the same marriage differ quite markedly. Undoubtedly marriage involves some form of status passage and public avowal of recognising other(s) as of particular importance in one way or another, yet it does not occur universally between two people, nor between two people of the opposite sex, nor is it always viewed as linked to reproduction. Marriage, in the way in which we think of it, is therefore not universal.

Similarly, definitions of sexuality with regard to incest have not been universal or unchanging. In medieval Europe it was considered incestuous to have sexual relations with anyone less than a seventh cousin, and marriage between cousins was proscribed. Now it is possible to marry first cousins. In Egypt during the Pharaonic and Ptolemaic period, sibling marriages were permitted, and, in some cases, father–daughter marriages. This was seen as a way of preserving the purity of royalty and was not endorsed for the whole of society—although it was permitted for everyone after the Roman conquest of Egypt.

Incestuous marriages were also permitted among royal families in Hawaii and Peru. The Mormons of Utah allowed incest (and polygamy) as a means of ensuring marriage within their church; this was not banned until 1892 (Renvoize 1982:32). Obviously these examples are more related to marriage customs and inheritance or descent problems, but serve to illustrate that even an incest taboo cannot be taken as a universal defining characteristic of families: "who could Adam's sons marry except their sisters?" (ibid., p. 32). Nevertheless, the almost universal existence of some form of incest taboo is a useful illustration of the fact that all societies do, in a myriad of ways, have some form of social organisation of sexuality, mating and reproduction.

Murdock's definition does not take adequate account of the diversity of ways in which co-residence, economic relations, sexuality and reproduction can be organised. Various theorists have made amendments and refinements to Murdock's definition of the family, but all tend to make similar errors. In particular, they translate contemporary western (and usually middle-class) ideas and ideals of what a family should be into what they assume it is everywhere.

Far more precise attempts at definition and analysis have been made by anthropologists who prefer the term kinship to that of family. A feminist anthropologist recently defined kinship as "the ties which exist between individuals who are seen as related both through birth (descent) and through mating (marriage). It is thus primarily concerned with the ways in which mating is socially organised and regulated, the ways in which parentage is assigned, attributed and recognised, descent is traced, relatives are classified, rights are transferred across generations and groups are formed" (Edholm 1982:166). This definition of kinship is a vast improvement on functionalist definitions of family because, first, it stresses the fact that kinship is a social construction, and, second, it emphasises the variability of kinship depending on how it is defined. The social nature of kinship has been stressed by many others elsewhere,[2] and yet there remains a strong common-sense belief that kinship is in fact a quite straightforward biological relationship. It is not.

We assume that because we (think we) know who our parents are and how they made us that kinship is therefore a biological fact. Consider, however, stories we have all heard about children who were brought up by parent(s) for perhaps twenty years, who all along believed their parents were their biological parents, but then discovered that they had in fact been adopted. Such people often suffer severe "identity crises" because they no longer know "who they are" or who their parents are. Their suffering is caused by the way in which we define kinship in our society, namely, in strictly biological terms, differentiating clearly between a "biological" and a "social" parent. The biological parent is always seen by our society as the "real" parent with whom a child should have the strongest ties and bonds. Knowledge of parenthood through families is the central way in which individuals are "located" socially and economically in western society. This, however, is a culturally and historically specific way of defining parenthood and kinship. Other cultures and groups in modern society believe that the person who rears a child is by definition the real parent, regardless of who was involved in the actual reproduction process.

In many poor families in Western Europe and America well into this century it was not uncommon for children to be raised by a grandparent, other kin, or friend, and such children often thought of those who raised them as their parents, even though acknowledging that they also had biological parents who were different. R. T. Smith (1978) found such practices common in Guyana and Jamaica, and reports how "close and imperishable bonds are formed through the act of 'raising' children, irrespective of genetic ties. . . . What is erroneously termed 'fictive kinship' is a widespread phenomenon. . . . While a father may be defined minimally as the person whose genetic material mingled with that of the mother in the formation of the child during one act of sexual intercourse, the father 'role' varies a good deal in any but the most homogeneous societies" (p. 353).

Others have shown the ways in which kinship is a social construction, and how those who are not biologically related to one another come to define themselves as kin: "Liebow, Stack, Ladner and others describe fictive kinship, by which friends are turned into family. Since family is supposed to be more reliable than friendship, 'going for brothers,' 'for sisters,' 'for cousins,' increases the commitment of a relationship, and makes people ideally more responsible for one another. Fictive kinship is a serious relationship" (Rapp 1980:292). It is possible to argue that this is how all kinship began and becomes constructed. Kinship, whether we choose to label it as "biological," "social" or "fictive," is a way of identifying others as in some way special from the rest, people to whom the individual or collectivity feel responsible in certain ways. It is a method of demarcating obligations and responsibility between individuals and groups.

It is thus essential to get away from the idea that kinship is a synonym for "blood" relations—*even though it may often be expressed in those terms*—and to think of it as a social construction which is highly variable and flexible. Some anthropologists recently have argued that kinship is no more and no less than a system of meanings and symbols and that it is "absolutely distinct from a biological system or a system of biological reproduction. Animals reproduce, mate, and undoubtedly form attachments to each other, but they do not have kinship systems" (Smith 1978:351). Indeed, just as Marx argued that it is labour that distinguishes people from animals, it could equally be argued that it is kinship systems that do just that.

This is not to say that many kinship relations do not have some sort of biological base—many do—but the fact that not all of them do, and that the type of base is highly variable, means that it cannot be assumed that there is some universal biological base to kinship. There is not. As Edholm (1982) argues: "notions of blood ties, of biological connection, which to us seem relatively unequivocal, are highly variable. Some societies of which we have anthropological record recognize only the role of the father or of the mother in conception and procreation. . . . Only one parent is a 'relation,' the other is not. In the Trobriand Islands . . . it is believed that intercourse is not the cause of conception, semen is not seen as essential for conception . . . (but) from the entry of a spirit child into the womb . . . it is the repeated intercourse of the same partner which 'moulds' the child" (p. 168).

Because fatherhood is always potentially unknown, and always potentially contestable, it is therefore also always a social category. Motherhood, on the other hand, is always known. Yet apart from carrying and giving birth to a child, the biological base of motherhood stops there. The rest is socially constructed, although it may be—and often is—attributed to biology or "maternal instinct." Whether or not women breastfeed their children has been historically and culturally variable. Baby bottles are no modern invention, but were used in ancient Egypt and in other cultures since. Historians have noted the number of babies given to "wet nurses" in earlier times in Europe as a sign of lack of love and care for infants on the part of mothers. But we can never really know the emotions felt by people hundreds of years ago or their motivations for their practices. The most we can do is to note that their customs were different. To use our own ideology of motherhood and love and apply it universally to all cultures is a highly ethnocentric and narrow way of trying to understand other societies.

Notions of motherhood and "good mothering" are highly variable:

> In Tahiti young women often have one or two children before they are considered, or consider themselves to be, ready for an approved and stable relationship. It is considered perfectly acceptable for the children of this young woman to be given to her parents or other close kin for adoption. . . . The girl can decide what her relationship to the children will be, but there is no sense in which she is forced into "motherhood" because of having had a baby. (Edholm 1982:170)

Who cares for children and rears them is also variable, although in most cases it is women who do so rather than men. Often those women who rear children may well claim some kinship tie to the biological mother—for example, grandmother or aunt—but this tie may simply be created as a result of rearing another woman's child. Motherhood, therefore, if taken to mean both bearing and rearing children, is not universal and is not a biological "fact."

Nor can it be argued that there is such a thing as maternal "instinct," although it is commonly believed to exist. Women are capable of conceiving children today from the age of 13 or 14, and can continue to bear children approximately every two years until they are 45 or 50. This could mean producing around eighteen or nineteen children (although fecundity declines as women age), and this, of course, seldom occurs. Few women in western society marry before they are 18 or 19, and few women in contemporary society have more than two or three children. Contraceptives control conception, not instincts, and unless it were argued that women are forced to use contraceptives,[3] there is little scope to argue for such a thing as maternal instinct.

Consider further that women who conceive babies now when they are *not* married are not hailed as true followers of their natural instinct, but are considered as "immoral," "loose," "whores," and so on. As Antonis (1981) notes: "maternal instinct is ascribed to *married women* only" (p. 59). That women can conceive and bear children is a universal phenomenon; that they do so by instinct is a fallacy. So is the notion that they always raise them. From the moment of birth, motherhood is a social construction.

Sociological and historical studies of the family have tended to pay most attention to the vertical relationships between parents and children. Less attention is paid to the lateral relationships between siblings. Yet in other cultures, and in Western Europe in earlier times, the sibling tie has often formed the basis of households and may be seen as more important than that between parent and child. Among the poorer sectors of western society until quite recently it was common for the eldest daughter to take responsibility for supervising and caring for younger siblings from quite an early age, thereby freeing her mother to engage in waged or domestic work. This remains common in many contemporary societies. In Morocco, for instance, girls "from the age of about four onwards look after younger siblings, fetch and carry, clean and run errands. The tasks themselves are arranged in a hierarchy of importance and attributed to women and girls according to their authority within the household. . . . Boys tend to be freed from domestic tasks and spend their time in groups of peers who play marbles or trap birds" (Maher 1981:73–74).

The content and importance of sibling ties varies, and this is partly a result of different interpretations of reproduction. In societies where the role of the male is seen as peripheral or unimportant—or even non-existent—in reproduction, then his children by another woman are not seen as having any relation to those of the first mother, or vice versa if the mother's role is seen as unimportant. The salience of sibling ties also depends on the organisation of kinship generally. The relative neglect of studying sibling ties as an important aspect of—or even basis of—kinship betrays our own assumptions about the primacy of parenthood in families and, particularly, the assumption that reproduction is the "essence" of kinship, with the mother and child forming the universal core of kinship. As Yanagisako (1977) points out in writing about Goodenough: "while he is undoubtedly right that in every human society mothers and children can be found, to view their *relationship* as the universal nucleus of the family is to attribute to it a social and cultural significance that is lacking in some cases" (pp. 197–98).

Implicit in definitions of kinship is a way of perceiving the social organisation of reproduction and mating, at the centre of which therefore is an organisation of relations between the sexes. The organisation of, and differentiation between, male and female takes many different forms, but all societies do have a social construction of the sexes into gender. Gender is an inherent part of the manner in which all societies are organised and is also a crucial part of the different ways in which kinship has been constructed and defined. The social, economic and political organisation of societies has been initially at least based on kinship—and thus also on gender. Understanding society means understanding the ways in which a society organised kinship and gender, and how these influence one another. Gender and kinship are universally present—as are mothers and children—but the content of them, and the meanings ascribed to them, is highly variable.

The most basic divisions of labour within any society, as pointed out by Durkheim (1933) and others, are based on age and sex. While age as a category can eventually be achieved, sex is ascribed, permanent, and immutable. The biological differences between men and women are such that only women can conceive and lactate; only men can impregnate. In spite of these obvious differences, none of them is great enough to be adequate grounds for allocating one kind of work to women and another to men. Indeed, cross-culturally and historically there are very few jobs that can be claimed to be specifically and universally performed by either men or women. Women have ploughed and mined and still do; men have laundered, gathered fruit and minded children. Hunting and warfare have almost always been male activities, while care of the young and sick has usually been a female activity. But allocation of tasks is also strongly based on age, so it is important to remember that it may be *young* men who hunt and *old* men or women who care for children; old women may be responsible for cooking, while both young men and women may work in the fields or mines.

Age is an important factor to consider in trying to understand the organisation of kinship and households. Nobody remains the same age—contrary to contemporary images in the media of the "happy family" where the couple is permanently 30 and the children forever 8 and 6. As individuals age, so the composition and structure of the unit in which they live change. Consider the ways in which the household composition and resources of a couple change as, first, aged 20, they marry and both work; second, aged 25, they have had two children and the wife has left the labour market for a few years to rear the children until they attend school; third, at 30, one partner leaves or dies and one parent is left with total care of the children; fourth, at 35, one or both may remarry someone who perhaps has three children from an earlier marriage, or may take in an elderly parent to care for, and so on. The number of wage earners and dependants changes over a household's cycle, just as it changes for the individuals within the household.

Thinking in terms of "the" family leads to a static vision of how people actually live and age together and what effects this process has on others within the household in which they live. Moreover, the environment and conditions in which any household is situated are always changing, and these changes can and often do have important repercussions on individuals and households. As Tamara Hareven (1982) points out, it is important when analysing families to differentiate between individual time, family time, and historical time. Thus in considering the structure and meaning of "family" in any society it is important to understand how definitions of dependency and individual time vary and change, how patterns of interaction between individuals and households change, and how historical developments affect all of these.

The notion of there being such a thing as "the family" is thus highly controversial and full of ambiguities and contradictions. Childbearing, childrearing, the construction of gender, allocation of resources, mating and marriage, sexuality and ageing all loosely fit into our idea of family, and yet we have seen how all of them are variable over time, between cultures and between social sectors. The claim that "the family" is universal has been especially problematic because of the failure by most to differentiate between how small groups of people live and work together, and what the ideology of appropriate behaviour for men, women and children within families has been.

Imbued in western patriarchal ideology, as discussed previously, are a number of important and culturally specific beliefs about sexuality, reproduction, parenting and the power relationships between age groups and between the sexes. The sum total of these beliefs makes up a strong *symbol-system which is labelled as the family*. Now while it can be argued that all societies have beliefs and rules on mating, sexuality, gender and age relations, the content of rules is culturally and historically specific and variable, and in no way universal. Thus to claim that patriarchy is universal is as meaningless as claiming that the family is universal.

If defining families is so difficult, how do we try to understand how and why people live, work and form relationships together in our own society? First, we need to acknowledge that while what we may think of as families are not universal, there are still trends and patterns specific to our culture which, by careful analysis, we can understand more fully. Second, we can accept that while there can be no perfect definition, it is still possible to discover certain defining characteristics which can help us to understand changing patterns of behaviour and beliefs. Finally, and most important, we can "deconstruct" assumptions usually made about families by questioning what exactly they mean. Before doing this, however, it is useful to attempt some definition of what is meant by "family" in western society.

Problematic though it may be, it is necessary to retain the notion of co-residence, because most people have lived, and do live, with others for much of their lives. Thus "household" is useful as a defining characteristic, while bearing in mind that it does not necessarily imply sexual or intimate relationships, and that, moreover, relationships *between* households are a crucial aspect of social interaction. "Household" should not be interpreted as a homogeneous and undivided unit. Virtually all households will have their own division of labour, generally based on ideals and beliefs, as well as the structure, of age and sex. There will always tend to be power relationships within households, because they will almost invariably be composed of different age and sex groups and thus different individuals will have differential access to various resources.

Because the essence of any society is interaction, a society will always be composed of a myriad of relationships between people, from the most casual to the most intimate. Relationships are formed between people of the same sex, the opposite sex, the same age group, different age groups, the same and different classes, and so on. Some of these relationships will be sexual—and sexual relations can occur in any type of relationship. Some relationships will be affectionate and loving, others will be violent or hostile. They may be made up of very brief encounters or may extend over the best part of a person's life-cycle. Thus while relationships are extremely varied in the ways in which they are formed, their nature and duration, *ideologically* western society has given highest status to long-term relationships between men and women, and between parents and children. Ideologically, such relationships are sup-posed to be loving and caring, though in reality many are not. They are pre-sented as "natural," but as we have seen, they are not. These ideals have become reified and sanctified in the notion of "family," virtually to the ex-clusion of all other long-term or intimate relationships.

Ideals of family relationships have become enshrined in our legal, social, religious and economic systems which, in turn, reinforce the ideology and pe-nalise or ostracise those who transgress it. Thus there are very real pressures on people to behave in certain ways, to lead their lives according to accept-able norms and patterns. Patriarchal ideology is embedded in our socio-economic and political institutions, indeed, in the very language we use, and as such encourages, cajoles and pressurises people to follow certain paths. Most of these are presented and defined in terms of "the family," and the fam-ily is in turn seen as the bulwark of our culture. The pressures of patriarchal ideology are acted out—and reacted against—in our interpersonal relation-ships, in marriage and non-marriage, in love and hate, having children and not having children. In short, much of our social behavior occurs in, and is judged on the basis of, the ideology of "the family."

Relationships are universal, so is some form of co-residence, of intimacy, sexuality and emotional bonds. But the *forms* these can take are infinitely vari-able and can be changed and challenged as well as embraced. By analysing the ways in which culture has prescribed certain, and proscribed other, forms of behaviour, it should be possible to begin to see the historical and cultural specificity of what is really meant when reference is made to "the family."

ENDNOTES

1. Murdock quoted in Morgan (1975), p. 20.
2. Notably C. C. Harris, J. Goody, W. Goode.
3. For a full discussion of power relationships between men and women with regard to contraceptive practice see Gittins (1982).

REFERENCES

Antonis, B. 1981. "Motherhood and Mothering." In *Women and Society,* edited by Cam-bridge Women's Study Group. London: Virago.
Bender, D. R. 1979. "A Refinement of the Concept of Household: Families, Co-residence and Domestic Functions." *American Anthropologist* 69.
Bernard, Jessie. 1973. *The Future of Marriage.* London: Souvenir Press.
Durkheim, Emile. 1933. *The Division of Labour in Society.* London: Collier-Macmillan.

Edholm, F. 1982. "The Unnatural Family." In *The Changing Experience of Women,* edited by Whitelegg et al. Oxford: Martin Robertson.

Gittins, Diana. 1982. *Fair Sex: Family Size and Structure, 1900–1939.* London: Hutchinson.

Goode, William J. 1975. "Force and Violence in the Family." In *Violence in the Family,* edited by Steinmetz and Straus. New York: Harper & Row.

Goody, J. 1972. "The Evolution of the Family." In *Household and Family in Past Time,* edited by Laslett and Wall. Cambridge: Cambridge University Press.

———. 1976. "Inheritance, Property and Women: Some Comparative Considerations." In *Family and Inheritance: Rural Society in Western Europe, 1200–1800,* edited by J. Goody, J. Thirsk, and E. P. Thompson. Cambridge: Cambridge University Press.

Goody, J., J. Thirsk, and E. P. Thompson, eds. 1976. *Family and Inheritance: Rural Society in Western Europe, 1200–1800.* Cambridge: Cambridge University Press.

Gutman, Herbert. 1976. *The Black Family in Slavery and Freedom, 1750–1925.* Oxford: Basil Blackwell.

Hareven, Tamara. 1982. *Family Time and Industrial Time.* New York: Cambridge University Press.

Harris, B. 1976. "Recent Work on the History of the Family: A Review Article." *Feminist Studies* (Spring).

Maher, V. 1981. "Work, Consumption and Authority within the Household: A Moroccan Case." In *Of Marriage and Market,* edited by Young et al. London: CSE Books.

Mead, Margaret. 1971. *Male and Female.* Harmondsworth: Penguin.

Morgan, D. H. J. 1975. *Social Theory and the Family.* London: Routledge & Kegan Paul.

Murdock, George. 1949. *Social Structure.* New York: Macmillan.

Rapp, Rayna. 1980. "Family and Class in Contemporary America: Notes Towards an Understanding of Ideology." *Science and Society* 42.

Renvoize, J. 1982. *Incest: A Family History.* London: Routledge & Kegan Paul.

Smith, R. T. 1978. "The Family and the Modern World System: Some Observations from the Caribbean." *Journal of Family History* 3.

Soliende de Gonzalez, N. 1965. "The Consanguineal Household and Matrifocality." *American Anthropologist* 67.

Stack, Carol. 1974. *All Our Kin: Strategies for Survival in a Black Community.* New York: Harper & Row.

Yanagisako, Sylvia J. 1977. "Family and Household: The Analysis of Domestic Groups." *Annual Review of Anthropology* 8.

2

FEMINIST RETHINKING
FROM RACIAL–ETHNIC FAMILIES

MAXINE BACA ZINN

U nderstanding diversity remains a pressing challenge for family scholars. Innumerable shortcomings in dominant social science studies
render much thinking ill-suited to the task. The growing diversity
movement in women's studies, together with new thinking on racial-ethnic
groups, holds the promise of a comprehensive understanding of family life.

The Family Transformation in Western Feminism

Two decades of feminist thinking on the family have demystified the idea of
the natural and timeless nuclear family. "By taking gender as a basic category
of analysis" (Thorne 1992:5), feminist theory has produced new descriptions
of family experience, new conceptualizations of family dynamics, and identified new topics for investigation. The following themes show how conventional notions of the family have been transformed:

1. The family is socially constructed. This means that it is not merely a biological arrangement but is a product of specific historical, social, and
   material conditions. In other words, it is shaped by the social structure.
2. The family is closely connected with other structures and institutions
   in society. Rather than being a separate sphere, it cannot be understood in isolation from outside factors. As a result, "the family" can be
   experienced differently by people in different social classes and of different races, and by women and men.
3. Since structural arrangements are abstract and often invisible, family
   processes can be deceptive or hidden. Many structural conditions make
   family life problematic. Therefore, families, like other social institutions, require changes in order to meet the needs of women, men, and
   children.

These themes have made great strides in challenging the myth of the
monolithic family, "which has elevated the nuclear family with a breadwin-

---

ner husband and a full time wife and mother as the only legitimate family form" (Thorne 1992:4). Viewing family life within wider systems of economic and political structures has uncovered great complexity in family dynamics and important variation among families within particular racial and ethnic groups. Despite these advances, women of color theorists contend that Western feminists have not gone far enough in integrating racial differences into family studies.

Differing Feminist Perspectives on the Family

Issues that are rooted in racial (and class) differences have always produced debates within feminist scholarship. Racial differences have evoked deeply felt differences among feminists about the meaning of family life for women. Rayna Rapp's description of a typical feminist meeting about the family captured well the essence of the debate in the late 1960s and early 1970s:

> Many of us have been at an archetypical meeting in which someone stands up and asserts that the nuclear family ought to be abolished because it is degrading and constraining to women. Usually, someone else (often representing a third world position) follows on her heels, pointing out that the attack on the family represents a white middle-class position and that other women need their families for support and survival. (Rapp 1982:168)

Women of color feminists have disagreed with several feminist notions about the meaning of family life for women. As Patricia Zavella recounts the differences:

> In particular, we had problems with the separatist politics (automatically uncooperative with men) in some early women's organizations, and with the white middle-class focus of Americans' feminism, a focus implicitly and sometimes explicitly racist. . . . Both the lack of race and class consciousness in much 1970s feminist political and scholarly work came in for severe criticism. (Zavella 1991:316)

Western feminism became more contextual in the 1980s. As women of color continued to challenge the notion that gender produced a universal woman's family experience, feminism in general worked to broaden feminist studies beyond issues important to White, middle-class, heterosexual women (Ginsburg and Tsing 1990:3). Although gender remains the basic analytical category, scholars now acknowledge the relationships between families and other social divisions (Thorne 1992). The discovery that families are differentiated by race and class has had limited impact on family theorizing across groups. Feminist social scientists now routinely note the importance of race and class differences in family life. Yet we have been more successful in offering single studies of particular groups of families and women than in providing systematic comparisons of families in the same society. Although

Western feminist thought takes great care to underscore race and class differences, it still marginalizes racial-ethnic families as special "cultural" cases. In other words, when it comes to thinking about family patterns, diversity is treated as if it were an intrinsic property of groups that are "different," rather than as being the product of forces that affect all families, but affect them in different ways. Feminism has taken on the challenge of diversity, yet it continues to treat race as epiphenomenal—in other words, to treat racial inequality and the social construction of race as secondary to gender (Zavella 1989:31). So far, mainstream feminism has failed to grapple with race as a power system that affects families throughout society and to apply that understanding to "the family" writ large. As Evelyn Nakano Glenn (1987) says, "Systematically incorporating hierarchies of race and class into the feminist reconstruction of the family remains a challenge, a necessary next step into the development of theories of family that are inclusive" (p. 368).

Inclusive Feminist Perspectives on Race and Family

Families and household groups have changed over time and varied with social conditions. Distinctive political and economic contexts have created similar family histories for people of color. Composite portraits of each group show them to have family arrangements and patterns that differ from those of White Americans. Although each group is distinguishable from the others, African Americans, Latinos, and Asians share some important commonalities (Glenn with Yap 1993). These include an extended kinship structure and informal support networks spread across multiple households. Racial-ethnic families are distinctive not only because of their ethnic heritage but also because they reside in a society where racial stratification shapes family resources and structures in important ways.

New thinking about racial stratification provides a perspective for examining family diversity as a structural aspect of society. Race is a socially constructed system that assigns different worth and unequal treatment to groups on the basis of its definition of race. While racial definitions and racial meanings are always being transformed (Omi and Winant 1986), racial hierarchies operate as fundamental axes for the social location of groups and individuals and for the unequal distribution of social opportunities. Racial and ethnic groups occupy particular social locations in which family life is constructed out of widely varying social resources. The uneven distribution of social advantages and social costs operates to strengthen some families while simultaneously weakening others.

By looking at family life in the United States across time and in different parts of the social order, we find that social and economic forces in society have produced alternative domestic arrangements. The key to understanding family diversity lies in the relationship between making a living and maintaining life on a daily basis. Feminist scholars call these activities productive and reproductive labor (Brenner and Laslett 1986:117).

Productive Labor

Historically, racial differences in how people made a living had crucial implications for domestic life. In short, they produced different family and household arrangements on the part of slaves, agricultural workers, and industrial workers. European ethnics were incorporated into low-wage industrial economies of the North, while Blacks, Latinos, Chinese, and Japanese filled labor needs in the colonial labor system of the economically backward regions of the West, Southwest and South. These colonial labor systems, while different, created similar hardships for family life. They required women to work outside of the home in order to maintain even minimal levels of family subsistence. Women's placement in the larger political economy profoundly influenced their family lives.

Several women of color theorists have advanced our understanding of the shaping power of racial stratification, not only for families of color but also for family life in general. For example, Bonnie Thornton Dill (1994) uncovers strong connections in the way racial meanings influence family life. In the antebellum United States, women of European descent received a certain level of protection within the confines of the patriarchal family. There is no doubt that they were constrained as individuals, but family life among European settlers was a highly valued aspect of societal development, and women—to the extent that they contributed to the development of families and to the economic growth of the nation—were provided institutional support for those activities. Unlike White migrants, who came voluntarily, racial-ethnics either were brought to this country or were conquered to meet the need for a cheap and exploitable labor force. Little attention was given to their family and community life. Labor, and not the existence or maintenance of families, was the critical aspect of their role in building the nation.

Women of color experienced the oppression of a patriarchal society (public patriarchy) but were denied the protections and buffering of a patriarchal family (private patriarchy). Thus, they did not have the social structural supports necessary to make their families a vital element in the social order. Family membership was not a key means of access to participation in the wider society. Families of women of color sustained cultural assaults as a direct result of the organization of the labor systems in which their groups participated. The lack of social, legal, and economic support for racial-ethnic families intensified and extended women's reproductive labor, created tensions and strains in family relationships, and set the stage for a variety of creative and adaptive forms of resistance.

Dill's study suggests a different conceptualization of the family, one that is not so bound by the notion of separate spheres of male and female labor or by the notion of the family as an emotional haven, separate and apart from the demands of the economic marketplace. People of color experienced no separation of work and family, no haven of private life, no protected sphere of domesticity. Women's work outside of the home was an extension of their family responsibilities, as family members—women, men, and children—pooled their resources to put food on the table (Du Bois and Ruiz 1990:iii). What we see here are families and women who are buffeted by the demands of the labor force and provided no legal or social protection other than the maintenance of their ability to work. This research on women of color demonstrates that protecting one's family from the demands of the market is strongly related to the distribution of power and privilege in the society. The majority of White settlers had the power to shelter their members from the market (especially their women and children), and to do so with legal and social support. People of color were denied these protections, and their family members were exploited and oppressed in order to maintain the privileges of the powerful. As Leith Mullings (1986) has said, "It was the working class and enslaved men and women whose labor created the wealth that allowed the middle class and upper middle class domestic lifestyles to exist" (p. 50).

Despite the harsh conditions imposed on family life by racial labor systems, families did not break down. Instead, they adapted as best they could. Using cultural forms where possible, and creating new adaptations where necessary, racial-ethnics adapted their families to the conditions thrust upon them. These adaptations were not exceptions to a "standard" family form. They were produced by forces of inequality in the larger society. Although the White middle-class model of the family has long been defined as the rule, it was neither the norm nor the dominant family type. It was, however, the measure against which other families were judged.

Reproductive Labor

Racial divisions in making a living shape families in important ways. They also determine how people maintain life on a daily basis. Reproductive labor is strongly gendered. It includes activities such as purchasing household goods, preparing and serving food, laundering and repairing clothing, maintaining furnishings and appliances, socializing children, providing care and emotional support for adults, and maintaining kin and community ties (Glenn 1992:1). According to Evelyn Nakano Glenn, reproductive labor has divided along racial as well as gender lines. Specific characteristics of the division have varied regionally and changed over time—shifting parts of it from the household to the market:

> In the first half of the century racial-ethnic women were employed as servants to perform reproductive labor in white households, relieving white middle-class women of onerous aspects of that work; in the second half of the century, with the expansion of commodified services (services turned into commercial products or activities), racial-ethnic women are disproportionately employed as service workers in institutional settings to carry out lower-level "public" reproductive labor, while cleaner white collar supervisory and lower professional positions are filled by white women. (Glenn 1992:3)

The activities of racial-ethnic women in "public" reproductive labor suggest new interpretations of family formation. Knowing that reproductive labor has divided along racial lines offers an understanding of why the idealized family has often been a luxury of the privileged.

Family Patterns as Relational

The distinctive place assigned to racial-ethnic women in the organization of reproductive labor has far-reaching implications for thinking about racial patterns in family diversity. Furthermore, insights about racial divisions apply to White families as well as racial-ethnic families. The new research reveals an important *relational* dimension of family formation. "Relational means that race/gender categories are positioned and that they gain meaning in relation to each other" (Glenn 1992:34). As Bonnie Thornton Dill (1986) puts it, when we examine race, class, and gender simultaneously, we have a better understanding of a social order in which the privileges of some people are dependent on the oppression and exploitation of others (p. 16). This allows us to grasp the benefits that some women derive from their race and their class while also understanding the restrictions that result from gender. In other words, such women are subordinated by patriarchal family dynamics. Yet race and class intersect to create for them privileged opportunities, choices, and lifestyles. For example, Judith Rollins (1985) uses the relationships between Black domestics and their White employers to show how one class and race of women escapes some of the consequences of patriarchy by using the labor of other women. Her study, *Between Women,* highlights the complex linkages among race, class, and gender as they create both privilege and subordination. These are simultaneous processes that enable us to look at women's diversity from a different angle.

The relational themes of privilege and subordination appear frequently in studies of domestic service (Romero 1992). Victoria Byerly (1986) found that White women who worked in the Southern textile mills hired African Americans as domestic workers. The labor of these domestics enabled the White women to engage in formal work. Vicki Ruiz (1988) describes how Mexican American women factory workers in Texas have eased their housework burdens by hiring Mexican domestic workers (Ward 1990:10–11). These studies highlight some of the ways in which race relations penetrate households, intersecting with gender arrangements to produce varied family experiences.

Theorizing across Racial Categories

Historical and contemporary racial divisions of productive and reproductive labor challenge the assumption that family diversity is the outgrowth of different cultural patterns. Racial stratification creates distinctive patterns in the way families are located and embedded in different social environments. It structures social opportunities differently, and it constructs and positions groups in systematic ways. This offers important lessons for examining current economic and social changes that are influencing families, and influencing them differently. Still, the knowledge that family life differs significantly by race does not preclude us from theorizing across racial categories.

The information and service economy continues to reshape family life by altering patterns associated with marriage, divorce, childbearing, and household composition. A growing body of family research shows that although some families are more vulnerable than others to economic marginalization, none are immune from the deep structural changes undermining "traditional" families. Adaptation takes varying forms, such as increased divorce rates, female-headed households, and extended kinship units. Although new patterns of racial formation will affect some families more than others, looking at social contexts will enable us to better understand family life in general.

The study of Black families can generate important insights for White families (Billingsly 1988). Families may respond in a like manner when impacted by larger social forces. To the extent that White families and Black families experience similar pressures, they may respond in similar ways, including the adaptation of their family structures and other behaviors. With respect to single-parent families, teenage parents, working mothers, and a host of other behaviors, Black families serve as barometers of social change and as forerunners of adaptive patterns that will be progressively experienced by the more privileged sectors of U.S. society.

On the other hand, such insights must not eclipse the ways in which racial meanings shape social perceptions of family diversity. As social and economic changes produce new family arrangements, some alternatives become more tolerable. Race plays an important role in the degree to which alternatives are deemed acceptable. When alternatives are associated with subordinate social categories, they are judged against "the traditional family" and found to be deviant. Many alternative lifestyles that appear new to middle-class Americans are actually variant family patterns that have been traditional within Black and other ethnic communities for many generations. Presented as the "new lifestyles of the young mainstream elite, they are the same lifestyles that have in the past been defined as pathological, deviant, or unacceptable when observed in Black families" (Peters and McAdoo 1983:228). As Evelyn Brooks Higginbotham (1992) observes, race often subsumes other sets of social relations, making them "good" or "bad," "correct" or "incorrect" (p. 255). Yet, many of the minority family patterns deemed "incorrect" by journalists, scholars, and policymakers are logical life choices in a society of limited social opportunities.

Growing Racial Diversity and "the Family Crisis"

Despite the proliferation of studies showing that families are shaped by their social context, conservative rhetoric is fueling a "growing social and ideological cleavage between traditional family forms and the emerging alternatives"

(Gerson 1991:57). This is complicated further by the profound demographic transformation now occurring in the United States. The unprecedented growth of minority populations is placing a special spotlight on family diversity.

Racial minorities are increasing faster than the majority population. During the 1980s Asians more than doubled, from 3.5 million to 7.3 million, and Hispanics grew from 14.6 to 22.4 million. The Black increase was from 16.5 to 30.0 million. The result of these trends is that whereas Whites in 1980 were 80 percent of the population, they will be only 70 percent by 2000 (Population Reference Bureau 1989:10). Immigration now accounts for a large share of the nation's population growth. The largest ten-year wave of immigration in U.S. history occurred during the 1980s, with the arrival of almost 9 million people. More immigrants were admitted during the 1980s than any decade since 1900–1910. By 2020, immigrants will be more important to the U.S. population growth than natural increase (Waldrop 1990:23). New patterns of immigration are changing the racial composition of society. Among the expanded population of first-generation immigrants, "the Asian-born now outnumber the European-born. Those from Latin America—predominantly Mexican—outnumber both" (Barringer 1992:2). This contrasts sharply with what occurred as recently as the 1950s, when two-thirds of legal immigrants were from Europe and Canada.

Changes in the racial composition of society are creating new polarizations along residential, occupational, educational, and economic lines. Crucial to these divisions is an ongoing transformation of racial meaning and racial hierarchy. Family scholars must be alert to the effects of these changes because the racial repositioning will touch families throughout the racial order.

New immigration patterns will escalate the rhetoric of family crises as immigrant lifestyles and family forms are measured against a mythical family ideal. Inevitably, some interpretations of diversity will revert to cultural explanations that deflect attention from the social opportunities associated with race. Even though pleas for "culturally sensitive" approaches to non-White families are well-meaning, they can unwittingly keep "the family" ensnared in a White middle-class ideal. We need to find a way to transcend the conflict among the emerging array of "family groups" (Gerson 1991:57). The best way to do this is to abandon all notions that uphold one family form as normal and others as "cultural variations." Immigration will undoubtedly introduce alternative family forms; they will be best understood by treating race as a fundamental structure that situates families differently and thereby produces diversity.

REFERENCES

Barringer, Felicity. 1992. "As American as Apple Pie, Dim Sum or Burritos." *New York Times,* May, sec. 4, p. 2.

Billingsly, Andrew. 1988. "The Impact of Technology on Afro-American Families." *Family Relations* 7:420–25.

Brenner, Johanna and Barbara Laslett. 1986. "Social Reproduction and the Family." In *The Social Reproduction of Organization and Culture,* edited by Ulf Himmelstrand. Newbury Park, CA: Sage.

Byerly, Victoria. 1986. *Hard Times Cotton Mill Girls*. Ithaca, NY: ILR Press.

Dill, Bonnie Thornton. 1986. *Our Mothers' Grief: Racial Ethnic Women and the Mainte-nance of Families*. Research Paper No. 4. Memphis, TN: Center for Research on Women, Memphis State University.

———. 1994. "Fictive Kin, Paper Sons, and Compadrazgo: Women of Color and the Struggle for Family Survival." In *Women of Color in U.S. Society*, edited by Maxine Baca Zinn and Bonnie Thornton Dill. Philadelphia: Temple University Press.

Du Bois, Ellen Carol and Vicki L. Ruiz, eds. 1990. "Introduction." In *Unequal Sisters: A Multicultural Reader in U.S. Women's History*. New York: Routledge.

Gerson, Kathleen. 1991. "Coping with Commitment: Dilemmas and Conflicts of Fam-ily Life." In *America at Century's End*, edited by Alan Wolfe. Berkeley: University of California Press.

Ginsburg, Faye and Anna Lowenhaupt Tsing. 1990. *Uncertain Terms: Negotiating Gen-der in American Culture*. Boston: Beacon Press.

Glenn, Evelyn Nakano. 1987. "Gender and the Family." In *Analyzing Gender*, edited by Beth B. Hess and Myra Marx Ferree. Newbury Park, CA: Sage.

———. 1992. "From Servitude to Service Work: Historical Continuities in the Racial Division of Paid Reproductive Labor." *Signs: Journal of Women in Culture and Society* 18(1):1–43.

Glenn, Evelyn Nakano, with Stacey H. Yap. 1993. "Chinese American Families." In *Minority Families in the United States: Comparative Perspectives*, edited by Ronald L. Taylor. Englewood Cliffs, NJ: Prentice-Hall.

Higginbotham, Evelyn Brooks. 1992. "African-American Women's History and the Metalanguage of Race." *Signs: Journal of Women in Culture and Society* 17(2):251–74.

Mullings, Leith. 1986. "Uneven Development: Class, Race, and Gender in the United States Before 1900." In *Women's Work*, edited by Eleanor Leacock and Helen I. Safa. New York: Bergin and Garvey.

Omi, Michael and Howard Winant. 1986. *Racial Formation in the United States*. London: Routledge & Kegan Paul.

Peters, Marie and Harriette P. McAdoo. 1983. "The Present and Future of Alternative Lifestyles in Ethnic American Cultures." In *Contemporary Families and Alternative Lifestyles*, edited by Eleanor D. Macklin and R. H. Rubin. Beverly Hills, CA: Sage.

Population Reference Bureau. 1989. *America in the 21st Century: Human Resource De-velopment*. Washington, DC: Population Reference Bureau.

Rapp, Rayna. 1982. "Family and Class in Contemporary America: Notes toward an Understanding of Ideology." In *Rethinking the Family: Some Feminist Questions*, edited by Barrie Thorne and Marilyn Yalom. New York: Longman.

Rollins, Judith. 1985. *Between Women: Domestics and Their Employers*. Philadelphia: Temple University Press.

Romero, Mary. 1992. *Maid in the U.S.A.* New York: Routledge.

Ruiz, Vicki. 1988. "By the Day or the Week: Mexican Domestic Workers in El Paso." In *Women in the U.S.-Mexico Border*, edited by Vicki Ruiz and Susan Tiano. Boston: Allen & Unwin.

Thorne, Barrie. 1992. "Feminism and the Family: Two Decades of Thought." In *Re-thinking the Family: Some Feminist Questions*, 2d ed., edited by Barrie Thorne and Marilyn Yalom. Boston: Northeastern University Press.

Waldrop, Judith. 1990. "You'll Know It's the 21st Century When . . ." *American Demo-graphics* 13 (December):22–27.

Ward, Kathryn. 1990. *Women Workers and Global Restructuring*. Ithaca, NY: Cornell Uni-versity Press.

Zavella, Patricia. 1989. "The Problematic Relationship of Feminism and Chicana Stud-ies." *Women's Studies* 17:25–36.

———. 1991. "Mujeres in Factories: Race and Class Perspectives on Women, Work, and Family." In *Gender at the Crossroads of Knowledge*, edited by Micaela di Leonardo. Berkeley: University of California Press.

3

EXILES FROM KINSHIP

KATH WESTON

*Indeed, it is not so much identical conclusions that prove minds to be
related as the contradictions that are common to them.*

ALBERT CAMUS

For years, and in an amazing variety of contexts, claiming a lesbian or
gay identity has been portrayed as a rejection of "the family" and a departure from kinship. In media portrayals of AIDS, Simon Watney (1987)
observes that "we are invited to imagine some absolute divide between the
two domains of 'gay life' and 'the family,' as if gay men grew up, were educated, worked and lived our lives in total isolation from the rest of society"
(p. 103). Two presuppositions lend a dubious credence to such imagery: the
belief that gay men and lesbians do not have children or establish lasting relationships, and the belief that they invariably alienate adoptive and blood
kin once their sexual identities become known. By presenting "the family" as
a unitary object, these depictions also imply that everyone participates in
identical sorts of kinship relations and subscribes to one universally agreed-
upon definition of family.

Representations that exclude lesbians and gay men from "the family" invoke what Blanche Wiesen Cook (1977:48) has called "the assumption that
gay people do not love and do not work," the reduction of lesbians and gay
men to sexual identity, and sexual identity to sex alone. In the United States,
sex apart from heterosexual marriage tends to introduce a wild card into social relations, signifying unbridled lust and the limits of individualism. If heterosexual intercourse can bring people into enduring association via the
creation of kinship ties, lesbian and gay sexuality in these depictions isolates
individuals from one another rather than weaving them into a social fabric.
To assert that straight people "naturally" have access to family, while gay
people are destined to move toward a future of solitude and loneliness, is not
only to tie kinship closely to procreation, but also to treat gay men and lesbians as members of a nonprocreative species set apart from the rest of humanity (cf. Foucault 1978).

It is but a short step from positioning lesbians and gay men somewhere
beyond "the family"—unencumbered by relations of kinship, responsibility,
or affection—to portraying them as a menace to family and society. A person
or group must first be outside and other in order to invade, endanger, and

threaten. My own impression from fieldwork corroborates Frances Fitz-Gerald's (1986) observation that many heterosexuals believe not only that gay people have gained considerable political power, but also that the absolute number of lesbians and gay men (rather than their visibility) has increased in recent years. Inflammatory rhetoric that plays on fears about the "spread" of gay identity and of AIDS finds a disturbing parallel in the imagery used by fascists to describe syphilis at mid-century, when "the healthy" confronted "the degenerate" while the fate of civilization hung in the balance (Hocquenghem 1978).

A long sociological tradition in the United States of studying "the family" under siege or in various states of dissolution lent credibility to charges that this institution required protection from "the homosexual threat." Proposition 6 (the Briggs initiative), which appeared on the ballot in California in 1978, was defeated only after a massive organizing campaign that mobilized lesbians and gay men in record numbers. The text of the initiative, which would have barred gay and lesbian teachers (along with heterosexual teachers who advocated homosexuality) from the public schools, was phrased as a defense of "the family" (in Hollibaugh 1979:55):

> One of the most fundamental interests of the State is the establishment and preservation of the family unit. Consistent with this interest is the State's duty to protect its impressionable youth from influences which are antithetical to this vital interest.

Other antigay legislative initiative campaigns adopted the slogans "save the family" and "save the children" as their rallying cries. In 1983 the *Moral Majority Report* referred obliquely to AIDS with the headline "Homosexual Diseases Threaten American Families" (Godwin 1983). When the *Boston Herald* opposed a gay rights bill introduced into the Massachusetts legislature, it was with an eye to "the preservation of family values" (Allen 1987).

Discourse that opposes gay identity to family membership is not confined to the political arena. A gay doctor was advised during his residency to discourage other gay people from becoming his patients, lest his waiting room become filled with homosexuals. "It'll scare away the families," warned his supervisor (Lazere 1986). Discussions of dual-career families and the implications of a family wage system usually render invisible the financial obligations of gay people who support dependents or who pool material resources with lovers and others they define as kin. Just as women have been accused of taking jobs away from "men with families to support," some lesbians and gay men in the [San Francisco] Bay Area recalled co-workers who had condemned them for competing against "people with families" for scarce employment. Or consider the choice of words by a guard at that "all-American" institution, Disneyland, commenting on a legal suit brought by two gay men who had been prohibited from dancing with one another at a dance floor on the grounds: "This is a family park. There is no room for alternative lifestyles here" (Mendenhall 1985).

Scholarly treatments are hardly exempt from this tendency to locate gay men and lesbians beyond the bounds of kinship. Even when researchers are sympathetic to gay concerns, they may equate kinship with genealogically calculated relations. Manuel Castells' and Karen Murphy's (1982) study of the "spatial organization of San Francisco's gay community," for instance, frames its analysis using "gay territory" and "family land" as mutually exclusive categories.

From New Right polemics to the rhetoric of high school hallways, "recruitment" joins "reproduction" in allusions to homosexuality. Alleging that gay men and lesbians must seduce young people in order to perpetuate (or expand) the gay population because they cannot have children of their own, heterosexist critics have conjured up visions of an end to society, the inevitable fate of a society that fails to "reproduce."[1] Of course, the contradictory inferences that sexual identity is "caught" rather than claimed, and that parents pass their sexual identities on to their children, are unsubstantiated. The power of this chain of associations lies in a play on words that blurs the multiple senses of the term *reproduction*.

Reproduction's status as a mixed metaphor may detract from its analytic utility, but its very ambiguities make it ideally suited to argument and innuendo.[2] By shifting without signal between reproduction's meaning of physical procreation and its sense as the perpetuation of society as a whole, the characterization of lesbians and gay men as nonreproductive beings links their supposed attacks on "the family" to attacks on society in the broadest sense. Speaking of parents who had refused to accept her lesbian identity, a Jewish woman explained, "They feel like I'm finishing off Hitler's job." The plausibility of the contention that gay people pose a threat to "the family" (and, through the family, to ethnicity) depends upon a view of family grounded in heterosexual relations, combined with the conviction that gay men and lesbians are incapable of procreation, parenting, and establishing kinship ties.

Some lesbians and gay men in the Bay Area had embraced the popular equation of their sexual identities with the renunciation of access to kinship, particularly when first coming out. "My image of gay life was very lonely, very weird, no family," Rafael Ortiz recollected. "I assumed that my family was gone now — that's it." After Bob Korkowski began to call himself gay, he wrote a series of poems in which an orphan was the central character. Bob said the poetry expressed his fear of "having to give up my family because I was queer." When I spoke with Rona Bren after she had been home with the flu, she told me that whenever she was sick, she relived old fears. That day she had remembered her mother's grim prediction: "You'll be a lesbian and you'll be alone the rest of your life. Even a dog shouldn't be alone."

Looking backward and forward across the life cycle, people who equated their adoption of a lesbian or gay identity with a renunciation of family did so in the double-sided sense of fearing rejection by the families in which they had grown up, and not expecting to marry or have children as adults. Although few in numbers, there were still those who had considered "going straight" or getting married specifically in order to "have a family." Vic Kochifos thought he understood why:

> It's a whole lot easier being straight in the world than it is being gay. . . . You have built-in loved ones: wife, husband, kids, extended family. It just works easier. And when you want to do something that requires children, and you want to have a feeling of knowing that there's gonna be someone around who cares about you when you're 85 years old, there are thoughts that go through your head, sure. There must be. There's a way of doing it gay, but it's a whole lot harder, and it's less secure.

Bernie Margolis had been sexually involved with men since he was in his teens, but for years had been married to a woman with whom he had several children. At age 67 he regretted having grown to adulthood before the current discussion of gay families, with its focus on redefining kinship and constructing new sorts of parenting arrangements:

> I didn't want to give up the possibility of becoming a family person. Of having kids of my own to carry on whatever I built up. . . . My mother was always talking about she's looking forward to the day when she would bring her children under the canopy to get married. It never occurred to her that I wouldn't be married. It probably never occurred to me either.

The very categories "good family person" and "good family man" had seemed to Bernie intrinsically opposed to a gay identity. In his fifties at the time I interviewed him, Stephen Richter attributed never having become a father to "not having the relationship with the woman." Because he had envisioned parenting and procreation only in the context of a heterosexual relationship, regarding the two as completely bound up with one another, Stephen had never considered children an option.

Older gay men and lesbians were not the only ones whose adult lives had been shaped by ideologies that banish gay people from the domain of kinship. Explaining why he felt uncomfortable participating in "family occasions," a young man who had no particular interest in raising a child commented, "When families get together, what do they talk about? Who's getting married, who's having children. And who's not, okay? Well, look who's not." Very few of the lesbians and gay men I met believed that claiming a gay identity automatically requires leaving kinship behind. In some cases, people described this equation as an outmoded view that contrasted sharply with revised notions of what constitutes a family.

Well-meaning defenders of lesbian and gay identity sometimes assert that gays are not inherently "antifamily," in ways that perpetuate the association of heterosexual identity with exclusive access to kinship. Charles Silverstein (1977), for instance, contends that lesbians and gay men may place more importance on maintaining family ties than heterosexuals do because gay people do not marry and raise children. Here the affirmation that gays and lesbians are capable of fostering enduring kinship ties ends up reinforcing the implication that they cannot establish "families of their own," presumably because the author regards kinship as unshakably rooted in heterosexual alliance and procreation. In contrast, discourse on gay families cuts across the politically loaded couplet of "profamily" and "antifamily" that places gay men and lesbians in an inherently antagonistic relation to kinship solely on the basis of their nonprocreative sexualities. "Homosexuality is not what is breaking up the Black family," declared Barbara Smith (1987), a black lesbian writer, activist, and speaker at the 1987 Gay and Lesbian March on Washington. "Homophobia is. My Black gay brothers and my Black lesbian sisters are members of Black families, both the ones we were born into and the ones we create."

At the height of gay liberation, activists had attempted to develop alternatives to "the family," whereas by the 1980s many lesbians and gay men were struggling to legitimate gay families as a form of kinship. When Armistead Maupin spoke at a gathering on Castro Street to welcome home two gay men who had been held hostage in the Middle East, partners who had stood with arms around one another upon their release, he congratulated them not only for their safe return, but also as representatives of a new kind of family. Gay or chosen families might incorporate friends, lovers, or children, in any combination. Organized through ideologies of love, choice, and creation, gay families have been defined through a contrast with what many gay men and lesbians in the Bay Area called "straight," "biological," or "blood" family. If families we choose were the families lesbians and gay men created for themselves, straight family represented the families in which most had grown to adulthood.

What does it mean to say that these two categories of family have been defined through contrast? One thing it emphatically does *not* mean is that heterosexuals share a single coherent form of family (although some of the lesbians and gay men doing the defining believed this to be the case). I am not arguing here for the existence of some central, unified kinship system vis-à-vis which gay people have distinguished their own practice and understanding of family. In the United States, race, class, gender, ethnicity, regional origin, and context all inform differences in household organization, as well as differences in notions of family and what it means to call someone kin.[3]

In any relational definition, the juxtaposition of two terms gives meaning to both.[4] Just as light would not be meaningful without some notion of darkness, so gay or chosen families cannot be understood apart from the families lesbians and gay men call "biological," "blood," or "straight." Like others in their society, most gay people in the Bay Area considered biology a matter of "natural fact." When they applied the terms "blood" and "biology" to kinship, however, they tended to depict families more consistently organized by procreation, more rigidly grounded in genealogy, and more uniform in their conceptualization than anthropologists know most families to be. For many lesbians and gay men, blood family represented not some naturally given unit that provided a base for all forms of kinship, but rather a procreative principle that organized only one possible *type* of kinship. In their descriptions they

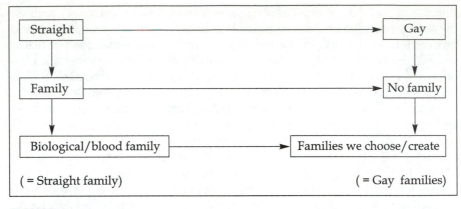

FIGURE 1

situated gay families at the opposite end of a spectrum of determination, subject to no constraints beyond a logic of "free" choice that ordered membership. To the extent that gay men and lesbians mapped "biology" and "choice"
onto identities already opposed to one another (straight and gay, respectively),
they polarized these two types of family along an axis of sexual identity.[5]

The chart in Figure 1 recapitulates the ideological transformation generated as lesbians and gay men began to inscribe themselves within the domain
of kinship. What this chart presents is not some static substitution set, but a
historically motivated succession.[6] To move across or down the chart is to
move through time. Following along from left to right, time appears as process, periodized with reference to the experience of coming out. In the first
opposition, coming out defines the transition from a straight to a gay identity. For the person who maintains an exclusively biogenetic notion of kinship,
coming out can mark the renunciation of kinship, the shift from "family" to "no
family" portrayed in the second opposition. In the third line, individuals who
accepted the possibility of gay families after coming out could experience
themselves making a transition from the biological or blood families in which
they had grown up to the establishment of their own chosen families.

Moving from top to bottom, the chart depicts the historical time that in-
augurated contemporary discourse on gay kinship. "Straight" changes from
a category with an exclusive claim on kinship to an identity allied with a specific kind of family symbolized by biology or blood. Lesbians and gay men,
originally relegated to the status of people without family, later lay claim to
a distinctive type of family characterized as families we choose or create.
While dominant cultural representations have asserted that straight is to gay
as family is to no family (lines 1 and 2), at a certain point in history gay people
began to contend that straight is to gay as blood family is to chosen families
(lines 1 and 3).

What provided the impetus for this ideological shift? Transformations in
the relation of lesbians and gay men to kinship are inseparable from sociohistorical developments: changes in the context for disclosing a lesbian or

gay identity to others, attempts to build urban gay "community," cultural inferences about relationships between "same-gender" partners, and the lesbian baby boom associated with alternative (artificial) insemination. If Pierre
Bourdieu (1977) is correct, and kinship is something people use to act as well
as to think, then its transformations should have unfolded not only on the
"big screen" of history, but also on the more modest stage of day-to-day life,
where individuals have actively engaged novel ideological distinctions and
contested representations that would exclude them from kinship. . . .

Kinship and Procreation

Since the time of Lewis Henry Morgan, most scholarly studies of familial relations have enthroned human procreation as kinship's ultimate referent. According to received anthropological wisdom, relations of blood (consanguinity)
and marriage (affinity) could be plotted for any culture on a universal genealogical grid. Generations of fieldworkers set about the task of developing
kinship charts for a multitude of "egos," connecting their subjects outward
to a network of social others who represented the products (offspring) and
agents (genitor/genetrix) of physical procreation. In general, researchers occupied themselves with investigations of differences in the ways cultures
arranged and divided up the grid, treating blood ties as a material base underlying an array of cross-cultural variations in kinship organization.

More recently, however, anthropologists have begun to reconsider the
status of kinship as an analytic concept and a topic for inquiry. What would
happen if observers ceased privileging genealogy as a sacrosanct or objective
construct, approaching biogenetic ties instead as a characteristically Western
way of ordering and granting significance to social relations? After a lengthy
exercise in this kind of bracketing, David Schneider (1972, 1984) concluded
that significant doubt exists as to whether non-Western cultures recognize
kinship as a unified construct or domain. Too often unreflective recourse to
the biogenetic symbolism used to prioritize relationships in Anglo-European
societies subordinates an understanding of how particular cultures construct
social ties to the project of cross-cultural comparison. But suppose for a moment that blood is not intrinsically thicker than water. Denaturalizing the genealogical grid would require that procreation no longer be postulated as
kinship's base, ground, or centerpiece.

Within Western societies, anthropologists are not the only ones who have
implicitly or explicitly subjected the genealogical grid to new scrutiny. By re-
working familiar symbolic materials in the context of nonprocreative relationships, lesbians and gay men in the United States have formulated a critique of
kinship that contests assumptions about the bearing of biology, genetics, and
heterosexual intercourse on the meaning of family in their own culture. Unlike Schneider, they have not set out to deconstruct kinship as a privileged
domain, or taken issue with cultural representations that portray biology as a
material "fact" exclusive of social significance. What gay kinship ideologies

challenge is not the concept of procreation that informs kinship in the United States, but the belief that procreation *alone* constitutes kinship, and that "non-biological" ties must be patterned after a biological model (like adoption) or forfeit any claim to kinship status.

In the United States, the notion of biology as an indelible, precultural substratum is so ingrained that people often find it difficult to take an anthropological step backward in order to examine biology as symbol rather than substance. For many in this society, biology is a defining feature of kinship: they believe that blood ties make certain people kin, regardless of whether those individuals display the love and enduring solidarity expected to characterize familial relations. Physical procreation, in turn, produces biological links. Collectively, biogenetic attributes are supposed to demarcate kinship as a cultural domain, offering a yardstick for determining who counts as a "real" relative. Like their heterosexual counterparts, lesbians and gay men tended to naturalize biology in this manner.

Not all cultures grant biology this significance for describing and evaluating relationships. To read biology as symbol is to approach it as a cultural construct and linguistic category, rather than a self-evident matter of "natural fact." At issue here is the cultural valuation given to ties traced through procreation, and the meaning that biological connection confers upon a relationship in a given cultural context. In this sense, biology is no less a symbol than choice or creation. Neither is inherently more "real" or valid than the other, culturally speaking.

In the United States, Schneider (1968) argues, "sexual intercourse" is the symbol that brings together relations of marriage and blood, supplying the distinctive features in terms of which kinship relations are defined and differentiated. A relationship mediated by procreation binds a mother to a daughter, a brother to a sister, and so on, in the categories of genitor or genetrix, offspring, or members of a sibling set. Immediately apparent to a gay man or lesbian is that what passes here for sex per se is actually the *hetero*sexual union of two differently gendered persons. While all sexual activity among heterosexuals certainly does not lead to the birth of children, the isolation of heterosexual intercourse as a core symbol orients kinship studies toward a dominantly procreative reading of sexualities. For a society like the United States, Sylvia Yanagisako's and Jane Collier's (1987) call to analyze gender and kinship as mutually implicated constructs must be extended to embrace sexual identity.

The very notion of gay families asserts that people who claim nonprocreative sexual identities and pursue nonprocreative relationships can lay claim to family ties of their own without necessary recourse to marriage, childbearing, or child rearing.[7] By defining these chosen families in opposition to the biological ties believed to constitute a straight family, lesbians and gay men began to renegotiate the meaning and practice of kinship from within the very societies that had nurtured the concept. Theirs has not been a proposal to number gay families among variations in "American kinship," but a more comprehensive attack on the privilege accorded to a biogenetically grounded mode of determining what relationships will *count* as kinship.

It is important to note that some gay men and lesbians in the Bay Area agreed with the view that blood ties represent the only authentic, legitimate form of kinship. Often those who disputed the validity of chosen families were people whose notions of kinship were bound up with their own sense of racial or ethnic identity. "You've got one family, one biological family," insisted Paul Jaramillo, a Mexican American man who did not consider his lover or friends to be kin.

> *They're very good friends and I love them, but I would not call them family. Family to me is blood. . . . I feel that Western Caucasian culture, that it's much more broken down, and that they can deal with their good friends and neighbors as family. But it's not that way, at least in my background.*

Because most individuals who expressed this view were well aware of the juxtaposition of blood family with families we choose, they tended to address gay kinship ideologies directly. As Lourdes Alcantara explained:

> *I know a lot of lesbians think that you choose your own family. I don't think so. Because, as a Latin woman, the bonds that I got with my family are irreplaceable. They can't be replaced. They cannot. So my family is my family, my friends are my friends. My friends can be more important than my family, but that doesn't mean they are my family. . . . 'Cause no matter what, they are just friends — they don't have your blood. They don't have your same connection. They didn't go through what you did. For example, I starved with my family a lot of times. They know what it is like. If I talk to my friends, they will understand me, but they will never feel the same.*

What Lourdes so movingly described was a sense of enduring solidarity arising from shared experience and symbolized by blood connection. Others followed a similar line of reasoning (minus the biological signifier) when they contended that a shared history testifies to enduring solidarity, which can provide the basis for creating familial relationships of a chosen, or nonbiological, sort.

In an essay on disclosing a lesbian or gay identity to relatives, Betty Berzon (1979) maintains that "from early on, being gay is associated with going against the family" (p. 89). Many people in the Bay Area viewed families as the principal mediator of race and ethnicity, drawing on folk theories of cultural transmission in which parents hand down "traditions" and identity (as well as genes) to their children [8] If having a family was part of what it meant to be Chicana or Cherokee or Japanese American, then claiming a lesbian or gay identity could easily be interpreted as losing or betraying that cultural heritage, so long as individuals conceived kinship in biogenetic terms (cf. Clunis and Green 1988:105; Tremble et al. 1989). Kenny Nash had originally worried that coming out as a gay man would separate him from other African Americans.

> *Because I related to the black community a lot as far as politics, and . . . unfortunately, sexual politics in some parts of the black movement are not very good. Just as there is this continuing controversy about feminism and*

*black women in the women's movement. It's a carry-over, I think, into [ideas]
about gay people, gay men and lesbians. Because there are some people who
think of [being gay] as the antithesis of building strong family institutions,
and that's what we need: role models for people, bringing up children, and
all that stuff.*

Condemnations of homosexuality might picture race or ethnicity and gay
identity as antagonists in response to a history of racist attributions of "weak"
family ties to certain groups (e.g., blacks), or in response to anything that appeared to menace the legacy of "strong" kinship bonds sometimes attributed
to other categories of people (e.g., Latinos, Jews). In either case, depicting lesbian or gay identity as a threat to ethnic or racial identity depended upon
the cultural positioning of gay people outside familial relations. The degree
to which individuals construct racial identity *through* their notions of family
remains a relatively unexplored aspect of why some heterosexuals of color reject gay or lesbian identity as a sign of assimilation, a "white thing."

Not all lesbians and gays of color or whites with a developed ethnic identity took issue with the concept of chosen families. Many African Americans,
for instance, felt that black communities had never held to a strictly biogenetic interpretation of kinship. "Blacks have never said to a child, 'Unless
you have a mother, father, sister, brother, you don't have a family'" (Height
1989:137).[9] Discourse and ideology are far from being uniformly determined
by identities, experiences, or historical developments. Divergent perceptions
of the relation between family ties and race or ethnicity are indicative of a
situation of ideological flux, in which procreative and nonprocreative interpretations vie with one another for the privilege of defining kinship. As the
United States entered the final decade of the twentieth century, lesbians and
gay men from a broad spectrum of racial and ethnic identities had come to
embrace the legitimacy of gay families.

From Biology to Choice

Upon first learning the categories that framed gay kinship ideologies, heterosexuals sometimes mentioned adoption as a kind of limiting case that appeared to occupy the borderland between biology and choice. In the United
States, adopted children are chosen, in a sense, although biological offspring
can be planned or selected as well, given the widespread availability of birth
control. Yet adoption in this society "is only understandable as a way of creating the social fiction that an actual link of kinship exists. Without biological
kinship as a model, adoption would be meaningless" (Schneider 1984:55).
Adoption does not render the attribution of biological descent culturally irrelevant (witness the many adopted children who, later in life, decide to search
for their "real" parents). But adoptive relations — unlike gay families — pose no
fundamental challenge to either procreative interpretations of kinship or the
culturally standardized image of a family assembled around a core of par-
ent(s) plus children.

Mapping biological family and families we choose onto contrasting sexual identities (straight and gay, respectively) places these two types of family in a relation of opposition, but *within* that relation, determinism implicitly differentiates biology from choice and blood from creation. Informed by contrasting notions of free will and the fixedness often attributed to biology in this culture, the opposition between straight and gay families echoes old dichotomies such as nature versus nurture and real versus ideal. In families we choose, the agency conveyed by "we" emphasizes each person's part in constructing gay families, just as the absence of agency in the term "biological family" reinforces the sense of blood as an immutable fact over which individuals exert little control. Likewise, the collective subject of families we choose invokes a collective identity—who are "we" if not gay men and lesbians? In order to identify the "we" associated with the speaker's "I," a listener must first recognize the correspondence between the opposition of blood to choice and the relation of straight to gay.

Significantly, families we choose have not built directly upon beliefs that gay or lesbian identity can be chosen. Among lesbians and gay men themselves, opinions differ as to whether individuals select or inherit their sexual identities. In the aftermath of the gay movement, the trend has been to move away from the obsession of earlier decades with the etiological question of what "causes" homosexuality. After noting that no one subjects heterosexuality to similar scrutiny, many people dropped the question. Some lesbian-feminists presented lesbianism as a political choice that made a statement about sharing their best with other women and refusing to participate in patriarchal relations. In everyday conversations, however, the majority of both men and women portrayed their sexual identities as either inborn or a predisposition developed very early in life. Whether or not to act on feelings already present then became the only matter left to individual discretion. "The choice for me wasn't being with men or being a lesbian," Richie Kaplan explained. "The choice was being asexual or being with women."

In contrast, parents who disapproved of homosexuality could convey a critical attitude by treating gay identity as something elective, especially since people in the United States customarily hold individuals responsible for any negative consequences attendant upon a "free choice." One man described with dismay his father's reaction upon learning of his sexual identity: "I said, 'I'm gay.' And he said, 'Oh. Well, I guess you made your choice.'" According to another, "My father kept saying, 'Well, you're gonna have to live by your choices that you make. It's your responsibility.' What's there to be responsible [about]? I was who I *am*." When Andy Wentworth disclosed his gay identity to his sister:

> She asked me, how could I choose to do this and to ignore the health risks . . . implying that this was a conscious, "Oh, I'd like to go to the movies today" type of choice. And I told her, I said, "Nobody in their right mind would go through this hell of being gay just to satisfy a whim." And I explained to her what it was like growing up. Knowing this other side of yourself that you

can't tell anybody about, and if anybody in your family knows they will be
upset and mortified.

Another man insisted he would never forget the period after coming out when he realized that he felt good about himself, and that he was not on his way to becoming "the kind of person that they're portraying gay people to be." What kind of person is that? I asked. "Well, you know, wicked, evil people who *decide* that they're going to be evil."

Rather than claiming an elective gay identity as its antecedent, the category "families we choose" incorporates the meaningful *difference* that is the product of choice and biology as two relationally defined terms. If many gay men and lesbians interpreted blood ties as a type of social connectedness organized through procreation, they tended to associate choice and creativity with a total absence of guidelines for ordering relationships within gay families. Although heterosexuals in the Bay Area also had the sense of creating something when they established families of their own, that creativity was often firmly linked to childbearing and child rearing, the *pro* in procreation. In the absence of a procreative referent, individual discretion regulated who would be counted as kin. For those who had constructed them, gay families could evoke utopian visions of self-determination in the absence of social constraint. . . .

Certainly lesbians and gay men, with their range of backgrounds and experiences, did not always mean the same thing or advance identical cultural critiques when they spoke of blood and chosen families. Ideological contrasts utilized and recognized by all need not have the same significance for all.[10] Neither can an examination of ideology alone explain why choice should have been highlighted as organizing principle of gay families. Only history, material conditions, and context can account for the specific content of gay kinship ideologies, their emergence at a particular point in time, and the variety of ways people have implemented those ideologies in their daily lives. In themselves, gay families comprise only a segment of the historical transformation sequence that mapped the contrast between straight and gay first onto "family/no family," and then onto "biological family/families we choose." Gone are the days when embracing a lesbian or gay identity seemed to require a renunciation of kinship. The symbolic groundwork for gay families, laid during a period when coming out to relatives witnessed a kind of institutionalization, has made it possible to claim a sexual identity that is not linked to procreation, face the possibility of rejection by blood or adoptive relations, yet still conceive of establishing a family of one's own.

ENDNOTES

1. See Godwin (1983) and Hollibaugh (1979).
2. For an analysis that carefully distinguishes among the various senses of reproduction and their equivocal usage in feminist and anthropological theory, see Yanagisako and Collier (1987).
3. On the distinction between family and household, see Rapp (1982) and Yanagisako (1979).

4. On relational definition and the arbitrariness of signs, see Saussure (1959).
5. For Lévi-Strauss (1963:88), most symbolic contrasts are structured by a mediating third term. Apparently conflicting elements incorporate a hidden axis of commonality that allows the two to be brought into relationship with one another. Here sexual identity is the hidden term that links "straight" to "gay," while kinship mediates the oppositions further down in the chart. This sort of triadic relation lends dynamism to opposition, facilitating ideological transformations while ensuring a regulated, or structured, relationship between the old and the new.

   My overall analysis departs from a Lévi-Straussian structuralism by historically situating these relations, discarding any presumption that they form a closed system, and avoiding the arbitrary isolation of categories for which structuralism has justly been criticized in the past (see Culler 1975; Fowler 1981; Jenkins 1979). The symbolic oppositions examined in this chapter incorporate indigenous categories in all their specificity (e.g., straight versus gay), rather than abstracting to universals of increasing generality and arguably decreasing utility (e.g., nature versus culture). Chronicled here is an ideological transformation faithful to history, process, and the perceptions of the lesbians and gay men who themselves identified each opposition included in the chart. For the deployment of these categories in everyday contexts, read on.
6. Notice how the contrasts in the chart map a relationship of difference (straight/gay) first onto a logical negation (family/no family, or A/NA), and then onto another relation of difference (biological [blood] family/families we choose [create], or A:B). On the generative potential of dichotomies that are constituted as A/B rather than A/NA, see N. Jay (1981:44).
7. See Foucault (1978) on the practice of grouping homosexuality together with other nonprocreative sex acts, a historical shift that supplanted the earlier classification of homosexuality with adultery and offenses against marriage. According to Foucault, previous to the late eighteenth century acts "contrary to nature" tended to be understood as an extreme form of acts "against the law," rather than something different in kind. Only later was "the unnatural" set apart in the emerging domain of sexuality, becoming autonomous from adultery or rape. See also Freedman (1982): "Although the ideological support for the separation of [erotic] sexuality and reproduction did not appear until the twentieth century, the process itself began much earlier" (p. 210).
8. See di Leonardo (1984), who criticizes the transmission model for its lack of attention to the wider socioeconomic context that informs the ways people interpret the relation of kinship to ethnicity.
9. See also Joseph and Lewis (1981:76), Kennedy (1980), McAdoo (1988), and Stack (1974). For a refutation and historical contextualization of allegations that African Americans have developed "dysfunctional" families, or even no families at all, see Gresham (1989).
10. Abercrombie et al. (1980) lay out many of the objections to treating culture as a shared body of values and knowledge determinative of social relations. For theoretical formulations critical of the assumption that ideology mechanically reflects a more fundamental set of material conditions, see Jameson (1981), Lichtman (1975), and R. Williams (1977). For different approaches to examining the influence of context, embodiment, and power relations on the formulation and interpretation of cultural categories, see Rosaldo (1989), Vološinov (1973), and Yanagisako (1978, 1985).

REFERENCES

Abercrombie, Nicholas, Stephen Hill, and Bryan S. Turner. 1980. *The Dominant Ideology Thesis.* Boston: Allen & Unwin.
Allen, Ronnie. 1987. "Times Have Changed at the *Herald.*" *Gay Community News,* June 28–July 4.

Berzon, Betty. 1978. "Sharing Your Lesbian Identity with Your Children." Pp. 69–74 in *Our Right to Love: A Lesbian Resource Book,* edited by Ginny Vida. Englewood Cliffs, NJ: Prentice-Hall.

———. 1979. "Telling the Family You're Gay." Pp. 88–100 in *Positively Gay,* edited by Betty Berzon and Robert Leighton. Los Angeles: Mediamix Associates.

Bourdieu, Pierre. 1977. *Outline of a Theory of Practice.* New York: Cambridge University Press.

Castells, Manuel and Karen Murphy. 1982. "Cultural Identity and Urban Structure: The Spatial Organization of San Francisco's Gay Community." Pp. 237–59 in *Urban Policy under Capitalism,* edited by Norman I. Fainstein and Susan S. Fainstein. Beverly Hills, CA: Sage.

Clunis, D. Merilee and G. Dorsey Green. 1988. *Lesbian Couples.* Seattle, WA: Seal Press.

Cook, Blanche Wiesen. 1977. "Female Support Networks and Political Activism: Lillian Wald, Crystal Eastman, Emma Goldman." *Chrysalis* 3:44–61.

Culler, Jonathan. 1975. *Structuralist Poetics: Structuralism, Linguistics and the Study of Literature.* Ithaca, NY: Cornell University Press.

di Leonardo, Micaela. 1984. *The Varieties of Ethnic Experience: Kinship, Class, and Gender among California Italian-Americans.* Ithaca, NY: Cornell University Press.

FitzGerald, Frances. 1986. *Cities on a Hill: A Journey through Contemporary American Cultures.* New York: Simon & Schuster.

Foucault, Michel. 1978. *The History of Sexuality.* Vol. 1. New York: Vintage Books.

Fowler, Roger. 1981. *Literature as Social Discourse: The Practice of Linguistic Criticism.* Bloomington: University of Indiana Press.

Freedman, Estelle B. 1982. "Sexuality in Nineteenth-Century America: Behavior, Ideology, and Politics." *Reviews in American History* 10:196–215.

Godwin, Ronald S. 1983. "AIDS: A Moral and Political Time Bomb." *Moral Majority Report,* July.

Gresham, Jewell Handy. 1989. "The Politics of Family in America." *The Nation,* July 24–31, pp. 116–22.

Height, Dorothy. 1989. "Self-Help—A Black Tradition." *The Nation,* July 24–31, pp. 136–38.

Hocquenghem, Guy. 1978. *Homosexual Desire.* London: Alison & Busby.

Hollibaugh, Amber. 1979. "Sexuality and the State: The Defeat of the Briggs Initiative and Beyond." *Socialist Review* 9(3):55–72.

Jameson, Frederic. 1981. *The Political Unconscious: Narrative as a Socially Symbolic Act.* Ithaca, NY: Cornell University Press.

Jay, Nancy. 1981. "Gender and Dichotomy." *Feminist Studies* 7(1):38–56.

Jenkins, Alan. 1979. *The Social Theory of Claude Lévi-Strauss.* New York: St. Martin's Press.

Joseph, Gloria I. and Jill Lewis. 1981. *Common Differences: Conflicts in Black and White Feminist Perspectives.* Garden City, NY: Anchor/Doubleday.

Kennedy, Theodore R. 1980. *You Gotta Deal with It: Black Family Relations in a Southern Community.* New York: Oxford University Press.

Lazere, Arthur. 1986. "On the Job." *Coming Up!,* June.

Lévi-Strauss, Claude. 1963. *Totemism.* Boston: Beacon Press.

Lichtman, Richard. 1975. "Marx's Theory of Ideology." *Socialist Revolution* 5(1):45–76.

McAdoo, Harriette P. 1988. *Black Families.* 2d ed. Newbury Park, CA: Sage.

Mendenhall, George. 1985. "Mickey Mouse Lawsuit Remains Despite Disney Dancing Decree." *Bay Area Reporter,* August 22.

Rapp, Rayna. 1982. "Family and Class in Contemporary America: Notes toward an Understanding of Ideology." Pp. 168–87 in *Rethinking the Family,* edited by Barrie Thorne with Marilyn Yalom. New York: Longman.

Rosaldo, Renato. 1989. *Culture and Truth: The Remaking of Social Analysis.* Boston: Beacon Press.

Saussure, Ferdinand de. 1959. *Course in General Linguistics.* New York: McGraw-Hill.

Schneider, David M. 1968. *American Kinship: A Cultural Account.* Englewood Cliffs, NJ: Prentice-Hall.

————. 1972. "What Is Kinship All About? In *Kinship Studies in the Morgan Centennial Year,* edited by Priscilla Reining. Washington, DC: Anthropological Society of Washington.

————. 1984. *A Critique of the Study of Kinship.* Ann Arbor: University of Michigan Press.

Silverstein, Charles. 1977. *A Family Matter: A Parents' Guide to Homosexuality.* New York: McGraw-Hill.

Smith, Barbara. 1987. "From the Stage." *Gay Community News,* November 8–14.

Stack, Carol B. 1974. *All Our Kin: Strategies for Survival in a Black Community.* New York: Harper & Row.

Tremble, Bob, Margaret Schneider, and Carol Appathurai. 1989. "Growing Up Gay or Lesbian in a Multicultural Context." Pp. 253–64 in *Gay and Lesbian Youth,* edited by Gilbert Herdt. New York: Haworth Press.

Vološinov, V. N. 1973. *Marxism and the Philosophy of Language.* New York: Seminar Press.

Watney, Simon. 1987. *Policing Desire: Pornography, AIDS, and the Media.* Minneapolis: University of Minnesota Press.

Williams, Raymond. 1977. *Marxism and Literature.* New York: Oxford University Press.

Yanagisako, Sylvia J. 1978. "Variance in American Kinship: Implications for Cultural Analysis." *American Ethnologist* 5(1):1529.

————. 1979. "Family and Household: The Analysis of Domestic Groups." *Annual Review of Anthropology* 8:161–205.

————. 1985. *Transforming the Past: Tradition and Kinship among Japanese Americans.* Stanford, CA: Stanford University Press.

Yanagisako, Sylvia Junko and Jane Fishburne Collier. 1987. "Toward a Unified Analysis of Gender and Kinship." Pp. 14–50 in *Gender and Kinship: Essays toward a Unified Analysis,* edited by Jane Fishburne Collier and Sylvia Junko Yanagisako. Stanford, CA: Stanford University Press.

4

THE STATE OF THE AMERICAN FAMILY

ARLENE SKOLNICK

The American family does not exist. Rather, we are creating many American families, of diverse styles and shapes. . . . We have fathers working while mothers keep house; fathers and mothers both working away from home; single parents; second marriages bringing together people from unrelated backgrounds; childless couples; unmarried couples, with and without children; gay and lesbian parents. We are living through a period of historic change in American family life.

— "The 21st Century Family"
Newsweek (1990)

The feminist revolution of this century has provided the most powerful challenge to traditional patterns of marriage. Yet paradoxically, it may also have strengthened the institution by giving greater freedom to both partners, and by allowing men to accept some of the traditionally female values.
— HELGE RUBENSTEIN
The Oxford Book of Marriage

The debate about whether the family in America is falling apart, here to stay, or better than ever has continued unabated since the 1970s, like an endless cocktail party conversation. There is of course no way of resolving the issue. "Most of us," observes Joseph Featherstone, "debate these matters from our general instinct of where history is tending, from our own lives and those of our friends. . . . One of the difficult things about the family as a topic is that everyone in the discussion feels obliged to defend a particular set of choices."[1]

While the argument shows no signs of reaching a resolution, some of the debaters have wandered away. Others have switched sides. Most of the radical voices who celebrated the death of the family have disappeared. Those who denounced the family as an oppressive institution and lamented its persistence have also passed from the scene, although continuing critical attacks have granted them a kind of immortality. Meanwhile, the ranks of the optimists who think the family is alive and well have thinned considerably. Recently, one family researcher did publish a book entitled *The Myth of Family Decline,* but generally there is less talk of family decline and decay in the media and more of it among social scientists.[2]

There is no doubt that the family transformations of recent times have left a great deal of disruption in their wake. But those who lament "the decline of the family" lump together an array of serious problems, as well as changes that are not necessarily problems at all: divorce, the sexual revolution, working mothers, the rising age of marriage, teenage pregnancy, abortion, childhood poverty, child abuse, domestic violence, the economic effects of no-fault divorce for women and children, the failure of many divorced fathers to pay child support and maintain contact with their children, an increase in the percentage of people living alone, young people "postponing" adulthood and refusing to leave home, latchkey children, the "dysfunctional family," drug use in the ghettos and suburbs, problems of minority families.

Wrapping these issues in one big package labeled "decline of the family" muddles rather than clarifies our understanding of family change. Some of these problems arise out of the old plague of poverty, which has grown worse over the past decade; others are by-products of an American economy afflicted by recession, inflation, and industrial decline and dislocation.

Change does not equal problem.

Still other difficulties are a result of the mismatch between the new realities of family life and social arrangements based on earlier family patterns. For example, the problem of "latchkey children" could be remedied if we had the will to do so—through afterschool programs, or a lengthening of the school day, or flexible work schedules for parents. And at least some of the painful consequences of divorce are products of the legal policies and practices governing the dissolution of marriage. No-fault divorce is a classic case of unintended consequences: what looked like reform of an unfair, degrading way of dealing with marital breakdown turned into an economic disaster for older homemakers and mothers with young children. Yet here, too, the worst features of the system can be remedied—for example, by postponing the sale of the family home until children are grown.

some solutions to the problems.

Moralistic cries about declining families and eroding values hinder public discussion about the kinds of modifications that can be made in other social institutions to alleviate current strains in family life. Framing the issue in terms of "the declining family" also leads to an overemphasis on personal and moral failings as the source of family and social problems, and draws attention away from the social sources of family change that have been discussed throughout [my research]: the economic and demographic factors that have drawn women into the workplace, the life-course revolutions that have reshaped families as well as the processes of growing up and growing old, and so on. The popularity of recent critiques of individualism reflects a strong American tradition of blaming serious social problems on individual moral character rather than on institutions and economic structures. For example, there was a tendency in the early 1930s—given voice by F. Scott Fitzgerald—to blame the Great Depression on the hedonism and immorality of the jazz age.

Without an economic catastrophe or government takeover by religious extremists, as in *The Handmaid's Tale*, women are not going to return to full-time domesticity, and unhappy couples will seek to remedy their unhappiness through divorce. Most people no longer feel there is a conflict between the family and the feminist search for equality. We need less hand wringing and more social ingenuity to help the families we do have work better. As E. J. Dionne has recently suggested, the American public is ready for a new "center" that makes peace between the liberal values of the 1960s and the work and family values of the 1980s.[3]

Individualism versus Attachment

It is not clear why social scientists have become so much more pessimistic than they used to be. The deepening gloom does not correspond to marked shifts in demographic trends. In the 1980s, for example, such vital indicators of family life as divorce rates and birthrates, which had changed sharply in the 1970s, leveled off. Toward the end of the 1980s, new births reached baby-boom levels, confounding the expectations of demographers. As a 1990 review of trends in family life put it, "Predictions of childlessness and large-scale abandonment of family life for this generation, a generation supposedly obsessed with individual fulfillment and achievement, will not be realized."[4]

Some family scholars may have been reacting against their overly optimistic assessments of family change in the 1970s. Responding to alarm about the impending "death of the family," many researchers, pointing to demographic and survey evidence of persisting commitments to family life, argued that the family was "here to stay." Emphasizing the benefits of recent trends—more freedom from the constraints of sex roles, greater opportunities for women, closer and more satisfying marriages—they tended to downplay the costs and hardships that come with changes. As if to compensate for that optimism, in the 1980s they stressed the negative.

But family scholars in recent years also seem to have been influenced by the pessimistic views of American character and culture that began to dominate intellectual discourse in the mid-1970s. The landmark work in this genre during the 1980s was the widely acclaimed, widely discussed, best-selling book *Habits of the Heart,* by Robert Bellah and his colleagues. Six years after *The Culture of Narcissism,* this new work continued the critique of individualism that had become prominent in the 1970s. . . .

Speaking to widely shared anxieties about social and cultural change, the book has played a surprisingly large role in the newly pessimistic discourse about the family on the part of social scientists. It is not uncommon to find works presenting hard statistical data on family trends that cite *Habits of the Heart* as evidence for a corrosive new individualism that can explain the trends. . . .

The fact that these recent attacks on individualism strike such responsive chords in the American public suggests that moral and communitarian values are alive and well. American culture has always been marked by an ambivalent yearning for autonomy on the one hand and attachment to family and community on the other.[5] It is not simply that Americans are individualistic or communitarian, but that the tension between these impulses is a central theme in American culture. Yet most writings on American character ignore this duality and the psychological and social tensions it creates. And aiming criticism at personal and moral failings not only is in keeping with American religiosity—we are the most religious of Western countries,[6] in both belief and churchgoing—but promises that we can solve our problems through changes of heart rather than through the difficult and divisive route of political and social change. But the problems of family life are located less in the realm of personal defects and declining values and more in the difficulties of making and maintaining families in a time of sweeping social change, in a society that is neglectful of families and their needs.

The most recent extended argument for the decline of the family from a family scholar has been put forth by David Popenoe. Popenoe is precise about what he means by "family decline." Since the 1960s, he argues, four major trends have signaled a "flight" from the traditional nuclear family as both ideal and reality: declining birthrates, the sexual revolution, the movement of mothers into the workplace, and the divorce revolution. Citing *Habits of the Heart*, Popenoe suggests that the trends toward expressive individualism and the therapeutic attitude have contributed to family decline. He is also precise about what he means by "traditional nuclear family": it is "focused on the procreation of children" and consists of "a legal, lifelong, sexually exclusive, heterosexual, monogamous marriage, based on affection and companionship, in which there is a sharp division of labor (separate spheres) *with the female as full-time housewife and the male as primary provider and ultimate authority*" (italics added).[7]

Def- of trad. nuclear family

Popenoe's argument illustrates that the debate over the declining family is often not so much about the decline of family life as about preference for a particular pattern of family and gender arrangements. He is certainly correct in claiming that what he defines as the traditional nuclear family is no longer dominant. Yet his definition is an essentially nineteenth-century portrait of family and gender roles, today favored by conservatives and the New Right but no longer shared by a majority of Americans. Clearly, the two-worker nuclear family is becoming the new cultural norm, and, while most people describe themselves as strongly pro-family, they favor a more symmetrical version of marriage.

Traditionalists like Popenoe place too much emphasis on family structure and not enough on the emotional quality of family life. Structural characteristics like divorce or maternal employment, as another researcher observes, "are weak predictors of the consequences most of us really care about: personal and family well-being, economic mobility, educational attainment, children's health."[8] . . .

Beyond Nostalgia and Moral Panic

How, then, can we make sense of the shifts in family life over the past several decades? We need a more complex and historically grounded account of the changes than we now have. The central argument I am advancing here is that the key to understanding the recent changes is not to be found in moral decay or in some deep flaw in the American character. Rather, because of the demographic, economic, and social changes that have transformed America and other advanced industrial countries in the twentieth century, we confront unprecedented circumstances. We live in a world unique in human history, a world our ancestors could hardly have imagined.

changes in the family based on shifts in society, not a moral decline

These changes have altered basic aspects of the human condition—from the facts of life and death, to the length and stages of the individual life course, to the kind of work we do, to the way we think and feel. The changes in our hearts and minds are responses to large-scale social change, rather than a fall from moral grace. Thus, family arrangements that made sense in 1800 or 1900 or even 1950 have little relevance for how we live today.

This is not the first time Americans have had to come to grips with unsettling new realities. As the historian Page Smith points out, "future shock" has been part of the American experience since the Pilgrims landed.[9] Yet in certain eras in our history, future shock has imposed a greater than usual strain on American consciousness. In such times, rapid and far reaching economic and social change has ushered in a period of cultural confusion and personal stress; there has been an uncomfortable mismatch between cultural norms and images and the ways people are actually living their lives.[10] These dislocations show up early in the family, as the behavior of large numbers of husbands and wives, parents and children, departs from expectations.

Sources of Social Transformation

The changes in larger society, as well as their reverberations in the family, call into question basic assumptions about the nature of American society, its family arrangements, and Americans themselves. A "cultural struggle" ensues as people debate the meaning of change.[11] One of these periods of cultural upheaval occurred in the early decades of the nineteenth century; a second occurred in the decades just before and after the turn of the twentieth century. For the last thirty years, we have been living through another such wave of social change.

Three related structural changes seem to have set the current cycle of family change in motion: first, the shift into a "postindustrial" information and service economy; second, a demographic revolution that not only created mass longevity but reshaped the individual and family life course, creating life stages and circumstances unknown to earlier generations; third, a process I call "psychological gentrification," which involves an introspective approach to experience, a greater sense of one's own individuality and subjectivity, a concern with self-fulfillment and self-development. This is the change misdiagnosed as narcissism.

The Postindustrial Revolution

To most Americans, the "traditional" family consists of a breadwinner-father and a mother who stays home to care for the children and the household. When New Right politicians and preachers speak of the biblical, Christian, or Judeo-Christian family, this is the family pattern they have in mind.[12] Yet in historical and international perspective, the breadwinner/housewife form of family is, as the sociologist Kingsley Davis observes, an uncommon and short-lived arrangement—an "aberration that arose in a particular stage of development and tends to recur in countries now undergoing development."[13]

The breadwinner family is actually the first form of the modern family, associated with the early stages of the Industrial Revolution. For most of human history, work was a household enterprise in which all family members took part. The shift of the workplace from the home that came with industry had a profound effect on gender as well as on parent and child roles.

If the early stages of modernization helped to create the breadwinner/housewife family, the later stages helped to undo it. Davis has tracked the rise and fall of the breadwinner system in the United States and other countries at various stages of industrialism. With the onset of industrialization, the new family pattern develops slowly, eventually reaching a climax in which few wives are employed, then declines as a steadily growing number of married women find white-collar jobs as file clerks, secretaries, teachers, and the like. In America, the breadwinner system peaked in 1890.

Since 1945 the United States, along with other highly advanced societies, has been shifting from a goods-producing to a service-producing economy, from the factory to the office, from blue-collar work to white-collar work. The term "postindustrial society" is often used to describe this shift. Yet, as a number of writers have suggested, the changes seem more a continuation of industrial society—a high-tech era based on an increasingly complex division of labor, the further application of science and technology to increase productivity. If the steam engine, the steel plant, and the automobile assembly line symbolize the old order, the computer, VCR, satellite broadcasting, CAT scanners, and genetic engineering symbolize the new.[14] One could also argue that the invention of the typewriter marks the onset of the postindustrial era, symbolizing the beginning of the service and information economy and the coming feminization of the work force.

The historical shift of women into the workplace has been going on for a century, but did not reach a critical mass until the 1970s. The long-term impact of postindustrialism on family life was magnified by the effects of inflation. The shift in the economy was reducing the number of high-paying blue-collar jobs for auto and steel workers, and creating a demand for the low-paying pink-collar jobs like typist and file clerk. Also, since the mid-1960s, the costs of food, housing, education, and other goods and services have risen faster than the average male breadwinner's income. Despite their lower pay, married women's contributions to the family income became critical to maintaining living standards in both middle- and working-class families.

It was this quiet revolution of women's steady march into the workplace that set the stage for the feminist revival of the 1970s. There is no evidence that feminist ideas led the mass of married women to work in the first place.[15] Nevertheless, the impact of both the feminist movement and the new realities of working women has shifted the cultural ideal of marriage in a more egalitarian or symmetrical direction. At the moment, we are in a painful period of "cultural lag"[16] or "stalled revolution."[17] Women have changed, but social arrangements—and men—have not kept pace.

The postindustrial shift of women into the workplace has led to other changes in family life: it has increased the "opportunity costs" of pregnancy and child rearing—that is, the money lost when women leave their jobs to bear and raise children—fostering lower fertility rates. There is also some evidence that the increasing employment of women makes divorce more likely, by reducing a woman's dependence on her husband's income, making it easier for her to leave an unhappy marriage.[18]

Finally, the shift to a service and information economy has had effects on family life besides those linked to gender. For young people, the coming of the postindustrial society has made adolescence and the transition to adult-hood more complex and problematic, exacerbating a dilemma that arose in the nineteenth century with the decline of the family economy. A greater amount of schooling is now necessary not only to maintain middle-class sta-tus but even to find jobs in the manufacturing sector. Until the 1970s, there was a supply of moderately well-paying jobs that did not require a high school diploma. High school graduates could find an array of decent jobs open to them. More schooling was necessary for a middle-class career, but there were alternative paths to making a living.

The high-tech postindustrial economy has changed all that. Today all roads to a successful livelihood lead through the classroom. Recent decades have seen a plummeting demand for unskilled labor and a sharp decline in the kind of well-paying blue-collar job that used to form the backbone of the American economy. A young working-class man who in the 1950s could have found an unskilled job paying enough to support a family now faces radi-cally curtailed economic prospects. These vast changes in the economy led to shifts in family behavior that paralleled those due to cultural change—later marriage, lower fertility, women flooding into the workplace. For many peo-ple, these choices reflected economic pressures, not new values.

The Life-Course Revolution

The breadwinner/housewife family was a response not only to nineteenth-century working conditions but to nineteenth-century demographic circum-stances. Because people lived shorter lives and had more children, a woman could expect to live her entire life with children in the home. Today, the av-erage woman can expect to live more than thirty-three years after her last child has left the house. The traditional nuclear unit of parents and small chil-dren exists for only a small proportion of the life of an individual or a family. Shifts in the length and patterning of the life course have made the conditions of modern existence unimaginably different from those that existed only a century ago.

Nostalgic images of family stability in past times typically leave out the terrible facts of high mortality rates in infancy and early adulthood. Before the twentieth century, death was as much a hovering presence in the home as divorce is today. While the death of a baby or small child was almost a typ-ical experience of parents down to the early decades of the twentieth century, the loss of a father or mother was also a common event of childhood and ado-lescence. The biography of almost any Victorian conveys the vulnerability of even the upper classes to untimely death.

In historical perspective, these changes have been remarkably sudden. Only in the twentieth century could a majority of people expect to live out the normal life course of growing up, marrying, having children, and surviving with one's spouse until age fifty.[19] The changes in life chances between the 1920s and the 1950s have been as rapid as in the years between 1880 and 1920.[20]

In advanced societies today, death strikes few youngsters and few adults between their twenties and fifties. Couples in enduring marriages will spend most of their married life together without having young children in the home. The shrinking of the active parental phase of the life course is also one of the reasons women have entered the work force in increasing numbers since the 1950s. Domesticity is not enough to fill a life span of almost eighty years. Little wonder then that marriage has become more of a personal and sexual relationship than it was in the past.

The emergence of old age as an expectable part of the life course is, as Ronald Blyth points out, one of the essential ways we differ from our ancestors; today's elders are among the first generations in which the mass of the population, not just the hardy few, survive long enough to experience the aging process, that "destruction of the physical self" so familiar to us now.[21] People over eighty-five are the fastest-growing age group today. But for much of old age, people are not *old* in the traditional sense but healthy and active.

Our lives have become not just longer but more complicated. Stages of life that scarcely existed a hundred years ago have become part of the average person's experience: adolescence, middle age, empty nest, retirement. Also, in recent years, the life course has grown more fluid; people experience more transitions than earlier generations did, not just because of rising divorce rates but because of changes in the workplace. In an age of rapidly changing technology and market conditions, few employees can count on being "organization" men or women the way people did in the 1950s.

Ironically, the demographic and social changes that lengthened and reshaped the life course were desired themselves, yet are responsible for some of the major problems besetting family life today. Before mass longevity, the aged were not a problem population because there were so few of them. Mixed-up adolescents were rare when adult work began in childhood and formal education ended, if it ever began, in grade school. Identity was not a problem when a person's place in society was decided at birth. In the past, middle-aged men and women were not sandwiched between the needs of their adolescent children and their aging parents; nor when life expectancy was forty-nine or fifty did they have to confront the issue of what to do with the rest of their lives. Even though the "woman question" was an issue during most of the nineteenth century, women then did not confront the reality that the active phase of mothering would usually involve only a small portion of their lives.

All of this possibility for change created new sources of stress. Transitions can be problematic periods in which both individual identities and family relations have to be redefined and renegotiated. The emergence of a focus on the self and the idea of development as applied to adults is not just a fantasy of pop psychology. The popularity of books like Gail Sheehy's *Passages* reflects genuine changes in the structure of individual experience across the life course.[22] The emergence of a heightened sense of self is a natural by-product of this more complicated life course.

Psychological Gentrification

The third major transformation is in part a product of the changes in the nature of work and in the shape of the life course. But it is also a product of other social and cultural changes, especially rising levels of education and increases in the standard of living and leisure time. In the past, few jobs required learning or personal development. Working hours were long—about fifty-three hours a week at the turn of the century—and there was little time for leisure or extended vacations. Thus men's lives were dominated by the job; women's, by domesticity.

The affluent, postindustrial society of the postwar era involved more than an increase in living standards. Despite persisting inequality, the decades since the end of World War II were years of remarkable progress for masses of Americans. The democratization that began in the 1940s when the G.I. Bill opened up educational opportunity and the possibilities of home ownership eventually led to "the democratization of personhood" —the opportunity for large numbers of ordinary people to "take themselves seriously . . . to make a sustained project of the ordinary self."[23]

At a time when jeremiads about the decline of the American mind appear on the best-seller lists, it is easy to forget that during the postwar decades higher education became a reality for the first time to millions of Americans. In 1940 only 15 percent of young people between eighteen and twenty-two went to college; a college education was one of those rarely crossed boundaries separating the upper middle class from those below them. By the middle of the 1960s nearly half of young Americans went to college. By the end of the decade the number of college students was four times what it had been in the 1940s.[24]

The explosion of education was due not only to the demand of a new middle class for what it saw as key to success for its children; it was also due to the need of a postindustrial economy for a more educated work force. However pragmatic and instrumental the motivation for increased education, rising educational levels have had a profound influence on American culture. Middle-class Americans became, as the sociologist Todd Gitlin observes, "cultural omnivores," traveling abroad, going to concerts, museums, and theaters, joining book clubs, in growing numbers.[25] Everyday life in America has become "internationalized," as Americans become more familiar with and appreciative of other cultures. "We have grown from a nation of meat-and-potato eaters to a nation of sushi samplers," observes Walter Mead, "and we like it that way."[26]

Another result of this increasing cosmopolitanism is that avant-garde ideas that had once shocked the bourgeoisie in earlier generations, from cubist painting to bohemian sexual mores to Freudian psychology, diffused to college students in the 1960s and then to the middle-class masses in the 1970s. This diffusion can be clearly seen in the comparison of the results of national surveys conducted in 1957 and 1976 by the University of Michigan's Institute of Social Research. Aimed at assessing the state of American mental health, the studies delved into a wide range of questions concerning satisfactions and dissatisfactions with self, family relations, and work.

Comparisons of the two surveys reveal striking insights into the recent changes in American culture. In *The Inner American*, Joseph Veroff, Elizabeth Douvan, and Richard Kulka suggest that a "psychological revolution" took place between 1957 and 1976. Over the course of two decades, Americans had become more introspective, more attentive to inner experience, more willing to admit to marital and personal problems than in the past, and yet more satisfied with their marriages. Above all, they became more attentive to the emotional quality of relationships, not just in the family but at work as well. Increasingly, people wanted friendly, warm relationships at work and intimacy and closeness in the family.[27]

Paradoxically, the new emphasis on warmth and intimacy can place new burdens on family relationships and create discontents that didn't exist when family life was a matter of conformity to social roles and rituals. But the results of this study, carried out at the height of the so-called Me Decade, show no evidence that we have become a nation of narcissistic, unattached individuals. Family ties were shown to be even more important than in the past, especially for men. Despite high divorce rates and a willingness to admit marital problems, the study found an overwhelming preference for being married, and many more men and women were happy about their marriages than they had been in 1957.[28]

The Michigan studies provide clear documentation for the process of psychological gentrification. The habit of introspection, the psychological approach to life and preoccupation with warmth and intimacy, was not new in the 1970s. In the 1950s, however, it was found almost exclusively among the most highly educated. Twenty years later this way of looking at the self and the world had become "common coin."[29]

Conclusion

As a result of all the changes I discussed in this chapter, the realities of life in late-twentieth-century America and other advanced societies are unlike those faced by any earlier generation. No other people ever lived longer or healthier lives, or exercised so much choice about life's central dramas: work, marriage, parenthood. Many of the troubles and anxieties confronting the American family today arise out of benefits few of us would undo if we could—lower mortality rates, reliable birth control, mass education, the democratization of American life.

The metaphor of an earthquake, often invoked to describe the social and cultural upheavals of the 1960s and 1970s, turns out to be a fairly good model of what actually did happen during those years. No other natural cataclysm— hurricanes, tornadoes, floods—strikes less randomly than earthquakes; they occur at fairly regular intervals, along clearly detectable fault lines.

The seismic forces at work in the social and cultural earthquake were, on the one side, locked-in cultural norms about family structure, gender roles, and sexuality and, on the other, a set of long-term changes that include the demographic, economic, and structural trends I have discussed. For example, the sexual revolution of the 1960s was also a product of a long trend away from Victorian sexual restrictions; premarital sex had been increasing gradually since the early decades of the twentieth century. As a result of these trends, social reality was increasingly at odds with the prevailing assumptions that "all brides are virgins, all marriages are first marriages, all wives are housewives."

The reality of everyday experience was at odds not only with the rigidity of middle-class norms but also with the cultural images of family happiness that were supposed to result from holding on to those norms. All during the silent 1950s, these discontents were simmering below the surface. In the 1960s and 1970s the upheavals of the Vietnam War and racial tensions called established cultural norms into question. Pressure continued to build up along the fault line, the trends reaching what the sociologist Jessie Bernard calls "tipping points."[30] Behavior that had formerly been practiced only by a minority approached, or became, majority behavior. In a time of political turbulence, the two sides of the fault line jolted apart. We are still digging out of the rubble, but there is no way of going back to where we were before.

ENDNOTES

1. See Joseph Featherstone, "Family Matters," *Harvard Educational Review* 49 (1979): 20–52.
2. See Edward L. Kain, *The Myth of Family Decline: Understanding Families in a World of Rapid Social Change* (Lexington, MA: Lexington Books, 1990); Norval D. Glenn, "Continuity vs. Change, Sanguineness vs. Concern: Views of the American Family in the Late 1980s," *Journal of Family Issues* 8(4) (1987): 348–54; and Graham Spanier, "Bequeathing Family Continuity," *Journal of Marriage and the Family* 51 (February 1989): 3–13.
3. E. J. Dionne, 1991.
4. Suzanne M. Bianchi, "America's Children: Mixed Prospects," *Population Bulletin* 45(1) (1990).
5. Rupert Wilkinson, *The Pursuit of American Character* (New York: Harper & Row, 1988); and John P. Hewitt, *Dilemmas of the American Self* (Philadelphia: Temple University Press, 1989).
6. Seymour Martin Lipset, "Failures of Extremism," *Transaction/Society* 20(1) (1982): 48–58.
7. See David Popenoe, *Disturbing the Nest: Family Change and Decline in Modern Societies* (New York: Aldine de Gruyter, 1988/1989), p. 1.
8. See Dennis K. Orthner, "The Family in Transition," in *Rebuilding the Nest: A New Commitment to the American Family,* ed. David Blankenhorn, Steven Bayme, and Jean Bethke Elshtain (Milwaukee: Family Service America, 1990), p. 34.
9. Carroll Smith-Rosenberg, *Disorderly Conduct: Visions of Gender in Victorian America* (New York: Knopf, 1985).
10. William McLoughlin, *Revivals, Awakenings, and Reform* (Chicago: University of Chicago Press, 1978).
11. This discussion is based on McLoughlin, *Revivals, Awakenings, and Reform;* Neil J. Smelser and Sydney Halpern, "The Historical Triangulation of Family, Economy,

and Education," *American Journal of Sociology* 84 (1978); and Smith-Rosenberg, *Disorderly Conduct.*

12. James Davison Hunter, *Evangelicalism: The Coming Generation* (Chicago: University of Chicago Press, 1987).
13. See Kingsley Davis, "Wives and Work: A Theory of the Sex-Role Revolution and Its Consequences," in *Feminism, Children, and the New Families,* ed. Sanford M. Dornbusch and Myra H. Strober (New York: Guilford Press, 1988), p. 74.
14. Raymond Williams, *The Long Revolution* (New York: Columbia University Press, 1961).
15. Maxine L. Margolis, *Mothers and Such: Views of American Women and Why They Changed* (Berkeley: University of California Press, 1984).
16. William F. Ogburn, *Social Change* (New York: Viking Press, 1950).
17. Arlie Hochschild with Anne Machung, *The Second Shift: Working Parents and the Revolution at Home* (New York: Viking/Penguin, 1989).
18. G. C. Kitson, K. B. Babri, and M. J. Roach, "Who Divorces and Why: A Review," *Journal of Family Issues* 6(3) (1985): 255–93.
19. Peter Uhlenberg, "Death and the Family," *Journal of Family History* 5(3) (1980): 313–20.
20. See Robert V. Wells, *Revolutions in Americans' Lives: A Demographic Perspective on the History of Americans, Their Families, Their Society* (Westport, CT: Greenwood Press, 1982), p. 221.
21. Ronald Blythe, *The View in Winter* (New York: Harcourt Brace Jovanovich, 1979).
22. Gail Sheehy, *Passages* (New York: Bantam Books, 1976).
23. Peter Clecak, *America's Quest for the Ideal Self: Dissent and Fulfillment in the 60's and 70's* (New York: Oxford University Press, 1983).
24. William H. Chafe, *The Unfinished Journey: America since World War II* (New York: Oxford University Press, 1986).
25. Todd Gitlin, *The Sixties: Years of Hope, Days of Rage* (New York: Bantam Books, 1987).
26. See Walter Russell Mead, *Mortal Splendor: The American Empire in Transition* (Boston: Houghton Mifflin, 1987), p. 181.
27. J. Veroff, G. Douvan, and R. A. Kulka, *The Inner American: A Self-Portrait from 1957–1976* (New York: Basic Books, 1981).
28. Ibid., p. 24.
29. Ibid., p. 25.
30. Jessie Bernard, "Adolescence and the Socialization for Motherhood," in *Adolescence and the Life Cycle,* ed. S. E. Dragastin and G. H. Elder (New York: Wiley, 1975), pp. 227–52.

PART II

Historical Changes
and Family Variations

In this section, we examine the diverse history of American families and the variety of family forms and experiences that have occurred across cultural groups. The study of the history of the family is important in order to understand the contemporary family. Remember the argument from Part I that there is no one universal family form; instead, the family is socially constructed. The historical study of the family helps us to see how the family is socially constructed over time and across different cultures. Moreover, it enables us to deconstruct notions of the white, middle-class family as the dominant family form. By examining diverse family forms, including those of different racial-ethnic, cultural, and social class groups, we begin to understand the plurality of families that have historically coexisted and still coexist within the United States today. Thus, the study of family history shows that family forms and experiences vary distinctively between groups, and that many myths and assumptions we hold about families are historically inaccurate. Finally, studying the history of the family helps us to understand how the institution of the family is shaped by other institutions, including the economy, law, politics, and religion.

Tamara K. Hareven, a historian of the family, has argued that recent historical research on the family has challenged some myths and generalizations about family life and society. But the current work of doing historical research is much more complicated due to a recognition that families, themselves, are continually changing. She states:

> Contemporary historians of the family have sought to reintroduce human experience into historical research and to emphasize the complexity of historical change. The challenge for such scholars is the reconstruction of a multi-tiered reality — the lives of individual families and their interactions with major social, economic, and political forces. This enterprise is complicated by our increasing appreciation of the changing and diverse nature of "the family," rendered fluid by shifts in internal age and gender configurations across regions and over time. The formidable goal is to understand the family in various contexts of change, while allowing the levels of complexity to play themselves out at different points in historical time. In short, it represents an effort to understand the interrelationship between individual time, family time, and historical time. (Hareven 1994:13–14)

Thus, Hareven argues that contemporary historians must be aware of not only the microexperience of interactions within families, but also the macroexperience of how families are being shaped by other social, economic, and political forces. This research is challenging because the family is continually in flux based on changes both internal and external to the institution.

The challenge of studying the diversity of family history is addressed in the first reading in this section, "Historical Perspectives on Family Diversity," by Stephanie Coontz. Coontz is a social historian at Evergreen State College in Olympia, Washington, and she has written several books on the social history of the American family, including *The Way We Never Were: American Families and the Nostalgia Trap* (1992) and *The Way We Really Are: Coming to Terms with America's Changing Families* (1997). In both books, Coontz shatters many of the myths we have about families. The selection included here continues her use of history to challenge myths and misconceptions about family diversity in Europe and in the United States. Similar to Diana Gittins (see Reading 1), Coontz argues that there is no universal definition of family. Instead, there are many different historical definitions of family, and the experience of family varies greatly in different societies and time periods. Thus, not only do the forms and definition of family vary over time and across cultures, but so do the emotional meanings attached to families. In this selection, Coontz focuses her analysis primarily on the diversity of American families, including Native American families, African American slave families, Mexican and Chicano families, and the families of European immigrants.

One important theme of Coontz's article is her linking of family history to the history of economic systems. That is, in any given time period, the economy shapes the institution of the family, and as the institution of the economy changes, the institution of the family also changes. Thus, as societies move from subsistence economies, to agrarian economies, to early industrialization, to global capitalism, the family is forced to adapt to and to accommodate changes in economic incentives and structures. Family scholars continually ask: How is the economy affecting the family? How does capitalism shape the family? Historical analysis helps us to understand this interrelationship between the economy and the family. For example, while historically the family was a site for both production and consumption, today, both the productive and reproductive labor done within families has changed. The family not only is shaped by who is in the paid workforce, but it also serves as a site for consumerism. As the next reading shows, this historical relationship between the economy and the family is central to the diversity of forms and experiences of African American families.

African American Families

The second reading in this section, "Interpreting the African Heritage in Afro-American Family Organization," by Niara Sudarkasa, builds on many arguments made by Coontz in the first reading. Sudarkasa is a professor of anthropology and currently the president of Lincoln University in Pennsylvania. She has published extensively on women, trade, and family organization among the Yoruba of Nigeria and other parts of Africa. In this selection,

Sudarkasa also echoes Diana Gittins' argument about the incorrect assumption that there is a universal family. There is no one ideal family form that explains family variation across racial-ethnic and social class lines in the United States. Sudarkasa argues that in order to understand contemporary African American families, scholars must examine both the historical legacy of slavery and the cultural traditions brought from Africa. One important distinction between the historical influences that African and European heritages have on the institution of the family is that whereas European families emphasize affinal ties, especially conjugal (marriage) relationships, African families emphasize consanguineal (parent–child) relationships. These differences continue to affect family arrangements in the United States.

Mexican American Families

The third reading in this section, "*La Familia:* Family Cohesion among Mexican American Families in the Urban Southwest, 1848–1900," is by Richard Griswold del Castillo, a professor of Mexican American Studies at San Diego University. Griswold del Castillo wrote this essay as one of a series of chapters for his book *La Familia: Chicano Families in the Urban Southwest, 1848 to the Present* (1984). For this essay, Griswold del Castillo used historical statistics to study extended-family formation as an expression of family solidarity. Trained as a humanist scholar at UCLA in the 1960s, he became fascinated with computer analyses of historical data, spending long hours at his terminal trying to figure out statistical methods. Griswold del Castillo became convinced that illustrating historical trends with quantitative data was useful only if the user was sophisticated about levels of significance and tests of association. Thus, this reading demonstrates some of the limitations of using census data to study family patterns. It also demonstrates the application of sociological theory about families, especially life course analysis, to a historical era. By coincidence, Griswold del Castillo finds that his own personal life has followed virtually the same patterns he discerned for Mexican Americans in the 19th century—he now lives in a family that any census taker would consider to be extended, but that is, in fact, a stepfamily.

Chinese American Families

The fourth reading in this section extends our understanding of racial ethnic diversity by examining Chinese American families. The reading, "Split Household, Small Producer, and Dual Wage Earner: An Analysis of Chinese American Family Strategies," is by Evelyn Nakano Glenn. A professor of womens studies at the University of California at Berkeley, Glenn has studied Asian American families for over 25 years. Building on Hareven's arguments mentioned earlier, Glenn utilizes a macroperspective to challenge cultural analyses of Chinese American families. Glenn argues that, instead of utilizing a cultural approach, one needs to use an institutional approach to better understand the historical realities of Chinese American family life. In particular, Glenn states that "a fuller understanding of the Chinese American family must begin with an examination of the changing constellation of economic, legal, and political constraints that have shaped the Chinese experience in America." She argues that these constraints have shaped Chinese family life and have led Chinese Americans to create a number of family strategies that have enabled them to survive as immigrants in the United States. Thus, this selection is similar to Niara Sudarkasa's (Reading 6) in challenging Eurocentric analyses of family. It also builds on Stephanie Coontz's (Reading 5) arguments about how the economy and other social institutions shape the family.

REFERENCES

Coontz, Stephanie. 1992. *The Way We Never Were: American Families and the Nostalgia Trap*. New York: Basic Books.
————. 1997. *The Way We Really Are: Coming to Terms with America's Changing Families*. New York: Basic Books.
Griswold del Castillo, Richard. 1984. *La Familia: Chicano Families in the Urban Southwest, 1848 to the Present*. Notre Dame, IN: University of Notre Dame Press.
Hareven, Tamara K. 1994. "Recent Research on the History of the Family." Pp. 13–43 in *Time, Family and Community: Perspectives on Family and Community History*, edited by Michael Drake. Cambridge, MA: Blackwell.

5

HISTORICAL PERSPECTIVES
ON FAMILY DIVERSITY

STEPHANIE COONTZ

Variability in the European
and American Historical Record

In the ancient Mediterranean world, households and kin groupings were so disparate that no single unit of measurement or definition could encompass them. By the late 14th century, however, the English word *family*, derived from the Latin word for a household including servants or slaves, had emerged to designate all those who lived under the authority of a household head. The family might include a joint patrilocal family, with several brothers and their wives residing together under the authority of the eldest, as was common in parts of Italy and France before 1550, as well as in many Eastern European communities into the 19th century. Or it might be a stem family, in which the eldest son brought his bride into his parents' home upon marriage, and they lived as an extended family until the parents' deaths. The son's family then became nuclear in form, until the eldest son reached the age of marriage. Owing to late marriages and early mortality, most such families would be nuclear at any particular census, but most of them would pass through an extended stage at some point in their life cycle (Berkner 1972; Coontz 1988; Hareven 1987).

Until the early 19th century, most middle-class Europeans and North Americans defined *family* on the basis of a common residence under the authority of a household head, rather than on blood relatedness. This definition thus frequently included boarders or servants. Samuel Pepys began his famous 17th-century English diary with the words: "I lived in Axe Yard, having my wife, and servant Jane, and no more in family than us three." In 1820 the publisher Everard Peck and his wife, of Rochester, New York, childless newlyweds, wrote home: "We collected our family together which consists of seven persons and we think ourselves pleasantly situated" (Coontz 1988; Hareven 1987).

Among the European nobility, an alternative definition of family referred not to the parent–child grouping, but to the larger descent group from which claims to privilege and property derived. Starting in the late 17th century, other writers used the word to refer exclusively to a man's offspring, as in the phrase *his family and wife*. Not until the 19th century did the word *family* commonly describe a married couple with their coresident children, distinguished from household residents or more distant kin. This definition spread widely during the 1800s. By the end of the 19th century, the restriction of the word to the immediate, coresidential family was so prevalent that the adjective *extended* had to be added when people wished to refer to kin beyond the household (Williams 1976).

Diversity in Emotional and Sexual Arrangements

. . . [Family diversity extends] not just to forms and definitions, but to the emotional meanings attached to families and the psychological dynamics within them. Whereas 17th-century Mediterranean families were organized around the principle of honor, which rested largely on the chastity of the family's women, other groups did not traditionally distinguish between "legitimate" and "illegitimate" children. When Jesuit missionaries told a Montagnais-Naskapi Indian that he should keep tighter control over his wife to ensure that the children she bore were "his," the man replied: "Thou hast no sense. You French people love only your own children; but we love all the children of our tribe" (Leacock 1980: 31; see also Gutierrez 1991).

What is considered healthy parent–child bonding in our society may be seen as selfishness or pathological isolation by cultures that stress the exchange and fostering of children as ways of cementing social ties. The Zinacantecos of southern Mexico do not even have a word to distinguish the parent–child relationship from the house, suggesting that the emotional saliency of the cooperating household unit is stronger than that of blood ties per se. In Polynesia, eastern Oceania, the Caribbean, and the West Indies (and in 16th-century Europe), to offer your child to friends, neighbors, or other kin for adoption or prolonged coresidence was not considered abandonment but a mark of parental love and community reciprocity (Collier, Rosaldo, and Yanigasako 1982; Peterson 1993; Stack 1993).

Modern Americans stress the need for mother–daughter and father–son identification, but in matrilineal societies, where descent is reckoned in the female line, a man usually has much closer ties with his nephews than with his sons. Among the Trobriand Islanders, for instance, a child's biological father is considered merely a relation by marriage. The strongest legal and emotional bonds are between children and their maternal uncles. Conversely, among the patrilineal Cheyenne, mother–daughter relations were expected to be tense or even hostile, and girls tended to establish their closest relationships with their paternal aunts (Collier et al. 1982).

What counts as healthy family dynamics or relationships also varies *within* any given society. Research on contemporary families has demonstrated that parenting techniques or marital relationships that are appropriate to middle-class white families are less effective for families that must cope with economic deprivation and racial prejudice (Baumrind 1972; Boyd-Franklin and Garcia-Preto 1994; Knight, Virdin, and Roosa 1994).

Values about the proper roles and concerns of mothers and fathers differ as well. Today women tend to be in charge of family rituals, such as weddings and funerals. In colonial days, however, this was a father's responsibility, while economic activities were far more central to a colonial woman's identity (and occupied much more of her time) than was child rearing. Contemporary American thought posits an inherent conflict between mothering and paid work, but breadwinning is an integral part of the definition of mothering in many cultural traditions. One study found that "traditional" Mexicanas in the United States experience *less* conflict or guilt in integrating the worlds of home and paid employment than do their Chicana counterparts who have internalized the notions of good mothering portrayed in the American mass media (Calvert 1992; Gillis 1996).

Even something as seemingly "natural" as sexual behavior and identity shows amazing variation across time and cultures. Categories of gender and sexuality have not always been so rigidly dichotomous as they are in modern Euro-American culture. Among many Native American societies, for instance, the *berdache* has a spiritual, social, economic, and political role that is distinct from either men's or women's roles. Neither he nor the female counterparts found in other Native American groups can be accurately described by the sexual identity we know as homosexual. Similarly, in traditional African culture, a person's sexual identity was not separable from his or her membership and social role in a family group (Herdt 1994; Jeater 1993; Schnarch 1992; Williams 1986).

Ever since the spread of Freudian psychiatric ideas at the beginning of the 20th century, Europeans and North Americans have tended to see a person's sexual behavior as the wellspring or driving force of his or her identity. The ancient Greeks, in contrast, thought that dreams about sex were "really" about politics. Until comparatively recently in history, a person's sexual acts were assumed to be separate from his or her fundamental character or identity. Indeed, the term *homosexual* did not come into use until the end of the 19th century. A person could commit a sexual act with a person of the same sex without being labeled as having a particular sexual "orientation." This lack of interest in identifying people by their sexual practices extended to heterosexual behavior as well. In mid-17th century New England, Samuel Terry was several times convicted for sexual offenses, such as masturbating, in public, but this behavior did not prevent his fellow townspeople from electing him town constable (D'Emilio and Freedman 1988; Padgug 1989).

Since the early 20th century, most American experts on the family have insisted on the importance of heterosexual intimacy between husband and wife in modeling healthy development for children, yet in the 19th century, no one saw any harm in the fact that the closest bonds of middle-class women were with other women, rather than with their husbands. Men were often secondary in women's emotional lives, to judge from the silence or nonchalance about them in women's diaries and letters, which were saturated with expressions of passion that would immediately raise eyebrows by modern standards of sexual categorization. Although the acceptability of such passionate bonds may have provided cover for sexual relations between some women, these bonds were also considered compatible with marriage. Men, too, operated in a different sexual framework than today. They talked matter-of-factly about sleeping with their best friends, embracing them, or laying a head on a male friend's bosom—all without any self-consciousness that their wives or fiancées might misinterpret their "sexual orientation" (Duberman, Vicinus, and Chauncey 1989; Faderman 1981; Rotundo 1993; Smith-Rosenberg 1985). . . .

Families in the Cauldron of Colonization

At the time of European exploration of the New World, Native American families in North America orbited around a mode of social reproduction based on kinship ties and obligations. Kinship provided Native Americans with a system of assigning rights and duties on the basis of a commonly accepted criterion—a person's blood relationship (although this relationship might have been fictive) to a particular set of relatives. Kinship rules and marital alliances regulated an individual's place in the overall production and distribution of each group's dominant articles of subsistence and established set patterns in the individual's interactions with others.

Among groups that depended on hunting and gathering, such as those of the northern woods or Great Basin, marriage and residence rules were flexible and informal. In other Native American societies, typically those that had extensive horticulture, people were grouped into different sections, moieties or phratries, and clans, each of which was associated with different territories, resources, skills, duties, or simply personal characteristics. Exogamy, the requirement that an individual marry out of his or her natal group into a different clan or section, ensured the widest possible social cooperation by making each individual a member of intersecting kin groups, with special obligations to and rights in each category of relatives. Marriage and residence rules also organized the division of labor by age and gender (Coontz 1988; Leacock and Lurie 1971; Spicer 1962).

Unlike a state system, which makes sharp distinctions between family duties and civil duties, domestic functions and political ones, North American Native Americans had few institutions (prior to sustained contact with Europeans) that were set up on a basis other than kinship. Some groups, such as the Cherokee, might have had a special governing body for times of war, and the influence of such groups was invariably strengthened once Native Americans engaged in regular conflicts with settlers, but most of the time village elders made decisions. There was no opposition between domestic or "private" functions and political or public ones. North American Native Americans had no institutionalized courts, police, army, or other agencies to tax or coerce labor. Kin obligations organized production, distributed surplus products, and administered justice. Murder, for example, was an offense not against the state but against the kin group, and, therefore, it was the responsibility and right of kin to punish the perpetrator. To involve strangers in this punishment, as modern state judicial systems deem best, would have escalated the number of groups and individuals involved in the conflict (Anderson 1991; Coontz 1988).

The nuclear family was not a property-holding unit, since resources and land were either available to all or were held by the larger kin corporation, while subsistence tools and their products were made and owned by individuals, rather than families. Its lack of private property meant that the nuclear family had less economic autonomy vis-á-vis other families than did European households. The lack of a state, on the other hand, gave Native American families more political autonomy because people were not bound to follow a leader for any longer than they cared to do so. However, this political autonomy did not seem to create a sense of exclusive attachment to one's "own" nuclear family. The nuclear family was only one of many overlapping ties through which individuals were linked. It had almost no functions that were not shared by other social groupings (Leacock and Lurie 1971; Spicer 1962).

Native American kinship systems created their own characteristic forms of diversity. North American Indians spoke more than 200 languages and lived in some 600 different societies with a wide variety of residence, marital, and genealogical rules. Among nomadic foragers, residence rules were flexible and descent was seldom traced far back. Horizontal ties of marriage and friendship were more important in organizing daily life than were vertical ties of descent. More settled groups tended to have more extensive lineage systems, in which rights and obligations were traced through either the female or the male line of descent. Most of the Great Plains and prairie Indians were patrilineal; matrilineal descent was common among many East Coast groups; the Creeks, Choctaws, and Seminoles of the South; and the Hopi, Acoma, and Zuni groups of the Southwest (Axtell 1981, 1988; Catlin 1973; Coontz 1988; Gutierrez 1991; Leacock and Lurie 1971; Mindel, Habenstein, and Wright 1988; Peters 1995; Snipp 1989).

Native American family systems produced land-use and fertility patterns that helped maintain the abundance of game and forests that made the land so attractive to European settlers. But they also made the Native Americans vulnerable to diseases brought by the Europeans and their animals, as well as to the Europeans' more aggressive and coordinated methods of warfare or political expansion (Axtell 1985, 1988; Cronon 1983).

The impact of European colonization on Native American family systems was devastating. Massive epidemics, sometimes killing 60%–90% of a group's members, devastated kin networks and hence disrupted social continuity. Heightened warfare elevated the role of young male leaders at the expense of elders and women. In most cases, the influence of traders, colonial political officials, and Christian missionaries fostered the nuclear family's growing independence from the extended household, kinship, and community group in which it had traditionally been embedded. In other instances, as with Handsome Lake's revival movement among the Iroquois, Native Americans attempted to adapt European family systems and religious values to their own needs. Either way, gender and age relations were often transformed, while many Native American groups were either exterminated or driven onto marginal land that did not support traditional methods of social organization and subsistence. Native American collective traditions, however, were surprisingly resilient, and Euro-Americans spent the entire 19th century trying to extinguish them (Adams 1995; Anderson 1991; Calloway 1997; Coontz 1988; Mindel et al. 1988; Peters 1995).

The European families that came to North America were products of an international mercantile system whose organizing principles of production, exchange, ownership, and land use were on a collision course with indigenous patterns of existence. Europeans also had the support of a centralized state apparatus whose claims to political authority and notion of national interests had no counterweight among Native Americans. Colonial families had far more extensive property and inheritance rights than did Native American families, but they were also subjected to far more stringent controls by state and church institutions. The redistribution duties of wealthy families, however, were much more limited than those of Native Americans, so there were substantial differences in wealth and resources among colonial families, with the partial exception of those in the New England colonies right from the beginning (Coontz 1988; Mintz and Kellogg 1988).

These features of colonial society led to a different kind of family diversity than that among Native Americans. In addition to differences connected to the national, class, and religious origins of the settlers, the sex ratio of different colonizing groups, and the type of agriculture or trade they were able to establish, the colonies were also characterized by larger disparities in the wealth and size of households. Poorer colonists tended to concentrate in propertied households as apprentices, servants, or temporary lodgers.

At the same time as European settlers were destroying the Native American kinship system, they were importing an African kinship system, which they also attempted to destroy. But because the colonists depended on African labor, they had to make some accommodations to African culture and to African American adaptations to the requirements of surviving under slavery. The slaves were at once more subject to supervision and manipulation of their families and more able than Native Americans to build new kinship networks and obligations. They adapted African cultural traditions to their new realities, using child-centered, rather than marriage-centered, family systems; fictive kin ties; ritual coparenting or godparenting; and complex naming patterns that were designed to authenticate extended kin connections, all in the service of building kin ties within the interstices of the slave trade and plantation system. But African American families also had their own characteristic forms of diversity, depending on whether they lived in settlements of free blacks, on large plantations with many fellow slaves, or on isolated small farms in the South (Franklin 1997; Gutman 1976; Stevenson 1996).

Slave families were not passive victims of the traffic in human beings nor organized in imitation of or deference to their masters' values. However, they could never be free of the constraints imposed by their white owners. They emerged out of a complex set of struggles and accommodations between both groups. But slaveowners' families were *also* derived from the dialectic of slavery. Anxieties about social control and racial-sexual hierarchies, fears of alliances between blacks and poor whites, and attempts to legitimate slavery in the face of Northern antislavery sentiment created a high tolerance for sexual hypocrisy; pervasive patterns of violence within white society, as well as against slaves; and elaborate rituals of patriarchy, both in family life and in the community at large (Edwards 1991; Isaacs 1982; McCurry 1995; Mullings 1997; Stevenson 1996).

Families in the Early Commercial and Industrializing Economy

From about the 1820s, a new constellation of family systems emerged in the United States, corresponding to the growth of wage labor, a national market economy, and the specialization of many occupations and professions. Merchants, manufacturers, and even many farmers consolidated production and hired employees to work for a set number of hours, rather than purchased supplies or raw materials from independent producers. Such producers, along with the apprentices and journeymen whom wage workers replaced, lost older routes to self-employment or accession to family farms. At the same time, married women's traditional household production was taken over by unmarried girls working in factories.

In an attempt to avoid becoming wage laborers and to find new professions or sources of self-employment for them and their children, a growing number of middle-class families developed a more private nuclear family orientation, keeping their children at home longer instead of sending them away for training or socialization elsewhere. Meanwhile, immigrants from Europe poured into the growing towns to work in factories or tenement workshops, while westward expansion drew new Mexican and Native American groups into the economy. Such trends in the early development of American capitalism reshaped ethnic traditions and class relations and led to the emergence of "whiteness" as a category that European immigrants could use to differentiate themselves from other groups near the bottom of the economic hierarchy (Johnson 1978; Jones 1997; Roediger 1988; Ryan 1981).

The gravitational force that was pulling families into new orbits in this period was the emergence of wage labor in the context of competing older values and an inadequately developed set of formal supporting institutions for capitalist production—schools, credit associations, unions, and even a developed consumer industry. Families who sought to escape wage labor by moving west, setting up small businesses, or trying to compete with factory-made goods through household production were just as surely affected by the progress of capitalism as were families who either owned or had to work

in the larger workshops and factories that increasingly supplanted appren-
ticeship arrangements in separate households or farms. At the same time, few
families could yet free themselves from some reliance on household production or community sponsorship and social ties.

The gradual separation of work and home—market production and
household reproduction—created new tensions between family activities and
"economic" ones. Households could no longer get by primarily on things they
made, grew, or bartered. However, they could not yet rely on ready-made
purchased goods. Even in middle-class homes, the labor required to make purchased goods usable by the families was immense (Strasser 1982).

These competing gravitational pulls produced a new division of labor
among middle-class families and many workers. Men (and in working-class
families, children as well) began to specialize in paid work outside the home.
Wives took greater responsibility for child care and household labor. A new ideology of parenting placed mothers at the emotional center of family life and romanticized the innocence of children, stressing the need to protect them within
the family circle. What allowed middle-class white families to keep children at
home longer and to divert the bulk of maternal attention from the production
of clothes and food to child rearing was the inability of many working-class
families to adopt such domestic patterns. The extension of childhood and the
redefinition of motherhood among the middle class required the foreshorten-
ing of childhood among the slaves or sharecropping families who provided
cotton to the new textile mills, the working-class women and children whose
long hours in the factory made store-bought clothes and food affordable, and
the Irish or free African American mothers and daughters who left their
homes to work in what their mistresses insisted in defining as a domestic
sanctuary, rather than a workplace. In addition to its class limitations, domesticity (along with its corollary, female purity) was constructed in opposition to the way that women of color were defined (Baca Zinn and Eitzen 1990;
Dill 1998; Glenn 1992).

Even as many wives gave up their traditional involvement in production
for sale or barter, others followed their domestic tasks out of the household
and into the factories or small workshops that made up "the sweated trades."
Still, as wage labor increasingly conflicted with domestic responsibilities, most
families responded by trying to keep one household member near home. Although most wives of slaves and freed blacks continued to participate in the
labor force, wives in most other racial and ethnic groups were increasingly
likely to quit paid work outside the home after marriage. After the Civil War,
freed slaves also attempted to use new norms of sexually appropriate work
to resist gang labor, in a struggle with their former masters and current land-
lords that helped produce the sharecropping system in the South (Franklin
1997; Hareven 1976; Jones 1985; Lerner 1969; Mullings 1997).

But these superficially similar family values and gender-role behaviors
masked profound differences, since working-class families continued to depend on child labor and support networks of neighbors beyond the family
and the work of women within the home or neighborhood varied immensely

by class. For example, "unemployed" wives among the working class frequently took in boarders or lodgers, made and sold small articles or foodstuffs, and otherwise kept far too busy with household subsistence tasks to act like the leisured ladies of the upper classes or the hovering mothers of the middle classes (Boydston 1990; Hareven 1987).

Among the wealthy, fluid household membership and extended family ties remained important in mobilizing credit, pooling capital, and gaining political connections. In the working class, family forms diverged. Single-person and single-parent households multiplied among the growing number of transient workers. But the early factory system and its flip side, the sweated trades, reinforced the notion of the family as a productive unit, with all members working under the direction of the family head or turning their wages over to him.

After the Civil War, industrialization and urbanization accelerated. As U.S. families adapted to the demands and tensions of the industrializing society, different groups behaved in distinctive ways, but some trends could be observed. It was during this period that American families took on many of the characteristics associated with "the modern family." They became smaller, with lower fertility rates; they revolved more tightly around the nuclear core, putting greater distance between themselves and servants or boarders; parents became more emotionally involved in child rearing and for a longer period; couples oriented more toward companionate marriage; and the separation between home and work, both physically and conceptually, was sharpened (Coontz 1988; Mintz and Kellogg 1988).

Yet these trends obscure tremendous differences among and within the changing ethnic groups and classes of the industrializing United States. Between 1830 and 1882, more than 10 million immigrants arrived from Europe. After the Civil War, new professions opened up for middle-class and skilled workers, while job insecurity became more pronounced for laborers. Class distinctions in home furnishings, food, and household labor *widened* in the second half of the 19th century. There was also much more variation in family sequencing and form than was to emerge in the 20th century. Young people in the 19th century exhibited fewer uniformities in the age of leaving school and home, marrying, and setting up households than they do today. No close integration between marriage and entry into the workforce existed: Young people's status as children, rather than marriage partners, determined when and where they would start work. Family decisions were far more variable and less tightly coordinated throughout the society than they would become in the 20th century (American Social History Project 1992; Baca Zinn and Eitzen 1990; Graff 1987; Modell 1989).

In addition to this diversity in the life cycle, family forms and household arrangements diverged in new ways. The long-term trend toward nuclearity slowed between 1870 and 1890 when a number of groups experienced an increase in temporary coresidence with other kin, while others took in boarders or lodgers. American fertility fell by nearly 40% between 1855 and 1915, but this average obscures many differences connected to occupation, region, race, and ethnicity. The fertility of some unskilled and semiskilled workers actually *rose* during this period (Coontz 1988; Hareven 1987).

Another form of family and gender-role diversity in the late 19th century stemmed from mounting contradictions and conflicts over sexuality, which was increasingly divorced from fertility. In the middle class, birth control became a fact of life, despite agitated attempts of conservatives, such as Anthony Comstock, to outlaw information on contraceptives. In the working class, fertility diverged from sexuality, in another way—not only in the growth of prostitution in the cities, but with the emergence of a group of single working women who socialized with men outside a family setting. The opportunities for unsupervised sexual behavior in the cities also increased the possibilities for same-sex relationships, and even entire subcultures, to develop (D'Emilio and Freedman 1988).

The changes that helped produce more "modern" family forms, then, started in different classes, meant different things to families who occupied different positions in the industrial order, and did not proceed in a unilinear way. The "modernization" of the family was the result not of some general evolution of "the" family, as early family sociologists originally posited, but of *diverging* and *contradictory* responses that occurred in different areas and classes at various times, eventually interacting to produce the trends we now associate with industrialization. As Katz, Doucet, and Stern (1982) pointed out:

> The five great changes in family organization that have occurred are the separation of home and work place; the increased nuclearity of household structure; the decline in marital fertility; the prolonged residence of children in the home of their parents; and the lengthened period in which husbands and wives live together after their children have left home. The first two began among the working class and among the wage-earning segment of the business class (clerks and kindred workers). The third started among the business class, particularly among its least affluent, most specialized, and most mobile sectors. The fourth began at about the same time in both the working and business class, though the children of the former usually went to work and the latter to school. (P. 317)

The fifth trend did not occur until the 20th century and represented a reversal of 19th-century trends, as did the sixth major change that has cut across older differences among families: the reintegration of women into productive work, especially the entry of mothers into paid work outside the home and the immediate neighborhood.

The Family Consumer Economy

Around the beginning of the 20th century, a new constellation of family forms and arrangements took shape, as a consolidated national industrial system and mass communication network replaced the decentralized production of goods and culture that had prevailed until the 1890s. The standardization of economic production, spread of mass schooling into the teenage years, abolition of child labor, growth of a consumer economy, and gradual expansion of U.S. international entanglements created new similarities and differences in people's experience of family life.

In the 1920s, for the first time, a bare majority of children came to live in a male-breadwinner, female-homemaker family, in which the children were in school rather than at work. Numerous immigrant families, however, continued to pull their children out of school to go to work, often arousing intense generational conflicts. African American families kept their children in school longer than any immigrant group, but their wives were much more likely than other American women to work outside the home (Hernandez 1993).

A major reorientation of family life occurred in the middle classes and in the dominant ideological portrayals of family life at that time. For the 19th-century middle class, the emotional center of family life had become the mother–child link and the wife's networks of female kin and friends. Now it shifted to the husband–wife bond. Although the "companionate marriage" touted by 1920s sociologists brought new intimacy and sexual satisfaction to married life, it also introduced two trends that disturbed observers. One was increased dissatisfaction with what used to be considered adequate relationships. Great expectations, as the historian May (1980) pointed out, could also generate great disappointments. These disappointments took the form of a jump in divorce rates and a change in the acceptable grounds for divorce (Coontz 1996; May 1980; Mintz and Kellogg 1988; Smith-Rosenberg 1985).

The other was the emergence of an autonomous and increasingly sexualized youth culture, as youths from many different class backgrounds interacted in high schools. The middle-class cult of married bliss and the new romance film industry led young people increasingly to stress the importance of sexual attractiveness and romantic experimentation. At the same time, the model of independent courting activity provided by working-class youths and the newly visible African American urban culture helped spread the new institution of "dating" (Bailey 1989; D'Emilio and Freedman 1988).

Another 20th-century trend was the state's greater intervention into the economy in response to the growth of the union movement, industry's need to regulate competition, the expanding international role of the United States, and other related factors. Families became increasingly dependent on the state and decreasingly dependent on neighborhood institutions for regulating the conditions under which they worked and lived. This change created more zones of privacy for some families but more places for state intervention in others. Sometimes the new state institutions tried to impose nuclear family norms on low-income families, as when zoning and building laws were used to prohibit the coresidence of augmented or extended families or children were taken away from single parents. But in other cases, state agencies imposed a female-headed household on the poor, as when single-parent families were the only model that entitled people to receive governmental subsidies (Gordon 1988; Zaretsky 1982).

Diversity, however, continued to be a hallmark of American family life. Between 1882 and 1930, more than 22 million immigrants came to America, many of them from southern and Eastern Europe, rather than from the traditional Western European suppliers of labor to the United States. They brought a whole range of new customs, religions, and traditions that interacted with their point of entry into the U.S. economy and with the new ethnic prejudices they encountered. By 1910 close to a majority of all workers in heavy industry were foreign born (Baca Zinn and Eitzen 1990).

These immigrants enriched urban life and changed the nature of industrial struggle in the United States. They neither "assimilated" to America nor retained their old ways untouched; rather, they used their cultural resources selectively to adapt to shifting institutional constraints and opportunities. For many groups, migration to America set up patterns of life and interaction with the larger mainstream institutions that forged a new cultural identity that was quite different from their original heritage. But this identity, in turn, changed as the socioeconomic conditions under which they forged their family lives shifted (Baca Zinn and Eitzen 1990; Glenn 1983; Sanchez 1993).

Space does not permit me to develop the history of diversity in 20th-century families, but one of the backdrops to the current debate about family life is that for some years there was a seeming reduction in family diversity, especially after restrictions on immigration in the 1920s began to take effect. For the first two-thirds of the 20th century, there was a growing convergence in the age and order in which young people of all income groups and geographic regions left home, left school, found jobs, and got married. The Great Depression, World War II, and the 1950s contributed to the impression of many Americans, even those in "minority" groups, that family life would become more similar over the course of the 20th century. Most families were hurt by the Great Depression, although the impact differed greatly according to their previous economic status. Marriage and fertility rates fell during the 1930s for all segments of the population; desertion rates and domestic violence increased. World War II spurred a new patriotism that reached across class and racial lines. It also disrupted or reshuffled families from all social and ethnic groups, albeit in different ways, ranging from the removal of Japanese Americans to internment camps to the surge in divorce rates as GIs came home to wives and children they barely knew (American Family History Project 1992; Coontz 1992; Graff 1987; Mintz and Kellogg 1988).

At the end of the 1940s, for the first time in 60 years, the average age of marriage and parenthood fell, the proportion of marriages ending in divorce dropped, and the birth rate soared. The percentage of women remaining single reached a 100-year low. The percentage of children being raised by breadwinner fathers and homemaker mothers and staying in high school until graduation reached an all-time high. The impression that the United States was becoming more homogeneous was fostered by the intense patriotism and anticommunism of the period, by the decline in the percentage of foreign-born persons in the population, and by powerful new media portrayals of the "typical" American family (Coontz 1992; May 1988; Skolnick 1991).

We now know, of course, that the experience of many families was literally "whited out" in the 1950s. Problems, such as battering, alcoholism, and incest, were swept under the rug. So was the discrimination against African Americans and Hispanics, women, elders, gay men, lesbians, political dissidents, religious minorities, and the handicapped. Despite rising real wages, 30% of American children lived in poverty, a higher figure than today. African American married-couple families had a poverty rate of nearly 50%, and there was daily violence in the cities against African American migrants from the South who attempted to move into white neighborhoods or use public parks and swimming areas (Coontz 1992, 1997; May 1988).

Yet poverty rates fell during the 1950s as new jobs opened up for blue-collar workers and the government gave unprecedented subsidies for family formation, home ownership, and education of children. Forty percent of the young men who started families at the end of World War II were eligible for veterans' benefits. Combined with high rates of unionization, heavy corporate investment in manufacturing plants and equipment, and an explosion of housing construction and financing options, these subsidies gave young families a tremendous economic jump start, created predictable paths out of poverty, and led to unprecedented increases in real wages. Sociologists heralded the end of the class society, and the popular media proclaimed that almost everyone was now "middle class." Even dissidents could feel that social and racial differences were decreasing. The heroic struggle of African Americans against Jim Crow laws, for example, finally compelled the federal government to begin to enforce the Supreme Court ruling against "separate but equal" doctrines.

Despite these perceptions, diversity continued to prevail in American families, and it became more visible during the 1960s, when the civil rights and women's liberation movements exposed the complex varieties of family experiences that lay behind the Ozzie and Harriet images of the time. In the 1970s, a new set of divisions and differences began to surface. The prolonged expansion of real wages and social benefits came to an end in the 1970s. By 1973, real wages were falling for young families in particular, and by the late 1970s, tax revolts and service cuts had eroded the effectiveness of the government's antipoverty programs that had proliferated in the late 1960s and brought child poverty to an all-time low by 1970. A new wave of immigrants began to arrive, but this time the majority were from Asian, Latin American, and Caribbean countries, rather than from Europe. By the 1980s, racial and ethnic diversity was higher than it had been since the early days of colonization, while it was obvious to most Americans that the reports of the death of class difference had been greatly exaggerated (Coontz 1992, 1997; Skolnick 1991).

Race relations were also no longer as clear-cut as in earlier times, despite the persistence of racism. They had evolved "from a strictly enforced caste system," in which there was unequivocal subordination of all blacks to whites to a more complex "system of power relations incorporating elements of social status, economics, and race" (Allen and Farley 1986:285). Although long-term residential segregation and discrimination in employment ensured that the deterioration of the country's inner cities would hit African Americans especially hard, resulting in deepening and concentrated poverty, some professional African Americans made impressive economic progress in the decades after the 1960s, leading to a shift in the coding of racism and often to the rediscovery of white ethnicity by Americans who were seeking to roll back affirmative action (Coontz, Parson, and Raley 1998; Rubin 1994; Wilson 1978, 1996).

In one important way, family life has changed in the same direction among all groups. In 1950 only a quarter of all wives were in the paid labor force, and just 16% of all children had mothers who worked outside the home. By 1991 more than 58% of all married women in the United States, and nearly two-thirds of all married women with children, were in the labor force, and 59% of children, including a majority of preschoolers, had mothers who worked outside the home. Women of color no longer have dramatically higher rates of labor force participation than white women, nor do lower-income and middle-income groups differ substantially in the labor force participation of wives and mothers. Growing numbers of women from all social and racial-ethnic groups now combine motherhood with paid employment, and fewer of them quit work for a prolonged period while their children are young (Spain and Bianchi 1996).

But the convergence in women's participation in the workforce has opened up new areas of divergence in family life. Struggles over the redivision of household labor have created new family conflicts and contributed to rising divorce rates, although they have also led to an increase in egalitarian marriages in which both spouses report they are highly satisfied. Women's new economic independence has combined with other social and cultural trends to produce unprecedented numbers of divorced and unwed parents, cohabitating couples (whether heterosexual, gay, or lesbian), and blended families. Yet each of these family types has different dynamics and consequences, depending on such factors as class, race, and ethnicity (Coontz 1997; Cowan, Cowan, and Kerig 1993; Gottfried and Gottfried 1994; Morales 1990). . . .

Implications of Historical Diversity for Contemporary Families

The amount of diversity in U.S. families today is probably no larger than in most periods of the past. But the ability of so many different family types to demand social recognition and support for their existence is truly unprecedented. Most of the contemporary debate over family forms and values is not occasioned by the *existence* of diversity but by its increasing *legitimation*.

Historical studies of family life can contribute two important points to these debates. First, they make it clear that families have always differed and that no one family form or arrangement can be understood or evaluated outside its particular socioeconomic context and relations with other families.

Many different family forms and values have worked (or not worked) for various groups at different times. There is no reason to assume that family forms and practices that differ from those of the dominant ideal are necessarily destructive.

Second, however, history shows that families have always been fragile, vulnerable to rapid economic change, and needful of economic and emotional support from beyond the nuclear family. *All* families experience internal contradictions and conflicts, as well as external pressures and stresses. Celebrating diversity is no improvement over ignoring it unless we analyze the changing social conditions that affect families and figure out how to help every family draw on its potential resources and minimize its characteristic vulnerabilities.

REFERENCES

Adams, D. 1995. *Education for Extinction: American Indians and the Boarding School Experience, 1877–1928.* Lawrence: University Press of Kansas.

Allen, W. and R. Farley. 1986. "The Shifting Social and Economic Tides of Black America, 1950–1980." *American Review of Sociology* 12:277–306.

American Social History Project. 1992. *Who Built America? Working People and the Nation's Economy, Politics, Culture, and Society.* Vols. 1 and 2. New York: Pantheon.

Anderson, K. 1991. *Chain Her by One Foot: The Subjugation of Women in Seventeenth-Century New France.* New York: Routledge.

Axtell, J. 1981. *The Indian Peoples of Eastern America: A Documentary History of the Sexes.* New York: Oxford University Press.

————. 1985. *The Invasion Within: The Contest of Cultures in Colonial America.* New York: Oxford University Press.

————. 1988. *After Columbus: Essays in the Ethnohistory of Colonial North America.* New York: Oxford University Press.

Baca Zinn, M. 1990. "Feminism, Family, and Race in America." *Gender & Society* 4:68–82.

————. 1994. "Feminist Thinking from Racial-Ethnic Families." In *Women of Color in U.S. Society,* edited by M. B. Zinn and B. T. Dill. Philadelphia: Temple University Press.

Baca Zinn, M. and S. Eitzen. 1990. *Diversity in American Families.* New York: Harper-Collins.

Bailey, B. 1989. *From Front Porch to Back Seat: Courtship in Twentieth-Century America.* Baltimore: Johns Hopkins University Press.

Baumrind, D. 1972. "An Exploratory Study of Socialization Effects on Black Children: Some Black-White Comparisons." *Child Development* 43:261–67.

Berkner, L. 1972. "The Stem Family and the Developmental Cycle of the Peasant Household." *American Historical Review* 77:398–418.

Boyd-Franklin, N. and N. Garcia-Preto. 1994. "Family Therapy: The Cases of African American and Hispanic Women." Pp. 239–64 in *Women of Color: Integrating Ethnic and Gender Identities in Psychotherapy,* edited by L. Lomas-Diaz and B. Greene. New York: Guilford Press.

Boydston, J. 1990. *Home and Work: Housework, Wages, and the Ideology of Love in the Early Republic.* New York: Oxford University Press.

Calloway, C. 1997. *New Worlds for All: Indians, Europeans, and the Remaking of Early America.* Baltimore: Johns Hopkins University Press.

Calvert, K. 1992. *Children in the House.* Boston: Northeastern University Press.

Catlin, G. 1973. *Letters and Notes on the Manners, Customs and Conditions of the North American Indians.* New York: Dover.

Collier, J., M. Rosaldo, and S. Yanigasako. 1982. "Is There a Family? New Anthropological Views." Pp. 25–39 in *Rethinking the Family,* edited by B. Thorne. White Plains, NY: Longman.

Coontz, S. 1988. *The Social Origins of Private Life: A History of American Families, 1600–1900.* London: Verso.

———. 1992. *The Way We Never Were: American Families and the Nostalgia Trap.* New York: Basic Books.

———. 1996. "Where Are the Good Old Days?" *Modern Maturity* 34:36–43.

———. 1997. *The Way We Really Are: Coming to Terms with America's Changing Families.* New York: Basic Books.

Coontz, S., M. Parson, and G. Raley, eds. 1998. *American Families: A Multicultural Reader.* New York: Routledge.

Cowan, P., C. Cowan, and P. Kerig, eds. 1993. *Family, Self, and Society: Toward a New Agenda for Family Research.* Hillsdale, NJ: Lawrence Erlbaum.

Cronon, W. 1983. *Changes in the Land: Indians, Colonists, and the Ecology of New England.* New York: Hill & Wang.

D'Emilio, J. and E. Freedman. 1988. *Intimate Matters: A History of Sexuality in America.* New York: Harper & Row.

Dill, B. T. 1998. "Fictive Kin, Paper Sons, and *Compadrazgo:* Women of Color and the Struggle for Family Survival." Pp. 2–19 in *American Families,* edited by S. Coontz, M. Parson, and G. Raley. New York: Routledge.

Duberman, M., M. Vicinus, and G. Chauncey. 1989. *Hidden from History: Reclaiming the Gay and Lesbian Past.* New York: New American Library.

Edwards, L. 1991. "Sexual Violence, Gender, Reconstruction, and the Extension of Patriarchy in Granville County, North Carolina." *North Carolina Historical Review* 68:237–60.

Faderman, L. 1981. *Surpassing the Love of Men: Romantic Friendship and Love between Women from the Renaissance to the Present.* New York: William Morrow.

Franklin, D. 1997. *Ensuring Inequality: The Structural Transformation of the African-American Family.* New York: Oxford University Press.

Gillis, J. 1996. *A World of Their Own Making: Myth, Ritual, and the Quest for Family Values.* New York: Basic Books.

Glenn, E. N. 1983. "Split Household, Small Producer, and Dual Wage-Earner." *Journal of Marriage and the Family* 45:35–46.

———. 1992. "From Servitude to Service Work: Historical Continuities in Racial Division of Paid Reproductive Labor." *Signs* 18:1–43.

Gordon, L. 1988. *Heroes of Their Own Lives: The Politics and History of Family Violence, Boston 1880–1960.* New York: Viking.

Gottfried, A. and A. Gottfried. 1994. *Redefining Families: Implications for Children's Development.* New York: Plenum.

Graff, H., ed. 1987. *Growing Up in America: Historical Experiences.* Detroit: Wayne State University Press.

Gutierrez, R. 1991. *When Jesus Came, the Corn Mothers Went Away: Marriage, Sexuality, and Power in New Mexico, 1500–1846.* Stanford, CA: Stanford University Press.

Gutman, H. 1976. *The Black Family in Slavery and Freedom, 1750–1925.* New York: Pantheon.

Hareven, T. 1976. "Women and Men: Changing Roles." Pp. 93–118 in *Women and Men: Changing Roles, Relationships and Perceptions Report of a Workshop,* edited by L. A. Cater, A. F. Scott, and W. Martyna. Palo Alto, CA: Aspen Institute for Humanistic Studies.

———. 1987. "Historical Analysis of the Family." In *Handbook of Marriage and the Family,* edited by M. B. Sussman and S. K. Steinmetz. New York: Plenum.

Hawkes, J. 1973. *The First Great Civilizations: Life in Mesopotamia, the Indus Valley, and Egypt.* New York: Alfred A. Knopf.

Herdt, G., ed. 1994. *Third Sex, Third Gender: Beyond Sexual Dimorphism in Culture and History.* New York: Zone.

Hernandez, D. 1993. *America's Children: Resources from Family, Government, and the Economy*. New York: Russell Sage Foundation.

Howard, E. A., R. Heighton, C. Jordan, and R. Gallimore. 1970. "Traditional and Modern Adoption Patterns in Hawaii. In *Adoption in Eastern Oceania*, edited by V. Carroll. Honolulu: University of Hawaii Press.

Ingoldsby, B. and S. Smith, eds. 1995. *Families in Multicultural Perspective*. New York: Guilford Press.

Isaacs, R. 1982. *The Transformation of Virginia, 1740–1790*. Chapel Hill: University of North Carolina Press.

Jeater, D. 1993. *Marriage, Perversion, and Power: The Construction of Moral Discourse in Southern Rhodesia, 1894–1930*. New York: Oxford University Press.

Johnson, P. 1978. *A Shopkeeper's Millennium: Society and Revivals in Rochester, New York, 1815–1837*. New York: Hill & Wang.

Jones, J. 1985. *Labor of Love, Labor of Sorrow: Black Women, Work, and the Family from Slavery to the Present*. New York: Basic Books.

———. 1997. *American Work: Four Centuries of Black and White Labor*. New York: W. W. Norton.

Katz, M., M. Doucet, and M. Stern. 1982. *The Social Organization of Industrial Capitalism*. Cambridge, MA: Harvard University Press.

Knight, G. P., L. M. Virdin, and M. Roosa. 1994. "Socialization and Family Correlates of Mental Health Outcomes among Hispanic and Anglo-American Children." *Child Development* 65:212–24.

Leacock, E. 1980. "Montagnais Women and the Program for Jesuit Colonization." In *Women and Colonization: Anthropological Perspectives*, edited by M. Etienne and E. Leacock. New York: Praeger.

Leacock, E. and N. O. Lurie. 1971. *North American Indians in Historical Perspective*. New York: Random House.

Leibowitz, L. 1978. *Females, Males, Families: A Biosocial Approach*. North Scituate, MA: Duxbury Press.

Lerner, G. 1969. "The Lady and the Mill Girl: Changes in the Status of Women in the Age of Jackson, 1800–1840." *Midcontinent American Studies Journal* 10:5–14.

May, E. T. 1980. *Great Expectations: Marriage and Divorce in Post-Victorian America*. Chicago: University of Chicago Press.

———. 1988. *Homeward Bound: American Families in the Cold War Era*. New York: Basic Books.

McCurry, S. 1995. *Masters of Small Worlds: Yeoman Households, Gender Relations, and the Political Culture of the Antebellum South Carolina Low Country*. New York: Oxford University Press.

Mindel, C., R. Habenstein, and R. Wright, eds. 1988. *Ethnic Families in America: Patterns and Variations*. New York: Elsevier.

Mintz, S. and S. Kellogg. 1988. *Domestic Revolutions: A Social History of American Family Life*. New York: Free Press.

Modell, J. 1989. *Into One's Own: From Youth to Adulthood in the United States, 1920–1975*. Berkeley: University of California Press.

Morales, E. S. 1990. "Ethnic Minority Families and Minority Gays and Lesbians." Pp. 217–39 in *Homosexuality and Family Relations*, edited by F. W. Bozett and M. B. Sussman. New York: Harrington Park Press.

Morris, P. 1993. "Incest or Survival Strategy? Plebian Marriage within the Prohibited Degrees in Somerset, 1730–1835." In *Forbidden History: The State, Society, and the Regulation of Sexuality in Modern Europe*, edited by J. C. Fout. Chicago: University of Chicago Press.

Mullings, L. 1997. *On Our Own Terms: Race, Class, and Gender in the Lives of African-American Women*. New York: Routledge.

Padgug, R. 1989. "Sexual Matters: Rethinking Sexuality in History." Pp. 54–64 in *Hidden From History: Reclaiming the Gay and Lesbian Past*, edited by M. B. Duberman, M. Vicinus, and G. Chauncey Jr. New York: New American Library.

Peters, V. 1995. *Women of the Earth Lodges: Tribal Life on the Plains*. North Haven, CT: Archon Books.

Peterson, J. 1993. "Generalized Extended Family Exchange: A Case from the Philippines." *Journal of Marriage and the Family* 55:570–84.

Roediger, D. 1988. *The Wages of Whiteness: Race and the Making of the American Working Class*. London: Verso.

Rotundo, A. 1993. *American Manhood*. New York: Basic Books.

Rubin, L. 1994. *Families on the Fault Line*. New York: Basic Books.

Ryan, M. 1981. *Cradle of the Middle Class: The Family in Oneida County, New York*. New York: Cambridge University Press.

Sanchez, G. 1993. *Becoming Mexican-American: Ethnicity, Culture, and Identity in Chicano Los Angeles, 1900–1945*. New York: Oxford University Press.

Schnarch, B. 1992. "Neither Man nor Woman: Berdache – A Case for Non-dichotomous Gender Construction." *Anthropologica* 34:106–21.

Skolnick, A. 1991. *Embattled Paradise: The American Family in an Age of Uncertainty*. New York: Basic Books.

Smith-Rosenberg, C. 1985. *Disorderly Women: Visions of Gender in Victorian America*. New York: Oxford University Press.

Snipp, M. 1989. *American Indians: The First of This Land*. New York: Russell Sage Foundation.

Spain, D. and S. M. Bianchi. 1996. *Balancing Act: Motherhood, Marriage, and Employment among American Women*. New York: Russell Sage Foundation.

Spicer, E. H. 1962. *Cycles of Conquest: The Impact of Spain, Mexico, and the United States on the Indians of the Southwest, 1533–1960*. Tucson: University of Arizona Press.

Stack, C. 1993. "Cultural Perspectives on Child Welfare." Pp. 344–49 in *Family Matters: Readings on Family Lives and the Law*, edited by M. Minow. New York: New Press.

Stevenson, B. E. 1996. *Life in Black and White: Family and Community in the Slave South*. New York: Oxford University Press.

Strasser, S. 1982. *Never Done: A History of American Housework*. New York: Pantheon.

Wilson, W. J. 1978. *The Declining Significance of Race: Blacks and Changing American Institutions*. Chicago: University of Chicago.

———. 1996. *When Work Disappears: The World of the New Urban Poor*. New York: Alfred A. Knopf.

Williams, R. 1976. *Keywords: A Vocabulary of Culture and Society*. New York: Oxford University Press.

Williams, W. L. 1986. *The Spirit and the Flesh: Sexual Diversity in American Indian Culture*. Boston: Beacon Press.

Zaretsky, E. 1982. "The Place of the Family in the Origins of the Welfare State." Pp. 188–224 in *Rethinking the Family*, edited by B. Thorne. White Plains, NY: Longman.

6

INTERPRETING THE AFRICAN HERITAGE IN AFRO–AMERICAN FAMILY ORGANIZATION

NIARA SUDARKASA

Whereas it is generally agreed that the history of the family in Europe is pertinent to an understanding of European-derived family organization in America (and throughout the world), many—if not most—scholars working on Black American families have argued or assumed that the African family heritage was all but obliterated by the institution of slavery. This view has retained credence, despite the accumulation of evidence to the contrary, in large measure because E. Franklin Frazier (1939), the most prestigious and prolific student of the Black American family, all but discounted the relevance of Africa in his analyses.

This chapter takes its departure from W. E. B. Du Bois (1908[1969]), Carter G. Woodson (1936), and M. J. Herskovits (1958), all of whom looked to Africa as well as to the legacy of slavery for explanations of African American social institutions. Herskovits is the best-known advocate of the concept of African survivals in African American family life, but Du Bois was the first scholar to stress the need to study the Black American family against the background of its African origins. In his 1908 study of the Black family, Du Bois (1969) prefaced his discussions of marriage, household structure, and economic organization with observations concerning the African antecedents of the patterns developed in America.

> In each case an attempt has been made to connect present conditions with the African past. This is not because Negro-Americans are Africans, or can trace an unbroken social history from Africa, but because there is a distinct nexus between Africa and America which, though broken and perverted, is nevertheless not to be neglected by the careful student. (P. 9)

Having documented the persistence of African family patterns in the Caribbean, and of African derived wedding ceremonies in Alabama, Du Bois noted:

> Careful research would doubtless reveal many other traces of the African family in America. They would, however, be traces only, for the effectiveness of the slave system meant the practically complete crushing out of the African clan and family life. (P. 21)

With the evidence that has accumulated since Du Bois wrote, it is possible to argue that even though the constraints of slavery did prohibit the replication of African lineage ("clan") and family life in America, the principles on which these kin groups were based, and the values underlying them, led to the emergence of variants of African family life in the form of the extended families which developed among the enslaved Blacks in America. Evidence of the Africanity to which Du Bois alluded is to be found not only in the relatively few "traces" of direct *institutional transfer* from Africa to America, but also in the numerous examples of *institutional transformation* from Africa to America.

No discussion of the relevance of Africa for understanding Afro-American family organization can proceed without confronting the issue of the "diversity" of the backgrounds of "African slaves" (read "enslaved Africans") brought to America. Obviously for certain purposes, each African community or each ethnic group can be described in terms of the linguistic, cultural, and/or social structural features which distinguish it from others. At the same time, however, these communities or ethnic groups can be analyzed from the point of view of their similarity to other groups.

It has long been established that the Africans enslaved in the United States and the rest of the Americas came from the Western part of the continent where there had been a long history of culture contact and widespread similarities in certain institutions (Herskovits 1958, chaps. 2 and 3). For example, some features of kinship organization were almost universal. Lineages, large co-resident domestic groups, and polygynous marriages are among the recurrent features found in groups speaking different languages, organized into states as well as "segmentary" societies, and living along the coast as well as in the interior (Fortes 1953; Onwuejeogwu 1975; Radcliffe-Brown 1950).

When the concept of "African family structure" is used here, it refers to those organizational principles and patterns which are common to the different ethnic groups whose members were enslaved in America. These features of family organization are known to have existed for centuries on the African continent and are, therefore, legitimately termed a part of the African heritage.

African Family Structure: Understanding the Dynamics of Consanguinity and Conjugality

African families, like those in other parts of the world, embody two contrasting bases for membership: *consanguinity,* which refers to kinship that is commonly assumed or presumed to be biologically based and rooted in "blood ties," and *affinity,* which refers to kinship created by law and rooted "in-law." *Conjugality* refers specifically to the affinal kinship created between spouses (Marshall 1968). Generally, all kinship entails a dynamic tension between the operation of the contrasting principles of consanguinity and affinity. The comparative study of family organization led Ralph Linton (1936:159–63) to observe that in different societies families tend to be built either around a conjugal core or around a consanguineal core. In either case, the other principle is subordinate.

According to current historical research on the family in Europe, the principle of conjugality appears to have dominated family organization in the Western part of that continent (including Britain) at least since the Middle Ages, when a number of economic and political factors led to the predominance of nuclear and/or stem families built around married couples. Certainly for the past three or four hundred years, the conjugally based family has been the ideal and the norm in Western Europe (Shorter 1975; Stone 1975; Tilly and Scott 1978). Whether or not the European conjugal family was a structural isolate is not the issue here. The point is that European families, whether nuclear or extended (as in the case of stem families), tended to emphasize the conjugal relationship in matters of household formation, decision making, property transmission, and socialization of the young (Goody 1976).

African families, on the other hand, have traditionally been organized around consanguineal cores formed by adult siblings of the same sex or by larger same-sex segments of patri- or matrilineages. The groups which formed around these consanguineally related core members included their spouses and children, and perhaps some of their divorced siblings of the opposite sex. This co-resident *extended family* occupied a group of adjoining or contiguous dwellings known as a compound. Upon marriage, Africans did not normally form new isolated households, but joined a compound in which the extended family of the groom, or that of the bride, was already domiciled (Sudarkasa 1980:38–49).

African extended families could be subdivided in two ways. From one perspective, there was the division between the nucleus formed by the consanguineal core group and their children and the "outer group" formed by the in-marrying spouses. In many African languages, in-marrying spouses are collectively referred to as "wives" or "husbands" by both females and males of the core group. Thus, for example, in any compound in a patrilineal society, the in-marrying women may be known as the "wives of the house." They are, of course, also the mothers of the children of the compound. Their collective designation as "wives of the house" stresses the fact that their membership in the compound is rooted in law and can be terminated by law, whereas that of the core group is rooted in descent and is presumed to exist in perpetuity.

African extended families may also be divided into their constituent conjugally based family units comprised of parents and children. In the traditional African family, these conjugal units did not have the characteristics of the typical "nuclear family" of the West. In the first place, African conjugal families normally involved polygynous marriages at some stage in their developmental cycle. A number of Western scholars have chosen to characterize the polygynous conjugal family as several distinct nuclear families with one husband/father in common (Colson 1962; Murdock 1949:2; Rivers 1924:12). In the African conception, however, whether a man had one wife and children or many wives and children, his was *one* family. In the case of polygynous families, both the husband and the senior co-wife played important roles in integrating the entire group (Fortes 1949, chaps. 3 and 4; Sudarkasa 1973, chap. 5; Ware 1979). The very existence of the extended family as an "umbrella" group for the conjugal family meant that the latter group differed from the Western nuclear family. Since, for many purposes and on many occasions, *all* the children of the same generation within the compound regarded themselves as brothers and sisters (rather than dividing into siblings versus "cousins"), and since the adults assumed certain responsibilities toward their "nephews" and "nieces" (whom they term sons and daughters) as well as toward their own offspring, African conjugal families did not have the rigid boundaries characteristic of nuclear families of the West.

The most far-reaching difference between African and European families stems from their differential emphasis on consanguinity and conjugality. This difference becomes clear when one considers extended family organization in the two contexts. The most common type of European extended family consisted of two or more nuclear families joined through the parent–child or sibling tie. It was this model of the stem family and the joint family that was put forth by George P. Murdock (1949:23, 33, 39–40) as the generic form of the extended family. However, the African data show that on that continent, extended families were built around consanguineal cores and the conjugal components of these larger families differed significantly from the nuclear families of the West.

In Africa, unlike Europe, in many critical areas of family life the consanguineal core group rather than the conjugal pair was paramount. With respect to household formation, I have already indicated that married couples joined existing compounds. It was the lineage core that owned (or had the right of usufruct over) the land and the compound where families lived, farmed, and/or practiced their crafts. The most important properties in African societies — land, titles, and entitlements — were transmitted through the lineages, and spouses did not inherit from each other (Goody 1976).

Within the extended family residing in a single compound, decision making centered in the consanguineal core group. The oldest male in the compound was usually its head, and all the men in his generation constituted the elders of the group. Together they were ultimately responsible for settling internal disputes, including those that could not be settled within the separate conjugal families or, in some cases, by the female elders among the wives (Sudarkasa 1973, 1976). They also made decisions, such as those involving the allocation of land and other resources, which affected the functioning of the constituent conjugal families.

Given the presence of multiple spouses within the *conjugal* families, it is not surprising that decision making within them also differed from the model associated with nuclear family organization. Separate rather than joint decision making was common. In fact, husbands and wives normally had distinct purviews and responsibilities within the conjugal family (Oppong 1974; Sudarkasa 1973). Excepting those areas where Islamic traditions overshadowed indigenous African traditions, women had a good deal of control over the fruits of their own labor. Even though husbands typically had ultimate authority over wives, this authority did not extend to control over their wives' properties (Oppong 1974; Robertson 1976; Sudarkasa 1976). Moreover, even though women were subordinate in their roles as wives, as mothers and sisters they wielded considerable authority, power, and influence. This distinction in the power attached to women's roles is symbolized by the fact that in the same society where wives knelt before their husbands, sons prostrated before their mothers and seniority as determined by age, rather than gender, governed relationships among siblings (Sudarkasa 1973, 1976).

Socialization of the young involved the entire extended family, not just the separate conjugal families, even though each conjugal family had special responsibility for the children (theirs or their relatives') living with them. It is important to note that the concept of "living with" a conjugal family took on a different meaning in the context of the African compound. In the first place, husbands, wives, and children did not live in a bounded space, apart from other such units. Wives had their own rooms or small dwellings, and husbands had theirs. These were not necessarily adjacent to one another. (In some matrilineal societies, husbands and wives resided in separate compounds.) Children ordinarily slept in their mothers' rooms until they were of a certain age, after which they customarily slept in communal rooms allocated to boys or girls. Children usually ate their meals with their mothers, but they might also eat some of these meals with their fathers' co-wives (assuming that no hostility existed between the women concerned) or with their grandmothers. Children of the same compound played together and shared many learning experiences. They were socialized by all the adults to identify themselves collectively as sons and daughters of a particular lineage and compound, which entailed a kinship, based on descent, with all the lineage ancestors and with generations unborn (Radcliffe-Brown and Forde 1950; Sudarkasa 1980; Uchendu 1965).

The stability of the African extended family did not depend on the stability of the marriage(s) of the individual core group members. Although traditional African marriages (particularly those in patrilineal societies) were more stable than those of most contemporary societies, marital dissolution did not have the ramifications it has in nuclear family systems. When divorces did occur, they were usually followed by remarriage. Normally, all adults other than those who held certain ceremonial offices or who were severely mentally or physically handicapped lived in a marital union (though not necessarily the same one) throughout their lives (for example, Lloyd 1968). The children of a divorced couple were usually brought up in their natal compound (or by members of their lineage residing elsewhere), even though the in-marrying parent had left that compound.

Several scholars have remarked on the relative ease of divorce in some traditional African societies, particularly those in which matrilineal descent was the rule (for example, Fortes 1950:283). Jack Goody (1976:64) has even suggested that the rate of divorce in precolonial Africa was higher than in parts of Europe and Asia in comparable periods as a corollary of contrasting patterns of property transmission, contrasting attitudes toward the remarriage of women (especially widows), and contrasting implications of polygyny and monogamy. If indeed there was a higher incidence of divorce in precolonial Africa, this would not be inconsistent with the wide-ranging emphasis on consanguinity in Africa as opposed to conjugality in Europe.

Marriage in Africa was a contractual union which often involved long-lasting companionate relationships, but it was not expected to be the all-encompassing, exclusive relationship of the Euro-American ideal type. Both men and women relied on their extended families and friends, as well as on their spouses, for emotionally gratifying relationships. Often, too, in the context of polygyny women as well as men had sexual liaisons with more than one partner. A woman's clandestine affairs did not necessarily lead to divorce because, in the absence of publicized information to the contrary, her husband was considered the father of all her children (Radcliffe-Brown 1950). And in the context of the lineage (especially the patrilineage), all men aspired to have as many children as possible.

Interpersonal relationships within African families were governed by principles and values which I have elsewhere summarized under the concepts of respect, restraint, responsibility, and reciprocity. Common to all these principles was a notion of commitment to the collectivity. The family offered a network of security, but it also imposed a burden of obligations (Sudarkasa 1980:49–50). From the foregoing discussion, it should be understandable that, in their material form, these obligations extended first and foremost to consanguineal kin. Excepting the gifts that were exchanged at the time of marriage, the material obligations entailed in the conjugal relationship and the wider affinal relationships created by marriage were of a lesser magnitude than those associated with "blood" ties.

Afro–American Family Structure: Interpreting the African Connection

Rather than start with the question of what was *African* about the families established by those Africans who were enslaved in America, it would be more appropriate to ask what was *not* African about them. Most of the Africans who were captured and brought to America arrived without any members of their families, but they brought with them the societal codes they had learned regarding family life. To argue that the trans-Atlantic voyage and the trauma of enslavement made them forget, or rendered useless their memories of how they had been brought up or how they had lived before their capture, is to argue from premises laden with myths about the Black experience (Elkins 1963:101–2; see also Frazier 1966, chap. 1).

Given the African tradition of multilingualism and the widespread use of lingua francas (Maquet 1972:18–25)—which in West Africa would include Hausa, Yoruba, Djoula, and Twi—it is probable that many more of the enslaved Africans could communicate among themselves than is implied by those who remark on the multiplicity of "tribes" represented among the slaves. As Landman (1978) has pointed out:

> In many areas of the world, individuals are expected to learn only one language in the ordinary course of their lives. But many Africans have been enculturated in social systems where multiple language or dialect acquisition have been regarded as normal. (P. 80)

The fact that Africans typically spoke three to five languages also makes it understandable why they quickly adopted "pidginized" forms of European languages as lingua francas for communicating among themselves and with their captors.

The relationships which the Blacks in America established among themselves would have reflected their own backgrounds *and* the conditions in which they found themselves. It is as erroneous to try to attribute what developed among them solely to slavery as it is to attribute it solely to the African background. Writers such as Herbert Gutman (1976), who emphasize the "adaptive" nature of "slave culture," must ask what it was that was being adapted as well as in what context this adaptation took place. Moreover, they must realize that adaptation does not necessarily imply extensive modification of an institution, especially when its structure is already suited (or "pre-adapted") to survival in the new context. Such an institution was the African extended family, which had served on that continent, in various environments and different political contexts, as a unit of production and distribution; of socialization, education, and social control; and of emotional and material support for the aged and the infirm as well as the hale and hearty (Kerri 1979; Okediji 1975; Shimkin and Uchendu 1978; Sudarkasa 1975b).

The extended family networks that were formed during slavery by Africans *and their descendants* were based on the institutional heritage which the Africans had brought with them to this continent, and the specific forms they took reflected the influence of European-derived institutions as well as the political and economic circumstances in which the enslaved population found itself.

The picture of Black families during slavery has become clearer over the past decade, particularly as a result of the wealth of data in Gutman's justly heralded study. Individual households were normally comprised of a conjugal pair, their children, and sometimes their grandchildren, other relatives, or nonkin. Marriage was usually monogamous, but polygynous unions where the wives lived in separate households have also been reported (Blassingame 1979:171; Gutman 1976:59, 158; Perdue, Barden, and Phillips 1980:209).

Probably only in a few localities did female-headed households constitute as much as one-quarter of all households (Gutman 1976, esp. chaps. 1–3). The rarity of this household type was in keeping with the African tradition whereby women normally bore children within the context of marriage and lived in monogamous or polygynous conjugal families that were part of larger extended families. I have tried to show elsewhere why it is inappropriate to apply the term "nuclear family" to the mother–child dyads within

African polygynous families (Sudarkasa 1980:43–46). In some African societies—especially in matrilineal ones—a small percentage of previously married women, or married women living apart from their husbands, might head households that were usually attached to larger compounds. However, in my view, on the question of the origin of female-headed households among Blacks in America, Herskovits was wrong, and Frazier was right in attributing this development to conditions that arose during slavery and in the context of urbanization in later periods (Frazier 1966; Furstenberg, Hershbert, and Modell 1975; Herskovits 1958).

Gutman's data suggest that enslaved women who had their first children out of wedlock did not normally set up independent households, but rather continued to live with their parents. Most of them subsequently married and set up neolocal residence with their husbands. The data also suggest that female-headed households developed mainly in two situations: (1) A woman whose husband died or was sold off the plantation might head a household comprised of her children and perhaps her grandchildren born to an unmarried daughter; (2) a woman who did not marry after having one or two children out of wedlock but continued to have children (no doubt often for the "master") might have her own cabin built for her (Gutman 1976, chaps. 1–3).

It is very important to distinguish these two types of female-headed households, the first being only a phase in the developmental cycle of a conjugally headed household, and the second being a case of neolocal residence by an unmarried female. The pattern of households headed by widows was definitely not typical of family structure in Africa, where normally a widow married another member of her deceased husband's lineage. The pattern of neolocal residence by an unmarried woman with children would have been virtually unheard of in Africa. Indeed, it was also relatively rare among enslaved Blacks and in Black communities in later periods. Before the twentieth-century policy of public assistance for unwed mothers, virtually all young unmarried mothers in Black communities continued to live in households headed by other adults. If in later years they did establish their own households, these tended to be tied into transresidential family networks.

The existence during slavery of long-lasting conjugal unions among Blacks was not a departure from African family tradition. Even with the relative ease of divorce in matrilineal societies, most Africans lived in marital unions that ended only with the death of one of the spouses. In the patrilineal societies from which most American Blacks were taken, a number of factors, including the custom of returning bridewealth payments upon the dissolution of marriage, served to encourage marital stability (Radcliffe-Brown 1950:43–54). Given that the conditions of slavery did not permit the *replication* of African families, it might be expected that the husband and wife as elders in the household would assume even greater importance than they had in Africa, where the elders within the consanguineal core of the extended family and those among the wives would have had major leadership roles within the compound.

When the distinction is made between family and household—and, following Bender (1967), between the composition of the co-resident group and the domestic functions associated with both households and families—it becomes apparent that the question of who lived with whom during slavery (or later) must be subordinate to the questions of who was doing what for whom and what kin relationships were maintained over space and time. In any case, decisions concerning residence per se were not always in the hands of the enslaved Blacks themselves, and space alone served as a constraint on the size, and consequently to some extent on the composition, of the "slave" cabins.

That each conjugally based household formed a primary unit for food consumption and production among the enslaved Blacks is consistent with domestic organization within the African compound. However, Gutman's data, and those reported by enslaved Blacks themselves, on the strong bonds of obligation among kinsmen suggest that even within the constraints imposed by the slave regime, transresidential cooperation—including that between households in different localities—was the rule rather than the exception (Gutman 1976, esp. pp. 131–38; Perdue et al. 1980, esp. pp. 26, 256, 323). One might hypothesize that on the larger plantations with a number of Black families related through consanguineal and affinal ties, the households of these families might have formed groupings similar to African compounds. Certainly we know that in later times such groupings were found in the South Carolina Sea Islands and other parts of the South (Agbasegbe 1976, 1981; Gutman 1976; Johnson 1934, chap. 2; Powdermaker 1939, chap. 8).

By focusing on extended families (rather than simply on households) among the enslaved Blacks, it becomes apparent that these kin networks had many of the features of continental African extended families. These Afro-American groupings were built around consanguineal kin whose spouses were related to or incorporated into the networks in different degrees. The significance of the consanguineal principle in these networks is indicated by Gutman's statement that "the pull between ties to an immediate family and to an enlarged kin network sometimes strained husbands and wives" (1976:202; see also Frazier 1966, pt. 2).

The literature on Black families during slavery provides a wealth of data on the way in which consanguineal kin assisted each other with child rearing, in life crisis events such as birth and death, in work groups, in efforts to obtain freedom, and so on. They maintained their networks against formidable odds and, after slavery, sought out those parents, siblings, aunts, and uncles from whom they had been torn (Blassingame 1979; Genovese 1974; Gutman 1976; Owens 1976). Relationships within these groups were governed by principles and values stemming from the African background. Respect for elders and reciprocity among kinsmen are noted in all discussions of Black families during slavery. The willingness to assume responsibility for relatives beyond the conjugal family and selflessness (a form of restraint) in the face of these responsibilities are also characteristics attributed to the enslaved population.

As would be expected, early Afro-American extended families differed from their African prototypes in ways that reflected the influence of slavery and of Euro-American values, especially their proscriptions and prescriptions regarding mating, marriage, and the family. No doubt, too, the Euro-American emphasis on the primacy of marriage within the family reinforced conjugality among the Afro-Americans even though the "legal" marriage of enslaved Blacks was prohibited. As Du Bois noted at the turn of the century, African corporate lineages could not survive intact during slavery. Hence, the consanguineal core groups of Afro-American extended families differed in some ways from those of their African antecedents. It appears that in some of these Afro-American families membership in the core group was traced bilaterally, whereas in others there was a unilineal emphasis without full-fledged lineages.

Interestingly, after slavery, some of the corporate functions of African lineages reemerged in some extended families which became property-owning collectivities. I have suggested elsewhere that "the disappearance of the lineage principle or its absorption into the concept of extended family" is one of the aspects of the transformation of African family organization in America that requires research (Sudarkasa 1980:57). Among the various other issues that remain to be studied concerning these extended families are these: (1) Did members belong by virtue of bilateral or unilineal descent from a common ancestor or because of shared kinship with a living person? (2) How were group boundaries established and maintained? (3) What was the nature and extent of the authority of the elder(s)? (4) How long did the group last and what factors determined its span in time and space?

Conclusion

. . . Obviously, Black families have changed over time, and today one would expect that the evidence for African "retentions" (Herskovits 1958:xxii–xxiii) in them would be more controvertible than in the past. Nevertheless, the persistence of some features of African family organization among contemporary Black American families has been documented for both rural and urban areas. Although this study cannot attempt a full-scale analysis of these features and the changes they have undergone, it is important to make reference to one of them, precisely because it impacts upon so many other aspects of Black family organization, and because its connection to Africa has not been acknowledged by most contemporary scholars. I refer to the emphasis on consanguinity noted especially among lower-income Black families and those in the rural South. Some writers, including Shimkin and Uchendu (1978), Agbasegbe (1976, 1981), Aschenbrenner (1973, 1975, 1978), Aschenbrenner and Carr (1980), and the present author (1975a, 1980, 1981), have dealt explicitly with this concept in their discussions of Black family organization. However, without labeling it as such, many other scholars have described some aspects of the operation of consanguinity within the Black family in their discussions of "matrifocality" and "female-headed households." Too often, the origin of this consanguineal emphasis in Black families, which can be manifest even in households with both husband and wife present, is left unexplained or is "explained" by labeling it an "adaptive" characteristic.

In my view, historical realities require that the derivation of this aspect of Black family organization be traced to its African antecedents. Such a view does not deny the adaptive significance of consanguineal networks. In fact, it helps to clarify why these networks had the flexibility they had and why they, rather than conjugal relationships, came to be the stabilizing factor in Black families. The significance of this principle of organization is indicated by the list of Black family characteristics derived from it. Scrutiny of the list of Black family characteristics given by Aschenbrenner (1978) shows that 12 of the 18 "separate" features she lists are manifestations of the overall strength and entailments of consanguineal relationships.

Some writers have viewed the consanguineally based extended family as a factor of *instability* in the Black family because it sometimes undermines the conjugal relationships in which its members are involved. I would suggest that historically among Black Americans the concept of "family" meant first and foremost relationships created by "blood" rather than by marriage. (R. T. Smith [1973] has made substantially the same point with respect to West Indian family organization.) Children were socialized to think in terms of obligations to parents (especially mothers), siblings, and others defined as "close kin." Obligations to "outsiders," who would include prospective spouses and in-laws, were definitely less compelling. Once a marriage took place, if the demands of the conjugal relationship came into irreconcilable conflict with consanguineal commitments, the former would often be sacrificed. Instead of interpreting instances of *marital* instability as prima facie evidence of family instability, it should be realized that the fragility of the conjugal relationship could be a consequence or corollary of the *stability* of the consanguineal family network. Historically, such groups survived by nurturing a strong sense of responsibility among members and by fostering a code of reciprocity which could strain relations with persons not bound by it.

Not all Black families exhibit the same emphasis on consanguineal relationships. Various factors, including education, occupational demands, aspirations toward upward mobility, and acceptance of American ideals concerning marriage and the family, have moved some (mainly middle- and upper-class) Black families toward conjugally focused households and conjugally centered extended family groupings. Even when such households include relatives other than the nuclear family, those relatives tend to be subordinated to the conjugal pair who form the core of the group. This contrasts with some older types of Black families where a senior relative (especially the wife's or the husband's mother) could have a position of authority in the household equal to or greater than that of one or both of the spouses. Children in many contemporary Black homes are not socialized to think in terms of the parent–sibling group as the primary kin group, but rather in terms of their future spouses and families of procreation as the main source of their future emotional and material satisfaction and support. Among these Blacks, the nuclear household tends to be more isolated in terms of instrumental functions, and such extended family networks as exist tend to be clusters of nuclear families conforming to the model put forth by Murdock (1949, chaps. 1 and 2).

For scholars interested in the heritage of Europe as well as the heritage of Africa in African American family organization, a study of the operation of the principles of conjugality and consanguinity in these families would provide considerable insight into the ways in which these two institutional traditions have been interwoven. By looking at the differential impact of these principles in matters of household formation, delegation of authority, maintenance of solidarity and support, acquisition and transmission of property, financial management, and so on (Sudarkasa 1981), and by examining the political and economic variables which favor the predominance of one or the other principle, we will emerge with questions and formulations that can move us beyond debates over "pathology" and "normalcy" in Black family life.

ENDNOTE

Author's note: I wish to thank Tao-Lin Hwang for his assistance with the research for this chapter, and Bamidele Agbasegbe Demerson for his helpful comments.

REFERENCES

Agbasegbe, B. 1976. "The Role of Wife in the Black Extended Family: Perspectives from a Rural Community in Southern United States." Pp. 124–38 in *New Research on Women and Sex Roles,* edited by D. McGuigan. Ann Arbor: Center for Continuing Education of Women, University of Michigan.

———. 1981. "Some Aspects of Contemporary Rural Afroamerican Family Life in the Sea Islands of Southeastern United States." Presented at the Annual Meeting of the Association of Social and Behavioral Scientists, Atlanta, March 1981.

Allen, W. R. 1978. "The Search for Applicable Theories of Black Family Life." *Journal of Marriage and the Family* 40 (February):117–29.

———. 1979. "Class, Culture, and Family Organization: The Effects of Class and Race on Family Structure in Urban America." *Journal of Comparative Family Studies* 10 (Autumn):301–13.

Aschenbrenner, J. 1973. "Extended Families among Black Americans." *Journal of Comparative Family Studies* 4:257–68.

———. 1975. *Lifelines: Black Families in Chicago.* New York: Holt, Rinehart & Winston.

———. 1978. "Continuities and Variations in Black Family Structure." Pp. 181–200 in *The Extended Family in Black Societies,* edited by D. B. Shimkin, E. M. Shimkin, and D. A. Frate. The Hague: Mouton.

Aschenbrenner, J. and C. H. Carr 1980. "Conjugal Relationships in the Context of the Black Extended Family." *Alternative Lifestyles* 3 (November):463–84.

Bender, D. R. 1967. "A Refinement of the Concept of Household: Families, Co-residence, and Domestic Functions." *American Anthropologist* 69 (October):493–504.

Billingsley, A. 1968. *Black Families in White America.* Englewood Cliffs, NJ: Prentice-Hall.

Blassingame, J. W. 1979. *The Slave Community.* New York: Oxford University Press.

Colson, E. 1962. "Family Change in Contemporary Africa." *Annals of the New York Academy of Sciences* 96 (January):641–52.

Du Bois, W. E. B. [1908] 1969. *The Negro American Family.* New York: New American Library.

Elkins, S. [1959] 1963. *Slavery: A Problem in American Intellectual Life.* New York: Grosset & Dunlap.

English, R. 1974. "Beyond Pathology: Research and Theoretical Perspectives on Black Families." Pp. 39–52 in *Social Research and the Black Community: Selected Issues and Priorities,* edited by L. E. Gary. Washington, DC: Institute for Urban Affairs and Research, Howard University.

Fortes, M. 1949. *The Web of Kinship among the Tallensi.* London: Oxford University Press.

———. 1950. "Kinship and Marriage among the Ashanti." Pp. 252–84 in *African Systems of Kinship and Marriage,* edited by A. R. Radcliffe-Brown and D. Forde. London: Oxford University Press.

———. 1953. "The Structure of Unilineal Descent Groups." *American Anthropologist* 55 (January–March):17–41.

Frazier, E. [1939] 1966. *The Negro Family in the United States.* Chicago: University of Chicago Press.

Furstenberg, F., T. Hershbert, and J. Modell. 1975. "The Origins of the Female-Headed Black Family: The Impact of the Urban Experience." *Journal of Interdisciplinary History* 6 (Autumn):211–33.

Genovese, E. D. 1974. *Roll Jordan Roll: The World the Slaves Made.* New York: Random House.

Goody, J. 1976. *Production and Reproduction: A Comparative Study of the Domestic Domain.* Cambridge: Cambridge University Press.

Gutman, H. 1976. *The Black Family in Slavery and Freedom: 1750–1925.* New York: Random House.

Herskovits, M. J. [1941] 1958. *The Myth of the Negro Past.* Boston: Beacon Press.

Johnson, C. S. 1934. *Shadow of the Plantation.* Chicago: University of Chicago Press.

Kerri, J. N. 1979. "Understanding the African Family: Persistence, Continuity, and Change." *Western Journal of Black Studies* 3 (Spring):14–17.

Landman, R. H. 1978. "Language Policies and Their Implications for Ethnic Relations in the Newly Sovereign States of Sub-Saharan Africa." Pp. 69–90 in *Ethnicity in Modern Africa,* edited by B. M. duToit. Boulder, CO: Westview Press.

Linton, R. 1936. *The Study of Man.* New York: Appleton-Century-Crofts.

Lloyd, P. C. 1968. "Divorce among the Yoruba." *American Anthropologist* 70 (February): 67–81.

Maquet, J. 1972. *Civilizations of Black Africa.* London: Oxford University Press.

Marshall, G. A. [Niara Sudarkasa.] 1968. "Marriage: Comparative Analysis." In *International Encyclopedia of the Social Sciences.* Vol. 10. New York: Macmillan/Free Press.

Murdock, G. P. 1949. *Social Structure.* New York: Macmillan.

Nobles, W. 1974a. "African Root and American Fruit: The Black Family." *Journal of Social and Behavioral Sciences* 20:52–64.

———. 1974b. "Africanity: Its Role in Black Families." *The Black Scholar* 9 (June):10–17.

———. 1978. "Toward an Empirical and Theoretical Framework for Defining Black Families." *Journal of Marriage and the Family* 40 (November):679–88.

Okediji, P. A. 1975. "A Psychosocial Analysis of the Extended Family: The African Case." *African Urban Notes,* Series B 1(3):93–99. (African Studies Center, Michigan State University.)

Onwuejeogwu, M. A. 1975. *The Social Anthropology of Africa: An Introduction.* London: Heinemann.

Oppong, C. 1974. *Marriage among a Matrilineal Elite: A Family Study of Ghanaian Senior Civil Servants.* Cambridge: Cambridge University Press.

Owens, L. H. 1976. *This Species of Property: Slave Life and Culture in the Old South.* New York: Oxford University Press.

Perdue, C. L., Jr., T. E. Barden, and R. K. Phillips, eds. 1980. *Weevils in the Wheat: Interviews with Virginia Ex-Slaves.* Bloomington: Indiana University Press.

Powdermaker, H. 1939. *After Freedom: A Cultural Study in the Deep South.* New York: Viking Press.

Radcliffe-Brown, A. R. 1950. "Introduction." Pp. 1–85 in *African Systems of Kinship and Marriage,* edited by A. R. Radcliffe-Brown and D. Forde. London: Oxford University Press.

Radcliffe-Brown, A. R. and D. Forde, eds. 1950. *African Systems of Kinship and Marriage.* London: Oxford University Press.

Rivers, W. H. R. 1924. *Social Organization.* New York: Knopf.

Robertson, C. 1976. "Ga Women and Socioeconomic Change in Accra, Ghana." Pp. 111–33 in *Women in Africa: Studies in Social and Economic Change,* edited by N. J. Hafkin and E. G. Bay. Stanford, CA: Stanford University Press.

Shimkin, D., E. M. Shimkin, and D. A. Frate, eds. 1978. *The Extended Family in Black Societies.* The Hague: Mouton.

Shimkin, D. and V. Uchendu. 1978. "Persistence, Borrowing, and Adaptive Changes in Black Kinship Systems: Some Issues and Their Significance." Pp. 391–406 in *The Extended Family in Black Societies,* edited by D. Shimkin, E. M. Shimkin, and D. A. Frate. The Hague: Mouton.

Shorter, E. 1975. *The Making of the Modern Family.* New York: Basic Books.

Smith, R. T. 1973. "The Matrifocal Family." Pp. 121–44 in *The Character of Kinship,* edited by J. Goody. Cambridge: Cambridge University Press.

Stack, C. 1974. *All Our Kin.* New York: Harper & Row.

Staples, R. 1971. "Toward a Sociology of the Black Family: A Decade of Theory and Research." *Journal of Marriage and the Family* 33 (February):19–38.

——, ed. 1978. *The Black Family: Essays and Studies.* Belmont, CA: Wadsworth.

Stone, L. 1975. "The Rise of the Nuclear Family in Early Modern England: The Patriarchal Stage." Pp. 13–57 in *The Family in History,* edited by C. E. Rosenberg. Philadelphia: University of Pennsylvania Press.

Sudarkasa, N. 1973. *Where Women Work: A Study of Yoruba Women in the Marketplace and in the Home.* Anthropological Papers No. 53. Ann Arbor: Museum of Anthropology, University of Michigan.

——. 1975a. "An Exposition on the Value Premises Underlying Black Family Studies." *Journal of the National Medical Association* 19 (May):235–39.

——. 1975b. "National Development Planning for the Promotion and Protection of the Family." *Proceedings of the Conference on Social Research and National Development,* edited by E. Akeredolu-Ale. The Nigerian Institute of Social and Economic Research, Ibadan, Nigeria.

——. 1976. "Female Employment and Family Organization in West Africa." Pp. 48–63 in *New Research on Women and Sex Roles,* edited by D. G. McGuigan. Ann Arbor: Center for Continuing Education of Women, University of Michigan.

——. 1980. "African and Afro-American Family Structure: A Comparison." *The Black Scholar* 11 (November/December):37–60.

——. 1981. "Understanding the Dynamics of Consanguinity and Conjugality in Contemporary Black Family Organization." Presented at the Seventh Annual Third World Conference, Chicago, March 1981.

Tilly, L. A. and J. W. Scott. 1978. *Women, Work, and Family.* New York: Holt, Rinehart & Winston.

Uchendu, V. 1965. *The Igbo of South-Eastern Nigeria.* New York: Holt, Rinehart & Winston.

Ware, H. 1979. "Polygyny: Women's Views in a Transitional Society, Nigeria 1975." *Journal of Marriage and the Family* 41 (February):185–95.

Woodson, C. G. 1936. *The African Background Outlined.* Washington, DC: Association for the Study of Negro Life and History.

7

LA FAMILIA

Family Cohesion among Mexican American Families in the Urban Southwest, 1848–1900

RICHARD GRISWOLD DEL CASTILLO

You didn't have to ask for anyone's help. They would just come to you. Whenever my mother had a child, the house would be filled with other women who would take care of us children, cook for her, bathe her and the baby, help her in every possible way.

> —Reminiscence of a Woman from South Texas in Foley,
> Mota, Post, and Lozano, *from Peones to Politicos:*
> *Ethnic Relations in a South Texas Town 1900–1977*, p. 59.

Contemporary sociologists studying the Mexican American family have found that *la familia* among the Spanish speaking is often a broad and encompassing term, not one limited to a household or even to biologically related kin. Close bonds of affection and assistance among members of the family household and a wide network of kinfolk have been found to be one of the most important characteristics of Mexican American family life.[1] The network of *la familia* usually includes a number of *compadres*, or coparents, established through rituals of *compadrazgo* (god parenthood). This family, conceived in its broadest sense, is often an important source of emotional and economic support. Family members are expected to be warm and nurturing, and to be willing to provide security for one another throughout their lives. Individuals, as members of a family, whether in a nuclear household or as members of an extended network, are expected to place their personal welfare second only to the welfare of *la familia*.[2] While there is some debate over the exact structural form this extended *familia* has taken in present-day Mexican American society, most experts agree that it is a pervasive characteristic of familial life.[3]

This chapter is concerned with the interplay of economic and cultural forces as they have affected kinship networks and family solidarity. The approach taken here is . . . an attempt to compare the ideology of family solidarity with the empirical evidence of household structures. The Mexican American experience within the extended family is contrasted with that of Anglo Americans and offered as a way to evaluate significant differences and similarities between the two groups.

Without entering into an analysis of contemporary sociological literature regarding Mexican American family solidarity and kinship support, my concern here is rather to describe something of this phenomenon in times past. [My future research] will discuss contemporary aspects of Chicano family life in comparison to what we know about the nineteenth century.

The Origins and Development of Familism

Some have argued that familism, or the values, attitudes, beliefs, and behaviors associated with the Mexican American extended family, has it roots in the pre-Hispanic social world. The Mexica-Aztec family emphasized the individual's subordination to community-defined norms of behavior. Rigid sex roles were determined at birth, and women were regarded as subordinate to men and morally weak. The emphasis in rhetorical orations was on the family's role in promoting proper ritual behavior, maintaining honor, and fostering self-control.[4] The community *calpulli* system of clan organization and the Aztec-Nahua teachings regarding male and female family obligations influenced the Mestizo family, which emerged as a result of mixture with Europeans.[5] Indeed, in many respects the Mexica-Aztec attitudes surrounding family life closely resembled the Iberian-Spanish. The social transitions under Spanish domination in the succeeding centuries reinforced the older pre-Columbian values, while accommodations resulted in a renewed sense of the importance of the Indian community.[6]

Iberian-Spanish family ideology also influenced Mexican and subsequently Mexican American values regarding familism. A 700-year-long conflict with the Moors, who invaded and occupied Spain in the eighth century, heightened the importance of family honor and pure lineage. Struggles between Spanish families over the privileges, titles, and lands that were gained during the reconquest reinforced the importance of family solidarity. A close and prolonged contact with the Moors and Jews in Spain loaded a family's claim to *limpieza de sangre,* or pure blood, with religious and political connotations. In the New World the Spanish attempted to preserve their concept of honor and pure descent by regulating racial mixture. By the laws embodied in the *Regim de Castas* they ranked various degrees of race and ethnic mixture with the supposedly pure Spanish. Family status came to be associated with the degree to which its members had intermarried with "inferior" castes.[7]

The psychological and social meanings of kinship and family bonds differed according to a family's class position. For the landed aristocracy in Mexico and in Spain a continuity in the inheritance of real property, titles, and social status was of utmost importance. For the landless poor the extended *familia* served more as a form of social insurance against hard times. On Mexico's far northern frontier the paternalistic hacienda system was less well established, and the benevolent institutions of the church and state were not well funded or organized. For the poor in this agrarian and pastoral society family solidarity was a necessity, involving the widest possible links with members of the community. The extended family was essential to provide for protection in a hostile environment.[8]

One way that families enlarged their ties to others in the community was through *compadrazgo*. The custom of god parenthood made nonbiologically related individuals of a community members of the extended family. *Compadrazgo* evolved in Mediterranean folk custom as a formal ritual sanctioned by the Catholic Church. Godparents were required for the celebration of the major religious occasions in a person's life: baptism, confirmation, first communion, and marriage. At these times *padrinos, or godfathers,* and *madrinas, or godmothers,* entered into special religious, social, and economic relationships with the godchild, or *ahiado,* as well as with the parents of the child with whom they became *compadres* or *comadres.*[9] In the ideal, *padrinos* acted as co-parents to their *ahiados,* providing discipline and emotional and financial support when needed. They could expect from their godchildren obedience, respect, and love in return. As *compadres* they were expected to become the closest friends of the parents and integral members of the extended family.

Historical evidence of *compadrazgo* is scattered throughout the letters and reminiscences of the Spanish-Mexican frontier aristocracy in the nineteenth century. In 1877, for example, Antonio Coronel in Los Angeles remembered that "the obligations of the godparents was that they should take the place of the parents should they (the parents) die."[10] In their private correspondence the aristocracy sometimes referred to their *padrinos* and *madrinos* as mother (*madre*) and father (*padre*). They expressed obligations to behave toward these kinfolk much in the same manner as they would toward their biological parents. Frequent visits, celebration of namesake saint days (*mañanitas*), anniversaries, and intimate communications with godparents were part of an *ahiado's* normal family life.[11]

Visiting between *comadres* was an important social activity among women, especially in the more isolated rural regions. They often took care of one another's children and had a good deal of authority over them. A teenage diarist in San Antonio during the 1880s told of numerous visits of her mother's *comadre*. Often the *comadre,* Adina de Zavala, stayed with the girl's family for many days.[12] These visits of relatives, *comadres,* and their families were, for this young girl, high points in what she thought was a drab and cloistered life. And so it must have been for many others in a frontier society where so many were so poor and where there were so few amusements for women outside the home environment. Visiting among the families of friends and relatives was perhaps the major form of recreation.

Extended family members including *compadres* and *comadres* also were important during times of crisis. When a woman gave birth or a family member took seriously ill, *comadres* and female relatives automatically came to each other's assistance. Sometimes they even moved their own families into the stricken household on a temporary basis.[13] James Tafolla, living in South Texas during the 1870s and 1880s, recalled that on more than one occasion relatives came to live with his family when he and his wife were sick.[14] And Juan Bandini sadly noted in his diary of having to send his two daughters to live with his sister during a period of personal financial hardship.[15] In these cases and in others it was expected and often true that extended family members would help when needed. Adina de Zavala, a San Antonio matron, expressed this feeling in her journal entry of 1882 when she wrote: "My life is only for my family. My whole life shall be worth while [sic] if I can render happy and comfortable the declining years of my parents and see my brothers safely launched on life's troubled seas."[16]

An important way that families strengthened their support networks outside the immediate kinship arena was through their participation in *mutualistas,* or mutual-aid societies. In both rural and urban areas Mexican Americans sought to insure themselves against the tragedies of death and economic disaster by forming societies where they could pool their meager resources. Most often these *mutualistas* became sources of emergency loans as well. Families often used *mutualistas* like community banks. The mutual-aid societies frequently became a focal point for the community's social life by organizing dances, fiestas, fund raisers, and the like. Occasionally, in conjunction with the Mexican consular offices, they played an important role in helping labor unions during strikes. They also provided help for recent Mexican immigrants by providing temporary housing, food, and job assistance.[17]

The *mutualista* movement among Mexican Americans appears to have been particularly strong in the cities and towns of the Southwest during the late nineteenth century. In Los Angeles, La Sociedad Hispano Americana de Beneficia Mutual was established in 1875 and La Sociedad Progresista Mexicana in 1883. In San Antonio, Mexicanos organized La Sociedad de la Unión in 1886 and La Sociedad de Protección Mutua de Trabajadores Unidos in 1890. These are only a few examples of the many mutual-aid associations which sprang up throughout the last part of the nineteenth century.

A detailed examination of the books of at least one mutual-aid society, that of La Sociedad de la Unión in San Antonio in 1886, reveals that members paid monthly dues of about one dollar and that the average accumulated savings ran between 80 and 90 dollars. Members of La Unión frequently borrowed small sums against their accumulated dues.[18] Thus, the society and others like it acted as community banks, extending credit to persons who normally would have found it difficult to get loans from banks.

Perhaps the largest and longest-lived *mutualista* was La Alianza Hispano Americana in Tucson.[19] Organized in 1894 by Carlos Ignacio Velasco, editor of *El Fronterizo,* and Mariano Samaniego, a wealthy freighter and rancher, La Alianza grew rapidly from a dozen or so subscribers to over 17,000 members in eight states. Like the other mutual-aid societies of that era, La Alianza was at first exclusively a men's organization, but families also participated in the social activities. By 1913 La Alianza began to admit women to equal membership in the organization.

Mutual-aid societies proved to be very popular among the Mexican immigrants who had regular wage-paying jobs. As fraternal societies they provided the kind of support that was often difficult for poor families to provide — a guarantee of a decent funeral was important for the Catholic immigrants.

The societies also provided an important source of entertainment and social activities for members of the working class. They were often a common meeting ground for the immigrant and the native-born Mexican Americans. Not incidentally the *mutualistas* provided status and some economic security for those who were considered aliens by the majority society.

Familism and the Extended Household

Anglo Americans were frequently impressed by the warmth and closeness they found in Mexican American families. Frederick Law Olmstead in 1858 observed that "their manners toward one and another is engaging and that of the children and the parents most affectionate." A Protestant missionary in South Texas wrote that the "Tejanos were kindly in home life, particularly to the aged, and clannish to a degree whole families of several generations occupying one hut."[20] A closeness of affection characterized Mexican American families in the nineteenth century. The roots of this family cohesion, as an emotional reality, lay in religious ideologies and folk customs, as well as in a common poverty.

Family cohesion among the poorer classes can best be studied by analyzing household structures in the nineteenth-century censuses. The surviving documents, letters, and diaries of the Spanish speaking are usually cryptic and incomplete. In any case they reflect the experience of only a handful of upper-class individuals. The degree to which families were willing and able to provide food and shelter for relatives can be viewed as a significant indicator of how families realized, in part, their commitment to a larger extended network. While almost everyone, except the recent immigrants from Mexico, had kin who lived in the same town, only a few were likely to have, at any given moment, a household which they shared with relatives. Extended family households were a temporary and impermanent creation of circumstance arising out of old age, sickness, death, or economic misfortune. Nevertheless, the incidence of extended-family household structures in the general population is one way to determine how families interacted with their *familia*.

Mexican American households may be defined in several ways. Not all households were composed of married couples with or without children (termed "nuclear families"). It was quite common in the nineteenth century for there to be a wide variety of "others" living in households. Boarders, adopted and visiting children, friends, *compadres,* and servants often shared dwellings with married couples. The "extended-family household" was an ideal type, where nuclear families lived with other individuals who were clearly related to the head of the household. These relatives were not always adults, but more often teenagers and children who had come to live with relatives for a variety of reasons. Extended-family households often had "others" such as relatives on the wife's side of the family, servants, boarders, and friends as well as multiple families. Nuclear families who lived in homes without clearly determined relatives but with these "others" may be called the "nuclear-plus-other" type of household. Those households where apparently none of the individuals were related I have termed "no-family" households.

Within these ideal types a good deal of variation in composition and relationship was possible. A couple could be married, sharing the same last name, or live in *unión libre*. Widows and widowers could live alone, with others, or with relatives (a stem family in the last case). Older brothers and sisters could live together with or without children from previous marriages. And a great variety of adults in varying numbers and related by *compadrazgo* or distant kinship could be present in all types of households.

An analysis of the proportions of extended households in comparison to "no-family" households is one way to assess the changing patterns of familism. No-family households were groups of individuals who were obviously living separate from their extended families. The members of these no-family households may have participated in an extended-family network located in the same town or a nearby village or farm. Some may have had nuclear families of their own living in Mexico or elsewhere in the Southwest. But their household status, as boarders, travelers, visitors, transients, or simply unattached individuals, meant that they had weaker ties to family than those individuals who reside with kin. Table 1 shows the relative proportions of extended-family households in comparison to no-family households in the urban Southwest.

Generally, the proportions of extended-family households declined throughout the period. A notable exception to this trend occurred in San Antonio in 1860, where extended households exceeded 27 percent, representing a huge jump from the previous decade. A possible explanation for this unusual increase would be the decade of civil strife in South Texas and Mexico. A series of anti-Mexican riots, the Cart War of 1857, the Cortina rebellion in the Matamoros–Brownsville area in 1859, and the wars of the reform in Mexico (1857–1862) displaced hundreds of families from their ancestral homes in Mexico and the South Texas region.[21] Many Mexicans fleeing the violence in the surrounding countryside may have sought safety with relatives and friends in the comparative security of the large city of San Antonio.

Los Angeles also had a slight increase in extended family households in 1870. This was probably caused by the sudden collapse of the ranching industry in Southern California, which increased unemployment and put pressures on families to consolidate their resources.[22] Barbara Laslett in her study of Los Angeles has found that by 1870 those families that owned real and personal property were more likely to live in extended households than in any others. This had not been the case earlier, indicating that economic pressures were at work.[23]

It should be noted that in Los Angeles and Santa Fe the extended-family household remained about as prevalent in 1880 as it had been in 1850 despite the very different socioeconomic histories of the two towns. Only in San Antonio and Tucson was there a big decline in extended-family households. The expected effect of variations in regional economic development thus did not appear to have an influence on extended-family formation. Indeed, no single set of variables appears to account for these patterns; this underscores

TABLE 1   Proportions of Extended and No-Family Households, 1850–1880

	1850	1860	1870	1880
Los Angeles				
No-family	14.4	26.9	20.6	22.8
Extended	11.5	10.1	15.2	10.2
Tucson				
No-family	—	—	23.9	16.2
Extended	—	—	15.3	10.3
Santa Fe				
No-family	11.8	21.7	30.9	14.4
Extended	15.8	15.2	9.4	13.3
San Antonio				
No-family	17.0	17.8	11.1	18.7
Extended	14.0	27.7	13.2	3.7

the truism that family solidarity was a complex of beliefs, attitudes, and customs that varied often irrespective of the economic cycle.

The pattern of no-family households presents a similar problem of explanation. Generally, at any given census year there were proportionally more unattached individuals than people living in extended families. San Antonio, Santa Fe, and Los Angeles had a net increase in no-family households over the forty-year period. There were progressively more unattached "family-less" individuals in the Mexican American population. This suggests a probable decline in the cohesiveness of the family unit, especially when seen in conjunction with the net decline in extended-family households.

The pattern could also have been caused by increased geographic mobility and by economic pressures. Young men and women left their families of origin to seek adventure and fortune or perhaps in the hope of helping their families to survive. The patterns of the two types of households, the no-family and the extended, seem to have been related. The number of no-family households rose when the proportion of extended households declined. No-family households declined in years when extended households were increasing. It appears that familism, as measured in terms of household organization, acted as a safety valve for temporary dislocations. In Laslett's theoretical view . . . the formation of extended families was a strategy for family survival.

The Formation of Extended–Family Households

The formation of extended-family households among Mexican Americans was influenced by a number of factors: socioeconomic class, nativity, age, sex, and marital status of the head of household. Over the forty-year period most extended families were headed by married, lower-working-class, native-born men

under the age of twenty-five. As the decades progressed, Mexican-born immigrants established more and more extended families, and this indicated a
progressive stabilization of immigrant family life. Little wonder that extended-
family living was most prevalent among the poor and young: both were more
likely to be dependent on relatives for support. The stem family, with young
newly married couples living with older parents, existed hardly at all among
the Mexican Americans. Early in the American era single parents with children
did not tend to live in extended families. The majority of extended households
were of heads of nuclear families with children. A noticeable trend later in the
century was for more and more extended families to be headed by single, unmarried individuals without children. Obviously, the nature of family solidarity changed during the decades—away from the nuclear core families to other
more complex family relationships.

One case history points out this process. In 1860 Francisco Solano lived
in Tucson with his wife, Ramona. The census marshall in that year recorded
that they had six children. Four years later the territorial census taker listed
them as having thirteen children, all with the same last name as the father.
Six years later, in 1870, the Solanos had only seven children, a housekeeper,
and a married son with his common-law wife.[24] Without an exhausting and
probably fruitless genealogical search we will probably never know how the
Solano family mysteriously expanded and contracted during these years. In
only ten years the Solanos had progressed from being a purely nuclear family to being one more complex.

In analyzing the question of why individuals entered into extended-
family relationships, it is useful to compare the Anglo American population
with the Mexican American. Through this comparison we get a better idea of
the role of culture in family solidarity.

Table 2 shows the decennial proportions of household types in the four
towns for Mexican Americans and Anglo Americans. As might be expected,
given the value of *la familia* in Mexican culture, Mexican Americans regularly
had larger proportions of extended-family households and fewer no-family
households than did the Anglo Americans. There was very little difference,
however, with regard to other forms of household organization. Anglo American as well as Mexican immigrants, most of whom were recent arrivals
to these southwestern towns, were unlikely to have many extended-family
members and more likely to be single and unattached. The native-born Spanish speaking, however, had historic kinship ties in the region. For them
extended-family households accounted for a significant proportion of all types
of households until 1880. Over the decades, Mexican Americans and Anglo
Americans became more similar in their family structures. This was largely
due to the fact that more and more Anglo Americans formed extended families, while the proportions of Mexican Americans who lived in these kinds
of households remained the same.

Notwithstanding the possibility that it was more difficult for Anglos to
create large extended families on the frontier, their proportions of these
types exceeded the national averages in the rest of the country except in 1880.

TABLE 2   Distribution of Mexican American (MA) and Anglo
American (AA) Households, 1850–1880 (expressed as a percentage)

	1850		1860		1870		1880	
	MA	AA	MA	AA	MA	AA	MA	AA
N in Sample	(385)	(106)	(687)	(218)	(756)	(376)	(986)	(299)
No-Family	14.5	34.0	24.9	28.0	21.4	30.3	19.8	27.1
Nuclear Family	50.2	42.4	40.9	43.5	45.6	44.7	48.4	45.8
Nuclear plus Other	22.3	17.9	20.8	20.2	19.2	17.0	18.4	20.1
Extended	13.0	5.7	13.4	8.3	13.8	8.0	9.9	7.0

Carl Degler, studying the families who migrated west in the late nineteenth
century, found some evidence to show that many Anglo Americans either
brought kinfolk with them or financed a serial migration of relatives from
back east.[25] During the late nineteenth century the eastern seaboard cities
underwent rapid urbanization and industrialization. The industrial Northeast had the highest percentages of extended families in the nation.

Rudy Ray Seward, who studied this unusual occurrence, believed that
economic and residential pressures in these eastern cities sometimes forced
families to lure wage-paying relatives to come and live with them.[26] The population east of the Mississippi also felt the demographic effects of the Civil
War, which created many broken households and resulted in higher inci-
dences of extended households. Moreover, in the industrial cities newly arriving European migrants tended to cluster along Old World family and town
lines, often sharing the same tenements, apartments, or neighborhoods.

By 1880 the proportions of extended families east of the Mississippi
reached high levels. These same high levels had existed among Mexican
Americans in the urban Southwest for thirty years prior to that time. It is not
at all clear that the prevalence of extended families among the Spanish speaking was due to the same factors that were operating in the East. Of all the
forms of household organization the extended family in the southwestern
cities was most related to ethnicity.[27]

Cultural Factors in Extended–Family Formation

In considering why it was that Mexican Americans tended to have more extended households than did Anglo Americans, inevitably the problem of cultural determinism arises. The question of causation is not easily dismissed by
simply arguing that because of their cultural traditions Mexican Americans
preferred to live with their kin rather than alone or in other types of arrangements. If this were indeed the case, we should have trouble explaining why
it was that at no point in the late nineteenth century did the majority of the

Spanish speaking live in extended-family households. Most lived separate from kin.

One would expect that the kinship organizations of both Americans and Mexican Americans would be disrupted by geographic mobility. Evidence from nineteenth-century western towns on this point suggests that both groups tended to be highly transient. In San Antonio only 32 percent of the total population continued to live in the town between 1880 and 1890.[28] Geographic mobility was most related to socioeconomic status, with the laboring classes being the period 1870–1900, found that only 7 percent of the skilled and unskilled workers continued to live in the city. The rates of persistence were much higher for the middle and upper classes.[29] In Los Angeles only about 11 percent of the Spanish-surnamed population remained in the town during the twenty-year period 1860–1880. Only twenty-two heads of households remained in the town between 1850 and 1880.[30]

There were systematic differences in the composition of Mexican American and Anglo American extended families. Mexican Americans differed most from Anglo Americans with regard to age and occupational status. After 1860 young Mexican Americans tended to be overrepresented in extended households. For Anglos age was not as important. The young were as likely as the aged to be the relatives residing in households. As can be seen in Table 3, the overwhelming majority of Mexican American extended-family members were under twenty-nine years of age in every census year. This was not the case for Anglo Americans.

That so many young people should have been relatives in these Spanish-speaking families seems unusual given our contemporary notions about the family as a collective source of economic support. Few of these young people could contribute much in the way of wages to the households. Some of the older teenagers and young adults worked outside the home to supplement their family's income. But in the census the majority of the young adults were classified as unemployed. Of course there were other ways a young person could help the family, even though not employed in a full-time occupation. He or she could take part-time care for younger children and perform housework, freeing others to enter the job market.

Some of these young relatives probably were newly married spouses who were just starting out and who needed a place to live. In the Spanish and Mexican eras it had been a custom for newlyweds to reside with the bride's parents for a period of time.[31] Other young members of extended households were probably relatives who may have been visitors or orphans.

Indeed, visiting was probably responsible for a significant number of these child relatives. The great distances which sometimes separated extended-family members led to protracted visits whenever they got together. In the early 1900s, for example, Dolores Aguirre sent her daughter to visit relatives in El Paso, Texas. Lupe stayed with her aunt Dolores P. de Bennet three weeks and then was sent to visit her cousins in Juárez for another month.[32] Many of the wealthier families had guest rooms that they used to put up friends and relatives during their stays. The Ochoa family in Tucson, for example, had

TABLE 3 Age Characteristics of Mexican American and Anglo American
Relatives Living in Extended Households, 1850–1880 (expressed as a percentage)

Age Categories	1850		1860		1870		1880	
	MA	AA	MA	AA	MA	AA	MA	AA
1–19	55.2	25.0	57.5	56.5	58.6	19.2	57.9	50.0
20–29	23.2	37.5	24.6	21.7	14.8	19.2	22.2	7.1
30–49	17.3	37.5	11.0	13.1	19.5	34.6	11.1	14.3
50–	4.3	0	6.0	8.7	7.1	27.0	8.8	28.6

three or four rooms set aside for this purpose. The house was reportedly always full of friends and relatives, who visited for long periods of time.[33] A general ethic of hospitality and sharing was traditional in Spanish-speaking society. This had the domestic result of reducing isolation and integrating family members with a great variety of others. Mutual respect and formality ensured a degree of privacy. By and large the family's home was available and open to almost everyone of good will. To be sure, the ability of a family to support visitors depended on its economic resources, although even the poorer classes were quick to share their meager food and humble abodes with visitors and relatives.

It may be stretching the point to call these households "extended" when many had this structure only because of the presence of young visitors, cousins, siblings, adopted children, stepchildren, and distant kinfolk. The presence of these youthful relatives also suggests that some nuclear families were unable to provide a supporting home environment for children.

Judge Benjamin Hayes recounted one example of how children came to be displaced from a nuclear family. In 1856 he told the story of a native California woman who came to him for legal advice. Months earlier she had applied for a divorce from her husband, who had been mistreating her. At this time the husband along with the children moved into his mother's home. Subsequently the couple had been reconciled, but the mother-in-law refused to forgive her son's wife, and she would not allow her to have her children back. "This mother (the mother-in-law) fired with wrath whenever the subject was mentioned, and warned the son that if he received his repentant wife she would give him her malediction, a mother's curse, a wish that he might go out upon the earth in rags, with neither bread to eat nor water to drink, a dire malediction dreaded by the son with a terror he cannot overcome, for it appears that Religion had no exorcismal value."[34]

The story of the wrathful mother-in-law indicates how much influence parents in Mexican American society had over their married children's lives. From the mother-in-law's perspective, her son's wife had violated a taboo against divorce and thus was not worthy of raising her own children. Stories like this illustrate the importance of tradition and ideology in family life. It also points out the occasional role that culture, and not incidentally emotion, played in breaking up nuclear families.

Comparisons with Other Extended Households

Economic factors seem to have been relatively more important in the formation and maintenance of Anglo American extended households. Most relatives in Mexican American extended households were unemployed or under the age of 19. But in every census year except 1880 proportionally more Anglo relatives tended to have wage-paying jobs. Thus Anglo American extended households tended to benefit economically from the incomes of their relatives. This was not true of the majority of Mexican American households. For Anglo relatives, joining a nuclear family appeared to be more a matter of individual choice and, perhaps, negotiation. Both the individual and the receiving family stood to benefit. The American extended families appeared less to be the result of crises than economic and perhaps residential convenience.

This point of view is strengthened by evidence from studies of extended families in industrial cities in both America and England during the late nineteenth century. Howard Chudacoff and Tamara Hareven studied Essex County, Massachusetts, between 1860 and 1889 and found that it became progressively more difficult for young people to find inexpensive housing. Newly married couples and young people who were anxious to leave home were pressured by the difficulty of finding suitable housing. For economic reasons they continued to live with their parents. During their prolonged stay they contributed to the family by having jobs. The "empty nest" syndrome was less common among Americans in these cities than later in the twentieth century.[35] . . .

The evidence surrounding family solidarity among Mexican Americans suggests that the kinship network functioned primarily as a support system during times of crisis. It seems to have served the same function among blacks. In Herbert Gutman's view, "extended and augmented families were important 'adaptive strategies' to deal with the poverty most Blacks knew." Indeed the proportions of extended and augmented families among blacks seem to have increased when more and more families moved to the cities. In 1880 approximately 36 percent of all black households in Mobile and Richmond were extended or augmented. By 1900 samples from the same urban areas showed rates of family extension as high as 59 percent.[36]

In the nineteenth century the extended-family household among Mexican Americans was an important institution, much more so then than now. It functioned primarily as a place to take care of displaced children. Contrary to the contemporary ideal conceptualizations of the Chicano family, there were very few aged *abuelos and abuelitas* (grandfathers and grandmothers) who lived with nuclear families. In fact, the probability that the aged would find shelter with the families of their children was greater for Anglo Americans than it was for Mexican Americans.

Extended households among the Spanish speaking were more important as emotional support systems than was true for other Americans in the West. They were vital to ensure the proper rearing of children and were less important as a means of economic security for adults.

The Diversity of Household Organization

Neither the majority of Anglo Americans nor of Mexican Americans lived in extended or in nuclear households. In fact, a great diversity of living arrangements characterized both groups. Table 2 illustrated four different types of households found among Mexican Americans and Anglo Americans. Throughout the decades there were few differences between the two groups with respect to the proportions of households containing nuclear, nuclear-plus-other families, or "no-family" households. The most important differences, those that relate how the culture and the economy affected Mexican Americans, were the higher numbers of female-headed households and extended households among the Spanish speaking. The former seems to have resulted primarily from economic pressures, while the latter, the extended-family household, from cultural patterns.

Given the wide diversity of household types and a lack of geographic stability for both Anglo Americans and Mexican Americans, it seems likely that family solidarity was realized in a great variety of settings, not just in extended-household situations. Fluid and dynamic family structures changed to meet the needs of individuals. The kinds of support and degree of interaction between kin and the members of households varied according to a great variety of factors: the residential proximity of kinfolk, the social status and economic class of the family in relation to kinfolk, the type of relationship to the head of household (biological or fictive), generational differences, and the personality preferences of individuals.

In sum, it appears that the economic changes in the nineteenth-century urban Southwest did not clearly alter the role of *la familia* as a support network, particularly among the working classes. In fact, for the poorest members of Mexican American society economic insecurities may have resulted in strengthened bonds of family unity. This was despite the fact that the economy also worked to disrupt traditional familistic behavior, mainly by creating broken homes. The existence of extended households which had little economic support from resident kin was evidence that cultural ideals of familism continued to provide strategies for survival during hard times.

ENDNOTES

1. Jaime Sena-Rivera, "Extended Kinship in the United States: Competing Models and the Case of La Familia Chicana," *Journal of Marriage and the Family* 41(1) (February 1979): 121–29; Oscar Ramírez and Carlos H. Arce, "The Contemporary

Chicano Family: An Empirically Based Review," in *Explorations in Chicano Psychology,* ed. Augustine Barron, Jr. (New York: Praeger, 1981), pp. 3–28.

2. Nathan Murillo, "The Mexican American Family," in *Chicanos: Social and Psychological Perspectives,* ed. Nathaniel N. Wagner and Marsha Haug (St. Louis: Mosby, 1971), p. 102; Alfredo Mirandé, "The Chicano Family: A Reanalysis of Conflicting Views," *Journal of Marriage and the Family* 39(4) (November 1977): 751–52.
3. See, for example, Ramírez and Arce, "The Contemporary Chicano Family," pp. 9–11, for a review of the literature on the extended family and its importance.
4. For a full discussion of the Nahuatl attitudes and practices regarding family matters, see Colin M. MacLachlan and Jaime E. Rodríguez, *The Forging of the Cosmic Race: A Reinterpretation of Colonial Mexico* (Berkeley: University of California Press, 1980), pp. 45–50.
5. Ramírez and Arce, "The Contemporary Chicano Family," p. 10; Alfredo Mirandé and Evangelina Enríquez, *La Chicanas: The Mexican-American Woman* (Chicago and London: University of Chicago Press, 1979), pp. 17–23.
6. MacLachlan and Rodríguez, *The Forging of the Cosmic Race,* p. 206.
7. Ramón Gutiérrez, "Marriage, Sex and the Family: Social Change in Colonial New Mexico, 1680–1848" (Ph.D. dissertation, history, University of Wisconsin–Madison, 1980), pp. 93–95, 108.
8. The importance of family ties on the frontier is documented in the histories of Frances Leon Swadesh, *Los Primeros Pobladores: Hispanic Americans of the Ute Frontier* (Notre Dame and London: University of Notre Dame Press, 1974); David J. Weber, ed., *Foreigners in Their Native Land: Historical Roots of the Mexican Americans* (Albuquerque: University of New Mexico Press, 1973); and Father Angélico Chávez, *Origin of New Mexico Families in the Spanish Colonial Period* (Santa Fe: Gannon, 1975).
9. Margaret Clark, *Health in the Mexican American Culture: A Community Study* (Berkeley: University of California Press, 1959), pp. 157–58.
10. Antonio Coronel, "Cosas de California" (ms., Bancroft Library, Berkeley, CA), p. 231.
11. See, for example, Josefa del Valle to her father (ms., May 29, 1876, Coronel Collection, Los Angeles County Museum of Natural History).
12. "Diary of a Young Child," (ms., Adina de Zavala Collection, Benson Library, University of Texas, Austin, 1889).
13. Douglas Foley, Clarice Mota, Donald E. Post, and Ignacio Lozano, *From Peones to Politicos: Ethnic Relations in a South Texas Town, 1900–1977,* University of Texas Monograph No. 3 (Center for Mexican American Studies, 1979), pp. 52, 59.
14. James Tafolla, "Nearing the End of the Trail" (typescript), p. 65.
15. Juan Bandini, *Diary* (typescript, H. E. Huntington Library, San Marino, CA).
16. Adina de Zavala, *Journal,* January 15, 1882 (ms., Benson Library, University of Texas, Austin).
17. See David Maciel, *La Clase Obrera en la Historia de Mexico: Al Norte del Rio Bravo (pasado inmediato) (1930–1980),* Vol. 17 (Mexico DF: Siglo Veintiuno, 1982), for a detailed discussion of *mutualista* activity in relation to the labor movement. See also José Amaro Hernández, *Mutual Aid for Survival: The Case of the Mexican American* (Malabar, FL: Krieger, 1983).
18. Sociedad de la Unión, *Membership Books* (ms., Catholic Archives of San Antonio, Books 1–4 [1886–1935]).
19. Kay Lynn Briegal, "La Alianza Hispano Americana, 1894–1965: A Mexican American Fraternal Insurance Society" (Ph.D. dissertation, history, University of Southern California, 1974).
20. Arnoldo De Leon, *The Tejano Community, 1830–1900* (Albuquerque: University of New Mexico Press, 1982), pp. 127–30.
21. Frederick Law Olmstead, *A Journey through Texas: Or, A Saddle-Trip on the Southwestern Frontier* (1857; reprint edition, Austin: University of Texas Press, 1978), p. 164; Acūna, *Occupied America,* pp. 46–50; Weber, *Foreigners in Their Native Land,* pp. 152–53.

22. Richard Griswold del Castillo, *The Los Angeles Barrio* (Berkeley: University of California Press, 1980), pp. 41–50.
23. Barbara Laslett, "Social Change and the Family: Los Angeles, California, 1850–1870," *American Sociological Review* 42(2) (April 1977): 227.
24. Francisco Solano, "Historical Address" (ms., Arizona Historical Society).
25. Carl Degler, *At Odds: Women and the Family in America from the Revolution to the Present* (New York: Oxford University Press, 1980), p. 105.
26. Rudy Ray Seward, *The American Family: A Demographic History* (Beverly Hills: Sage, 1978), pp. 130–31; this explanation of the increases in urban industrial extended families also has been advanced by Michael Anderson, who has studied the industrial towns of Lancashire, England. See Michael Anderson, "Family, Household and the Industrial Revolution," in *The American Family in Sociohistorical Perspective*, 2d ed., ed. Michael Gordon (New York: St. Martin's Press, 1978), pp. 67, 82.
27. The statistical association of ethnicity with extended-family households (Anglos = 1, Mexican Americans = 0) was a Lambda of −.639 with family-type dependent. For all household types the association was a Tau C score of .051 at a significance level of .0001 ($\chi^2 = 101.8$, sig. .0001).
28. Stephen Thernstrom, *The Other Bostonians: Poverty and Progress in an American Metropolis* (Cambridge, MA: Harvard University Press, 1973), pp. 222–23.
29. Alwyn Barr, "Occupational and Geographic Mobility in San Antonio, 1870–1900," *Social Science Quarterly* 5(2) (September 1970): 401.
30. Griswold del Castillo, *The Los Angeles Barrio*, pp. 36–38.
31. Ibid., p. 65.
32. Dolores P. de Bennet to Dolores Aguirre (ms., Samaniego Collection, Arizona Historical Society, Tucson, 1910).
33. Mrs. Juana Armizo, "Reminiscences of Juana Armizo" (typescript, Arizona Historical Society, Tucson).
34. Judge Benjamin Hayes, *Pioneer Notes from the Diaries of Judge Benjamin Hayes, 1849–1878* (Los Angeles: privately printed, 1929), p. 153.
35. Howard P. Chudacoff and Tamara K. Hareven, "Family Transitions into Old Age" in *Transitions: The Family and Life Course in Historical Perspective*, ed. Tamara K. Hareven (New York: San Francisco: Academic Press, 1976), pp. 217–43.
36. Herbert Gutman, *The Black Family in Slavery and Freedom, 1750–1925* (New York: Pantheon Books, 1976), pp. 448–49.

8

SPLIT HOUSEHOLD, SMALL PRODUCER, AND DUAL WAGE EARNER: AN ANALYSIS OF CHINESE AMERICAN FAMILY STRATEGIES

EVELYN NAKANO GLENN

Most research on family patterns of black and other urban poor minorities points to the decisive impact of larger institutional structures. Particular attention has been paid to structures that lock certain classes of people into marginal employment and/or chronic unemployment (Drake and Cayton 1962; C. Valentine 1968). It has been argued that many characteristics of family organization—for example, reliance on female-based kinship networks—represent strategies for coping with the chronic poverty brought about by institutional racism (Stack 1974; Valentine 1978). Structural factors are considered sufficiently powerful to outweigh the influence of cultural tradition, especially in the case of blacks.

Chinese Americans, despite their historical status as an economically exploited minority, have been treated in almost exactly opposite terms. Studies of the Chinese American family have largely ignored social and economic conditions. They focus on purely cultural determinants, tracing characteristics of family life to Chinese values and traditions. The resulting portrayal of the Chinese American family has been highly favorable; the family is depicted as stable and problem-free—low in rate of divorce (Huang 1976), delinquency (Sollenberger 1969), and welfare dependency (Light 1972). These virtues are attributed to the family-centered values of Chinese society.

Given this positive assessment, the absence of challenge to the cultural approach is understandable. Still, the case of the Chinese cannot be disengaged from controversies involving other minority groups. The apparent fortitude of the Chinese has been cited as evidence supporting the view of black and Hispanic families as disorganized. Along with other "model" minorities, notably the Japanese and Cubans, the Chinese seem to have offered proof that some groups possess cultural resources that enable them to resist the demoralizing effects of poverty and discrimination. By implication, the diffi-

Evelyn Nakano Glenn, "Split Household, Small Producer, and Dual Wage Earner: An Analysis of Chinese American Family Strategies," reprinted from *Journal of Marriage and the Family*, Vol. 45, No. 1 (1983), pp. 35–46. Copyright © 1983 by the National Council on Family Relations, 3989 Central Avenue N.E., Suite 550, Minneapolis, MN 55421. Reprinted by permission.

culties experienced by blacks and Hispanics are due in some measure to the cultural weaknesses of these groups.

On the basis of an historical review and informant interviews,[1] this study argues that a purely cultural analysis does not adequately encompass the historical realities of Chinese American family life. It argues furthermore, that a fuller understanding of the Chinese American family must begin with an examination of the changing constellation of economic, legal, and political constraints that have shaped the Chinese experience in America. When followed by an analysis of the strategies adopted to cope with these constraints, such an examination reveals the many institutionally created problems the Chinese have confronted in forming and maintaining family life, and the variety of strategies they have used to overcome limitations. By positing a more or less passive cultural determinism and a continuity of Chinese culture, the cultural approach used up to now by many writers tends to obscure not only the problems and struggles of Chinese American families but also their heterogeneity over time.

Cultural vs. Institutional Approaches to the Chinese American Family

The cultural approach grows out of the dominant assimilative perspective in the race- and ethnic-relations field (Gordon 1964; Park 1950). This perspective focuses on the initial cultural and social differences among groups and attempts to trace the process of assimilation over time; much literature on Chinese Americans is framed in these terms (Hirata 1976). The rather extreme emphasis on traditional *Chinese* culture, however, seems to require further explanation. The emphasis may be due in part to the prevailing conception of the Chinese as perpetual foreigners or "strangers" (Wolfe 1950). The image of the Chinese as strange, exotic, and different seems to have preceded their actual arrival in the United States (Miller 1969). Since arriving, their marginal position in the larger society, combined with racist ideology, has served to perpetuate and popularize the image. First, laws excluding the Chinese from citizenship and preventing them from bringing over spouses and children ensured that for over 130 years a large proportion of the Chinese American population consisted of non–English-speaking alien residents. Second, discriminatory laws and practices forced the Chinese to congregate in ethnic ghettos and to concentrate in a narrow range of enterprises such as laundries, restaurants, and tourist-oriented businesses (Light and Wong 1975) that simultaneously reinforced and exploited their foreignness. Moreover, because of distinctive racial features, Americans of Chinese ancestry have been lumped together in the public mind with Chinese foreign nationals and recent immigrants, so that third-, fourth- or even fifth-generation Americans are assumed to be culturally as well as racially Asian. It is not surprising, therefore, to find that until recently studies of Chinese Americans interpreted social and community organizational patterns as products of Chinese culture rather than as responses to economic and social conditions in the United States (Lyman 1974 is an exception; see also Hirata 1976 and Kwong 1979 for related critiques).

Studies of family life follow in this same mold. Authors typically begin by examining traditional Chinese family patterns, then attempt to show how these patterns are expressed in a new setting and undergo gradual change through acculturation (e.g., Haynor and Reynolds 1937; Hsu 1971; Kung 1962; Sung 1971; Weiss 1974). The features identified as typical of Chinese American families and as evidence of cultural continuity are (a) stable family units as indicated by low rates of divorce and illegitimacy; (b) close ties between generations, as shown by the absence of adolescent rebellion and juvenile delinquency; (c) economic self-sufficiency, demonstrated by avoidance of welfare dependency; and (d) conservatism, expressed by retention of Chinese language and customs in the home.

Each of these characteristics is interpreted in terms of specific aspects of Chinese culture. For example, the primacy of the family unit over the individual in Chinese society is credited for the rarity of divorce. Similarly, the principles of Confucianism (filial piety, respect for elders, and reverence for tradition) are cited as the philosophical bases for close control over children by parents and retention of Chinese language and customs in the home; and the family-based production system in the Chinese agricultural village is seen as the precedent for immigrants' involvement in family enterprise and economic self-sufficiency.

An institutional approach starts at a different point, looking not at Chinese society but at conditions in the United States. More specifically, it focuses on the legal and political restrictions imposed on the Chinese, particularly with respect to immigration, citizenship, residential mobility, and economic activity. The Chinese were the first group excluded on racial grounds for legally immigrating, starting in 1882 and continuing until the mid-1950s. When they were allowed entry, it was under severe restrictions which made it difficult for them to form and maintain families in the United States. They also were denied the right to become naturalized citizens, a right withheld until 1943. This meant that for most of their 130-year history in the United States, the Chinese were categorically excluded from political participation and entrance into occupations and professions requiring citizenship for licensing (see Konvitz 1946). In addition, during the latter part of the nineteenth century and through the early twentieth, California and other western states in which the Chinese were concentrated imposed head taxes and prohibited Chinese from carrying on certain types of businesses. The Chinese were routinely denied most civil rights, including the right to testify in court, so they had no legal recourse against injury or exploitation (Jacobs and Landau 1971; Wu 1972). Having initially worked in railroad building, agriculture, and mining, the Chinese were driven out of smaller towns, rural areas, and mining camps during the late nineteenth century and were forced to congregate in urban ghettos (Lyman 1977). The effect of these various restrictions was to keep the Chinese in the status of alien guests or commuters going back and forth between China and America. In addition, the restrictions led to a population made up disproportionately of male adults, concentrated in Chinatowns, and limited to a few occupations and industries.

These circumstances provide an alternative explanation for some of the features previously described as originating in Chinese culture: (a) low divorce rates result when spouses are forced to stay together by the lack of economic options outside of family enterprises; (b) low delinquency rates may reflect the demographic composition of the population which, up to the mid-1950s, contained few adolescents who, therefore, could be more effectively controlled by community sanctions; (c) avoidance of welfare is necessitated by the illegal status of many immigrants and the lack of access to sources outside the community; (d) retention of Chinese language and custom is a logical outcome of ghetto life and denial of permanent membership in American society.

Being able to generate plausible explanations does not itself constitute support for one approach over the other. However, in addition to offering alternative interpretations, the two approaches lead to quite different expectations regarding the degree of types of changes which the Chinese American family has undergone over time. By tracing family patterns to a specific cultural system, the *cultural approach* implies a continuity in family organization over time, with change occurring gradually and linearly via acculturation. By connecting family patterns to contemporaneous institutional structures, the *institutional approach* implies that family organization could and probably would undergo dramatic change with alteration in external constraints. A related point is that the cultural approach suggests that Chinese American family patterns are unique to this group, while the institutional approach suggests that other groups with differing cultural traditions might display similar patterns under parallel conditions.

The analysis that follows tests these expectations against the historical evidence by documenting the existence of qualitatively different family forms among Chinese Americans in different historical periods, with occasional reference to similar family forms among other groups in comparable circumstances. Three distinct family types are identified, corresponding to three periods demarcated by shifts in institutional constraints.

The Split–Household Family

For the first seventy years of Chinese presence in the United States, from 1850 to 1920, one can hardly speak of family life, since there were so few women or children (Lyman 1968; Nee and Nee 1974). As Table 1 shows, from the late nineteenth to the early twentieth century, the ratio of males to females ranged from 13:1 to 20:1. In 1900 less than 4 percent of the Chinese population consisted of children fourteen years and under, compared to 37.4 percent of the population of whites of native parentage (U.S. Census 1902).

TABLE 1   Chinese Population in the United States, by Sex, Sex Ratio, Percentage Foreign Born, and Percentage Under Age 15, 1860–1970

Year	Total	Male	Female	Male/Female Ratio	% Foreign Born	% Aged 14 or Under
1860	34,933	33,149	1,784	18.58		
1870	63,199	58,633	4,566	12.84	99.8	
1880	105,465	100,686	4,779	21.06	99.0	
1890	107,475	103,607	3,868	26.79	99.3	
1900	89,863	85,341	4,522	18.87	90.7	3.4
1910	71,531	66,856	4,675	14.30	79.3	
1920	61,639	53,891	7,748	6.96	69.9	12.0
1930	74,954	59,802	15,152	3.95	58.8	20.4
1940	77,504	57,389	20,115	2.85	48.1	21.2
1950	117,140	76,725	40,415	1.90	47.0	23.3
1960	236,084	135,430	100,654	1.35	39.5	33.0
1970	431,583	226,733	204,850	1.11	46.9	26.6

Source: U.S. Censuses for the years 1872, 1883, 1895, 1902, 1913, 1922, 1933, 1943, 1953, 1963, and 1973. List of specific tables available upon request.

The first thirty-two years, from 1850 to 1882, was a period of open immigration, when over 300,000 Chinese left Guangdong Province to work in California and the West (Lyman 1974). Most were able-bodied young men, recruited for labor on the railroads and in agriculture, mining, and manufacturing. Although some men of the merchant class came and brought wives or concubines, the vast majority of immigrants were laborers who came alone, not intending to stay; over half left wives behind in China (Coolidge 1909). Many were too impoverished to pay for passage and came on the credit ticket system, which obligated them to work for a fixed term, usually seven years, to pay for transport (Ling 1912). These "birds of passage" labored to send remittances to relatives and to accumulate capital to enable them to acquire land in China. Two-thirds apparently succeeded in returning, as there were never more than 110,000 Chinese in the United States at any one time.

It is possible that, like other Asian immigrants, Chinese laborers eventually would have sent for wives, had open immigration continued. The passage of the Chinese Exclusion Act of 1882 precluded this possibility. The Act barred laborers and their relatives but exempted officials, students, tourists, merchants, and relatives of merchants and citizens. Renewals of the Act in 1892 and 1902 placed further restrictions on entry and return. Finally, the Immigration Act of 1924 cut off all immigration from Asia (Wu 1972). These acts achieved their aim, which was to prevent the Chinese from settling in the United States. With almost no new immigration and the return of many sojourners to China, the Chinese population dwindled from a high of 107,000 in 1890 to 61,000 in 1920. Chinese men of the laboring class—faced with an unfavorable sex ratio, forbidden as non-citizens from bringing over wives, and prevented by laws in most western states from marrying whites—had three choices: (a) return permanently to China; (b) if single, stay in the United States as bachelors; or (c) if married, remain separated from families except for occasional visits.

Faced with these alternatives, the Chinese nevertheless managed to take advantage of openings in the law; if they had not, the Chinese population in the United States would have disappeared. One category for which entry was still allowed was relatives of citizens. Men born in the United States could return to China, marry, and father children, who were then eligible for entry. The 1906 earthquake and fire in San Francisco that destroyed most municipal records proved a boon for the large Chinese population of that area. Henceforth, residents could claim American birth without officials being able to disprove the contention (Sung 1971). It became common practice for American-born Chinese (actual or claimed) to visit China, report the birth of a son, and thereby create an entry slot. Years later the slot could be used by a relative, or the papers could be sold to someone wanting to immigrate. The purchaser, called a "paper son," simply assumed the name and identity of the alleged son.

Using these openings, many families adopted a strategy of long-term sojourning. Successive generations of men emigrated as paper sons. To ensure loyalty to kin, young men were married off before leaving. Once in America, they were expected to send money to support not only wives and children but also parents, brothers, and other relatives. In some villages, overseas remittances constituted the main source of income. It has been estimated that between 1937 and 1940 overseas Chinese remitted more than $2 billion, and that an average of $7 million per annum was sent from the United States in the years between 1938 and 1947 (Lyman 1968; Sung 1971). In one typical family history, recounted by a 21-year-old college student, great-grandfather arrived in the United States in the 1890s as a paper son and worked for about twenty years as a laborer. He then sent for the grandfather, who helped great-grandfather run a small business. Great-grandfather subsequently returned to China, leaving grandfather to carry on the business and forward remittances. In the 1940s grandfather sent for father. Up to this point, none of the wives had left China; finally, in the late 1950s, father returned to China and brought back his wife, so that after nearly seventy years, a child was finally born in the United States.

The sojourning strategy led to a distinctive family form, the *split-household family*. A common sociological definition of a family is: a group of people related by blood or marriage, cooperating to perform essential domestic tasks such as production, consumption, reproduction, and socialization. In the split-household family, production would be separated from other functions and carried out by a member living far away (who, of course, would be responsible for his own consumption needs). The other functions—reproduction, socialization, and the rest of consumption—would be carried out by the wife and other relatives in the home village. The family would remain an interdependent, cooperative unit, thereby fulfilling the definition of a family, despite geographic separation. The split-household form made possible the maximum exploitation of the worker. The labor of prime-age male workers could be bought relatively cheaply, since the cost of reproduction and family maintenance was borne partially by unpaid subsistence work of women and old people in the village. The sojourner's remittances, though small by U.S. standards, afforded a comfortable standard of living for family members in China.

The split household is not unique to the Chinese and, therefore, cannot be explained as a culturally preferred pattern. Sojourning occurs where there are (a) large differences in the level of economic development of receiving vs. sending regions, and (b) legal/administrative barriers to integration of the sending group. Three examples of the phenomenon are guest workers in Western Europe (Castles and Kosack 1973); gold-mine workers in South Africa (Boserup 1970); and Mexican braceros in the American Southwest (Power 1979). In all three cases, prime-age workers from disadvantaged regions are issued limited-duration permits to reside in regions needing low-wage labor but are prevented from bringing relatives or settling permanently. Thus, the host country benefits from the labor of sojourners without having to incorporate them into the society. Although the persistence of sojourning for several generations makes the Chinese somewhat unusual, there is evidence that legal restrictions were critical to maintaining the pattern. Other societies to which the Chinese immigrated did not prohibit intermarriage or limit economic competition — for example, Peru and the Philippines. In these societies, a high proportion of the Chinese intermarried with the native population (Hunt and Walker 1974; Wong 1978).

The life of the Chinese sojourner in the United States has been described in sociological and historical studies (see Lyman 1977; Nee and Nee 1974). Employed as laborers or engaged in small enterprises, the men lived in rented rooms alone or with other "bachelors." In place of kin ties, they relied on immigrant associations based on fictive clan relationships. As is common in predominantly male societies, many sojourners found outlets in gambling, prostitution, and drugs. Those successful enough or frugal enough to pay for passage returned periodically to China to visit and to father more children. Others, as a result of bad luck or personal disorganization, could never save enough to return. Even with movement back and forth, many sojourners gradually came to feel remote from village ties, and attached to life in the Chinese American colony. Thus, they ended up staying in the United States more or less by choice (Siu 1952).

The situation of wives and relatives in China has not been documented in the literature. According to informants, wives generally resided with in-laws; and remittances were sent to the husband's kin, usually a brother or son, to ensure that wives remained chaste and subject to the ultimate control of their husbands. Despite the lack of formal authority, most wives had informal influence and were consulted on major decisions. An American-born informant, the daughter of an herbalist and his concubine, was sent as a young girl to be raised by her father's first wife in China. This first wife never wanted to join her husband, as she lived quite comfortably in the village; with remittances from her husband, she maintained a large house with two servants and oversaw substantial landholdings and investments. The father's concubine led an arduous life in the United States, raising several children, running the household, and working long hours in the shop.

Parent–child relations were inevitably affected by separation. The mother–child tie was strengthened by the absence of the father. The mother's tie with her eldest son, normally an important source of leverage within an extended-kin household, became particularly close. In contrast, prolonged absence made the father's relationship with his children more formal and distant. The long periods between visits meant that the children were spaced far apart, and the father was often middle-aged or elderly by the time the youngest child was born. The age gap between fathers and later children added to the formality of the relationship.

The Small–Producer Family

Despite obstacles to family formation, the presence of families was evident in the major U.S. Chinatowns by the 1920s. As Table 1 shows, the male–female ratio fell, and the proportion of children nearly doubled between 1920 and 1930. These early families were started primarily by small entrepreneurs, former laborers who had accumulated enough capital to start a small business alone or in partnership. Due to occupational restrictions and limited capital, the enterprises were confined to laundries, restaurants, groceries, and other small shops. Once in business they could register as merchants, return to China, and bring over wives and children. There was an economic incentive to bring over families; besides providing companionship and affection, women and children were a source of free labor for the business.

The number of families grew steadily, then jumped dramatically during the 1950s due to changes in immigration regulations. The first small opening was created in 1943 with the repeal of the Chinese Exclusion Act. In recognition of China's position as an ally in World War II, a token quota of 105 entrants per year was granted, and permanent residents were declared eligible for citizenship. A larger opening was created by the "Brides Act" of 1946, which permitted entry to wives and children of citizens and permanent residents, and by the Immigration Act of 1953, which gave preference to relatives of citizens (Lee 1956; Li 1977b). For the first time in over sixty years, sizable legal immigration flowed from China; and for the first time in history, the majority of entrants were women. The women fell into two general categories: wives separated from their husbands for periods ranging up to thirty years or more, and brides of servicemen and other citizens who took advantage of the 1946 and 1953 laws to visit China and get married (Lee 1956). The marriages were usually arranged hastily; Chinese families were eager to have eligible daughters married to Americans, so the men had no problem finding prospects on short notice. At the same time, parents of American-born men often preferred Chinese-born brides (Lee 1956). An American-born woman explained why; she once had an engagement broken off because her fiancé's parents objected to the marriage:

> *They thought American girls will be bossy; she'll steal the son and go out freely. They said, "She will ruin your life. She'll be free spending with money." Also, she won't support the parents the rest of their life. They want a typical Chinese girl who will do what the father wants.* [Interview with subject]

At his parent's urging, the fiancé later visited China and brought back a wife.

During the period from about 1920 to the mid-1960s, the typical immigrant and first-generation family functioned as a productive unit in which all members, including children, worked without wages in a family business. The business was profitable only because it was labor-intensive and members put in extremely long hours. Often, for reasons of thrift, convenience, or lack of options, the family's living quarters were located above or behind the shop; thus, the workplace and home were physically joined.

Some flavor of the close integration of work and family life is seen in this description of the daily routine in a family laundry, provided by a woman who grew up in Boston's Chinatown during the 1930s and 1940s. The household consisted of the parents and four children. The work day started at 7:00 in the morning and did not end until midnight, six days a week. Except for school and a short nap in the afternoon, the children worked the same hours as the parents, doing their homework between midnight and 2:00 A.M. Each day's routine was the same. All items were marked or tagged as they were brought in by customers. A commercial cleaner picked up the laundry, washed it, and brought it back wet. The wet laundry was hung to dry in a back room heated by a coal burner. Next, items were taken down, sprinkled, starched, and rolled for ironing. Tasks were allocated by age and sex. Young children of six or seven performed simple tasks such as folding socks and wrapping parcels. At about age ten they started ironing handkerchiefs and underwear. Mother operated the collar and cuff press, while father hand-ironed shirts and uniforms. Only on Sunday did the family relax its hectic regimen to attend church in the morning and relax in the afternoon.

This family may have been unusually hard working, but this sort of work-centered family life was common among the generation that grew up between 1920 and 1960. In fact, the close-knit small-business family was portrayed in several popular autobiographies covering this period (Kingston 1976; Lowe 1943; Wong 1950). These accounts describe a life of strict discipline, constant toil, and frugality. Family members constantly interacted, but communication tended to revolve around concrete details of work. Parents directed and admonished the children in Chinese as they worked, so that the American-born Chinese became fluent in Chinese as well as in English, which they learned in school. Education was stressed, so that children's time was fully occupied by studying, working, and caring for younger siblings. Not so apparent in these accounts was the high incidence of disease, including tuberculosis, due to overcrowding and overwork (Lee et al. 1969).

The small-producer family had several distinct characteristics. First was the lack of any clear demarcation between work and family life. Child care, domestic maintenance, and income-producing activities occurred simultaneously in time and in the same location. Second was the self-contained nature of the family as a production and consumption unit. All members contributed to family income and domestic maintenance, including the children. Third was the division of labor by age and gender, with gradations of responsibility according to capacity and experience. Elder siblings were responsible for disciplining and taking care of younger siblings, who in turn were expected to defer to their older brothers and sisters. Finally, there was an emphasis on the collectivity over the individual. With so many individuals working in close quarters for extended periods of time, a high premium was placed on cooperation. Self-expression, which might engender conflict, had to be curbed.

While these features are in some way similar to those found in Chinese peasant families, they do not necessarily represent carryovers of Chinese patterns; they can be attributed equally to the particular material and social conditions arising from the family's involvement in small enterprise, an involvement dictated by limited economic options. There is evidence that these features are common to small-producer families in various societies and times (see, for example, Demos' 1970 account of the early Puritan families of the Massachusetts Bay Colony). Moreover, the Chinese American small-producer family had some features that differed from those of rural Chinese families due to circumstances of life in America. Of great significance was the family's location in a society whose dominant language and customs differed greatly. Children had the advantage in this regard. Once they started school, children quickly learned to speak and write English, while parents were rarely able to acquire more than rudimentary English. The parents came to depend on their children to act as mediators in relation to the outside society. As a result, children gained a great deal of status at an early age, in contrast to the subordinate position of children in China. American-born Chinese report that, starting at age eight or nine, they helped their parents in business and domestic matters by reading documents and contracts, accompanying them to the bank to fill out slips, negotiating with customers, and translating notices in stores.

A second circumstance was the age composition of immigrant communities, which were made up primarily of childbearing-aged men, and later, women. In the initial period of family formation, therefore, there were no grandparents; and households tended to be nuclear in form. In China the preferred pattern was for sons to live with parents, and wives were required to defer to mothers-in-law. The young immigrant mother, however, did not have to contend with in-laws. As a result of this, and the fact that she was an equal producer in the family economy, the wife had more autonomy. Many informants recall their mothers as the disciplinarians and central figures in the household.

The Dual Wage Earner Family

Following World War II, particularly after the Civil Rights Movement of the 1960s, discrimination against Asian Americans eased. College-educated Chinese Americans were able to enter white-collar occupations and industries formerly barred to them and to move into previously restricted neighborhoods. Among these socially mobile families, the parents still shop and visit friends in Chinatown; but their children tend not to have ties there. The lowering of barriers also speeded the integration of the so-called scholar-professional immigrants. Educated in Hong Kong, mainland China or Taiwan, many are Mandarin-speaking, in contrast to the Cantonese-speaking resident population. The older segment of this group arrived as students in the 1940s and 1950s and stayed, while the younger segment entered under the 1965 immigration act, which did away with national quotas and gave preference to relatives of citizens and permanent residents and to those in needed occupations. Employed as professionals, this group tends to live in white neighborhoods and to have little connection with Chinatown. Thus, for the socially mobile American-born and the scholar/professional immigrants, the trend has been toward assimilation into the mainstream of American society.

At the same time, however, there has been a countertrend that has re-Sinicized the Chinese American population. The same immigration law that brought in professionals and scholars has brought in an even larger influx of working-class Chinese. Under the liberalized law, over 20,000 Chinese have entered the United States each year since 1965, primarily via Hong Kong (U.S. Department of Justice 1977).[2] About half the immigrants can be classified as working class, having been employed as service workers, operatives, craftsmen, or laborers in Hong Kong (Nee and Nee 1974). After arrival, moreover, a significant proportion of professional, managerial, and white-collar immigrants experience a drop in occupational status into blue-collar and service jobs because of language and licensing difficulties (U.S. Department of Health, Education, and Welfare 1974).

Unlike the earlier immigrants who came over as individuals, most new immigrants come over in family groups — typically a husband, wife, and unmarried children (Li 1977a). The families have pulled up stakes in order to gain greater political security, economic opportunity, and educational advantages for their children. Since the law gives preference to relatives, most families use kinship ties with previous immigrants to gain entry. Frequently, the ties are used in a chainlike fashion (Li 1977b). For example, a couple might sponsor the wife's sister, her husband, and her children; the sister's husband in turn sponsors his parents, who later bring over one of their children, and so forth. In this way an extended-kin network is reunited in the United States.

Initially, the new immigrants usually settle in or near Chinatown so that they can trade in Chinese-speaking stores, use bilingual services, and find employment. They are repopulating and stimulating growth in Chinatowns at a time when these communities are experiencing declines due to the mobility of American-born Chinese (Hong 1976). The new immigrants have less dramatic adjustments to make than did earlier immigrants, having lived for some years in an urban society that exposed them to Western goods and lifestyles. In addition, although bilingual social services are frequently inadequate, municipal and county agencies now provide medical care, advice on immigration problems, family counseling, and the like. The immigrants rely on these public services rather than on the clan associations which, thus, have lost their old influence.

Despite the easier adjustment and greater opportunities for mobility, problems of language, and discrimination in small trade, construction and craft unions still affect immigrants who are not professionally trained. Having given up property, businesses or jobs, and having exhausted their resources to pay for transportation and settlement, they must quickly find a way to make a living and establish their families in a highly industrialized economy. The strategy most families have adopted is for husband and wife to find employment in the secondary labor market, the labor-intensive, low-capital service and small manufacturing sectors. The wage each earns is low, but by pooling income a husband and wife can earn enough to support a family. The typical constellation is a husband, who works as a waiter, cook, janitor, or store helper, and a wife who is employed in a small garment shop (Ikels and Shiang 1979; Nee and Nee 1974; "Tufts' lease . . ." 1981; cf. Lamphere, Silva, and Sousa 1980 for parallels with Azorean immigrants).

Although many women have been employed in Hong Kong, for most it is a new experience to juggle full-time work outside the home with child care and housework. In Hong Kong, mothers could do piecework at home, stitching or assembling plastic flowers during spare hours (Ikels and Shiang 1979). In the United States, employment means a long complicated day involving dropping off children at school, going to work in a shop for a few hours, picking up children from school, preparing food, and returning for a few more hours of work in the shop. Another change in many families is that the women's earnings comprise a greater share of family income in the United States. The pay differential between men and women, which is large in Hong Kong, becomes less or even reversed because of the downward shift in the husband's occupation (Hong 1980). Wives and husbands become more or less coequal breadwinners.

Perhaps the most striking feature of the dual-worker family is the complete segregation of work and family life. As a result, in contrast to the round-the-clock togetherness of the small-producer family, parents and children in the dual-worker family are separated for most of the day. While apart they inhabit totally different worlds. The parents' lives are regulated by the discipline of the job, while children lead relatively unstructured and unsupervised lives, often in the company of peers whose parents also work (Nee and Nee 1974). Furthermore, although mothers are usually at home by early evening, the father's hours may prevent him from seeing the children at all. The most common shift for restaurant workers runs from 2:00 in the afternoon until 11:00 at night. The sons and daughters of restaurant workers reported that they saw their fathers only on their days off.

The parents' fatigue, the long hours of separation, and the lack of common experiences combine to undermine communication. Children complain
that their parents are not around much and, when they are, are too tired to
talk. One young student notes, "We can discuss things, but we don't talk that
much. We don't have that much to say." In addition, many parents suffered
serious trauma during World War II and the Chinese Revolution, which they
refuse to discuss. This refusal causes blocks to intimacy between parents and
children since certain topics become taboo. For their part, parents complain
that they have lost control over their children. They attribute the loss of influence to the fact that children adjust to American ways and learn English
much more quickly than parents. Over a period of years, a language barrier
frequently develops. Since parents are not around to direct and speak to children in Chinese, the children of wage-earning parents lost the ability (or willingness) to speak Chinese. When they reach adolescence, moreover, children
can find part-time employment, which gives them financial independence as
well as money to spend on outside recreation.

The absence of a close-knit family life among dual-worker families has
been blamed for the eruption of youth rebellion, delinquency, and gang violence in Chinatowns during the 1960s and 1970s (Lyman 1974; Nee and Nee
1974). While the change in family patterns undoubtedly has been a factor,
other demographic and social changes have contributed to the surfacing of
youth problems (Light and Wong 1975). Adolescents make up a higher proportion of the new immigrants than they did in previous cohorts, and many
immigrants arriving as adolescents encounter difficulties in school because of
the language barrier. When they leave school they face unemployment or the
prospect of low-wage service jobs. Similar obstacles were faced by the early
immigrants, but they take on a new meaning in the present era when expectations are higher and when there is more awareness of institutional racism.

In a similar vein, dual-worker families are beset by the chronic difficulties that plagued Chinese American families in the past—rundown crowded
housing, low incomes, immigration problems, and language difficulties; but
their impact is different now that the family faces them in a less unified fashion. Social workers employed in Chinatown report that the immigrant family is torn by a multiplicity of problems.[3] Ironically, the resilience of the Chinese
American family until recently has retarded efforts at relief. It has taken the
visible outbreak of the youth unrest mentioned above to dramatize the fact
that the Chinese American family cannot endure any and all hardships without support. For the first time, social services, housing programs, and other
forms of support are being offered to Chinese American families.

Summary and Conclusions

This sociohistorical examination of the Chinese American immigrant family
has emphasized three main points: first, throughout their history in the United
States, Chinese Americans have faced a variety of economic, social and polit-

ical constraints that have had direct effects on family life. Second, Chinese American families have displayed considerable resourcefulness in devising strategies to overcome structural obstacles and to take advantage of the options open to them. Third, the strategies adopted have varied according to the conditions prevailing during given historical periods, resulting in three distinct family types. . . .

The split-household type, prevalent until 1920, adopted the strategy of sending married men abroad to specialize in income-producing activities. This created two separate households, one in the United States consisting of a primary individual—or, in some cases, a pair of related males such as a father and son—and another in China, consisting of the relatives of the sojourner—wife, children, parents, and brothers and their wives. Production was separated from the rest of family life, with the husband/father engaging in paid work abroad while the other relatives engaged in subsistence activities (e.g., small-scale farming) and carried out other domestic functions. Husband and wife, therefore, led completely separate existences, with the husband's relation to parents taking precedence over his relation to his wife, and the wife forming her primary attachment with children.

The small-producer type succeeded the split-household type around 1920 and became more common after the late 1940s when women were allowed to join their spouses in the United States. The economic strategy was to engage in small-scale enterprises that relied on the unpaid labor of husband, wife, and children. The nuclear household was the basic unit, with no separation between production and family life, and was focused around work. Close parent–child relations resulted from the enforced togetherness and the constant interaction required to carry on the business. The economic roles of husband and wife were basically parallel, and most daily activities were shared in common.

Finally, the dual-wage type, which has predominated among immigrants arriving after 1965, is based on a strategy of individual wage work, with husband and wife engaged in low-wage employment. The pooling of two wages provides sufficient income to support the family. The household is primarily nuclear, with production and family life separate, as is common in industrial society. The clearest division of labor is between parents and children, with parents specializing in income-producing activities while children are economically inactive. The roles of husband and wife are symmetrical; that is, they engage in similar proportions of paid and unpaid work but in separate settings (cf. Young and Wilmott 1973). Because parent's employment schedules often keep them away from home, there is little shared activity. The parent–child tie becomes attenuated, with children involved in a separate world of peers.

The existence of three distinctly different family types corresponding to different historical periods calls into question the adequacy of purely cultural explanations of Chinese American family patterns. If cultural patterns were the sole or primary determinants, we would expect to find greater continuity in family patterns over time; instead, we find discontinuities associated with shifts in institutional conditions. These discontinuities underline the importance of the larger political economic structures in which the family is embedded.

At the same time, the family is shown as actively striving to survive and maintain ties within the constraints imposed by these structures. The persistence of ties and the variety of strategies adopted by Chinese American families testify to their resilience and resourcefulness in overcoming obstacles. Further insights into the relationships among and between culture, larger institutional structures, and family strategies might be gained through comparative historical analysis of different racial and ethnic groups.

ENDNOTES

The author is grateful to Gloria Chun, Judy Ng, and Yee Mei-Wong for discussions that provided valuable insights; and to Ailee Chin, Gary Glenn, Larry Hong, Charlotte Ikels, Peter Langer, S. M. Miller, T. Scott Miyakawa, and Barbara Vinick for comments on earlier drafts. A previous version of this paper was presented at the meetings for the Study of Social Problems, Toronto, August, 1981.

1. The analysis is based on review of the English-language literature on Chinese Americans and informant interviews of twenty-nine individuals of varying ages, nativity, and family status, mainly residing in the Boston area. Informants were interviewed about family immigration histories, economic activities, household composition, residence, and relations among family members. Social and community workers provided broader information on typical tensions and problems for which help was sought.
2. Although the immigrants enter via Hong Kong, they mostly originate from the same region of southern China as the earlier immigrants. They or their parents fled Guangdong during the Sino-Japanese War or during the land reform following the Communist victory. Hence, they tend to have kinship ties with earlier immigrants.
3. According to community workers and government agencies, the most common problems are low, though not poverty-level, family income; substandard and dilapidated housing; language difficulties; legal problems with immigration; and unresolved past traumas, including separation between family members.

REFERENCES

Billingsley, A. 1968. *Black Families in White America*. Englewood Cliffs, NJ: Prentice-Hall.

Boserup, E. 1970. *Women's Role in Economic Development*. New York: St. Martin's Press.

Castles, S. and G. Kosack. 1973. *Immigrant Workers and Class Structure in Western Europe*. London: Oxford University Press.

Coolidge, Mary. 1909. *Chinese Immigration*. New York: Henry Holt.

Demos, John. 1970. *A Little Commonwealth*. London: Oxford University Press.

Drake, S. C. and H. R. Cayton. 1962. *Black Metropolis*. Rev. ed. New York: Harper and Row.

Frazier, E. F. 1939. *The Negro Family in the United States*. Rev. ed. New York: Macmillan.

Gordon, M. M. 1964. *Assimilation in American Life: The Role of Race, Religion, and National Origin*. New York: Oxford University Press.

Haynor, N. S. and C. N. Reynolds. 1937. "Chinese Family Life in America." *American Sociological Review* 2:630–37.

Herskovits, M. 1958. *The Myth of the Negro Past*. Boston: Beacon Press.

Hill, R. A. 1971. *The Strengths of Black Families*. New York: Emerson Hall.

Hirata, L. C. 1976. "The Chinese American in Sociology." Pp. 20–26 in *Counterpoint: Perspectives on Asian Americans*, edited by E. Gee. Los Angeles: Asian American Studies Center, University of California, Los Angeles.

Hong, L. K. 1976. "Recent Immigrants in the Chinese American Community: Issues of Adaptations and Impacts." *International Migration Review* 10 (Winter):509–14.

———. 1980. Personal communication.

Hsu, F. L. K. 1971. *The Challenge of the American Dream: The Chinese in the United States.* Belmont, CA: Wadsworth.

Huang, L. J. 1976. "The Chinese American Family." Pp. 124–47 in *Ethnic Families in America,* edited by C. H. Mindel and R. W. Habenstein. New York: Elsevier.

Hunt, C. I. and L. Walker. 1974. "Marginal Trading Peoples: Chinese in the Philippines and Indians in Kenya." Chap. 4 in *Ethnic Dynamics: Patterns of Intergroup Relations in Various Societies.* Homewood, IL: Dorsey Press.

Ikels, P. and J. Shiang. 1979. "The Chinese in Greater Boston." Interim Report to the National Institute of Aging.

Jacobs, P. and S. Landau. 1971. *To Serve the Devil.* Vol. 2, *Colonials and Sojourners.* New York: Vintage Books.

Kingston, M. H. 1976. *The Woman Warrior.* New York: Knopf.

Konvitz, M. G. 1946. *The Alien and Asiatic in American Law.* Ithaca, NY: Cornell University Press.

Kung, S. W. 1962. *Chinese in American Life: Some Aspects of Their History, Status, Problems, and Contributions.* Seattle: University of Washington Press.

Kwong, P. 1979. *Chinatown, New York: Labor and Politics, 1930–1950.* New York: Monthly Review Press.

Lamphere, L., F. M. Silva, and J. P. Sousa. 1980. "Kin Networks and Family Strategies; Working Class Portuguese Families in New England." Pp. 219–45 in *The Versatility of Kinships,* edited by L. S. Cordell and S. Beckerman. New York: Academic Press.

Lee, L. P., A. Lim, and H. K. Wong. 1969. Report of the San Francisco Chinese Community Citizen's Survey and Fact Finding Committee (abridged ed.). San Francisco: Chinese Community Citizen's Survey and Fact Finding Committee.

Lee, R. H. 1956. "The Recent Immigrant Chinese Families of the San Francisco-Oakland Area." *Marriage and Family Living* 18 (February):14–24.

Levine, L. W. 1977. *Black Culture and Black Consciousness.* New York: Oxford University Press.

Li, P. S. 1977a. "Occupational Achievement and Kinship Assistance among Chinese Immigrants in Chicago." *Sociological Quarterly* 18(4):478–89.

———. 1977b. "Fictive Kinship, Conjugal Tie and Kinship Claim among Chinese Immigrants in the United States." *Journal of Comparative Family Studies* 8(1):47–64.

Light, I. 1972. *Ethnic Enterprise in America.* Berkeley and Los Angeles: University of California Press.

Light, I. and C. C. Wong. 1975. "Protest or Work: Dilemmas of the Tourist Industry in American Chinatowns." *American Journal of Sociology* 80:1342–68.

Ling, P. 1912. "The Causes of Chinese Immigration." *Annals of the American Academy of Political and Social Sciences* 39 (January):74–82.

Lowe, P. 1943. *Father and Glorious Descendant.* Boston: Little, Brown.

Lyman. S. M. 1968. "Marriage and the Family among Chinese Immigrants to America, 1850–1960." *Phylon* 29(4):321–30.

———. 1974. *Chinese Americans.* New York: Random House.

———. 1977. "Strangers in the City: The Chinese in the Urban Frontier." In *The Asians in North America.* Santa Barbara, CA: ABC Clio Press.

Miller, S. C. 1969. *The Unwelcome Immigrant: The American Image of the Chinese, 1785–1882.* Berkeley: University of California Press.

Moynihan, D. P. 1965. *The Negro Family: The Case for National Action.* Washington, DC: U.S. Department of Labor, Office of Planning and Research (reprinted in Lee Rainwater and William Yancey, *The Moynihan Report and the Politics of Controversy.* Cambridge, MA: MIT Press, 1967).

Nee, V. G. and B. Nee. 1974. *Longtime Californ'.* Boston: Houghton Mifflin.

Park, R. E. 1950. *Race and Culture.* Glencoe, IL: The Free Press.

Power, J. 1979. *Migrant Workers in Western Europe and the United States.* Oxford: Pergamon Press.

Siu, P. C. T. 1952. "The Sojourners." *American Journal of Sociology* 8 (July):32–44.

Sollenberger, R. T. 1968. "Chinese American Childbearing Practices and Juvenile Delinquency." *Journal of Social Psychology* 74 (February):13–23.

Stack, C. B. 1974. *All Our Kin: Strategies for Survival in a Black Community.* New York: Harper and Row.

Sung, B. L. 1971. *The Story of the Chinese in America.* New York: Collier Books.

"Tufts' Lease on Two Kneeland Street Buildings Threatens Over 600 Jobs in Chinatown." 1981. *Sampan,* May.

U.S. Bureau of the Census. 1872. *Ninth Census. Vol. I: The Statistics of the Population of the United States.* Washington, DC: Government Printing Office.

————. 1883. *Tenth Census. Statistics of the Population of the United States.* Washington, DC: Government Printing Office.

————. 1895. *Eleventh Census. Report on Population of the United States, Part I.* Washington, DC: Government Printing Office.

————. 1902. *Twelfth Census of the United States Taken in the Year 1900. Census Reports, Vol. II: Population, Part II.* Washington, DC: United States Census Office.

————. 1913. *Thirteenth Census of the United States Taken in the Year 1910. Vol. I: Population, General Report and Analysis.* Washington, DC: Government Printing Office.

————. 1922. *Fourteenth Census Taken in the Year 1920. Vol. II: Population, General Report and Analytic Tables.* Washington, DC: Government Printing Office.

————. 1933. *Fifteenth Census of the United States: 1930. Population, Vol. II: General Report, Statistics by Subject.* Washington, DC: Government Printing Office.

————. 1943. *Sixteenth Census of the Population: 1940. Population Characteristics of the Non-White Population by Race.* Washington, DC: Government Printing Office.

————. 1953. *U.S. Census of the Population: 1950. Vol. IV: Special Reports, Part 3, Chapter B, Non-White Population by Race.* Washington, DC: Government Printing Office.

————. 1963. *U.S. Census of the Population: 1960. Subject Reports. Nonwhite Population by Race. Final Report PC(2)-1C.* Washington, DC: Government Printing Office.

————. 1973. *Census of Population: 1970. Subject Reports. Final Report PC(2)-1G, Japanese, Chinese and Filipinos in the United States.* Washington, DC: Government Printing Office.

U.S. Department of Health, Education, and Welfare. 1974. *A Study of Selected Socioeconomic Characteristics of Ethnic Minorities Based on the 1970 Census, Vol. II: Asian Americans.* HEW Publication No. (OS) 75–121. Washington, DC: U.S. Department of Health, Education, and Welfare.

U.S. Department of Justice. 1977. *Immigration and Naturalization Service Annual Report.* Washington, DC: U.S. Department of Justice.

Valentine, B. L. 1978. *Hustling and Other Hard Work.* New York: The Free Press.

Valentine, C. 1968. *Culture and Poverty: Critique and Counter-proposals.* Chicago: University of Chicago Press.

Weiss, M. S. 1974. *Valley City: A Chinese Community in America.* Cambridge, MA: Schenkman.

Wolff, K. 1950. *The Sociology of Georg Simmel.* Glencoe, IL: The Free Press.

Wong, B. 1978. "A Comparative Study of the Assimilation of the Chinese in New York City, and Lima, Peru." *Comparative Studies in Society and History* 20 (July):335–58.

Wong, J. S. 1950. *Fifth Chinese Daughter.* New York: Harper and Brothers.

Wu, C. 1972. *"Chink": A Documentary History of Anti-Chinese Prejudice in America.* New York: Meridian.

Young, M. and P. Wilmott. 1973. *The Symmetrical Family.* London: Routledge and Kegan Paul.

PART III
Courtship, Dating, and Power

How do we select a marriage or life partner? Traditionally, courtship and dating were the processes used to select a mate. But courtship and dating are about numerous things in addition to screening for potential marriage partners and for finding romantic love. Courtship and dating are also about economic relationships, family control (or the lack thereof), power dynamics, competition, popularity, having sex, recreation, and consumption patterns. In this section we examine the history of courtship in Western societies to discover when it evolved into a modern pattern of dating. This history reveals that courtship and, later, dating reflect changing norms about who controls mate selection. Over time, Western societies have moved from collective/community control over marriage selection to increased family/parental control to individual control. Moreover, this history of courtship and dating practices shows changing gender norms and power dynamics. In particular, it reveals the changing status of women and the changing social norms concerning relationships and sexuality. In this section, we examine the history of courtship and its more contemporary counterpart: dating. We also examine power dynamics in dating relationships and whether the U.S. society is a postdating culture.

History of Courtship

Historically, courtship and mating were *not* distinctive from marriage. Courtship, with or without premarital sex, had the sole purpose of finding a spouse. Love was not the basis of marriage; instead, relationships were based on economic and family considerations. Because marriage was a financial arrangement between two families, parents often exercised control over their children's choice of mates. Arranged marriages are an excellent example of this premise. Parents or village elders would select prospective spouses via financial and status concerns. A bride price or dowry may be arranged as well to reaffirm the economic nature of this relationship. In some societies, if love developed after an arranged marriage occurred, that was considered to be a bonus. However, in other societies, romantic love was seen as problematic in a marriage relationship because it interfered with the work that needed to be done. Instead, romantic love occurred outside of marriage. In medieval Europe, for example, knights tried to seduce married ladies and sonnets were written to strangers about undying love. Thus, romantic love was *not* always central to courtship activities.

Today, the United States is often described as a culture with a "romantic love complex." That is, compared to many other societies, the U.S. culture places a high value on romance as a precondition for relationships. Some scholars argue that our expectations for romantic love are so extreme, relationships have a difficult time matching this ideal and thus we have high divorce rates. Moreover, most Americans expect love prior to marriage and look down on those who marry for reasons other than love. The recent *Who Wants to Marry a Millionaire* television program is an excellent example of cultural condemnation of individuals who would marry for money instead of love. In this program, 50 women competed with each other (somewhat like a beauty contest) to win the approval of a wealthy man, who asked the winner to marry him at the end of the "contest."

Dating

Unlike courtship, dating is more romanticized and also ensures more individual choice in the selection of a partner. The first article in this section, "Choosing Mates—The American Way," by Martin King Whyte, focuses on this transition from courtship to dating that occurred around the turn of the century in the United States. Whyte, a professor of sociology at George Washington University, argues that, in the late 1800s, an intermediary practice termed "calling" often occurred in middle- and upper-class families. A male suitor would ask a woman to have the privilege of "calling" on her. If the woman said yes, he would visit her home and spend time socializing with her. Their interaction was often supervised and controlled by a parent, usually the mother. Thus, little premarital intimacy could occur. A popular young woman would have several male suitors calling on her, and she would have to select which one to marry. Thus, the purpose of calling was for the woman to select a marriage partner. Whyte's article then focuses on how individuals select the person they will marry in a more modern dating context and why dating is *not* a good predictor of marital success.

Moreover, dating has other purposes than just finding a marriage partner (Laner 1995). In fact, many people will argue that dating is not about looking for a life partner. Instead, dating is supposed to be for fun and recreation. Young people are expected to fall in love at earlier ages, but they are also expected to marry later. Thus, dating is supposed to fill in the gap of time between one's teen years and the time one marries, if she or he does. Sociologist Willard Waller (1937) argues that dating is not for fun or recreation; rather, it serves as a status sorting device. Waller, who studied dating at Penn State in the 1930s, found that young people rank their peers as more or less desirable. This ranking system varies between youths and adults and between the sexes. In particular, Waller found that men and women rank potential dating partners in terms of their physical and personality characteristics. Only a few individuals are placed at the top of the ranking system, and they are the highest in demand for dates. Waller called this system the "campus rating complex," and it rates individuals on a scale of 1 to 10, with 10 being the most desirable. Variations of this rating and dating system are common in each high school or peer group. Thus, Waller argued that dating has much more to do with competition and popularity than with romantic love or finding a marriage partner.

Economic changes, such as the rise of capitalism and consumerism, also have greatly influenced dating patterns. For example, Beth Bailey argues in her research on dating, *From the Front Porch to the Back Seat* (1988), that the development of the automobile, drive-in movies, and other technologies, such as contraceptives, greatly altered the content and meaning of dating in the 20th century. Economic influences on courtship and dating patterns can be seen in the second article in this section, "Men Are Gone, Off to U.S., But Courtship Continues," by Alfredo Corchado. Corchado, a journalist, reports on what happens to courtship in a Mexican village when the men migrate north to the United States to find employment.

Power in Dating Relationships

One important theme in the literature on courtship and dating is *power*. Power dynamics are found in all human relationships but are especially evident in family relationships. For example, there is power in the person who controls whom you can date and whom you can marry. Historically, this power resided in the parents, especially in the patriarchal father, to determine who their children could court or date. Today, we have more individual control over dating and marriage choices. Thus, dating reflects a movement from family control over mate selection to individual control. Instead of parents overseeing dating rituals, peers have more control over dating. As Whyte argues in his article (Reading 9), this movement from family to individual control over dating also has been paralleled by another change, the movement from women having more power in a calling or dating relationship to men having more power. Thus, the control over courtship and dating has shifted from parents, to individual women, to men, to peers.

The changing balance of power in dating relationships is addressed in the third article in this section, "The Balance of Power in Dating," by Letitia Anne Peplau and Susan Miller Campbell. Peplau and Campbell assert that power relations are at the core of all romantic relationships. They define power as "one person's ability to influence the behavior of another to achieve personal goals." In their examination of power within intimate relationships, they studied college-aged, heterosexual students, a sample that is predominantly white, middle class, and educated. They found their subjects to be either traditional or nontraditional in terms of adherence to sex-role norms and the power play in their relationship. They also found that the distribution of power in a relationship correlates with sex-role attitudes, balance of involvement, personal resources, future plans, and attractiveness.

The power dynamics in dating relationships can bring about conflicts related to sexuality, birth control, and sexually transmitted diseases. Moreover, there is growing concern about the frequency of violence, including date rape, in dating relationships. Parental fears about dating violence and the lack of parental control over dating are reflected in Vicki Crompton's (1991) "A Parent's Story." In this narrative, Crompton shares what happened to her daughter and family when her daughter, Jenny, first began to date. Crompton describes how she and her husband attempted to oversee Jenny's dating experiences by setting clear guidelines. Crompton also had frank and open communication with Jenny about sexual intimacy and other dating issues. But she did not realize that the man her daughter was seeing was controlling and abusive. Jenny hid this fact from her parents and, instead, sought help from her friends. She thought she had the situation under control. However, the violence that erupted after Jenny broke up with this man was, sadly, a frequent experience of many women in dating relationships. Jenny's boyfriend stalked her and killed her. After her daughter's death, Crompton became a public speaker on dating violence, and she travels to high schools and colleges to educate young people about the abuse of power in dating relationships.

Postdating Society

Is the United States a postdating society? Teenagers and college students say they do not go out on formal dates anymore, whereby one person asks another to go out. Instead, they hang out together in groups, or a couple may "go" with each other, that is, spend additional time together and "hook up" (Taylor 1996). However, going with someone does not imply commitment or an intention to marry that person. In addition, going with someone does not necessarily mean you are going somewhere, as in a traditional date where a couple would go out to dinner or the movies or partake in some other activity. Many scholars attribute the change in dating relationships to changing gender roles, especially the increase in closer platonic relationships between males and females; to changing peer culture, where young people spend more time in group-oriented social activities; and to increased fears of relationship failures and the unknown. Given the high incidence rates of dating violence and sexually transmitted diseases, it makes sense that people are more cautious about dating today.

Simon Rodberg, a student at Yale University, comments on the lack of romantic love on college campuses today. Rodberg argues that college students feel nostalgia for the ideal of the pre-1960s dating scene where parties had "dance cards, big bands, and good wine rather than keg beer." Instead of the Friday night dating scene, college life today is marked by random hook-ups.

> Hook-ups, Mr. Rodberg and his classmates suggest, are the easiest, most physically gratifying way to find refuge from the pressures of finding and maintaining the ever-elusive "relationship." That, he notes, is because those relationships are an enormous source of pressure, especially for students accustomed to analyzing, deconstructing, planning, and achieving—particularly in the era of AIDS and high divorce rates. The

fundamental problem, Mr. Rodberg writes, is that "history and popular culture promised us true love and great sex, but reality taught us how much we could get hurt." (Academe Today 1999)

Thus, many young people are more cautious and pessimistic about dating.

Dating has changed in other ways as well. People have busier schedules now, and it is difficult for many single adults to meet each other, especially after the completion of high school or college. People look for dating partners through newspaper or Internet personal ads or through dating services that attempt to match people based on their interests and values. Most newspapers now carry personal ads categorized by sexual preference where individuals advertise what they are looking for in a relationship. The Right One, a national dating service, advertises services in 53 U.S. cities and 5 cities in Canada. Their promotion materials state:

> At The Right One, our professional Membership Consultants will spend time talking with you about your background, your relationship history, your work, what you like to do in your free time, and what you are looking for in a potential partner. This one-on-one personal approach helps us introduce you to the type of people you are compatible with—which makes dating more comfortable and enjoyable. *It's sensible, safer, and it works!* (The Right One 1999)

It is interesting to note that this dating service emphasizes how logical and safe this route to dating is. Members are led to believe that the service is screening out the potentially dangerous or unbecoming alternatives. The Right One costs a couple of thousand dollars per person to join. For that amount, the individual receives six introductions over a period of time. Each introduction has been carefully matched based on the answers clients give to a survey of questions on their values, hobbies, and relationship preferences. The success rate of dating services in helping people find a long-term mate is debatable.

REFERENCES

Academe Today. 1999. "Nostalgia for Collegiate Romance." From the Daily Report of the *Chronicle for Higher Education,* May 5. <daily@chronicle.com>

Bailey, Beth. 1988. *From the Front Porch to the Back Seat.* Baltimore: Johns Hopkins University Press.

Crompton, Vicki. 1991. "A Parent's Story." Pp. 21–27 in *Dating Violence: Young Women in Danger,* edited by Barry Levy. Seattle, WA: Seal Press.

Laner, Mary Riege. 1995. *Dating: Delights, Discontents, and Dilemmas.* 2d. ed. Salem, WI: Sheffield Publishing Company.

Taylor, Matthew. 1996. "Hanging Out Together Replaces Going Out on Dates." *Des Moines Register,* November 21, p. 3T.

The Right One. 1999, Fall. Promotional materials mailed to single adults. <www.therightone.com>

Waller, Willard. 1937. "Rating and Dating Complex." *American Sociological Review* 2:737–39.

9

CHOOSING MATES – THE AMERICAN WAY

MARTIN KING WHYTE

As America's divorce rate has been soaring, popular anxieties about marriage have multiplied. Is it still possible to "live happily ever after," and if so, how can this be accomplished? How can you tell whether a partner who leaves you breathless with yearning will, as your spouse, drive you to distraction? Does "living together" prior to marriage provide a realistic assessment of how compatible you and your partner might be as husband and wife? Questions such as these suggest a need to examine our American way of mate choice. How do we go about selecting the person we marry, and is there something wrong with the entire process?

For most twentieth-century Americans, choosing a mate is the culmination of a process of dating. Examination of how we go about selecting mates thus requires us to consider the American dating culture. Dating is a curious institution. By definition it is an activity that is supposed to be separate from selecting a spouse. Yet, dating is expected to provide valuable experience that will help in making a "wise" choice of a marital partner. Does this combination work?

How well dating "works" may be considered in a number of senses of this term. Is it easy or difficult to find somebody to go out with? Do dates mostly lead to enjoyable or painful evenings? However, these are not the aspects of dating I wish to consider. The issue here is whether dating works in the sense of providing useful experience that helps pave the way for a successful marriage.

Dating is a relatively new institution. The term, and the various practices associated with it, first emerged around the turn of the century. By the 1920s dating had more or less completely displaced earlier patterns of relations among unmarried Americans. Contrary to popular assumptions, even in colonial times marriages were not arranged in America. Parents were expected to give their approval to their children's nuptial plans, a practice captured in our image of a suitor asking his beloved's father for her hand in marriage. Parental approval, especially among merchants and other prosperous classes, put some constraint on the marriages of the young. For example, through the eighteenth century, children in such families tended to marry in birth order and marriage to cousins was not uncommon. (Both practices had declined sharply by the nineteenth century.) However, parents rarely directly arranged the marriages of their children. America has always exhibited "youth-driven"

Martin King Whyte, "Choosing Mates — The American Way" from *Society*, Vol. 29 No. 3, March/April 1992, pp. 71–77. © 1992 by Transaction Publishers, Inc. Reprinted by permission.

patterns of courtship. Eligible males and females took the initiative to get to know each other, and the decision to marry was made by them, even if that decision was to some degree contingent on parental approval. (Of course, substantial proportions of later immigrant groups from Southern and Eastern Europe, Asia, and elsewhere brought with them arranged marriage traditions, and contention for control over marriage decisions was often a great source of tension in such families.)

How did young people get to know one another well enough to decide to marry in the era before dating? A set of customs, dominant for the two centuries, preceded the rise of the dating culture. These activities came to be referred to as "calling" and "keeping company." Young people might meet in a variety of ways—through community and church socials, informally in shops or on the street, on boat and train trips, or through introductions from friends or relatives. (America never developed a system of chaperoning young women in public, and foreign observers often commented on the freedom unmarried women had to travel and mix socially on their own.) Usually young people would go to church fairs, local dances, and other such activities with family, siblings, or friends, rather than paired off with a partner. Most activities would involve a substantial degree of adult and community supervision. Nonetheless, these gatherings did encourage some pairing off and led to hand holding, moonlit walks home, and other romantic exploration.

As relationships developed beyond the platonic level, the suitor would pay visits to the home of the young woman. By the latter part of the nineteenth century, particularly among the middle and upper classes, this activity assumed a formal pattern referred to as "calling." Males would be invited to call on the female at her home, and they were expected to do so only if invited. (A bold male could, however, request an invitation to call.) Invitations might be extended by the mother of a very young woman, but eventually they would come from the young woman herself. Often a woman would designate certain days on which she would receive callers. She might have several suitors at one time, and thus a number of men might be paying such calls. A man might be told that the woman was not at home to receive him, and he would then be expected to leave his calling card. If this happened repeatedly, he was expected to get the message that his visits were no longer welcome.

Initiative and control in regard to calling were in the hands of women (the eligible female and her mother). Although some variety in suitors was possible, even in initial stages the role of calling in examining potential marriage partners was very clear to all involved. The relatively constrained and supervised nature of calling make it certain that enjoyment cannot have been a primary goal of this activity. (During the initial visits the mother was expected to remain present; in later visits she often hovered in an adjacent room.) If dating is defined as recreational and romantic pairing off between a man and a woman, away from parental supervision and without immediate consideration of marriage, then calling was definitely not dating.

The supervised and controlled nature of calling should not, however, lead us to suppose that propriety and chastity were always maintained until marriage. If the relationship had deepened sufficiently, the couple might progress from calling to "keeping company," a precursor of the twentieth-century custom of "going steady." At this stage, the primary activity would still consist of visits by the suitor to the woman's home. However, now she would only welcome calls from one man, and he would visit her home on a regular basis. Visits late into the evening would increasingly replace afternoon calls. As the relationship became more serious, parents would often leave the couple alone. Nineteenth-century accounts mention parents going off to bed and leaving the young couple on the couch or by the fireplace, there to wrestle with, and not infrequently give in to, sexual temptation.

Even though some women who headed to the altar toward the end of the nineteenth century had lost their virginity prior to marriage, premarital intimacy was less common than during the dating era. (The double standard of the Victorian era made it possible for many more grooms to be non-virgins at marriage than brides. Perhaps 50 percent or more of men had lost their virginity prior to marriage, as opposed to 15 to 20 percent of women, with prostitutes and "fallen women" helping to explain the differential.) What is less often realized is that the formalization of the calling pattern toward the end of the nineteenth century contributed to a decline in premarital sexual intimacy compared to earlier times. America experienced not one but two sexual revolutions — one toward the end of the eighteenth century, at the time of the American Revolution, and the other in the latter part of the twentieth century.

The causes of the first sexual revolution are subject to some debate. An influx of settlers to America who did not share the evangelical puritanism of many early colonists, the expansion of the population into the unsettled (and "unchurched") frontier, the growth of towns, and the individualistic and freedom-loving spirit of the American Revolution may have contributed to a retreat from the fairly strict emphasis on premarital chastity of the early colonial period. Historians debate the extent to which the archetypal custom of this first sexual revolution, bundling (which allowed an unmarried couple to sleep together, although theoretically fully clothed and separated by a "bundling board"), was widespread or largely mythical. Whatever the case, other evidence is found in studies of communities, such as those by Daniel Scott Smith and Michael Hindus, which found that the percentage of married couples whose first births were conceived premaritally increased from about 11 percent before 1700 to over 33 percent in the last decades of the eighteenth century.

This first sexual revolution was reversed in the nineteenth century. The reasons for its demise are also not clear. The closing of the frontier, the rise of the middle class, the defensive reactions of that new middle class to new waves of immigrants, the growth of Christian revivalism and reform movements, and the spread of models of propriety from Victorian England (which were in turn influenced by fear of the chaos of the French Revolution) — all these have been suggested as having contributed to a new sexual puritanism in the nineteenth century. According to Smith and Hindus, premarital conceptions decreased once again to about 15 percent of first births between 1841 and 1880.

It was in the latter time period that the customs of calling and keeping company reached their most formal elaboration — calling, in less ritualized forms, can be traced back to the earliest colonial period. Not long after reaching the formal patterns described, calling largely disappeared. In little more than a generation, dating replaced calling as the dominant custom.

Dating involved pairing off of couples in activities not supervised by parents, with pleasure rather than marriage as the primary goal. The rules governing dating were defined by peers rather than by adults. The initiative, and much of the control, shifted from the female to the male. The man asked the woman out, rather than waiting for her invitation to call. The finances and transportation for the date were also his responsibility. The woman was expected to provide, in turn, the pleasure of her company and perhaps some degree of romantic and physical intimacy. By giving or withholding her affection and access to her body, she exercised considerable control over the man and the date as an event. Nonetheless, the absence of parental oversight and pressure to respond to a man's initiatives placed a woman in a weaker position than she was in the era of calling.

The man might pick up the woman at her home, but parents who tried to dictate whom their daughters dated and what they did on dates generally found such efforts rejected and evaded. Parents of a son might not even know where junior was going or whom he was dating. Dates were conducted mostly in the public arena, and in some cases — such as at sporting events or school dances — adults might be present. But dates often involved activities and venues where no adults were present or where young people predominated — as at private parties or at local dance halls. Or in other cases the presence of adults would have little inhibiting effect, as in the darkened balconies of movie theaters. American youths also developed substantial ingenuity in finding secluded "lovers' lanes" where they could escape the supervision of even peers. (Localities varied in the places used for this purpose and how they were referred to. In locales near bodies of water, young people spoke of "watching submarine races"; in the rural area of upstate New York where I grew up, the phrase was "exploring tractor roads.") Community dances and gatherings for all generations and ages practically disappeared in the dating era.

Greater privacy and autonomy of youths promoted romantic and physical experimentation. Not only kissing but petting was increasingly accepted and widespread. Going beyond petting to sexual intercourse, however, involved substantial risks, especially for the female. This was not simply the risk of pregnancy in the pre-pill era. Dating perpetuated the sexual double standard. Men were expected to be the sexual aggressors and to try to achieve as much intimacy as their dates would allow. But women who "went too far" risked harming their reputations and their ability to keep desirable men interested in them for long. Women were expected to set the limits, and they had to walk a careful line between being too unfriendly (and not having males wanting to date them at all) and being too friendly (and being dated for the "wrong reasons").

During the initial decades of the dating era, premarital intimacy increased in comparison with the age of calling, but still a majority of women entered marriage as virgins. In a survey in the greater Detroit metropolitan area, I found that of the oldest women interviewed (those who dated and married prior to 1945), about one in four had lost her virginity prior to marriage. (By the 1980s, according to my survey, the figure was closer to 90 percent.) Escape from parental supervision provided by dating weakened, but did not immediately destroy, the restraints on premarital intimacy.

When Americans began dating, they were primarily concerned with enjoyment, rather than with choosing a spouse. Indeed, "playing the field" was the ideal pursued by many. Dates were not suitors or prospects. Seeing different people on successive nights in a hectic round of dating activity earned one popularity among peers. One of the early students and critics of the dating culture, Willard Waller, coined the term "rating and dating complex" to refer to this pattern. After observing dating among students at Pennsylvania State University in the 1930s, Waller charged that concern for impressing friends and gaining status on campus led to superficial thrill-seeking and competition for popularity, and eliminated genuine romance or sincere communication. However, Waller has been accused of both stereotyping and exaggerating the influence of this pattern. Dating was not always so exploitative and superficial as he charged.

Dating was never viewed as an endless stage or an alternative to courtship. Even if dates were initially seen as quite separate from mate selection, they were always viewed as only the first step in a progression that would lead to marriage. By the 1930s, the stage of "going steady" was clearly recognized, entailing a commitment by both partners to date each other exclusively, if only for the moment. A variety of ritual markers emerged to symbolize the increased commitment of this stage and of further steps toward engagement and marriage, such as wearing the partner's high school ring, being lavaliered, and getting pinned.

Going steady was a way-station between casual dating and engagement. Steadies pledged not to date others, and they were likely to become more deeply involved romantically and physically than casual daters. They were not expected explicitly to contemplate marriage, and the majority of women in our Detroit survey had several steady boyfriends before the relationships that led to their marriages. If a couple was of a "suitable age," though, and if the steady relationship lasted more than a few months, the likelihood increased of explicit talk about marriage. Couples would then symbolize their escalated commitment by getting engaged. Dating arose first among middle and upper middle class students in urban areas, and roughly simultaneously at the college and high school levels. The practice then spread to other groups—rural young people, working class youths, to the upper class, and to employed young people. But what triggered the rapid demise of calling and the rise of dating?

One important trend was prolonged school attendance, particularly in public, co-educational high schools and colleges. Schools provided an arena in which females and males could get to know one another informally over many years. Schools also organized athletic, social, and other activities in which adult supervision was minimal. College campuses generally allowed a more total escape from parental supervision than high schools.

Another important influence was growing affluence in America. More and more young people were freed from a need to contribute to the family economy and had more leisure time in which to date. Fewer young people worked under parental supervision, and more and more fathers worked far from home, leaving mothers as the primary monitors of their children's daily activities. These trends also coincided with a rise in part-time and after-school employment for students, employment that provided pocket money that did not have to be turned over to parents and could be spent on clothing, makeup, movie tickets, and other requirements of the dating culture. Rising affluence also fueled the growth of entire new industries designed to entertain and fill leisure time—movies, popular music recording, ice cream parlors, amusement parks, and so on. Increasingly, young people who wanted to escape from supervision of their parents found a range of venues, many of them catering primarily to youth and to dating activities.

Technology also played a role, and some analysts suggest that one particular invention, the automobile, deserves a lion's share of the credit. Automobiles were not only a means to escape the home and reach a wider range of recreation spots. They also provided a semiprivate space with abundant romantic and sexual possibilities. New institutions, such as the drive-in movie theater, arose to take advantage of those possibilities. As decades passed and affluence increased, the borrowed family car was more and more replaced by cars owned by young people, advancing youth autonomy still further.

All this was part of a larger trend: the transformation of America into a mass consumption society. As this happened, people shifted their attention partially from thinking about how to work and earn to pondering how to spend and consume. Marketplace thinking became more and more influential. The image of the individual as *homo economicus* and of modern life typified by the rational application of scientific knowledge to all decisions became pervasive. The new ideological framework undermined previous customs and moral standards and extended to the dating culture.

Dating had several goals. Most obviously and explicitly, dates were expected to lead to pleasure and possibly to romance. It was also important, as Waller and others have observed, in competition for popularity. But a central purpose of dating was to gain valuable learning experience that would be useful later in selecting a spouse. Through dating young people would learn how to relate to the opposite sex. Dating would increase awareness of one's own feelings and understanding of which type of partner was appealing and which not. Through crushes and disappointments, one would learn to judge the character of people. And by dating a variety of partners and by increasingly intimate involvement with some of them, one would learn what sort of person one would be happy with as a marital partner. When it came time to marry, one would be in a good position to select "Mr. Right" or "Miss Right." Calling, which limited the possibilities of romantic experimentation, often to only one partner, did not provide an adequate basis for such an informed choice.

What emerged was a "marketplace learning viewpoint." Selecting a spouse is not quite the same as buying a car or breakfast cereal, but the process was seen as analogous. The assumptions involved in shopping around and test driving various cars or buying and tasting Wheaties, Cheerios, and Fruit Loops were transferred to popular thinking about how to select a spouse.

According to this marketplace learning viewpoint, getting married very young and without having acquired much dating experience was risky, in terms of marital happiness. Similarly, marrying your first and only sweetheart was not a good idea. Neither was meeting someone, falling head over heels in love, and marrying, all within the course of a month. While Americans recognized that in some cases such beginnings could lead to good marriages, the rationale of our dating culture was that having had a variety of dating partners and then getting to know one or more serious prospects over a longer period of time and on fairly intimate terms were experiences more likely to lead to marital success.

Eventually, this marketplace psychology helped to undermine America's premarital puritanism, and with it the sexual double standard. The way was paved for acceptance of new customs, and particularly for premarital cohabitation. Parents and other moral guardians found it increasingly difficult to argue against the premise that, if sexual enjoyment and compatibility were central to marital happiness, it was important to test that compatibility before marrying. Similarly, if marriage involved not just hearts and flowers, but also dirty laundry and keeping a budget, did it not make sense for a couple to live together prior to marriage to see how they got along on a day-to-day basis? Such arguments on behalf of premarital sex and cohabitation have swept into popular consciousness in the United States, and it is obvious that they are logical corollaries of the marketplace learning viewpoint.

Our dating culture thus is based upon the premise that dating provides valuable experience that will help individuals select mates and achieve happy marriages. But is this premise correct? Does dating really work? What evidence shows that individuals with longer dating experience, dates with more partners, or longer and more intimate acquaintances with the individuals they intend to marry end up with happier marriages? Surprisingly, social scientists have never systematically addressed this question. Perhaps this is one of those cherished beliefs people would prefer not to examine too closely. When I could find little evidence on the connection between dating and other premarital experiences and marital success in previous studies, I decided to conduct my own inquiry.

My desire to know whether dating experiences affected marriages was the basis for my 1984 survey in the Detroit area. A representative sample of 459 women was interviewed in three counties in the Detroit metropolitan area (a diverse, multi-racial and multi-ethnic area of city and suburbs containing about 4 million people in 1980). The women ranged in ages from 18 to 75, and all had been married at least once. (I was unable to interview their husbands, so unfortunately marriages in this study are viewed only through the eyes of women.) The interviewees had first married over a sixty-year span of time, between 1925 and 1984. They were asked to recall a variety of things about their dating and premarital experiences. They were also asked a range of questions about their marital histories and (if currently married) about the positive and negative features of their relations with their husbands. The questionnaire enabled us to test whether premarital experiences of various types were related to marital success, a concept which in turn was measured in several different ways. (Measures of divorce and of both positive and negative qualities in intact marriages were used.)

The conclusions were a surprise. It appears that dating does not work and that the "marketplace learning viewpoint" is misguided. Marrying very young tended to produce unsuccessful marriages. Premarital pregnancy was associated with problems in marriage. However, once the age of marriage is taken into account, none of the other measures—dating variety, length of dating, length of courtship or engagement, or degree of premarital intimacy with the future husband or others—was clearly related to measures of marital success. A few weak tendencies in the results were contrary to predictions drawn from the marketplace learning viewpoint. Women who had dated more partners or who had engaged in premarital sex or cohabited were slightly less likely to have successful marriages. This might be seen as evidence of quite a different logic.

Perhaps there is a "grass is greener" effect. Women who have led less sheltered and conventional lives prior to marriage may not be as easily satisfied afterward. Several other researchers have found a similar pattern with regard to premarital cohabitation. Individuals who had been living together prior to marriage were significantly less likely to have successful marriages than those who did not.

In the Detroit survey, these "grass is greener" patterns were not consistent or statistically significant. It was not that women with more dating experience and greater premarital intimacy had less successful marriages; rather, the amount and type of dating experience did not make a clear difference one way or the other.

Women who had married their first sweethearts were just as likely to have enduring and satisfying marriages as women who had married only after considering many alternatives. Similarly, women who had married after only a brief acquaintance were no more (nor less) likely to have a successful marriage than those who knew their husbands-to-be for years. And there was no clear difference between the marriages of women who were virgins at marriage and those who had had a variety of sexual partners and who had lived together with their husbands before the wedding.

Dating obviously does not provide useful learning that promotes marital success. Although our dating culture is based upon an analogy with consumer purchases in the marketplace, it is clear that in real life selecting a spouse is quite different from buying a car or breakfast cereal. You cannot actively consider several prospects at the same time without getting your neck broken and being deserted by all of them. Even if you find Ms. Right or Mr. Right, you may be told to drop dead. By the time you are ready to marry, this special someone you were involved with earlier may no longer be available, and you may not see anyone on the horizon who comes close to being as desirable. In addition, someone who is well suited at marriage may grow apart from you or find someone else to be with later. Dating experience might facilitate marital success if deciding whom to marry was like deciding what to eat for breakfast (although even in the latter regard tastes change, and toast and black coffee may replace bacon and eggs). But these realms are quite different, and mate selection looks more like a crap-shoot than a rational choice.

Is there a better way? Traditionalists in some societies would argue that arranged marriages are preferable. However, in addition to the improbability that America's young people will leave this decision to their parents, there is the problem of evidence. The few studies of this topic, including one I have been collaborating on in China, indicate that women who had arranged marriages were less satisfied than women who made the choice themselves. So having Mom and Dad take charge is not the answer. Turning the matter over to computerized matchmaking also does not seem advisable. Despite the growing sophistication of computers, real intelligence seems preferable to artificial intelligence. As the Tin Woodman in *The Wizard of Oz* discovered, to have a brain but no heart is to be missing something important.

Perhaps dating is evolving into new patterns in which premarital experience will contribute to marital success. Critics form Waller onward have claimed that dating promotes artificiality, rather than realistic assessment of compatibility. Some observers suggest that the sort of superficial dating Waller and others wrote about has become less common of late. Dating certainly has changed significantly since the pre–Second World War era. Many of the rigid rules of dating have broken down. The male no longer always takes the initiative; neither does he always pay. The sexual double standard has also weakened substantially, so that increasingly Americans feel that whatever a man can do a woman should be able to do. Some writers even suggest that dating is going out of style, replaced by informal pairing off in larger groups, often without the prearrangement of "asking someone out." Certainly the terminology is changing, with "seeing" and "being with" increasingly preferred to "dating" and "going steady." To many young people the latter terms have the old-fashioned ring that "courting" and "suitor" had when I was young.

My daughter and other young adults argue that current styles are more natural and healthier than the dating experienced by my generation and the generation of my parents. Implicit in this argument is the view that, with formal rules and the "rating and dating" complex in decline, it should be possible to use dating (or whatever you call it) to realistically assess compatibility and romantic chemistry. These arguments may seem plausible, but I see no evidence that bears them out. The youngest women we interviewed in the Detroit survey should have experienced these more informal styles of romantic exploration. However, for them dating and premarital intimacy were, if anything, less closely related to marital success than was the case for the older women. The changes in premarital relations do not seem to make experience a better teacher.

While these conclusions are for the most part quite negative, my study leads to two more positive observations. First, marital success is not totally unpredictable. A wide range of features of how couples structure their day-to-day marital relations promote success—sharing in power and decision-making, pooling incomes, enjoying similar leisure-time activities, having similar values, having mutual friends and an active social life, and other related qualities. Couples are not "doomed" by their past histories, including their dating histories, and they can increase their mutual happiness through the way they structure their marriages.

Second, there is something else about premarital experience besides dating history that may promote marital success. We have in America not one, but two widely shared, but quite contradictory, theories about how individuals should select a spouse: one based on the marketplace learning viewpoint and another based on love. One viewpoint sees selecting a spouse as a rational process, perhaps even with lists of criteria by which various prospects can be judged. The other, as songwriters tell us, is based on the view that love conquers all and that "all you need is love." Love is a matter of the heart (perhaps with some help from the hormonal system) and not the head, and love may blossom unpredictably, on short notice or more gradually. Might it not be the case, then, that those couples who are most deeply in love at the time of their weddings will have the most successful marriages? We have centuries of poetry and novels, as well as love songs, that tell us that this is the case.

In the Detroit study, we did, in fact, ask women how much they had been in love when they first married. And we did find that those who recalled being "head over heels in love" then, had more successful marriages. However, there is a major problem with this finding. Since we were asking our interviewees to recall their feelings prior to their weddings—in many cases weddings took place years or even decades earlier—it is quite possible and even likely that these answers are biased. Perhaps whether or not their marriage worked out influenced these "love reports" from earlier times, rather than having the level of romantic love then explain marital success later. Without either a time machine or funds to interview couples prior to marriage and then follow them up years later, it is impossible to be sure that more intense feelings of love lead to more successful marriages. Still, the evidence available does not question the wisdom of poets and songwriters when it comes to love. Mate selection may not be a total crap-shoot after all, and even if dating does not work, love perhaps does.

REFERENCES

Bailey, Beth. 1988. *From Front Porch to Back Seat*. Baltimore: Johns Hopkins University Press.

Burgess, Ernest W. and Paul Wallin. 1953. *Engagement and Marriage*. Chicago: Lippincott.

Modell, John. 1983. "Dating Becomes the Way of American Youth." In *Essays on the Family and Historical Change*, edited by Leslie P. Moch and Gary Stark. College Station: Texas A&M University Press.

Rothman, Ellen K. 1984. *Hands and Hearts: A History of Courtship*. New York: Basic Books.

Smith, Daniel S. and Michael Hindus. 1975. "Premarital Pregnancy in America, 1640–1971: An Overview and Interpretation." *Journal of Interdisciplinary History* 4:537–70.

Waller, Willard. 1937. "Rating and Dating Complex." *American Sociological Review* 2:737–39.

Whyte, Martin King. 1990. *Dating, Mating, and Marriage*. New York: Aldine de Gruyter.

10

MEN ARE GONE, OFF TO U.S., BUT COURTSHIP CONTINUES

ALFREDO CORCHADO

In San Miguel, in matters of love you can't lose your head. You must also be practical and realistic. Jobs in the United States get in the way of love.
— NANCY LOZANO VEGA, 18, whose boyfriend left Mexico

San Miguel el Alto, Mexico — The pretty women looking for love in this city walk in circles around the local square in the timeless tradition of the serenata.

But these days, they're competing with an unlikely rival: Uncle Sam.

Prospective suitors in Jalisco state have been lured away, not by other women, but by jobs in places such as Texas, California, and Colorado.

Alfredo Corchado, "Men Are Gone, Off to U.S., But Courtship Continues" from the *Dallas Morning News*, August 4, 1996. Reprinted by permission of the Dallas Morning News.

"Americans say that our men take jobs away from them," said Erica Ortiz Munoz, 17, whose boyfriend works as a busboy in Pomona, Calif. "Americans forget that they, too, take our men away from us."

Across Mexico, communities such as San Miguel el Alto, population 50,000, are nearly deserted by their youngest, boldest and most ambitious men.

Faced with a lack of jobs, many of these men take the hearts and hopes of their prospective brides with them on their trek north.

Here in San Miguel el Alto, surrounded by rugged hills, many of the wives and girlfriends left behind care for the town, harvest the fields, milk the cows, train horses and toil in textile factories, all the while awash in memories and longing for their husbands, sons and fiances.

"In the evening, I sadly miss my boyfriend and pray for his safe return," said Nancy Lozano Vega, 18, who works at a local factory. "But during the day, I know that life has to go on, with or without him. We have to face reality, no matter how harsh or lonely it may be."

Fortunately for many, their loneliness does not last long. Across this striking region of cactus and mesquite trees known as Los Altos de Jalisco, or the Heights of Jalisco, the ritual of courtship known as the serenata thrives, despite the exodus of local men.

Many of the women have well-founded doubts that their loved ones will indeed return for good, so they look for other opportunities.

Every Sunday, eager suitors from across Mexico are lured by the romance of the serenata. Some drive for hours in the hope of finding their dream girl.

As dusk settles over San Miguel el Alto, shadows fall over striking homes of pink stonework, setting the stage for romance. Live music blares. Young men with bags of confetti and fresh red roses strategically line the main square.

At promptly 8 P.M., following a final blessing from the local priest, women promenade around the square, timidly exchanging glances with their male counterparts.

If a woman catches a young man's eye, he will toss confetti on her head. On the next turn, the man will offer a red rose. By the third turn, if the attraction remains mutual, the woman will accept the man's invitation for a stroll around the plaza.

"Once you walk around a few times, the rules aren't as confusing," quipped 21-year-old Jedsmin Gonzalez, who helps her parents on their ranch while her brothers work in the United States. "We arrive home looking like Christmas trees, our hair filled with confetti and rosebuds."

The big test comes at 10 P.M. when local policemen circle the plaza and order people to go home. If sparks fly and the woman allows the man to walk her home, love may well be in full bloom. Plans are made for the following serenata.

A good-night kiss, however, is strictly taboo—"impossible," stressed Gonzalez's sister, Jakeline, 18, "especially during courtship."

The serenata can be traced back centuries to the provinces of Spain. Although it is still practiced in many smaller communities across Mexico, it is a rapidly disappearing custom.

But in San Miguel el Alto, most of the people live traditional lives. They abide by unspoken rules, such as attending church regularly, dressing conservatively and abstaining from any intense physical contact with their sweethearts.

This year alone, Catholic Church officials and parents pressured two nightclubs and one disco in the town to shut down because "sinful activities" had been reported there. At one bar, a couple had been observed doing more than holding hands — they were necking.

Still, many San Miguel el Alto women dismiss the idea that they're missing out on life. They say they follow tradition out of respect for their elders.

"When I'm in the big city, or when my relatives from the United States visit, I feel grateful for the simple life I lead," explained Norma Encino, an ice cream vendor. "What is wrong with wanting to find a supportive husband to raise a family with? It's not a question of ambition, or lack of it, but a matter of priorities."

When San Miguel el Alto's men return from the United States, many have changed, some of the town's women complain. The men mostly brood about the lack of local jobs and pout over the strangers who steal their girlfriends, the women say.

Once humble and forthright, they have been tainted by life in the United States, the women say.

"They're arrogant, flaunting their cash, their shiny new cars, new clothes, boasting of streets filled with dollars," Gonzalez said.

"They're no longer fun," added Estela Manriquez, 20. "My boyfriend became boring, wanting only one thing — sex. Can you believe that?"

Meanwhile, Lozano, while insisting her heart still belongs to her boyfriend Antonio, concedes that she keeps her options open.

"In San Miguel, in matters of love you can't lose your head. You must also be practical and realistic. Jobs in the United States get in the way of love."

11

THE BALANCE OF POWER IN DATING

LETITIA ANNE PEPLAU • SUSAN MILLER CAMPBELL

Americans are sentimental about love. In thinking about romance, we emphasize intimacy and caring; we like to view our lover and the relationship as unique. We tend to neglect a crucial aspect of love relationships — power. This chapter investigates the nature of power in dating . . . and analyzes factors that can tip the balance of power away from equality.

The traditional formula for male–female relationships prescribes that the man should be the leader. In dating, he should take the initiative by asking the woman out, by planning activities, by providing transportation, and by paying the bills. In marriage, he should be the "head" of household, who has final say about major family decisions. Our society's concept of "male superiority" dictates that a woman should "look up" to the significant man in her life, a stance that is often facilitated by his being taller, older, better educated, and more experienced.

Feminists have severely criticized the idea that men should have the upper hand in love relationships. In *Sexual Politics*, Kate Millett[1] argues that patriarchal norms are pervasive and insidious. Male domination may be seen most easily in business, education, religion, and politics, but it also extends to personal relationships between the sexes. The family mirrors the power relations of the society at large and also perpetuates this power imbalance by teaching children to accept the superior status of men. In Millett's analysis, romantic love does not "put women on a pedestal" or elevate women's social status. Rather, the ideology of love hides the reality of women's subordination and economic dependence on men. As television commercials readily illustrate, "love" can be used for the emotional manipulation of women. It is "love" that justifies household drudgery, as well as deference to men. Thus, true equality would require basic changes in the intimate relationships of women and men.

Although traditional views of romantic relationships are being challenged, proponents of the old pattern remain strong. A striking example is provided by Helen Andelin,[2] author of *Fascinating Womanhood* and an advocate of a benevolent form of male dominance. Andelin urges women to accept and enjoy traditional sex roles. Male leadership is a key element. According to Andelin, women should defer to men and take pleasure in being cared for. The man is "the undisputed head of the family." The woman has a "submissive role, a supporting role and sometimes an active role. . . . But, first she must accept him as her leader, support and obey him." The popularity of *Fascinating Womanhood* and similar books suggests that many women endorse this traditional view.

Young couples today are confronted with alternative models for romantic relationships. Traditional sex roles prescribe that the man should take the lead. But contemporary thinking favors a more equal balance of power. This chapter examines the balance of power in dating . . . today. We begin by describing in depth a study of power in the dating relationships of college students. We explore attitudes about power, consider how to assess the actual balance of power in a relationship, and analyze factors that determine whether or not couples actually achieve equal power in their relationships. . . .

College Couples in Love:
A Study of Power in Dating Relationships

A study by Zick Rubin, Anne Peplau, and Charles Hill[3] explored in detail the issue of power in dating relationships. This research, known as the Boston Couples Study, recruited 231 college-age couples from four colleges and universities located in the Boston area. These included a small private nonsectarian university, a large private nonsectarian university, a Jesuit university, and a state college enrolling commuter students. Participants were typically middle class in background, and virtually all were white. To be eligible for the study, a couple had to indicate that they were "going with" each other and that both partners were willing to participate. The typical couple had been going together for about eight months when the study began. Couples were studied intensively over a two-year period. In 1972, and again in 1973 and 1974, each partner in the couple independently completed lengthy questionnaires about their relationship. We found that the college students in our sample were strong supporters of an egalitarian balance of power. When we asked, "Who do you think should have more say about your relationship, your partner or you?" 95 percent of women and 87 percent of men indicated that dating partners should have "exactly equal say." Although male dominance may once have been the favored pattern of male–female relations, it was overwhelmingly rejected by the students in this study. It is possible that some students gave the answer they considered socially desirable, rather than their own true opinion. In either case, however, responses indicated a striking change in the type of male–female relationship considered appropriate.

Although students advocated equality, they seldom reported having grown up in an egalitarian family. As one student explained:

> When I was growing up, my father was the Supreme Court in our family. He ran the show. My relationship with Betsy is very different. We try to discuss things and reach consensus. And that's the way I think it should be.

Only 18 percent of the students reported that their parents shared equally in power. A 53 percent majority indicated that their father had more say; the remaining 29 percent reported that their mother had more say. Clearly, most college students were seeking a different type of relationship from the model set by their parents. Our next question was whether these student couples would be successful in achieving the equal-power relationship they desired.

Assessing the Balance of Power

Although the word *power* suggests a phenomenon that is obvious and easy to study, this is not the case. Power is often elusive, especially in close relationships. Consider a woman who appears to dominate her boyfriend by deciding what to do on dates, determining which friends the couple sees, and even selecting her boyfriend's new clothes. Is it reasonable to infer that she has a good deal of power in the relationship? Not necessarily. Further investigation might reveal that her boyfriend, a busy pre-med student, disdains such "trivial" matters, and cheerfully delegates decision making in these areas to his girlfriend. In addition, he may retain veto power on all decisions but rarely exercise it, because his girlfriend scrupulously caters to his preferences. In this instance, greater power may actually reside with the man, who delegates responsibility, rather than with the woman, who merely implements his preference.[4]

Power—one person's ability to influence the behavior of another to achieve personal goals—cannot be observed directly, but must be inferred from behavior.[5] The context in which an action occurs and the intentions of the participants largely determine the meaning of the act. Especially in close personal relationships, judgments about power may be difficult to make. One reason for this is that people can exert influence in subtle and indirect ways. Indeed, traditional sex roles have dictated that men and women should use different influence tactics—he should be direct, even bold in his leadership; she should be tactful and covert. *Fascinating Womanhood* offers several suggestions about how women should give "feminine advice":

> *Ask leading questions:* A subtle way of giving advice is to ask leading questions, such as "Have you ever thought of doing it this way?" . . . The key word is *you*. In this way you bring him into the picture so the ideas will seem like his own.
>
> *Insight:* When expressing your viewpoint use words that indicate insight such as "I feel." Avoid the words "I think" or "I know."
>
> *Don't appear to know more than he does:* Don't be the all-wise, all-knowing wife who has all the answers and surpasses her husband in intelligence.
>
> *Don't talk man to man:* Don't "hash things over" as men do and thereby place yourself on an equal plane with him. . . . Keep him in the dominant position so that he will feel needed and adequate as the leader.[6]

Sociologists have taken note of these possible differences in male and female styles of power. In fact, Jessie Bernard suggests that in many marriages male control may be only an illusion:

From time immemorial, despite the institutional pattern conferring authority on husbands, whichever spouse had the talent for running the show did so. If the wife was the power in the marriage, she exerted her power in a way that did not show; she did not flaunt it, she was satisfied with the "power-behind-the-throne" position.[7]

For these reasons, measuring the actual balance of power in relationships can be tricky.

To assess power in our couples, we asked very general questions about the overall balance of power, as well as more specific questions about particular situations and events. For instance, we asked, "Who do you think has more of a say about what you and your partner do together — your partner or you?" Subjects responded on a five-point scale from "I have much more say" to "My partner has much more say," with "exactly equal" as the midpoint. All these measures involved self-reports; that is, we asked students to describe the balance of power in their relationship as they perceived it. Most studies of power in close relationships have also used self-reports, assuming that, in the final analysis, participants in a relationship are the best judges of their own personal experiences of power.

Our results were somewhat surprising. Despite their strong support for equality, only 49 percent of the college women and 42 percent of the men in our study reported equal power in their current dating relationship. This represents a large proportion of the students, but is much less than the 91 percent who said they favored equal power. When the relationship was unequal, it was usually the man who had more say. About 45 percent of the men and 35 percent of the women reported that the man had more say, compared to 13 percent and 17 percent, respectively, who said the woman had more say. There are two points to be made about these results. First, there was much variation in students' views of the relationships. Although many students did report power equality, other patterns were also found. Second, these results suggest that at least some students who said that they wanted equal power in their relationship were not able to achieve this goal.

Tipping the Balance of Power

Why is it that some people who want an egalitarian relationship are not successful in creating one? Research has identified three important factors that affect the balance of power in relationships: the social norms dictating who "should" be more powerful, the psychological dependency of each partner in the couple, and the personal resources that partners bring to their relationship [8]

Social Norms   Historically, social norms or rules of conduct have specified that the man should be the "boss" in male–female relationships. If couples endorse traditional roles for their relationship — believing, for example, that the man's career should be more important than the woman's, and that the woman should look up to the man as a leader — the balance of power is likely to tip away from gender equality. Our study of dating couples included a

ten-item Sex-Role Attitude Scale. Students indicated their agreement or disagreement with such statements as "If a couple is going somewhere by car,
it's better for the man to do most of the driving," and "If both husband and
wife work full-time, her career should be just as important as his in determining where the family lives." Responses indicated that some students
advocated strongly traditional positions, others endorsed strongly feminist
positions, and many fell somewhere in between. Dating partners generally
held similar attitudes; it was unusual to find an ardent feminist dating a very
traditional partner.

   We found that endorsement of traditional sex roles was often associated
with unequal power in dating relationships. For example, 59 percent of the
men who had traditional sex-role attitudes believed they had greater say than
did their girlfriend, compared to only 25 percent of the men with nontraditional (profeminist) attitudes. However, exceptions to this pattern did occur.
For instance, over one-third of the most traditional couples reported equal
power, as Paul and Peggy illustrate. For them, power was not a prominent issue. Whereas Peggy was considered the expert on cooking and social skills,
Paul made decisions about what to do on dates. They divided responsibilities in a traditional way but believed that overall they had equal power. Most
often, however, sex-role attitudes did have an important impact on the balance of power. Believing that men and women can perform similar tasks, acknowledging that the woman's career is as important as the man's, and other
nontraditional attitudes can foster an equal-power relationship. At the same
time, it is also likely that having an egalitarian relationship encourages nontraditional sex-role attitudes. The link between attitudes and power can work
both ways.

Imbalance of Involvement   Social psychological theory suggests that power
in a couple is affected by each partner's dependence on the relationship. In
some relationships, both partners are equally in love, or equally disinterested.
In other cases, however, the partners' degree of involvement differs. One
partner may be passionately in love, while the other partner may have only
a lukewarm interest in the relationship. Such imbalances of involvement are
likely to affect the balance of power.[9] Sociologist Willard Waller[10] described
this phenomenon as the "principle of least interest," which predicts that the
person who is least involved or interested in a relationship will have greater
influence. The more involved person, eager to maintain the relationship, de-
fers to the partner's wishes. Thus, the less interested partner is better able
to set the terms of the relationship and exert control. Being deeply in love is
a wonderful experience. But unless love and commitment are reciprocated,
they make a person especially vulnerable to their partner's influence.

   Our questionnaire contained several measures of love and involvement.
One question asked straightforwardly, "Who do you think is more involved
in your relationship—your partner or you?" Less than half the students reported that their relationship was equal in involvement. The principle of least

TABLE 1　Power and Involvement in Dating Relationships

	Relative Involvement		
Relative Power	Women Less Involved (60 couples)	Equal (57 couples)	Man Less Involved (100 couples)
Man more say	23%	54%	70%
Equal say	28	20	20
Woman more say	49	26	10

interest was strongly supported by our data, as can be seen in Table 1. In couples where the man was the least involved, it was most common for the man to have more power. In contrast, when the woman was the least involved, nearly half the couples reported that the woman had greater power.

Attraction to a partner and involvement in a relationship are affected by many factors. The degree to which we find our partner desirable and rewarding is very important, as is our assessment of the possible alternative relationships available to both of us. If our present partner is more desirable than the available alternatives, our attraction should remain high. Thus, such personal resources as physical attractiveness, intelligence, a sense of humor, loyalty, prestige, or money can affect the balance of power.

Findings concerning physical attractiveness illustrate this point. Although we may like to think that inner qualities are more important than physical appearance, there is ample evidence that beauty can be a valuable resource in interpersonal relations, at least among younger adults. As part of our study, we took full-length color photos of each participant, and then had these photos rated on physical attractiveness by a panel of student judges. As predicted, if one person was judged much more attractive than her or his partner, she or he was likely to have more power in the relationship.

Another important determinant of dependency on a relationship is the likelihood that a person could find another partner if the current relationship ended. The more options a person has about alternative dating relationships, the less dependent he or she is on a single partner. We asked students whether they had either dated or had sexual intercourse with someone other than their primary partner during the past two months. We also inquired whether there was a "specific other" they could be dating at present. For both men and women, having dating alternatives was related to having greater power in the current relationship.

Our analysis suggests that a possible way to increase one's relative power in a relationship is to acquire new personal resources or greater options. This message is conveyed, in highly different forms, by both traditionalists and feminists. *Fascinating Womanhood* promises that women can have a happier marriage by learning to be more "feminine." Women are encouraged to improve their appearance, become better cooks, learn to be more sexually alluring, pay more attention to their husband, and, in general, improve their "feminine" skills. By increasing her own desirability, the woman may indirectly increase her husband's interest in their relationship. As a result, the husband may be more willing to defer to his wife's wishes and concerns. While endorsing a pattern of male leadership and control, *Fascinating Womanhood* nonetheless suggests ways for women to work within the traditional pattern to increase their personal influence and to achieve their own goals.

Contemporary feminists have rejected inequality between the sexes and have encouraged women to become less dependent on men. Women can achieve this independence by developing closer relationships with other women and by learning new skills, especially "masculine" skills such as car repair or carpentry. The greatest emphasis has been given to women's gaining financial independence through paid employment. In the next section, data from our study bearing on the impact of women's careers on power in dating relationships are presented.

Women's Career Goals   Traditionally, men divide their interest and energy between personal relationships and paid work. For women, in contrast, a family and a career have often been viewed as incompatible goals. Typically, women have given far higher priority to personal and family relationships than to paid employment. Many of the college students in our study rejected the idea that the woman's place is in the home; both men and women tended to support careers for women. What impact does this have on power in male–female relationships?

Full-time paid employment makes women more similar to men in several ways. Work provides women with additional skills and expertise, with important interests outside the relationship, and with additional resources such as income or prestige. For all these reasons, it seems likely that a woman's employment might affect power in a dating relationship.

Leonard and Felicia, two participants in our study, illustrate this effect. They met and were married in college, where both majored in music. The couple agreed that while Felicia is a competent musician, Leonard is a musical genius on his way to becoming a famous composer. After college, Felicia took a job as a music teacher to put her husband through graduate school. She acknowledged his superior ability and was willing to support his career by working. But she viewed her job strictly as a necessity. Her primary involvement was in her marriage. Leonard's job attitude was completely different. Felicia said bluntly: "For him, music comes first and I'm second. If he had to move to New York to be famous and I wouldn't go, he'd leave me." In part because of this imbalance of involvement, Leonard had greater power in their relationship. He determined where they lived, for instance, and required Felicia to tolerate his sexual infidelities.

When we reinterviewed Leonard and Felicia a year later, we learned that there had been a great deal of strain in their relationship. Partly because of this tension, Felicia took a summer-school course in a new method of teaching music. She found the course exciting, and during the summer she gained greater confidence in her abilities as a music teacher. She became seriously interested in teaching as a career. With the support of other women in the class, Felicia decided to apply for admission to a graduate program in the new instructional method. In long talks with other women, she reexamined her ideas about marriage, sex roles, and her career. She realized that "the fantasy of having a man fulfill a woman is a dangerous myth. You have to fulfill yourself." Despite some objections from Leonard, Felicia intended to start graduate school the next year. She felt that these changes had already helped her marriage and changed the balance of power. "If I'd gone on working this year to support him, as Len wanted me to, he'd be the more dominant. . . . If I hadn't decided to go to school, he'd be taking the money and running the show." Having made her decision, Felicia felt less dominated and exploited by her husband. She hoped that, as she gained more respect for her own abilities, Len would gain respect for her, too.

This is only one example. We asked all the couples about their educational and career plans. Nearly 70 percent of both men and women said they planned to go to graduate school. Among those seeking advanced degrees, women were more likely than men to desire only a master's degree (50 percent of women versus 32 percent of men). Men were more likely than women to aspire to a doctorate or the equivalent (38 percent of men versus 19 percent of women). Additional questions probed students' attitudes about full-time employment for women and their personal interest in having a dual-career marriage in which both spouses have full-time careers.

As expected, the women's educational and career plans were significantly related to the balance of power in the current relationship. For instance, in one analysis we examined the relationship between the highest degree the woman aspired to and the balance of power. The results were striking. When the woman aspired to less than a bachelor's degree, 87 percent of students reported that the man had more power in their relationship. When the woman planned to complete her bachelor's degree, about half (45 percent) reported that the man had more power. And, when the woman planned on an advanced degree, only about 30 percent reported that the man had more say. As the woman's educational aspirations increased, the likelihood of a male-dominant relationship decreased sharply. In contrast, no association was found between the man's educational aspirations or career plans and power.

In summary, we have found that power in a dating relationship is related to sex-role attitudes, to the balance of involvement, and to personal resources such as the woman's career plans. For college women in our sample, these three factors were interrelated. Women who planned on graduate school reported relatively less involvement in their current relationship, had more liberal sex-role attitudes (and tended to date men who were also more liberal), and often planned to make a major commitment to a full-time career, as well as to marriage.

For college men in our sample, educational plans, sex-role attitudes, and relative involvement were *not* interrelated. Liberal and traditional men did not differ in their educational goals or in their relative involvement in the current relationship. In American society, all men are expected to have jobs. This is as true for men who reject traditional roles as for men who support them. Although the man's educational plans did not affect the balance of power, his own sex-role attitudes and his relative involvement in the relationship were important determinants of power.

Although many women in our sample wanted to pursue a career, they did not see this as a substitute for marriage. About 96 percent of women and 95 percent of men said they expected to marry eventually, although not necessarily this partner. Further, 90 percent of women and 93 percent of men said they wanted to have one or more children. What distinguished traditional and liberal women was not their intention to marry but rather their orientation toward employment.

Finally, we should note that couples can achieve equal power in different ways. Some, perhaps most often nontraditional couples, attempt to share all decision making completely. Ross and Betsy told us that they always make joint decisions—they shop together, discuss entertainment and vacation plans together, and reach mutual solutions to conflicts. Other couples, perhaps most often traditionalists, adopt a pattern in which each partner has specific areas of responsibility. Diane told us that she and Alan have equal power, but explained that "in almost every situation, one of us is more influential. There are very few decisions that are fifty–fifty." For instance, Diane picked their new apartment, but Alan decided about moving the furniture. Diane said, "I make the aesthetic decisions and Alan makes the practical ones." Dividing areas of responsibility, sharing decision making totally, or some mixture of the two are all possible avenues to equal power in relationships.

Power and Satisfaction in Dating Relationships

Fascinating Womanhood proposed that the acceptance of traditional sex roles and male leadership is essential to a happy male–female relationship. Feminists argue that traditional sex roles oppress women and make honest male–female relationships difficult. What impact do sex-role attitudes and the balance of power have on the success of a dating relationship? Our surprising answer is that they seem to have little impact on the happiness or survival of dating relationships.

We found no association between sex-role attitudes and satisfaction with the current relationship. Liberal and traditional couples rated themselves equally satisfied with their relationships and indicated that they felt equally close to their partners. Liberal and traditional couples did not differ in reports of the likelihood of eventually marrying the current partner, of love for their partner, or of the number of problems they anticipated in the relationship. Data from our two-year followup indicated that liberal and traditional couples were equally likely to break up.

To understand these findings, we must remember that dating partners usually had similar sex-role beliefs. Sharing attitudes and values may be much more crucial to the success of a relationship than is the content of the attitudes. Mismatching on sex-role attitudes can create problems for couples, and such differences may be most important when a couple first begins to date. Since all the students in our study were already "going with" their partner, we do not have information about the impact of sex roles on first meetings or casual dating. Couples in our study had all survived the beginning of a relationship, perhaps partly because they agreed about sex roles or had managed to reconcile their differences.

Since students were nearly unanimous in their endorsement of an egalitarian ideal of power, we might expect the balance of power to affect couple satisfaction or survival. In fact, equal-power and male-dominant couples did not differ in their reports of satisfaction and closeness, or in the likelihood of breaking up by the time of our two-year followup. In contrast, however, both men and women reported *less* satisfaction in relationships where the woman had more say. It is apparently easier to follow a traditional pattern or to adhere to the new pattern of equality than to experience a female-dominant relationship.

Currently, there is much controversy over proper behavior for men and women. Whether to adopt traditional standards, to attempt to modify them, or to reject old patterns outright are decisions we all must face. The results of this study suggest that traditional and egalitarian patterns are equally likely to lead to a satisfactory dating relationship or to a miserable one. Consensus between a woman and a man may be more important for couple happiness than is the particular pattern a couple follows. Feminists, however, might raise a further question. Even if individuals are able to find personal happiness in unequal relationships, is it good for society to perpetuate male dominance in marriage?

ENDNOTES

Author's note: We are grateful for the help of Monique Watson and Eileen Davis in preparing this manuscript. We received valuable bibliographic suggestions from Steven Gordon, Vickie Mays, Hector Myers, Amado Padilla, and Belinda Tucker.

1. Kate Millett, *Sexual Politics* (Garden City, NY: Doubleday, 1970).
2. Helen Andelin, *Fascinating Womanhood* (New York: Bantam Books, 1963), pp. 134–35.
3. For more information on this large-scale study, see Charles T. Hill, Zick Rubin, Letitia A. Peplau, and Susan G. Willard, "The Volunteer Couple: Sex Differences, Couple Commitment and Participation in Research on Interpersonal Relationships," *Social Psychology Quarterly* 42(4) (1979): 415–20; and Letitia A. Peplau, Zick Rubin, and Charles T. Hill, "The Sexual Balance of Power," *Psychology Today* (November 1976): 142.
4. Constantina Safilios-Rothschild, "The Study of Family Power Structure: A Review 1960–1969," *Journal of Marriage and the Family* 32 (1970): 539–52.
5. Ted L. Huston, "Power," in *Close Relationships*, ed. Harold H. Kelley et al. (New York: Freeman, 1983), pp. 169–219.
6. Andelin, *Fascinating Womanhood*, pp. 145–46.
7. Jessie Bernard, *The Future of Marriage* (New York: Bantam Books, 1972), p. 155.
8. For other discussions of factors affecting the balance of power, see Sharon S. Brehm, *Intimate Relationships* (New York: Random House, 1985); Huston, "Power";

Gerald W. McDonald, "Family Power: The Assessment of a Decade of Theory and Research, 1970–1979," *Journal of Marriage and the Family* 42(4) (1980): 841–54.
9. Constantina Safilios-Rothschild, "A Macro- and Micro-Examination of Family Power and Love: An Exchange Model," *Journal of Marriage and the Family* 38 (1976): 355–62.
10. Willard Waller, *The Family: A Dynamic Interpretation* (New York: Cordon, 1938).

PART IV

Cohabitation, Marriage, and Partnership

In this section, we examine various forms of family formation, namely cohabitation, marriage, and partnership. These three family forms are examples of *coupling:* how couples come together to form a family relationship. It should be noted, however, that there are additional types of coupling and family formation, such as communes, where a group of people live together as a family; polygamy, whereby an individual marries more than one spouse; and polyamorous relationships, in which more than two people are involved in a love relationship. There are also a number of people who will never marry and, possibly, who will never cohabit but are in ongoing relationships. Thus, as students of the family, we need to recognize the diversity of family forms that exist in our society and in other societies beyond traditional, heterosexual marriage. We also need to recognize that the personal experience of any one family form is also diverse depending on a person's race-ethnicity, social class, gender, and sexual orientation.

Given that diversity, what is known about cohabitation, marriage, and partnership?

Cohabitation

In the United States, even though cohabitation has existed for centuries, it is a fairly modern alternative to heterosexual marriage. The numbers of cohabiting couples in the United States did not begin to rapidly grow until after 1960. According to the U.S. Bureau of the Census (1998), the number of couples cohabiting increased from 439,000 in 1960 to 4,236,000 in 1998.[1] Prior to 1960, cohabitation was considered to be socially deviant. Couples were thought to be "living in sin" or "shacking up" together. Social attitudes about cohabitation began to change during the 1960s and 1970s due to the influences of the sexual revolution and the feminist movement, which brought renewed attention to sexual freedom and to the traditional and often oppressive gender roles in marriage. During this time period, many "anti-marriage" groups began to form as part of the anti-establishment movement. Divorce rates also began to rise, and with the increasing public criticism of marriage,

---

[1] Note that these data reflect the numbers of heterosexual couples living together and not those cohabitors who are same-sex couples. The U.S. Bureau of the Census did not begin to collect data on same-sex couples sharing a household until the 1990 census. Moreover, in general, most of the research on cohabitation focuses on heterosexual couples.

more young couples chose to live together either as an alternative to marriage or as a trial marriage. Today, cohabitors are usually one of three types: (1) couples planning to marry, but living together first; (2) couples cohabiting as a temporary alternative to marriage; and (3) couples cohabiting as a permanent alternative to marriage.

Unlike many other areas of study on the family, there is not as much research on cohabitation (Bumpass and Sweet 1989). Most of the research on cohabitation focuses on how cohabitation affects marriage rates or marital stability. There is also some research on how cohabitation affects divorce rates and on the role cohabitation plays in relationships formed after a divorce. In fact, a growing number of cohabitors are individuals over age 45 who, after experiencing a divorce, would rather cohabit than remarry. These individuals do not want to bear the legal and emotional complications of marrying again. Another area of study within the cohabitation literature is the influence cohabitation has on children. Manning and Lichter (1996) estimate that more than 2.2 million, or roughly 1 in 7, children live in the household of a cohabiting couple. This research examines the emotional and financial well-being of children in cohabiting households versus that of children in married households.

The first article in this section, "The Role of Cohabitation in Declining Rates of Marriage," by Larry L. Bumpass, James A. Sweet, and Andrew Cherlin, examines the relationship between cohabitation and the declining rates of marriage in the United States. Bumpass and Sweet are social demographers at the Center for Demography and Ecology at the University of Wisconsin at Madison. Andrew Cherlin is a professor of sociology at Johns Hopkins University. As social scientists, they are interested in studying the changes in family-formation patterns and household living arrangements caused by more people never marrying or choosing to cohabit after a divorce instead of remarrying. In this reading, the authors address several important questions: Are people, in fact, cohabiting more and marrying less? What are the characteristics of cohabiting couples, and how can they be distinguished from couples who choose to marry? Do cohabiting couples expect to marry, and how does cohabiting prior to marriage affect marital relationships?

Marriage

Even with the increasing numbers of individuals who choose to cohabit or to never marry, the majority of individuals in the United States eventually marry. Unlike cohabitation, however, there is abundant research on the institution of marriage (the macrolevel) and on the personal experience of marriage (the microlevel). At the macrolevel, marriage is a social institution that is influenced by other institutions, including the legal, religious, economic, and political institutions. Norval D. Glenn, a well-known family scholar, has argued that marriage is an institution of social control because it regulates individual behavior. Glenn (1996) also has studied the paradox that, while marriage is important to most adult Americans, the proportion of Americans ever-married has declined and the proportion successfully married has declined even more. Why are people choosing not to marry? And, if people do choose to marry, what are they looking for in a spouse?

This latter question is the focus of the second reading in this section, "In Search of the Right Spouse: Interracial Marriage among Chinese and Japanese Americans," by Colleen Fong and Judy Yung. Fong and Yung interviewed 19 women and 24 men who, as Asian Americans, were currently married to or had been married to Whites. In particular, Fong and Yung are interested in what preconditions allowed for interracial love and marriage. How did the timing of the relationship and the availability of other Asian partners affect this intermarriage? Do they have an aversion of marrying someone from their same race? Fong and Yung explore these and other questions about their respondents' lives prior to marriage and after marriage. Of particular interest in their study is the separate interviews and analysis of women and men. Fong and Yung provide the women's perspective and men's perspective in order to show how interracial relationships are gendered.

The third article in this section, "Peer Marriage" by Pepper Schwartz, is an excerpt from Schwartz's book *Peer Marriage: How Love between Equals Really Works* (1995). Since her graduate school days at Yale, Schwartz has studied gender, relationships, and power dynamics. Schwartz chose to study peer marriage because everyone said it couldn't exist, but she knew it could because she has been in a peer marriage for more than 15 years and knows other couples in peer marriages. She says she has always believed that equality and equity are important principles for respect and happiness. Regarding her research, Schwartz also says:

> It was and is important for me to show that men and women do not have to be in a hierarchical relationship — and that women, in particular, do not have to settle for anything less than a fair deal in a loving partnership. (Personal Interview 1997)

Schwartz divides her respondents into three groups: traditional couples, Near Peer Couples, and Peer Couples. Each type of marital coupling has strengths and weaknesses, including the fact that in order to have a peer or egalitarian marriage requires a great deal of work on the couple's part. Peer Couples have to work every day on sustaining the power balance and communication in their relationship.

Partnership

Many individuals, regardless of sexual orientation, decide that marriage is not for them and decide, instead, to form commitments called "partnerships." The meaning and recognition of these partnerships varies because the government primarily recognizes legal, heterosexual marriages. Thus, some couples try to form domestic partnerships through employment or local governments to give their relationships recognition and rights similar to those of married couples. Later in this book, Reading 43, by Wisensale and Heckart, examines domestic partnerships. Other couples are less concerned about the legal recognition of their relationship, but want to have a committed relationship outside of marriage. They may decide to create a private or public commitment ceremony to honor their relationship to each other. In recent years, there has been increased research on the commitment ceremonies of gay and lesbian couples, including Suzanne Sherman's book *Lesbian and Gay Marriage: Private Commitments, Public Ceremonies* (1992); Ellen Lewin's book *Recognizing Ourselves: Ceremonies of Lesbian and Gay Commitment* (1998); and Gretchen A. Stiers' book *From This Day Forward: Commitment, Marriage, and Family in Lesbian and Gay Relationships* (1999).

In the final article in this section, "Gay and Lesbian Families Are Here," Judith Stacey examines the partnerships formed by gay couples in their efforts to create families. In particular, Stacey, the Streisand Professor of Contemporary Gender Studies and professor of sociology at the University of Southern California, argues that many social institutions deny gay families certain rights. Legislatures do not recognize their committed relationships, adoption agencies often deny gay and lesbian parents the right to adopt, and single and lesbian women often have difficulty gaining access to alternative insemination. The specific focus of Stacey's article is on same-sex marriage. Stacey provides both the pro and con arguments to this debate, which is still being waged in many states. A number of states have passed "Defense of Marriage" Acts that will make same-sex marriages contracted elsewhere illegal in their state. As this book was going to press, the state of Vermont was debating legal recognition of same-sex relationships. The House of Representatives in Vermont argued that the legislature must recognize civil unions to ensure that same-gender marriage is legal or provide an alternative whereby these couples would be afforded the same rights as married couples now have. The House in Vermont passed the resolution and it was sent to the Senate, where it was passed into law in April 2000. The issue of same-sex marriage is not going away, however, as is evidenced by calls to repeal the Vermont law, which gives legal rights to gay couples, and by the 1,000 gay couples who participated in a mass wedding during the Millennium March on Washington for Equality on April 29, 2000.

REFERENCES

Bumpass, Larry L. and James A. Sweet. 1989. "National Estimates of Cohabitation." *Demography* 26(4):615–25.

Glenn, Norval D. 1996. "Values, Attitudes, and the State of American Marriage." Pp. 15–33 in *Promises to Keep: Decline and Renewal of Marriage in America,* edited by David Popenoe, Jean Bethke Elshtain, and David Blankenhorn. Lanham, MD: Rowman and Littlefield.

Lewin, Ellen. 1998. *Recognizing Ourselves: Ceremonies of Lesbian and Gay Commitment.* New York: Columbia University Press.

Manning, Wendy and Daniel Lichter. 1996. "Parental Cohabitation and Children's Economic Well-Being." *Journal of Marriage and the Family* 58:998–1010.

Schwartz, Pepper. 1995. *Peer Marriage: How Love between Equals Really Works.* New York: The Free Press.

Sherman, Suzanne, ed. 1992. *Lesbian and Gay Marriage: Private Commitments, Public Ceremonies.* Philadelphia: Temple University Press.

Stiers, Gretchen A. 1999. *From This Day Forward: Commitment, Marriage, and Family in Lesbian and Gay Relationships.* New York: St. Martin's Press.

U.S. Bureau of the Census. 1998. "Marital Status and Living Arrangements: March 1998." *Current Population Reports,* Series P20-514. Washington, DC: U.S. Bureau of the Census.

12

THE ROLE OF COHABITATION
IN DECLINING RATES OF MARRIAGE

LARRY L. BUMPASS • JAMES A. SWEET

ANDREW CHERLIN

It is by now well known that recent cohorts of young adults in the United States and most other Western nations have been postponing marriage relative to the cohorts that entered adulthood in the period from 1945 to 1965. It is also well known that the number of cohabiting couples has increased greatly since about 1970. It is the connection between these two developments that we address in this analysis. In particular, we compare trends in marriage and remarriage to trends in these variables when cohabitation is included, and examine education differences in the rise of cohabitation. We then document the characteristics of cohabiting couples in terms of the duration of the union, presence of children, perceived stability, marriage plans, and opinions about cohabitation. Finally, we analyze several marriage-related attitude items among all unmarried persons under age 35. . . .

Until recently there have not been adequate data for an assessment of the relationship between changing marriage and cohabitation [patterns] in the United States. Fortunately, we are now able to do this with the recently completed National Survey of Families and Households (NSFH).

The National Survey of Families and Households

The NSFH is a national sample survey of 13,017 respondents, conducted in 1987–88. In addition to a main sample of 9,643 persons aged 19 and over, we oversampled certain population subgroups. The oversample included households containing single-parent families, stepfamilies, recently married couples, cohabiting couples, blacks, Chicanos, or Puerto Ricans. In each selected household, a randomly selected adult was interviewed. A self-administered form was also filled out by the spouse (or cohabiting partner), and by a householder in cases in which the primary respondent was a relative of the householder (such as an adult child in a parent's household or an elderly parent in a child's household). Interviews averaged about one hour and forty minutes in length.

From "The Role of Cohabitation in Declining Rates of Marriage" by Larry Bumpass, James A. Sweet, and Andrew Cherlin. *Journal of Marriage and the Family*, Vol. 53, November 1991, pp. 913–927. Reprinted by permission of the authors.

The NSFH was designed to provide detailed information on many aspects of family life in order to permit analyses of relationships among various family domains (see Sweet, Bumpass, and Call 1988). Because of the importance of cohabitation for understanding the changing meaning of marital unions, we devoted considerable attention to the relationships between cohabitation and marriage, including the following components:

1. Detailed measurement of cohabitation histories in the context of marriage and separation histories.
2. A sequence on attitudes relating to marriage and cohabitation asked of never-married and previously married respondents under age 35.
3. A series of questions concerning the nature and quality of the relationship between partners in both married and cohabiting couples.
4. A self-administered interview with the spouse or partner of the main respondent.
5. A few questions relating to attitudes toward marriage and cohabitation asked of all respondents.

While the present study is only exploratory, it draws on each of these initiatives to provide information on the relationship between cohabitation and marriage in the United States. . . .

Marital and Nonmarital Union Formation

The Formation of First Unions

In the United States, the proportion of persons who lived with a partner before marrying for the first time increased from 11 percent around 1970 (Bumpass and Sweet 1989a) to nearly half for recent first marriages (Bumpass 1990). Figures 1 and 2 illustrate (for males and females, respectively) the effect of cohabitation in offsetting the decline in marriage rates. The oldest of these cohorts, aged 40–44 at interview, reached age 20 during the mid-1960s; the most recent reached age 20 in the mid-1980s. Because of the low levels of cohabitation for the oldest cohorts, there is little difference between the proportions ever married and the proportions ever in a union. For these cohorts, age at marriage was a reasonable indicator of age at first union. This is clearly no longer so. In the absence of cohabitation, there would have been a substantial decline in the proportions setting up housekeeping before ages 20 and 25. However, when first cohabitation is included with first marriage, we find only a very slight decline in age at first union over these cohorts.

Note that, for women, the proportion experiencing a union before age 20 did not decline until the cohorts centered on 1960 reached adulthood—which was in the 1980s. Even then, the decline was slight, and the proportion experiencing a union before age 25 has yet to decline substantially. . . .

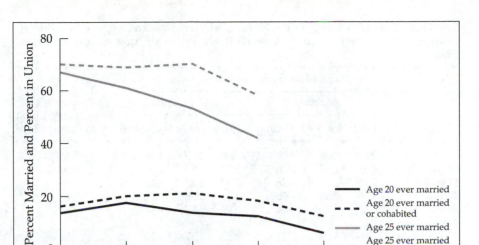

FIGURE 1   **Percentage Married, and Percentage in Union, before Ages 20 and 25: Males**

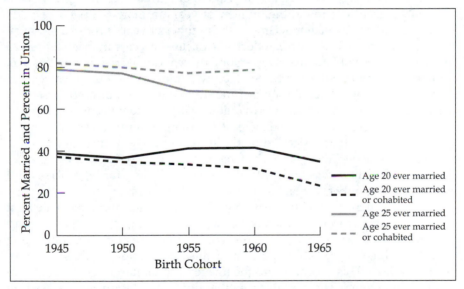

FIGURE 2   **Percentage Married, and Percentage in Union, before Ages 20 and 25: Females**

About 40 percent of cohabiting unions in the United States break up without the couple getting married, and this tends to occur rather quickly. By about one and one-half years, half of cohabiting couples have either married or broken up (Bumpass and Sweet 1989a). Consequently, the number of years in a union before age 25 may have declined even when the experience of a

TABLE 1   Relative Change in the Number of Years in Marriage, and Number of Years in a Union, before Age 25: Cohorts Reaching These Ages around 1970 and 1985

	Mean Number of Years before Age 25						
	Married			In Any Union			% Change Married −% Change Union/
Category	1970	1985	% Change	1970	1985	% Change	% Change Married
Total	2.90	2.05	−29%	3.05	2.59	−15%	48%
Males	2.15	1.37	−36	2.27	1.84	−19	47
Females	3.68	2.63	−28	3.83	3.23	−16	43
Whites	2.97	2.08	−30	3.10	2.56	−17	43
Blacks	2.43	1.36	−44	2.60	2.17	−17	61
Education							
0–11 years	3.89	3.08	−21	4.32	3.87	−10	52
12 years	3.32	2.52	−24	3.33	3.11	−07	71
College	2.24	1.42	−37	2.34	1.86	−21	43

union by that age has remained relatively stable. Table 1 shows the number of years in marriage and number of years in any union before age 25. There was a 29 percent decline in the number of years in marriage before age 25, compared to the 15 percent decline in the number of years ever in a union by this age. Part of this, of course, reflects the decline in years married by age 25 as a consequence of later marriage among those who married before this age, and part also reflects the decreased stability of marital unions. However, it is also the case that cohabitation offset the decline in years in union less than the decline in the proportion ever in union by age 25 (48 percent as compared to 67 percent). Nonetheless, the increase in young adult years spent "single" is only about half that suggested by declining marriage rates.

Though the decline in number of years married before age 25 was greater among blacks, there was an identical 17 percent decline for both blacks and whites in the number of years in a union before that age.

It is clear that cohabitation has compensated for declining marriage least among persons who have attended college. For example, it offsets 84 percent of the decline in marriages before age 25 among persons not completing high school, compared to 63 percent of this decline among those who attended college. This is contrary to the image of cohabitation as a college student phenomenon. The popular treatment of cohabitation has focused on college graduates or college students in urban areas — rather than on the consensual unions that were more common among the lower class. Thus there was the impression that cohabitation was an innovation of college students in the 1960s, which then spread during the 1970s and 1980s to the rest of the population. Taking into account "common-law" marriages in the lower class, we might expect that cohabitation was rare outside the lower class before it was adopted by well-educated young adults in large metropolitan areas and then diffused widely across the middle and working classes. Evidence relating to this model has been slim. One Swedish study reports, to the contrary, that rates of consensual union formation were consistently higher among young working-class women than among young women from the bourgeoisie across birth cohorts, and consistently higher among nonstudents than among students (Hoem 1986). . . .

At all times, the percentage cohabiting before 25 was least for the college-educated. This group did experience a surge in cohabitation during the 1970s, so the claim that they were radically changing their behavior was correct. But so was everyone else. It seems likely that college students attracted the attention of the media and academics because they were the most visible component of a widespread phenomenon. College graduates have not been the innovators in the spread of cohabitation, but rather the imitators. This leaves more unsettled than ever the question of just why the transformation of union formation occurred. The inverse relationship with education does suggest, however, that one component may be the substitution of cohabitation for marriage in the early years of a union when there are economic constraints. We will see some related evidence on this point subsequently.

Postmarital Union Formation

Because of our high levels of marital instability, large proportions of the population experience separation or divorce. At the same time, rates of remarriage have fallen rapidly. We have seen that cohabitation has offset much of the decline in first marriage rates; to what extent has it also compensated for declining rates of remarriage?

We know that cohabitation is even more common among separated and divorced persons than among the never-married. Sixty percent of persons who remarried between 1980 and 1987 lived with a partner before remarriage—46 percent only with the person they then married and 14 percent with someone else (Bumpass and Sweet 1989a). . . . Although the proportion marrying within five years of separation declined 16 percent between 1970 and the early 1980s, the proportion who had formed a new union within five years actually increased slightly. Hence, cohabitation has compensated fully for the fall in remarriage. There has been no decline in the pace of union formation following marital dissolution, although an increasing proportion of these unions are nonmarital.

Characteristics of Cohabitors

As outlined earlier, the NSFH provides a wealth of data on cohabiting couples that allow comparisons to married couples on the one hand and to other unmarried persons on the other. In this section we explore some preliminary clues about the nature of cohabiting relationships.

TABLE 2   Duration of Cohabitation, by Whether Respondent Was Ever Married

	Ever Married		
Duration	Yes	No	Total
Less than 1 year	30%	39%	36%
1–1.9 years	17	19	18
2–2.9 years	12	11	11
3–3.9 years	9	8	8
4–4.9 years	9	5	7
5+ years	23	17	20
Total	100	100	100

TABLE 3   Presence of Children in Household of Cohabiting Respondents, by Whether Respondent Was Ever Married

	Ever Married		
Children	Yes	No	Total
No children	53%	65%	60%
Couple's	7	16	12
One partner's	39	22	27
Total	100	100	100

Duration and Presence of Children

We have already noted that cohabitation tends to be a very short-lived state. Only about 1 out of 10 remain cohabiting after five years without either marrying or breaking up. Nonetheless, this does not mean that there are few cohabitations of long duration at any point in time. Longer cohabitations tend to "accumulate" in the population, so there are more in the cross-section than we might expect from a cohort perspective. As we can see from Table 2, 20 percent of cohabiting couples have lived together for five or more years. The duration of cohabiting unions is longer among previously married persons, among whom only 30 percent began living together in the last year, compared to 39 percent among the never-married. We would expect marriage rates to be lower among the previously married because of their older age distribution. Whether there is a further disinclination to marry associated with having been previously married is a topic that warrants further examination, and one on which we will see more evidence subsequently.

The common image of cohabiting couples as college students, or at least young couples, does not usually include a family with children. Yet, 4 of every 10 such couples have children present (Table 3). This proportion is one-third among the never-married and almost half among the previously married.

TABLE 4   Age of Youngest Child in Household of Cohabiting Respondents, by Whether Respondent Was Ever Married

| | Ever Married | | |
Children	Yes	No	Total
No children	54%	64%	60%
0–4	16	24	21
5–9	14	7	10
10–17	16	5	10
Total	100	100	100

One-sixth of never-married cohabiting couples have a child that was born since they began living together. As we noted in an earlier analysis of children's single-parent experience, this represents a significant component of unmarried births (about a quarter) that are not born into single-parent households (Bumpass and Sweet 1989a).

Further, the children in cohabiting households are not all young children. In Table 4 we see that one-quarter of the households with children have children age 10 or older, mostly living with previously married parents. In thinking about the meaning of cohabitation and the dynamics of cohabiting households, it is critical to keep in mind that issues of parenting and step-parenting are very much a part of the picture.

Attitudes toward Cohabitation

We turn now to several attitudinal items that relate to differences and similarities between cohabitation and marriage. One such sequence was a series of questions concerning how important various factors are in thinking about whether or not to live with someone without being married. Responses were on a 7-point scale ranging from "not at all important" to "very important." Table 5 shows the percentage of cohabitors who responded in the two categories at each end of the scale.

The only item that was regarded as "important" by a majority of the respondents was "couples can be sure they are compatible before marriage." A quarter of the respondents reported that opportunity to "share living expenses" was important.

Though the idea of cohabitation as a testing ground for marriage includes an explicit tentativeness about such relationships, issues of lower personal commitment or greater personal independence are not reported as important by very large proportions (only about 15 percent to 20 percent). These cohabiting couples may be rationalizing their current status, but there is very little concern with cohabitation being a moral issue or with the disapproval of parents and friends.

TABLE 5   Views on Reasons for and Against Cohabitation: Cohabitors under Age 35

Reasons why a person might WANT to live with someone of the opposite sex without being married. How important is each reason to YOU?

Response	Important		Not Important	
	Male	Female	Male	Female
a. It requires less personal commitment than marriage.	14%	18%	46%	48%
b. It is more sexually satisfying than dating.	17	18	49	59
c. It makes it possible to share living expenses.	28	26	32	29
d. It requires less sexual faithfulness than marriage.	12	10	64	69
e. Couples can be sure they are compatible before marriage.	51	56	18	16
f. It allows each partner to be more independent than marriage.	17	19	36	41

Reasons why a person might NOT want to live with someone of the opposite sex without being married. How important is each reason to YOU?

Response	Important		Not Important	
	Male	Female	Male	Female
a. It is emotionally risky.	13%	18%	47%	44%
b. My friends disapprove.	4	4	84	82
c. My parents disapprove.	8	11	71	61
d. It is morally wrong.	6	9	75	60
e. It is financially risky.	7	7	64	55
f. It requires more personal commitment than dating.	19	25	43	40
g. It requires more sexual faithfulness than dating.	24	28	42	43

How Married Life Would Be Different

Cohabitors were asked, "How do you think your life would be different if you were married now?" There were five response categories, ranging from "much worse" to "much better." Table 6 shows the percentage of cohabiting men and women responding in the two "better" and the two "worse" categories to each of these items.

The striking thing about these measures is that the majority response category for each of these items is that things would not change, that is, that they would be "the same." When differences are perceived, with few exceptions, more of the cohabitors believe that each of these conditions would improve rather than deteriorate if they were married. The most important exception is that nearly a third of men, but only about a sixth of the women, report that

TABLE 6   Views on How Being Married Would Change Their Life: Cohabitors under Age 35

Aspect of Life	Better		Same		Worse	
	Male	Female	Male	Female	Male	Female
a. Standard of living	19	18	74	76	7	6
b. Economic security	24	32	67	61	9	7
c. Overall happiness	30	36	57	57	13	7
d. Freedom to do what you want	11	9	59	74	30	17
e. Economic independence	11	10	75	78	14	12
f. Sex life	22	14	68	81	10	5
g. Friendships with others	14	12	73	80	13	6
h. Relations with parents	22	24	71	72	7	4
i. Emotional security	28	38	63	57	9	5

Note: Cohabiting respondents age 35 and younger were asked, "How do you think your life might be different if you were married now?" A 5-point scale was used for responses. The "better" category above includes "somewhat better" and "much better." "Worse" includes "somewhat worse" and "much worse."

their "freedom to do what they want" would be worse if they were married. Apparently, this item captures an element of concern with independence that is not tapped by the measures on the importance of various considerations in Table 5.

A fairly sizable proportion of cohabiting respondents, especially women, report that their economic security and emotional security would be better if they were married.

A third of the respondents say that their overall happiness would improve if they were married now; a somewhat higher proportion of women than men report this. The meaning of this response is not clear. To the extent that the couple is not married because of some constraint (employment instability or low income, an impending move associated with finishing school, or the fact that one of the partners is not yet divorced from a previous marriage), it may be that it is not the marriage itself that would make the person happier, but the change in conditions that would make marriage possible.

Perceived Stability

While we do not have much evidence yet on the reasons, we know that cohabiting unions are much less stable than those of marriages (Balakrishnan et al. 1987; Bennett, Blanc, and Bloom 1988; Booth and Johnson 1988). Forty percent will disrupt before marriage, and marriages that are preceded by living together have 50 percent higher disruption rates than marriages without premarital cohabitation (Bumpass and Sweet 1989b). Several factors may be at work. On the one hand, it may just be that persons who are willing to cohabit are less traditional in their family values, and hence, at the same level of marital unhappiness, more likely to accept divorce as a solution (Booth and Johnson 1988). For example, among unions of 10 or fewer years duration, cohabitors are much less likely to agree that "marriage is a lifetime relationship and should never be ended except under extreme circumstances." Fifty-five percent agree with this statement, compared to 71 percent among married persons, net of duration and age differences.

It may also be that cohabiting unions are less well adjusted, other things being equal, either as a cause or as a consequence of cohabitation. On the one hand, there may well be a selection into cohabitation of persons more tentative about their relationship. Indeed, while some may be testing whether they should marry their partner, others may have no intention of marrying this partner. Some, perhaps because of experiences in their first marriage or personal problems of one sort or another, may not want to marry ever again. And, for those for whom cohabitation may be a substitute for marriage because of delaying circumstances, whether financial or a still existing marriage to someone else, those circumstances may have a negative impact on adjustment. At the same time, it is at least plausible that cohabitation could have a direct causal impact on adjustment after marriage if, for example, habits of relating to each other (that seem appropriate to the unmarried) persist into marriage.

Marriage Expectations

In Table 7, we see the marriage expectations of our cohabiting respondents. Slightly less than half say they have definite plans to marry their partner, and 74 percent either have definite plans or think they will marry this person. These figures are somewhat higher among those who have never been married—81 percent expect to marry their partner, compared with 61 percent among previously married cohabitors. On the other hand, a fifth of cohabiting persons do not expect to marry anyone; almost a third, among the previously married.

We can examine couple data for those cases in which the cohabiting partner completed the self-administered questionnaire. Not surprisingly, response rates of partners were higher for couples in which marriage was seen as more likely (80 percent of the primary respondents in these couples expected marriage, compared with 73 percent among all primary respondents). Among the couples for which we have joint data, there is a fairly high level of agreement about marriage expectations. Sixty-nine percent agree that they either plan or expect marriage, and 13 percent agree that they do not expect to marry each other. At the same time, this means that there is disagreement over whether marriage is expected in about one-fifth of the couples in which at least one partner expects marriage. Hence, the relatively high instability of cohabiting unions is not surprising when we consider that about a third either disagree about marriage or do not expect marriage.

As we might expect, cohabitors are not unaware of the potential shakiness of their relationship. Almost half say that they have thought that their

TABLE 7   Marriage Plans of Cohabiting Respondents, by Whether Respondent Was Ever Married

Marriage Plans	Ever Married		Total
	Yes	No	
Definite plans	40%	50%	47%
Think will marry	21	31	27
Marry someone	6	6	6
Not marry anyone	30	13	20
Total	100	100	100

relationship might be in trouble in the last year—and in three of every four cohabiting relationships, at least one partner reports having thought the relationship was in trouble. Clearly, there is a good deal of uncertainty among cohabitors about the potential stability of their union. Compared with married respondents and adjusted for duration and age differences, cohabitors are almost twice as likely to report that they have thought their relationship was in trouble over the past year.

Our data provide information on differences among cohabitors with respect to whether they have thought their relationship might be in trouble, whether they think they will marry their partner, and whether they think they will ever marry.

. . . Relationships of over a year duration are *more*, rather than less, likely to agree to the "trouble" measure, while those of three or more years duration are less likely to expect to marry the partner and particularly likely to say they will never marry. Apparently the dominant selection process with increasing duration is associated with marriages of better-adjusted couples. In addition, some subset of longer-duration couples who plan never to marry may represent more traditional "common-law" marriages.

There is surprisingly little variation in these items by education, though the "trouble" measure peaks among those with some college and then declines, and expectations of never marrying are lowest among those who completed college. Females are more likely than males to report trouble in the relationship, less likely to expect to marry the partner, and more likely to expect ever to marry, net of the other factors.

We might have expected that women would be reluctant to enter cohabiting relationships except for relationships believed to be a prelude to marriage. In fact, cohabiting women seem more tentative about marriage than cohabiting men.

Despite the higher levels of marital disruption among blacks, cohabiting blacks are less likely than cohabiting whites to report trouble in the relationship, and Mexican Americans are least likely to do so. Mexican Americans are also more likely to say that they will never marry, perhaps again reflecting traditions of consensual unions.

It seems clear that it is not just the presence of children, but whose children they are, that affects the relationship. Partner's children that are not the respondent's increase the report of trouble, and decrease marriage expectations, whereas if the respondent has children in the household that are not the partner's, it markedly increases the expectation of marriage and decreases the expectation of never marrying. There is surely an element of wishful thinking in this pattern, reflecting the associated economic and social costs. . . .

The age patterns in these variables are not as large or as consistent as we might have thought.

Cohabitors who have been married before are considerably less likely to expect to marry, either their partner or ever. This may be the beginnings of the pattern noted for Scandinavia by Blanc (1987), where cohabitation substitutes for remarriage for a majority of those experiencing marital disruption.

Attitudes toward Marriage among Never-Married Persons

Finally in this exploration of the connections between marriage and cohabitation, we turn to comparisons between cohabitors and other unmarried persons with respect to five items relating to marriage. . . .

Contrary to the "coercive pronatalism" themes of the early 1970s (Blake 1972), parental pressure to marry does not seem particularly salient. Only 30 percent of this sample agree that their parents would prefer it if they were married. The proportion increases markedly after age 25, but only reaches one-half among those in their late 30s. Never-married cohabitors are most likely to say that their parents would rather they were married, whereas previously married cohabitors are least likely (37 percent vs. 24 percent, respectively, net of other factors). The latter is somewhat surprising — perhaps parents are less likely to express opinions about their children's marriage choices after a separation or divorce.

Cohabitation is clearly a step between marriage and dating with respect to the constraints it places on individual freedom. Cohabitors feel marriage would make less difference in this respect than do others. Net of other factors, about a quarter of the cohabitors say that their freedom to do what they want would be worse if they were married, compared to about two-fifths of persons not cohabiting. As we observed for this item among cohabiting couples in Table 6, men seem much more concerned about the effect of marriage on their independence than women (49 percent vs. 31 percent).

Several years ago, Thornton and Freedman (1982) reported trends in attitudes concerning the relative merits of marriage and singleness. One startling aspect of that report from the Detroit Area Study was that only a third agreed that "it's better for a person to get married than to go through life being single." At the same time, two-thirds also disagreed that being single was better. Thornton and Freedman put an optimistic face on this, emphasizing that most seemed to think that it should be a matter of personal choice. That in itself is startling in the context of traditional norms concerning marriage, but we can also note that a third either were indifferent or thought it preferable to remain unmarried.

We repeated the first item and also find that only a third agree that marriage is better; indeed, a quarter explicitly disagree. There is also surprisingly little difference by either cohabitational or previous marital status. While the difference is not large, it is notable that males are more likely to agree that marriage is better than are females (37 percent compared to 30 percent).

We asked a similar item concerning whether "it's better for a person to have a child than to go through life childless." Only 29 percent agreed with this, and 25 percent explicitly disagreed.

Finally, the last item considered concerns the issue of bearing children out of wedlock. One-quarter of recent births were to unmarried mothers; rates among white women have more than doubled since the mid-1970s. As we noted earlier, children are frequently born to cohabiting couples. A third of unmarried persons under age 35 agree that "it would be all right for me to have children without being married" if they had plans to marry; a quarter disagreed with this. Over a quarter thought it would be all right even if they did not have plans to marry.

Summary and Conclusions

The large increases in the proportion never-married among persons in their early twenties is commonly interpreted to mean that young people are staying single longer. Because of cohabitation, however, being unmarried is not synonymous with being single. Young people are setting up housekeeping with partners of the opposite sex at almost as early an age as they did before marriage rates declined. Three-quarters of the decline in the proportion of women married for the first time by age 25 was offset by increased cohabitation. Nor does the decline in remarriage mean that separated and divorced persons are staying single longer. All of the decline in the proportion of separated and divorced persons who remarried within five years was offset by increased cohabitation.

Contrary to the popular image of cohabitation as a college student phenomenon, the trend toward cohabitation has been led by the least educated segment of the population, and the role of cohabitation in replacing early marriage is most pronounced for persons who have not completed high school. We have examined a number of characteristics of current cohabitors to shed more light on the nature and meaning of cohabitation. Cohabiting relationships tend to have been formed recently, though one in five have been cohabiting for five years or more. Further, 40 percent of cohabiting households include children. Thus in many ways currently cohabiting couples resemble married families. Most cohabitors expect to marry their partners, though we find a surprisingly high level of disagreement between partners about whether they will marry, and a high proportion are concerned about the stability of their relationship.

Attitudes concerning cohabitation and marriage suggest that while most expect to marry, normative pressures toward marriage are not very high.

Indeed, one-fifth of cohabiting persons do not expect ever to marry (or marry again). Among all unmarried persons, only a minority agree that it is better to marry than to go through life single. One-third say it would be all right for them to have a child without being married. While most expect to marry and have children, normative pressures toward marriage and childbearing and against unmarried childbearing appear very weak.

Thus the picture that is emerging is that cohabitation is very much a family status, but one in which levels of certainty about the relationship are lower than in marriage. This is partially a result of the use of cohabitation as a testing ground for marriage. We will never be able to determine the proportion of current cohabitators who would have been married at the same stage in their relationship under the regime of the late 1960s. Nonetheless, it is clear that we must include cohabitation along with marriage if we are to understand family life in modern societies.

REFERENCES

Balakrishnan, T. R., K. V. Rao, E. Lapierre-Adamcyk, and K. J. Krotki. 1987. "A Hazard Model Analysis of the Covariates of Marriage Dissolution in Canada." *Demography* 24:395–406.

Bennett, Noel G., Ann Klimas Blanc, and David E. Bloom. 1988. "Commitment and the Modern Union: Assessing the Link between Premarital Cohabitation and Subsequent Marital Stability." *American Sociological Review* 53:127–38.

Blake, Judith. 1972. "Coercive Pronatalism and American Population Policy." In *Aspects of Population Growth Policy,* Vol. 6, edited by Robert Parke and Charles F. Westoff. Washington, DC: Commission on Population Growth and the American Future.

Blanc, Ann Klimas. 1987. "The Formation and Dissolution of Second Unions: Marriage and Cohabitation in Sweden and Norway." *Journal of Marriage and the Family* 49:391–400.

Booth, Alan and David Johnson. 1988. "Premarital Cohabitation and Marital Success." *Journal of Family Issues* 9:255–72.

Bumpass, Larry. 1990. "What's Happening to the Family? Interactions between Demographic and Institutional Change." Presidential address, annual meeting of the Population Association of America. *Demography* 27:483–98.

Bumpass, Larry L. and James A. Sweet. 1989a. "Children's Experience in Single-Parent Families: Implications of Cohabitation and Marital Transitions." NSFH Working Paper No. 3, Center for Demography and Ecology, University of Wisconsin.

———. 1989b. "National Estimates of Cohabitation: Cohort Levels and Union Stability." *Demography* 25:615–25.

Hoem, Jan M. 1986. "The Impact of Education on Modern Family-Union Formation." *European Journal of Population* 2:113–33.

Sweet, James A., Larry L. Bumpass, and Vaughn R. A. Call. 1988. "The Design and Content of the National Survey of Families and Households." NSFH Working Paper No. 1, Center for Demography and Ecology, University of Wisconsin.

Thornton, Arland and Deborah Freedman. 1982. "Changing Attitudes toward Marriage and Single Life." *Family Planning Perspectives* 14:297–303.

13

IN SEARCH OF THE RIGHT SPOUSE
Interracial Marriage among Chinese and Japanese Americans

COLLEEN FONG • JUDY YUNG

Through in-depth interviews with Chinese and Japanese American women and men who are or have been married to Whites, this study examines factors involved in contemporary Asian-white heterosexual marriages. We chose to focus on Chinese and Japanese because they have a long presence in the United States and were the first Asian Americans to outmarry, usually to Whites, in the largest numbers. Specifically, we wanted to find out what factors were involved in their decision to outmarry—which factors were shared by both the women and the men and which were unique—and why a higher proportion of women than men outmarried.

This research broadens the parameters of existing work on Asian American outmarriage in several ways. First, it is gender-comparative, looking at both Asian American women and men who have outmarried. Much of the recent interest in Asian intermarriage focuses only on the pairing of Asian women and white men. While this can be explained in part because higher proportions of contemporary Asian American women than men have outmarried, the gap is closing.[1] Furthermore, the focus on women has at times been divisive, racist, and sexist, as indicated by the record number of letters sent to the editor following the publication of one such article.[2] Second, our research draws from qualitative interview data and fleshes out the demographic profiles of outmarried Asian Americans provided by most other studies on the topic.[3] Finally, our work goes beyond the assimilationist interpretation of outmarriage, which posits that once the physical and social distance between members of different racial groups is minimized, romantic love and marriage will follow.[4] While our findings support the view that intermarriage is facilitated by the dismantling of racial barriers and the assimilation process, they also indicate other factors are involved, such as aversion to Asian patriarchy; overbearing Asian mothers; cultural and economic compatibility, particularly with Jewish Americans, upward mobility; and media representations of beauty and power. Thus, intermarriage may be tied to racial and gender power relations in our society.

Interracial marriage, as we know it today, is a relatively recent phenomenon. Anti-miscegenation laws, which date back to the 1660s, were an outgrowth of slavery that reinforced a racial/class/gender hierarchy with white,
male property holders at the top.[5] In California, marriage between Chinese
and Whites was deemed illegal in 1880. By 1933 the statute had been amended
to include all other "Mongolians" (namely Japanese, Koreans, and Indians—
predominantly Sikhs) and "Malays" (namely Filipinos). In 1948, California
repealed its anti-miscegenation law, after Congress amended the War Bride's
Act of 1945, which permitted the entry of Japanese brides married to American soldiers. But it was not until 1967, at the height of the civil rights movement, that the U.S. Supreme Court declared all anti-miscegenation laws
unconstitutional.[6] As a result of these legal actions and improved racial relations in this country, marriages between Asian and white Americans first
occurred in noticeable numbers during the post–World War II period and
increased dramatically in the post–civil rights era.[7] In 1980 the majority of
Asian Americans in the state of California were married within their own
ethnic groups; however, 25 percent of married Asian American women and
14.4 percent of married Asian American men were intermarried, compared
to 8.2 percent for other racial/ethnic groups. Of the Asian American wives,
73 percent had white spouses compared to 54 percent of Asian American
husbands.[8] . . .

Methodology

A total of nineteen women and twenty-four men were interviewed for this
study. Most of the interviewees were born in the 1940s or 1950s, representing
the generation most affected by the repeal of anti-miscegenation laws and the
civil rights movement. Most interviewees live in the greater San Francisco
Bay Area, where Chinese Americans and Japanese Americans have consistently resided since the beginning of their immigration in the mid-nineteenth
century. Among the women are thirteen of Chinese descent (six foreign-born)
and six of Japanese descent (all U.S.-born). Among the men are thirteen of
Chinese descent (six foreign-born) and eleven of Japanese descent (three
foreign-born). All except one has attended college and most hold professional
occupations, thus corresponding to the middle-class background of Asian
Americans who have outmarried, according to statistical studies. . . .

The interviews were usually conducted in the homes of the subjects and
averaged two hours in length. Asian American female interviewers were used
to interview the women and Asian American male interviewers for the men.
Interviewees were assured that their confidentiality would be protected, and
all names used here are pseudonyms. Open-ended questions were asked about
family background, childhood, education, and social life prior to marriage,
and most important, interviewees were asked to describe their lives at the
time they met their partners and decided to marry. Finally, interviewees were
asked about their married lives, children (if applicable), in-laws, and so forth.

Proximity: A Precondition for Marrying for Love and Compatibility

Most men and women interviewed met their spouses at school or at work and described their marriages as the outgrowth of compatibility, love, and trust — factors which are based primarily on romantic love.[9] Chinese American Byron Woo and his wife met in college in the 1970s through mutual friends. They started dating and after a year or so moved in together. Upon graduation they purchased a house together. Once co-owners of a house, Byron says, "In essence we were married." A few years after buying the house they decided to get married. The marriage appears to be the culmination of a long-term relationship. They had been a couple for so long the wedding ceremony itself was, in Byron's words, "no big deal." They went to Reno to get married.

Third-generation Japanese American Kevin Osuga met his wife, Susan, at an academic conference while they were both graduate students in the early 1980s. After an intellectually stimulating plenary session, Kevin and Susan went out with a large group of people. The next day they attended a number of sessions together and continued their intellectual conversation. At the end of the conference he headed back to the East Coast and she to the South. Even though they were both involved with other people at the time, they broke off these relationships and Susan arranged to study on the East Coast. Kevin comments on the strength of their relationship, "We're both academics. We're both interested in the same kinds of things — theoretical stuff, political things, involved in the same kind of work. We share those kinds of struggles in terms of understanding the nature of the pressure [of academic work]. We laugh because in the first part of our relationship it was fun to go to a bookstore and browse for hours. That was a cheap date!"

These are examples of interracial marriages that seem to have grown out of mutual attraction and love. As third-generation Chinese American Daniel Chan comments, "I meet who I meet. I get along with who I get along with. The cards fell where they did." Born in 1954 in Hawaii, Daniel's comment reflects his age cohort in that when he began dating in the early 1970s, legalized segregation had been outlawed and anti-miscegenation laws had been repealed. In this sense these interviews can be used as evidence of the assimilationist understanding of outmarriage in that without prior "contact" between members of different races these love relationships could not have developed. While this is a legitimate explanation for the increasing rate of outmarriage among Asian Americans, responses in our interviews indicate that other factors are also involved

Timing and Unavailability of Asian American Partners

Timing is an important factor in the decision to marry. Some interviewees were more cognizant of this than others. Third-generation Chinese American Marcia Ong was in her late thirties when she was interviewed. She said she finally felt ready to commit herself to marriage after "pretty much" accomplishing what she wanted professionally and personally. No doubt she would have married an Asian American in the 1970s because being a part of the Ethnic Studies movement then, that was all she dated. But she had "outgrown" that "anti-white" phase and was now dating a "Jewish, white guy." Women in particular mentioned they were getting older and felt the time was right. Whom they married sometimes seemed less significant than their readiness. These women believed that if they did not marry soon they would "lose" the opportunity. In 1976 Chinese American Diana Prentice was twenty-eight and still living with her immigrant parents close to San Francisco Chinatown when she met Dan at work. She admits she was not attracted to him at all because he had "long hair, a beard, and always wore sandals." But after he showed interest in her and other co-workers told her he was "nice," she accepted a date with him. She says, "I was feeling kind of bad that I was getting so old and I hadn't really dated and been around men much. That [her experience] really bothered me." Dating Dan prompted Diana to move out of her parents' home. They dated for seven years and then married.

Some Asian American men and women married Whites because Asian American partners were not available in the geographic areas in which they grew up or in their places of work or professional fields. Wes Gin, born in 1943, grew up in a small, coastal California town where he had little contact with other Chinese Americans. The pool of women from which he dated were white, and it is no surprise that both his first and present wife are white. Lorelei Fong was born and raised in a large metropolitan area full of other Chinese Americans, but she found herself having less contact with Chinese American men as she became more involved in her field as a performing artist. Although she went to a college with many other Chinese Americans, she says they were not in her field and "I just wasn't interested in dating Chinese engineering students at that time in my life—I was into the arts!" At age twenty-eight when she met her future Jewish American husband, she had not had an Asian American boyfriend for a number of years. "The kinds of things I was doing [professionally] just didn't expose me to Asian American men. . . . You can look at the field today and see how many Asian American men are there and of the ones who are there, they're usually married to white women."

Cultural Affinity: The Jewish Connection; The Hawaiian Propensity

Although Lorelei married a white man she married a white, Jewish man, and it appears that there is a propensity for our interviewees to meet and date Jews in college or in their professional fields and marry them. Eighteen percent of the Chinese and Japanese American women and men we interviewed were married to Jewish partners. Five described how they shared a cultural affinity with their Jewish spouses; most often they mentioned how both cultures valued strong family ties and educational achievement. Interviewees also described their Jewish spouses as having a sense of "ethnic tradition" and an immigrant legacy found lacking in non-Jewish whites they had known or dated. Calvin Jung pointed out that both he and his wife were third generation and how her grandfather, an immigrant from Russia, enjoyed trading stories with Calvin about his Chinese immigrant grandparents. Similarly, Nellie Tsui, born in Boston in 1950, reported she and her Jewish husband often joke about possibly being "related" since his grandfather traded on the Chinese silk road. Marcia Ong says her husband, who is aware of the history of anti-Semitism, understands her sense of racial justice. "I don't have to explain it," she says. In all of these cases, there is also the added factor of economic compatibility in that both spouses shared similar middle-class values and socialized in the same professional circles.

There also seems to be a propensity for individuals who grew up in Hawaii to outmarry. Unlike the mainland, Hawaii has a long history of marital mixing.[10] Japanese American Mary Fujimoto, who lived in Hawaii from age fifteen to twenty-five, said she was used to being around people of all different backgrounds and in fact always considered "hapa [racially mixed] children cuter." She dated Asians and Whites before marrying her white, college sweetheart. Third-generation Chinese American Timothy Tom grew up in a multiracial Hawaiian neighborhood of Japanese, Portuguese, Hawaiian, Puerto Rican and other Chinese. He believes it was this environment that provided him with an openness to other groups and most importantly an openness to Whites who do not occupy the same dominant position as they do on the mainland. He later chose to marry a white classmate he met and dated while attending college on the mainland.

Aversion to Marrying within the Same Race

Even when potential Asian American spouses were available, many of the Asian American men and women we interviewed found them "less attractive" than the white partners they eventually chose. Analysis of these interviews reveals both men and women had formed negative opinions and feelings about Asian Americans of the opposite sex. On the one hand, cultural attributes such as a patriarchal family structure, an overbearing mother, or growing up in an ethnically insulated neighborhood turned them away from seeking Asian American partners. On the other hand, the media promotion of white beauty and power encouraged them to date and marry white Americans.

A number of our interviewees grew up in repressive family situations where one or both parents were unbearably domineering and manipulative and where negative reinforcement and strict discipline were practiced. They said this resulted in views of their parents as anti-role models and an aversion to marrying within the same race. "I knew I didn't want to marry someone like my father [or mother]," was one of the more common responses from women who described their fathers as too patriarchal, insensitive, and nonexpressive and from men who characterized their mothers as manipulative and complaining. Hoping to escape what they perceived to be unhappy marriages of their parents', interviewees placed great emphasis on marriages based on romantic love and grounded in mutual respect and equality.

The Women's Perspective

Mimi Kato, a third-generation Japanese American woman born in the early 1940s, was very aware of both the patriarchal oppression in her mother's two in-marriages and the status mobility to be gained by marrying someone white. Mimi's father walked out on the family when she was five, and her stepfather was physically abusive to both her and her mother. She knew at an early age that she did not want to end up victimized like her mother and powerless to resist the abuse. Mimi dated Japanese American men but found them too protective and the relationships "suffocating." While most of the interviewees' parents had strong objections to interracial dating and marriage, Mimi's mother encouraged her in that direction for reasons of class mobility. Media messages that "white is right, beautiful, and acceptable" also encouraged Mimi to date white men who shared her interest in art and literature. In searching for her "white knight," someone who would be the kind father she never had, she settled upon Dave, her teaching assistant in a literature class. As she admitted some twenty years after their divorce:

> He was very sensitive, very bright, very very good as a writer, and he was really kind and very tolerant. He was the kind of person that I would really want to be the father of my child. I think I had decided at that time that I wanted a child that was half-white [because] . . . I was raised with all the values that white was infinitely more attractive, infinitely more acceptable, infinitely more powerful. And I wanted my child to have half the power, to have all that that dream represented, all that that program represented.

However, as with a number of other interviewees, when Mimi became politicized by the Third World strike at San Francisco State University,[11] she reassessed her motivations for marriage and the marriage ended in divorce.

The women interviewed reported that Asian American men tended not to treat them as equals. This they learned from either observing real situations in their own families or through firsthand dating experiences. Born in Hong Kong in 1950, Nellie Tsui came from a well-to-do family. She remembers that while her brother was groomed to follow in the footsteps of their father, a successful businessman with a Harvard degree, she was expected to marry and become a housewife like her mother. When she immigrated to the United States after high school, Nellie's parents expected her to date and marry Chinese. She consciously dated Chinese American men in college with that in mind, but found them unattractive or thought they found her unattractive because she was tall, dark, and had a tendency to be outspoken. In the end, she married a white, Jewish colleague who offered her what she found lacking in Chinese men like her own father. "Bill was very feminine, very caring, and very verbal," she says. "He's a great cook, and he's always done the dishes no matter who cooks." As she told her mother right after she met Bill, "I said I think I met the man I'm going to marry, and I said jokingly, 'He has my martini ready for me when I come home from work.' And that was the kind of person he was. There's no way my father would do that. You know, it's too demeaning." Upon further analysis, Nellie realized that her father's cultural upbringing and insecurities — which stemmed from his awareness of his racial minority status — prevented him from being more giving and encouraging. Whereas her father had devalued her, Bill always made her feel good about being an Asian woman.

We found that Asian American interviewees who identified as feminists had the hardest time accepting sexist attitudes and behavior. Their coming to a new sense of consciousness as a result of the growing women's liberation movement of the 1970s no doubt contributed to the increased rate of intermarriage among these women. As feminists, they were much more aware of patriarchy and less willing to tolerate it. Alice Stein, who grew up in China after the 1949 Revolution, had feminist beliefs even before she came to the United States. Upon arrival as a foreign student in 1980, she was immediately struck by the sexism that pervaded American culture and the attitudes of the Chinese American men she met:

> *I guess growing up in a Communist society, at least the Communist Party advocates equality a lot between men and women. That's one thing that I was hit [with] the minute I got here. Everything is so sexually oriented, putting women on such a degrading [level]. All the selling of cars and everything has a woman perched on it. I felt it very strong among Chinese American men, not only among the two that I met but even with other Chinese American men that I talked to. So I sort of got turned off real fast.*

Having experienced an unhappy marriage in China, Alice was determined not to marry until the right person came along however badly she needed a green card to stay in the United States. What drew her to marry Joseph — a white, Jewish man — was his non-sexist attitude. He had an appreciation for Chinese culture and for her as a person. "He was very open, very equal, and communication with him was very easy," she says.

While the women recognized certain positive characteristics in Asian American men — well-educated, stable, reliable — these qualities were evidently not enough for them. As Marcia Ong says of Terrence, her Asian American boyfriend of many years, "He was the kind an Asian woman would really like. He's educated, polite, generous, kind, and tall. My mother really loved him." But like her father, he was not expressive or nurturing enough. According to Marcia:

> *I would say, "I need to hear from you. I know you care, but you're just like my Dad." He would show me by being reliable and doing things for me, but I would say, "You have to TELL me. I need to hear it. I need more. Do you care about me? How do you feel about me?" It was not okay because I had to ask. I wanted him to volunteer to talk about it. It was difficult. As I have*

become better at expressing myself, I've expected my partners to be good at expressing themselves.

What Marcia found lacking in Terrence she found in Clarence and John, her African American and white, Jewish boyfriends respectively. Both were good about expressing their appreciation of her, their feelings about what they liked or disliked, and unlike Terrence, they had a sense of humor. Also unlike most Asian American men she had known, neither Clarence nor John were threatened by her tough personality and her outspokenness. Both men saw and appreciated what she called her "compliant" self underneath her "tough" exterior. "With Asian guys, I would have to pursue them," says Marcia. "Black and white men take the chance. They are persistent. John said if we hadn't been introduced he would have found a way to meet me." This difference in courtship patterns can be deemed an indication of where the racial power lies in our society because like their male counterparts, white women were reportedly more aggressive than Asian American women in pursuing men—four of the male interviewees admitted to being pursued or "pushed into marriage" by their white girlfriends.

The Men's Perspective

The male interviewees talked in similar ways about Asian cultural attributes in women they wanted to avoid in a marital relationship. Although they may have been favored as sons, they too found their family environments oppressive, with one or both parents too domineering and manipulative. While the Asian patriarchy no doubt benefited them in some ways, they wanted no part in it. At all costs, they did not want their marriages to end up like their parents', and so they consciously looked for partners whom they felt were kind, sensitive, and egalitarian. These spouses turned out to be white women.

Third-generation Japanese American Vincent Kaneko describes his father as "abusive, domineering, and cheap," and his mother as "very shy, giving, loving, and tolerant." It was an unhappy marriage that lasted fifty-two years "only because my mother was the most tolerant person in the world." He admired and loved his mother as much as he despised his father. Knowing that his mother did not approve of interracial dating or marriage, he chose to date and marry a Japanese American woman whom he thought would be like his mother. Vincent was eighteen years old at the time; the year was 1963. But his wife turned out to be more like his father, "the grouchiest Japanese woman I've ever known in my whole life." They divorced eleven years later, and he swore he would never date another Japanese American woman as long as he lived. To get himself out of what he called "the syndrome of marrying [his] father," Vincent turned to dating white women. As he admits, he had been conditioned by television and magazines to regard "the white female body as the best overall." What surprised and pleased him, because he had been teased as a youngster about being short and nerdy, was that white women found him sexually attractive. This boosted his self-esteem and male confidence. After a number of relationships, Vincent married again. His second wife was a white, Jewish woman who proved to be very unlike the mother figure he was searching for. Not only was she aggressive and outspoken, but she was in his words a "confirmed lesbian." At the time of the interview, they had just divorced after a stormy marriage and he was engaged to a Chicana he had met at work.

Born in 1960, fifth-generation Chinese American Winston Fong cites his troubled family background as a factor contributing to his outmarriage. In his words, his father was a "spoiled, rotten brat" who was used to having his way. He controlled his wife and children "out of fear, not out of respect or love or anything like that." He had violent fits and would not think twice about hitting his children at the dinner table if he felt like it. His mother "was pretty screwed up" too, often lying to the children in order to manipulate them. Pressured to date and marry Chinese, Winston's first serious relationship was with Pearl, a Chinese American classmate from high school. But she was too much like his father. "I was not about to go through life with someone who throws tantrums and calls everyone stupid," says Winston. "She was a pretty spoiled kid, fairly well taken care of throughout life." Although he dated other Chinese American women and had every intention of finding one who was soft, outgoing, energetic, and family oriented, he ended up marrying his colleague Betty, who was white. They lived together for five years before the wedding. He reported that unlike his parents, they had an equal relationship and hardly fought despite their differences; they could communicate well and had common interests and goals.

In at least two cases, Chinese American men reported they could not consider dating or marrying a Chinese American woman because it would be like marrying their own sister—incestuous. Wes Gin, born in 1943, grew up in a tight-knit Chinese American family in a predominantly white community. In high school Wes dated Japanese American women. After college, as soon as anti-miscegenation attitudes began to change in the mid-1960s, he dated white women. Wes married twice, both times to white women. He said his first wife, Grace, resembled the media stereotype of feminine beauty. After nine years of marriage they divorced. His second wife, Leah, was "calm, intelligent, dependable," and Jewish—someone who shared his values and goals in life. "It seems like I'm enough different from Leah where it doesn't feel like it's hugging my sister or myself," he replied when asked why he married her.

Although Calvin Jung spent his childhood years in San Francisco Chinatown, he shared Wes Gin's sentiments about not wanting to marry someone who was Chinese American like him:

> The Chinese [American] women that I knew growing up I knew all my life, sort of like your sisters—[beginning in] first grade. And I keep running into these people now, you don't really think of them as marriage partners. They're too close. They remind you of your mother—voice, intonation, and the ease in which they operate in Chinatown. All the things I was running from. They were just what I was trying to escape. Also, you were so familiar with them, it was almost like incest.

His family was the first Chinese American family to move into a white sub-urb outside of San Francisco. It was 1950 and his parents wanted their children to assimilate and lose their Chinatown accents, but not to go so far as to risk eliciting white racism by dating or marrying a white woman. So Calvin went steady with a Japanese American classmate throughout high school:

> *Anyway, we looked right. We were the cute couple and all that. She was bright and we were all headed for [the University of California at] Berkeley. She was going to be an English teacher and I was going to be the dentist. And every-thing was going to work out just fine.*

By the time Calvin attended college in the early 1960s, he discovered that white attitudes had changed and he began to date white women. Also, living in Europe for a year opened up doors to him in terms of interracial romance. "Gee, you got to know [white] girls and go out and be civilized and all that," said Calvin. "So by the time I got back to school again, I had finally outgrown my insularity." Calvin was also aware of the empowerment resulting from re-lationships with white women. As he says,

> *You have more access in the society if you're connected with the majority. I realized that very early on. I don't think it was any conscious thing that I was only going to date white in order to get into these places, but in fact, you operate in a fashion where you take chances you wouldn't take. I don't have to protect, be in a position of being responsible for my Chinese [Ameri-can] wife if someone calls her a Chink or [threatens] to beat her up. You're connected to the majority. That dynamic is very real.*

As it turned out, Calvin married Jean—a white, Jewish woman who shared his interest in the fine arts. Although Calvin's sense of ethnic pride and soli-darity was awakened by the Third World strikes at San Francisco State and the University of California at Berkeley in 1968–69, he did not abandon his marriage as a result. His wife, Jean, was supportive and encouraged his po-litical activism while she went off to pursue her own interests in theater. . . .

Conclusions

Our data indicate that Asian American outmarriage is not simply the "nat-ural" outcome of more contact with white Americans, as assimilationists would have us believe, but also the result of a number of complex factors, some of which have been raised by Spickard, Shinagawa and Pang, and Sung. While proximity is a necessary precondition to interracial marriage, other factors intimately tied to issues of race and gender power relations are also involved. Interviewees who grew up in Hawaii, where interracial mar-riage was not as negatively sanctioned as on the mainland, seemed to be more open to outmarriage in general. Other interviewees were attracted to Jewish Americans because they shared certain middle-class values and traditions. A few admitted they married Whites for some measure of upward mobility—clear cases of hypergamy. Both male and female interviewees stated outright that they had an aversion to marrying a member of their own group because they wanted to avoid replicating their parents' marriages. Finally, both men and women complained that their Asian American dates were too out of touch with the popular youth culture of the time—music, literature, fashion—and overburdened with the protocol dictated by traditional Chinese or Japanese culture. Aware of the race/class/gender hierarchy in American society, they opted to marry white Americans over Asian Americans who were equally acculturated into the dominant lifestyle. Likewise, they chose Whites over other groups such as Hispanic or African Americans because of the racial hierarchy of preference ingrained in them through their parents and popular media.[12]

Despite the overwhelming overlap in motivation shared by the women and men, some differences do stand out. Asian American women, in particular, seemed to have outmarried in part to escape from what they perceived as Asian patriarchy. These women reported that Asian American men treated them in less egalitarian ways than men of other races and they wanted equal partners in a marriage. This combined, with the fact that Asian American women have been "positively" depicted in the mass media while Asian American men have been "negatively" depicted, provides some insight into why Asian American women outmarry at higher proportions than men. Timing also played a more crucial role for women who outmarried than men. Women more often felt they were running out of time or getting too old to be considered marriageable. Asian American men reported that white women appreciated their economic stability and emotional support. They also said that dating and marrying white women, upon which standards of beauty are based, boosted their self-esteem. Some who grew up in predominantly white areas discussed their aversion to marrying Asian American women as rooted in the incest taboo. Dating other Asian American members of the community—families that had considered themselves like fictive kin for decades—seemed incestuous.

Clearly the complexity of the factors involved in outmarriage uncovered by this study indicates that beyond simple proximity lies a whole host of factors. Future research in this area might explore some of the more interesting findings of this project such as the cultural affinity and economic compatibility between Asian and Jewish Americans; Asian American aversion to Asian patriarchy and matriarchy; the perception of in-marriage as a violation of the incest taboo; and the impact of political activism and ethnic consciousness on marital choice in the 1960s, particularly between the various Asian groups and between Asians and other groups of color. Other topics we hope to explore in future studies include war brides and military wives; foreign students; mail-order brides; those who married during the anti-miscegenation era; views of white partners married to Asian Americans; the current generation of marriage-age Asian Americans; gay/lesbian couples; and racially mixed Asian Americans.

ENDNOTES

Author's note: Both authors contributed equally to this work; the order of the authors is alphabetical. We wish to acknowledge Elaine Kim for initiating this research project, the CSUH Affirmative Action Faculty Development Program for partial funding, and Pat Guthrie, Rivka Polatnick, Ann Lane, Warren Lane, Deborah Woo, Rudy Busto, and Peggy Pascoe for their helpful comments. We are also grateful to the interviewees who took part in this study.

1. See Larry Shinagawa and Gin Yong Pang, "Intraethnic, Interethnic, and Interracial Marriages among Asian Americans in California, 1980," *Berkeley Journal of Sociology* 33 (1986): 95–114; and Betty Lee Sung, *Chinese American Intermarriage* (Staten Island, NY: Center for Migration Studies, 1990).
2. See reaction to Joan Walsh, "Asian Women, Caucasian Men: The New Demographics of Love," *Image, San Francisco Examiner/Chronicle,* December 2, 1990, in the January 6 and 13, 1991 issues.
3. See Sharon M. Lee and Keiko Yamanaka, "Patterns of Asian American Intermarriage and Marital Assimilation," *Journal of Comparative Family Studies* 21(2) (1990): 287–305; Shinagawa and Pang, "Intraethnic, Interethnic, and Interracial Marriages"; Akemi Kikumura and Harry H. L. Kitano, "Interracial Marriage: A Picture of the Japanese Americans," *Journal of Social Issues* 29(2) (1973): 67–81; Harry H. L. Kitano and Lynn Chai, "Korean Interracial Marriage," *Marriage and Family Review* 5 (1982): 75–89; Harry H. L. Kitano and Wai-tsang Yeung, "Chinese Interracial Marriage," *Marriage and Family Review* 5 (1982): 35–48; and Harry H. L. Kitano, Wai-tsang Yeung, Lynn Chai, and Herbert Hatanaka, "Asian-American Interracial Marriage," *Journal of Marriage and the Family* 46 (1984): 179–90.
4. See D. Yuan, "Significant Demographic Characteristics of Chinese Who Intermarry in the United States," *California Sociologist* 3 (Summer, 1980): 184–96; John N. Tinker, "Intermarriage and Ethnic Boundaries: The Japanese American Case," *Journal of Social Issues* 29 (1973): 49–66; Donna Lockwood Leonetti and Laura Newell-Morris, "Exogamy and Change in the Biosocial Structure of a Modern Urban Population," *American Anthropologist* 84 (1982): 19–36; C. K. Cheng and Douglas S. Yamamura, "Interracial Marriage and Divorce in Hawaii," *Social Forces* 36(1) (1957): 77–84. . . .
5. The first anti-miscegenation law was passed in the colony of Maryland in 1664. Some forty states and colonies did likewise; sixteen of which still had anti-miscegenation laws in force when the U.S. Supreme Court ruled them unconstitutional in 1967. See David Fowler, *Northern Attitudes toward Interracial Marriage* (Garland, 1987), xi. For a discussion of interracial marriage as an issue of both race and gender relations, see Peggy Pascoe, "Race, Gender, and Intercultural Relations: The Case of Interracial Marriage," *Frontiers: A Journal of Women Studies* 12(1) (1991): 5–18.
6. See *Loving v. Virginia* 388 U.S. 1 (1967); Megumi Dick Osumi, "Asians and California's Anti-Miscegenation Laws," in *Asian and Pacific American Experiences: Women's Perspectives,* edited by Nobuya Tsuchida (Minneapolis: Asian/Pacific American Learning Resource Center and General College, University of Minnesota, 1982), 1–37; and Anselm Strauss, "Strain and Harmony in American-Japanese War-Marriages," *Marriage and Family Living* 16 (1954): 99–106. Strauss estimates that between 1947 and 1952, 10,517 U.S. citizens, mostly white military personnel, married Japanese women.
7. For studies of increased outmarriages among Chinese Americans and Japanese Americans during the 1960s and 1970s, see D. Yuan, "Significant Demographic Characteristics of Chinese Who Intermarry in the United States"; Tinker, "Intermarriage and Ethnic Boundaries: The Japanese American Case"; Russell Endo and

Dale Hirokawa, "Japanese American Intermarriage," *Free Inquiry in Creative Sociology* 11(2) (1983): 159–62, 66; and Leonetti and Newell-Morris, "Exogamy and Change in the Biosocial Structure of a Modern Urban Population."

8. Shinagawa and Pang, "Intraethnic, Interethnic, and Interracial Marriages," 103. National statistics drawn from the 1980 U.S. Census, as presented in Lee and Yamanaka, "Patterns of Asian American Intermarriage and Marital Assimilation," gave a comparable picture: 25.4 percent of Asian Americans were intermarried (31.5 percent among Asian American women and 16.6 percent among Asian American men), 76 percent of them to white spouses (pp. 290, 294).

9. A few interviewees mentioned other factors in the decision to marry: pregnancy, leaving for the armed services, and a strong taboo against "living together" among both sets of parents.

10. But, as Spickard points out in *Mixed Blood,* the intermarriage rate among Japanese Americans in Hawaii is lower than that of the mainland because the large Japanese community in Hawaii works to discourage outmarriage (pp. 73–84). For a discussion of intermarriage patterns in Hawaii, see also Labov and Jacobs, "Intermarriage in Hawaii, 1950–1983."

11. In November 1968, students of color at San Francisco State University, inspired by the civil rights movement, went on strike to demand the establishment of an autonomous Ethnic Studies program. See Karen Umemoto, "'On Strike!' San Francisco State College Strike, 1968–69: The Role of Asian American Students," *Amerasia Journal* 15(1) (1989): 3–41; and William Wei, *The Asian American Movement* (Philadelphia: Temple University Press, 1993), 15–24.

12. . . . Responses from our interviewees about their racial preferences in spouses prior to their marriages concur with the aggregate findings in Shinagawa and Pang that was based on a cross-tabulation of actual and expected frequencies of marriages between certain racial/ethnic groups ("Intraethnic, Interethnic, and Interracial Marriages among Asian Americans in California, 1980," pp. 101–103). Asian Americans' first choice of spouse was a member of their own ethnic group; second choice, other Asian/Pacific Islanders; third choice, Whites; and fourth choice, Hispanic and African Americans. In anticipation as well as in actuality, there appears to be a low incidence of intermarriage between Asian Americans and other groups of color. We attribute this to proximity and assimilation, but more important, the low socioeconomic status of a high proportion of Hispanic, African, and Native Americans.

14

PEER MARRIAGE

PEPPER SCHWARTZ

When I told people that I was beginning a research study of couples who evenly divided parenting and housework responsibilities, the usual reaction was mock curiosity—how was I going to find the three existing egalitarian couples in the universe? Despite several decades of dissecting the sexism and inequities inherent in traditional marriage, as a society, we have yet to develop a clear picture of how more balanced marital partnerships actually work. Some critics even argue that the practice of true equality in marriage is not much more common today than it was 30 years ago. In fact, authors like Arlie Hochschild have suggested that women's liberation has made prospects for equity worse. The basic theme of her provocative book, *The Second Shift*, is that women now have two jobs—their old, traditional marital roles and their new responsibilities in the work force. A look at the spectacular divorce rates and lower marriage rate for successful women provides further fuel for the argument that equality has just brought wives more, not less, burdens.

All of this figured heavily in my own commitment to exploring the alternative possibilities for marital partnership. Ten years ago this began with *American Couples: Money, Work and Sex*, a study I did with Philip Blumstein that compared more than 6,000 couples—married, cohabiting, gay males and lesbians—looking for, among other things, what aspects of gendered behavior contributed to relationship satisfaction and durability. This study contained within it a small number of egalitarian couples, who fascinated and inspired me. We discussed them rather briefly in the book, but our editor encouraged us to make them the subject of a second study that would examine how couples manage to sustain an egalitarian partnership over time. Unfortunately, my co-author was not able to continue the project and it was not until three years ago that I began the research on what I came to call Peer Marriage. I began looking for couples who had worked out no worse than a 60-40 split on childrearing, housework and control of discretionary funds and who considered themselves to have "equal status or standing in the relationship."

I started out interviewing some of the couples originally studied for *American Couples* and then, using what sociologists call a "snowball sample," I

---

asked those couples if they knew anyone else like themselves that I could interview. After talking to a few couples in a given network, I then would look
for a different kind of couple (different class, race, educational background,
etc.) in order to extend the range of my sample. I interviewed 57 egalitarian
couples, but even after the formal study was over, I kept running into couples
that fit my specifications and did 10 more partial interviews.

While initially my design included only Peer Marriages, I also began to
interview a lot of couples who others thought to be egalitarian, but who
did not meet my criteria. Instead of throwing them out of the sample, I used
them as a base of comparison, dividing them into two additional categories:
"Traditionals" and "Near Peers." Traditionals were couples in which the man
usually had veto power over decision-making (except with the children) and
in which the wife felt that she did not have—nor did she want—equal status. The Near Peers were couples who, while they believed in equality, felt
derailed from their initial goal of an egalitarian marriage because of the realities of raising children and/or the need or desire to maximize male income.
As a result, the husband could not be anywhere near as participatory a father
as the couple had initially envisioned. These two groups proved to be a for-
tuitous addition to the design. It is sometimes hard to understand what peer
couples are doing that allows them to fulfill an egalitarian agenda without
understanding what keeps other couples from doing the same.

Even though I consider myself to be in a Peer Marriage, I found many
surprises among the Peer Couples I studied. Of course, as a researcher, one is
never supposed to extrapolate from one's own experience, but it is almost impossible not to unconsciously put one's presuppositions into the hypothesis
phase of the research. Clearly, people make their marital bargains for many
different reasons, and face different challenges in sustaining them. Here are
some of the discoveries I made that I thought might be of use to therapists
[and to other family scholars].

I assumed most couples would, like myself, come to egalitarianism out
of the women's movement or feminist ideology. Nevertheless, while approximately 40 percent of the women and about 20 percent of the men cited
feminism and a desire to be in a nonhierarchical relationship, the majority of
couples mentioned other reasons. These included a desire to avoid parental
models that they found oppressive in their own upbringing, the *other* partner's strong preference for an egalitarian marriage, some emotional turmoil
that had led to their rethinking their relationship, or an intense desire for co-
parenting. Women in particular often mentioned their own parents as a negative model. One woman said, "*I want a husband who knows how to pack his
own suitcase, who puts away his own clothes, who can't tell me to shut up at will.
. . . My mother may have been happy with this kind of marriage, but I'm still angry
at my father for treating my mother like that—and angry at her for letting him.*"
A 25-year-old husband told me, on a different theme, "*My main objective in
having an equal relationship was not to be the kind of father I had. I want my kids*

to know me before they are adults. I want them to be able to talk to me. I want them to run to me if they hurt themselves. I want our conversations to be more than me telling them they could do better on a test or that I was disappointed they didn't make the team. I want to be all the things to my kids that my dad was not. I want us to have hugged many, many times and not just on birthdays or their wedding day."

Quite a few men in Peer Marriages said they really had no strong feelings about being in either traditional or egalitarian marriages, but had merely followed their wives' lead. Typical of this group was a high school basketball coach who said he had had a very traditional first marriage because that was the only arrangement that he and his wife could envision even when it wasn't working. But when he met his current wife, a policewoman who had been single quite a while, her demands for equality seemed perfectly reasonable to him. He just, more or less, fell into line with his future wife's ideas about the relationship. Many of these men told me they had always expected a woman to be the emotional architect of a relationship and were predisposed to let her set the rules.

Most of the couples, however, did have strong ideas about marriage and placed particular emphasis on equity and equality. Even if they didn't start out with a common agenda, most ended up sharing a high degree of conscious purpose. People's particular personal philosophies about marriage mattered less than the fact that their philosophies differentiated their family from a culture that reinforced the general belief that equality is neither possible nor even in the long-term interests of couples. Many people talked about how easy it is to slide into old and familiar roles or follow economic opportunities that started to whittle away at male participation in childrearing. It takes an intense desire to keep a couple on the nontraditional track and a clear sense of purpose to justify the economic sacrifices and daily complications it takes to co-parent. As one wife of 10 years said, *"We always try to make sure that we don't start getting traditional. It's so easy to do. But we really want this extraordinary empathy and respect we have. I just know it wouldn't be there if we did this marriage any other way."*

Important as relationship ideology is, Peer Marriages depend at least as much on coordinating work with home and childraising responsibilities and not letting a high earner be exempt from daily participation. Previous research had shown me the connection between a husband's and wife's relative income and their likelihood of being egalitarian. So I assumed that most of the couples I interviewed would be working couples and have relatively similar incomes. This was mostly true, although I was struck by the couples who were exceptions. Four husbands in the study had non-working wives. The men didn't want to dominate those relationships because they felt very strongly that money did not legitimately confer power. For example, one husband had inherited a great deal of money but didn't feel it was any more his than his wife's. She stayed at home with the children, but he took over in the late afternoon and on weekends. He also was the primary cook and cleaner. In another case, a husband who earned a good deal more than his wife put all the money in a joint account and put investments in her name as well as his. Over time, she had assets equal to his. While these triumphs over income differentials were exceptions, it did make me respect the fact that truly determined couples could overcome being seduced by the power of economic advantage.

However, many Peer Marriages had a significant income differential and husbands and wives had to negotiate a lot just to make sure they didn't fall into the trap of letting the higher earner be the senior decision-maker. Even more tricky, according to many, was not letting work set the emotional and task agenda of the household. The couples needed to keep their eyes on what was the tail and what was the dog so that their relationship was not side-tracked by career opportunities or job pressures. Many Peer Couples had gone through periods in which they realized that they were beginning to have no time for each other, or that one of them was more consistently taking care of the children while the other was consumed with job demands. But what distinguished those couples from more traditional marriages was that they had a competing ideology of economic or career success that guided them when their egalitarianism began to get out of kilter.

One husband, who had an architectural practice designing and building airports, had begun to travel for longer and longer periods of time until it was clear that he was no longer a true co-parent or a full partner in the marriage. After long and painful discussions, he quit his job and opened up a home office so he could spend more time with his wife and children. Both partners realized this would cause some economic privations and, in fact, it took the husband five years to get a modestly successful practice going while the wife struggled to support the family. Without minimizing how tough this period had been, the couple felt they had done the right thing. "After all," the husband said, "we saved our marriage."

This attitude helped explain another surprise in this study. I had presumed that most of the Peer Marriages I would find would be yuppie or post-yuppie couples, mostly young or baby boom professionals who were "having it all." In fact, most of them were solidly middle class: small-business owners, social workers, schoolteachers, health professionals (but not doctors). Apparently, people on career fast tracks were less willing to endanger their potential income and opportunities for promotion. There may be childrearing Peer Marriages out there comprised of litigators, investment bankers and brain surgeons—but I didn't find them. The closest I came to finding fast trackers in a Peer Marriage and family were high-earning women who had husbands who were extremely pleased with their partner's success and were willing to be the more primary parent in order to support her career.

When these women negotiated issues with their husbands in front of me, they seemed more sensitive about their husbands' feelings than men of comparable accomplishment with lower earning wives. For example, they did not interrupt as much as high-earning men in traditional marriages, and they seemed to quite consciously not pull rank when I asked them jointly to solve a financial problem. They told me, however, that they consciously had to work at being less controlling than they sometimes thought they deserved to be. A very successful woman attorney, married to another, significantly-less-prominent attorney, told me that they had some problems because he wasn't used to picking up the slack when she was called away suddenly to represent a Fortune 500 company. She found herself battling her own ambitions in order to be sensitive to his desire for her to let up a bit. As she noted, *"We [women] are not prepared to be the major providers and it's easy to want all the privileges and leeway that men have always gotten for the role. But our bargain to raise the kids together and be respectful of one another holds me back from being like every other lawyer who would have this powerful a job. Still, it's hard."*

The other fast-track exception was very successful men in their second marriages who had sacrificed their first in their climb to the top. Mostly these were men who talked about dependent ex-wives, their unhappiness at paying substantial support and their determination not to repeat the mistakes of their first marriages. One 50-year-old man, who had traveled constantly in his first marriage raising money for pension funds, told me he was through being the high earner for the company and wanted more family time in the second part of his life. As he put it, *"I consciously went looking for someone who I could spend time with, who I had a lot in common with, who would want me to stop having to be the big earner all the time. I don't want to die before I've been a real partner to somebody who can stand on her own two feet . . . and I've been a real father."*

When I first realized how often the desire to co-parent led couples into an egalitarian ideology, I thought this might also lead couples to prioritize their parenting responsibilities over their husband-and-wife relationship. But these were not marriages in which husbands and wives called each other "Mom" and "Dad." For the most part, these couples avoided the rigidly territorial approach I saw in Traditional and Near Peer marriages. In both of these types of couples, I observed mothers who were much more absorbed in their children, which both partners regarded as a primarily female responsibility. As a result, women had sole control over decisions about their children's daily life and used the children as a main source of intimacy, affection and unshared secrets. They related stories about things the children told them that "they would never dare tell their father." While quite a few of the mothers talked about how "close" their husbands were with their children, they would also, usually in the same story, tell me how much closer their children were with them. What surprised me was that while these traditional moms complained about father absence, very few really wanted to change the situation. Most often, it was explained that, while it would be great to have their husband home, they "couldn't afford it." But of course "afford" is a relative term and I sensed that the women really did not want the men interfering with their control over parenting. Or they would have liked more fatherly engagement but definitely not at the cost of loss of income. One young, working Near Peer Couple with four kids was discussing the husband's lesser parenting responsibilities with me when he said, "*You know, I could come home early and get the kids by 3:30. I'd like to do that.*" The wife's response was to straightforwardly insist that with four kids going to private school, his energies were best used paying for their tuitions. She preferred a double shift to a shared one because her financial priorities and her vision of what most profited her children were clear.

But there was an unexpected downside for the couples who did manage to co-parent. I was unprepared for how often Peer Couples mentioned serious conflict over childrearing. Because each partner felt very strongly about the children's upbringing, differences of opinion were not easily resolved. As one peer wife said, "*We are both capable of stepping up to the line and staying there screaming at each other.*" Another husband said, "*If you only talked to us about how we deal with disagreements about the kids, you might think we were a deeply conflicted marriage. We're not. But unfortunately, we have very different ideas about discipline and we can get pretty intense with one another and it might look bad. We went to counseling about the kids and this therapist wanted to look at our whole relationship and we had to say, 'You don't get it. This really is the only thing we argue about like this.'*"

Peers may, in fact, have more conflict about children than more Traditional partners because unlike Traditional Marriage, there is no territory that is automatically ceded to the other person and conflict cannot be resolved by one person claiming the greater right to have the final word. Still, while a majority of Peer Couples mentioned fights over child-related decisions, there were only a few Peer Marriages where I wondered if these arguments threatened the relationship. In the majority of them, the couples talked about how they ultimately, if not in the heat of battle, followed their usual pattern of talking until agreement was reached. What usually forced them to continue to communicate and reach a joint answer was their pledge to give the other partner equal standing in the relationship. Occasionally, a few people told me, they just couldn't reach a mutually satisfying answer and let their partner "win one" out of trust in his or her good judgment, not because they agreed on a given issue.

The couples that I felt might be in more trouble had recurring disagreements that they were never able to resolve over punishments, educational or religious choices or how much freedom to give kids. Furthermore, in each instance at least one partner said that the other partner's approach was beginning to erode the respect that made their relationship possible. Moreover, this particular kind of conflict was deeply troubling since many of them had organized their marriage around the expectation of being great co-parents. It may be that co-parenting requires that parenting philosophies be similar or grow together. Co-parents may have a particular need for good negotiating and communication skills so that they can resolve their differences without threatening the basis of their relationship.

In contrast with traditional or Near Peer Couples, the partners in Peer Marriages never complained about lack of affection or intimacy in their relationships. What they did mention, that other couples did not, was the problem of becoming so familiar with each other that they felt more like siblings than lovers. Some researchers have theorized that sexual arousal is often caused or intensified by anxiety, fear and tension. Many others have written about how sexual desire depends on "Yin" and "Yang" — mystery and difference. And quite a few women and men I talked to rather guiltily confessed that while they wanted equal partners, all their sexual socialization had been to having sex in a hierarchical relationship: Women had fantasies of being "taken" or mildly dominated; men had learned very early on that they were expected to be the orchestrators of any given sexual encounter and that masculinity required sexual directiveness. For men, sexual arousal was often connected with a strong desire to protect or control.

Peer couples complained that they often forgot to include sex in their daily lives. Unlike Traditional or Near Peers, their sexual frequency did not slow down because of unresolved issues or continuing anger, at least not in any systematic ways. These couples may start to lose interest in sex even more than the other kinds of marriages because sex is not their main way of getting close. Many Traditional and some Near Peer Couples mentioned that the only time they felt that they got through to each other was in bed. Perhaps the more emotional distance couples feel with one another, the larger the role sexuality plays in helping them feel they still have the capacity for intimacy. Being less dependent on this pathway to intimacy, partners in Peer Marriage may be more willing to tolerate a less satisfactory sexual relationship.

One husband, who worked with his wife in their own advertising firm, even talked about having developed "an incest taboo," which had led to the couple entering therapy. They were such buddies during the daytime, he had trouble treating her as anything else in the evening. The therapist this couple consulted encouraged them to assume new personas in the bedroom. For example, he told them to take turns being the dominant partner, to create scenarios where they created new characters and then behaved as they thought the person they were impersonating would behave. He gave them "homework," such as putting themselves in romantic or sexy environments and allowing themselves to imagine meeting there the first time. The wife was encouraged to dress outrageously for bed every now and then; the husband occasionally to be stereotypically directive. The therapist reminded both partners that their emotional bargain was safe: they loved and respected each other. That meant they could use sex as recreation, release and exploration. They were good pupils and felt they had really learned something for a lifetime.

In another couple, it was the wife who mentioned the problem. Her husband had been the dominant partner in his previous marriage and had enjoyed that role in bed. However, she liked more reciprocity and role-sharing in sex, so he tried to be accommodating. However, early on in the relationship he began treating her, as she put it, *"too darn respectfully . . . it was almost as if we were having politically correct sex. . . . I had to remember that he wasn't my brother and it was okay to be sexually far out with him."*

On the other hand, Peer Couples with satisfying sexual relationships often mentioned their equality as a source of sexual strength. These couples felt their emotional security with one another allowed them to be more uninhibited and made sex more likely since both people were responsible for making it happen. Women with unhappy sexual experiences with sexist men mentioned that for the first time in their lives they could use any sexual position without worrying about any larger meaning in the act. Being on the bottom just meant being on the bottom; it was not about surrendering in more cosmic ways. Being a sex kitten was a role for the evening—and not part of a larger submissive persona.

Many of the Peer Couples I interviewed had terrific sexual lives. The women, especially, felt they had finally met men with whom they could be vulnerable and uninhibited. As one woman said, *"I used to be a real market for women's books. I wanted men who fit the stereotype of Clark Gable or Kevin Costner—few words, and when they are delivered, they are real ringers, and there is a lot of eye contact and passion, and that's about as much talking as you get. Maybe it was dating all these guys who were really like that, but even as fantasy objects, I got tired of men who didn't want to explore a feeling or who were only loving when they had a hard-on. I fell in love the first time sharing* Prince of Tides *with the guy I was dating, and fell in love with Eric [her husband] over a discussion of* Eyes on the Prize. *The sexy thing was the conversation and the quality of our minds. . . . I can't imagine anything more boring or ultimately unsexy than a man—and I don't care if he looked like Robert Redford and earned like Donald Trump—who had nothing to say or if he did, didn't get turned on by what I was saying."*

Equality brings with it the tools to have a great erotic relationship and also, at the same time, the pitfalls that can lead to sexual boredom. If couples learn that their sexual lives need not be constrained by any preconceived idea of what is "egalitarian sex" or appropriate sexual roles, there is no reason that their equality can't work for them. But couples who cannot separate their nights and days, who cannot transcend their identities in everyday life, may need guidance from a knowledgeable counselor.

What enables couples to sustain a style of egalitarian relationship in a world that encourages families to link their economic destiny with the male's career and casts women in an auxiliary worker role so that they can take responsibility for everyday childcare and household chores? In Peer Couples, a sense of shared purpose helps guide the couple back to why they are putting up with all the problems that come from putting together a new model of relationship without societal or familial supports.

Otherwise, it is all too easy for mothers to fall in love with their children and assume primary responsibility for their upbringing or for men to allow their careers to sweep them out of the home, away from their children and back into the more familiar territory they have been trained to inhabit. When this begins to happen, a couple's ideology, almost like an organization's mission statement, helps remind them what their central goal is: the marital intimacy that comes from being part of a well-matched, equally empowered, equally participatory team.

But avoiding traditional hierarchy involves a constant struggle to resist the power of money to define each partner's family roles. Peer Couples continually have to evaluate the role of work in their lives and how much it can infringe on parenting and household responsibilities. If one partner earns or starts to earn a lot more money, and the job starts to take up more time, the couple has to face what this means for their relationship—how much it might distort what they have set out to create.

Peer Couples check in with each other an extraordinary amount to keep their relationship on track. They each have to take responsibility for making sure that they are not drifting too far away from reciprocity. Peer Couples manage to maintain equity in small ways that make sure the balance in their marriage is more than an ideology. If one person has been picking up the kids, the other is planning their summer activities and getting their clothes. Or if one partner has been responsible lately for making sure extended family members are contacted, the other person takes it over for a while. If one partner really decides he or she likes to cook, then the other partner takes on some other equally functional and time-consuming job. There's no reason that each partner can't specialize, but both are careful that one of them doesn't take over all the high-prestige, undemanding jobs while the other ends up with the classically stigmatized assignments (like cleaning bathrooms, or whatever is personally loathed by that person).

Besides monitoring jobs and sharing, couples have to monitor their attitude. Is the wife being treated as a subordinate? Does one person carry around the anger so often seen in someone who feels discounted and unappreciated? Is one person's voice considered more important than the other person's? Is the relationship getting distant, and is the couple starting to lead parallel lives? Do they put in the time required to be best friends and family collaborators? Are they treating each other in the ways that would support a non-romantic relationship of freely associating friends?

There is nothing "natural" or automatic about keeping Peer Marriages going. There will be role discomfort when newly inhabiting the other gender's world. That is why some research shows that men who start being involved with a child from prenatal classes on show more easy attachment and participation in childrearing activities later. While men become comfortable with mothering over time, some need a lot of help. Children will sense who is the primary parent and that will be the person to whom they run, make demands, and from whom they seek daily counsel. One direct way of helping fathers evaluate how they are doing is to help the partners measure how much the children treat them as equally viable sources of comfort and help.

Likewise, being a serious provider is a responsibility some women find absolutely crushing. Most middle-class women were raised to feel that working would be voluntary. After they have made a bargain to do their share of keeping the family economically afloat, they may regret the pressures it puts on them. The old deal of staying at home and being supported can look pretty good after a bad day at the office. But only the exceptional relationship seems to be able to make that traditional provider/mother deal for very long and still sustain a marriage where partners have equal standing in each other's eyes. Couples have to keep reminding themselves how much intimacy, respect and mutual interest they earn in exchange for learning new roles and sustaining the less enjoyable elements of new responsibilities.

Couples who live as peers often attract others like themselves, and the building of a supportive community can modify the impact of the lack of support in the larger world. Like-minded others who have made similar decisions help a lot, especially when critical turning points are reached: such as re-evaluating a career track when it becomes painfully clear that it will not accommodate Peer Family life.

This study yielded no single blueprint for successful Peer Marriage. As in all couples, partners in Peer Marriages require a good measure of honesty, a dedication to fair play, flexibility, generosity and maturity. But most of all, they need to remember what they set out to do and why it was important, at least for them. If they can keep their eyes and hearts on the purpose of it all — if we help them do that — more Peer Marriages will endure and provide a model for others exploring the still-uncharted territory of egalitarian relationships.

15

GAY AND LESBIAN FAMILIES ARE HERE

JUDITH STACEY

In 1992 in Houston, I talked about the cultural war going on for the soul of America. And that war is still going on! We cannot worship the false god of gay rights. To put that sort of relationship on the same level as marriage is a moral lie.

— PAT BUCHANAN, February 10, 1996

Homosexuality is a peculiar and rare human trait that affects only a small percentage of the population and is of little interest to the rest.
—JONATHAN RAUCH, 1994

I came to Beijing to the Fourth World Conference of Women to speak on behalf of lesbian families. We are part of families. We are daughters, we are sisters, we are aunts, nieces, cousins. In addition, many of us are mothers and grandmothers. We share concerns for our families that are the same concerns of women around the world.
—BONNIE TINKER, *Love Makes a Family*, September 1995

Until but a short time ago, gay and lesbian families seemed quite a queer concept, even preposterous, if not oxymoronic, not only to scholars and the general public, but even to most lesbians and gay men. The grassroots movement for gay liberation that exploded into public visibility in 1969, when gays resisted a police raid at the Stonewall bar in New York City, struggled along with the militant feminist movement of that period to liberate gays and women *from* perceived evils and injustices represented by the family, rather than *for* access to its blessings and privileges. During the early 1970s, marches for gay pride and women's liberation flaunted provocative, countercultural banners, like "Smash The Family" and "Smash Monogamy." Their legacy is a lasting public association of gay liberation and feminism with family subversion. Yet how "queer" such antifamily rhetoric sounds today, when gays and lesbians are in the thick of a vigorous profamily movement of their own.

Gay and lesbian families are indisputably here. In June of 1993, police chief Tom Potter joined his lesbian, police officer daughter in a Portland, Oregon, gay pride march for "family values." By the late 1980s an astonishing "gay-by boom" had swelled the ranks of children living with gay and lesbian parents to between six and fourteen million.[1] *Family Values* is the title of a popular 1993 book by and about a lesbian's successful struggle to become a legal second mother to one of these "turkey-baster" babies, the son she and his biological mother have co-parented since his birth.[2] In 1989 Denmark became the first nation in the world to legalize a form of gay marriage, termed "registered partnerships," and its Nordic neighbors, Norway and Sweden, soon followed suit. In 1993, thousands of gay and lesbian couples participated in a mass wedding ceremony on the Washington Mall during the largest demonstration for gay rights in U.S. history. Three years later, on March 25, 1996, mayor of San Francisco Willie Brown proudly presided over a civic ceremony to celebrate the domestic partnerships of nearly 200 same-sex couples. "We're leading the way here in San Francisco," the mayor declared, "for the rest of the nation to fully embrace the diversity of people in love, regardless of their gender or sexual orientation."[3] By then thousands of gay and lesbian couples across the nation were eagerly awaiting the outcome of *Baehr v. Lewin*, cautiously optimistic that Hawaii's Supreme Court will soon order the state to become the first in the United States, and in the modern world, to grant full legal marriage rights to same-sex couples. As this work went to press in May 1996, the Republican party had just made gay marriage opposition a wedge issue in their presidential campaign.

Gay and lesbian families are undeniably here, yet they are not queer, if one uses the term in the sense of "odd" to signify a marginal or deviant population.[4] It is nearly impossible to define this category of families in a manner that could successfully distinguish all of their members, needs, relationships, or even their values, from those of all other families. In fact, it is almost impossible to define this category in a satisfactory, substantive way at all. What should count as a gay or lesbian family? Even if we bracket the thorny matter of how to define an individual as gay or lesbian and rely on self-identification, we still face a jesuitical challenge. Should we count only families in which every single member is gay? Clearly there are not very many, if even any, of these. Or does the presence of just one gay member color a family gay? Just as clearly, there are very many of these, including those of Ronald Reagan, Colin Powell, Phyllis Schlafly and Newt Gingrich.[5] More to the point, why would we want to designate a family type according to the sexual identity of one or more of its members? No research, as we will see, has ever shown a uniform, distinctive pattern of relationships, structure, or even "family values," among families that include self-identified gays. Of course, most nongays restrict the term *gay family* to units that contain one or two gay parents and their children. However, even such families that most commonsensically qualify as gay or lesbian are as diverse as are those which do not.

Gay and lesbian families come in different sizes, shapes, ethnicities, races, religions, resources, creeds, and quirks, and even engage in diverse sexual practices. The more one attempts to arrive at a coherent, defensible sorting principle, the more evident it becomes that the category "gay and lesbian family" signals nothing so much as the consequential social fact of widespread, institutionalized homophobia.[6] The gay and lesbian family label marks the cognitive dissonance, and even emotional threat, that much of the nongay public experiences upon recognizing that gays can participate in family life at all. What unifies such families is their need to contend with the particular array of psychic, social, legal, practical, and even physical challenges to their very existence that institutionalized hostility to homosexuality produces. Paradoxically, the label "gay and lesbian family" would become irrelevant if the nongay population could only "get used to it."

In this chapter I hope to facilitate such a process of normalization, ironically, perhaps, to allow the marker "gay and lesbian" as a family category once again to seem queer—as queer, that is, as it now seems to identify a *family*, rather than an individual or a desire, as heterosexual. . . . Gay and lesbian families represent such a new, embattled, visible and necessarily self-conscious, genre of postmodern kinship, that they more readily expose the widening gap between the complex reality of postmodern family forms and the simplistic modern family ideology that still undergirds most public rhetoric, policy and law concerning families. In short, I hope to demonstrate that, contrary to Jonathan Rauch's well-meaning claim in the second epigraph above, the experience of "homosexuals"[7] should be of immense interest to everyone else. Nongay families, family scholars and policymakers alike can learn a great deal from examining the experience, struggles, conflicts, needs, and achievements of contemporary gay and lesbian families. . . .

A More, or Less, Perfect Union?

Much nearer at hand . . . than most ever dared to imagine has come the momentous prospect of legal gay marriage. The idea of same-sex marriage used to draw nearly as many jeers from gays and lesbians as from nongays. As one lesbian couple recalls, "In 1981, we were a very, very small handful of lesbians who got married. We took a lot of flak from other lesbians, as well as heterosexuals. In 1981, we didn't know any other lesbians, not a single one, who had had a ceremony in Santa Cruz [in northern California], and a lot of lesbians live in that city. Everybody was on our case about it. They said, What are you doing, How heterosexual. We really had to sell it."[8]

Less than a decade later, gay and lesbian couples could proudly announce their weddings and anniversaries, not only in the gay press, which now includes specialized magazines for gay and lesbian couples, like *Partners Magazine,* but even in such mainstream, Midwestern newspapers as the *Minneapolis Star and Tribune.*[9] Jewish rabbis, Protestant ministers, Quaker meetings, and even some Catholic priests regularly perform gay and lesbian wedding or commitment ceremonies. This phenomenon is memorialized in cultural productions within the gay community, like "Chicks in White Satin," a documentary about a Jewish lesbian wedding which won prizes at recent gay film festivals, but it has also become a fashionable pop culture motif. In December 1995, the long-running TV sitcom program "Roseanne" featured a gay male wedding in a much-hyped episode called "December Bride." Even more provocative, however, was a prime-time lesbian wedding that aired one month later on "Friends," the highest rated sitcom of the 1995–1996 television season. Making a cameo appearance on the January 18, 1996, episode, Candice Gingrich, the lesbian half-sister of right-wing Speaker of the House Newt Gingrich, conducted a wedding ceremony which joined the characters who play a lesbian couple on the series "in holy matrimony" and pronounced them "wife and wife."

When the very first social research collection about gay parents was published in 1987, not even one decade ago, its editor concluded that however desirable such unions might be, "It is highly unlikely that marriages between same-sex individuals will be legalized in any state in the foreseeable future."[10] Yet, almost immediately thereafter, precisely this specter began to exercise imaginations across the political spectrum. A national poll reported by the *San Francisco Examiner* in 1989 found that 86 percent of lesbians and gay men supported legalizing same-sex marriage.[11] However, it is the pending *Baehr v. Lewin* court decision concerning same-sex marriage rights in Hawaii that has thrust this issue into escalating levels of front-page and prime-time prominence. Amidst rampant rumors that thousands of mainland gay and lesbian couples were stocking their hope chests with Hawaiian excursion fares, poised to fly to tropical altars the instant the first gay matrimonial bans falter, right-wing Christian groups began actively mobilizing resistance. Militant antiabortion leader Randall Terry of Operation Rescue flew to Hawaii in February 1996 to fight "queer marriage," and right-wing Christian women's leader and radio broadcast personality Beverly LaHaye urged her "Godly" listeners to fight gay marriage in Hawaii.[12]

Meanwhile, fearing that Hawaii will become a gay marriage mecca, state legislators have rushed to introduce bills that exclude same-sex marriages performed in other states from being recognized in their own, because the "full faith and credit" clause of the U.S. Constitution obligates interstate recognition of legal marriages. While fourteen states had rejected such bills by May 1995, eight others had passed them, and contests were underway in numerous others, including California.[13] On May 8, 1996, gay marriage galloped onto the nation's center political stage when Republicans introduced the Defense of Marriage Act (DOMA) which defines marriage in exclusively heterosexual terms, as "a legal union between one man and one woman as husband and wife."[14] The last legislation that Republican presidential candidate Bob Dole co-sponsored before he resigned from the Senate to pursue his White House bid full throttle, DOMA exploits homophobia to defeat President Clinton and the Democrats in November 1996. With Clinton severely bruised by the political debacle incited by his support for gay rights in the military when he first took office, but still dependent upon the support of his gay constituency, the President indeed found himself "wedged" between a rock and a very hard place. Unsurprisingly, he tried to waffle. Naming this a "time when we need to do things to strengthen the American family," Clinton publicly opposed same-sex marriage at the same time that he tried to reaffirm support for gay rights and to expose the divisive Republican strategy.[15]

Polemics favoring and opposing gay marriage rights now proliferate in editorial pages and legislatures across the nation, and mainstream religious bodies find themselves compelled to confront the issue. In March 1996 the Vatican felt called upon not merely to condemn same-sex marriage as a "moral disorder," but also to warn Catholics that they would themselves risk "moral censure" if they were to support "the election of the candidate who has formally promised to translate into law the homosexual demand."[16] Just one day after the Vatican published this admonition, the Central Conference of American Rabbis, which represents the large, generally liberal wing of Judaism, took a momentous action in direct opposition. The Conference resoundingly endorsed a resolution to "support the right of gay and lesbian couples to share fully and equally in the rights of civil marriage." Unsurprisingly, Orthodox rabbis immediately condemned the action as prohibited in the Bible and "another breakdown in the family unit."[17] One week later, in another historic development, a lead editorial in the *New York Times* strongly endorsed gay marriage.[18]

As with child custody, the campaign for gay marriage clings to legal footholds carved by racial justice pioneers. It is startling to recall how recently it was that the Supreme Court finally struck down antimiscegenation laws. Not until 1967, that is, only two years before Stonewall, did the high court, in *Loving v. Virginia,* find state restrictions on interracial marriages to be unconstitutional. (Twenty states still had such restrictions on the books in 1967, only one state fewer than the twenty-one which currently prohibit sodomy.) A handful of gay couples quickly sought to marry in the 1970s through appeals to this precedent, but until three lesbian and gay male couples sued Hawaii in *Baehr v. Lewin* for equal rights to choose marriage partners without restrictions on gender, all U.S. courts had dismissed the analogy. In a historic ruling in 1993, the Hawaiian state Supreme Court remanded this suit to the state, requiring it to demonstrate a "compelling state interest" in prohibiting same-sex marriage, a strict scrutiny standard that few believe the state will be able to meet. Significantly, the case was neither argued nor adjudicated as a gay rights issue. Rather, just as ERA opponents once had warned and advocates had denied, passage of an equal rights amendment to Hawaii's state constitution in 1972 paved the legal foundation for *Baehr.*[19]

Most gay activists and legal scholars anticipate a victory for gay marriage when *Baehr* is finally decided early in 1997, but they do not all look forward to this prospect with great delight. Although most of their constituents desire the right to marry, gay activists and theorists continue to vigorously debate the politics and effects of this campaign. Refining earlier feminist and socialist critiques of the gender and class inequities of marriage, an articulate, vocal minority seeks not to extend the right to marry, but to dismantle an institution they regard as inherently, and irredeemably, hierarchical, unequal, conservative, and repressive. Nancy Polikoff, one of the most articulate lesbian legal activist-scholars opposed to the marriage campaign, argues that

> advocating lesbian and gay marriage will detract from, and even contradict, efforts to unhook economic benefits from marriage and make basic health care and other necessities available to all. It will also require a rhetorical strategy that emphasizes similarities between our relationships and heterosexual marriages, values long-term monogamous coupling above all other relationships, and denies the potential of lesbian and gay marriage to transform the gendered nature of marriage for all people. I fear that the very process of employing that rhetorical strategy for the years it will take to achieve its objective will lead our movement's public representatives, and the countless lesbians and gay men who hear us, to believe exactly what we say.[20]

A second perspective supports legal marriage as one long-term goal of the gay rights movement, but voices serious strategic objections to making this a priority before there is sufficient public support to sustain a favorable ruling in Hawaii or the nation. Such critics fear that a premature victory will prove pyrrhic, because efforts to defend it against the vehement backlash it has already begun to incite are apt to fail, after sapping resources and time better devoted to other urgent struggles for gay rights. Rather than risk a major setback for the gay movement, they advise an incremental approach to establishing legal family status for gay and lesbian kin ties through a multi-faceted struggle for family diversity.[21]

However, the largest, and most diverse, contingent of gay activist voices now supports the marriage rights campaign, perhaps because gay marriage can be read to harmonize with virtually every hue on the gay ideological spectrum. Pro-gay marriage arguments range from profoundly conservative to liberal humanist to radical and deconstructive. Conservatives, like those radicals who still oppose marriage, view it as an institution that promotes monogamy, commitment and social stability, along with interests in private property, social conformity and mainstream values. They likewise agree that legalizing gay marriage would further marginalize sexual radicals by segregating counter-cultural gays and lesbians from the "whitebread" gay couples who could then choose to marry their way into Middle America. Radicals and conservatives, in other words, envision the same prospect, but regard it with inverse sentiments.[22]

Liberal gays support legal marriage, of course, not only to affirm the legitimacy of their relationships and help sustain them in a hostile world, but as a straightforward matter of equal civil rights. As one long-coupled gay man expresses it: "I resent the fact that married people get lower taxes. But as long as there is this institution of marriage and heterosexuals have that privilege, then gay people should be able to do it too."[23] Liberals also recognize that marriage rights provide access to the social advantages of divorce law. "I used to say, 'Why do we want to get married? It doesn't work for straight people,' one gay lawyer comments. 'But now I say we should care: They have the privilege of divorce and we don't. We're left out there to twirl around in pain.'"[24]

Less obvious or familiar, however, are cogent arguments in favor of gay marriage that some feminist and other critical gay legal theorists have developed in response to opposition within the gay community. Nan Hunter, for example, rejects feminist legal colleague Nancy Polikoff's belief that marriage is an unalterably sexist and heterosexist institution. Building upon critical theories that reject the notion that social institutions or categories have inherent, fixed meanings apart from their social contexts, Hunter argues that legalized same-sex marriage would have "enormous potential to destabilize the gendered definition of marriage for everyone."[25]

Evan Wolfson, director of the Marriage Project of the gay legal rights organization Lambda Legal Defense, who has submitted a brief in support of *Baehr*, pursues the logic of "anti-essentialism" even more consistently. The institution of marriage is neither inherently equal nor unequal, he argues, but depends upon an ever-changing cultural and political context.[26] (Anyone who doubts this need only consider such examples as polygamy, arranged marriages, or the same-sex unions in early Western history documented by the late Princeton historian, John Boswell.) Hoping to use marriage precisely to change its context, gay philosopher Richard Mohr argues that access to legal marriage would provide an opportunity to reconstruct its meaning by serving "as a nurturing ground for social marriage, and not (as now) as that which legally defines and creates marriage and so precludes legal examination of it." For Mohr, social marriage represents "the fused intersection of love's sanctity and necessity's demands," and does not necessarily depend upon sexual monogamy.[27]

Support for gay marriage, not long ago anathema to radicals and conservatives, gays and nongays, alike, now issues forth from ethical and political perspectives as diverse, and even incompatible, as these. The cultural and political context has changed so dramatically since Stonewall that it now seems easier to understand why marriage has come to enjoy overwhelming support in the gay community than to grasp the depth of resistance to the institution that characterized the movement. Still, I take seriously many of the strategic concerns about the costly political risks posed by a premature campaign. Although surveys and electoral struggles suggest a gradual growth in public support for gay rights, that support is tepid, uneven and fickle, as the debacle over Clinton's attempt to combat legal exclusion of gays from the military made distressingly clear. Thus, while 52 percent of those surveyed in a 1994 *Time* magazine/CNN poll claimed to consider gay lifestyle acceptable, 64 percent did not want to legalize gay marriages or to permit gay couples to adopt children.[28]

Gay marriage, despite its apparent compatibility with mainstream family values sentiment, raises far more threatening questions than does military service about gender relations, sexuality and family life. Few contemporary politicians, irrespective of their personal convictions, display the courage to confront this contradiction, even when urged to do so by gay conservatives. In *Virtually Normal: An Argument about Homosexuality*, New Republic editor Andrew Sullivan develops the "conservative case for gay marriage," that he earlier published as an op-ed, which stresses the contribution gay marriage could make to a conservative agenda for family and political life. A review of Sullivan's book in the *New Yorker* points out that, "here is where the advocates of gay rights can steal the conservatives' clothes."[29] The epigraph to this chapter by Jonathan Rauch about the insignificance of the homosexual minority comes from a *Wall Street Journal* op-ed he wrote to persuade Republicans that they should support legal gay marriage, not only because it is consistent with conservative values, but to guard against the possibility that gay rights advocates will exploit the party's inconsistency on this issue to political advantage.[30]

The logic behind the conservative case for gay marriage strikes me as compelling. Most importantly, gay marriage would strengthen the ranks of those endangered two-parent, "intact," married-couples families whose praises conservative, "profamily" enthusiasts never seem to tire of singing. Unsurprisingly, however, the case has won few nongay conservative converts to the cause. After all, homophobia is a matter of passion and politics, not logic. The religious right regards homosexuality as an abomination, and it has effectively consolidated its influence over the Republican party. For example, in

1994, Republicans in the Montana state senate went so far as to pass a bill that would require anyone convicted of homosexual acts to register for life as a violent sex offender. They reversed their vote in response to an outpouring of public outrage.[31] It was not long afterward, however, that Republican presidential contender Robert Dole returned the thousand-dollar campaign contribution from the gay Log Cabin Republicans in the name, of course, of family values. Nor have figures prominent in the centrist, secular neo-family-values campaign or the communitarian movement, whose professed values affirm both communal support for marital commitment and for tolerance, displayed much concern for such consistency. And even when, in the 1995 fall preelection season, President Clinton sought to "shore up" his standing among gays and lesbians by announcing his administration's support of a bill to outlaw employment discrimination against gays, he specifically withheld his support from gay marriage.[32] First Lady Hillary Rodham Clinton's [1996] book, *It Takes a Village*, ostensibly written to challenge "false nostalgia for family values," fails even to mention gay marriage or gay families, let alone to advocate village rights and resources for children whose parents are gay.[33]

Despite my personal political baptism in the heady, antifamily crucible of early second-wave feminism, I, for one, have converted to the long-term cause. A "postmodern" ideological stew of discordant convictions enticed me to this table. Like Wolfson, Mohr, and Hunter, I have come to believe that legitimizing gay and lesbian marriages would promote a democratic, pluralistic expansion of the meaning, practice, and politics of family life in the United States. This could help to supplant the destructive sanctity of *the family* with respect for diverse and vibrant *families*.

To begin with, the liberal implications of legal gay marriage are far from trivial, as the current rush by the states and Congress to nullify them should confirm. The Supreme Court is certain to have its docket flooded far into the next century with constitutional conflicts that a favorable decision in Hawaii, or elsewhere, will unleash. Under the "full faith and credit" provision of the Constitution, which requires the 50 states to recognize each other's laws, legal gay marriage in one state could begin to threaten antisodomy laws in all the others. Policing marital sex would be difficult to legitimate, and differential prosecution of conjugal sex among same-sex couples could violate equal protection legislation. Likewise, if gay marriages were legalized, the myriad state barriers to child custody, adoption, fertility services, inheritance, and other family rights that lesbians and gay men currently suffer could also become subject to legal challenge. Moreover, it seems hard to overestimate the profound cultural implications for the struggle against the pernicious effects of legally condoned homophobia that would ensue were lesbian and gay relationships to be admitted into the ranks of legitimate kinship. In a society that forbids most public school teachers and counselors even the merest expression of tolerance for homosexuality, while lesbian and gay youth attempt suicide at rates three to five times greater than other youth,[34] granting full recognition to even just whitebread lesbian and gay relationships could have dramatic, and salutary, consequences.

Of course, considerations truer to some of my earlier, more visionary feminist convictions also invite me to join the gay wedding procession. For while I share some of Polikoff's disbelief that same-sex marriage can in itself dismantle the patterned gender and sexual injustices of the institution, I do believe it could make a potent contribution to those projects, as the research on gay relationships I discuss below seems to indicate. Moreover, as Mohr suggests, admitting gays to the wedding banquet invites gays and nongays alike to consider the kinds of place settings that could best accommodate the diverse needs of all contemporary families.

Subjecting the conjugal institution to this sort of heightened democratic scrutiny could help it to assume varied creative forms. If we begin to value the meaning and quality of intimate bonds over their customary forms, there are few limits to the kinds of marriage and kinship patterns people might wish to devise. The "companionate marriage," a much celebrated, but less often realized, ideal of modern sociological lore, could take on new life. Two friends might decide to marry without basing their bond on erotic or romantic attachment, as Dorthe, a prominent Danish lesbian activist who had initially opposed the campaign for gay marriage, fantasized after her nation's parliament approved gay registered partnerships: "If I am going to marry it will be with one of my oldest friends in order to share pensions and things like that. But I'd never marry a lover. That is the advantage of being married to a close friend. Then, you never have to marry a lover!"[35] Or, more radical still, perhaps some might dare to question the dyadic limitations of Western marriage and seek some of the benefits of extended family life through small-group marriages arranged to share resources, nurturance and labor. After all, if it is true that "The Two-Parent Family Is Better"[36] than a single-parent family, as family-values crusaders like David Popenoe tirelessly proclaim, might not three-, four-, or more-parent families be better yet, as many utopian communards have long believed?

While conservative advocates of gay marriage surely would balk at such radical visions, they correctly realize that putative champions of committed relationships and of two-parent families who oppose gay marriage can be charged with gross hypocrisy on this score. For access to legal marriage not only would promote long-term, committed intimacy among gay couples, but also would afford invaluable protection to the children of gay parents, as well as indirect protection to closeted gay youth who reside with nongay parents. Clearly, only through a process of massive denial of the fact that millions of children living in gay and lesbian families are here, and here to stay, can anyone genuinely concerned with the best interests of children deny their parents the right to marry.

In the face of arguments for legalizing gay marriage as compelling and incongruent as these, it is hard to dispute Evan Wolfson's enthusiastic claim that "the brilliance of our movement's taking on marriage is that marriage is, at once and truly, both conservative and transformative, easily understood in basic human terms of equality and respect, and liberating in its individual and social potential."[37]

EPIGRAPH SOURCES

Buchanan quoted in Susan Yoachum and David Tuller, "Right Makes Might in Iowa,"
    San Francisco Chronicle, February 12, 1996, pp. A1, 11.
Rauch (see References).
Bonnie Tinker, "Love Makes a Family," presentation to 1995 United Nations Inter-
    national Women's Conference, Beijing, September 14.

ENDNOTES

1. The estimate that at least six million children were living with a gay parent by
    1985 appeared in Schulenberg, *Gay Parenting,* and has been accepted or revised
    upwards by most scholars since then. See, for example, Bozett, *Gay and Lesbian
    Parents,* p. 39; Patterson, "Children of Lesbian and Gay Parents"; Allen and Demo,
    "The Families of Lesbians and Gay Men: A New Frontier in Family Research."
2. Burke, *Family Values: A Lesbian Mother's Fight for Her Son.*
3. Goldenberg, "Virtual Marriages for Same-Sex Couples."
4. Many gay activist groups and scholars, however, have begun to reclaim the term
    "queer" as a badge of pride, in much the same way that the black power move-
    ment of the 1960s reclaimed the formerly derogatory term for blacks.
5. Reagan and Schlafly both have gay sons, Powell has a lesbian daughter, and
    Gingrich has a lesbian half-sister.
6. For a sensitive discussion of the definitional difficulties involved in research on
    gay and lesbian families, see Allen and Demo, "Families of Lesbians and Gay Men,"
    pp. 112–13.
7. Most gay and lesbian scholars and activists reject the term "homosexual" because
    it originated within a medical model that classified homosexuality as a sexual per-
    version or disease and because the term emphasizes sexuality as at the core of the
    individual's identity. In this chapter, I follow the generally preferred contempo-
    rary practice of using the terms "lesbians" and "gay men," but I also occasionally
    employ the term "gay" generically to include both women and men. I also play with
    the multiple, and currently shifting, meanings of the term "queer," by specifying
    whether I am using the term in its older pejorative sense, in its newer sense of
    proudly challenging fixed notions of gender and sexuality, or in its more collo-
    quial sense of simply "odd."
8. Quoted in Sherman, ed., *Lesbian and Gay Marriage,* p. 191.
9. Ibid., p. 173.
10. Bozett, epilogue to *Gay and Lesbian Parents,* p. 232.
11. Cited in Sherman, *Lesbian and Gay Marriage,* p. 9, n. 6. A more recent poll con-
    ducted by *The Advocate* suggests that the trend of support for gay marriage is in-
    creasing. See Wolfson, "Crossing the Threshold," p. 583.
12. Terry announced his plans January 24, 1996, on "Randall Terry Live," and LaHaye
    made her pitch the next day, January 25, 1996, on "Beverly LaHaye Live."
13. Dunlap, "Some States Trying to Stop Gay Marriages Before They Start," p. A18;
    Dunlap, "Fearing a Toehold for Gay Marriage, Conservatives Rush to Bar the Door,"
    p. A7. Lockhead, "GOP Bill Targets Same-Sex Marriages," *San Francisco Chronicle,*
    May 9, 1996, pp. A1, 15.
14. Ibid, p. A1.
15. Press briefing by Mike McCurry, White House, May 14, 1996, Office of the Press
    Secretary.
16. "Vatican Denounces Gay-Marriage Idea," *New York Times,* March 29, 1996, p. A8.
17. Dunlap, "Reform Rabbis Vote to Back Gay Marriage," p. A8.
18. "The Freedom to Marry," *New York Times,* April 7, 1996, Editorials/Letters, p. 10.
19. The decision stated that the sexual orientation of the parties was irrelevant, be-
    cause same-sex spouses could be of any sexual orientation. It was the gender

discrimination involved in limiting one's choice of spouse that violated the state constitution. See Wolfson, "Crossing the Threshold," p. 573.

20. Polikoff, "We Will Get What We Ask For: Why Legalizing Gay and Lesbian Marriage Will Not 'Dismantle the Legal Structure of Gender in Every Marriage.'"
21. Law professor Thomas Coleman, who is executive director of the Family Diversity Project in California, expresses these views in Sherman, pp. 128–29.
22. Sullivan, "The Conservative Case for Gay Marriage"; Rauch, "A Pro-Gay, Pro-Family Policy."
23. Tede Matthews in Sherman, *Lesbian and Gay Marriage*, p. 57.
24. Kirk Johnson quoted in Wolfson, "Crossing the Threshold," p. 567.
25. Hunter, "Marriage, Law, and Gender," p. 12.
26. Wolfson, "Crossing the Threshold."
27. Mohr, *A More Perfect Union*, pp. 41, 48, 50.
28. "Some Progress Found in Poll on Gay Rights," *San Francisco Chronicle*, June 20, 1994.
29. Ryan, "No Easy Way Out," p. 90; Sullivan, "Here Comes the Groom."
30. Rauch, "Pro-Gay, Pro-Family Policy."
31. Herscher, "After Reconsidering, Montana Junks Gay Sex Bill," p. A2.
32. Clinton, according to his senior adviser George Stephanopoulos, "thinks the proper role for the government is to work on the fight against discrimination, but he does not believe we should support (gay) marriage." Quoted in Sandalow and Tuller, "White House Tells Gays It Backs Them," p. A2.
33. Clinton, *It Takes a Village*, book jacket copy.
34. Remafedi, *Death by Denial*.
35. Quoted in Miller, *Out in the World*, p. 350.
36. This is the title and central argument of Popenoe's *New York Times* op-ed.
37. Wolfson, "Crossing the Threshold," p. 599.

REFERENCES

Allen, Katherine R. and David H. Demo. 1995. "The Families of Lesbians and Gay Men: A New Frontier in Family Research." *Journal of Marriage and the Family* 57 (February):111–27.

Bozett, Frederick W., ed. 1987. *Gay and Lesbian Parents*. New York: Praeger.

Burke, Phyllis. 1993. *Family Values: A Lesbian Mother's Fight for Her Son*. New York: Random House.

Clinton, Hillary Rodham. 1996. *It Takes a Village: And Other Lessons Children Teach Us*. New York: Simon & Schuster.

Dunlap, David W. 1995. "Some States Trying to Stop Gay Marriages Before They Start." *New York Times*, March 15, p. A18.

Goldberg, Carey. 1996. "Virtual Marriages for Same-Sex Couples." *New York Times*, March 26, p. A8.

Herscher, Elaine. 1995. "After Reconsidering, Montana Junks Gay Sex Bill." *San Francisco Chronicle*, March 24.

Hunter, Nan D. 1991. "Marriage, Law, and Gender: A Feminist Inquiry." *Law & Sexuality* 1(1):9–30.

Miller, Neil. 1992. *Out in the World: Gay and Lesbian Life from Buenos Aires to Bangkok*. New York: Random House.

Mohr, Richard. 1994. *A More Perfect Union. Why Straight America Must Stand Up for Gay Rights*. Boston: Beacon Press.

Patterson, Charlotte J. 1992. "Children of Lesbian and Gay Parents." *Child Development* 63:1025–42.

Polikoff, Nancy. 1993. "We Will Get What We Ask For: Why Legalizing Gay and Lesbian Marriage Will Not 'Dismantle the Legal Structure of Gender in Every Marriage.'" *Virginia Law Review* 79:1549–50.

Popenoe, David. 1992. "The Controversial Truth: The Two-Parent Family Is Better." *New York Times*, December 26, p. 13.

Rauch, Jonathan. 1994. "A Pro-Gay, Pro-Family Policy." *Wall Street Journal*, November 29, p. A22.

Remafedi, Gary. 1994. *Death by Denial*. Boston: Alyson.

Ryan, Alan, ed. 1995. "No Easy Way Out." *New Yorker*, September 11, p. 90.

Sandalow, Marc and David Tuller. 1995. "White House Tells Gays It Backs Them." *San Francisco Chronicle*, October 21, p. A2.

Sherman, Suzanne, ed. 1992. *Lesbian and Gay Marriage: Private Commitments, Public Ceremonies*. Philadelphia: Temple University Press.

Sullivan, Andrew. 1989. "Here Comes the Groom: A (Conservative) Case for Gay Marriage." *New Republic* 201(9):20–21.

Wolfson, Evan. 1994–95. "Crossing the Threshold: Equal Marriage Rights for Lesbians and Gay Men and the Intra-Community Critique." *Review of Law & Social Change* 21:3.

PART V
Parents and Children

In this section, we examine parent–child relationships from a variety of perspectives. Parenting remains the central focus of the sociological study of the family. Ideally, research on parenting should include both the perspectives of parents and the perspectives of children. However, until recently, more research has been done on parenthood and the perspectives of parents than on childhood and the perspectives of children. Granted, it is much easier to gain research access with adults than it is with children. Still, more research on children and childhood is needed. Family scholars are working to rectify this limitation, and we are beginning to see separate courses and books on children and childhood. One recent example is William A. Corsaro's book, *The Sociology of Childhood* (1997), in which he examines childhood based on his cross-cultural experiences in Italy. To date, research on parenting covers a range of topics from studies on who becomes parents, to the transition to parenthood, to how people parent (types of discipline, values, etc.), to what are the consequences of parenting (e.g., how do children change people's lives, and what effects does parenting have on the marital relationship?). Research on children tends to focus on socialization, day care, the effects of parental employment on children, and the effects of divorce/remarriage on children. We begin our investigation with the historical conceptions of parent–child relationships before examining issues specifically related to parenting (i.e., fertility and single-parent families) and issues specifically related to children (i.e., children's household labor and the effects of divorce on children).

Historical Perspectives

To understand contemporary parenting, we need to have a historical perspective. Robert LeVine and Merry White (1987), for example, in their research on the social transformation of parenthood and childhood, argue that childhood has changed more in the past 200 years than it has in 9 millennia. This transformation of childhood has occurred on many levels, including ideological changes, socioeconomic changes, demographic changes, and educational changes. On an ideological level, LeVine and White argue that the meanings of children have changed. In Western urban areas, the economic utility of children has declined, and children have become more valued sentimentally. In addition, there is more public interest in children today, especially evident in discussions concerning children's rights and policies affecting children. On a socioeconomic level, childhood was affected by the shift from agrarian to urban-industrial economies. Families experienced socioeconomic improvement, and parents could now invest unilaterally in their children's lives.

209

LeVine and White point out that this socioeconomic improvement led to improved diets, sanitation, water, and housing, which resulted in decreased mortality and fertility. Arlene Skolnick (1994) argues that this increased longevity has encouraged stronger emotional bonds between parents and children and lengthened the duration of parent–child relationships. Moreover, as we shall see in Reading 33, increased longevity also has made grandparenthood a more common life experience. According to LeVine and White (1987), the final transformative change of childhood occurred with the rise of mass schooling and the public school movement in the United States. By 1890, most children were attending schools, which limited the amount of control parents had over their children. Children were kept out of full-time productive work, and they required more resources in order to attend school.

These historical changes provide a background for the first reading on parenting, Maris A. Vinovskis' "Historical Perspectives on Parent–Child Interactions." In this reading, Vinovskis, a family historian, summarizes the major changes in parent–child relationships during the past 400 years. This summary is important because it shows that parenthood is socially constructed; that is, what is considered important and relevant to parenting changes across cultures and across time. Moreover, the various factors that influence the relationship between parents and children also change over time. Vinovskis focuses his analysis on the changes in perceptions and treatment of children, and on the changes in parent–child relationships since the Middle Ages. In particular, Vinovskis examines changes in parents' love of children, the intellectual capabilities of young children, and the recognition of adolescence. His discussion of parent–child relations assesses historical changes in parental responsibility for early child care and in parental control of children.

Fertility

Over the past 200 years, birthrates have declined dramatically in the United States. In 1800 an adult woman had an average of 7 births during her lifetime. By 1995 this average had dropped to 1.7 births per adult woman. Many factors contributed to this decline in fertility, including women's increased education and workforce participation, people marrying later and divorcing more, the increased cost of raising children, the increased availability of birth control and legalized abortion, and a decrease in religious and societal pressures to have children. A key factor in the declining birthrate is a change in the ideal family size. Whereas large families were considered to be ideal in earlier centuries, today, the majority of Americans think the ideal family size is two children. There also has been a significant change in attitudes toward childlessness. Prior to 1960, most Americans (85 percent) agreed with the statement that "all married couples should have children." By the mid-1980s, the percentage of Americans who agreed with this statement was 43 percent. These data indicate that more people are separating the institution of marriage from the institution of parenthood. Societal attitudes have changed: Not all married people are expected to have children. Moreover, an increasing number of people plan to be voluntarily childless, or child free. For example, the percentage of Americans who said they expect to remain childless increased from 5 percent in 1960 to 10 percent by the mid-1980s. Thus, more people are defining their social roles in adulthood as separate from parenting.

Even though there is an increase in voluntary childlessness, we are still a pronatalist society, which means that our society encourages people to have children. However, while many people are influenced by pronatalism and want children, an increasing number of Americans are attempting to control the timing of childbirth in their lives. For example, prior to 1970, 80 percent of women under 25 years of age had experienced childbirth. By 1989, only 50 percent of women under 25 had experienced childbirth. Today, more and more women are delaying childbirth until their thirties, and some women are delaying it into their forties (Ventura 1999). This delay has numerous consequences, both positive and negative. Couples who delay childbearing tend to be more established in their careers and have more financial resources for raising children. However, delayed childbearing also means there is a larger age gap between the parents and children, and some people are concerned that older parents may have less energy to devote to children. On the other hand, others argue that older parents tend to be more patient with children.

One important consequence of delaying childbirth is its effect on birthrates: More people will not have children at all. Moreover, while most people (90 percent) still want to have children, due to delayed childbearing, a substantial percentage (20 percent) will have some difficulty having children biologically. In fact, 15 percent of all heterosexual couples are infertile, meaning they have been unable to get pregnant after trying for over a year. Historically and medically, the primary focus has been on female infertility. Now, fertility treatments and reproductive technologies focus on both men and women. Judith N. Lasker and Susan Borg, in their article "In Search of Parenthood: Coping with Infertility and High-Tech Conception," examine infertile couples' drive to biologically bear children. Many couples have such a great desire to have biological children that they are turning to expensive and intrusive reproductive technologies to achieve their goals. Lasker and Borg interview infertile couples who have tried using alternative or artificial insemination (AI) or in vitro fertilization (IVF). The couples talk about their personal experiences with infertility and the internal and external pressures they feel to have children. Lasker and Borg also ask their respondents if they have considered adoption and how long they will keep trying to have a biological child.

Single–Parent Families

Using reproductive technologies is not limited to married, heterosexual couples who are experiencing infertility. An increasing number of single, heterosexual women and lesbians are also using these technologies to get pregnant.

This trend is another example of how, as mentioned earlier, parenting is increasingly separate from marriage. In addition, there are a growing number of children being raised by never-married women and by divorced, separated, or widowed parents. The rise in single parenthood is often a subject of public debate. Many conservatives see these families as problematic because they believe they are financially dependent on welfare or inferior to the two-parent family. The last article on parenting examines the myths and realities of single-parent families in the United States. Stephen D. Sugarman's "Single-Parent Families" provides an overview of the diversity of demographic types of single-parent families. Not only are there single-parent families headed by men, but single-parent families vary in terms of marital status, socioeconomic status, race-ethnicity, and employment. Sugarman also examines the changes over time in social policies pertaining to single-parent families.

Children and Childhood

Two articles present research on children. The first, by Frances K. Goldscheider and Linda J. Waite, is "Children's Share in Household Tasks." As the title suggests, Goldscheider and Waite examine the labor or work that children do in families. Of particular interest to the authors is how children's experiences with household labor in childhood and early adulthood influence the families they form later on. A critical question is whether household tasks are gender-typed from an early age. Goldscheider and Waite use data from the National Longitudinal Studies of Young Women and Mature Women to answer the following research questions: Under what circumstances, if any, are children more involved in household tasks, and in which families are children's tasks becoming more egalitarian? Have parents' experiences of nontraditional family forms in childhood and young adulthood influenced the way the parents share household labor with their own children? And are divorce and remarriage changing the involvement of children in household tasks?

The second reading on children and childhood, "Life-Span Adjustment of Children to Their Parents' Divorce," is by Paul R. Amato, who has been researching divorce for several years. In this article, he reviews all the research related to the effects of divorce on children. This research is important because there is a great deal of debate in the family literature concerning the effects divorce has on children. A large proportion of this debate depends on what variables the researcher is studying because the experience of divorce varies so widely in families. Clearly, parents and children experience divorce in multiple ways, and how parents manage the divorce transition greatly affects their parenting and their children. Key variables that need to be examined are short-term versus long-term effects, and how the effects vary between girls and boys and between older and younger children. Amato discusses the differences between these effects and how divorce affects children's well-being. He concludes by suggesting policy changes that would improve the lives of children after divorce.

REFERENCES

Corsaro, William A. 1997. *The Sociology of Childhood.* Thousand Oaks, CA: Pine Forge Press.

LeVine, Robert A. and Merry White. 1987. "Parenthood in Social Transformation." Pp. 271–93 in *Parenting across the Life Span: Biosocial Dimensions,* edited by Jane B. Lancaster, Jeanne Altmann, Alice S. Rossi, and Lonnie R. Sherrod. New York: Aldine de Gruyter.

Skolnick, Arlene S. 1994. "The Life Course Revolution." Pp. 62–71 in *Family in Transition,* edited by Arlene S. Skolnick and Jerome H. Skolnick. New York: HarperCollins.

Ventura, Stephanie J. et al. 1999. "Highlights of Trends in Pregnancies and Pregnancy Rates by Outcome: Estimates for the United States, 1976–96." *National Vital Statistics Reports,* vol. 47, no. 29. Washington, DC: U.S. Department of Health and Human Services.

16

HISTORICAL PERSPECTIVES ON PARENT–CHILD INTERACTIONS

MARIS A. VINOVSKIS

Overview

The perception and treatment of children and parent–child relationships have experienced major changes during the past 300 or 400 years. While most Western families have always been small and nuclear, the sharp boundary between the modern American family and the rest of society is a recent development. Although parents have historically been responsible for their children, they were not always closely attached to them as infants. Nor have young children been perceived and treated the same throughout history. Whether or not children were once seen as miniature adults, it is clear that they were regarded as capable of considerable intellectual training at a very early age. Furthermore, while historians differ among themselves on the existence or meaning of adolescence in earlier times, most of them agree that the life course of youth has changed considerably during the past several hundred years.

Parent–child relationships have also changed over time. Parental involvement in early child care has grown considerably since the Middle Ages, but the role of the father in the catechizing and educating of young children has diminished. At the same time, parental control over children has been greatly diminished in areas such as sexual behavior or choice of a career or spouse.

The relationship between parents and children is influenced by many factors and can vary over time. Alterations in the composition and size of the household as well as its interactions with the outside can affect the experiences of children growing up within it. Similarly, changes in the roles of parents or servants, for example, may affect the socialization of the young by that household. And any changes in the perceptions of the nature of children or their appropriate role in society is likely to influence their dealings with parents and other adults.

During the past 20 years, historians have reexamined the nature of the family as it once was as well as the changes in the perception and treatment

Reprinted with permission from Jane B. Lancaster, Jeanne Altman, Alice S. Rossi, and Lonnie R. Sherrod, editors. *Parenting Across the Life Span: Biosocial Dimensions* (New York: Aldine de Gruyter). Copyright © 1987 Social Science Research Council.

of children (Degler 1980b; Vinovskis 1977, 1983a). Most of these efforts, however, have been focused on some particular aspect of the family of the child, with less attention paid to their interaction. This chapter will attempt to bring together some of these diverse studies and suggest how parenting and child development may have been different in the past than it is today. Although this analysis will draw upon historical examples from all of Western Europe since the 16th century, its primary focus will be on 17th-, 18th-, and 19th-century England and America. Furthermore, while there are many different possible definitions of family, throughout this chapter, family will refer to members of the same kin living under one roof (Stone 1977).

Nature of the Family and Household in the Past

The social context of parenting and child development is very much affected by the nature of the residence in which the child is reared. The traditional assumption (Parsons 1943; Wirth 1938) is that most children in the past grew up in extended households. After marriage, they continued to live with their parents and supported them in their old age. As a result, young children frequently grew up in large households where their grandparents as well as their parents played an important role in their upbringing.

Accordingly, the extended Western preindustrial household was transformed into an isolated nuclear one as the result of the disruptive impact of urbanization and industrialization (often incorrectly combined under the term "modernization") in the 19th and 20th centuries. While this new nuclear household was supposedly better suited to the needs of the modern economy in terms of providing a more mobile and less kin-oriented labor force, the tasks of child rearing and care of the elderly were seen to have suffered in the process.

Recent historical research has cast considerable doubt on the idea that the Western family evolved from extended to nuclear due to the onset of urbanization and industrialization. As Laslett (1972) and his associates have argued, most households in preindustrial Western Europe were already nuclear and therefore could not have been transformed by any recent economic changes. While some variations did exist in household size, these were surprisingly small and mainly due to the presence or absence of servants or boarders and lodgers rather than relatives. Furthermore, instead of the nostalgic view of children growing up in large families, Laslett (1972) contends that most households were actually quite small (mean household size was about 4.75).

Critics (Berkner 1972, 1973) of the use of a mean household size point out that studying the average size of families at any given moment is misleading and incorrect because individual families increase and decrease in size and complexity over time. While only a small proportion are extended at any particular instance, a much larger proportion of them may have been extended at some point. Berkner (1972) in particular notes the prevalence of the stem family in Austria, where one of the male children continues to live with the parents after he marries and then inherits the farm after the father dies.

Although the critics of the use of mean household size are correct in questioning its conceptual and analytical utility, it is not likely that many families in preindustrial England or America had married children routinely living with them (Degler 1980a; Vinovskis 1977, 1983a). While single servants or boarders and lodgers frequently resided in the same household (Demos 1970; Modell and Hareven 1973), it was expected that married couples would establish their own separate, independent households. In some parts of Western Europe, however, such as southern France (Flandrin 1979) or the Baltic provinces (Plakens 1975), multigenerational households were more common. Furthermore, while mean household size was usually quite small in Western Europe (Laslett 1972), it was considerably larger in colonial New England (Greven 1972) because of the higher fertility and lower mortality in that region.

Even if most Western European families had always been small and nuclear, it does not mean that the social context in which children were brought up in a household remained the same. As Aries (1962) has pointed out, the medieval family was very different from its modern counterpart in that the boundary between the household and the larger society was not as rigidly drawn and the role of parents, servants, or neighbors in the socialization of children was not as differentiated and clear-cut. Stone's (1977) analysis of the late medieval and early 16th century English family confirms and expands upon many of Aries's findings. While Stone acknowledges that his categorization and periodization of the changes in English families is limited by the sources and the overlapping of these ideal family types to some degree in practice, his framework provides a useful point of departure for this analysis.

The English in the late medieval period maintained only weak boundaries between their families and the rest of society, and family members were oriented more toward kin relationships among the upper classes and toward neighbors among their poorer counterparts (Stone 1977). Marriage among property-owning classes in 16th-century England was a collective decision involving not only the family but also other kin. Individual considerations of happiness and romantic love were subservient to the need to protect the long-term interests of the lineage. Relationships within the nuclear family were not much closer than those with neighbors, relatives, or other friends.

According to Stone (1977), this open lineage family gave way to a restricted patriarchal nuclear family that predominated from 1580 to 1640, during which time loyalties to lineage, kin, and local community declined as allegiances to the state and church and kin within the household increased. As a result, the boundary between the nuclear family and the other members of society increased, while the authority of the father as head of the household within that family was enhanced. Both the state and the church provided new theoretical and practical support for patriarchy within the family, which was coupled with a new interest in children. Fathers now had added incentive to ensure that their offspring internalized the values of submissiveness to them even if it meant breaking their will at an early age. This drive toward parental dominance was particularly characteristic of the Puritans, who tended to be especially anxious about their children's upbringing. Concern about children continued as they developed, and upper-class parents sought to control their choices of both a career and a spouse.

Finally, Stone (1977) sees the growth of the closed domesticated nuclear family after the mid-17th century among the upper bourgeoise and squirarchy caused by the rise of affective individualism. The family was now increasingly organized around the principle of personal autonomy and bound together by strong affective ties. The separation between the members of the nuclear family and their servants or boarders and lodgers widened, along with the distance between the household and the rest of society. Physical privacy became more important, and the idea of the individual's right to pursue his own happiness became more acceptable.

While the causes of the changes or the exact timing among the different social classes of the move from the open lineage family to the closed domesticated nuclear family are not always clear or agreed upon (Trumbach 1978), the occurrence of that shift is generally accepted. Children growing up in 15th-century England, for example, encountered a very different social environment in their homes and neighborhoods from those in the 18th and 19th centuries. Thus, the close-knit affective nuclear family that is most prevalent today is really only the latest stage in the longer evolution of households and family life in Western Europe in the past 500 years.

Throughout most of the preindustrial period the household also functioned as the central productive unit of society. Children received training in their own homes regarding their future occupations or were employed in someone else's household (Mitterauer and Sieder 1982). But as the economic functions of the household were transferred in the late 18th- and 19th centuries to the shop or the factory, the home environment in which the children were raised changed. Rather than being closely integrated into neighborhood activities and serving as an economic focal point, the household increasingly became a haven or escape from the outside world (Cott 1977; Lasch 1977). Furthermore, as members of the nuclear family increasingly distanced themselves from others, they came to expect and cherish more from each other emotionally (Mitterauer and Sieder 1982). As a result, whereas children growing up in the 15th century were expected and encouraged to interact closely with many other adults besides their own parents, those in the 18th and 19th centuries came to rely more upon each other and their own parents for their emotional needs.

While major changes in the nature of the family occurred in Western Europe, such changes were less dramatic in America due to the fact that when the New World was settled the closed domesticated nuclear family was already prevalent in England (Stone 1977). The families that migrated to the New World, especially the Puritans, brought with them the ideal of a close and loving family (Demos 1970; Morgan [1944] 1966). While the economic functions of the American household were altered in the 19th century, the over-all change was less than the shift from an open lineage family to the closed domesticated nuclear family in Western Europe. Thus, although the relation-ship between parents and their children, for example, has not remained con-stant in America during the past 300 years, the extent of that change is probably less than in Western Europe.

Changing Perceptions and Treatment of Children

Having surveyed some of the changes in the nature of the household and the way they might affect the environment in which children were raised, the way those children were perceived and treated will now be considered. Because it is impossible, of course, to survey child development in its entirety, the focus will be confined to only three aspects: (1) parental love of children, (2) intel-lectual capabilities of young children, and (3) youth.

Parental Love of Children

It is commonly assumed that one of the basic characteristics of human beings is the close and immediate attachment between the newborn child and the parents—especially the mother. Consequently, child abandonment or abuse today is puzzling to many Americans, since these practices seem to contradict what is perceived to be a deeply ingrained feeling toward one's own children.

Maternal indifference to infants, however, may have been common dur-ing the Middle Ages (Aries 1962; Stone 1977). Parents did not pay much at-tention to newborn infants and did not display much grief if they died. According to Aries, the lack of affection toward and attention to infants con-tinued until the 16th and 17th centuries, and Shorter (1975) argues that it per-sisted into the 18th and 19th centuries among the ordinary people of Western Europe. A few studies (Pollock 1983), however, question the extent of mater-nal indifference and inattention in the past and thereby tend to minimize any of the more recent changes perceived by other historians.

As evidence of parental indifference to infants, scholars point to the ca-sualness with which deaths of young children were accepted and sometimes seemingly encouraged or at least tolerated. Although overt infanticide was frowned upon and increasingly prosecuted in the 16th century, it still may have been quite common in parts of Western Europe (Langer 1975). There also seems to be agreement that the practice of leaving infants at foundling hospi-tals or with rural wet nurses during the 17th, 18th, and 19th centuries resulted in very high mortality rates (Badinter 1981). The prevalence of wet-nursing is indicated by the fact that in the first two decades of the 19th century approx-imately half of the infants born in Paris were nursed commercially, even though this often resulted in more than one quarter of those infants dying (Sussman 1977). In addition, the natural children of the wet nurses also suffered and were more apt to die because they did not receive sufficient nour-ishment (Lehning 1982). Whether the decision to abandon an infant to a char-itable institution or to a wet nurse was mainly the result of the mother's economic desperation, the difficulty of raising an out-of-wedlock child, or a lack of attachment for the young infant is not clear. But the fact that many well-to-do, married women casually chose to give their infants to wet nurses, de-spite the apparent higher risks of mortality, suggests that not every-one using this form of child care was driven to it by dire circumstances (Shorter 1975).

While the practice of overt infanticide and child abandonment may have been relatively widespread in parts of Western Europe (such as France), it does not seem to have been as prevalent in either England or America (Hoffer and Hull 1981; Stone 1977). Indeed, authorities in both those countries prosecuted cases of infanticide in the 16th and 17th centuries more vigorously than most other forms of murder and emphasized the importance of maternal care of the young child. Furthermore, the use of wet nurses (employed by upper-class English women) became unfashionable by the end of the 18th century (Trumbach 1978).

Although there is considerable disagreement on the extent and timing of parental indifference to infants in Western Europe, almost everyone is agreed on its presence as well as its subsequent demise. Though few individuals (Pollock 1983) have begun to challenge this interpretation — at least in its more extreme forms — most observers still concur that by the 17th and 18th centuries (or perhaps even later among French peasants and workers) par-ents expressed more interest in and affection for their children (Demos 1970; Morgan 1966; Stone 1977; Trumbach 1978). Indeed, the deep affection and attachment to one's own children became one of the major characteristics of the closed domesticated nuclear family. By the 19th century, many observers began to even criticize parents for being too child-centered (Wishy 1968).

While the gradual change in the reactions of parents to their newborn undoubtedly improved the situation of children generally, parents still could, if they chose, abuse their own children as long as such abuse did not result in death. Gradually, however, the state began to intervene to protect the child from harm inflicted at the workplace or at home. Yet it was not until the late 19th century that reformers in England were able to persuade lawmakers to pass legislation to protect children from abusive parents, since the parent–child relationship was regarded as sacred and beyond state intervention (Behlmer 1982). Ironically, efforts to prevent cruelty against animals preceded those to ac-complish the same ends for children by nearly half a century (Turner 1980).

Intellectual Capabilities of Young Children

Child developmentalists sometimes portray the nature and capabilities of the young as invariant across cultures and over time, without taking into con-sideration how much of the behavior of those children can be explained by parental and societal expectations. Yet historically the perceptions and treat-ment of the child have been quite varied.

Some of the earliest studies (Earle 1899) of children in colonial America yielded the observation that a distinct phase of childhood did not exist. Children were expected to think and behave as adults from a very early age. As Fleming (1933) noted, "Children were regarded simply as miniature adults" (p. 60). This perception of children received strong reinforcement from Aries (1962), who argued that medieval society in general did not distinguish between children and adults and that the idea of childhood as a separate and distinct stage did not emerge until the 16th and 17th centuries.

Some recent scholars (Demos 1970, 1974; Zuckerman 1970) of the colonial American family have continued the idea that children were perceived and treated as miniature adults. But others (Axtell 1974; Kaestle and Vinovskis 1978, 1980; Stannard 1975, 1977) have questioned this interpretation by pointing out that the New England Puritans were aware that children had different abilities and temperaments from adults and that child rearing should be molded to those individual differences (Moran and Vinovskis 1983).

Young children in colonial America, however, were perceived as being more capable intellectually at an early age than their counterparts today. The Puritans believed that children should be taught to read the Bible as soon as possible because it was essential for everyone's salvation. The importance of early reading was reinforced for them by their expectation that children were likely to die at any moment and therefore had to be spiritually prepared for this eventuality (Slater 1977; Stannard 1975, 1977; Vinovskis 1972, 1976, 1981b). Indeed, the notion that children could and should learn to read as soon as they could talk was so commonly accepted by educators (Locke 1964) that they did not feel the need to elaborate upon it in their writings (Kaestle and Vinovskis 1978, 1980).

The idea of early childhood learning received a powerful boost in the first third of the 19th century, when the infant school movement swept the United States (Kaestle and Vinovskis 1978, 1980; May and Vinovskis 1977). The focus on special classes for very young children was imported from England, where infant schools had been created to help disadvantaged poor children. While most infant schools in America were initially intended to help poor children, they were quickly adopted by middle-class parents once it became evident that they were useful in helping children to develop. By the 1830s and 1840s in Massachusetts, for example, nearly 40–50 percent of 3-year-old children were attending schools and learning to read. Although some infant-school teachers were reluctant to focus on intellectual activities such as reading, pressures from parents forced most of them to provide such instruction.

During the first two centuries of settlement in the New World, the idea that 3- and 4-year-old children were intellectually capable of learning to read had gone virtually unchallenged in theory as well as practice and was reinforced by the infant-school movement of the late 1820s. Yet in the 1830s this viewpoint became strongly and successfully contested. Amariah Brigham, a prominent physician, published a popular book (1833) in which he argued that the early intellectual training of children seriously and permanently physically weakened their growing young minds and often led to insanity in later life. His dire warnings were accepted and repeated by educators as well as writers of child-rearing manuals. As a result, crucial financial support for the infant schools from the middle-class reformers dropped precipitously, and many such institutions were forced to close. Although parents were much slower than physicians and educators in abandoning early childhood education, by the 1850s and 1860s virtually no very young children (3- or 4-year-olds) could be found in Massachusetts schools. Interestingly, when the kindergarten movement was popularized in the United States in the 1860s and 1870s by Mary Peabody, a former Massachusetts infant-school teacher, it was restricted to children at least 5 or 6 years old and deliberately avoided intellectual activities such as reading.

This example of the changing attitudes on when a child could and should learn to read illustrates how alterations in the perception of children can greatly affect the type of socialization provided for them in early life. It also demonstrates how sudden and dramatic shifts in the perceptions of the child can alter the basic pattern of child care that had been accepted unquestioningly for several centuries. One might even speculate that as society becomes increasingly willing to incorporate the latest scientific and medical findings in the care of the young, and as social institutions such as the schools become more willing and able to determine how and when parents educate their children, the likelihood of frequent swings in child-rearing practices may increase.

Youth

Although the historical study of youth is now attracting more research (Gillis 1974; Kett 1977), there is still little agreement among scholars on the changes that occur in this phase of the life course. The recognition of adolescence as a particular stage of development in the past, for example, has not been conclusively demonstrated. Some historians (Demos and Demos 1969) see its emergence only in the late 19th or early 20th century, as a result of the introduction of more career choices and the sharper discontinuities in young people's lives due to urban-industrial development. Others (Hiner 1975) have challenged that interpretation by arguing for the presence of adolescence in the early 18th century. Some individuals (Kett 1977) have moved away from the issue of adolescence as a particular stage and focused instead on the changes in the lives of youth as they move from a state of dependence to one of independence, signaled by the establishment of their own household.

Rather than trying to analyze the individual emotional turmoil and tension that is often associated with adolescence today, many historians are studying other aspects of teenage development, such as patterns of school attendance and labor force participation. Here the debate, usually among economic and educational historians, revolves not around the life course experiences of the individual, but on those differences in the experiences among various ethnic groups or classes (Vinovskis 1983). Scholars like Thernstrom (1964) argue that early school leaving in 19th century America was mainly the result of ethnic rather than class differences, as Irish parents were more willing to have their children leave school in order to help the family earn enough money to purchase their own home. Other historians (Bowles and Gintis 1976; Katz and Davey 1978) reject this ethnic interpretation and contend that the real cause of variations in school attendance was class differences. Finally, some analysts (Kaestle and Vinovskis 1980) offer a more pluralistic interpretation that recognizes the importance of both the ethnicity and class of the parents as well as the type of community in which the children are raised.

While historians may be moving toward more agreement on the patterns of school attendance and labor force participation among youth, they are simultaneously beginning to disagree on the importance of that education. Whereas Thernstrom (1964) and most other social historians simply assumed that education was an important factor in the social functioning and mobility of 19th-century teenagers, Graff (1979) questions the benefits and necessity of literacy and education altogether. Thus, historians who have been content to analyze the patterns and causes of teenage school attendance are now being forced to reexamine its actual meaning and impact on the lives of those children.

Although American historians have tried to analyze the patterns of school attendance and labor force participation of teenagers in the past as well as the existence of adolescence as a stage of the life course, surprisingly little has been done to explore the changes in teenage sexuality, pregnancy, or childbearing (Vinovskis 1982). This is somewhat surprising, since the issue of the so-called "epidemic" of adolescent pregnancy has become so visible and symbolically important to policymakers in Washington today (Vinovskis 1981a).

In early America, adolescent sexuality, pregnancy, and childbearing were not perceived to be particular problems (Vinovskis 1982). Although the age of menarche in colonial New England biologically was low enough for teenage parenting to occur, few became pregnant because of the stringent 17th-century prohibitions against premarital sexual relations and the fact that few women married in their early teens. Even if teenage girls were sexually active and did become pregnant, their age was less of a factor in how society reacted than their general behavior. In other words, early Americans were more concerned about premarital sexual relations in general than the age of the women involved. Only in the late 19th and early 20th centuries is there differentiation between teenage and adult sexual behavior, with a more negative connotation attached to the former.

Throughout most of the 17th, 18th, and 19th centuries, there was little onus attached to teenage marriages as long as the couple was self-supporting. Because opportunities for careers for single or married women outside the home were limited, the handicaps currently associated with early childbearing did not seem as severe. Furthermore, the relatively small number of teenage marriages during these years compared to the situation today also minimized the attention that was paid to teenage childbearing in the past.

Indeed, only in the post–World War II period has the issue of teenage pregnancy and childbearing become such a major public concern. Ironically, the greatest attention to it has come during the late 1970s and early 1980s, even though the rates of teenage pregnancy and childbearing peaked in the United States in the late 1950s (Vinovskis 1981a).

Parent–Child Relations

Thus far this chapter has dealt with changes in the . . . perception and treatment of children over time. Two issues in the relationship between parents and children—(1) parental responsibility for early child care and (2) parental control of children—should also be considered.

Parental Responsibility for Early Child Care

In modern American society, it is assumed that the parents have the primary responsibility for child care until the children are enrolled in schools where they will receive most of their educational instruction. When the behavior of parents seriously threatens the well-being of the young child, the state can intervene to protect it, but this does not occur frequently. Furthermore, the physical care and early socialization of the child is almost always the responsibility of the mother—even if both parents are employed.

Historically, the primary responsibility for the upbringing of young children belonged almost exclusively to the parents, especially the father. Although in some periods and societies, such as 17th- and 18th-century New England (Moran and Vinovskis 1983), the state or church intervened in order to ensure that the children were properly catechized and instructed, it was not until the late 19th and early 20th centuries that the state was willing to remove the young child from the direct supervision of negligent or abusive parents (Behlmer 1982). It should also be noted, however, that although the state valued the family in the past, it was not irrevocably committed to it when that family was incapable of supporting its own members. Thus, in early America destitute families were sometimes disbanded and the children placed in other households in order to reduce the welfare costs to the rest of the community (Rosenkrantz and Vinovskis 1977).

If the responsibility for early child care usually resided with the parents, they did not always provide that care themselves. In the medieval household, for example, servants as well as neighbors complemented the care given the young child by the parents or their older siblings (Aries 1962; Stone 1977). In addition, as was discussed previously, many women in the past willingly or out of economic necessity relinquished the nurturing of their infants to a wet nurse (Shorter 1975; Sussman 1977).

By the 17th and 18th centuries, particularly in England and America, parents increasingly cared for their own young children and began to limit assistance from nonfamily members (Morgan 1966; Stone 1977). This trend was caused in large part by the growing affection and self-centeredness among the immediate family members in the closed domesticated nuclear family. Furthermore, parental involvement in the upbringing of their own children was especially evident among the Puritans, who insisted on the importance of the family in providing for the spiritual as well as the physical needs of the young child (Moran and Vinovskis 1982, 1983).

As the family began to play a more active role in the care of its young children, there was often a division of labor between the parents. The mother provided for the physical needs of the child while the father, as head of the household, attended to its spiritual and educational development. Indeed, the Puritans saw the father as the primary catechizer of children and household servants (Moran and Vinovskis 1983).

The importance in these areas of the Puritan father was reversed in the 18th and 19th centuries, as men stopped joining churches and therefore were deemed less suitable for overseeing the religious upbringing of their children (Moran 1979, 1980). New England Puritans came to rely more upon the mothers who, although they were less literate than the husbands, continued to join the churches. By the end of the 18th and early 19th centuries, the mother's role in early childhood care and socialization was clearly established (Kuhn 1947; Moran and Vinovskis 1983). The only major change thereafter was the growing role of the schools in the provision of formal education for the young child, as parents usually willingly relinquished that task to reluctant schoolteachers who had tried to limit the entry of young children into their classrooms (Kaestle and Vinovskis 1980).

Thus, although parents have usually been assigned the primary responsibility for the care and socialization of the young child in Western society, they have not always provided those services themselves. During the past 300 or 400 years, however, parents have increasingly nurtured and socialized, at least to some degree and frequently with the assistance of specialized institutions such as schools or churches, their own children. While the direct involvement of parents in early child care and education has grown, that of other non-related members of the household or of the neighbors has diminished; the family today is more private and self-centered than its medieval counterpart. Finally, although the father played a more important role in the catechizing and educating of young children in certain time periods and cultures, the primary provider of care and affection for the young child was usually the mother or her female substitute. The mother's role in the upbringing of the young child increased during the 18th and 19th centuries as fathers became too busy or uninterested in sharing more fully in the raising of their young offspring. While child-rearing manuals continued to acknowledge the importance of the father for the care of the young, they also recognized that the mother had become the major figure in the performance of that task (Demos 1982).

Parental Control of Children

Throughout most of Western development, parents exercised considerable control over children as long as they remained in the home. Children were expected to be obedient to their parents and to contribute to the well-being of the family. During much of this time parents arranged the marriages of their children and greatly influenced their choice of careers.

In the medieval period, the interests of the lineage and kin were more important than those of the individual (Aries 1962; Stone 1977). Children were expected not only to acquiesce to the requests of parents, but also to the interests of the larger kinship network. Marriages were arranged in order to further the goals of the family and its kindred.

The emergence of the restricted patriarchal nuclear family weakened the claims of the lineage and kin on the allegiances of the children as the nuclear family grew closer together. The emphasis on the authority of the father as the head of the household, however, reinforced parental control over the children.

It was not until the arrival of the closed domesticated nuclear family that the rights of children as individuals were clearly recognized and acknowledged. Increasingly, children were allowed not only to veto an unsatisfactory marriage partner, but even to choose someone they loved (Stone 1977; Trumbach 1978). While dating this erosion of parental power in the selection of a child's mate may vary from one society to another, it probably occurred in America between the late 18th and 19th centuries (Smith 1973).

Parents tried to determine not only whom children should marry, but also when. According to Greven (1970), the second generation in 17th-century Andover, Massachusetts were prevented from early marriages by the unwillingness of their fathers to relinquish legal control over the land they had set aside for their sons. While this argument is plausible, Greven has been unable to establish it statistically (Vinovskis 1971). Indeed, while there is little doubt that parents often tried to influence the timing as well as the partner of their child's marriage, very few of the existing historical studies are able to ascertain the relative importance of the role of the parents—especially since many of the children may have willingly acquiesced in this process anyway. Yet the idea that a child has rights independent of and superior to those of the parents is a relatively recent development in Western society.

In Western Europe, children were also expected to turn over almost all their earnings directly to the parents—sometimes even after they had left home (Shorter 1975). Under these circumstances, the economic value of children to the family was considerably enhanced, since the additional labor or revenue from a grown child could be substantial. Although children frequently contributed some of their outside earnings to their parents in the United States, it does not seem to have been as common as in Western Europe—especially among the native-born population (Dublin 1979). This difference in parental control over the earnings of children probably reflects both the greater individuality and freedom of the child in the 19th- century American family and the fact that these families were not as economically destitute as their European counterparts. Certainly among some immigrant groups in the United States there seems to have been a stronger tradition of children, particularly girls, turning over their pay envelopes to the parents (Hareven 1982).

Over time parental control of children has been significantly diminished. Whereas in the medieval and early modern periods parents had almost unlimited control over the behavior of their children in their own households, such is no longer the case. Although parents may still influence the choice of a child's mate or career, they cannot determine them. In addition, the idea of a child giving most of his/her outside wages to the parents seems anachronistic and inappropriate today. Indeed, the development of children's rights has proceeded so far and rapidly that society is in the midst of a backlash as efforts are being made to reassert parental rights in areas such as the reproductive behavior of minor children.

Conclusion

This brief historical survey of the nature of the family and household, the perception and treatment of children, and parent–child relationships suggests that major changes have occurred in these areas during the past 300 to 400 years. While most Western families have always been small and nuclear, the sharp boundary between the modern American family and the rest of society is a recent development.

Although parents have been responsible for their children, they were not always closely attached to them as infants. Nor were young children perceived and treated the same throughout history. Whether or not children were once seen as miniature adults, it is clear that they were regarded as capable of considerable intellectual training at a very early age. Furthermore, while historians differ among themselves on the existence or meaning of adolescence in the past, most of them agree that the life course of youth has drastically changed during the past several hundred years.

Finally, parent–child relationships have changed over time as well. Parental involvement in early child care has grown greatly since the Middle Ages, but the role of the father in the catechizing and educating of young children has diminished. At the same time, parental control over the behavior of children has been greatly diminished in areas such as sexual behavior or choice of a career or spouse.

Although there have been major changes in the way society treats children, it would be very difficult to agree on the costs and benefits of those trends from the viewpoint of the child, the parents, or society. While many applaud the increasing individualism and freedom for children within the family, others lament the loss of family responsibility and individual discipline. While an historical analysis of parents and children cannot resolve such issues, it can provide us with a better appreciation of the flexibility and resilience of the family as an institution for raising the young.

ENDNOTES

Author's note: Research was supported by the Program in American Institutions at the University of Michigan.

REFERENCES

Aries, P. 1962. *Centuries of Childhood: A Social History of Family Life.* Translated by R. Baldick. New York: Vintage Books.

Axtell, J. 1974. *The School upon a Hill: Education and Society in Colonial New England.* New Haven, CT: Yale University Press.

Badinter, E. 1981. *Mother Love: Myth & Reality.* New York: Macmillan.

Behlmer, G. K. 1982. *Child Abuse and Moral Reform in England, 1870–1908.* Stanford, CA: Stanford University Press.

Berkner, L. K. 1973. "Recent Research on the History of the Family in Western Europe." *Journal of Marriage and the Family* 35:395–405.

———. 1972. "The Stem Family and the Developmental Cycle of the Peasant Household: An Eighteenth-Century Austrian Example." *American Historical Review* 77: 398–418.

Bowles, S. and H. Gintis. 1976. *Schooling in Capitalist America: Educational Reform and the Contradictions of Economic Life.* New York: Basic Books.

Brigham, A. 1833. *Remarks on the Influence of Mental Cultivation and Mental Excitement upon Health.* 2d ed. Boston, MA: Marsh, Capen and Lyon.

Cott, N. F. 1977. *The Bonds of Womanhood: "Woman's Sphere" in New England, 1780–1835.* New Haven, CT: Yale University Press.

Degler, C. 1980a. *At Odds: Women and the Family in America from the Revolution to the Present.* New York: Oxford University Press.

———. 1980b. "Women and the Family." Pp. 308–26 in *The Past Before Us: Contemporary Historical Writings in the United States,* edited by M. Kammen. Ithaca, NY: Cornell University Press.

Demos, J. 1970. *A Little Commonwealth: Family Life in Plymouth Colony.* New York: Oxford University Press.

———. 1974. "The American Family in Past Time." *American Scholar* 43:422–46.

———. 1982. "The Changing Faces of Fatherhood: A New Exploration in American Family History." Pp. 425–50 in *Father and Child: Developmental and Clinical Perspectives,* edited by S. H. Cath, A. R. Gurwitt, and J. M. Ross. Boston, MA: Little, Brown.

Demos, J. and V. Demos. 1969. "Adolescence in Historical Perspective." *Journal of Marriage and the Family* 31:632–38.

Dublin, T. 1979. *Women at Work: The Transformation of Work and Community in Lowell, Massachusetts, 1826–1860.* New York: Columbia University Press.

Earle, A. M. 1899. *Child Life in Colonial Days.* New York: Macmillan.

Flandrin, J. L. 1979. *Families in Former Times: Kinship, Household and Sexuality in Early Modern France.* Translated by R. Southern. Cambridge: Cambridge University Press.

Fleming, S. 1933. *Children and Puritanism: The Place of Children in the Life and Thought of the New England Churches, 1620–1847.* New Haven, CT: Yale University Press.

Gillis, J. R. 1974. *Youth and History.* New York: Academic Press.

Graff, H. J. 1979. *The Literacy Myth: Literacy and Social Structure in the Nineteenth-Century City.* New York: Academic Press.

Greven, P. J. 1972. "The Average Size of Families and Households in the Province of Massachusetts in 1764 and in the United States in 1790: An Overview." Pp. 545–60 in *Household and Family in Past Time,* edited by P. Laslett. Cambridge: Cambridge University Press.

———. 1970. *Four Generations: Population, Land, and Family in Colonial Andover, Massachusetts.* Ithaca, NY: Cornell University Press.

Hareven, T. K. 1982. *Family Time & Industrial Time: The Relationship between the Family and Work in a New England Industrial Community.* Cambridge: Cambridge University Press.

Hiner, N. R. 1975. "Adolescence in Eighteenth-Century America." *History of Childhood Quarterly* 3:253–80.

Hoffer, P. C. and N. E. H. Hull. 1981. *Murdering Mothers: Infanticide in England and New England, 1558–1803.* New York: New York University Press.

Kaestle, C. F. and M. A. Vinovskis. 1978. "From Apron Strings to ABCs: Parents, Children, and Schooling in Nineteenth-Century Massachusetts." Pp. 539–580 in *Turning Points: Historical and Sociological Essays on the Family*, edited by J. Demos and S. S. Boocock. Chicago: University of Chicago Press.

———. 1980. *Education and Social Change in Nineteenth-Century Massachusetts*. Cambridge: Cambridge University Press.

Katz, M. B. and I. E. Davey. 1978. "School Attendance and Early Industrialization in a Canadian City: A Multivariate Analysis." *History of Education Quarterly* 18:271–94.

Kett, J. F. 1977. *Rites of Passage: Adolescence in America, 1790 to the Present*. New York: Basic Books.

Kuhn, A. L. 1947. *The Mother's Role in Childhood Education*. New Haven, CT: Yale University Press.

Langer, W. 1975. "Infanticide: A Historical Survey." Pp. 55–68 in *The New Psychohistory*, edited by L. DeMause. New York: The Psychohistory Press.

Lasch, C. 1977. *Haven in a Heartless World: The Family Besieged*. New York: Basic Books.

Laslett, P., ed. 1972. *Household and Family in Past Time*. Cambridge: Cambridge University Press.

Lehning, J. R. 1982. "Family Life and Wetnursing in a French Village." *Journal of Interdisciplinary History* 12:645–56.

Locke, J. 1964. *Some Thoughts Concerning Education*. Abridged and edited by F. W. Garforth. Woodbury, NY: Barron.

May, D. and M. A. Vinovskis. 1976. "A Ray of Millennial Light: Early Education and Social Reform in the Infant School Movement in Massachusetts, 1826–1840." Pp. 62–99 in *Family and Kin in American Urban Communities, 1800–1940*, edited by T. K. Hareven. New York: Watts.

Mitterauer, M. and M. Sieder. 1982. *The European Family: From Patriarchy to Partnership*. Translated by K. Oosterveen and M. Horzinger. Chicago: University of Chicago Press.

Modell, J. and T. K. Hareven. 1973. "Urbanization and the Malleable Household: An Examination of Boarding and Lodging in American Families." *Journal of Marriage and the Family* 35:467–79.

Moran, G. F. 1980. "Sisters in Christ: Women and the Church in Seventeenth-Century New England." Pp. 47–64 in *Women in American Religion*, edited by J. W. James. Philadelphia: University of Pennsylvania Press.

———. 1979. "Religious Renewal, Puritan Tribalism, and the Family in Seventeenth-Century Milford Connecticut." *William and Mary Quarterly*, 3rd Series, 36:236–54.

Moran, G. F. and M. A. Vinovskis. 1982. "The Puritan Family and Religion: A Critical Reappraisal." *William and Mary Quarterly*, 3rd Series, 39:29–63.

———. 1983. "The Great Care of Godly Parents: Early Childhood in Puritan New England." Paper presented at Biennial Meeting of the Society for Research in Child Development, Detroit, April.

Moran, E. S. 1966. *The Puritan Family: Religion and Domestic Relations in Seventeenth-Century New England*. New York: Harper and Row.

Parsons, T. 1943. "The Kinship System of the Contemporary United States." *American Anthropologist* 45:22–38.

Plakens, A. 1975. "Seigneurial Authority and Peasant Family Life: The Baltic Area in the Eighteenth Century. *Journal of Interdisciplinary History* 4:629–54.

Pollock, L. 1983. *Forgotten Children: Parent–Child Relations from 1500 to 1900*. Cambridge: Cambridge University Press.

Rosenkrantz, B. G. and M. A. Vinovskis. 1977. "Caring for the Insane in Anti-bellum Massachusetts: Family, Community, and State Participation." Pp. 187–218 in *Kin and Communities: Families in America*, edited by A. J. Lichtman and J. R. Challinor. Washington, DC: Smithsonian Institution Press.

Shorter, E. 1975. *The Making of the Modern Family*. New York: Basic Books.

Slater, P. G. 1977. *Children in the New England Mind: In Death and in Life*. Hamden, CT: Archon Books.

Smith, D. S. 1973. "Parental Power and Marriage Patterns: An Analysis of Historical Trends in Hingham, Massachusetts." *Journal of Marriage and the Family* 35:406–18.

Stannard, D. E. 1975. "Death and the Puritan Child." Pp. 9–29 in *Death in America,* edited by D. E. Stannard. Philadelphia: University of Pennsylvania Press.

———. 1977. *The Puritan Way of Death: A Study in Religion, Culture, and Social Change.* New Haven, CT: Yale University Press.

Stone, L. 1977. *The Family, Sex and Marriage in England, 1500–1800.* New York: Oxford University Press.

Sussman, G. D. 1977. "Parisian Infants and Norman Wet Nurses in the Early Nineteenth Century: A Statistical Study." *Journal of Interdisciplinary History* 7:637–54.

Thernstrom, S. 1964. *Poverty and Progress: Social Mobility in a Nineteenth-Century City.* Cambridge, MA: Harvard University Press.

Trumbach, R. 1978. *The Rise of the Egalitarian Family: Aristocratic Kinship and Domestic Relations in Eighteenth-Century England.* New York: Academic Press.

Turner, J. 1980. *Reckoning with the Beast: Animals, Pain, and Humanity in the Victorian Mind.* Baltimore: Johns Hopkins Press.

Vinovskis, M. A. 1971. "American Historical Demography: A Review Essay." *Historical Methods Newsletter* 4:141–48.

———. 1972. "Mortality Rates and Trends in Massachusetts before 1860." *Journal of Economic History* 32:184–213.

———. 1976. "Angels, Heads and Weeping Willows: Death in Early America." *Proceedings of the American Antiquarian Society:* 86:273–302.

———. 1977. "From Household Size to the Life Course: Some Observations on Recent Trends in Family History." *American Behavioral Scientist* 21:263–87.

———. 1981a. "An Epidemic of Adolescent Pregnancy? Some Historical Considerations. *Journal of Family History* 6:205–30.

———. 1981b. *Fertility in Massachusetts from the Revolution to the Civil War.* New York: Academic Press.

———. 1982. "Adolescent Sexuality, Pregnancy, and Childbearing in Early America: Some Preliminary Speculations." Paper presented at the SSRC Conference on School-Age Pregnancies and Parenthood, Belmont Conference Center, Maryland, May.

———. 1983a. "American Families in the Past." Pp. 115–37 in *Ordinary People and Everyday Life: Perspectives on the New Social History.* Nashville, TN: American Association for State and Local History.

———. 1983b. "Quantification and the Analysis of Antebellum Education." *Journal of Interdisciplinary History* 13:761–86.

Wirth, L. 1938. "Urbanism as a Way of Life." *American Journal of Sociology* 44:1–24.

Wishy, B. 1968. *The Child and the Republic.* Philadelphia: University of Pennsylvania Press.

Zuckerman, M. 1970. *Peaceable Kingdoms: New England Towns in the Eighteenth Century.* New York: Alfred A. Knopf.

17

IN SEARCH OF PARENTHOOD
Coping with Infertility and High–Tech Conception

JUDITH N. LASKER • SUSAN BORG

*We'll sell the car, the house even, if it comes to it. . . . There was nothing
I wouldn't give up if it meant we could have a child.*[1]

Over and over we have heard such words of desperation, of willingness
to endure any pain or expense, even to risk one's life, all in order to
have a child. The search for parenthood by infertile people has been
compared to a terminal cancer victim's quest for a cure. But infertility, though
painful, is not life threatening. Why are people so driven in their efforts?

Personal and Social Pressures

Gail is a thirty-four-year-old woman who has been through eight cycles of
AIH (artificial insemination with her husband's sperm) and four attempts at
IVF (test-tube fertilization) in the last five years, all without success. Gail is a
calm, good-natured person, but she describes herself as "driven" to keep trying to get pregnant:

> *It's worth it all to know you've done everything that you can do. I don't want
> to always be wondering if we should have pushed a little harder or tried some-
> thing else. At least I know my inability to conceive is not from lack of trying.*

What is it about conceiving and bearing children that is so crucial to infertile people like Gail, that makes them willing to try almost anything? Some
scientists, agreeing with Harvard sociobiologist Edward O. Wilson's theories,
claim that people's desire to reproduce is innate, perhaps even programmed
into their genes. Although there may be a biological component to wanting to
bear children, no one has yet been able to prove or measure it. On the contrary,
a great deal of evidence shows that social and psychological pressures to have
children are at least as powerful, if not more so, than the biological pressures.[2]

Gail's desire for children is like that of many other people. She talks about
feelings of emptiness, the sense that her family is not yet complete. She and

her husband Bill have been married for nine years, and they are eager to share their love with children. They yearn for the pleasure of cuddling babies and playing with them as they grow. They want to pass on their values, to see themselves as living on in the future through the lives of their children.

Gail and Bill's own internal drive to be parents is strongly reinforced by external pressures. They believe they have made their own choice to have children, but it is obvious that this choice would be greatly approved by others. Gail described the pressures from her family and friends:

> When I was little, my parents talked a lot about what it would be like when I grew up and became a mother. "Growing up" and "becoming a mother" seemed like the same thing. After I got married, the comments started coming in from my friends as well as my parents — "Well, when are you going to have a family?" they kept asking us. They were all having kids, and we felt very left out. I'm sure this all had an impact on our wish for children.
>
> It isn't just my relatives and friends. I think it's in the air, almost like an epidemic. Everywhere I go there are pregnant women and babies, in the stores, on TV, just walking along the street. It makes you feel abnormal not to be pushing a stroller or buying the newest kind of diaper.

The pressures to have children go beyond comments from others and commercials on television. They are deeply embedded in the culture, supported by powerful social norms.

Every culture has its ideal image of what a man and a woman should be like, and for the woman, the cultural ideal is almost always focused on motherhood. People who do not have children are generally considered selfish and maladjusted, a harsh judgment from society.[3]

The influence of social pressures becomes most obvious when a shift in fertility trends occurs. In the United States, for example, there have been dramatic changes over the last few decades in the number of children per family. In the aftermath of World War II, women were encouraged to have large families, and the birth rate rose sharply. Then, in the late 1960s and early 1970s, fertility dropped steadily. Childlessness became more acceptable, and small families were preferred. In the 1980s, the pressures seem to have gone in the opposite direction once again. Children of the postwar baby boom are now having children, and the result is a rise in the number of babies being born and a great deal of public attention to pregnancy and childbirth.[4]

These changes are responses to the economic and political climate of the time, not simply the accumulation of millions of individual decisions. We all like to think that such important decisions as whether or not to have children and how many to have are made by ourselves, independently. Yet our behavior, consciously or unconsciously, is often strongly influenced by prevailing social trends.

The pressures to have children affect not only married couples. A growing number of single women are turning to technological means of conception because of their desire to have children.[5]

The demands of others also affect those who already have one child. If having no children is selfish, having one and denying him or her the chance to have siblings is said to be cruel. "Only children" are stereotyped as spoiled and maladjusted, despite considerable evidence to the contrary. In fact, a study by sociologist Nancy Russo found that the plan to have one child is almost as unpopular among Americans as the goal of having none. This attitude makes the frequent situation of secondary infertility even more difficult for people who are trying so hard to have another child.[6]

Why should it be necessary to pressure people to have children? If the notion were true that children bring the ultimate fulfillment (especially for women), then no one would need encouragement. But having children can be a very risky business.

National surveys all agree that couples without children are happier with their marriages than those who do have children. Satisfaction with marriage starts to drop shortly after the first child arrives, increasing again only after the last child leaves home.[7]

Women, paradoxically, suffer the most from having children. Mothers are more likely to be depressed than nonmothers. And women who, without children, are equal to their husbands in almost every way in their marriage, quickly discover that the arrival of a child sharply reduces their power in marital decision making. Even women who continue working outside of the home lose power as they become defined as primary caretaker and homemaker.[8]

Of course there is another very different reality — that children can be wonderful, that parenting can be the most satisfying experience in one's life. Having children is neither pure heaven nor total hell but some combination of both. The vast majority of people keep their eyes fixed on the positive, the beautiful, and take the risk. They count on the miracle of new life and the love that children bring. They cannot imagine going through life without them.

It is understandable why many people like Gail who cannot have children are so desperate. They have failed to fulfill their own desires, their expectations of what their lives would be like. They have also failed to fulfill the powerful mandate of society, but not by any choice of their own. And they feel the stigma attached to anyone who deviates from the most central norms of society. It is no wonder some people are willing to undergo enormous stress and risk to become parents.[9]

Why Not Adopt?

If the goal were primarily to be parents, it should not matter so much where the children come from. Gail told us she is asked by some of her friends, "Why not just adopt?"

> *They don't seem to understand why, for me, adoption is still a last resort. It just is not the same as having a biological child.*

The social norm is not only to be a parent; it is to be a biological parent. We are urged to create new life, to perpetuate the species.

Most of the people who responded to our questionnaires and interviews indicated that they had indeed considered adoption or were already on a waiting list. The fact remains, however, that almost all of them (including some who had already adopted one child) were still pursuing other alternatives. Why don't they give up on trying to conceive, especially after repeated failures? Why do they reject adoption or turn to it only as a last resort?

Adoption is risky and difficult. Waiting lists for healthy infants are long. The costs are exorbitant. Adoption agency caseworkers ask many personal questions, make judgments, and have excessive control over one's life. Some people simply are not eligible. These are the reasons people gave us for not wanting to pursue adoption.

But infertility procedures are often described in exactly the same terms. Programs are impersonal; waiting for results is unbearable. Failure rates are high, and costs are prohibitive for many. Even so, most people prefer to try infertility treatments, with all their problems, rather than face the difficulties of adoption. There is one very basic reason for this choice: Most people want a biological child.

All those who filled out our questionnaire and said they had rejected adoption as an alternative cited the desire for a biological child as the reason. Those who try the reproductive alternatives go through all of the trouble and stress not only to be parents, but to create their "own" children.[10]

Becoming parents is very closely tied, in the minds of many, to the proper functioning of their bodies. A man sees a biological child as proof of his virility. For a woman, a biological child means being able to experience pregnancy, birth, and breast-feeding. For both, the inability to produce a child is a threat to their sexual identity.

For many people, genes are the key issue. As Bill said:

> Gail is really smart and pretty, and I feel good about myself. It would be neat to see our qualities passed on to a child. And we worry about how healthy or intelligent an adopted child would be. At least with our own, we think we'd have a pretty good idea of what we'd be getting.

Some people worry about the effects of adoption on children, especially foreign-born or biracial children. Having "one's own" seems so much less complicated. It is certainly more acceptable to the world around us.

A child is the most visible demonstration of a couple's love for each other, a miraculous creation that comes out of the intimate union of two people. One woman expressed her regret at losing this possibility:

> The hardest part of all of this has been dealing with the idea of our love-making not producing a little part of ourselves, melted together. I still miss my husband's smile or his eyes in our adopted son, although I love him dearly.

Men usually appear to be the driving force behind the preference for a biological child. Many women told us they would be happy to adopt, but that their husbands wanted a genetic connection. The men agreed. Why the difference?

Genes are the biggest contribution men make to the creation of a child. They cannot carry, birth, or nurse a baby. In addition, they are rarely the major caregiver. Women can "mother" in many ways. Many men, especially those who have not yet experienced the daily caring and loving that fathering can entail, focus on the biological connection.

Gail explained her husband's reluctance to adopt:

> *Bill thought he would feel more comfortable with a child that was ours biologically. He says he just couldn't accept an adopted child on his own.*

Men may also be more concerned with carrying on the family name and heritage. One man who learned he was infertile explained:

> *The hardest part was telling my father. I felt like I had failed him. I had broken the chain, the idea of continuity from the past to the future which still seems so important in some primitive part of ourselves.*

When adoption was easier, it may have been a more acceptable solution. In any case, it was often the only alternative to childlessness. Today, the situation is dramatically different. People keep trying to have biological children not only because they want them and not only because of social pressures, but also because infertility specialists are promising new alternatives. It has become increasingly difficult for infertile people to say no to this new set of pressures.

The Pressure to Keep Trying

An individual's desire to keep trying to have a baby is powerfully reinforced from the outside—from media accounts of miracle babies, from acquaintances who have been successful, and from friends who encourage one to try a new method they have heard about. One woman told us she felt overly pressured by optimistic news reports:

> *If I see one more article or book that says "You can have a baby," or "New hope for childless couples," I think I'll scream. Sure it's good for the public to know, but the message seems to be that if you just try hard enough or go to the right doctor you're sure to get pregnant. I wish it were so easy!*

The most direct pressure, and the hardest for many to resist, comes from physicians. Almost everyone we surveyed who attempted conception through AIH or AID (artificial insemination with a donor's sperm) cited a doctor's recommendation as the reason. The choice of IVF (in vitro fertilization) was explained as "our last hope," "our only choice," a message that is strongly reinforced by the medical community.

A staff member of an IVF program described the pressure to try alternatives:

> *More and more it has become a matter of "all roads lead to in vitro." More and more physicians around the country are saying to couples, "Well, there's always IVF."*

People who do decide to try a new method are usually very persistent, very driven to succeed.[11] They are people, like Gail, who feel compelled to keep going:

> *For someone who doesn't gamble and hates the idea of getting on a roller coaster, it was quite an effort to decide to try IVF. But at the same time, I found the idea of quitting most frightening. It was as if all the tests, operations, and medication through the years would have been for nothing. I just could not face the idea of failure.*

Gail is accurate in describing her decision as a gamble, a high-risk venture into the unknown. Gamblers make pacts with themselves (pacts that are often broken) about how much longer they will try to win or how much more money they will spend on each game. Infertile people do the same. They often "hedge their bets" by getting onto adoption lists while trying to conceive. They promise themselves that they will try just "one more time," or "one more year," or until the money runs out.

Every new technique creates new options and new pressures, added possibilities, increased risks. It is hard to decide whether it is worth all of the risks one has to take to pursue another alternative. Is it worth the problems of having a child who is biologically related to only one parent? Is it worth the money? Is it worth the personal stress and physical pain? And most of all, is it worth taking the risk of failing once again?

Many people, despite all of the pressures, eventually decide they have had enough. It is not worth it to them to keep trying, to keep hurting and hoping. They discover that their lives can be fulfilling in ways other than parenting, or that adopted children bring them every joy they had hoped for.

Others decide it is worth the risks, the trouble, the stresses of the treatment. Their commitment to having a biological child compels them to go on, overshadowing other goals. Not being able to have children makes them so unhappy that some are willing to try anything that might help. Theirs is a grief that is often overwhelming, a sense of loss that only success, it seems, can erase.

ENDNOTES

1. Lesley Brown and John Brown, with Sue Freeman, *Our Miracle Called Louise: A Parents' Story* (New York and London: Paddington Press, 1979).
2. Edward O. Wilson, *Sociobiology: The New Synthesis* (Cambridge: Harvard University Press, 1975); Jessie Bernard, *The Future of Motherhood* (New York: Penguin, 1974);

Diana Burgwyn, *Marriage without Children* (New York: Harper and Row, 1981); Betty Friedan, *The Feminine Mystique: Twentieth Anniversary Edition* (New York: Norton, 1983); Ellen Peck and Judith Senderowitz, eds., *Pronatalism; The Myth of Mom and Apple Pie* (New York: Thomas Y. Crowell, 1974); J. Richard Udry, "The Effect of Normative Pressures on Fertility," *Population and Environment: Behavioral and Social Issues* 5 (Summer 1982): 109–22; Jean Veevers, "Voluntary Childlessness: A Review of Issues and Evidence," *Marriage and Family Review* 2 (1979): 1–26.

3. P. H. Jamison, Louis R. Franzini, and Robert M. Kaplan, "Some Assumed Characteristics of Voluntary Childfree Women and Men," *Psychology of Women Quarterly* 4 (1979): 266–73; Marcia Ory, "The Decision to Parent or Not: Normative and Structural Components," *Journal of Marriage and the Family* 40 (August 1978): 531–39.

4. Charles Westoff, "Fertility in the United States," *Science*, October 31, 1986, 554–59.

5. Judy Klemesrud, "Single Mothers by Choice: Perils and Joys," *New York Times*, May 2, 1983, 35; Maureen McGuire and Nancy Alexander, "Artificial Insemination of Single Women," *Fertility and Sterility* 43 (February 1985): 182–84.

6. Nancy Felipe Russo, "The Motherhood Mandate," *Journal of Social Issues* 32 (1976): 143–53.

7. Norval D. Glenn, "Psychological Well-Being in the Post-Parental Stage: Some Evidence from National Surveys," *Journal of Marriage and the Family* 37 (February 1975): 105–10; Norval Glenn and Sara McLanahan, "Children and Marital Happiness: A Further Specification of the Relationship," *Journal of Marriage and the Family* 44 (February 1982): 63–72; Sharon Houseknecht, "Childlessness and Marital Adjustment," *Journal of Marriage and the Family* 41 (May 1979): 259–65; Richard Lerner and Spanier Graham, eds., *Child Influences on Marital and Family Interaction* (New York: Academic Press, 1978).

8. Elaine Hilberman Carmen, N. F. Russo, and J. B. Miller, "Inequality and Women's Mental Health: An Overview," *American Journal of Psychiatry* 138 (October 1981): 1319–30; Walter Gove and M. Hughes, "Possible Causes of the Apparent Sex Difference in Physical Health," *American Sociological Review* 44 (1979): 126–46; Walter Gove and J. F. Tudor, "Adult Sex Roles and Mental Illness," *American Journal of Sociology* 78 (1973): 50–73; Holly Waldron and Donald Routh, "The Effect of the First Child on the Marital Relationship," *Journal of Marriage and the Family* 43 (November 1981): 785–88.

9. Erving Goffman, *Stigma* (Englewood Cliffs, NJ: Prentice Hall, 1963); Charlene Miall, "The Stigma of Involuntary Childlessness," *Social Problems* 33 (1986): 268–82; Jean Veevers, "The Violation of Fertility Mores: Voluntary Childlessness as Deviant Behavior," in Craig Boydell, Craig F. Grindstaff, and Paul C. Whitehead, eds., *Deviant Behavior and Societal Reaction* (New York: Holt, Rinehart and Winston, 1973).

10. Edmond J. Farris and Mortimer Garrison, "Emotional Impact of Successful Donor Insemination," *Obstetrics and Gynecology* 3 (1954): 19–20.

11. Jeannette E. Given, G. S. Jones, and D. L. McMillen, "A Comparison of Personality Characteristics between In Vitro Fertilization Patients and Other Infertile Patients," *Journal of In Vitro Fertilization and Embryo Transfer* 2 (1985): 49–54.

18

SINGLE–PARENT FAMILIES

STEPHEN D. SUGARMAN

What do the former First Lady Jackie Kennedy, the chief prosecutor in the O. J. Simpson case, Marcia Clark, the pop star Madonna, and the TV character Murphy Brown have in common? They all are, or at one time were, single mothers—unmarried women caring for their minor children. This chapter concerns public policy and the single-parent family, a family type dominated by single mothers.

Because these four women are fitting subjects for *Lifestyles of the Rich and Famous,* they are a far cry from what most people have in mind when the phrase "single mother" is used. Many picture, say, a nineteen-year-old high school dropout living on welfare in public housing. Hence, just mentioning these four prominent women vividly demonstrates the diversity of single mothers. These four also illustrate the major categories of single mothers—the widowed mother, the divorced or separated mother, and the single woman who bears her child outside of marriage. (Women in this last category are often misleadingly called "never married" even though approximately one-fourth of the women who are unmarried at the birth of their child had been married at an earlier time.[1])

One further distinction should also be made here. The usual picture of the single mother is of a woman living *alone* with her children—Jackie Kennedy, Marcia Clark, and Murphy Brown. But those we call "cohabitants" are also single mothers as a legal matter, even though their children are living in two-adult households. Indeed, where the woman is cohabiting with the father of her child—Madonna—while the mother is single, from the child's perspective it is an intact family.

As with single mothers generally, these four prominent women arouse a wide range of feelings, from support to dismay, in the public at large. Jackie Kennedy surely gained the maximum empathy of our foursome when her husband was murdered in her presence. Even those women who are widowed in less horrifying ways have long been viewed as victims of cruel fate and strongly deserving of community compassion.

Not too long ago, having been divorced was by itself thought to disqualify those seeking public office or other positions of public prominence.

That no longer holds, as Ronald Reagan's presidency made clear. As a result, when the spotlight of fame first shined on Marcia Clark, she probably appeared to most Americans as one of many of today's divorced professional women who had the challenging task of having to balance the pursuit of her career with raising a child on her own. The grueling pressures of prosecuting her most notorious case and her subsequent publicly revealed squabbles with her former husband did, however, bring to the fore our society's general uneasiness about how well children fare in these settings, as well as our uncertainty about the appropriate roles of divorced fathers as providers of both cash and care.

In Sweden today, Madonna's family structure is commonplace. There, a very large number of men and women live together and have children together, but do not go through the formalities of marriage. Lately, in America as well, the cohabitation category, long ignored by the census, is rapidly growing. This is not to say that most Americans, unlike the Swedes, accept cohabitation as though it were marriage. Indeed, American public policy, as we will see, treats cohabitation very differently from marriage.

Perhaps because Murphy Brown is a fictional character, this has allowed those who are on the rampage against unmarried women who bear children to be candid about their feelings without having to be so openly nasty to a "real" person. Yet Murphy Brown is an awkward icon. To be sure, she flouted the conventional morality of an earlier era. She had sex outside of marriage and then decided to keep and raise her child once she discovered she had unintentionally become pregnant. Although many people in our society still rail against sex other than between married couples, sex outside of marriage has become such a widespread phenomenon that it is generally no longer a stigma. And while it would be easy to chastise Murphy Brown for carelessly getting pregnant, this also is so commonplace that it is barely remarkable any more. Indeed, Murphy Brown might have come in for more censure had she, as a single woman, deliberately become pregnant.

As for deciding to raise her child on her own, this *by itself* no longer arouses great public outcry. After all, it is not as though widowed mothers who make that decision are castigated for choosing not to remarry. As for the unmarried birth mother, shotgun weddings are seen to be less promising than they once were; abortion, while still a right, is hardly thought to be a duty; and while giving a child up for adoption is often commendable, today this is seen primarily as the route for women who do not want to, or cannot afford to, take care of their children themselves.

In short, the strongest objection by those who have assailed Murphy Brown is that she is a bad role model—in particular, that she is a bad role model for *poor* women who, unlike her, cannot provide for their children on their own, but go ahead and have them anyway, planning to turn to the state for financial and other assistance. In many quarters those single mothers are doubly condemned. First, they are seen to be prying money out of the rest of us by trading on our natural sympathy for their innocent children; yet this is said to leave taxpayers both unhappy because they have less money to spend on their own children and with the distasteful feeling that society is condoning, even promoting, the initial irresponsible and self-indulgent behavior by these poor single mothers. Then, these low-income women are rebuked as high-frequency failures as parents—for example, when their children disproportionately drop out of, or are disruptive at, school or turn to criminal behavior. Of course, not everyone disapproves of Murphy Brown or even those poor women who choose to have children on their own knowing that they will have to turn to the state for financial assistance. Many people believe that every American woman (at least if she is emotionally fit) ought to be able to be a mother if she wants to be.

These various types of single mothers are significant because they raise different issues, and, in turn, they have yielded very different policy solutions and proposals for reform. But before we turn to policy questions, some general demographic information is presented that, among other things, shows single-parent families to differ significantly from some common myths about them. The policy discussion that follows begins with a historical overview that demonstrates how American policies have changed sharply through the century. . . . The chapter concludes with a call to refocus public attention on the needs of the children in single-parent families.

Single–Parent Family Demographics: Myths and Realities

Father-Headed Single-Parent Families

In the first place, not all single-parent families are headed by women. In 1970, three-quarters of a million children living in single-parent families lived with their father (10 percent of such families); by 1992, more than two million children lived in father-headed single-parent families (an increase to 14 percent).[2]

These families are not the subject of much policy attention, however. First, most of them are headed by divorced (or separated) men; a few are widowers. It is rare, however, that the father of a child born outside of marriage will gain physical control of that child, and this takes custodial fathers largely outside the most controversial category of single parents. Furthermore, single fathers caring for their children tend to be financially self-supporting and therefore generally beyond the purview of welfare reformers. Finally, they tend to remarry fairly quickly and hence remain heads of single-parent families for only a short time. In fact, the main public policy controversy involving these men today concerns divorce custody law—in what circumstances should fathers be able to become heads of single-parent families in the first place?

Noncustodial fathers are quite another matter—whether divorced from or never married to the mothers of their children. As we will see, they are the subject of a great deal of public attention and concern.

Unmarried as Compared to Divorced and Widowed

Turning back to families headed by single mothers, one myth is that they are predominantly women who have never been married to the father of their child. Yet there are actually more divorced (and separated) single mothers. For example, in 1992, 60 percent of single mothers were divorced or separated, and another 5 percent were widowed.[3] Moreover, because of the predominance of widowed and divorced mothers, large numbers of women become single mothers, not at their child's birth, but later on in their child's life, often not until the child is a teenager. Hence, among the children in single-parent families, living one's entire childhood apart from one's father is by no means the norm.

Cohabitants

Cohabitants with children in their household are a complicated category, and, in turn, they complicate the data.[4] As noted earlier, although the women in these families are decidedly single mothers in a legal sense, in many respects these couples resemble married couples. So, many of these households are better described as two-parent, not single-parent, families. Some demographers have recently suggested that "cohabitation operates primarily as a precursor or a transitional stage to marriage among whites, but more as an alternative form of marriage among blacks."[5]

In any case, these cohabiting households come in several varieties. One first thinks of two biological parents not married to each other but living with their child — as exemplified by Madonna and the father of her child and the Swedish model. Cohabiting mothers in this situation still often show up in U.S. surveys as though they were never-married mothers living on their own, because survey instruments tend to categorize respondents only as married or single.

A second variety of cohabiting households includes a single mother with her child who is now living with, but not married to, a man who is *not* the child's father. These women are drawn out of the ranks of the never married, the divorced, and the widowed; they, too, are frequently counted in surveys as living on their own. Moreover, in this second category especially, it is often unclear to outsiders whether the man is a de facto spouse and stepparent, a casual boyfriend, or something in between.

Yet a third category of cohabiting households contains a homosexual couple (more often two women) in which one of the partners is the legal (usually biological) parent and the other is formally a stranger (although some lesbian couples of late have successfully become dual mothers through adoption).

Working and Not

Although the myth is that single mothers (especially never-married welfare moms) spend their time lounging around the house, watching TV, doing

drugs, and/or entertaining men, this is a wild exaggeration. A large proportion is in the paid labor force. Official data from 1993 show that about two-
thirds of *all* women with children are in the labor force. Married women's
rates are about 60 percent where the youngest child is under six and about
75 percent where the youngest child is six or older. Within the ranks of single mothers, divorced women work *more* than married women, whereas never-
married women are less likely to *report* working.[6]

Single mothers often feel compelled to work full time even when their
children are very young, although the official data again show a difference
between divorced and never-married women. According to 1993 figures, of
those women with a child under age six, 51 percent of divorced women and
26 percent of never-married women worked *full time,* on average this was
slightly higher than the rate for married women, 38 percent of whom were
working full time.[7]

Although fewer than 10 percent of single mothers who are receiving welfare officially acknowledge earning wages,[8] recent research by Kathryn Edin
suggests that, in fact, a high proportion of them is actually employed at least
part time.[9] They tend to work for cash in the underground (and sometimes
illegal) economy. According to Edin's findings, they do not typically do so to
be able to buy drugs or booze but, rather, in order to keep their households
from utter destitution or to avoid having to live in intolerably dangerous public housing projects. They keep this work a secret from the welfare authorities because if the authorities knew they would so cut back those women's
welfare benefits to make their wages from work nearly meaningless. Although
these women would be viewed by the welfare system as "cheaters," they
tend to remain living in fairly impoverished circumstances. As Edin puts it,
they feel compelled to break the law by the skimpiness of the welfare benefits they receive.

Poor and Nonpoor

Even with the receipt of government assistance, more than a third of family
households headed by single mothers officially live below the poverty level
(as compared with only 6.5 percent of families headed by a married couple).[10]
Although this is a distressingly high number, to the extent that the myth is
that single mothers are poor and on welfare, the myth is false. A substantial
share of single mothers provides a reasonable level of material goods for their
children, and more than half of all single mothers are not on welfare. In 1992,
for example, about 44 percent of female-headed households with related children under age eighteen received means-tested cash assistance.[11]

Those who escape poverty for their families tend to do so primarily
through earnings and secondarily through child support and government
benefits (or through a combination of these sources)—although typically not
by receiving welfare. In 1992, *nonpoor* single mothers received about 80 percent of their income from earnings, 8 percent from child support and alimony,
and 7 percent from Social Security, pensions, unemployment compensation

and the like, and only just over 3 percent from welfare, food stamps, and housing assistance.[12] This is because nowhere in America today does welfare alone bring a family even close to the poverty level, and, as noted already, the rules governing welfare tend to reduce the amount of the welfare payment by nearly all the money the mother obtains from other sources. It is not surprising, then, that, in 1992, the poverty rate for single-parent families with children under age eighteen was 48.2 percent before the receipt of means-tested cash transfers and 45.2 percent after their receipt, a relatively modest reduction indeed. (Noncash benefits have a greater impact, reducing the rate to less than 40 percent.)[13] A different, and often more promising, route out of poverty for single mothers and their children is through marriage and thereby into a new family structure.

White and Nonwhite

The myth is that single mothers primarily come from racial and ethnic minorities. While it is true that these groups are disproportionately represented given their share of the population, in fact, these days more single mothers are white than any other group. For example, in 1993, 60 percent of nonmarital births were to whites and 36 percent to blacks.[14] On a cumulative basis, as of 1992 there were 5.8 million white, mother-headed family groups (including white Hispanics) as compared with three million black, mother-headed family groups (including black Hispanics) — even though 58 percent of all black family groups were headed by mothers and only 26 percent of all white family groups were headed by mothers.[15]

Change over Time

The demography of single parenting has changed a lot over the course of this century. There are many more single parents today than there were several generations ago, both in absolute numbers and, more importantly, in terms of the percentage of all children (or all parents) affected.

In 1900, the typical single parent was a widow. Male deaths through industrial and railway accidents were very visible. By contrast, divorce was then scarce (although desertion was a problem). And becoming a single mother by becoming pregnant outside of marriage was not very common, especially because so many who got pregnant promptly married the father.[16] Now, especially since the 1960s, all that is changed. Divorce is more frequent. "Illegitimacy" and cohabitation are also more prevalent than in earlier periods. For example, of women born between 1940 and 1944, only 3 percent had lived with a partner of the opposite sex by age twenty-five; of those born between 1960 and 1964, 37 percent had done so.[17] Moreover, the stigma of bearing a child outside of marriage and/or what some still call "living in sin" is much reduced.

Nonetheless, along with these changing characteristics of the single-parent family has come a change in public empathy. Earlier there was very widespread compassion for single parents and their children when single parents were mainly widows and divorcees, especially in the pre-no-fault era, when divorce usually was triggered (formally at least) by the misbehavior of the husband. Today, at least in some quarters, single mothers are loathed — those receiving welfare who have borne their children outside of marriage or who are suspected of bringing about the end of their marriages through their own selfishness. Currently, slightly more than half of those receiving welfare have had children outside of marriage as compared with but a trivial share in the 1930s and less than 30 percent as late as 1969.[18]

Changing Policies toward Single Parents

Widows

In 1909, President Theodore Roosevelt convened a historic first White House Conference on Children, which identified the poverty of widowed mothers and their children as a central policy problem. Then, if states and localities provided any assistance at all, it was too often through the squalid conditions of the "poor house" into which single-parent families might move — something of a counterpart to today's shelters for homeless families. The poor house itself was the successor to an earlier system in which desperate mothers farmed their children out to others, in effect providing young servants to those people who took these semiorphaned children into their homes, farms, and businesses. Reflecting the outlook of the social work profession that was then just getting under way, the White House Conference pushed instead for the adoption of Mothers' Pensions plans. Soon enacted, at least on paper, in most of the states, this new approach envisaged cash payments to single (primarily widowed) mothers who were certified by social workers as capable of providing decent parenting in their own homes if they only had a little more money in their pockets.[19]

Mothers' Pensions, the precursor to Aid to Families with Dependent Children (AFDC), reflected both the psychological perspective that it was best for the children to be raised in their own homes and the sociological outlook that it was appropriate for the mothers to stay at home and raise them (perhaps taking in other families' laundry or sewing, but not leaving their children to join the regular paid labor force).[20] As we will see, this benign attitude toward the payment of public assistance to single parents, which was reinforced by the adoption of AFDC in 1935 at the urging of President Franklin D. Roosevelt and maintained at least through the 1960s, is now rapidly disappearing.

Divorcees

Much earlier in the century, while widows were pitied, marital breakup was broadly frowned upon. Nonetheless, it was increasingly acknowledged that some spouses acted in intolerable ways and should be censured by allowing their spouses to divorce them. Adultery, spousal abuse, and desertion were the main categories of unacceptable marital conduct, and most of it seemed to be engaged in by husbands. As the decades rolled by, however, the divorce law requirement of severe wrongdoing by one spouse and innocence on the part of the complaining spouse soon ill-fit the attitudes of many couples themselves. Especially starting after World War II, and accelerating in the 1960s, many more couples came to realize that their marriages had simply broken down and they both wanted out. Until divorce law changed to reflect this new outlook, couples were prompted to engage in fraudulent charades (often involving the husband pretending to engage in adultery) so as to satisfy domestic relations law judges.

No-fault divorce law first emerged in California in 1970 and was rapidly followed by other states.[21] As a practical matter, not only did this reform allow couples amicably to obtain a divorce without having either one of them adjudicated as the wrongdoer but also, in most states, it permitted any dissatisfied spouse to terminate the marriage unilaterally. Whether no-fault divorce actually caused an increase in the divorce rate or merely coincided with (indeed, grew out of) the spiraling demand for divorce is unclear.[22] What is clear, however, is that divorce rates today are enormously greater than they were before 1970, thereby contributing to the great increase in single parenting.[23] As we will see, that state of affairs, in turn, has recently generated something of a backlash movement, one that seeks to reintroduce legal barriers to divorce in families with minor children.

Illegitimacy

Public policies toward illegitimacy (and, in turn, toward both abortion and teen pregnancy) have also changed significantly during this century. At an earlier time, children born outside of marriage were pejoratively labeled "bastards" and denied inheritance and other rights connected to their fathers, although their biological fathers did generally have the legal duty to support them.[24] If a single woman became pregnant, a standard solution was to promptly marry the child's father, perhaps pretending that the pregnancy arose during marriage after all. Adoption was available to some, who would be encouraged to go away before their pregnancies began to "show," only to return childless afterward as though nothing had happened. Pursuing an abortion instead then risked criminal punishment and subjected the woman to grave risks to her life and health.

Rather suddenly, a little more than two-thirds of the way through this century, policies in these areas turned around dramatically. For those who wanted it, abortion became legal. More important for our purposes, remaining unmarried and then keeping a child born out-of-wedlock became much more acceptable. For example, instead of expelling pregnant teens, schools adopted special programs for them. Fewer women gave up their newborns for adoption—for example, 19 percent of white, unmarried birth mothers did so in the 1960s, but only 3 percent did so in the 1980s.[25] The courts forced states to give many legal rights to illegitimates that had previously been enjoyed only by legitimates;[26] and many legislatures voluntarily expanded the inheritance rights and other entitlements of out-of-wedlock children. Soon, unmarried pregnant women far less often married the biological father during the course of the pregnancy—a drop of from 52 percent to 27 percent between 1960 and 1980.[27]

Women who had children outside of marriage were no longer casually labeled unsuitable mothers and, as noted previously, soon became the largest category of single mothers receiving welfare. In terms of public acceptability, something of a high-water mark may have been reached in the early 1970s with the conversion of welfare into a "right" by the federal courts, the elimination of welfare's "suitable home" requirement, and the end to one year waiting periods for newcomers seeking welfare.[28] This ignited an explosion of the welfare rolls,[29] and for the first time in many states, African American women gained reasonably secure access to benefits. At that time, Republican President Richard Nixon proposed turning AFDC from a complex state-federal program into a uniform national scheme.

[Near the end of the century, however, a policy backlash emerged.] Between 1967 and 1997, the proportion of African American children born outside of marriage skyrocketed from around 25 percent to nearly 70 percent; and the rate for white children is conceivably poised for a similar trajectory — and in any case has grown from 8 percent thirty years ago to around 25 percent today.[30] Now, curbing illegitimacy, or at least unmarried teen pregnancy, seems to be near the top of many politicians' lists. An indicator of how fast things have changed was Democratic President Bill Clinton's call to "end welfare as we know it" during his 1992 election campaign.

Child Support

It has been long understood that fathers have a moral obligation to provide for the financial support of their minor children. In the absent-parent context, this means paying "child support." For most of the century, however, a substantial proportion of men failed to pay the support they might have paid.[31] The default rate by divorced fathers has long been very high, and in out-of-wedlock births the father's paternity often was not even legally determined. (Stepfathers with no legal duties were frequently a more reliable source of support.) Moreover, in many states, even if noncustodial fathers paid all they owed, this was judged to be a pittance when compared with the child's reasonable needs. Deceased fathers were no more reliable, frequently dying with estates of trivial value and without life insurance.

Through the 1930s, AFDC and its predecessors were the main public response to these failures — providing means-tested cash benefits to poor children (and their mothers) deprived of the support of a breadwinner. In 1939, however, special privileged treatment was afforded widows and their children. The Social Security system was expanded so that, upon the death of the working father, "survivor" benefits would be paid to the children and their caretaker mother based upon the father's past wages.[32] This, in effect, created publicly funded life insurance for most widows and their children, with the result that today hardly any widowed mothers find it necessary to apply for welfare.

No comparable "child support insurance" was provided, however, so that divorced and never-married poor mothers have had to continue to turn to the socially less favored means-tested welfare programs instead of Social Security. On behalf of these families, the effort, much enlarged since the mid-1970s, has been to increase the amount of child support an absent father owes and to beef up child support enforcement efforts.[33] Notwithstanding those reforms, it is still estimated that more than five billion dollars of child support annually goes uncollected, and many custodial mothers are unable to collect any support for their children.[34]

Cohabitation

It appears that American society generally is becoming more accepting of cohabitation, even if it remains frowned upon in many circles. (Clearly, same-sex cohabitation continues to be highly controversial.) So far as public policy is concerned, however, marriage still makes a significant difference. For example, when children are involved and the cohabitants split up, the woman who keeps the children (as is typically the case) continues to be disadvantaged as compared with the woman who had married. Although she is entitled to support for her child, only in very special circumstances can she gain financial support for herself from her former partner. So, too, upon the death of her partner who was the father of her children, while her children can claim Social Security benefits, she does not qualify for the caretaker Social Security benefits that a legal widow would have obtained.[35] On the other hand, if she cohabits with a man who is not the father of her children, a mother and her children have been able to qualify for welfare; by contrast, were she married (or cohabiting with the father of her children), it has been extremely unlikely for them to obtain welfare. . . .

Refocusing the Policy Perspective

When it comes to single-parent families, much of our current policy focus is on parents: whether they divorce, whether they pay child support, whether they have children outside of marriage, whether they work, and so on. Suppose instead that policy attention was aimed at the *children* in single-parent families. For example, as we have seen, if a child's breadwinner parent dies, the government ordinarily assures that child far better financial security than it does if that child's breadwinner parent is simply absent from the home:

Social Security steps in to satisfy the deceased parent's obligation to have provided life insurance but not the absent parent's duty to provide child support.

Comparable treatment for the latter group implies some sort of publicly funded "child support insurance" scheme. Plans of this sort (including those that would expand Social Security in exactly this way) have in fact been proposed in recent years, most notably by Irwin Garfinkel, although so far at least they have not won widespread endorsement.[36] This sort of scheme could assure all children living in single-parent families with equal financial support—say, up to the poverty level. Or, like Social Security and private child support obligations, the benefits could be related to the absent parent's past wages. In either case, unlike the rules that have governed AFDC, earnings by the custodial parent could supplement rather than replace the child support benefit.

Such a plan could be financed by general revenues or Social Security payroll taxes. But it might also be funded, at least in substantial part, by absent parents, thereby making the plan one that guarantees that a suitable level of child support will actually be provided and makes up the shortfall when the collection effort fails. Were this second approach adopted, not only should it dramatically reduce our sense of the cost of the plan, but also it should offset any tendency that the plan might otherwise have to increase divorce.

It is important to emphasize that a plan like this would much improve the lot of both many children who in the past have been dependent on AFDC and large numbers of children with working-class and even middle-class mothers whose absent fathers now default on their child support obligations. It must be conceded, however, that in view of the direction of recent welfare reform, the prospects at the moment are not favorable for any new initiative to provide cash for children in single-parent families.

A different child-centered approach, therefore, is to try to assure all children with essential goods by means other than providing cash. Ought not all American youths live in decent housing, obtain a quality education, receive adequate food, have access to decent health care, and so on? This is not the place to detail the many alternative mechanisms by which these critical items might be delivered. What needs emphasizing, however, is that any program guaranteeing these sorts of things to all children would vastly disproportionately benefit children now living in single-parent families. Moreover, if we can keep the focus on the needy and innocent members of the next generation, perhaps we can escape ideological battles over the worthiness of these children's parents. This is possibly a naive hope, but one that may be enhanced when the thing delivered to the child's family is other than money: witness the greater public and legislative popularity of the federal food stamps program and federal aid to elementary and secondary education as compared with the now-decimated federal welfare program.

The many policy reforms discussed here are unlikely to have large impacts on people like Jackie Kennedy, Marcia Clark, Madonna, and Murphy Brown. But ordinary single mothers (and their children) who are in analogous situations have a great deal at stake.

ENDNOTES

1. Dore Hollander, "Nonmarital Childbearing in the United States: A Government Report," *Family Planning Perspectives* 28(1):30, 1996.
2. *Current Population Reports* P20, No. 468, "Marital Status and Living Arrangements," 1992:xii, Table G.
3. *Current Population Reports* P-20, No. 467, "Household and Family Characteristics," 1992(March):xiv.
4. Larry L. Bumpass and R. Kelly Raley, "Redefining Single-Parent Families: Cohabitation and Changing Family Reality," *Demography* 32(1):97, 1995.
5. Wendy D. Manning and Pamela J. Smock, "Why Marry? Race and the Transition to Marriage among Cohabitors," *Demography* 32(4):509, 1995. See also Ronald R. Rindfuss and Audrey Vandenheuvel, "Cohabitation: A Precursor to Marriage or an Alternative to Being Single?" *Population and Development Review* 16:703, 1990.
6. Committee on Ways and Means, U.S. House of Representatives, Overview of Entitlement Programs, 1994 Green Book (hereafter 1994 Green Book), Table 12-2, 534.
7. 1994 Green Book, Table 12-4, 536.
8. In 1992, for example, just over 2 percent of single mothers on AFDC reported working full time and another 4 percent reported working part time. Another 12 percent were said to be seeking work. 1994 Green Book, Table 10-28, 404.
9. More specifically, Edin found that about 15 percent were working full time (typically under another name) and many others were working part time. Kathryn Edin and Christopher Jencks, "Reforming Welfare," in Christopher Jencks, *Rethinking Social Policy: Race, Poverty and the Underclass*. Cambridge: Harvard University Press, 1992, 204–35.
10. *Current Population Reports* P-60, No. 188, "Income, Poverty and Valuation of Non-Cash Benefits," 1993:xvi, Table C.
11. *Current Population Reports* P-60, No. 185, "Poverty in the U.S.," 1992:xviii, Table F.
12. 1994 Green Book, Table G-32, 1144–45.
13. 1994 Green Book, Table H-12, 1174.
14. Hollander, "Nonmarital Childbearing," 29.
15. *Current Population Reports* P-20, No. 467, "Household and Family Characteristics." March 1992, xiv, Table F.
16. Mary Ann Mason, *Father's Property to Children's Rights*, New York: Columbia University Press, 1994, 11–16.
17. Hollander, "Nonmarital Childbearing," 30.
18. 1994 Green Book, Table 10-29, 401.
19. Winifred Bell, *Aid to Dependent Children*, New York: Columbia University Press, 1965.
20. Committee on Economic Security. Social Security in America, The Factual Background of the Social Security Act as Summarized from Staff Reports to the Committee on Economic Security, 1937.
21. Herma Hill Kay, "Beyond No-fault: New Directions in Divorce Reform," in Stephen Sugarman and Herma Hill Kay (eds), *Divorce Reform at the Crossroads*, New Haven: Yale University Press, 1990, 6–36.
22. H. Elizabeth Peters, "Marriage and Divorce: Information Constraints and Private Contracting," *American Economic Review* 76:437, 1986; Gary S. Becker, *A Treatise on the Family*, Cambridge: Harvard University Press, 1981, 228–29.
23. Centers for Disease Control and Prevention, National Center for Health Statistics, "Monthly Vital Statistics Report," 44(4), 1995.
24. Ira Mark Ellman, Paul M. Kurtz, and Katharine T. Bartlett, *Family Law: Cases, Text, Problems*, 2d ed., Charlottesville: Michie Law Publishers, 1991, 881–912.
25. Hollander, "Nonmarital Childbearing," 31.
26. Levy v. Louisiana, 391 U.S. 68 (1968); Weber v. Aetna Cas. & Sur. Co., 406 U.S. 164 (1972).

27. Hollander, "Nonmarital Childbearing," 31.
28. Goldberg v. Kelly, 397 U.S. 254 (1970); King v. Smith, 392 U.S. 309 (1968); and Shapiro v. Thompson, 394 U.S. 618 (1969).
29. 1994 Green Book, Table 10-1, 325.
30. Charles Murray, "The Coming White Underclass," *Wall Street Journal*, Oct. 29, 1993, A14.
31. David L. Chambers, *Making Fathers Pay: The Enforcement of Child Support*, Chicago: University of Chicago Press, 1979.
32. Stephen D. Sugarman, "Children's Benefits in Social Security," *Cornell Law Review* 65:836–908, 1980.
33. 1994 Green Book, 455–530.
34. 1994 Green Book, Table 11-4, 463.
35. This rule was unsuccessfully challenged in Boles v. Califano, 443 U.S. 282 (1979).
36. Irwin Garfinkel, *Assuring Child Support*, New York: Russell Sage Foundation, 1992; Stephen D. Sugarman, "Reforming Welfare Through Social Security," *University of Michigan Journal of Law Reform* 26:817–51, 1993; Stephen D. Sugarman, "Financial Support of Children and the End of Welfare as We Know It," *Virginia Law Review* 81:2523–73, 1995.

CHILDREN AND CHILDHOOD

19

CHILDREN'S SHARE IN HOUSEHOLD TASKS

FRANCES K. GOLDSCHEIDER • LINDA J. WAITE

Children growing up in America learn early that the home is not a very egalitarian place, far less even than the world of work. The roles of males and females in the home differ sharply. Although most mothers are working, like fathers, it is mothers who are primarily responsible for running the household, with few fathers taking more than a secondary role. Further, the tasks children do are still rigidly divided by gender in most families, with girls doing different and *more* tasks around the house than boys.

Sex typing of children's household tasks begins very early, so sharp differences have crystalized by adolescence. Girls tend to spend about twice as much time on housework as their brothers, mirroring the different levels of contribution by their mothers and fathers (Thrall 1978; White and Brinkerhoff 1981). However, their schools have relatively gender-free curricula (at least in theory) and they have working-mother role models, so most girls are being prepared for adult roles both in the workplace and in the home. In contrast, boys in most families receive almost no preparation for competence in any aspect of making a home.

It is often the case, however, that neither boys nor girls gain much experience doing household tasks, because in many families their mothers do almost all of them. As men's productive efforts were being withdrawn from the home with the growth of new urban, industrial jobs, children were also increasingly diverted from home tasks by a new definition of childhood that emphasized the importance of preparation for adult roles only in the workplace, not in the home. The old view that children should help their parents (and eventually support them in their old age) has given way to an expectation that parents must exert themselves to the utmost to ensure that their children grow up to be successes. As a result, the ideal American child has been transformed from a "useful child" to a "useless child" (Zelizer 1985). Few children would agree that their childhoods totally fit this new stereotype, thinking of the many onerous and resented tasks that diverted them from play; in fact, children do almost as much household work as their fathers. But young people learn early that claiming heavy school assignments will nearly always serve as an adequate excuse for the room uncleaned or the lawn unmowed. What has happened?

Children's Work in the Household

When mothers and fathers are asked *why* they expect their children to share some responsibility for household tasks, they give a variety of reasons, revealing the strong ambivalence parents in the United States feel about children's role in the household economy. Most parents respond that performing household work builds character and develops a sense of responsibility. Only a few report that they require the child's labor in running the house, and even fewer indicate that they view "chores" as a way to prepare the child for the performance of household tasks they will need as adults—learning to cook, do laundry, and clean up one's room—and this answer is most often given by families with daughters. Another minority response, most commonly given in large families, is that parents want children to feel they have a responsibility to participate in the work of the household enterprise. (Of course, since more than a third of parents *pay* children for work around the house, they are really reinforcing a view that such work is optional.)

Our premise in this study is that the experiences children have in childhood and early adulthood are extremely important for the families they later form. And it is clear that the experiences children have even in relatively modern families reinforce a traditional division of labor in the next generation. If children, particularly boys, have little experience with the tasks associated with maintaining a home, it is difficult to expect them to feel comfortable taking them on as adults.

This is a critical area for our understanding of future family trends: Will egalitarian roles be achieved only through a complete abandonment of family-centered activities, or can men and women achieve a redefined and more egalitarian combination of work and family life? However, systematic research on children's roles in the family that would help us understand how children are being prepared for future family roles is even more dramatically lacking than it is for men. For example, although we have learned in the last decade or so that married men are increasing their contribution to domestic tasks, we have no direct evidence for trends in the extent to which children have participated in household tasks, or trends in the proportions of boys and girls performing these tasks. There have been studies showing that youths growing up on farms have numerous duties that often require substantial numbers of hours (Light, Hertsgaard, and Martin 1985). We have also learned that families in urban areas depend less on their children's labor than those in more rural areas (Lawrence, Tasker, and Babcock 1983; Straus 1962). These findings imply that as families became increasingly urbanized and as fewer grew up on farms, children were involved less in family tasks. But we do not know how much change is really involved or which children have participated most in it. And it has now been decades—even generations—since urban life came to dominate American society.

What is happening to the roles of children in homemaking? Under what circumstances, if any, are children more involved in household tasks and in which families are children's tasks becoming more egalitarian? Have *parents'* experiences of nontraditional family forms in childhood and young adulthood influenced the way they share with their own children? And are divorce and remarriage changing the involvement of children in household tasks? To answer these questions, we will examine how much, and under what circumstances, children share in household work, taking into consideration the nature and amount of work needed to be done and the parents' attitudes and values, particularly those resulting from experience with nontraditional families in their own lives.

Measuring Children's Share
in the Division of Household Labor

The women included in the National Longitudinal Studies (NLS) of Young Women and Mature Women answered a series of questions about a variety of household chores, including cooking, cleaning, laundry, child care, dishes, yard work, grocery shopping, and paperwork. From the answers to these questions, we created a detailed scale of how much responsibility children took for seven of these tasks. (Children's share of family paperwork is not included.) In brief, the scale takes on a higher value the more tasks children do and the more responsibility they take for them, from a value of zero if children do no tasks at all to a high of 28 if children do all tasks completely by themselves.

In order to interpret the answers women gave, we translate them into percentage terms. So the range of answers (0–4) given for each task can be interpreted to mean that women who said that children did not share in a given task share none of that task with children; women who said their children shared "some but less than half" share about 25 percent; women who said they shared "about half" a task with children share 50 percent of that task with their children; and so on.

In our analysis, we consider only families with at least one child between the ages of six and eighteen, although they could have younger and older children, too.

How Much Do These Children Share?

Children take relatively little responsibility for most household tasks, although the list of tasks we consider includes some that are often shared with children as well as some that are virtually never shared. Overall (averaging children's sharing across the set of seven tasks), children contribute a relatively small proportion of total household labor — 15 percent; but their share is quite substantial for some tasks. Mothers report that their children take a good deal of responsibility for washing dishes and for cleaning the house, taking more than a quarter of the responsibility for these tasks (and more than their fathers do). Equally clearly, most families do not give children any responsibility for paperwork, or much responsibility for grocery shopping or child care. Laundry, cooking, and yard work fall in between, with children doing 12 to 15 percent of these tasks. Thus, children's participation in household tasks depends very much on *which* task.

Which Children Share?

The NLS questions on household labor allow a woman to report that her children share some responsibility for various household tasks, but they do not provide information on which of her children are actually sharing in these tasks. So two women could report identically that children have sole responsibility for the dishes and for the yard, but in one family, one of the children always does the dishes and the other always cuts the grass, and in the other family, the two children share equally in both tasks. The questions do not allow us to distinguish easily between these two women and their children.

But we want to know whether there are differences in the involvement of children, between younger and older children, and particularly between boys and girls. Previous research and common sense suggest that the age and composition of the children in the household will affect whether a woman shares tasks with any of her offspring.

These distinctions—male/female, preteen/teen—seem straightforward. However, the role of children who have reached adulthood in household tasks is less obvious. On one hand, they are adults and might be expected to take an adult's share of responsibilities. On the other hand, simply by reaching this age, the common justification for sharing—as a mechanism for character development—becomes inappropriate. Further, to the extent that grown children spend more time at work than they did at school, they are less available for household chores. Many parents may continue to feel responsibility for investing their own time (and money) in their child's future as long as he or she remains at home. They may reason that in early adulthood, even more than during high school, a social life is necessary to get married and starting careers is stressful; as a result, they may be unwilling to make demands on their grown children for help. So we need to examine sharing tasks with children in families with children of different ages and sexes, even adult "children."

What we found is that even though we cannot know exactly which children are actually sharing a given task with the mother, the pattern of sharing duties in families is responsive to both the number and type of children present. The more children in the family the more the mother reports sharing housework with children as a group. This is sensible, since the more potential workers there are the more likely some of them will be to pitch in.

The children's age and gender also influence the amount of task sharing, sometimes very clearly, sometimes not so clearly. Considering the younger children (under twelve), there are few differences among families that have only preteen children. It doesn't matter whether all children are ages six to eleven or whether some are younger. Based on our results that husbands share more tasks when there are toddlers in the household than when there are only older children, we had expected that the presence of very young children might increase sharing with older children. Babies and toddlers require extra work, and harassed mothers might press their older children into service (since each family in our analysis has at least one child between the ages of six and eighteen in the household).

Since it is families with children ages four to six who share tasks least of all, we infer that older children are helping a little with the toddlers, help that is not as necessary for somewhat older children. But the differences are small, in part because the level of sharing with children is low across all families that only have children in these ages.

As children get older, they clearly become more involved in household chores, indoors and outdoors. Families with teenage children share substantially more housework with their children than families with only preteens. Teenage children are most particularly helpful with yard work, with about equal amounts of task sharing from teenage boys and girls. But the biggest differences by age and sex are in "female" chores.

Families with teenage girls report sharing *five times more* of these other tasks with children than do families with boys of the same age. In fact, girls ages twelve to eighteen seem to carry the largest share of housework of all children. Mothers with a daughter age twelve to eighteen delegate essentially three-quarters of an entire task (most of the laundry, say, or most of the dishes) compared to mothers with children ages six to eleven. Although teenage girls do more of all household tasks (except paperwork) than their younger brothers and sisters, they seem to contribute especially large amounts toward doing dishes and cleaning the house, and to share substantially in cooking and laundry. Their teenage brothers, in contrast, share more than younger siblings overall, but only because they do significantly more yard work.

Turning to adult sons and daughters, girls seem to continue their contributions to the household economy as they reach young adulthood, sharing only slightly less after age eighteen than before. Older daughters shift their contributions to grocery shopping, child care, and laundry and away from dishes and cleaning, and they drop their share of yard work substantially. However, young adult males may contribute no more to housework than do preteen children, and substantially less than their sisters of the same age. In fact, grown sons do significantly less cooking and child care than children six to twelve years old. It is not that these young men contribute financially to the family, since most evidence suggests that adult children living at home keep their earnings (Goldscheider and Goldscheider 1988). Hence, grown sons are being subsidized by their parents both financially and in terms of household services, since although they certainly eat and require clean clothes, they rarely contribute to the performance of these tasks; yet someone has to provide these services to them. Unless grown daughters contribute even less of their earnings to the family than grown sons, staying at home after age eighteen seems to provide much less benefit for daughters than for sons. While sons provide virtually no help in housework (even in yard and home maintenance), daughters continue to contribute at a very high level after age eighteen.

These basic results show that families raising children in the early 1980s shared household tasks with them in very traditional ways, giving older children more responsibility than younger ones, girls more than boys, and dividing tasks up so that what are considered female adult tasks are shared with daughters and what are considered male adult tasks are primarily shared with sons. But what factors influence this division by gender? Are there any that increase young males' sharing in the central tasks involved in making a home?

New Family Experiences and Sharing with Children

Children perform sex-traditional tasks, learning to do—and to like—the tasks usually assigned to adults of their gender. Boys mostly help around the house by cutting the lawn or doing repairs, while watching their sisters cook meals and clean the house. This childhood socialization helps to reproduce the sex segregation of household labor found among husbands and wives. The family is a "gender factory," (Berk 1985) serving as a focal point where the importance—especially the symbolic importance—of the division of labor between the sexes is most strongly reinforced.

But for many families, "reproducing" the parental division of labor is not possible, since the traditional parental structure does not exist. The rise in divorce, together with the increase in out-of-wedlock parenthood, means that unmarried women are increasingly heading families with children. How might this influence the children's role in household tasks?

Women who head families alone face enormous pressures with relatively few resources. In many ways, they are the new "farms" in which the labor of children is once again a dire necessity. These families lack two elements generally available in married-couple families: the earning capacity and labor power of an adult male. So female-headed families tend to have much lower incomes than do families headed by married couples. Moreover, women who head families show higher rates of labor force participation than do married women, because these unmarried women are almost always responsible for their own support and that of their children (U.S. Bureau of the Census 1989). Families headed by unmarried women, then, have both less money and less of the mother's time at home than do families headed by couples; they are in effect squeezed in both directions. Under these circumstances, families may feel more need to turn to the labor power of the children, both in the home and in the market (Greif 1985; Sanik and Mauldin 1986; Tilly and Scott 1978).

The family's need for the children's contribution suggests that women who head families alone will share more tasks with children. In fact, many such mothers say they cannot function without the children's labor (Peters and Haldeman 1987). But this reasoning does not tell us *which* children will take on extra tasks. Perhaps teenage or young adult males take over only the household duties of the absent male head, increasing sharing in such traditionally male tasks as yard work, leaving girls to take over traditionally female tasks such as cooking, cleaning, and child care. This could lead to more task sharing in female-headed families, but no change in the traditional allocation of tasks between boys and girls. However, boys are the obvious candidates for extra responsibilities, even those normally done by females, since the household duties of the absent male head are usually not very onerous, and even in two-parent families, girls do much more work than boys. This situation provides the potential for a less-traditional allocation of household tasks among children in mother-only rather than in married-couple families.

If mother-only families are more egalitarian, it is also likely that children who spend some time in such a situation may become socialized to greater sharing and to exchanging tasks between the sexes. Even if their mother remarries, the recent experience that the mother and children had as a single-parent family may affect their division of household labor in the new blended family. The effect might extend even further, into the next generation of the children of divorce. Those who spend at least part of their childhood in a female-headed household may have received different training and social-ization in the levels and nature of children's participation in household tasks. If female-headed families share more with children than do married-couple families, as we expect, then those raised in such families may transfer this pattern of greater participation by children to their own families. This effect should appear regardless of the structure of the current family.

Mother-Only Families

Children who live in a mother-only family play a key role in the household economy: they share more overall and they share more in every single task. Comparing the children's share of household responsibilities in intact fami-lies and in mother-only families shows that children in mother-only families take nearly twice as much responsibility for household tasks as those in stan-dard nuclear (nonblended) families.

Children are drawn into the pool of family labor far more intensively in mother-only families than in any other type of family. This effect takes into account differences in the mother's hours of employment and family income, and so goes beyond the obvious stress that these two "shortages" tend to put on mother-only families. Clearly, children are central to the family economy in these households in a way that they are not in other families, and as a result, they are likely to feel needed and more responsible. Weiss (1979) spec-ulates that single parents develop a very different relationship with their children than do married couples, essentially forming partnerships in which children share responsibility with the parent for decision making and for getting tasks done.

Do all children do much more housework in mother-only than in intact families, or does the burden fall disproportionately on some? We find that both sons and daughters are drawn into more household chores in mother-only as compared to married couple families. Figure 1 shows that boys in mother-only families—both teenagers and young adults—take *much* more respon-sibility for housework than do sons in otherwise comparable families headed by two parents. Teenage boys only contribute more than younger children if they live in mother-only families.

We considered the argument that this increased participation results only from the greater involvement of these young men in traditionally male tasks, so that in some sense sons take over the chores that were the province of the absent father. This is the case, but it is not the whole story. Although teenage boys do about twice as much yard work and home maintenance in families headed by their mother only than they do in two-parent families, they also do more grocery shopping, more cooking, and more cleaning if they live with their unmarried mother (and the same result applies to dishes, child care, and paperwork). Similarly, young adult sons share more in every household task except yard work.

What about daughters in mother-only families? We find that teenage girls take more responsibility for housework when they live with a single mother

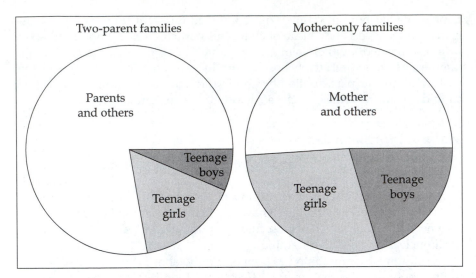

FIGURE 1   Effect of Living in a Mother-Only Family on Sharing Housework with Teenage Sons and Daughters

than they do in two-parent families. But the difference between the amount of housework done by children in mother-only and two-parent families is actually larger for teenage boys than for teenage girls, perhaps because girls do so much in all families, whereas boys in two-parent families do very little. As with boys, girls share significantly more of nearly every task when they live in a family headed by their mother alone than if they live with two parents. Indeed, teenage boys in mother-only families share considerably more housework than do teenage girls in two-parent families.

We found another surprise in our results: Adult daughters are the workhorses in mother-only families. These young women take twice as much responsibility for housework as do girls their age in two-parent families, including more of every household task but laundry and yard work. Mother-only families with young adult daughters allocate more to children by assigning complete responsibility for entire tasks—for example, dishes and cooking.

These results show very clearly that mothers heading families do not maintain the traditional segregation of household tasks by sex. Daughters in these families participate much more than girls the same age living with two parents, including greater participation in the two traditionally male tasks in our scale, yard work and paperwork. But these mothers also incorporate teenage boys into virtually all traditionally female household tasks, whereas boys participate very little in families headed by married couples.

Stepparent Families

Children who live with their mother and a stepfather take a greater role in household chores than do children who live with both their biological parents, primarily because they wash more dishes and do more child care. However, the differences between stepparent families and other two-parent families are much less than between mother-only and never-disrupted families.

Evidently, the increased involvement the children are likely to have experienced before the remarriage does not carry over very much in the new family constellation; perhaps the stepfather takes over many of their chores. It is likely that part of the difference between the effects of mother-only and stepparent families reflects the fact that most children in these stepparent families experienced a shorter period in a mother-only family and at a much younger age. Data that allow a detailed breakdown of when and how long children were exposed to a mother-only family are needed to see how much of the experience carries over into stepparent families.

We also examined whether the pattern of increased participation in household tasks by boys, established while they were living in a mother-only household, carried over into remarriage. We saw that children in general share more in such households than those living with their biological parents. It turns out that this is a general pattern, with few differences by age and sex of children. Not only do stepfathers create "Cinderellas," they seem to increase the household contribution of stepsons as well so that both are involved in the "extra" work. Stepdaughters are significantly more likely to take responsibility for child care, paralleling the finding that stepfathers seem less likely to share in the care of small children, even those likely to be theirs. This results in part because their stepdaughters are helping out more. Boys between the ages of twelve and eighteen share more in household tasks than younger children in stepfamilies, as they did in mother-only families; boys with two natural parents do not assume significantly more responsibility when they reach their teens.

The few stepchildren who remain in the household after they become adults, in contrast, do not help out much at all. Unlike adult daughters in mother-only families, otherwise comparable stepdaughters are particularly unlikely to participate in cooking, dishwashing, or shopping for groceries. This pattern also characterizes young adult stepsons, who pitched in when their family was headed only by their mother, but who are very unlikely to share in many tasks—particularly laundry, dishwashing, or household cleaning—when a stepfather is present.

Comparing these three types of families suggests very strongly that the composition of the household has a considerable influence on the exposure of children, and particularly of sons, to household tasks. It may be that women generally try to establish some feeling of teamwork in their approach to housework, but that they generally "team" with a spouse, when one is available. Perhaps women only feel that it is legitimate to divert children from schoolwork to take responsibility for housework when they *feel* they have no one else to turn to. What is clear at this point is that the current period of family disruption, characterized as it is by high proportions of children living at least for some period in mother-only families, is contributing strongly to household competence in men.

REFERENCES

Berk, Sarah Fenstermaker. 1985. *The Gender Factory.* New York: Plenum.

Goldscheider, Calvin and Frances K. Goldscheider. 1988. "The Intergenerational Flow of Income: Family Structure and the Status of Black Americans." Paper presented at the annual meetings of the Population Association of America, New Orleans.

Greif, Geoffrey L. 1985. "Children and Housework in the Single Father Family." *Family Relations* 34(3):353–57.

Lawrence, Frances Cogle, Grace E. Tasker, and Deborah K. Babcock. 1983. "Time Spent in Housework by Urban Adolescents." *Home Economics Research Journal* 12(2): 199–205.

Light, Harriet K., Doris Hertsgaard, and Ruth E. Martin. 1985. "Farm Children's Work in the Family." *Adolescence* 20(78):425–32.

Peters, Jeanne M. and Virginia A. Haldeman. 1987. "Time Used for Household Work." *Journal of Family Issues* 8(2):212–25.

Sanik, Margaret Mietus and Teresa Mauldin. 1986. "Single Versus Two-Parent Families: A Comparison of Mothers' Time." *Family Relations* 35(1):53–56.

Straus, Murray A. 1962. "Work Roles and Financial Responsibility in the Socialization of Farm, Fringe, and Town Boys." *Rural Sociology* 27(3):257–74.

Thrall, Charles A. 1978. "Who Does What: Role Stereotype, Children's Work, and Continuity Between Generations in the Household Division of Labor." *Human Relations* 31(3):249–65.

Tilly, Louise and Joan Scott. 1978. *Women, Work, and Family.* New York: Holt, Rinehart & Winston.

U.S. Bureau of the Census. 1989. "Money Income of Households, Families, and Persons in the United States: 1987." *Current Population Reports*, Series P-60, no. 162. Washington: U.S. Government Printing Office.

Weiss, Robert S. 1979. "Growing Up a Little Faster: The Experience of Growing Up in a Single-Parent Household." *Journal of Social Issues* 35(4):97–111.

White, Lynn K. and David B. Brinkerhoff. 1981. "The Sexual Division of Labor: Evidence from Childhood." *Social Forces* 60(1):170–81.

Zelizer, Viviana. 1985. *Pricing the Priceless Child: The Changing Social Value of Children.* New York: Basic Books.

20

LIFE–SPAN ADJUSTMENT OF CHILDREN TO THEIR PARENTS' DIVORCE

PAUL R. AMATO

C hildren have always faced the threat of family disruption. In the past, death was more likely to disrupt families than was divorce. Around the turn of the century in the United States, about 25 percent of children experienced the death of a parent before age 15, compared with 7 percent or 8 percent who experienced parental divorce.[1] As a result of the increase in longevity, the proportion of dependent children who lost a parent through death decreased during this century; currently, only about 5 percent of children are so affected. But the divorce rate increased over this same period, and at current rates, between two-fifths and two-thirds of all recent first marriages will end in divorce or separation.[2] The high rate of marital dissolution means that about 40 percent of children will experience a parental divorce prior to the age of 16.[3] Although a substantial risk of family disruption has always been present, today it is much more likely to be caused by divorce than by death.

Americans traditionally have believed that a two-parent family is necessary for the successful socialization and development of children. Consequently, it was assumed that parental death leads to many problems for children, such as delinquency, depression, and even suicide in later life — assumptions that appeared to be confirmed by early research.[4]

More recent studies indicate that, although parental death disadvantages children, the long-term consequences are not as severe as people once believed.[5] Nevertheless, many social scientists assumed that children who "lost" a parent through divorce experienced serious problems similar to those experienced by children who lost a parent through death. Furthermore, whereas the death of a parent is usually unintended and unavoidable, marital dissolution is freely chosen by at least one parent. Consequently, the question of the impact of divorce on children took on moral overtones. These concerns, combined with the dramatic increase in the rate of divorce during the last few decades, resulted in a proliferation of studies on the effects of divorce on children.

Paul R. Amato, "Life-Span Adjustment of Children to Their Parents' Divorce" from *The Future of Children*, Vol. 4, Spring 1994. © 1994 by the David & Lucille Packard Foundation. Reprinted by permission of the David & Lucille Packard Foundation.

This research literature does not always lead to firm conclusions. Many gaps exist in our knowledge, and weaknesses in study methodology mean that many findings are tentative at best. Nevertheless, a consensus is beginning to emerge among social scientists about the consequences of divorce for children. And, in spite of its limitations, this knowledge can help to inform policies designed to improve the well-being of children involved in parental marital dissolution. . . .

How Do Children of Divorce Differ from Other Children?

Those who delve into the published literature on this topic may experience some frustration, as the results vary a good deal from study to study. Many studies show that children of divorce have more problems than do children in continuously intact two-parent families.[6] But other studies show no difference,[7] and a few show that children in divorced families are better off in certain respects than children in two-parent families.[8] This inconsistency results from the fact that studies vary in their sampling strategies, choice of what outcomes to measure, methods of obtaining information, and techniques for analyzing data.

A technique known as *meta-analysis* was recently developed to deal with this situation.[9] In a meta-analysis, the results of individual studies are expressed in terms of an "effect size" which summarizes the differences between children in divorced and intact groups on each outcome. Because these effect sizes are expressed in a common unit of measure, it is possible to combine them across all studies to determine whether significant effects exist for each topic being reviewed. It is also possible to examine how design features of studies, such as the nature of the sample, might affect the conclusions.

In 1991, Amato and Keith pooled the results for 92 studies that involved more than 13,000 children ranging from preschool to college age.[10] This meta-analysis confirmed that children in divorced families, on average, experience more problems and have a lower level of well-being than do children in continuously intact two-parent families. These problems include lower academic achievement, more behavioral problems, poorer psychological adjustment, more negative self-concepts, more social difficulties, and more problematic relationships with both mothers and fathers.

To determine if there are also differences in adjustment when children of divorce grow into adulthood, Amato and Keith carried out a second meta-analysis of 37 studies in which they examined adult children of divorce.[11] These results, based on pooled data from 80,000 adults, suggest that parental divorce has a detrimental impact on the life course. Compared with those raised in intact two-parent families, adults who experienced a parental divorce had lower psychological well-being, more behavioral problems, less education, lower job status, a lower standard of living, lower marital satisfaction, a heightened risk of divorce, a heightened risk of being a single parent, and poorer physical health.

The view that children adapt readily to divorce and show no lingering negative consequences is clearly inconsistent with the cumulative research in this area. However, several qualifications temper the seriousness of this conclusion. First, the average differences between children from divorced and continuously intact families are small rather than large. This fact suggests that divorce is not as severe a stressor for children as are other things that can go wrong during childhood. For example, a recent meta-analysis of studies dealing with childhood sexual abuse revealed average effect sizes three to four times larger than those based on studies of children of divorce.[12] Second, although children of divorce differ, on average, from children in continuously intact two-parent families, there is a great deal of overlap between the two groups.

. . .

This diversity helps us to understand why the *average* effects of divorce are relatively weak. Divorce may represent a severe stressor for some children, resulting in substantial impairment and decline in well-being. But for other children, divorce may be relatively inconsequential. And some children may show improvements following divorce. In other words, to inquire about the effects of divorce, as if all children were affected similarly, is to ask the wrong question. A better question would be "Under what conditions is divorce harmful or beneficial to children?" This point is returned to below.

Variations by Gender of Child

Some researchers are interested in measuring differences in adjustment between children of divorce and children in intact families based on such variables as gender, ethnicity, age, and cohort membership in attempts to identify groups that may respond differently to divorce. Summarized below are the major findings with regard to the relationship between these variables and adjustment.

Several early influential studies found that boys in divorced families had more adjustment problems than did girls.[6] Because these studies have been widely cited, many have come to accept this finding as incontrovertible. Given that boys usually live with their mothers following family disruption, the loss of contact with the same-sex parent could account for such a difference. In addition, boys, compared with girls, may be exposed to more conflict, receive less support from parents and others (because they are believed to be tougher), and be picked on more by custodial mothers (because they resemble their fathers). Other observers have suggested that boys may be more psychologically vulnerable than girls to a range of stressors, including divorce.[13] However, a number of other studies have failed to find a gender difference in children's reactions to divorce,[8,14] and some studies have found that girls have more problems than do boys.[15]

Amato and Keith tried to clarify this issue in their meta-analytic studies by pooling the results from all studies that reported data for males and females separately.[10,11] For children, the literature reveals one major gender difference: The estimated negative effects of divorce on social adjustment are stronger for boys than for girls. Social adjustment includes measures of popularity, loneliness, and cooperativeness. In other areas, however, such as academic achievement, conduct, or psychological adjustment, no differences between boys and girls are apparent. Why a difference in social adjustment, in particular, should occur is unclear. Girls may be more socially skilled than boys, and this may make them less susceptible to any disruptive effects of divorce. Alternatively, the increased aggressiveness of boys from divorced families may make their social relationships especially problematic, at least in the short term.[16] Nevertheless, the meta-analysis suggests that boys do not always suffer more detrimental consequences of divorce than do girls.

The meta-analysis for adults also revealed minimal sex differences, with one exception: Although both men and women from divorced families obtain less education than do those from continuously intact two-parent families, this difference is larger for women than for men. The reason for the greater vulnerability of women is somewhat unclear. One possibility is that noncustodial fathers are less likely to finance the higher education of daughters than sons.

Variations by Ethnicity of Child

There is a scant amount of research on how divorce affects nonwhite children of divorce. For example, because relatively little research has focused on this population, Amato and Keith were unable to reach any conclusions about ethnic differences in children's reactions to divorce.[10] The lack of information on how divorce affects nonwhite children is a serious omission in this research literature.

With regard to African American children, some research has suggested that academic deficits associated with living with a single mother are not as pronounced for black children as for white children.[17]

In relation to adults, Amato and Keith show that African Americans are affected less by parental divorce than are whites. For example, the gap in socioeconomic attainment between adults from divorced and nondivorced families of origin is greater among whites than among African Americans. This difference may have to do with the fact that divorce is more common, and perhaps more accepted, among African Americans than among whites. Also, because extended kin relations tend to be particularly strong among African Americans, single African American mothers may receive more support from their extended families than do single white mothers.[18] Alternatively, given the large number of structural barriers that inhibit the attainment of African Americans, growing up in a divorced single-parent family may result in relatively little additional disadvantage.

We need additional research on divorce in different racial and ethnic groups, including African Americans, Asian Americans, Hispanics, and Native Americans. In addition to the adjustment of children of divorce, we need information on relationships between children and custodial and noncustodial parents, the role of extended kin in providing support, and, in general, how culture moderates the impact of marital dissolution on children.

Variations by Age of Child

Some of the best descriptions of how divorce affects children of different ages come from the work of Wallerstein and Kelly, who conducted detailed interviews with children and parents.[19] Although their sample appears to have overrepresented parents who had a difficult time adjusting to divorce, many of their conclusions about age differences have been supported by later studies. Observation of children during the first year after parental separation showed that preschool age children lack the cognitive sophistication to understand the meaning of divorce. Consequently, they react to the departure of one parent with a great deal of confusion. Because they do not understand what is happening, many become fearful. For example, a child may wonder, "Now that one parent is gone, what is to stop the other parent from leaving also?" Young children also tend to be egocentric, that is, they see themselves at the center of the world. This leads some children to blame themselves for their parents' divorce. For example, they may think, "Daddy left because I was bad." Regression to earlier stages of behavior is also common among very young children.

Children of primary school age have greater cognitive maturity and can more accurately grasp the meaning of divorce. However, their understanding of what divorce entails may lead them to grieve for the loss of the family as it was, and feelings of sadness and depression are common. Some children see the divorce as a personal rejection. However, because egocentrism decreases with age, many are able to place the blame elsewhere—usually on a parent. Consequently, older children in this age group may feel a great deal of anger toward one, or sometimes both, parents.

Adolescents are more peer-oriented and less dependent on the family than are younger children. For this reason, they may be impacted less directly by the divorce. However, adolescents may still feel a considerable degree of anger toward one or both parents. In addition, adolescents are concerned about their own intimate relationships. The divorce of their parents may lead adolescents to question their own ability to maintain a long-term relationship with a partner.

The work of Wallerstein and Kelly suggests that children at every age are affected by divorce, although the nature of their reactions differs. But are these reactions more disturbing for one group than for another? Wallerstein and Kelly found that preschool children were the most distressed in the period following parental separation. However, 10 years later, the children of preschool age appeared to have adjusted better than children who were older at the time of family disruption.[20]

Many other studies have examined age at the time of divorce to see if it is associated with children's problems. However, these studies have yielded mixed and often inconsistent results, and the meta-analyses of children and adults were unable to cast much light on these issues.[21] A common problem in many data sets is that age at divorce and time since divorce are confounded. In other words, for a group of children of the same age, the younger they were at the time of divorce, the more time that has elapsed. But if we examine children whose parents all divorced at about the same time, then the more time that has passed, the older children are at the time of the study. Similarly, if we hold constant the age of the child at the time of divorce, then length of time and current age are perfectly correlated. In other words, it is impossible to separate the effects of age at divorce, length of time since divorce, and current age. Given this problem, it is not surprising that research findings are unclear. Nevertheless, it is safe to say that divorce has the potential to impact negatively on children of all ages.

Year of Study

One additional noteworthy finding that emerged from the meta-analyses by Amato and Keith concerns the year in which the study was conducted. These researchers found that older studies tended to yield larger differences between children from divorced and intact families than studies carried out more recently. This tendency was observed in studies of children (in relation to measures of academic achievement and conduct) and in studies of adults (in relation to measures of psychological adjustment, separation and divorce, material quality of life, and occupational quality). The difference persisted when the fact that more recent studies are more methodologically sophisticated than earlier studies was taken into account.

This finding suggests that more recent cohorts of children are showing less severe effects of divorce than earlier cohorts. Two explanations are worth considering. First, as divorce has become more common, attitudes toward divorce have become more accepting, so children probably feel less stigmatized. Similarly, the increasing number of divorces makes it easier for children to obtain support from others in similar circumstances. Second, because the legal and social barriers to marital dissolution were stronger in the past, couples who obtained a divorce several decades ago probably had more serious problems and experienced more conflict prior to separation than do some divorcing couples today. Furthermore, divorces were probably more acrimonious before the introduction of no-fault divorce. Thus, children of divorce in the past may have been exposed to more dysfunctional family environments and higher levels of conflict than were more recent cohorts of children.

Why Does Divorce Lower Children's Well–Being?

Available research clearly shows an association between parental divorce and children's well-being. However, the causal mechanisms responsible for this association are just beginning to be understood. Most explanations refer to the absence of the noncustodial parent, the adjustment of the custodial parent, interparental conflict, economic hardship, and life stress. Variations in these factors may explain why divorce affects some children more adversely than others.

Parental Absence

According to this view, divorce affects children negatively to the extent that it results in a loss of time, assistance, and affection provided by the noncustodial parent. Mothers and fathers are both considered potentially important resources for children. Both can serve as sources of practical assistance, emotional support, protection, guidance, and supervision. Divorce usually brings about the departure of one parent—typically the father—from the child's household. Over time, the quantity and quality of contact between children and noncustodial parents often decreases, and this is believed to result in lower levels of adjustment for these children as compared with children from intact families.[22]

The parental-absence explanation is supported by several lines of research. For example, some studies show that children who experience the death of a parent exhibit problems similar to those of children who "lose" a parent through divorce.[23] These findings are consistent with the notion that the absence of a parent *for any reason* is problematic for children. Also consistent with a parental absence perspective are studies showing that children who have another adult (such as a grandparent or other relative) to fill some of the functions of the absent parent have fewer problems than do children who have no substitute for the absent parent.[24] In addition, although the results of studies in the area of access to the noncustodial parent and adjustment are mixed,[25] in general, studies show that a close relationship with both parents is associated with positive adjustment after divorce. One circumstance in which high levels of access may not produce positive adjustment in children is in high-conflict divorces. When conflict between parents is marked, frequent contact with the noncustodial parent may do more harm than good.[26]

Custodial Parental Adjustment and Parenting Skills

According to this view, divorce affects children negatively to the extent that it interferes with the custodial parents' psychological health and ability to parent effectively. Following divorce, custodial parents often exhibit symptoms of depression and anxiety. Lowered emotional well-being, in turn, is likely to impair single parents' child-rearing behaviors. Hetherington and colleagues found that, during the first year following separation, custodial parents were less affectionate toward their children, made fewer maturity demands, supervised them less, were more punitive, and were less consistent in dispensing discipline.[27]

Research provides clear support for this perspective. Almost all studies show that children are better adjusted when the custodial parent is in good mental health[28] and displays good child-rearing skills.[29] In particular, children are better off when custodial parents are affectionate, provide adequate supervision, exercise a moderate degree of control, provide explanations for rules, avoid harsh discipline, and are consistent in dispensing punishment. Also consistent with a parental adjustment perspective are studies showing that, when custodial parents have a good deal of social support, their children have fewer difficulties.

Interparental Conflict

A third explanation for the effects of divorce on children focuses on the role of conflict between parents. A home marked by high levels of discord represents a problematic environment for children's socialization and development. Witnessing overt conflict is a direct stressor for children. Furthermore, parents who argue heatedly or resort to physical violence indirectly teach children that fighting is an appropriate method for resolving differences. As such, children in high-conflict families may not have opportunities to learn alternative ways to manage disagreements, such as negotiating and reaching compromises. Failure to acquire these social skills may interfere with children's ability to form and maintain friendships. Not surprisingly, numerous studies show that children living in high-conflict two-parent families are at increased risk for a variety of problems.[30] It seems likely, therefore, that many of the problems observed among children of divorce are actually caused by the conflict between parents that precedes and accompanies marital dissolution.

Studies show that children in high-conflict intact families are no better off — and often are worse off — than children in divorced single-parent families.[31] Indeed, children in single-parent families may show improvements in well-being following divorce if it represents an escape from an aversive and dysfunctional family environment. Furthermore, a study by Cherlin and colleagues shows that many, but not all, of the difficulties exhibited by children of divorce, such as behavioral problems and low academic test scores, are present *prior* to parental separation, especially for boys.[32] This finding is consistent with the notion that the lowered well-being of children is partly attributable to the conflict that precedes divorce. In addition, conflict may increase around the time of the separation, and parents often continue to fight long after the divorce is final. Indeed, many studies show that children's adjustment is related to the level of conflict between parents following divorce.[33] It should be noted here that postdivorce adjustment may also be influenced by residual effects of conflict that occurred during the marriage.

Economic Hardship

Divorce typically results in a severe decline in standard of living for most custodial mothers and their children.[34] Economic hardship increases the risk of psychological and behavioral problems among children[35] and may negatively affect their nutrition and health.[36] Economic hardship also makes it difficult for custodial mothers to provide books, educational toys, home computers, and other resources that can facilitate children's academic attainment. Furthermore, economically pressed parents often move to neighborhoods where schools are poorly financed, crime rates are high, and services are inadequate.[37] Living under these circumstances may facilitate the entry of adolescents into delinquent subcultures. According to this view, divorce affects children negatively to the extent that it results in economic hardship.

Studies show that children's outcomes—especially measures of academic achievement—are related to the level of household income following divorce. For example, Guidubaldi and colleagues found that children in divorced families scored significantly lower than children in intact two-parent families on 27 out of 34 outcomes; taking income differences into account statistically reduced the number of significant differences to only 13.[38] Similarly, McLanahan found that income accounted for about half of the association between living in a single-parent family and high school completion for white students.[39] However, most studies show that, even when families are equated in terms of income, children of divorce continue to experience an increased risk of problems. This suggests that economic disadvantage, although important, is not the sole explanation for divorce effects.

Life Stress

Each of the factors noted above—loss of contact with the noncustodial parent, impaired child rearing by the custodial parent, conflict between parents, and a decline in standard of living—represents a stressor for children. In addition, divorce often sets into motion other events that may be stressful, such as moving, changing schools, and parental remarriage. And of course, parental remarriage brings about the possibility of additional divorces. Multiple instances of divorce expose children to repeated episodes of conflict, diminished parenting, and financial hardship.[40] For some children of divorce, stress accumulates throughout childhood.

Research generally supports a stress interpretation of children's adjustment following divorce. Divorces that are accompanied by a large number of other changes appear to have an especially negative impact on children.[41] Furthermore, parental remarriage sometimes exacerbates problems for children of divorce,[42] as does a second divorce.[43]

A General Perspective on How Divorce Affects Children

All five explanations for the effects of divorce on children appear to have merit, and a complete accounting for the effect of divorce on children must make reference to each. Because of variability in these five factors, the consequences of divorce differ considerably from one child to the next.

Consider a divorce in which a child loses contact with the father, the custodial mother is preoccupied and inattentive, the parents fight over child support and other issues, the household descends abruptly into poverty, and the separation is accompanied by a series of other uncontrollable changes. Under these circumstances, one would expect the divorce to have a substantial negative impact on the child. In contrast, consider a divorce in which the child continues to see the noncustodial father regularly, the custodial mother continues to be supportive and exercises appropriate discipline, the parents are able to cooperate without conflict, the child's standard of living changes little, and the transition is accompanied by no other major disruptions in the child's life. Under these circumstances, one would predict few negative consequences of divorce. Finally, consider a high-conflict marriage that ends in divorce. As the level of conflict subsides, the previously distant father grows closer to his child, and the previously distracted and stressed mother becomes warmer and more attentive. Assuming no major economic problems or additional disruptive changes, this divorce would probably have a positive impact on the child.

Overall, to understand how divorce affects children, it is necessary to assess how divorce changes the total configuration of resources and stressors in children's lives.[44] The five factors described above should also be considered when evaluating policy alternatives aimed at improving the well-being of children of divorce.

What Interventions Might Benefit Children of Divorce?

Concern for the well-being of children of divorce leads to a consideration of how various policies and interventions might reduce the risk of problems for them. The most commonly discussed interventions include lowering the incidence of divorce, joint custody, child-support reform, enhancing the self-sufficiency of single mothers, and therapeutic programs for children and parents. Interventions suggested in this article are considered in the light of available research evidence.

Lowering the Incidence of Divorce

In the United States during the twentieth century, divorce became increasingly available as the result of a series of judicial decisions that widened the grounds for divorce. In 1970, no-fault divorce was introduced in California; presently it is available in all 50 states.[45] Under most forms of no-fault divorce, a divorce can be obtained without a restrictive waiting period if one partner wants it even if the other partner has done nothing to violate the marriage contract and wishes to keep the marriage together. This fact raises an interesting question: If the law were changed to make marital dissolution more difficult to obtain, and if doing so lowered the divorce rate, would we see a corresponding improvement in the well-being of children?

Several considerations suggest that this outcome is unlikely. First, although legal divorces occurred less often in the past, informal separations and desertions were not uncommon, especially among minorities and those of low socioeconomic status.[46] From a child's perspective, separation is no better than divorce. If the legal system were changed to make divorce more difficult, it would most likely increase the proportion of children living in separated but nondivorced families. It would also increase the proportion of people who spend their childhoods in high-conflict, two-parent families. As noted above, high-conflict two-parent families present just as many problems for children as do divorced single-parent families, perhaps more so. Given that the legal system cannot stop married couples from living apart or fighting, changing the legal system to decrease the frequency of divorce is unlikely to improve the well-being of children.

Is it possible to lower the frequency of divorce by increasing marital happiness and stability? The government could enact certain changes toward this end, for example, by changing the tax code to benefit married parents. It is possible that such a policy would enhance the quality and stability of some marriages; however, providing these benefits to married-couple families would increase the relative disadvantage of single parents and their children, an undesirable outcome. Alternatively, the government could take steps to promote marriage preparation, enrichment, and counseling. Increasing the availability of such services would probably help to keep some marriages from ending in divorce. However, as Furstenberg and Cherlin suggest, the rise in divorce is the result of fundamental changes in American society, including shifts in personal values and the growing economic independence of women, factors that cannot be affected easily by government policies.[47] As such, any actions taken by government to strengthen marriage are likely to have only minor effects on the divorce rate.

Increasing the Incidence of Joint Physical Custody

The history of custody determination in the United States has changed over time primarily in response to societal influences. In the eighteenth century, fathers usually were awarded custody of their children as they were considered the dominant family figure and were most likely to have the financial means to care for them. In the nineteenth century, the preference for custody moved toward women. The reason for this shift was probably occasioned, in part, by the industrial revolution and the movement of men from the home to the workplace to earn a living. Women, in this circumstance, were needed to care for the children while men were at work and became the primary caretakers of children. At this time, child developmental theorists also focused on the importance of the mother–child relationship, and the assumption was that the children were usually better off under the custody of their mother. Recently, society has moved toward a dual-earner family, and child developmentalists have emphasized the importance of both parents to the child. These changes are currently reflected in the law which emphasizes the importance of maintaining relationships with both parents. The result has been an increased interest in joint custody, which is now available as an option in most states.[41] *Joint physical custody* provides legal rights and responsibilities to both parents and is intended to grant children substantial portions of time with each parent. *Joint legal custody,* which is more common, provides legal rights and responsibilities to both parents, but the child lives with one parent.

Joint legal custody may be beneficial to the extent that it keeps both parents involved in their children's lives. However, studies show few differences between joint legal and mother-custody families in the extent to which fathers pay child support, visit their children, and are involved in making decisions about their children, once parental income, education, and other pre-divorce parental characteristics are taken into account.[48] Although joint legal custody may have symbolic value in emphasizing the importance of both parents, it appears to make little difference in practice.

In contrast, joint physical custody is associated with greater father contact, involvement, and payment of child support.[49] Fathers also appear to be more satisfied with joint physical custody than with mother custody. For example, Shrier and colleagues found in 1991 that joint-custody fathers were significantly more satisfied than sole-maternal-custody fathers in two areas, including their legal rights and responsibilities as a parent and their current alimony and child support financial arrangements.[50] Joint physical custody may be beneficial if it gives children frequent access to both parents. On the other hand, residential instability may be stressful for some children. Although few studies are available, some show that children in joint physical custody are better adjusted than are children with other custody arrangements,[51] and other studies show no difference.[52]

However, these results may present a picture that is too optimistic. Courts are most likely to grant joint physical custody to couples who request it. A large-scale study by Maccoby and Mnookin in California showed that couples with joint physical custody, compared with those who receive sole custody, are better educated and have higher incomes; furthermore, couples who request joint custody may be relatively less hostile, and fathers may be particularly committed to their children prior to divorce.[53] These findings suggest that some of the apparent positive "effect" of joint custody is a natural result of the type of people who request it in the first place.

It is unlikely that joint physical custody would work well if it were imposed on parents against their will. Under these conditions, joint custody may lead to more contact between fathers and their children but may also maintain and exacerbate conflict between parents.[54] Maccoby and Mnookin found that, although conflict over custody is relatively rare, joint custody is sometimes used to resolve custody disputes. In their study, joint custody was awarded in about one-third of cases in which mothers and fathers had each initially sought sole custody; furthermore, the more legal conflict between parents, the more likely joint custody was to be awarded. Three and one-half years after separation, these couples were experiencing considerably more conflict and less cooperative parenting than couples in which both had wanted joint custody initially. This finding demonstrates that an award of joint custody does not improve the relationship between hostile parents.

As noted above, studies show that children's contact with noncustodial parents is harmful if postdivorce conflict between parents is high. To the extent that joint physical custody maintains contact between children and parents in an atmosphere of conflict, it may do as much (or more) harm than good.[55] Joint custody, therefore, would appear to be the best arrangement for children when parents are cooperative and request such an arrangement. But in cases where parents are unable to cooperate, or when one parent is violent or abusive, a more traditional custody arrangement would be preferable.

Does research suggest that children are better adjusted in mother- or father-custody households? From an economic perspective, one might expect children to be better off with fathers, given that men typically earn more money than do women. On the other hand, children may be cared for more competently by mothers than fathers, given that mothers usually have more child-care experience. Studies that have compared the adjustment of children in mother- and father-custody households have yielded mixed results, with some favoring mother custody, some favoring father custody, and others favoring the placement of the child with the same-sex parent.[21]

A recent and thorough study by Downey and Powell,[56] based on a large national sample of children, found little evidence to support the notion that children are better off with the same-sex parent. On a few outcomes, children were better off in father-custody households. However, with household income controlled, children tended to be slightly better off with mothers. This finding suggests that the higher income of single-father households confers certain advantages on children, but if mothers earned as much as fathers, children would be better off with mothers. The overall finding of the study, however, is that the sex of the custodial parent has little to do with the children's adjustment. In general, then, it does not appear that either mother or father custody is inherently better for children, regardless of the sex of the child.

Child Support Reform

It is widely recognized that noncustodial fathers often fail to pay child support. In a 1987 study by the U.S. Bureau of the Census, about one-third of formerly married women with custody had no child support award. And among those with an award, one-fourth reported receiving no payments in the previous year.[57] In the past, it has been difficult for custodial mothers to seek compliance with awards because of the complications and expense involved. New provisions in the 1988 Family Support Act allow for states to recover child support payments through the taxation system.[58] Starting in 1994, all new payments will be subject to automatic withholding from parents' paychecks.

Child support payments represent only a fraction of most single mothers' income, usually no more than one-fifth.[59] As such, stricter enforcement of child support payments cannot be expected to have a dramatic impact on children's standard of living. Nevertheless, it is usually highly needed income. As noted above, economic hardship has negative consequences for children's health, academic achievement, and psychological adjustment. Consequently, any policy that reduces the economic hardship experienced by children of divorce would be helpful. Furthermore, the extra income derived from child support may decrease custodial mothers' stress and improve parental functioning, with beneficial consequences for children. Consistent with this view, two studies show that regular payment of child support by noncustodial fathers decreases children's behavior problems and increases academic test scores.[60] Furthermore, in these studies, the apparently beneficial effect of child support occurred in spite of the fact that contact between fathers and children was not related to children's well-being.

Research indicates that the majority of fathers are capable of paying the full amount of child support awarded; in fact, most are capable of paying more. Based on these considerations, it would appear to be desirable to increase the economic support provided by noncustodial fathers to their children. This would include increasing the proportion of children with awards, increasing the level of awards, and enforcing child support awards more strictly. A guaranteed minimum child support benefit, in which the government sets a minimum benefit level and ensures full payment when fathers are unable to comply, would also improve the standard of living of many children.[61]

Requiring fathers to increase their economic commitment to children may also lead them to increase visitation, if for no other reason than to make sure that their money is being spent wisely. A number of studies have shown that fathers who pay child support tend to visit their children more often and make more decisions about them than do fathers who fail to pay.[62] If increasing the level of compliance increases father visitation, it may increase conflict between some parents. On the other hand, some children may benefit from greater father involvement. Overall, the benefits of increasing fathers' economic contribution to children would seem to outweigh any risks.

Economic Self-Sufficiency for Single Mothers

As noted above, stricter enforcement of child-support awards will help to raise the standard of living of single mothers and their children. However, even if fathers comply fully with child-support awards, the economic situation of many single mothers will remain precarious. To a large extent, the economic vulnerability of single mothers reflects the larger inequality between men and women in American society. Not only do women earn less than men, but many married women sacrifice future earning potential to care for children by dropping out of the paid labor force, cutting back on the number of hours worked, taking jobs with more-flexible hours, or taking jobs closer to home. Thus, divorcees are disadvantaged both by the lower wages paid to women and by their work histories. In the long run, single mothers and their children will achieve economic parity with single fathers only when women and men are equal in terms of earnings and time spent caring for children.

In the short term, however, certain steps can be taken to allow single mothers receiving public assistance to be economically self-sufficient. These steps would include the provision of job training and subsidized child care.[63] Although these programs operate at government expense, they are cost-effective to the extent that women and children become independent of further public assistance. Furthermore, many single mothers are "penalized" for working because they lose government benefits, such as health care and child care. Welfare reform that removes work disincentives by allowing women to earn a reasonable level of income without losing health-care and child-care benefits would be desirable. In fact, changes in these directions are being implemented as part of the Family Support Act of 1988.[64] Given that the employment of single mothers does not appear to be harmful to children and can provide a higher standard of living for children than does welfare, and given that economic self-sufficiency would probably improve the psychological well-being of single mothers, it seems likely that these changes will benefit children.

Therapeutic Interventions for Children

According to Cherlin, there are still no firm estimates on the proportion of children who experience harmful psychological effects from parental divorce.[2] Research suggests that, in many cases, children adjust well to divorce without the need for therapeutic intervention. However, our current understanding is that a minority of children do experience adjustment problems and are in need of therapeutic intervention. The type of therapeutic intervention suited for children varies according to the type and severity of the adjustment problems and the length of time they are expressed by the child. The major types of therapeutic interventions include child-oriented interventions and family-oriented interventions.[65]

Child-oriented interventions attempt to help children by alleviating the problems commonly experienced by them after divorce. Some intervention programs include private individual therapy. However, many single parents are unable to afford private therapy for their children and may enroll them in programs in which counselors work with groups of children.

Typically, in these sessions, children meet on a regular basis to share their experiences, learn about problem-solving strategies, and offer mutual support. Children may also view films, draw, or participate in role-playing exercises. Small groups are desirable for children of divorce for several reasons. Not only can they reach large numbers of children, but the group itself is therapeutic: Children may find it easier to talk with other children than with adults about their experiences and feelings. Most group programs are located in schools; such programs have been introduced in thousands of school districts across the United States.

Evaluations of these programs have been attempted, and in spite of some methodological limitations, most are favorable: Children from divorced families who participate, compared with those who do not, exhibit fewer maladaptive attitudes and beliefs about divorce, better classroom behavior, less anxiety and depression, and improved self-concept.[66] Although much of the evidence is positive, it is not entirely clear which components of these programs are most effective. For example, improvement may be brought about by a better understanding of divorce, newly acquired communication skills, or the support of other students. Although more evaluation research is needed, the evidence is positive enough to warrant further development and introduction of therapeutic programs for children.

In addition to child-focused interventions, there are *family-focused interventions* including both educational and therapeutic programs. These programs are aimed at divorcing parents, with the intention of either improving parenting skills or reducing the level of conflict over children.[67] In principle, therapeutic interventions that improve parental child-rearing skills or decrease the level of conflict between parents should benefit children, although this effect has not yet been demonstrated.

What Directions Should Future Research Take?

All things being equal, existing research suggests that a well-functioning nuclear family with two caring parents may be a better environment for children's growth and development than a divorced single-parent family. Children of divorce, as a group, are at greater risk than children from intact families, as a group, for many psychological, academic, and social problems. And adults raised in divorced single-parent families, as a group, do not achieve the same level of psychological and material well-being as those raised in continuously intact two-parent families. However, we need to keep in mind that many children are better off living in single-parent households than in two-parent families marked by conflict. Furthermore, we need to recognize that most single parents work hard to provide their children with a loving and structured family life. Many single-parent families function well, and most children raised in these settings develop into well-adjusted adults. Blaming single parents as a group for the problems experienced by children of divorce is a pointless exercise.

At this time, our knowledge about children and divorce needs to be expanded in certain directions. The long-term effect of divorce on children is the basic question that needs to be addressed. The answers to this question will inform social policy and the court system, shape models of intervention, and influence parental decision making. This type of information should be obtained from longitudinal and longitudinal-sequential designs. Needed are studies that begin prior to divorce, as well as studies that follow children of divorce through adolescence and into adulthood.[68]

Also needed are data on how a variety of factors — relations with parents, parental adjustment, economic well-being, conflict, and exposure to stressors — combine to affect children's response to divorce. This research should make it possible to determine which children lose the most through divorce, which children are relatively unaffected, and which children benefit.

Information on how divorce affects children in different racial and ethnic groups is another area of research that would be informative from the standpoint of both clinical and economic intervention.[18] And more evaluation of various interventions, both legal (joint custody, mediation, child support reform) and therapeutic, are also needed.

It is important to focus on establishing policies that will help narrow the gap in well-being between children of divorce and children from intact families. High divorce rates and single-parent families are facts of life in American society. If it is impossible to prevent children from experiencing parental divorce, steps must be taken to ease the transition.

ENDNOTES

1. Furstenberg Jr., F. F., and Cherlin, A. J. *Divided families: What happens to children when parents part.* Cambridge, MA: Harvard University Press, 1991, pp. 1–15; Uhlenberg, P. Death and the family. *Journal of Family History* (1980) 5:313–20.
2. Cherlin, A. *Marriage, divorce, remarriage.* Rev. ed. Cambridge, MA: Harvard University Press, 1992.
3. Bumpass, L. Children and marital disruption: A replication and update. *Demography* (1984) 21:71–82.
4. For examples, see the articles in *The child in his family: The impact of disease and death.* E. J. Anthony, ed. New York: Wiley, 1973.
5. Crook, T., and Eliot, J. Parental death during childhood and adult depression: A critical review of the literature. *Psychological Bulletin* (1980) 87:252–59.
6. See, for example, Guidubaldi, J., Cleminshaw, H. K., Perry, J. D. and McLoughlin, C. S. The impact of parental divorce on children: Report of the nationwide NASP study. *School Psychology Review* (1983) 12:300–23; Hetherington, E. M., Cox, M., and Cox, R. Effects of divorce on parents and children. In *Nontraditional families.* M. E. Lamb, ed. Hillsdale, NJ: Lawrence Erlbaum Associates, 1982, pp. 223–88.
7. See, for example, Baydar, N. Effects of parental separation and reentry into union on the emotional well-being of children. *Journal of Marriage and the Family* (1988) 50:967–81; Enos, D. M., and Handal, P. J. Relation of parental marital status and perceived family conflict to adjustment in white adolescents. *Journal of Consulting and Clinical Psychology* (1986) 54:820–24; Mechanic, D., and Hansell, S. Divorce, family conflict, and adolescents' well-being. *Journal of Health and Social Behavior* (1989) 30:105–16.
8. Amato, P. R., and Ochiltree, G. Child and adolescent competence in intact, one-parent, and stepfamilies. *Journal of Divorce* (1987) 10:75–96.
9. See Glass, G. V., McGaw, B., and Smith, M. L. An evaluation of meta-analysis. In *Meta-analysis in social research.* Newbury Park, CA: Sage, 1981.
10. Amato, P. R., and Keith, B. Parental divorce and the well-being of children: A meta-analysis. *Psychological Bulletin* (1991) 100:26–46.
11. Amato, P. R., and Keith, B. Parental divorce and adult well-being: A meta-analysis. *Journal of Marriage and the Family* (1991) 53:43–58.
12. Kendall-Tackett, K. A., Williams, L. M., and Finkelhor, D. Impact of sexual abuse on children: A review and synthesis of recent empirical studies. *Psychological Bulletin* (1993) 113:164–80.
13. Rutter, M. Sex differences in children's responses to family stress. In *The child in his family.* Vol. 1. E. J. Anthony and C. Koupernik, eds. New York: Wiley, 1970.

14. See, for example, Booth, A., Brinkerhoff, D. B., and White, L. K. The impact of parental divorce on courtship. *Journal of Marriage and the Family* (1984) 46:85–94; Smith, T. E. Parental separation and adolescents' academic self-concepts: An effort to solve the puzzle of separation effects. *Journal of Marriage and the Family* (1990) 52:107–18.

15. Slater, E., Steward, K. J., and Linn, M. W. The effects of family disruption on adolescent males and females. *Adolescence* (1983) 18:931–42.

16. See Peterson, J. L., and Zill, N. Marital disruption, parent–child relationships, and behavior problems in children. *Journal of Marriage and the Family* (1986) 48:295–307; Hetherington, E. M., and Chase-Lansdale, P. L. The impact of divorce on life-span development: Short and long term effects. In *Life-span development and behavior.* P. B. Baltes, D. L. Featherman, and R. M. Lerner, eds. Hillsdale, NJ: Lawrence Erlbaum Associates, 1990.

17. Hetherington, E. M., Camara, K. A., and Featherman, D. L. Achievement and intellectual functioning of children in one-parent households. In *Achievement and achievement motives.* J. T. Spence, ed. San Francisco: W. H. Freeman, 1983.

18. Del Carmen, R., and Virgo, G. N. Marital disruption and nonresidential parenting: A multicultural perspective. In *Nonresidential parenting: New vistas in family living.* C. Depner and J. Bray, eds. Newbury Park, CA: Sage, 1993, pp. 13–36.

19. Wallerstein, J. S., and Kelly, J. B. *Surviving the breakup: How children and parents cope with divorce.* New York: Basic Books, 1980.

20. Wallerstein, J. S., and Blakeslee, S. *Second chances: Men, women, and children a decade after divorce.* New York: Ticknor and Fields, 1989.

21. For a summary of these studies, see Amato, P. R. Children's adjustment to divorce: Theories, hypotheses, and empirical support. *Journal of Marriage and the Family* (1993) 55:23–38.

22. Furstenberg Jr., F. F., and Nord, C. W. Parenting apart: Patterns of child-rearing after marital disruption. *Journal of Marriage and the Family* (1985) 47:893–904; Selzer, J. A. Relationships between fathers and children who live apart: The father's role after separation. *Journal of Marriage and the Family* (1991) 53:79–101.

23. This trend was confirmed in the meta-analysis by Amato and Keith; see note no. 11. For examples of studies, see Amato, P. R., Parental absence during childhood and depression in later life. *Sociological Quarterly* (1991) 32:543–56; Gregory, I. Introspective data following childhood loss of a parent: Delinquency and high school dropout. *Archives of General Psychiatry* (1965) 13:99–109; Saucier, J., and Ambert, A. Parental marital status and adolescents' optimism about their future. *Journal of Youth and Adolescence* (1982) 11:345–53. Our meta-analysis also showed that, although children who experience parental death are worse off than those in intact two-parent families, they have higher levels of well-being than do children of divorce.

24. Cochran, M., Larner, M., Riley, D., et al. *Extending families: The social networks of parents and their children.* Cambridge, MA: Cambridge University Press, 1990; Dornbusch, S., Carlsmith, J. M., Bushwall, S. J., et al. Single parents, extended households, and the control of adolescents. *Child Development* (1985) 56:326–41.

25. Kelly, J. B. Current research on children's postdivorce adjustment: No simple answers. *Family and Conciliation Courts Review* (1993) 31:29–49.

26. Amato, P. R., and Rezac, S. J. Contact with nonresident parents, interparental conflict, and children's behavior. Paper presented at the Annual Meeting of the Midwest Sociological Society. Chicago, IL, 1993; Healy, Jr., J., Malley, J., and Stewart, A. Children and their fathers after parental separation. *American Journal of Orthopsychiatry* (1990) 60:531–43.

27. See Simons, R. L., Beaman, J., Conger, R. D., and Chao, W. Stress, support, and antisocial behavior traits as determinants of emotional well-being and parenting practices among single mothers. *Journal of Marriage and the Family* (1993) 55:385–98.

28. Kline, M., Tschann, J. M., Johnston, J. R., and Wallerstein, J. S. Children's adjustment in joint and sole physical custody families. *Developmental Psychology* (1989) 25:430–38. Guidubaldi, J., and Perry, J. D. Divorce and mental health sequelae for children: A two-year follow-up of a nationwide sample. *Journal of the American Academy of Child Psychiatry* (1985) 24:531–37; and Kalter, N., Kloner, A., Schreiser, S., and Olka, K. Predictors of children's postdivorce adjustment. *American Journal of Orthopsychiatry* (1989) 59:605–18.

29. Guidubaldi, J., Cleminshaw, H. K., Perry, J. D., et al. The role of selected family environment factors in children's postdivorce adjustment. *Family Relations* (1986) 35:141–51; see note no. 6, Hetherington, Cox, and Cox. See note no. 28, Kalter, Kloner, Schreiser, and Olka; see note no. 16, Peterson and Zill.

30. Emery, R. Interparental conflict and the children of discord and divorce. *Psychological Bulletin* (1982) 92:310–30; Grych, J. H., and Fincham, F. D. Marital conflict and children's adjustment: A cognitive-contextual framework. *Psychological Bulletin* (1990) 108:267–90.

31. See note no. 14, Booth, Brinkerhoff, and White. See note no. 7, Enos and Handal; and Mechanic and Hansell; Long, N., Forehand, R., Fauber, R., and Brody, G. H. Self-perceived and independently observed competence of young adolescents as a function of parental marital conflict and recent divorce. *Journal of Abnormal Child Psychology* (1987) 15:15–27; see note no. 16, Peterson and Zill.

32. Cherlin, A. J., Furstenberg Jr., F. F., Chase-Lansdale, P. L., et al. Longitudinal studies of effects of divorce on children in Great Britain and the United States. *Science* (1991) 252:1386–89. Similar findings were reported by Block, J. H., Block, J., and Gjerde, P. R. The personality of children prior to divorce. *Child Development* (1986) 57:827–40.

33. Johnston, J. R., Kline, M., and Tschann, J. M. Ongoing postdivorce conflict: Effects on children of joint custody and frequent access. *American Journal of Orthopsychiatry* (1999) 59:576–92; Kurdek, L. A., and Berg, B. Correlates of children's adjustment to their parents' divorces. In *Children and divorce*. L. A. Kurdek, ed. San Francisco: Jossey-Bass, 1983; Shaw, D. S., and Emery, R. E. Parental conflict and other correlates of the adjustment of school-age children whose parents have separated. *Journal of Abnormal Child Psychology* (1987) 15:269–81. It is also probable that children's problems, to a certain extent, exacerbate conflict between parents.

34. Duncan, G. J., and Hoffman, S. D. Economic consequences of marital instability. In *Horizontal equity, uncertainty, and economic well-being*. M. David and T. Smeeding, eds. Chicago: University of Chicago Press, 1985; Weitzman, L. J. *The divorce revolution: The unexpected social and economic consequences for women and children in America*. New York: Free Press, 1985.

35. McLeod, J. D., and Shanahan, M. J. Poverty, parenting, and children's mental health. *American Sociological Review* (1993) 58:351–66.

36. Williams, D. R. Socioeconomic differentials in health: A review and redirection. *Social Psychology Quarterly* (1990) 52:81–99.

37. McLanahan, S., and Booth, K. Mother-only families: Problems, prospects, and politics. *Journal of Marriage and the Family* (1989) 51:557–80.

38. See note no. 6, Guidubaldi, Cleminshaw, Perry, and McLoughlin.

39. McLanahan, S. Family structure and the reproduction of poverty. *American Journal of Sociology* (1985) 90:873–901.

40. For a review of the effects of serial marriages (involving three or more marriages) and divorces on child adjustment, see Brody, G. H., Neubaum, E., and Forehand, R. Serial marriage: A heuristic analysis of an emerging family form. *Psychological Bulletin* (1988) 103:211–22.

41. Hodges, W. F., Tierney, C. W., and Buchsbaum, H. K. The cumulative effects of stress on preschool children of divorced and intact families. *Journal of Marriage and the Family* (1984) 46:611–19; Stolberg, A. L., and Anker, J. M. Cognitive and

behavioral changes in children resulting from parental divorce and consequent environmental changes. *Journal of Divorce* (1983) 7:23–37.

42. See note no. 7, Baydar. Hetherington and her colleagues found that the remarriage of the custodial mother was associated with increased problems for girls but decreased problems for boys. Hetherington, E. M., Cox, M., and Cox, R. Long-term effects of divorce and remarriage on the adjustment of children. *Journal of the American Academy of Child Psychiatry* (1985) 24:518–30.

43. Amato, P. R., and Booth, A. The consequences of parental divorce and marital unhappiness for adult well-being. *Social Forces* (1991) 69:895–914.

44. For similar perspectives, see Hetherington, E. M. Coping with family transitions: Winners, losers, and survivors. *Child Development* (1989) 60:1–14; Kurdek, L. A. An integrative perspective on children's divorce adjustment. *American Psychologist* 36:856–66.

45. Glendon, M. A. *The transformation of family law: State, law, and family in the United States and Western Europe.* Chicago: University of Chicago Press, 1989. See note no. 34, Weitzman.

46. See note no. 45, Glendon; Sweet, J. A., and Bumpass, L. L. *American families and households.* New York: Russell Sage Foundation, 1990.

47. See note no. 1, Furstenberg and Cherlin.

48. Seltzer, J. Legal custody arrangements and children's economic welfare. *American Journal of Sociology* (1991) 96:895–929.

49. Arditti, J. A. Differences between fathers with joint custody and noncustodial fathers. *American Journal of Orthopsychiatry* (1992) 62:186–95; Bowman, M., and Ahrons, C. R. Impact of legal custody status on fathers' parenting postdivorce. *Journal of Marriage and the Family* (1985) 47:481–88; Dudley, J. R. Exploring ways to get divorced fathers to comply willingly with child support agreements. *Journal of Divorce* (1991) 14:121–33; Leupnitz, D. A comparison of maternal, paternal, and joint custody: Understanding the varieties of postdivorce family life. *Journal of Divorce* (1986) 9:1–12.

50. See note no. 49, Arditti; Little, M. A. The impact of the custody plan on the family: A five-year follow-up. *Family and Conciliation Courts Review* (1992) 30:243–51; Shrier, D. K., Simring, S. K., Shapiro, E. T., and Greif, J. B. Level of satisfaction of fathers and mothers with joint or sole custody arrangements. *Journal of Divorce and Remarriage* (1991) 16:163–69.

51. Buchanan, C. M., Maccoby, E. E., and Dornbusch, S. M. Adolescents and their families after divorce: Three residential arrangements compared. *Journal of Research on Adolescents* (1992) 2:261–91; Glover, R. J., and Steele, C. Comparing the effects on the child of postdivorce parenting arrangements. *Journal of Divorce* (1989) 12:185–201; Wolchik, S. A., Braver, S. L., and Sandler, I. N. Maternal versus joint custody: Children's postseparation experiences and adjustment. *Journal of Clinical Child Psychology* (1985) 14:5–10.

52. Kline, M., Tschann, J. M., Johnston, J. R., and Wallerstein, J. S. Children's adjustment in joint and sole physical custody families. *Developmental Psychology* (1988) 25:430–38; Leupnitz, D. *Child custody.* Lexington, MA: D. C. Heath, 1982; Pearson, J., and Thoennes, N. Custody after divorce: Demographic and attitudinal patterns. *American Journal of Orthopsychiatry* (1990) 60:233–49.

53. See note no. 49, Arditti; note no. 52, Pearson and Thoennes; Steinman, S. The experience of children in a joint custody arrangement: A report of a study. *American Journal of Orthopsychiatry* (1981) 24:554–62; Macoby, E. E., and Mnookin, R. H. *Dividing the child: Social and legal dilemmas of custody.* Cambridge, MA: Harvard University Press, 1992.

54. Nelson, R. Parental hostility, conflict, and communication in joint and sole custody families. *Journal of Divorce* (1989) 13:145–57.

55. Buchanan, C. M., Maccoby, E. E., and Dornbusch, S. M. Caught between parents: Adolescents' experience in divorced homes. *Child Development* (1991) 62:1008–29;

Johnston, J. R., Kline, M., and Tschann, J. M. Ongoing postdivorce conflict: Effects on children of joint custody and frequent access. *American Journal of Orthopsychiatry* (1989) 59:576–92.

56. Downey, D., and Powell, B. Do children in single-parent households fare better living with same-sex parents? *Journal of Marriage and the Family* (1993) 55:55–71.

57. U.S. Bureau of the Census. *Child support and alimony: 1987.* Current Population Reports, Series P-23, No. 167. Washington, DC: U.S. Government Printing Office, 1990.

58. Public Law No. 100-485, reprinted in *1988 U.S. Code Cong. & Admin. News,* 102 Stat. 2343.

59. See note no. 34, Duncan and Hoffman.

60. Furstenberg Jr., F. F., Morgan, S. P., and Allison, P. D. Paternal participation and children's well-being after marital dissolution. *American Sociological Review* (1987) 52:695–701; King, V. Nonresidential father involvement and child well-being: Can dads make a difference? Paper presented at the annual meeting of the Population Association of America. Cincinnati, OH, 1993.

61. For a discussion of child-support reform, see Garfinkel, I. *Assuring child support: An extension of Social Security.* New York: Russell Sage Foundation, 1992; Garfinkel, I., and McLanahan, S. S. *Single mothers and their children: A new American dilemma.* Washington, DC: Urban Institute Press, 1986.

62. Seltzer, J. A., and Bianchi, S. M. Children's contact with absent parents. *Journal of Marriage and the Family* (1988) 50:663–77; Seltzer, J., Schaeffer, N. C., and Charng, H. Families ties after divorce: The relationship between visiting and paying child support. *Journal of Marriage and the Family* (1989) 51:1013–32.

63. Britto, K. The Family Support Act of 1988 Welfare Reform (Public Law 100-485). Vol. 2, No. 3. National Conference of State Legislatures. Denver, CO, 1989.

64. Aldous, J. Family policy in the 1980s: Controversy and consensus. *Journal of Marriage and the Family* (1990) 52:1136–51.

65. Grych, J., and Fincham, F. D. Interventions for children of divorce: Toward greater integration of research and action. *Psychological Bulletin* (1992) 111:434–54.

66. Anderson, R. F., Kinney, J., and Gerler, E. R. The effects of divorce groups on children's classroom behavior and attitudes toward divorce. *Elementary School Guidance and Counseling* (1984) 19:70–76; Crosbie-Burnett, M., and Newcomer, L. L. Group counseling children of divorce: The effects of a multimodel intervention. *Journal of Divorce* (1989) 13:69–78. Pedro-Carroll, J., and Cowan, E. L. The children of divorce intervention program: An investigation of the efficacy of a school-based intervention program. *Journal of Consulting and Clinical Psychology* (1985) 53:603–11; Stolberg, A. J., and Garrison, K. M. Evaluating a primary prevention program for children of divorce. *American Journal of Community Psychology* (1985) 13:111–24.

67. Bloom, B. L., Hodges, W. F., and Caldwell, R. A. A preventive program for the newly separated: Initial evaluation. *American Journal of Community Psychology* (1982) 10:251–64; Bloom, B. L., Hodges, W. F., Kern, M. B., and McFaddin, S. C. A preventive intervention program for the newly separated: Final evaluations. *American Journal of Orthopsychiatry* (1985) 55:9–26; Zibbell, R. A. A short-term, small-group education and counseling program for separated and divorced parents in conflict. *Journal of Divorce and Remarriage* (1992) 18:189–203.

68. Wallerstein, J. S. The long-term effects of divorce on children: A review. *Journal of the American Academy of Child Adolescent Psychiatry* (1991) 30:349–60.

PART VI
Motherhood and Fatherhood

A "natural" mother is a person without further identity, one who can find her chief gratification in being alone all day with small children, living at a pace tuned to theirs; that the isolation of mothers and children living in the home must be taken for granted; that maternal love is and should be, quite literally selfless; that children and mothers are the "causes" of each others' suffering.

—ADRIENNE RICH [1976] 1986

A father is first biological. He takes care of the children he helped bring into this world. . . . By that I mean he sees to it that his children have what they need to stay healthy. For example, enough food to eat and a roof over their heads. He provides for their everyday needs.

—A single African American mother in Hamer 1998:88

In the previous section, we examined parenting and childhood; in this section, we examine more closely how parenting is gendered, that is, how parenting is similar and different between mothers and fathers. In fact, when people talk about parenthood, they are usually talking about motherhood, or they assume that mothers are the primary parent. By including separate articles on motherhood and fatherhood, I hope to correct this gender bias. Both motherhood and fatherhood need to be examined to fully understand the complexity of parenting. Moreover, as both parenthood and childhood are socially constructed, so are motherhood and fatherhood each socially constructed. That is, the expectations for and meanings of motherhood and fatherhood vary across cultures and across time. For example, as seen in the Adrienne Rich quote above, in Western culture, motherhood has been idealized to such an extent that mothers are often placed on a pedestal, but also blamed for everything that is wrong with children. Scott Coltrane (1998) argues that "our idealized view of motherhood assumes that a dominant maternal instinct will naturally emerge and guide women's parenting because mothering is their destiny" (p. 96). Thus, many people believe that mothers have a maternal instinct, a biological desire to have children and the innate knowledge of how to be a good mother. Instead, nothing could be further from the truth. Women's desires to become a parent and their knowledge about parenting are learned via gender socialization and other societal messages.

Motherhood

The first article in this section, "Shifting the Center: Race, Class, and Feminist Theorizing about Motherhood," by Patricia Hill Collins, challenges contemporary social constructions of motherhood. Collins, a professor of sociology and African American studies at the University of Cincinnati, has extensively researched the diverse meaning of motherhood in various racial-ethnic and social class groups. In this selection, Collins argues that scholars need to place the voices and experiences of women of color at the center of feminist theorizing about motherhood. She states that until scholars "shift the center" of family scholarship away from white, middle-class, heterosexual families, they cannot understand how families are constructed differently for people of color. For example, work and family have not always been separate and conflicting spheres for women of color as they have been for white, middle-class women. Collins argues that scholars also need to understand that "motherwork" and the provision for physical survival of children vary by the racial-ethnic and social class backgrounds of mothers. For instance, the motherwork done by women of color often includes teaching their children their racial-ethnic identity and helping them to understand their own culture and learn ways to survive in the dominant culture.

Similar to Collins, Michele Hoffnung (1995) argues that the contemporary construction of motherhood in the dominant culture is a powerful ideological force that shapes many of the conflicts women face in the United States. In particular, this construction of motherhood has created a "motherhood mystique," which upholds the following principles: (1) The ultimate fulfillment as a woman is achieved by becoming a mother; (2) the body of work assigned to mothers — caring for child, home, and husband — fits together in a noncontradictory manner; (3) to be a good mother, a woman must like being a mother and all the work that goes with it; and (4) a woman's intense exclusive devotion to mothering is good for her children (Hoffnung 1995). Hoffnung argues that the dominant culture in the United States defines motherhood and mothering too narrowly. This limited construction of mothering is harmful not only to women but also to men and children. It has both psychological and material costs, especially for daughters who grow up thinking they can "do it all."

The second article in this section, "The Mommy Wars: Ambivalence, Ideological Work, and the Cultural Contradictions of Motherhood," by Sharon Hays, builds on many of Hoffnung's arguments. Hays, an associate professor of sociology and women's studies at the University of Virginia, interviewed 38 mothers of two- to four-year-olds to find out how they perceived mothering and child rearing (Hays 1996). Drawing on ideas about mothering since the Middle Ages, on contemporary child-rearing manuals, and on these indepth interviews, Hays finds that a powerful ideology of "intensive mothering" exists in our culture. This ideology of intensive mothering exacerbates the inevitable tensions working mothers face. Women are expected to be nurturing and unselfish in their role as mothers but competitive and even ruthless at work. These unrealistic expectations of mothers reflect a deep cultural ambivalence about the pursuit of self-interest. Nowhere is this better illustrated than in the socially constructed tensions and conflicts between stay-at-home moms and working mothers. Hays analyzes these "mommy wars" and the reality of women's lives from both perspectives.

Fatherhood

The two readings on motherhood show how the construct of motherhood is ideologically laden. As motherhood is socially constructed, so is fatherhood. The second quote at the beginning of this section reflects one such construction of fatherhood that fathers are to be good providers for the family. The author of this quote argues that this role is biological when, in reality, it is social. The social roles of fathers are determined by the larger society. Thus, our understanding of fatherhood is influenced by a number of cultural shifts, including changes in the larger economy, changes in marriage patterns, and changes in gender roles. The social construction of fatherhood is currently in flux. Even the very definition of fatherhood has had to adapt due to an increasing divorce rate and the rise of reproductive technologies. No longer is the biological definition of fatherhood sufficient, if it ever was. This increasing complexity of fatherhood demands more research.

The current flux in the construction of fatherhood has led to a greater emphasis on father blaming in the larger society. Fathers are called many derogatory terms, including "deadbeat dads," absent fathers, and uninvolved fathers. The first reading on fatherhood, "Dilemmas of Involved Fatherhood," by Kathleen Gerson, attempts to balance these views that men are not involved enough in their children's lives. Gerson, a professor of sociology at New York University, has studied gender and families for over 20 years. The selection here is excerpted from Gerson's book *No Man's Land: Men's Changing Commitments to Family and Work* (1993). In this study, Gerson examines how and why men's lives are changing in the wake of the gender revolution at home and at work. Gerson argues that many fathers are now choosing to reject the traditional role of the father in favor of a much more involved father role. This method of fathering challenges gender roles and the gendered division of labor within the family to varying degrees of success. Some fathers are "mothers' helpers," more willing to contribute to child care and domestic chores than traditional fathers while still leaving the responsibility and much of the "dirty work" in the hands of the mothers. Other fathers are attempting to create an equal partnership or even to assume the majority of responsibility for what has traditionally been seen as the woman's sphere. Gerson explores the reasoning behind decisions to parent equally or to maintain some division of labor, explaining that equal partnership takes a great deal of effort and that many men feel as though their partners enjoy doing more of the parenting work. However, even those men whose contribution to parenting is unequal are still participating in a radical transformation of our understanding of the roles of fatherhood.

The second article on fatherhood, "Gay Men Choosing to Be Fathers," by Michael Shernoff, also challenges traditional definitions of fatherhood. Shernoff, a clinical social worker in private practice in Manhattan and an adjunct faculty member at Hunter College Graduate School of Social Work, decided to write this article after realizing that the topic of fatherhood was often raised by his gay clients during therapy sessions. Shernoff investigates those gay men who desire to become parents and have discussed wanting to father children without pretending to be heterosexual. Thus, he is studying gay men who are "out" about their sexuality and also are actively parenting children. Outside of heterosexual relationships, gay men become parents via adoption, foster parenting, and biological parenting with the help of a surrogate mother. Shernoff explores these various options of pathways to gay fatherhood and how gay men perceive the role of parent. He concludes his article with some suggestions on how to provide better social services for gay fathers.

REFERENCES

Coltrane, Scott. 1998. *Gender and Families.* Thousand Oaks, CA: Pine Forge Press.
Gerson, Kathleen. 1993. *No Man's Land: Men's Changing Commitments to Family and Work.* New York: Basic Books.
Hamer, Jennifer F. 1998. "The Definition of Fatherhood: In the Words of Never-Married African American Custodial Mothers and the Noncustodial Fathers of Their Children." *Journal of Sociology and Social Welfare.* 25:81–104.
Hays, Sharon. 1996. *The Cultural Contradictions of Motherhood.* New Haven, CT: Yale University Press.
Hoffnung, Michele. 1995. "Motherhood: Contemporary Conflict for Women." Pp. 162–81 in *Women: A Feminist Perspective,* 5th ed., edited by Jo Freeman. Mountain View, CA: Mayfield.
Rich, Adrienne. [1976] 1986. "Anger and Tenderness." Pp. 21–40 in *Of Woman Born: Motherhood Experience and Institution.* New York: W. W. Norton.

21

SHIFTING THE CENTER
Race, Class, and Feminist Theorizing about Motherhood

PATRICIA HILL COLLINS

I dread to see my children grow, I know not their fate. Where the white boy has every opportunity and protection, mine will have few opportunities and no protection. It does not matter how good or wise my children may be, they are colored.

— AN ANONYMOUS AFRICAN AMERICAN MOTHER IN 1904
(reported in Lerner 1972:158)

For Native American, African American, Hispanic, and Asian American women, motherhood cannot be analyzed in isolation from its context. Motherhood occurs in specific historical contexts framed by interlocking structures of race, class, and gender, contexts where the sons of white mothers have "every opportunity and protection," and the "colored" daughters and sons of racial ethnic mothers "know not their fate." Racial domination and economic exploitation profoundly shape the mothering context not only for racial ethnic women in the United States but for all women.[1]

Despite the significance of race and class, feminist theorizing routinely minimizes their importance. In this sense, feminist theorizing about motherhood has not been immune to the decontextualization in Western social thought overall.[2] Although many dimensions of motherhood's context are ignored, the exclusion of race and/or class from feminist theorizing generally and from feminist theorizing about motherhood specifically merits special attention (Spelman 1988).[3]

Much feminist theorizing about motherhood assumes that male domination in the political economy and the household is the driving force in family life and that understanding the struggle for individual autonomy in the face of such domination is central to understanding motherhood (Eisenstein 1983).[4] Several guiding principles frame such analyses. First, such theories posit a dichotomous split between the public sphere of economic and political discourse and the private sphere of family and household responsibilities. This juxtaposition of a public political economy to a private, noneconomic, and apolitical domestic household allows work and family to be seen as separate institutions. Second, reserving the public sphere for men as a "male" domain leaves the private domestic sphere as a "female" domain. Gender roles become tied to the dichotomous constructions of these two basic societal institutions—men work and women take care of families. Third, the public/ private dichotomy separating the family/household from the paid labor market shapes sex-segregated gender roles within the private sphere of the family. The archetypal white middle-class nuclear family divides family life into two oppositional spheres—the "male" sphere of economic providing and the "female" sphere of affective nurturing, mainly mothering. This normative family household ideally consists of a working father who earns enough to allow his spouse and dependent children to forgo participation in the paid labor force. Owing in large part to their superior earning power, men as workers and fathers exert power over women in the labor market and in families. Finally, the struggle for individual autonomy in the face of a controlling, oppressive "public" society or the father as patriarch constitutes the main human enterprise.[5] Successful adult males achieve this autonomy. Women, children, and less successful males—namely, those who are working class or from racial ethnic groups—are seen as dependent persons, as less autonomous, and therefore as fitting objects for elite male domination. Within the nuclear family, this struggle for autonomy takes the form of increasing opposition to the mother, the individual responsible for socializing children by these guiding principles (Chodorow 1978; Flax 1978).

Placing the experiences of women of color in the center of feminist theorizing about motherhood demonstrates how emphasizing the issue of father as patriarch in a decontextualized nuclear family distorts the experiences of women in alternative family structures with quite different political economies. While male domination certainly has been an important theme for racial ethnic women in the United States, gender inequality has long worked in tandem with racial domination and economic exploitation. Since work and family have rarely functioned as dichotomous spheres for women of color, examining racial ethnic women's experiences reveals how these two spheres actually are interwoven (Collins 1990; Dill 1988; Glenn 1985).

For women of color, the subjective experience of mothering/motherhood is inextricably linked to the sociocultural concerns of racial ethnic communities—one does not exist without the other. Whether under conditions of the labor exploitation of African American women during slavery and the ensuing tenant farm system, the political conquest of Native American women during European acquisition of land, or exclusionary immigration policies applied to Asian Americans and Latinos, women of color have performed motherwork that challenges social constructions of work and family as separate spheres, of male and female gender roles as similarly dichotomized, and of the search for autonomy as the guiding human quest. "Women's reproductive labor — that is, feeding, clothing, and psychologically supporting the male wage earner and nurturing and socializing the next generation — is seen as work on behalf of the family as a whole rather than as work benefiting men in particular," observes Asian American sociologist Evelyn Nakano Glenn (1986:192). The locus of conflict lies outside the household, as women and their families engage in collective effort to create and maintain family life in the face of forces that undermine family integrity. But this "reproductive labor" or "motherwork" goes beyond ensuring the survival of members of one's family. This type of motherwork recognizes that individual survival, empowerment, and identity require group survival, empowerment, and identity. . . .

. . . I use the term *motherwork* to soften the dichotomies in feminist theorizing about motherhood that posit rigid distinctions between private and public, family and work, the individual and the collective, identity as individual autonomy and identity growing from the collective self-determination of one's group. Racial ethnic women's mothering and work experiences occur at the boundaries demarking these dualities. "Work for the day to come" is motherwork, whether it is on behalf of one's own biological children, children of one's racial ethnic community, or children who are yet unborn. Moreover, the space that this motherwork occupies promises to shift our thinking about motherhood itself.

Shifting the Center: Women of Color and Motherwork

What themes might emerge if issues of race and class generally, and understanding racial ethnic women's motherwork specifically, became central to feminist theorizing about motherhood? Centering feminist theorizing on the concerns of white middle-class women leads to two problematic assumptions. The first is that a relative degree of economic security exists for mothers and their children. A second is that all women enjoy the racial privilege that allows them to see themselves primarily as individuals in search of personal autonomy instead of members of racial ethnic groups struggling for power. These assumptions allow feminist theorists to concentrate on themes such as the connections among mothering, aggression, and death, the effects of maternal isolation on mother–child relationships within nuclear family households, maternal sexuality, relations among family members, all-powerful mothers as conduits for gender oppression, and the possibilities of an idealized motherhood freed from patriarchy (Chodorow and Contratto 1982; Eisenstein 1983).

Although these issues merit investigation, centering feminist theorizing about motherhood in the ideas and experiences of African American, Native American, Hispanic, and Asian American women might yield markedly different themes (Andersen 1988; Brown 1989). This stance is to be distinguished from adding racial ethnic women's experiences to preexisting feminist theories without considering how these experiences challenge those theories (Spelman 1988). Involving much more than consulting existing social science sources, placing the ideas and experiences of women of color in the center of analysis requires invoking a different epistemology concerning what type of knowledge is valid. We must distinguish between what has been said about subordinated groups in the dominant discourse, and what such groups might say about themselves if given the opportunity. Personal narratives, auto-biographical statements, poetry, fiction, and other personalized statements have all been used by women of color to express self-defined standpoints on mothering and motherhood. Such knowledge reflects the authentic stand-point of subordinated groups. Placing these sources in the center and sup-plementing them with statistics, historical material, and other knowledge produced to justify the interests of ruling elites should create new themes and angles of vision (Smith 1990).[6]

Specifying the contours of racial ethnic women's motherwork promises to point the way toward richer feminist theorizing about motherhood. Issues of survival, power, and identity — these three themes form the bedrock of women of color's motherwork. The importance of working for the physi-cal survival of children and community, the dialectical nature of power and powerlessness in structuring mothering patterns, and the significance of self-definition in constructing individual and collective racial identity comprise three core themes characterizing the experiences of Native American, African American, Hispanic, and Asian American women. Examining survival, power, and identity reveals how racial ethnic women in the United States encounter and fashion motherwork. But it also suggests how feminist theorizing about motherhood might be shifted if different voices became central in femi-nist discourse.

Motherwork and Physical Survival

> *When we are not physically starving we have the luxury to realize psychic and emotional starvation.*
>
> — Moraga 1979:29

Physical survival is assumed for children who are white and middle class. Thus, examining their psychic and emotional well-being and that of their mothers appears rational. The children of women of color, many of whom are "physically starving," have no such assurances. Racial ethnic children's lives have long been held in low regard. African American children face an infant mortality rate twice that for white infants. Approximately one-third of His-panic children and one-half of African American children who survive infancy live in poverty. Racial ethnic children often live in harsh urban environments where drugs, crime, industrial pollutants, and violence threaten their survival. Children in rural environments often fare no better. Winona LaDuke reports that Native Americans on reservations frequently must use contaminated water. On the Pine Ridge Sioux Reservation in 1979, for example, 38 percent of all pregnancies resulted in miscarriages before the fifth month or in excessive hemorrhaging. Approximately 65 percent of the children who were born suffered breathing problems caused by underdeveloped lungs and jaundice (LaDuke 1988:63).

Struggles to foster the survival of Native American, Latino, Asian American, and African American families and communities by ensuring the survival of children are a fundamental dimension of racial ethnic women's motherwork. African American women's fiction contains numerous stories of mothers fighting for the physical survival both of their own biological children and of those of the larger-African American community.[7] "Don't care how much death it is in the land, I got to make preparations for my baby to live!" proclaims Mariah Upshur, the African American heroine of Sara Wright's 1986 novel *This Child's Gonna Live* (p. 143). The harsh climates that confront racial ethnic children require that their mothers, like Mariah Upshur, "make preparations for their babies to live" as a central feature of their motherwork.

Yet, like all deep cultural themes, the theme of motherwork for physical survival contains contradictory elements. On the one hand, racial ethnic women's motherwork for individuals and the community has been essential for their survival. On the other hand, this work often extracts a high cost for large numbers of women, such as loss of individual autonomy or the submersion of individual growth for the benefit of the group. Although this dimension of motherwork is essential, the question of whether women are doing more than their fair share of such work for community development merits consideration.

Histories of family-based labor have shaped racial ethnic women's motherwork for survival and the types of mothering relationships that ensue. African American, Asian American, Native American, and Hispanic women have all worked and contributed to family economic well-being (Dill 1988; Glenn 1985). Much of these women's experiences with motherwork stems from the work they performed as children. The commodification of children of color — from the enslavement of African children who were legally owned as property to the subsequent treatment of children as units of labor in agricultural work, family businesses, and industry — has been a major theme shaping motherhood for women of color. Beginning in slavery and continuing into the post–World War II period, African American children were put to work at young ages in the fields of southern agriculture. Sara Brooks began full-time work in the fields at age eleven and remembers, "We never was lazy cause we used to really work. We used to work like mens. Oh, fight sometime, fuss sometime, but worked on" (Collins 1990:54). Black and Latino children in contemporary migrant farm families make similar contributions to their family's economy. "I musta been almost eight when I started following the crops," remembers Jessie de la Cruz, a Mexican American mother with six grown children. "Every winter, up north. I was on the end of the row of prunes, taking care of my younger brother and sister. They would help me fill up the cans and put 'em in a box while the rest of the family was picking the whole row" (de la Cruz 1980:168). Asian American children spent long hours working in family businesses, child labor practices that have earned Asian Americans the dubious distinction of being "model minorities." More recently, the family-based labor of undocumented racial ethnic immigrants, often mother–child units doing piecework for the garment industry, recalls the sweatshop conditions confronting turn-of-the-century European immigrants.

A certain degree of maternal isolation from members of the dominant group characterizes the preceding mother–child units. For women of color working along with their children, such isolation is more appropriately seen as reflecting the placement of women of color and their children in racially and class-stratified labor systems than as resulting from patriarchal domination. The unit may be isolated, but the work performed by the mother–child unit closely ties the mothering experiences of women of color to wider political and economic issues. Children learn to see their work and that of their mother not as isolated from the wider society but as essential to their family's survival. Moreover, in the case of family agricultural labor or family businesses, women and children worked alongside men, often performing the same work. If isolation occurred, the family, not the mother–child unit, was the focus.

Children working in close proximity to their mothers received distinctive types of mothering. Asian American children working in urban family businesses report long days filled almost exclusively with work and school. In contrast, the sons and daughters of African American sharecroppers and migrant farm children of all backgrounds did not fare as well. Their placement in rural work settings meant that they had less access to educational opportunities. "I think the longest time I went to school was two months in one place," remembers Jessie de la Cruz. "I attended, I think, about forty-five schools. When my parents or my brothers didn't find any work, we wouldn't attend school because we weren't sure of staying there. So I missed a lot of school" (de la Cruz 1980:167–68). It was only in the 1950s that southern school districts stopped the practice of closing segregated African American schools during certain times of the year so that the children could work.

Work that separated women of color from their children also framed the mothering relationship. Until the 1960s, large numbers of African American, Hispanic, and Asian American women worked in domestic service. Even though women worked long hours to ensure their children's physical survival, that same work ironically denied the mothers access to their children. Different institutional arrangements emerged in African American, Latino, and Asian American communities to resolve the tension between maternal separation due to employment and the needs of dependent children. The extended family structure in African American communities endured as a flexible institution that mitigated some of the effects of maternal separation. Grandmothers are highly revered in African American communities, often because they function as primary caretakers of their daughters' and daughters-in-law's children (Collins 1990). In contrast, exclusionary immigration policies that mitigated against intergenerational family units in the United States led Chinese American and Japanese American families to make other arrangements (Dill 1988).

Some mothers are clearly defeated by this situation of incessant labor performed to ensure their children's survival. The magnitude of their mother-work overwhelms them. But others, even while appearing to be defeated, manage to pass on the meaning of motherwork for survival to their children. African American feminist thinker June Jordan (1985) remembers her perceptions of her mother's work:

> As a child I noticed the sadness of my mother as she sat alone in the kitchen at night. . . . Her woman's work never won permanent victories of any kind. It never enlarged the universe of her imagination or her power to influence what happened beyond the front door of our house. Her woman's work never tickled her to laugh or shout or dance. (P. 105)

But Jordan also sees her mother's work as being motherwork that is essential to individual and community survival.

> But she did raise me to respect her way of offering love and to believe that hard work is often the irreducible factor for survival, not something to avoid. Her woman's work produced a reliable home base where I could pursue the privileges of books and music. Her woman's work invented the potential for a completely new kind of work for us, the next generation of Black women: huge, rewarding hard work demanded by the huge, different ambitions that her perfect confidence in us engendered.

Motherwork and Power

> *How can I write down how I felt when I was a little child and my grandmother used to cry with us 'cause she didn't have enough food to give us? Because my brother was going barefooted and he was cryin' because he wasn't used to going without shoes? How can I describe that? I can't describe when my little girl died because I didn't have money for a doctor. And never had any teaching on caring for sick babies. Living out in labor camps. How can I describe that?*
>
> (de la Cruz 1980:177)

Jessie de la Cruz, a Mexican American woman who grew up as a migrant farm worker, experienced firsthand the struggle for empowerment facing racial ethnic women whose daily motherwork centers on issues of survival. A dialectical relation exists between efforts of racial orders to mold the institution of motherhood to serve the interests of elites, in this case, racial elites, and efforts on the part of subordinated groups to retain power over motherhood so that it serves the legitimate needs of their communities (Collins 1990). African American, Asian American, Hispanic, and Native American women have long been preoccupied with patterns of maternal power and powerlessness because their mothering experiences have been profoundly affected by this dialectical process. But instead of emphasizing maternal power in dealing either with father as patriarch (Chodorow 1978; Rich 1986) or with male dominance (Ferguson 1989), women of color are concerned with their power and powerlessness within an array of social institutions that frame their lives.

Racial ethnic women's struggles for maternal empowerment have revolved around three main themes. The struggle for control over their own bodies in order to preserve choice over whether to become mothers at all is one fundamental theme. The ambiguous politics of caring for unplanned children has long shaped African American women's motherwork. For example, the widespread institutionalized rape of African American women by white men both during slavery and in the segregated South created countless biracial children who had to be absorbed into African American families and communities (Davis 1981). The range of skin colors and hair textures in contemporary African American communities bears mute testament to the powerlessness of African American women in controlling this dimension of motherhood.

For many women of color, choosing to become a mother challenges institutional policies that encourage white middle-class women to reproduce and discourage low-income racial ethnic women from doing so, even penalizing them (Davis 1981). Rita Silk-Nauni, an incarcerated Native American woman, writes of the difficulties she encountered in trying to have additional children. She loved her son so much that she left him only when she went to work. "I tried having more after him and couldn't," she observes. "I went to a specialist and he thought I had been fixed when I had my Son. He said I would have to have surgery in order to give birth again. The surgery was so expensive but I thought I could make a way even if I had to work 24 hours a day. Now that I'm here, I know I'll never have that chance" (Brant 1988:94). Like Silk-Nauni, Puerto Rican and African American women have long had to struggle with issues of sterilization abuse (Davis 1981). More recently, efforts to manipulate the fertility of poor women dependent on public assistance speaks to the continued salience of this issue in the lives of racial ethnic women.

A second dimension of racial women's struggles for maternal empowerment concerns getting to keep the children that are wanted, whether they were planned for or not. For racial ethnic mothers like Jessie de la Cruz whose "little girl died" because she "didn't have money for a doctor," maternal separation from one's children becomes a much more salient issue than maternal isolation with one's children within an allegedly private nuclear family. Physical or psychological separation of mothers and children designed to disempower racial ethnic individuals forms the basis of a systematic effort to disempower their communities.

For both Native American and African American mothers, situations of conquest introduced this dimension of the struggle for maternal empowerment. In her fictional account of a Native American mother's loss of her children in 1890, Brant explores the pain of maternal separation. "It has been two days since they came and took the children away. My body is greatly chilled. All our blankets have been used to bring me warmth. The women keep the fire blazing. The men sit. They talk among themselves. We are frightened by this sudden child-stealing. We signed papers, the agent said. This gave them rights to take our babies. It is good for them, the agent said. It will make them civilized" (1988:101). A legacy of conquest has meant that Native American mothers on so-called reservations confront intrusive government institutions such as the Bureau of Indian Affairs in deciding the fate of their children. For example, the long-standing policy of removing Native American children from their homes and housing them in reservation boarding schools can be seen as an effort to disempower their mothers. In the case of African American women under slavery, owners controlled virtually all dimensions of their children's lives — they could be sold at will, whipped, even killed, all with no recourse by their mothers. In such a situation, simply keeping and rearing one's children becomes empowerment.

A third dimension of racial ethnic women's struggles for empowerment concerns the pervasive efforts by the dominant group to control their children's minds. In her short story "A Long Memory," Beth Brant juxtaposes the loss felt in 1890 by a Native American mother whose son and daughter were forcibly removed by white officials to the loss that Brant felt in 1978 when a hearing took away her custody of her daughter. "Why do they want our babies?" queries the turn-of-the-century mother. "They want our power. They take our children to remove the inside of them. Our power" (Brant 1988:105). This mother recognizes that the future of the Native American way of life lies in retaining the power to define that worldview through educating the children. By forbidding children to speak their native languages and in other ways encouraging them to assimilate into Anglo culture, external agencies challenge the power of mothers to raise their children as they see fit.

Schools controlled by the dominant group comprise one important location where this dimension of the struggle for maternal empowerment occurs. In contrast to white middle-class children, whose educational experiences affirm their mothers' middle-class values, culture, and authority, African American, Latino, Asian American and Native American children typically receive an education that derogates their mothers' perspective. For example, the struggles over bilingual education in Latino communities are about much more than retaining Spanish as a second language. Speaking the language of one's childhood is a way of retaining the entire culture and honoring the mother teaching that culture (Anzaldúa 1987; Moraga 1979).

Jenny Yamoto (1988) describes the stress of ongoing negotiations with schools regarding her part African American and part Japanese sons. "I've noticed that depending on which parent, Black mom or Asian dad, goes to school open house, my oldest son's behavior is interpreted as disruptive and irreverent, or assertive and clever. . . . I resent their behavior being defined and even expected on the basis of racial biases their teachers may struggle with or hold. . . . I don't have the time or energy to constantly change and challenge their teachers' and friends' misperceptions. I only go after them when the children really seem to be seriously threatened" (p. 24).

In confronting each of these three dimensions of their struggles for empowerment, racial ethnic women are not powerless in the face of racial and class oppression. Being grounded in a strong, dynamic, indigenous culture can be central in racial ethnic women's social constructions of motherhood. Depending on their access to traditional culture, women of color invoke alternative sources of power.[8] "Equality per se may have a different meaning for Indian women and Indian people," suggests Kate Shanley (1988). "That difference begins with personal and tribal sovereignty — the right to be legally recognized as people empowered to determine our own destinies" (p. 214). Personal sovereignty involves the struggle to promote the survival of a social structure whose organizational principles represent notions of family and motherhood different from those of the mainstream. "The nuclear family has little relevance to Indian women," observes Shanley. "In fact, in many ways, mainstream feminists now are striving to redefine family and community in a way that Indian women have long known."

African American mothers can draw upon an Afrocentric tradition where motherhood of varying types, whether bloodmother, othermother, or community othermother, can be invoked as a symbol of power. Many African American women receive respect and recognition within their local communities for innovative and practical approaches to mothering not only their own biological children but also the children in their extended family networks and in the community overall. Black women's involvement in fostering African American community development forms the basis of this community-based power. In local African American communities, community othermothers can become identified as powerful figures through furthering the community's well-being (Collins 1990).

Despite policies of dominant institutions that place racial ethnic mothers in positions where they appear less powerful to their children, mothers and children empower themselves by understanding each other's position and relying on each other's strengths. In many cases, children, especially daughters, bond with their mothers instead of railing against them as symbols of patriarchal power. Cherríe Moraga describes the impact that her mother had on her. Because she was repeatedly removed from school in order to work, Moraga's mother would be considered largely illiterate by prevailing standards. But her mother was also a fine storyteller and found ways to empower herself within dominant institutions. "I would go with my mother to fill out job applications for her, or write checks for her at the supermarket," Moraga (1979) recounts. "We would have the scenario all worked out ahead of time. My mother would sign the check before we'd get to the store. Then, as we'd approach the checkstand, she would say — within earshot of the cashier — 'oh honey, you go 'head and make out the check,' as if she couldn't be bothered with such an insignificant detail" (p. 28). Like Cherríe Moraga and her mother, racial ethnic women's motherwork involves collaborating to empower mothers and children within oppressive structures.

Motherwork and Identity

> *Please help me find out who I am. My mother was Indian, but we were taken from her and put in foster homes. They were white and didn't want to tell us about our mother. I have a name and maybe a place of birth. Do you think you can help me?*

(Brant 1988:9)

Like this excerpt from a letter to an editor, the theme of loss of racial ethnic identity and the struggle to maintain a sense of self and community pervade the remaining stories, poetry, and narratives in Beth Brant's volume, *A Gathering of Spirit*. Carol Lee Sanchez offers another view of the impact of the loss of self. "Radicals look at reservation Indians and get very upset about their poverty conditions," observes Sanchez. "But poverty to us is not the same thing as poverty is to you. Our poverty is that we can't be who we are. We can't hunt or fish or grow our food because our basic resources and the right to use them in traditional ways are denied us" (Brant 1988:165). Racial ethnic women's motherwork reflects the tensions inherent in trying to foster a meaningful racial identity in children within a society that denigrates people of color. The racial privilege enjoyed by white middle-class women makes unnecessary this complicated dimension of the mothering tradition of women of color. Although white children can be prepared to fight racial oppression, their survival does not depend on gaining these skills. Their racial identity is validated by their schools, the media, and other social institutions. White children are socialized into their rightful place in systems of racial privilege. Racial ethnic women have no such guarantees for their children. Their children must first be taught to survive in systems that would oppress them. Moreover, this survival must not come at the expense of self-esteem. Thus, a dialectical relation exists between systems of racial oppression designed to strip subordinated groups of a sense of personal identity and a sense of collective peoplehood, and the cultures of resistance to that oppression extant in various racial ethnic groups. For women of color, motherwork for identity occurs at this critical juncture (Collins 1990).

"Through our mothers, the culture gave us mixed messages," observes Mexican American poet Gloria Anzaldúa (1987). "Which was it to be—strong or submissive, rebellious or conforming?" (p. 18). Thus women of color's mother-work requires reconciling two contradictory needs concerning identity. First, preparing children to cope with and survive within systems of racial oppression is essential. The pressures for these children to assimilate are pervasive. In order to compel women of color to participate in their children's assimilation, dominant institutions promulgate ideologies that belittle people of color. Negative controlling images infuse the worlds of their male and female children (Collins 1990; Green 1990; Tajima 1989). Native American girls are encouraged to see themselves as "Pocahontases" and "squaws"; Asian American girls as "geisha girls" and "Suzy Wongs"; Hispanic girls as "Madonnas" and "hot-blooded whores"; and African American girls as "mammies," "matriarchs," and "prostitutes." Girls of all groups are told that their lives cannot be complete without a male partner and that their educational and career aspirations must always be subordinated to their family obligations.

This push toward assimilation is part of a larger effort to socialize racial ethnic children into their proper subordinate places in systems of racial and class oppression. But despite pressures to assimilate, since children of color can never be white, assimilation by becoming white is impossible. Thus, a second dimension of this mothering tradition involves equipping children with skills to challenge the systems of racial oppression. Girls who become women believing that they are capable only of being maids and prostitutes cannot contribute to racial ethnic women's motherwork. Mothers make varying choices in preparing their children to fit into, yet resist, systems of racial domination. Some mothers remain powerless in the face of external forces that foster their children's assimilation and subsequent alienation from their families and communities. Through fiction, Native American author Beth Brant (1988:102–103) explores the grief felt by a mother whose children had been taken away to live among whites. A letter arrives giving news of her missing son and daughter:

> *This letter is from two strangers with the names Martha and Daniel. They say they are learning civilized ways. Daniel works in the fields, growing food for the school. Martha is being taught to sew aprons. She will be going to live with the schoolmaster's wife. She will be a live-in girl. What is live-in girl? I shake my head. The words sound the same to me. I am afraid of Martha and Daniel. These strangers who know my name.*

Other mothers become unwitting conduits of the dominant ideology. "How many times have I heard mothers and mothers-in-law tell their sons to beat their wives for not obeying them, for being *hociconas* (big mouths), for being *callajeras* (going to visit and gossip with neighbors), for expecting their husbands to help with the rearing of children and the housework, for wanting to be something other than housewives," asks Gloria Anzaldúa (1987:16). Some mothers encourage their children to fit in for reasons of survival. "My mother, nursed in the folds of a town that once christened its black babies Lee, after Robert E., and Jackson, after Stonewall, raised me on a dangerous generation's old belief," remembers African American author Marita Golden (1983). "Because of my dark brown complexion, she warned me against wearing browns or yellow and reds. . . . And every summer I was admonished not to play in the sun 'cause you gonna have to get a light husband anyway, for the sake of your children'" (p. 24). To Cherríe Moraga's mother, "on a basic economic level, being Chicana meant being 'less.' It was through my mother's desire to protect her children from poverty and illiteracy that we became 'anglocized'; the more effectively we could pass in the white world, the better guaranteed our future" (Moraga 1979:28). Despite their mothers' good intentions, the costs to children taught to submit to racist and sexist ideologies can be high. Raven, a Native American woman, looks back on her childhood: "I've been raised in white man's world and was forbade more or less to converse with Indian people. As my mother wanted me to be educated and live a good life, free from poverty. I lived a life of loneliness. Today I am desperate to know my people" (Brant 1988:221). Raven's mother did what she thought best to help her daughter avoid poverty. But ultimately, Raven experienced the poverty of not being able to be who she was.

Still other mothers transmit sophisticated skills to their children of how one can appear to submit to yet simultaneously challenge oppression. Willi Coleman's mother used a Saturday-night hair-combing ritual to impart an African American women's standpoint to her daughters:

> Except for special occasions mama came home from work early on Saturdays. She spent six days a week mopping, waxing and dusting other women's houses and keeping out of reach of other women's husbands. Saturday nights were reserved for "taking care of them girls" hair and the telling of stories. Some of which included a recitation of what she had endured and how she had triumphed over "folks that were lower than dirt" and "no-good snakes in the grass." She combed, patted, twisted and talked, saying things which would have embarrassed or shamed her at other times. (Coleman 1987:34)

Historian Elsa Barkley Brown captures the delicate balance that racial ethnic mothers must achieve. Brown (1989) points out that her mother's behavior demonstrated the "need to teach me to live my life one way and, at the same time, to provide all the tools I would need to live it quite differently" (p. 929).

For women of color, the struggle to maintain an independent racial identity has taken many forms, all revealing varying solutions to the dialectical relation between institutions that would deny their children their humanity and their children's right to exist as self-defined people. Like Willi Coleman's mother, African American women draw upon a long-standing Afrocentric feminist worldview emphasizing the importance of self-definition and self-reliance, and the necessity of demanding respect from others (Collins 1990; Terborg-Penn 1986).

Poet and essayist Gloria Anzaldúa (1987) challenges many of the ideas in Latino cultures concerning women: "Though I'll defend my race and culture when they are attacked by non-mexicanos, . . . I abhor some of my culture's ways, how it cripples its women, *como burras*, our strengths used against us" (p. 21). Anzaldúa offers a trenchant analysis of the ways in which the Spanish conquest of Native Americans fragmented women's identity and produced three symbolic "mothers." *La Virgen de Guadalupe,* perhaps the single most potent religious, political, and cultural image of the Chicano people, represents the virgin mother who cares for and nurtures an oppressed people. *La Chingada (Malinche)* represents the raped mother, all but abandoned. A combination of the first two, *la Llorona*, symbolizes the mother who seeks her lost children. "Ambiguity surrounds the symbols of these three 'Our Mothers,'" claims Anzaldúa (1987). "In part, the true identity of all three has been subverted— *Guadalupe* to make us docile and enduring, *la Chingada* to make us ashamed of our Indian side, and *la Llorona* to make us a long-suffering people" (p. 31). For Anzaldúa (1987), the Spanish conquest that brought racism and economic subordination to Indian people and created a new mixed-race Latino people simultaneously devalued women:

> No, I do not buy all the myths of the tribe into which I was born. I can understand why the more tinged with Anglo blood, the more adamantly my colored and colorless sisters glorify their colored culture's values— to offset the extreme devaluation of it by the white culture. It's a legitimate reaction. But I will not glorify those aspects of my culture which have injured me and which have injured me in the name of protecting me. (P. 22)

Latino mothers face the complicated task of shepherding their children through the racism of the dominant society and the reactions to that racism framing cultural beliefs internal to Hispanic communities. Many Asian American mothers stress conformity and fitting in as a way to challenge the system. "Our parents are painted as hard workers who were socially uncomfortable and had difficulty expressing even the smallest opinion," observes Japanese American Kesaya Noda in her autobiographical essay "Growing Up Asian in America" (1989:246). Noda questioned this seeming capitulation on the part of her parents: "'Why did you go into those camps,' I raged at my parents, frightened by my own inner silence and timidity. 'Why didn't you do anything to resist?'" But Noda (1989) later discovers a compelling explanation as to why Asian Americans are so often portrayed as conforming: "I had not been able to imagine before what it must have felt like to be an American— to know absolutely that one is an American—and yet to have almost everyone else deny it. Not only deny it, but challenge that identity with machine guns and troops of white American soldiers. In those circumstances it was difficult to say, 'I'm a Japanese American.' 'American' had to do" (p. 247).

Native American women can draw upon a tradition of motherhood and woman's power inherent in Native American cultures (Allen 1986; Awiakta 1988). In such philosophies, "water, land, and life are basic to the natural order," says Winona LaDuke (1988). "All else has been created by the use and misuse of technology. It is only natural that in our respective struggles for survival, the native peoples are waging a war to protect the land, the water, and life, while the consumer culture strives to protect its technological lifeblood" (p. 65). Marilou Awiakta (1988) offers a powerful summary of the symbolic meaning of motherhood in Native American cultures: "I feel the Grandmother's power. She sings of harmony, not dominance. And her song rises from a culture that repeats the wise balance of nature: the gender capable of bearing life is not separated from the power to sustain it" (p. 126). A culture that sees the connectedness between the earth and human survival, and that sees motherhood as symbolic of the earth itself holds motherhood as an institution in high regard.

Concluding Remarks

Survival, power, and identity shape motherhood for all women. But these themes remain muted when the mothering experiences of women of color are marginalized in feminist theorizing about motherhood. The theories reflect a lack of attention to the connection between ideas and the contexts in which they emerge. Although such decontextualization aims to generate universal theories of human behavior, in actuality the theories routinely distort or omit huge categories of human experience.

Placing racial ethnic women's motherwork in the center of analysis re-contextualizes motherhood. Whereas the significance of race and class in shaping the context in which motherhood occurs is virtually invisible when white, middle-class women's experiences are the theoretical norm, the effects of race and class stand out in stark relief when women of color are accorded theoretical primacy. Highlighting racial ethnic mothers' struggles concerning their children's right to exist focuses attention on the importance of survival. Exploring the dialectical nature of racial ethnic women's empowerment in structures of racial domination and economic exploitation demonstrates the need to broaden the definition of maternal power. Emphasizing how the quest for self-definition is mediated by membership in different racial and social class groups reveals how the issue of identity is crucial to all motherwork.

Existing feminist theories of motherhood have emerged in specific intellectual and political contexts. By assuming that social theory will be applicable regardless of social context, feminist scholars fail to realize that they themselves are rooted in specific locations, and that the contexts in which they are located provide the thought-models of how they interpret the world. Their theories may appear to be universal and objective, but they actually are only partial perspectives reflecting the white middle-class context in which their creators live. Large segments of experience, those of women who are not white and middle class, have been excluded (Spelman 1988). Feminist theories of motherhood thus cannot be seen as *theories* of motherhood generalizable to all women. The resulting patterns of partiality inherent in existing theories—for example, the emphasis placed on all-powerful mothers as conduits for gender oppression—reflect feminist theorists' positions in structures of power. Such theorists are themselves participants in a system of privilege that rewards them for not seeing race and class privilege as important. Their theories can ignore the workings of class and race as systems of privilege because their creators often benefit from that privilege, taking it as a given and not as something to be contested.

Theorizing about motherhood will not be helped, however, by supplanting one group's theory with that of another—for example, by claiming that women of color's experiences are more valid than those of white middle-class women. Just as varying placement in systems of privilege, whether race, class, sexuality, or age, generates divergent experiences with motherhood, examining motherhood and mother-as-subject from multiple perspectives should uncover rich textures of difference. Shifting the center to accommodate this diversity promises to recontextualize motherhood and point us toward feminist theorizing that embraces difference as an essential part of commonality.

ENDNOTES

1. In this chapter, I use the terms *racial ethnic women* and *women of color* interchangeably. Grounded in the experiences of groups who have been the targets of racism, the term *racial ethnic* implies more solidarity with men involved in struggles against racism. In contrast, the term *women of color* emerges from a feminist background where racial ethnic women committed to feminist struggle aimed to distinguish their history and issues from those of middle-class white women. Neither term captures the complexity of African American, Native American, Asian American, and Hispanic women's experiences.
2. Positivist social science exemplifies this type of decontextualization. In order to create scientific descriptions of reality, positivist researchers aim to produce ostensibly objective generalizations. But because researchers have widely differing values, experiences, and emotions, genuine science is thought to be unattainable unless all human characteristics except rationality are eliminated from the research process. By following strict methodological rules, scientists aim to distance themselves from the values, vested interests, and emotions generated by their class, race, sex, or unique situation. By decontextualizing themselves, they allegedly become detached observers and manipulators of nature. Moreover, this researcher decontextualization is paralleled by comparable efforts to remove the objects of study from their contexts (Jaggar 1983).
3. Dominant theories are characterized by this decontextualization. Boyd's (1989) helpful survey of literature on the mother–daughter relationship reveals that though much work has been done on motherhood generally, and on the mother–daughter relationship, very little of it tests feminist theories of motherhood. Boyd identifies two prevailing theories—psychoanalytic theory and social learning theory—that she claims form the bulk of feminist theorizing. Both of these approaches minimize the importance of race and class in the context of motherhood. Boyd ignores Marxist-feminist theorizing about motherhood, mainly because very little of this work is concerned with the mother–daughter relationship. But Marxist-feminist analyses of motherhood provide another example of how decontextualization frames feminist theories of motherhood. See, e.g., Ann Ferguson's *Blood at the Root: Motherhood, Sexuality, and Male Dominance* (1989), an ambitious attempt to develop a universal theory of motherhood that is linked to the social construction of sexuality and male dominance. Ferguson's work stems from a feminist tradition that explores the relation between motherhood and sexuality by either bemoaning their putative incompatibility or romanticizing maternal sexuality.
4. Psychoanalytic feminist theorizing about motherhood, such as Nancy Chodorow's groundbreaking work *The Reproduction of Mothering* (1978), exemplifies how decontextualization of race and/or class can weaken what is otherwise strong feminist theorizing. Although I realize that other feminist approaches to motherhood exist—see, e.g., Eisenstein's (1983) summary—I have chosen to stress psychoanalytic feminist theory because the work of Chodorow and others has been highly influential in framing the predominant themes in feminist discourse.
5. The thesis of the atomized individual that underlies Western psychology is rooted in a much larger Western construction concerning the relation of the individual to

the community (Hartsock 1983). Theories of motherhood based on the assumption of the atomized human proceed to use this definition of the individual as the unit of analysis and then construct theory from this base. From this grow assumptions that the major process to examine is that between freely choosing rational individuals engaging in bargains (Hartsock 1983).

6. The narrative tradition in the writings of women of color addresses this effort to recover the history of mothers. Works from African American women's autobiographical tradition such as Ann Moody's *Coming of Age in Mississippi*, Maya Angelou's *I Know Why the Caged Bird Sings*, Linda Brent's *Incidents in the Life of a Slave Girl*, and Marita Golden's *The Heart of a Woman* contain the authentic voices of African American women centered on experiences of motherhood. Works from African American women's fiction include *This Child's Gonna Live*, Alice Walker's *Meridian*, and Toni Morrison's *Sula* and *Beloved*. Asian American women's fiction, such a Amy Tan's *The Joy Luck Club* and Maxine Kingston's *Woman Warrior*, and autobiographies, such as Jean Wakatsuki Houston's *Farewell to Manzanar*, offer a parallel source of authentic voice. Connie Young Yu (1989) entitles her article on the history of Asian American women "The World of Our Grandmothers" and recreates Asian American history with her grandmother as a central figure. Cherríe Moraga (1979) writes a letter to her mother as a way of coming to terms with the contradictions in her racial identity as a Chicana. In *Borderlands/La Frontera*, Gloria Anzaldúa (1987) weaves autobiography, poetry, and philosophy together in her exploration of women and mothering.

7. Notable examples include Lutie Johnson's unsuccessful attempt to rescue her son from the harmful effects of an urban environment in Ann Petry's *The Street*; and Meridian's work on behalf of the children of a small southern town after she chooses to relinquish her own child, in Alice Walker's *Meridian*.

8. Noticeably absent from feminist theories of motherhood is a comprehensive theory of power and an account of how power relations shape any theories actually developed. Firmly rooted in an exchange-based marketplace with its accompanying assumptions of rational economic decision making and white male control of the marketplace, this model of community stresses the rights of individuals, including feminist theorists, to make decisions in their own interest, regardless of the impact on larger society. Composed of a collection of unequal individuals who compete for greater shares of money as the medium of exchange, this model of community legitimates relations of domination either by denying they exist or by treating them as inevitable but unimportant (Hartsock 1983).

REFERENCES

Allen, P. G. 1986. *The Sacred Hoop: Recovering the Feminine in American Indian Traditions.* Boston: Beacon Press.

Andersen, M. 1988. "Moving Our Minds: Studying Women of Color and Reconstructing Sociology." *Teaching Sociology* 16(2):123–32.

Anzaldúa, G. 1987. *Borderlands/La Frontera: The New Mestiza.* San Francisco: Spinsters.

Awiakta, M. 1988. "Amazons in Appalachia." Pp. 125–30 in *A Gathering of Spirit*, edited by B. Brant. Ithaca, NY: Firebrand Books.

Boyd, C. J. 1989. "Mothers and Daughters: A Discussion of Theory and Research." *Journal of Marriage and the Family* 51:291–301.

Brant, B., ed. 1988. *A Gathering of Spirit: A Collection by North American Indian Women.* Ithaca, NY: Firebrand Books.

Brown, E. B. 1989. "African-American Women's Quilting: A Framework for Conceptualizing and Teaching African-American Women's History. *Signs* 14(4):921–29.

Chodorow, N. 1978. *The Reproduction of Mothering.* Berkeley: University of California Press.

Chodorow, N. and S. Contratto. 1982. "The Fantasy of the Perfect Mother." Pp. 54–74 in *Rethinking the Family: Some Feminist Questions,* edited by B. Thorne and M. Yalom. New York: Longman.

Coleman, W. 1987. "Closets and Keepsakes." *Sage: A Scholarly Journal on Black Women* 4(2):34–35.

Collins, P. H. 1990. *Black Feminist Thought: Knowledge, Consciousness and the Politics of Empowerment.* New York: Routledge.

Davis, A. Y. 1981. *Women, Race, and Class.* New York: Random House.

de la Cruz, J. 1980. Interview. In *American Dreams: Lost and Found,* edited by S. Terkel. New York: Ballantine Books.

Dill, B. T. 1988. "Our Mothers' Grief: Racial Ethnic Women and the Maintenance of Families." *Journal of Family History* 13(4):415–31.

Eisenstein, H. 1983. *Contemporary Feminist Thought.* Boston: Hall.

Ferguson, A. 1989. *Blood at the Root: Motherhood, Sexuality, and Male Dominance.* New York: Unwin Hyman/Routledge.

Flax, J. 1978. "The Conflict between Nurturance and Autonomy in Mother–Daughter Relationships and within Feminism." *Feminist Studies* 4(2):171–89.

Glenn, E. N. 1985. "Racial Ethnic Women's Labor: The Intersection of Race, Gender and Class Oppression." *Review of Radical Political Economics* 17(3):86–108.

———. 1986. *Issei, Nisei, War Bride: Three Generations of Japanese American Women in Domestic Service.* Philadelphia: Temple University Press.

Golden, M. 1983. *Migrations of the Heart.* New York: Ballantine Books.

Green, R. 1990. "The Pocohontas Perplex: The Image of Indian Women in American Culture." Pp. 15–21 in *Unequal Sisters,* edited by E. C. DuBois and V. Ruiz. New York: Routledge.

Hartsock, N. 1983. *Money, Sex and Power.* Boston: Northeastern University Press.

Jaggar, A. 1983. *Feminist Politics and Human Nature.* Totowa, NJ: Rowman & Allanheld.

Jordan, J. 1985. *On Call.* Boston: South End Press.

LaDuke, W. 1988. "They Always Come Back." Pp. 62–67 in *A Gathering of Spirit,* edited by B. Brant. Ithaca, NY: Firebrand Books.

Lerner, G., ed. 1972. *Black Women in White America: A Documentary History.* New York: Vintage Books.

Moraga, C. 1979. "La Guera." Pp. 27–34 in *This Bridge Called My Back: Writings by Radical Women of Color,* edited by C. Moraga and G. Anzaldúa. Watertown, MA: Persephone Press.

Noda, R. E. 1989. "Growing Up Asian in America." Pp. 243–50 in *Making Waves: An Anthology of Writings by and about Asian American Women,* edited by Asian Women United of California. Boston: Beacon Press.

Rich, A. 1986. *Of Woman Born: Motherhood as Institution and Experience.* New York: Norton.

Shanley, K. 1988. "Thoughts on Indian Feminism." Pp. 213–15 in *A Gathering of Spirit,* edited by B. Brant. Ithaca, NY: Firebrand Books.

Smith, D. E. 1990. *The Conceptual Practices of Power: A Feminist Sociology of Knowledge.* Boston: Northeastern University Press.

Spelman, E. V. 1988. *Inessential Woman: Problems of Exclusion in Feminist Thought.* Boston: Beacon Press.

Tajima, R. E. 1989. "Lotus Blossoms Don't Bleed: Images of Asian Women." Pp. 308–17 in *Making Waves: An Anthology of Writings by and about Asian American Women,* edited by Asian Women United of California. Boston: Beacon Press.

Terborg-Penn, R. 1986. "Black Women in Resistance: A Cross-Cultural Perspective." Pp. 188–209 in *In Resistance: Studies in African, Caribbean and Afro-American History,* edited by G. Y. Okhiro. Amherst: University of Massachusetts Press.

Wright, S. 1986. *This Child's Gonna Live.* Old Westbury, NY: Feminist Press.

Yamoto, J. 1988. "Mixed Bloods, Half Breeds, Mongrels, Hybrids." Pp. 22–24 in *Changing Our Power: An Introduction to Women's Studies,* edited by J. W. Cochran, D. Langston, and C. Woodward. Dubuque, IA: Kendall/Hunt.

Yu, C. Y. 1989. "The World of Our Grandmothers." Pp. 33–41 in *Making Waves: An Anthology of Writings by and about Asian American Women,* edited by Asian Women United of California. Boston: Beacon Press.

22

THE MOMMY WARS
Ambivalence, Ideological Work,
and the Cultural Contradictions of Motherhood

SHARON HAYS

I have argued that all mothers ultimately share a recognition of the ideology of intensive mothering. At the same time, all mothers live in a society where child rearing is generally devalued and the primary emphasis is placed on profit, efficiency, and "getting ahead." If you are a mother, both logics operate in your daily life.

But the story is even more complicated. Over half of American mothers participate directly in the labor market on a regular basis; the rest remain at least somewhat distant from that world as they spend most of their days in the home. One might therefore expect paid working mothers to be more committed to the ideology of competitively maximizing personal profit and stay-at-home mothers to be more committed to the ideology of intensive mothering. As it turns out, however, this is not precisely the way it works.

Modern-day mothers are facing two socially constructed cultural images of what a good mother looks like. Neither, however, includes the vision of a cold, calculating businesswoman — that title is reserved for childless career women. If you are a good mother, you *must* be an intensive one. The only "choice" involved is whether you *add* the role of paid working woman. The options, then, are as follows. On the one side there is the portrait of the "traditional mother" who stays at home with the kids and dedicates her energy to the happiness of her family. This mother cheerfully studies the latest issue of *Family Circle,* places flowers in every room, and has dinner waiting when her husband comes home. This mother, when she's not cleaning, cooking, sewing, shopping, doing the laundry, or comforting her mate, is focused on attending to the children and ensuring their proper development. On the other side is the image of the successful "supermom." Effortlessly juggling home and work, this mother can push a stroller with one hand and carry a briefcase in the other. She is always properly coiffed, her nylons have no runs, her suits are freshly pressed, and her home has seen the white tornado. Her children are immaculate and well mannered but not passive, with a strong spirit and high self-esteem.

Although both the traditional mom and the supermom are generally considered socially acceptable, their coexistence represents a serious cultural ambivalence about how mothers should behave. This ambivalence comes out in the widely available indictments of the failings of both groups of women. Note, for instance, the way Mecca, a welfare mother, describes these two choices and their culturally provided critiques:

> The way my family was brought up was, like, you marry a man, he's the head of the house, he's the provider, and you're the wife, you're the provider in the house. Now these days it's not that way. Now the people that stay home are classified, quote, "lazy people," we don't "like" to work.
>
> I've seen a lot of things on TV about working mothers and nonworking mothers. People who stay home attack the other mothers 'cause they're, like, bad mothers because they left the kids behind and go to work. And, the other ones aren't working because we're lazy. But it's not lazy. It's the lifestyle in the 1990s it's, like, too much. It's a demanding world for mothers with kids.

The picture Mecca has seen on television, a picture of these two images attacking each other with ideological swords, is not an uncommon one.

It is this cultural ambivalence and the so-called choice between these paths that is the basis for what Darnton (1990) has dubbed the "mommy wars." Both stay-at-home and paid working mothers, it is argued, are angry and defensive; neither group respects the other. Both make use of available cultural indictments to condemn the opposing group. Supermoms, according to this portrait, regularly describe stay-at-home mothers as lazy and boring, while traditional moms regularly accuse employed mothers of selfishly neglecting their children.

My interviews suggest, however, that this portrait of the mommy wars is both exaggerated and superficial. In fact, the majority of mothers I spoke with expressed respect for one another's need or right to choose whether to go out to work or stay at home with the kids. And, as I have argued, they also share a whole set of similar concerns regarding appropriate child rearing. These mothers have not formally enlisted in this war. Yet the rhetoric of the mommy wars draws them in as it persists in mainstream American culture, a culture that is unwilling, for various significant reasons, to unequivocally embrace either vision of motherhood, just as it remains unwilling to embrace wholeheartedly the childless career woman. Thus, the charges of being lazy and bored, on the one hand, or selfish and money-grubbing, on the other, are made available for use by individual mothers and others should the need arise.

What this creates is a no-win situation for women of childbearing years. If a woman voluntarily remains childless, some will say that she is cold, heartless, and unfulfilled as a woman. If she is a mother who works too hard at her job or career, some will accuse her of neglecting the kids. If she does not work hard enough, some will surely place her on the "mommy track" and her career advancement will be permanently slowed by the claim that her commitment to her children interferes with her workplace efficiency (Schwartz 1989). And if she stays at home with her children, some will call her unproductive and useless. A woman, in other words, can never fully do it right.

At the same time that these cultural images portray all women as somehow less than adequate, they also lead many mothers to feel somehow less than adequate in their daily lives. The stay-at-home mother is supposed to be happy and fulfilled, but how can she be when she hears so often that she is mindless and bored? The supermom is supposed to be able to juggle her two roles without missing a beat, but how can she do either job as well as she is expected if she is told she must dedicate her all in both directions? In these circumstances, it is not surprising that many supermoms feel guilty about their inability to carry out both roles to their fullest, while many traditional moms feel isolated and invisible to the larger world.

Given this scenario, both stay-at-home and employed mothers end up spending a good deal of time attempting to make sense of their current positions. Paid working mothers, for instance, are likely to argue that there are lots of good reasons for mothers to work in the paid labor force; stay-at-home mothers are likely to argue that there are lots of good reasons for mothers to stay at home with their children. These arguments are best understood not as (mere) rationalizations or (absolute) truths but rather as socially necessary "ideological work." Berger (1981) uses this notion to describe the way that all people make use of available ideologies in their "attempt to cope with the relationship between the ideas they bring to a social context and the practical pressures of day-to-day living in it" (p. 15). People, in other words, select among the cultural logics at their disposal in order to develop some correspondence between what they believe and what they actually do. For mothers, just like others, ideological work is simply a means of maintaining their sanity.

The ideological work of mothers, as I will show, follows neither a simple nor a straightforward course. First, as I have pointed out, both groups face two contradictory cultural images of appropriate mothering. Their ideological work, then, includes a recognition and response to both portraits. This duality is evident in the fact that the logic the traditional mother uses to affirm her position matches the logic that the supermom uses to express ambivalence about her situation, and the logic that the employed mother uses to affirm her position is the same logic that the stay-at-home mother uses to express ambivalence about hers. Their strategies, in other words, are mirror images, but they are also incomplete—both groups are left with some ambivalence. Thus, although the two culturally provided images of mothering help mothers to make sense of their own positions, they simultaneously sap the strength of mothers by making them feel inadequate in one way or the other. It is in coping with these feelings of inadequacy that their respective ideological strategies take an interesting turn. Rather than taking divergent paths, as one might expect, both groups attempt to resolve their feelings of inadequacy by returning to the logic of the ideology of intensive mothering.

The Frumpy Housewife
and the Push toward the Outside World

Some employed mothers say that they go out to work for pay because they need the income. But the overwhelming majority also say that they *want* to work outside the home. First, there's the problem of staying inside all day: "I decided once I started working that I need that. I need to work. Because I'll become like this big huge hermit frumpy person if I stay home." Turning into a "big huge hermit frumpy person" is connected to the feeling of being confined to the home. Many women have had that experience at one time or another and do not want to repeat it:

> When I did stay home with him, up until the time when he was ten months old, I wouldn't go out of the house for three days at a time. Ya know, I get to where I don't want to get dressed, I don't care if I take a shower. It's like, what for? I'm not going anywhere.

Not getting dressed and not going anywhere are also tied to the problem of not having a chance to interact with other adults:

> I remember thinking, "I don't even get out of my robe. And I've gotta stay home and breast-feed and the only adult I hear is on Good Morning America—and he's not even live!" And that was just for a couple of months. I don't even know what it would be like for a couple of years. I think it would be really difficult.

Interacting with adults, for many paid working mothers, means getting a break from the world of children and having an opportunity to use their minds:

> When I first started looking for a job, I thought we needed a second income. But then when I started working it was like, this is great! I do have a mind that's not Sesame Street! And I just love talking with people. It's just fun, and it's a break. It's tough, but I enjoyed it; it was a break from being with the kids.

If you don't get a break from the kids, if you don't get out of the house, if you don't interact with adults, and if you don't have a chance to use your mind beyond the *Sesame Street* level, you might end up lacking the motivation to do much at all. This argument is implied by many mothers:

> If I was stuck at home all day, and I did do that 'cause I was waiting for day care, I stayed home for four months, and I went crazy, I couldn't stand it. I mean not because I didn't want to spend any time with her, but because we'd just sit here and she'd just cry all day and I couldn't get anything done. I was at the end of the day exhausted, and feeling like shit.

Of course, it is exhausting to spend the day meeting the demands of children. But there's also a not too deeply buried sense in all these arguments that getting outside the home and using one's mind fulfill a longing to be part of the larger world and to be recognized by it. One mother made this point explicitly:

> [When you're working outside the home] you're doing something. You're using your mind a little bit differently than just trying to figure out how to make your day work with your kid. It's just challenging in a different way. So there's part of me that wants to be, like, recognized. I think maybe that's what work does, it gives you a little bit of a sense of recognition, that you don't feel like you get [when you stay home].

Most employed mothers, then, say that if they stay at home they'll go stir-crazy, they'll get bored, the demands of the kids will drive them nuts, they won't have an opportunity to use their brains or interact with other adults, they'll feel like they're going nowhere, and they'll lose their sense of identity in the larger world. And, for many of these mothers, all these points are connected:

> Well, I think [working outside is] positive, because I feel good about being able to do the things that I went to school for, and keep up with that, and use my brain. As they grow older, [the children are] going to get into things that they want to get into, they're going to be out with their friends and stuff, and I don't want to be in a situation where my whole life has been wrapped around the kids. That's it. Just some outside interests so that I'm not so wrapped up in how shiny my floor is. [She laughs.] Just to kind of be out and be stimulated. Gosh, I don't want this to get taken wrong, but I think I'd be a little bit bored. And the other thing I think of is, I kind of need a break, and when you're staying at home it's constant. It's a lot harder when you don't have family close by, [because] you don't get a break.

In short, paid working mothers feel a strong pull toward the outside world. They hear the world accusing stay-at-home moms of being mindless and unproductive and of lacking an identity apart from their kids, and they experience this as at least partly true.

Stay-at-home mothers also worry that the world will perceive them as lazy and bored and watching television all day as children scream in their ears and tug at their sleeves. And sometimes this is the way they feel about themselves. In other words, the same image that provides working mothers with the reasons they should go out to work accounts for the ambivalence that stay-at-home mothers feel about staying at home.

A few stay-at-home mothers seem to feel absolutely secure in their position, but most do not. Many believe that they will seek paid work at some point, and almost all are made uncomfortable by the sense that the outside world does not value what they do. In all cases, their expressions of ambivalence about staying at home mimic the concerns of employed mothers. For instance, some women who stay at home also worry about becoming frumpy: "I'm not this heavy. I'm, like, twenty-seven pounds overweight. It sounds very vain of me, in my situation. It's like, I'm not used to being home all the time, I'm home twenty-four hours. I don't have that balance in my life any-more." And some stay-at-home mothers feel as if they are physically confined inside the home. This mother, for example, seems tired of meeting the children's demands and feels that she is losing her sense of self:

> *There's a hard thing of being at home all the time. You have a lot of stress, be-cause you're constantly in the house. I think having a job can relieve some of that stress and to make it a lot more enjoyable, to want to come home all the time. . . . My outings are [limited]. I'm excited when I have to go grocery shop-ping. Everything I pick is what they eat, everything they like, or what they should eat. Me, I'm just there. I'm there for them. I feel that I'm here for them.*

Both of these stay-at-home mothers, like over one-third of the stay-at-home mothers in my sample, plan to go out to work as soon as they can find paid employment that offers sufficient rewards to compensate (both financially and ideologically) for sending the kids to day care. Most of the remaining mothers are committed to staying at home with the children through what they un-derstand as formative years. The following mother shares that commitment, while also echoing many paid working mothers in her hopes that one day she will have a chance to be around adults and further her own growth:

> *Well, we could do more, we'd have more money, but that's really not the biggest reason I'd go back to work. I want to do things for myself, too. I want to go back and get my master's [degree] or something. I need to grow, and be around adults, too. I don't know when, but I think in the next two years I'll go back to work. The formative years — their personality is going to develop until they're around five. It's pretty much set by then. So I think it's pretty critical that you're around them during those times.*

One mother stated explicitly that she can hardly wait until the kids are through their formative years:

> *At least talking to grown-ups is a little more fulfilling than ordering the kids around all day. My life right now is just all theirs. Sometimes it's a depressing thought because I think, "Where am I? I want my life back." . . . I mean, they are totally selfish. It's like an ice cream. They just gobble that down and say, "Let me have the cinnamon roll now."*
> *. . . [But] I had them, and I want them to be good people. So I've dedicated myself to them right now. Later on I get my life back. They won't always be these little sponges. I don't want any deficiency — well, nobody can cover all the loopholes — but I want to be comfortable in myself to know that I did everything that I could. It's the least I can do to do the best I can by them.*

Mothers, she seems to be saying, are like confections that the kids just gobble down — and then they ask for more.

Thus, many stay-at-home moms experience the exhaustion of meeting the demands of the children all day long, just as employed mothers fear they might. And many stay-at-home mothers also experience a loss of self. Part of the reason they feel like they are losing their identity is that they know the outside world does not recognize a mother's work as valuable. This woman, committed to staying at home until her youngest is at least three years old, explains:

> You go through a period where you feel like you've lost all your marbles. Boy, you're not as smart as you used to be, and as sharp as you used to be, and not as respected as you used to be. And those things are really hard to swallow. But that's something I've discussed with other mothers who are willing to stay home with their kids, and we've formed a support group where we've said, "Boy, those people just don't know what they're talking about." We're like a support group for each other, which you have to have if you've decided to stay at home, because you have so many people almost pushing you to work, or asking "Why don't you work? You're not somehow as good as anybody else 'cause you're staying at home; what you're doing isn't important. We have a lot of that in this society.

Another mother, this one determined to stay at home with her kids over the long haul, provides a concrete example of the subtle and not-so-subtle ways in which society pushes mothers to participate in the paid labor force, and of the discomfort such mothers experience as a result:

> As a matter of fact, somebody said to me (I guess it was a principal from one of the schools) . . . "Well, what do you do? Do you have a job?" And it was just very funny to me that he was so uncomfortable trying to ask me what it was in our society that I did. I guess that they just assume that if you're a mom at home that it means nothing. I don't know, I just don't consider it that way. But it's kind of funny, worrying about what you're gonna say at a dinner party about what you do.

And it's not just that these mothers worry about being able to impress school principals and people at cocktail parties, of course. The following mother worries about being "interesting" to other women who do not have children:

> I find myself, now that I'm not working, not to have as much in common [with other women who don't have children]. We don't talk that much because I don't have that much to talk about. Like I feel I'm not an interesting person anymore.

In short, the world presents, and mothers experience, the image of the lazy mindless, dull housewife—and no mother wants to be included in that image.

The Time–Crunched Career Woman and the Pull toward Home

Stay-at-home mothers use a number of strategies to support their position and combat the image of the frumpy housewife. Many moms who are committed to staying at home with their kids often become part of formal or informal support groups, providing them an opportunity to interact with other mothers who have made the same commitment. Others, if they can afford the cost of transportation and child care, engage in a variety of outside activities — as volunteers for churches, temples, and community groups, for instance, or in regular leisure activities and exercise programs. They then have a chance to communicate with other adults and to experience themselves as part of a larger social world (though one in which children generally occupy a central role).

But the primary way that stay-at-home mothers cope with their ambivalence is through ideological work. Like paid working mothers, they make a list of all the good reasons they do what they do. In this case, that list includes confirming their commitment to good mothering, emphasizing the importance of putting their children's needs ahead of their own, and telling stories about the problems that families, and especially children, experience when mothers go out to work for pay.

Many stay-at-home mothers argue that kids require guidance and should have those cookies cooling on the kitchen counter when they come home from school:

> *The kids are the ones who suffer. The kids need guidance and stuff. And with two parents working, sometimes there isn't even a parent home when they come home from school. And that's one thing that got me too. I want to be home and I want to have cookies on the stove when they come home from school. Now we eat meals together all the time. It's more of a homey atmosphere. It's more of a* home *atmosphere.*

Providing this homey atmosphere is difficult to do if one works elsewhere all day. And providing some period of so-called quality time in the evening, these mothers tell me, is not an adequate substitute. One mother elaborates on this point in response to a question about how she would feel if she was working outside the home:

> *Oh, guilty as anything. I know what I'm like after dinner, and I'm not at my best. And neither are my kids. And if that's all the time I had with them, it wouldn't be, quote, "quality time." I think it's a bunch of b.s. about quality time.*

And quality time, even if it *is* of high quality, cannot make up for children's lack of a quantity of time with their mothers. This argument is often voiced in connection with the problem of paid caregiver arrangements. Most mothers, whether they work for pay or not, are concerned about the quality of day care, but stay-at-home mothers often use this concern to explain their commitment to staying at home. This mother, for example, argues that children who are shuffled off to a series of day-care providers simply will not get the love they need:

> *I mean, if I'm going to have children I want to raise them. I feel really strongly about that. Really strongly. I wish more people did that. Myself,*

I think it's very underestimated the role the mother plays with the child. I really do. From zero to three [years], it's like their whole self-image. [Yet, working mothers will say,] "Well, okay, I've got a caretaker now," "Well, that nanny didn't work out." So by the time the children are three years old they've had four or five people who have supposedly said "I'll love you forever," and they're gone. I think that's really tough on the kids.

Since paid caregivers lack that deep and long-lasting love, I'm told, they won't ever be as committed to ministering to the child's needs as a mom will:

I don't think anybody can give to children what a mother can give to her own children. I think there's a level of willingness to put up with hard days, crying days, cranky days, whining days, that most mothers are going to be able to tolerate just a little bit more than a caretaker would. I think there's more of a commitment of what a mother wants to give her children in terms of love, support, values, etcetera. A caretaker isn't going to feel quite the same way.

Stay-at-home mothers imply that all these problems of kids who lack guidance, love, and support are connected to the problem of mothers who put their own interests ahead of the interests of their children. A few stay-at-home mothers will explicitly argue, as this one does, that employed mothers are allowing material and power interests to take priority over the well-being of their kids:

People are too interested in power, they just aren't interested in what happens to their kids. You know, "Fine, put them in day care." And I just feel sad. If you're so interested in money or a career or whatever, then why have kids? Why bring them into it?

Putting such interests ahead of one's children is not only somehow immoral; it also produces children with real problems. The following mother, echoing many stories about "bad mothers" that we have heard before, had this to say about her sister:

My sister works full-time—she's a lawyer. And her kids are the most obnoxious, whiny kids. I can't stand it. They just hang on her. She thinks she's doing okay by them because they're in an expensive private school and they have expensive music lessons and they have expensive clothes and expensive toys and expensive cars and an expensive house. I don't know. Time will tell, I guess. But I can't believe they're not going to have some insecurities. The thing that gets me is, they don't need it. I mean, he's a lawyer too. Basically, it's like, "Well, I like you guys, but I don't really want to be there all day with you, and I don't want to have to do the dirty work."

These are serious indictments indeed.

It is just these sorts of concerns that leave paid working mothers feeling inadequate and ambivalent about *their* position. Many of them wonder at times if their lives or the lives of their children might actually be better if they stayed at home with the kids. Above all, many of them feel guilty and wonder, "Am I doing it right?" or "Have I done all I can do?" These are the mothers who, we're told, have it all. It is impossible to have it all, however, when "all" includes two contradictory sets of requirements. To begin to get a deeper sense of how these supermoms do not always feel so super, two examples might be helpful.

Angela is a working-class mother who had expected to stay home with her son through his formative years. But after nine months she found herself bored, lonely, and eager to interact with other adults. She therefore went out and got a full-time job as a cashier. She begins by expressing her concern that she is not living up to the homemaking suggestions she reads in *Parenting* magazine, worrying that she may not be doing it right:

> I get *Parenting* *magazine and I read it. I do what is comfortable for me and what I can do. I'm not very creative. Where they have all these cooking ideas, and who has time to do that, except for a mother who stays home all day? Most of this is for a mother who has five, six hours to spend with her child doing this kind of thing. I don't have time for that.*
>
> *So then that's when I go back to day care. And I know that she's doing this kind of stuff with him, teaching him things. You know, a lot of the stuff that they have is on schooling kinds of things, flash cards, that kind of thing. Just things that I don't do. That makes me feel bad. Then I think, "I should be doing this" and "Am I doing the right thing?" I know I have a lot of love for him.*

Although Angela loves her son and believes that this is probably "the most important thing," she also feels guilty that she may not be spending a sufficient amount of time with him, simply because she gets so tired:

> I think sometimes that I feel like I don't spend enough time with him and that's my biggest [concern]. And when I am with him, sometimes I'm not really up to being with him. Even though I am with him, sometimes I want him to go away because I've been working all day and I'm exhausted. And I feel sometimes I'll stick him in bed early because I just don't want to deal with him that day. And I feel really guilty because I don't spend enough time with him as it is. When I do have the chance to spend time with him, I don't want to spend time with him, because I'm so tired and I just want to be with myself and by myself.

Even though Angela likes her paid work and does not want to give it up, the problems of providing both a quantity of time and the idealized image of quality time with her child, just like the challenge of applying the creative cooking and child-rearing ideas she finds in *Parenting* magazine, haunt her and leave her feeling both inadequate and guilty.

Linda is a professional-class mother with a well-paying and challenging job that gives her a lot of satisfaction. She spent months searching for the right preschool for her son and is relieved that he is now in a place where the caregivers share her values. Still, she worries and wonders if life might be better if she had made different choices:

> *I have a friend. She's a very good mom. She seems very patient, and I never heard her raise her voice. And she's also not working. She gets to stay home with her children which is another thing I admire. I guess I sort of envy that too. There never seems to be a time where we can just spend, like, playing a lot. I think that's what really bothers me, that I don't feel like I have the time to just sit down and, in a relaxing way, play with him. I can do it, but then I'm thinking "Okay, well I can do this for five minutes." So that's always in the back of my mind. Time, time, time. So I guess that's the biggest thing.*
>
> *And just like your question, "How many hours a day is he at preschool and how many hours do you spend per day as the primary caregiver?" just made me think, "Oh my gosh!" I mean they're watching him grow up more than I am. They're with him more than I am. And that makes me feel guilty in a way, and it makes me feel sad in a way. I mean I can just see him, slipping, just growing up before me. Maybe it's that quality-time stuff. I don't spend a lot of time, and I don't know if the time I do spend with him is quality.*
>
> *[But] if I just stay at home, I'll kind of lose, I don't know if I want to say my sense of identity, but I guess I'll lose my career identity. I'm afraid of that I guess. . . . My friend who stays at home, she had a career before she had her children, but I forget what it was. So that whole part of her, I can't even iden-tify it now.*

On the one hand, Linda envies and admires stay-at-home moms and worries about not spending enough quality time with her son, or enough play time. She is also upset that her day-care provider spends more hours with her son each day than she can. On the other hand, Linda worries that if she did stay at home she'd lose her identity as a professional and a member of the larger society. "Time, time, time," she says, there's never enough time to do it all— or at least to do it all "right."

The issue of time is a primary source of paid working mothers' ambiva-lence about their double shift. Attempting to juggle two commitments at once is, of course, very difficult and stressful. This mother's sense of how time pressures make her feel that she is always moving too fast would be recog-nizable to the majority of paid working mothers:

> *I can see when I get together with my sister [who doesn't have a paid job] . . . that she's so easygoing with the kids, and she takes her time, and when I'm with her, I realize how stressed out I am sometimes trying to get things done.*
>
> *And I notice how much faster I move when I shop. . . . She's so relaxed, and I think I kind of envy that.*

The problem of moving too fast when shopping is connected to the problem of moving too fast when raising children. Many paid working mothers envy those who can do such things at a more relaxed pace.

For a few employed mothers (two out of twenty in my sample) the problems of quality and quantity time outweigh the rewards of paid work, and they intend to leave their jobs as soon as they can afford to do so. This woman is one example:

> *I believe there's a more cohesive family unit with maybe the mother staying at home. Because a woman tends to be a buffer, mediator, you name it. She pulls the family together. But if she's working outside the home, sometimes there's not that opportunity anymore for her to pull everyone together. She's just as tired as the husband would be and, I don't know, maybe the children are feeling like they've been not necessarily abandoned but, well, I'm sure they accept it, especially if that's the only life they've seen. But my daughter has seen a change, even when I was only on maternity leave. I've seen a change in her and she seemed to just enjoy it and appreciate us as a family more than when I was working. So now she keeps telling me, "Mom, I miss you."*

When this mother hears her daughter say "I miss you," she feels a tremendous pull toward staying at home. And when she talks about the way a family needs a mother to bring its members together, she is pointing to an idealized image of the family that, like quality and quantity time, weighs heavily in the minds of many mothers.

The following paid working mother also wishes she could stay at home with the kids and wishes she could be just like the television mom of the 1950s who bakes cookies every afternoon. But she knows she has to continue working for financial reasons:

> *Yes. I want to be Donna Reed, definitely. Or maybe Beaver Cleaver's mother, [Barbara Billingsley]. Anybody in an apron and a pretty hairdo and a beautiful house. Yes. Getting out of the television set and making the most of reality is what I have to do. Because I'll always have to work.*

But the majority of paid working mothers, as I have stated, not only feel they need to work for financial reasons but also *want* to work, as Angela and Linda do. Nonetheless, their concerns about the effects of the double shift on their children match the concerns of those employed moms who wish they could stay at home as well as mimicking those of mothers who actually do stay at home. This mother, for instance, loves her paid work and does not want to give it up, but she does feel guilty, wondering if she's depriving her kids of the love and stimulation they need, particularly since she does not earn enough to justify the time she spends away:

> *Honestly, I don't make that much money. So that in itself brings a little bit of guilt, 'cause I know I work even though we don't have to. So there's some guilt associated. If kids are coming home to an empty house every day, they're not getting the intellectual stimulation [and] they're not getting the love and nurturing that other mothers are able to give their kids. So I think in the long run they're missing out on a lot of the love and the nurturing and the caring.*

And this mother does not want it to seem that she is putting her child second, but she feels pressure to live up to the image of the supermom:

> *I felt really torn between what I wanted to do. Like a gut-wrenching decision. Like, what's more important? Of course your kids are important, but you know, there's so many outside pressures for women to work. Every ad you see in magazines or on television shows this working woman who's coming home with a briefcase and the kids are all dressed and clean. It's such a lie. I don't know of anybody who lives like that.*
>
> *There's just a lot of pressure that you're not a fulfilled woman if you're not working outside of the home. But yet, it's just a real hard choice.*

This feeling of being torn by a gut-wrenching decision comes up frequently:

> *I'm constantly torn between what I feel I should be doing in my work and spending more time with them. . . . I think I would spend more time with them if I could. Sometimes I think it would be great not to work and be a mom and do that, and then I think, "well?"*
>
> *I think it's hard. Because I think you do need to have contact with your kid. You can't just see him in the morning and put him to bed at night because you work all day long. I think that's a real problem. You need to give your child guidance. You can't leave it to the schools. You can't leave it to churches. You need to be there. So, in some ways I'm really torn.*

The overriding issue for this mother is guidance; seeing the children in the morning and putting them to bed at night is just not enough.

This problem, of course, is related to the problem of leaving kids with a paid caregiver all day. Paid working mothers do not like the idea of hearing their children cry when they leave them at day care any more than any other mother does. They are, as we have seen, just as concerned that their children will not get enough love, enough nurturing, enough of the right values, enough of the proper education, and enough of the right kind of discipline if they spend most of their time with a paid caregiver. To this list of concerns, paid working mothers add their feeling that when the kids are with a paid caregiver all day, it feels as if someone else is being the mother. One woman (who stayed at home until her son was two years old) elaborates:

> *Well, I think it's really sad that kids have to be at day care forty hours a week. Because basically the person who's taking care of them is your day-care person. They're pretty much being the mother. It's really sad that this other person is raising your child, and it's basically like having this other person adopting your child. It's awful that we have to do that. I just think it's a crime basically. I wish we didn't have to do it. I wish everybody could stay home with their kids and have some kind of outlet. . . .*
>
> *And I think having a career is really important, but I think when it comes time to have children, you can take that time off and spend it with your kid. Because you can't go backwards, and time does fly with them. It's so sad. . . . I hear people say, "Oh, my day-care lady said that so-and-so walked today or*

> *used a spoon or something." I mean it's just so devastating to hear that you didn't get to see that.*

Leaving one's child with a paid caregiver for hours on end is therefore a potential problem not only because that "other mother" may not be a good mother but also because the real mother misses out on the joys that come from just being with the child and having a chance to watch him or her grow. This is a heartrending issue for many mothers who work outside the home.

Once again, the arguments used by stay-at-home mothers to affirm their commitment to staying home are mimicked by the arguments paid working mothers use to express their ambivalence about the time they spend away from their children. And again, though the reasoning of these women is grounded in their experiences, it is also drawn from a widely available cultural rhetoric regarding the proper behavior of mothers.

The Curious Coincidence of Paid Work and the Ideology of Intensive Mothering

Both paid working moms and stay-at-home moms, then, do the ideological work of making their respective lists of the reasons they should work for pay and the reasons they should stay at home. Yet both groups also continue to experience and express some ambivalence about their current positions, feeling pushed and pulled in two directions. One would assume that they would cope with their ambivalence by simply returning to their list of good reasons for doing what they do. And stay-at-home mothers do just that: They respond to the push toward work in the paid labor force by arguing that their kids need them to be at home. But, as I will demonstrate, working mothers do not use the mirror strategy. The vast majority of these women do not respond to the pull toward staying at home by arguing that kids are a pain in the neck and that paid work is more enjoyable. Instead, they respond by creating a new list of all the reasons that they are good mothers even though they work outside the home. In other words, the ideological work meant to resolve mothers' ambivalence generally points in the direction of intensive mothering.

Most paid working mothers cope with their ambivalence by arguing that their participation in the labor force is ultimately good for their kids. They make this point in a number of ways. For instance, one mother thinks that the example she provides may help to teach her kids the work ethic. Another says that with the "outside constraints" imposed by her work schedule, she's "more organized and effective" as a mom. Yet another mother suggests that her second child takes just as much time and energy away from her first child as her career does:

> *I think the only negative effect [of my employment] is just [that] generally when I'm overstressed I don't do as well as a mother. But work is only one of the things that gets me overstressed. In fact it probably stresses me less than some other things. I think I do feel guilty about working 'cause it takes time*

away from [my oldest daughter]. But it struck me that it's acceptable to have a second child that takes just as much time away from the other child. That I'm not supposed to feel guilty about. But in some ways this [pointing to the infant she is holding] takes my time away from her more than my work does. Because this is constant.

More often, however, paid working mothers share a set of more standard explanations for why their labor-force participation is actually what's best for their kids. First, just as Rachel feels that her income provides for her daughter's toys, clothing, outings, and education, and just as Jacqueline argues, "I have weeks when I don't spend enough time with them and they suffer, but those are also the weeks I bring home the biggest paychecks," many mothers point out that their paid work provides the financial resources necessary for the well-being of their children:

How am I supposed to send her to college without saving up? And also the money that I make from working helps pay for her toys, things that she needs, clothes. I never have to say, "Oh, I'm on a budget, I can't go buy this pair of shoes." I want the best for her.

Some mothers express a related concern—namely, what would happen to the family if they did not have paying jobs and their husbands should die or divorce them? One woman expressed it this way:

Well, my dad was a fireman, so I guess there was a little bit of fear, well, if anything happened to him, how are we gonna go on? And I always kind of wished that [my mother] had something to fall back on. I think that has a lot to do with why I continue to work after the kids. I've always just felt the need to have something to hold on to.

The second standard argument given by employed mothers is that paid caregiver arrangements can help to further children's development. With respect to other people's kids, I'm told, these arrangements can keep them from being smothered by their mothers or can temporarily remove them from bad family situations. With reference to their own children, mothers emphasize that good day care provides kids with the opportunity to interact with adults, gives them access to "new experiences" and "different activities," "encourages their independence," and allows them to play with other kids—which is very important, especially now that neighborhoods no longer provide the sort of community life they once did:

They do say that kids in preschool these days are growing up a little more neurotic, but I don't think that my daughter would have had a better life. In fact I think her life would have been a thousand times worse if I was a low-income mother who stayed home and she only got to play with the kids at the park. Because I think that preschool is really good for them. Maybe not a holding tank, but a nice preschool where they play nice games with them and they have the opportunity to play with the same kids over and over again. I think that's really good for them. Back in the 1950s, everybody stayed home and there were kids all over the block to play with. It's not that way now. The neighborhoods are deserted during the week.

Third, several mothers tell me that the quality of time they spend with their kids actually seems to increase when they have a chance to be away from them for a part of the day. Listen to these mothers:

— When I'm with them too long I tend to lose my patience and start yelling at them. This way we both get out. And we're glad to see each other when we come home.
— If women were only allowed to work maybe ten to fifteen hours a week, they would appreciate their kids more and they'd have more quality time with them, rather than having to always just scold them.
— I think I have even less patience [when I stay home with the children], because it's like, "Oh, is this all there is?" ... Whereas when I go to work and come home, I'm glad to see him. You know, you hear people say that they're better parents when they work because they spend more quality time, all those clichés, or whatever. For me that happens to be true.
— And now when I come home from work (although I wish I could get off earlier from work), I think I'm a better mom. There you go! Because when I come home from work, I don't have all *day, just being with the kids. It's just that when I'm working I feel like I'm competent, I'm a person!*

Getting this break from the kids, a break that reinforces your feeling of competence and therefore results in more rewarding time with your children is closely connected to the final way paid working mothers commonly attempt to resolve their ambivalence. Their children's happiness, they explain, is dependent upon their *own* happiness as mothers. One hears this again and again: "Happy moms make happy children"; "If I'm happy in my work, then I think I can be a better mom"; and "I have to be happy with myself in order to make the children happy." One mother explains it this way:

In some ways working is good. It's definitely got its positive side, because I get a break. I mean, now what I'm doing [working part-time] is perfect. I go to work. I have time to myself. I get to go to the bathroom when I need to go to the bathroom. I come home and I'm very happy to see my kids again. What's good for the mother and makes the mother happy is definitely good for the kids.

In all these explanations for why their participation in the paid labor force is actually good for their kids, these mothers want to make it clear that they still consider children their primary interest. They are definitely not placing a higher value on material success or power, they say. Nor are they putting their own interests above the interests of their children. They want the children to get all they need. But part of what children need, they argue, is financial security, the material goods required for proper development, some time away from their mothers, more quality time when they are with their mothers, and mothers who are happy in what they do. In all of these statements, paid working mothers clearly recognize the ideology of intensive mothering and testify that they are committed to fulfilling its requirements.

To underline the significance of this point, let me remind the reader that these paid working mothers use methods of child rearing that are just as child-centered, expert-guided, emotionally absorbing, labor-intensive, and financially expensive as their stay-at-home counterparts; they hold the child just as sacred, and they are just as likely to consider themselves as primarily responsible for the present and future well-being of their children. These are also the very same mothers who put a tremendous amount of time and energy into finding appropriate paid caregiver arrangements. Yet for all that they do to meet the needs of their children, they still express some ambivalence about working outside the home. And they still resolve this ambivalence by returning to the logic of intensive mothering and reminding the observer that ultimately they are most interested in what is best for their kids. This is striking.

Continuing Contradictions

All this ideological work is a measure of the power of the pushes and pulls experienced by American mothers today. A woman can be a stay-at-home mother and claim to follow tradition, but not without paying the price of being treated as an outsider in the larger public world of the market. Or a woman can be a paid worker who participates in that larger world, but she must then pay the price of an impossible double shift. In both cases, women are enjoined to maintain the logic of intensive mothering. These contradictory logics highlight the emotional, cognitive, and physical toll they take on contemporary mothers.

As I have argued, these strategies also highlight something more. The ways mothers explain their decisions to stay at home or work in the paid labor force, like the pushes and pulls they feel, run in opposite directions. Yet the ways they attempt to resolve the ambivalence they experience as a result of those decisions run in the *same* direction. Stay-at-home mothers, as I have shown, reaffirm their commitment to good mothering, and employed mothers maintain that they are good mothers even though they work. Paid working mothers do not, for instance, claim that child rearing is a relatively meaningless task, that personal profit is their primary goal, and that children are more efficiently raised in child-care centers. If you are a mother, in other words, although both the logic of the workplace and the logic of mothering operate in your life, the logic of intensive mothering has a *stronger* claim.

This phenomenon is particularly curious. The fact that there is no way for either type of mother to get it right would seem all the more reason to give up the logic of intensive mothering, especially since both groups of mothers recognize that paid employment confers more status than motherhood in the larger world. Yet images of freshly baked cookies and *Leave It to Beaver* seem to haunt mothers more often than the housewives' "problem that has no name" (Friedan 1963), and far more often than the image of a corporate manager with a big office, a large staff, and lots of perks. Although these mothers do not want to be defined as "mere" housewives and do want to achieve recognition in the outside world, most would also like to be there when the kids come home from school. Mothers surely try to balance their own desires against the requirements of appropriate child rearing, but in the world of mothering, it is socially unacceptable for them (in word if not in deed) to place their own needs above the needs of their children. A good mother certainly would never simply put her child aside for her own convenience. And placing material wealth or power on a higher plane than the well-being of children is strictly forbidden. It is clear that the two groups come together in holding these values as primary, despite the social devaluation of mothering and despite the glorification of wealth and power.

The portrait of the mommy wars, then, is overdrawn. Although the ideological strategies these groups use to explain their choice of home or paid work include an implicit critique of those "on the other side," this is almost always qualified, and both groups, at least at times, discuss their envy or admiration for the others. More important, as should now be abundantly clear, both groups ultimately share the same set of beliefs and the same set of concerns. Over half the women in my sample explicitly state that the choice between home and paid work depends on the individual woman, her interests, desires, and circumstances. Nearly all the rest argue that home is more important than paid work because children are simply more important than careers or the pursuit of financial gain. The paid working women in my sample were actually twice as likely as their stay-at-home counterparts to respond that home and children are more important and rewarding than paid work. Ideologically speaking, at least, home and children actually seem to become more important to a mother the more time she spends away from them.

There *are* significant differences among mothers— ranging from individual differences to more systematic differences of class, race, and employment. But in the present context, what is most significant is the commitment to the ideology of intensive mothering that women share in spite of their differences. In this, the cultural contradictions of motherhood persist.

The case of paid working mothers is particularly important in this regard, since these are the very mothers who, arguably, have the most to gain from redefining motherhood in such a way as to lighten their load on the second shift. As we have seen, however, this is not exactly what they do. It is true, as Gerson (1985) argues, that there are ways in which paid working mothers do redefine motherhood and lighten their load—for instance, by sending their kids to day care, spending less time with them than their stay-at-home counterparts, legitimating their paid labor-force participation, and engaging in any number of practical strategies to make child-rearing tasks less energy- and time-consuming. But, as I have argued, this does not mean that these mothers have given up the ideology of intensive mothering. Rather, it means that, whether or not they actually do, they feel they should spend a good deal of time looking for appropriate paid caregivers, trying to make up for the lack of quantity time by focusing their energy on providing quality time, and remaining attentive to the central tenets of the ideology of intensive child rearing. It also means that many are left feeling pressed for time, a little guilty, a bit inadequate, and somewhat ambivalent about their position. These stresses and the strain toward compensatory strategies should actually be taken as a measure of the persistent strength of the ideology of intensive mothering.

To deepen the sense of paradox further, one final point should be repeated. There are reasons to expect middle-class mothers to be in the vanguard of transforming ideas about child rearing away from an intensive model. First, middle-class women were historically in the vanguard of transforming child-rearing ideologies. Second, while many poor and working-class women have had to carry a double shift of wage labor and domestic chores for generations, middle-class mothers have had little practice, historically speaking, in juggling paid work and home and therefore might be eager to avoid it. Finally, one could argue that employed mothers in the middle class have more to gain from reconstructing ideas about appropriate child rearing than any other group — not only because their higher salaries mean that more money is at stake, but also because intensive mothering potentially interferes with their career trajectories in a more damaging way than is true of less high-status occupations. But, as I have suggested, middle-class women are, in some respects, those who go about the task of child rearing with the greatest intensity.

When women's increasing participation in the labor force, the cultural ambivalence regarding paid working and stay-at-home mothers, the particular intensity of middle-class mothering, and the demanding character of the cultural model of appropriate child rearing are taken together, it becomes clear that the cultural contradictions of motherhood have been deepened rather than resolved. The history of child-rearing ideas demonstrates that the more powerful the logic of the rationalized market became, so too did its ideological opposition in the logic of intensive mothering. The words of contemporary mothers demonstrate that this trend persists in the day-to-day lives of women.

REFERENCES

Berger, Bennett. 1981. *Survival of a Counterculture.* Berkeley: University of California Press.

Darnton, Nina. 1990. "Mommy vs. Mommy." *Newsweek,* June 4.

Friedan, Betty. 1963. *The Feminine Mystique.* New York: Dell.

Gerson, Kathleen. 1985. *Hard Choices: How Women Decide about Work, Career, and Motherhood.* Berkeley: University of California Press.

Schwartz, Felice. 1989. "Management Women and the New Facts of Life." *Harvard Business Review* 67(1):65–77.

23

DILEMMAS OF INVOLVED FATHERHOOD

KATHLEEN GERSON

Work's a necessity, but the things that really matter are spending time with my family. If I didn't have a family, I don't know what I would have turned to. That's why I say you're rich in a lot of ways other than money. I look at my daughter and think, "My family is everything."

— CARL, A THIRTY-FOUR-YEAR-OLD UTILITIES WORKER

As they looked for commitments beyond the workplace and became involved with women who desired and expected help in child rearing, involved fathers found unexpected pleasure in parenting. Spending time with their children became as important to them as contributing money. Becoming an involved father, however, meant trading some historically male advantages for the chance to ease some historically male burdens.

While all involved fathers wished to participate in family life more than their breadwinning and autonomous peers did, most resisted full equality in parenting. Almost 40 percent of all involved fathers became (or planned to become) genuinely equal or primary parents, but the remaining men are better described as "mothers' helpers." This chapter takes a close look at all involved fathers, with an eye toward understanding their dilemmas and conflicts, their strategies for limiting their burdens, and the differences among them. What helped or hindered a father's involvement once a desire to participate had emerged? Why did some involved fathers become mothers' helpers, while others became equal or primary caretakers? The answers to these questions help us to identify the social and ideological barriers that suppress equality as well as the social conditions that foster equal or primary parenting among men.

The Shape and Limits of Involved Fatherhood

Involved fathers rejected distinct boundaries between supporting a family and nurturing one, and defined neither as one person's domain. Carl, a utility repairman with a young daughter and a wife employed as a marketing manager, insisted:

> *It's not like "Give me your money, and/or you take my money." We put it in*
> *one pot and take care of whatever we need. . . . We pull the same weight. . . .*
> *As far as time and being around the house is concerned, I can stay home more*
> *than my wife can stay home. I come home in the afternoon, and I'm here with*
> *my daughter after school. My wife can come home at night to be with her. She*
> *likes her job, and she likes the sharing. She's got both worlds. So it's worked*
> *out good.*

Some men in dual-earner marriages take little responsibility for child rearing, defining their parental commitments in terms of breadwinning despite
being married to women who work outside the home. Similarly, while most
caretaking fathers were married to (or planned to marry) work-committed
women, about 5 percent of them had nonemployed wives and another 20 percent had wives or partners who were employed part-time. It is his participation in caring for his children that determines whether a man is an involved
father, not the shared breadwinning that typically accompanies it.

How do I define *participation*? The type and degree of activity varied
greatly among the involved fathers, but they all emphasized sharing and flexibility in parenting and domestic tasks. Lou, a sewage worker and father of a
young girl, and Theodore, a planner who is married but not yet a father,
sound remarkably similar despite differences in class and life stage:[2]

> *Patricia and I know how the other works. If one of us had a bad day, the other*
> *person will pick up the slack. If it's getting Hannah ready, teaching her writ-*
> *ing, spelling, or such, it's whoever is in a better frame of mind that day who*
> *handles it. We feed off each other's vibes. If we both have bad days, then who-*
> *ever had the better day takes care of her.*

> *One thing I learned: you can't take domestic jobs and say, "You do this, and*
> *I do that. You're the one who does the vacuuming and washing and ironing,*
> *and I'm the one who does the car and cleans the bathroom." I don't think that's*
> *right, and I think the same way with children. It's not going to be, "You're the*
> *one who changes the diapers while I burp the child." You do it together. If she's*
> *too tired, then I'll do it; and if I'm too tired, then she'll do it.*

Involved fathers are flexible. Just as they decline to accept a rigid division
between breadwinning and caretaking, they also reject rigid divisions in parenting itself. They do not distinguish "mothering" from "fathering." Vincent,
a businessman in his early thirties who planned to become involved when he
had children, explained:

> *I think you have obligations to your kid not as a husband or a father but as a*
> *parent. There is nothing as a male that I would not do. I never really changed*
> *a diaper before, but I'm sure I can learn how to do it.*

Clarence, a self-employed consultant, added:

> *It doesn't have to be fifty-fifty. It may be seventy-five–twenty-five where I do*
> *seventy-five and she does twenty-five, or where she does seventy-five and I*
> *do twenty-five. But there's nothing in the raising of a child that I can't see*

myself doing—changing diapers, getting up, or whatever has to be done—
all of that I'm ready to do.

Autonomous men could make work choices without taking the economic
needs of children into account. Primary breadwinners faced pressure to maximize their economic contribution, but they could also make choices about
work without concern for spending time at home. Men who wished to care
for their children, however, faced hard choices between freedom and commitment, career and parenthood, time spent with children and time spent
making money or pursuing leisure. In the past, such trade-offs appeared to
be the sole preserve of employed mothers; today they confront any adult who
tries to be both a committed parent and a committed worker.[3]

First, involved fathers faced a conflict between spending time making
money and spending time caring for their children. They felt torn between an
ideal of good parenting that stresses providing emotional sustenance and one
that stresses providing economic support. Michael, a therapist, had become
the custodial parent of his adolescent son and daughter. He worried about
how to meet both his emotional and economic obligations:

dilemma

> *I think there's an ideal in my head that I should be around more than I am.*
> *I try to be as available as I can be with the amount of time that I work, but*
> *there's something to be said for quantity, not just quality, of time.*

The sense that good parenting means devoting a lot of time to children
inevitably clashed with the equally urgent desire to provide a decent standard of living by working hard. Michael continued:

> *It's tough to maintain a standard of living in today's world—to live in a nice*
> *place and be able to send your kids to college or take vacations. And nobody*
> *pays you for doing nothing. They don't pay you unless you bust your neck.*
> *So it's difficult for me to make a choice, to spend the time I think I should with*
> *them. It makes the choices complicated, because you frequently are in situa-*
> *tions where you're damned if you do and damned if you don't.*

Another dilemma for involved fathers revolves around the contrasting
demands of nurturing a family and nurturing a career. Unlike the previous
problem, this one concerns how these men can meet their own needs as well
as their children's. Ernie, a physical therapist, explained how:

> *You always feel like you have to make a choice between a career versus family,*
> *and that's so unfair. I want a higher position where I can grow and be finan-*
> *cially okay, but I don't want to have to travel or be away on weekends. I don't*
> *want to sacrifice time with my family; it isn't worth it. I want my cake and eat*
> *it too. So that's why I have to struggle all the time, why I always have prob-*
> *lems making a decision.*

Third, even in the absence of a perceived conflict between family and career, involved fathers faced trade-offs between freedom and commitment,
privilege and participation, the ability to pursue personal interests and the

demands of family involvement. Neil, a graduate student, anticipated that he would have to sacrifice many treasured leisure activities when he became a father:

> *I think I can balance my career and a child, but it's the other personal things that will obviously suffer — leisure time, political activity. That's definitely starting to concern me.*

Involved fathers felt these conflicts more acutely than other men precisely because they defined "good fathering" in terms of active involvement. Benjamin, a social worker, and his wife faced the same overloaded schedule in caring for their toddler:

> *It's very exhausting to be a man today, especially a man with a young child. It's exhausting for everybody because if you're going to share the responsibility, which my wife and I have always done, it means there's just a lot to do. I don't want to make it sound too depressing, because you get into the rhythm of it, but I wonder now, "How do I do it? How do I get up at six-fifteen every morning when I used to love to sleep late? How do I get through the day on only six hours sleep?" The fact is that I do, and I'm not falling over, but it's tiring.*

How did these involved fathers cope with the responsibilities of parental participation and the attendant loss of privileges that other men retained?

Containing the Costs of Involvement

Involved fathers were flexible about what they would do, but their commitment not to rule anything out did not necessarily include a commitment to rule everything explicitly in. The stress on fluid, interchangeable responsibilities left unresolved the question of how much time they would commit and how much responsibility they would assume. They could use this vagueness to avoid certain tasks. Indeed, most were able to limit or pass on some of the costs of child rearing. These efforts eased involved fathers' personal binds, but they also reduced the chances that their parental involvement would take the form of full equality.

One way to limit the demands of parenthood and still play a significant role in child rearing is to keep the family small. Many involved fathers pushed for this, sometimes amid a wife's ambivalence. Norm, an attorney, insisted on stopping after he and his wife had two children:

> *I don't want another child. My wife does and doesn't. If we had another one, it would be too much of a burden. We had a lot of time with Becky. We were able to give her a lot, and I want to be able to do the same thing for the little one, not have a third child in there where they really have to share that.*

Some, like Frank, a banker, concluded that the work of rearing one child was more than enough:

My wife brings the matter up from time to time, "Aren't we foolish not to have another one? The first one has been such a joy and a pleasure." And she has been. But I take a more tempered view and say, "Well, as great a joy as she is, she still requires a great deal of time on both of our parts. Isn't our time spread pretty thin already?" She agrees with that logic.

On the other hand, some involved fathers found themselves settling for fewer children than they would have preferred. Warren, an engineer with an eight-year-old daughter, reluctantly accepted his wife's decision:

I want more children. She doesn't. She just feels one's enough. She's satisfied. I don't like it, but I've learned to live with it. I can't force her, and even if it were to come down to that, I wouldn't want her to carry a kid just for me. I feel she might be resentful, taking something away from her career.

Given the convergence of demands on both partners, it makes sense that involved fathers had fewer children than breadwinning fathers. Among primary breadwinners with children, 34 percent had at least three, 49 percent had two, and only 17 percent had only one child. In contrast, only 6 percent of involved fathers had more than two offspring, while 42 percent had only one. Even more telling, taking both current and planned fertility into account, 24 percent of involved fathers planned to limit their family size to one child, while only 10 percent of primary breadwinners held similar expectations. While 36 percent of breadwinners hoped to have at least three children, only 17 percent of involved fathers did. For almost a quarter of those who were (or planned to be) significantly involved in caretaking, one child appeared to be the best compromise between a desire to be involved and a countervailing desire to keep down the costs of involvement. Paradoxically, the men most oriented toward child rearing — those who expressed the most pleasure from taking care of children — were also the least likely to have a lot of them. Carlos, a social worker, said of his and his fiancée's plans:

Unless there was a radical change in our work style, having a second child would be an extreme hardship on both of us. And I don't think we would want to bring a child in and not be able to really meet that child's needs. I think having one child would meet our needs.

Although the one-child strategy helped resolve the dilemma of how to be an involved father without relinquishing too much freedom, this choice could also produce a sense of unfulfilled desires.[4] To cope with concerns about having a small family, caretaking fathers focused on the potentially dire consequences of having a larger one. In rejecting his sister's suggestion that he and his wife consider adoption when they discovered she could not bear another child, Ernie emphasized the toll a second child might take on his career, his family's financial security, and the time available for his daughter:

I wouldn't do it now because I feel we struggle as it is with one. There are times that I feel like I don't give enough to Annie, and I don't feel I can pro-

vide enough to her. She gets a lot of attention; she gets a lot of love, which to me is primary, and materialistic things are secondary. But I don't feel I could take in another person. I feel we're just managing with one.

The decision to have one child, then, also promoted greater involvement by limiting a father's financial burdens and allowing more time for family life.[5] For Dean, a park worker married to a waitress, having one child allowed him to avoid his father's pattern of working too much and parenting too little:

I always say, "It would be nice to have another one." I enjoy Joey so much. A couple of times I kid my wife, "Maybe tonight's the night." She'll say, "Don't talk crazy." The thing always crosses your mind, but it's really not feasible. I would rather have one child and really devote time to him than have three and be like my father, where he had to work and not get much time.

Limiting family size may seem an ironic response to the desire to be involved, but it lowered parenthood's emotional, physical, and financial demands. It did not, however, resolve all the dilemmas of involved fatherhood. As Benjamin found, even one child can take a significant toll. "Karen. . . . sleeps through the night; she's a really good baby. But it is still exhausting to have a child—just exhausting."

Because only a small proportion of involved fathers shared parental responsibilities with a nonemployed partner, most (over three-fourths) of these households relied on paid or unpaid help from an additional caretaker. Involved fathers knew this help was essential for their own well-being, but they tended to view paid baby-sitters, housekeepers, and even relatives as substitutes for their wives (or, in some cases, ex-wives) and not for themselves. Since even the most involved fathers did not consider their paid work responsibilities to be negotiable, the wife's decision to remain at work (or her absence from the home altogether) triggered the search for a "substitute mother." Nevertheless, Norm found that hiring a caretaker after the birth of his second daughter relieved him of many of the duties he had assumed with his first child:

Before the housekeeper, I got my older daughter ready every morning, fed her breakfast, made her lunch—because my wife left earlier than me. Now when my wife and I have to get ready for work, we bring the baby downstairs. The housekeeper'll give the baby breakfast, take care of her, dress her or whatever. So she does a lot of things I used to do.

Of course, the willingness and ability of parents to rely on "parent substitutes" vary. Working-class households were less likely than middle-class ones to use help. While 88 percent of middle-class families with involved fathers relied on some form of paid or unpaid help from a third party, 62 percent of the working-class families did so; 73 percent of middle-class families relied exclusively on paid help, while only 14 percent of working-class families did. But working-class families were more likely to rely on a web of interdependent relationships than were middle-class households.[6] Almost half of working-class involved fathers (and their wives) had help from relatives or friends (or, in the case of those who had not yet had a child, planned to do so).

Scott, a paramedic, and his wife, a nurse, "adopted" his mother-in-law to help with their two children while they both worked full-time:

> *We moved in with her mom, and she helped a lot with raising both children. She's been an integral member of the family right from the beginning. I feel she's more my mother than my mother-in-law. She even treats me like her son. I don't think we could exist as a family without her help.*

Extended kin allowed working-class fathers to get help without adding a significant new expense to an already strained family budget. It also allowed them to rely on someone they trusted. Todd, a construction worker married to a dancer, conceded the need for an extra caretaker, but did not wish to entrust his newborn daughter to a "stranger":

> *Looking for somebody to watch her or even a day-care center — it's expensive and a risk, too. It takes a great amount of awareness to take care of a child. But without some sort of child care, we would inevitably get on each other's nerves. We have to have some time, or our relationship would deteriorate. Luckily her folks are going to be retiring, so we can depend on them.*

In some cases, a friend became a caretaker. These arrangements eased concerns about the quality of a child's care; they also offered flexibility and economic savings. Larry, now a limousine driver, was relieved to find a friend to care for his daughter:

> *So many people have problems about baby-sitters, and some of them are real expensive, too. We're very lucky. We hired a friend and bring the baby to her house. She doesn't care if we drop the baby off at six in the morning or if we pick her up at night. I don't know any other baby-sitter we could do that with.*

Because involved fathers, by definition, wished to participate in child rearing, it is not surprising that they were ambivalent about depending on others, paid or unpaid, strangers or friends. While breadwinners gave little thought to the possible drawback of their daily absence, involved fathers were more likely to worry that the time they had to spend at work might not be good for their children. After Michael acquired custody of his son and daughter, he felt a nagging sense of guilt about relying on someone else to help care for them:

> *For the first couple of years, I had to have help in. I had an aunt, and then when she got sick, I had to hire a stranger. I didn't like it. It just exacerbated my guilt feelings that "Why wasn't I there? You're the absent man." And, you know, it wasn't realistic. The kids liked it. They were together. If I came home late, there was a regular dinner.*

To assuage these concerns, involved fathers looked to the benefits of such arrangements. Housekeepers, baby-sitters, and day-care centers, they argued, exposed their children to a range of experience that parents alone cannot offer. Charles, a lawyer married to a professor, had nothing but praise for his son's day-care center:

> *He's in the center three days a week in addition to the baby-sitter. He loves it. I don't know if it would work with every kid, but it's certainly worked with him. I think there's a need for social interaction besides the mother. It can be bad if the kid ends up being isolated, so the center is very important.*

Some involved fathers rejected the argument that either parent's daily absence is cause for concern. Rather, they felt able to parent better precisely because caretaking "backups" relieved the pressures on them. Like less involved fathers, they also focused on the quality of the time they spent with their children. Russell, a legal-aid attorney married to a public relations director, concluded that having an extra caretaker gave his two children more attention than they could receive under different circumstances:

> *We've had two housekeepers. The first one was wonderful; the current one is even better. If it were just our responsibility to take care of them, things wouldn't happen to the same extent. They get out and play; they're read to; they don't have problems with separating from their parents. And because we're not with them all the time, we're fresher when we are; we're able to spend productive time with them. They have plenty of exposure to their parents. I think it's a wonderful arrangement. It's definitely agreeing with them.*

Ultimately, of course, nonparental caretakers could provide involved fathers and their wives only limited assistance. To some extent, this stemmed from the scant social supports for child rearing. Neil complained:

> *I have no problems with day care. I don't think there's anything destructive at all. In fact, I see a lot of positive things. I'd like to see my child exposed to people of different racial, ethnic, religious backgrounds. Unfortunately, day-care systems are one of the things that nobody spends money on in this country.*

Yet involved fathers, like Clarence, wished to keep reliance on an "extra" parent within limits: "Raising a kid is like an investment, and I want to protect my investment. That means being involved as much as I can."

As any mother can attest, a great deal of caretaking work remains even after baby-sitting help is taken into account. As Benjamin put it, there are "countless errands in just the day-to-day running of a household. You throw a child in and, housekeeper or not, it's very tiring." And, while all involved fathers did more caretaking than breadwinning and autonomous men, most still relied on a woman to be the primary parent. Frank, the bank vice president, pointed out how he "helped" his wife, a public relations officer, in caring for their young daughter:

> *My participation is very extensive. I thoroughly enjoy my daughter's company. I regularly take her out on my own to allow Sharon time without the interruptions of a young child. And when she has got to go out of town on business—often for as much as a week or ten days at a time—I'm perfectly capable of stepping into her shoes.*

Some fathers, however, became genuinely equal—and, in rare cases, primary—parents. Thirty-nine percent of involved fathers (or 13 percent of the entire sample) went beyond being mothers' helpers, reflecting a limited but growing trend. Although it is not possible to know exactly what proportion of couples share equally, even conservative estimates suggest that it is on the rise. One study found that about twenty percent of dual-earning couples shared "the second shift" equally.[7] Todd, the construction worker, was one of them:

> With the baby, we do everything even steven. We're in this together; we both want to be an influence on the child. The next step is for both of us to spend time with her. It's not just a case of doing what you call extra things because you're taught to think in role models. I'm not doing extra things. This is what has to be done when you have a baby.

While all involved fathers faced trade-offs that other men do not, the degree and consequently the price of parental involvement varied among the group.[8] Why and how did some men become equal, or even primary, parents, while most remained mothers' helpers?

Resisting Full Equality: The Strategies of Mothers' Helpers

Mothers' helpers managed to evade what they considered the dirty work of child care even while embracing the more enjoyable activities. They tended to treat child care and housework as separate domains, so that even when they divided the former equally, the latter remained primarily their wives' duty. And, as I will explain, they avoided *responsibility* for domestic arrangements even when participating equitably in carrying out the tasks. Like breadwinning fathers and autonomous men, they also developed rationales for their selective involvement. In doing so, they contained the costs of involved fatherhood and reduced their unease about passing such costs onto their partners.

Avoiding the Dirty Work

Mothers' helpers devoted much time and energy to their children, but they avoided those activities that they deemed least attractive. Although Howard, a financial manager, spent his evenings and weekends sharing child care with his employed wife, he let himself off the hook when it came to certain responsibilities:

> I wouldn't say either of us expends ourselves greater in time or emotion. We have a baby-sitter who comes in full-time, but when she's not there maybe Marcia does a little bit more physically. She'll probably get up at night more than I will. I sleep heavier. I don't even hear the baby, and she's up in a snap, and I won't even know it in the morning.

Though still single, Barry, a church organist, anticipated the pleasures of having a child one day, pleasures he associated with affection, not work:

> *I'd probably hog certain parts of it—the rocking, the cuddling, and that sort of thing. I like children that much. I probably wouldn't care for changing diapers too much.*

What is deemed fun and what is deemed work is, of course, subjective. But the option to choose between desirable and undesirable tasks, which their wives did not possess, allowed most of these mothers' helpers to pass to someone else much of what they preferred not to do.

When they did share child care equally, these men did not share housework in the same way. William, an accountant, and Charles, the lawyer married to a professor, agreed:

> *With Danny, I'd say it's pretty shared. It's really whoever happens to be there. He feels very comfortable with both of us. In the evening, I'll give him a bath and put him to bed, change him. We share responsibilities for Danny probably more equally than household chores.*

> *It's much more equal in what I do with Pete than in the house. I enjoy looking after him; it's more fun than washing dishes or even than putting them in the dishwasher, which I'm still not very good at. I'm lazy about housework and stuff like that, and Rachel is compulsive enough that if it doesn't get done, she'll do it. And I take advantage of that.*

The pattern of men's avoiding housework while participating in child care appears to be widespread. One study of two-career families found that some men became equal sharers, but that others avoided housework even when they became involved in caretaking. In another, men's share of child care was shown to be substantially higher than their share of housework. And a third found that women do 83 percent of the housework in breadwinner–homemaker households and 70 percent of the housework in dual-earner families (with no significant differences between classes).[9]

Participating without Responsibility

Mothers' helpers were also reluctant to take responsibility even though they participated. Dean, the park worker, conceded that despite his extensive involvement in domestic work, he relied on his wife to assign the tasks: "Joan does a little more of the housework. We never actually sat down and said who should do what, but if she asks me to do something, I'll pretty much gladly do it."

Warren, the engineer, relied on his employed wife to make last-minute arrangements during unexpected emergencies, even when caused by his job:

> *Sometimes, like if I get stuck working overtime, she'll have to make arrangements for getting a baby-sitter. She always complains to me that I'm working the overtime and she gets stuck finding the baby-sitter because she has to go to work that night. So the pressure is put on her.*

Participation without responsibility placed mothers' helpers in the role of reactor rather than initiator. The job of seeing that tasks are distributed equitably — or of making sure they get done at all — fell to the mother. Yet mothers' helpers, unlike breadwinners, did acquiesce to requests for help. Frank, the banker, explained:

> *My wife sought out commitment from me in terms of how involved I would be, and I gave the commitment to do whatever was assigned. My own attitude was that whatever was reasonable for me to do I would do it. And I think I've been pretty much behaving myself.*

The husband who remained a helper placed limits on his wife's ability to secure equality. Ultimately, he decided if and when to participate, knowing that she would make up for his absence. The struggle to secure domestic equality became her job, not his.

Explaining Unequal Participation

All involved fathers took pride as well as pleasure in their participation, but those who remained mothers' helpers faced a contradiction between their beliefs and their behavior. Because they supported the ideal of gender equality, they harbored concerns that their resistance clashed with their ideological commitments. Scott, the paramedic married to a nurse, conceded:

> *What my opinion is and what we do are two different things. I feel that it should be shared equally, and if the situation warranted it, I could do more housework. I'm not afraid of getting my hands dirty.*

To reconcile their behavior with their egalitarian beliefs, mothers' helpers developed rationales to explain the domestic gap that remained even after their participation was taken into account. Their most prevalent rationale centered around housework: they argued that their wives had different standards of cleanliness and different timetables for getting chores done. From this perspective, inequality in housework resulted as much from their wives' choice to do more as from their own choice to do less. Having lived alone before marriage, Keith, a traffic engineer, felt comfortable cleaning.[10] His wife did more housework, he concluded, because she insisted on a "spotless" home:

> *As far as washing dishes, taking care of the kids, anything, it really doesn't bother me in the least. I lived alone for a number of years, so I know how to do things. But Barbara's more into cleaning — everything's got to be spotless. She irons my shirts; I never used to do that. If she wants to do it, it's okay with me. She doesn't have to, but that's the way she is.*

In these instances, the party willing to tolerate a messy home held the upper hand in any negotiation over domestic labor. The person with the higher standards necessarily lost, either by doing more work or by living with conditions she (or he) did not like. But this impasse could also discomfit the benefiting party. Tom, an editor, found his wife's lack of patience more decisive than his own reluctance, but he was nevertheless uncomfortable with the result:

> *I wish I did more, but our time reference is quite different. I'll say, "Okay, I'll do that, but let me do this first." But she will frequently get frustrated and just not be able to stand the thought that it's not done, and then go ahead and do it.*

Another way to cope with the unease that accompanied domestic inequality was to attribute the imbalance to difference in skills and capacities. Because involved fathers rejected the belief that men cannot nurture children, the mothers' helpers among them tended to rely on a version of the skills argument that isolated the specific tasks they wished to avoid. Wayne, a comptroller for a large company, contended that changing diapers, unlike cuddling and playing, required an ability he lacked: "I would try, but I think she'd wind up taking the diaper away from me. I'm not skilled at that."

This argument also helped draw attention to the work that mothers' helpers performed unassisted. For Howard, the financial manager, being responsible for household maintenance offset his reluctance to perform daily chores:

> *I have things around the house that Marcia doesn't do—yard work, painting, carpentry, repairs, or whatever—so there's still things that I do and still things that she does, and it isn't chauvinism. It's just practicality and experience.*

Whatever the reasons, the wives of these men assumed the larger share of domestic work. Men who became mothers' helpers thus discounted the costs to their partners, emphasized their partners' willingness to pay them, and avoided the question of who paid the higher price. Russell, the legal-aid attorney with two children and a live-in caretaker, downplayed his wife's greater career concessions:

> *Everything I've given up she's given up, plus she's had more at home and her career is more affected than mine. So I guess she's given up more, but with full knowledge of what she was doing and pleasure in doing so.*

Mothers' helpers also concluded that their involvement did not fall very far short of equality. By comparing themselves to other men rather than to their partners, they could and did view their participation as admirable and their sacrifices as significant. Considering how much less the average man contributes, it is hard to disagree with Dwight, a computer technician who planned to share caretaking with his wife, an upwardly mobile manager at a utilities company:

> *I guess we both have to do some sacrificing; that's basically what it is to be a parent. It's probably not going to be fifty-fifty. . . . I think the mother would have a tendency to do a little more. But even sixty-forty is pretty good compared to the average.*

While few of these men denied that their partners bore the larger share of family responsibilities, they attributed the gap to situational pressures more than personal preferences.

Tom was in graduate school when his first child was born. He was thus able to take primary responsibility for his infant son's care when his first wife returned to work. Since he was now employed full-time, however, he did not expect to be able to re-create that arrangement when he and his second wife had a child:

> *I think ideally the father should be just as responsible as the mother, should have just as much a share. So I think if it worked some other way this time, it is simply because of circumstances. Roz happens to work at home. If she had an office job, then it would be as equally shared as possible.*

Because a man's participation emerges from fragile social contexts rather than an "inherent" ability or desire, he may become an equal father in one situation and a mother's helper, a breadwinner, or even an autonomous father in another. If some fathers did become equal participants in child rearing, it is because they faced stronger incentives and met fewer obstacles than other men.

Beyond Helping: What Leads to Equal Parenting?

If most involved fathers resisted equal participation, a substantial minority did not. These "equal parents" shared what mothers' helpers eschewed. Ernie shared responsibility for making arrangements for the care of his young daughter:

> *I wanted to be there for the good times and the bad times. I wanted to share in making decisions, which was good for my wife, too. I don't want her to decide on a nursery school; let's decide together. . . . How can I say I want children and not take that kind of responsibility?*

Equal fathers also shared the dirty work of child care and housework. Lloyd, a sanitation worker with three children, drew few boundaries in dividing daily tasks with his wife, a chiropractor:

> *We've always shared breadwinning and caretaking right down the middle. That's from washing the floor, changing diapers, washing clothes, cleaning the house. I don't draw any lines as to what is men's work and women's work; work is work.*

Ernie and his wife specialized in certain household tasks, but did not divide them in a stereotypical way:

> *It's got to be done, so at least we try to divide up the things that we are better at. She couldn't deal with shopping, and I'm much better shopping because I do the cooking and know what we use, so I do the shopping. One time I used the washing machine and it broke, so I stay away from that now. We split on the cleaning. We split on Annie. We're pretty balanced.*

Some childless men planned to become equal fathers when they had children.[11] Carlos kept an immaculate apartment while living alone. He also cared for many nieces and nephews in his large, close-knit Hispanic family. He thus did not doubt he would share these aspects of domestic life once he married:

> *I've changed diapers, baby-sat, rocked children. I'm not afraid of infants. I've fed children, burped them, and got thrown up on. I don't think I would be the type of person to say, "Well, the baby's crying. Go take care of it." And I don't want one person to accept a load that would tire them out to the point that they can't respond to anything else. It's my responsibility as well as the other person's — a fifty-fifty deal.*

In rare but significant cases, a father's contribution exceeded his partner's.[12] Rich, a teacher, assumed the lion's share of caretaking when his wife, a librarian, returned to a more highly structured, nine-to-five job shortly after the birth of their first daughter:

> *For those first five years, I got the kids dressed and fed and everything. I always got up in the night with the first one. Always. It was ninety-nine percent me with the older one. With the second one, it was shared. We have experimented and continued to do so — not really much thinking of it as an experiment anymore.*

For many years, he also did the larger share of the housework:

> *I have always done about ninety percent of the grocery shopping and about half of the cooking. For five years, I did most of the laundry, which I hate. Housecleaning, to the extent it gets done, is now probably half and half.*

In these families, mothers became "fathers' helpers." Michael, the divorced therapist, explained:

> *We had joint custody, but I had the primary residence. They were with me all the time. I was very eager to take the kids. I knew that she would help out, in the sense of being somewhat available. They visit her when they want.*

By rejecting the path of least resistance, these men illumine the unusual circumstances that allow and promote equality and even primary parenting for men. They also underscore what deters most involved fathers from choosing full equality even when they might wish to do so.

ENDNOTES

1. Eighty percent of involved fathers were married or in a committed relationship.
2. Thirty-six percent of the college-educated men became involved fathers, while 31 percent of the working-class group did so. Given the small size of the sample, these differences are not significant.
3. My research on women's choices (Gerson 1985) found that both domestic and work-committed women confronted conflicts and social disapproval. Hertz (1986) also explores the dilemmas that both mothers and fathers face in dual-career marriages.
4. Before the rise of breadwinning, potency was considered an important measure of manhood. This made sense in a preindustrial context, where children contributed to their families' economic survival and large families meant more people to rely

on. As children became economic liabilities, however, family size declined and bearing many children receded as a measure of a man's masculinity. Today, procreative measures of manhood persist mainly in poor communities and "traditional" cultures, where men have little chance of meeting more modern standards based on economic and work success. As women join men in the labor force, usurping their hold on economic power, men may turn to sexuality to reassert a separate masculine identity. Connell (1991) points out that men use physical attributes such as size, strength, and sexual potency to assert power when economic control eludes them.

5. Even though dual-career couples may wish to keep family size down, Peterson and Gerson (1992) found that dual-earner couples who have large families are more likely than those with small families to share child-care responsibilities. In these cases, the larger workload makes it harder for a husband to avoid domestic work or pass it on to his wife.
6. A large body of research has found that working-class and poor communities are more likely to depend on informal networks of kin and friends to help care for their children. See, for example, Stack (1974) and Zinsser (1990). Hertz (1986) presents an excellent analysis of how dual-career professional couples use hired caretakers to lighten their child-care load.
7. Hochschild with Machung 1989.
8. Bielby and Bielby (1989) argue that family-oriented men do not make trade-offs in their identity as women do because men can combine family and work more easily. This is the case when involved fathers remain mothers' helpers, but not when they become equal or primary parents.
9. Berardo 1987; Gilbert 1985; Goldscheider and Waite 1991. Brines (1990) explores the factors that encourage men to participate in housework.
10. Goldscheider and Waite (1991) report that men and women who lived on their own before marriage were more likely to choose nontraditional family arrangements.
11. Among all involved fathers, the percentage of childless men who planned to become equal parents was 35 percent, not quite as high as the 41 percent of fathers who had already done so. This is a small difference, which is not significant for such a small number of cases.
12. Five men, four of whom were divorced, became the primary parent to their children.

REFERENCES

Berardo, Donna H. 1987. "The Housework Gap." *Journal of Marriage and the Family* 49:381–90.
Bielby, William T. and Denise D. Bielby. 1989. "Family Ties: Balancing Commitments to Work and Family in Dual Earner Households." *American Sociological Review* 54(5):776–89.
Brines, Julie. 1990. "What Makes Housework Men's Work? The Politics of Change and Its Lessons for Current Family Policy." Paper presented at the 85th annual meeting of the American Sociological Association, Washington, DC, August.
Connell, R. W. 1991. "Live Fast and Die Young: The Construction of Masculinity among Young Working-Class Men on the Margin of the Labour Market." *Australian and New Zealand Journal of Sociology* 27(2):141–71.
Gerson, Kathleen. 1985. *Hard Choices: How Women Decide about Work, Career, and Motherhood.* Berkeley: University of California Press.
Gilbert, Lucia A. 1985. *Men in Dual-Career Families: Current Realities and Future Prospects.* Hillsdale, NJ: Erlbaum.
Goldscheider, Frances K. and Linda J. Waite. 1991. *New Families, No Families? The Transformation of the American Home.* Berkeley: University of California Press.
Hertz, Rosanna. 1986. *More Equal Than Others: Women and Men in Dual-Career Marriages.* Berkeley: University of California Press.

Hochschild, Arlie R., with Anne Machung. 1989. *The Second Shift: Working Parents and the Revolution at Home.* New York: Viking Press.

Peterson, Richard R. and Kathleen Gerson. 1992. "Determinants of Responsibility for Child-Care Arrangements among Dual-Earner Couples." *Journal of Marriage and the Family* 54(3):527–36.

Stack, Carol B. 1974. *All Our Kin: Strategies for Survival in a Black Community.* New York: Harper & Row.

Zinsser, Caroline. 1990. *Born and Raised in East Urban: A Community Study of Informal and Unregulated Child Care.* New York: Center for Public Advocacy Research.

24

GAY MEN CHOOSING TO BE FATHERS

MICHAEL SHERNOFF

There currently are an estimated 1 to 3 million gay fathers in the United States (Gold et al. 1994), the majority of whom appear to have had children in heterosexual marriages prior to their coming out as gay (Bozett 1993). This figure probably underestimates the true total because many gay parents are reluctant to reveal their sexual orientation. Bozett (1993) provides a comprehensive review of the literature on gay fathers, all of which describes men who had children in traditional marriages. This article is not about gay men who fathered children during a heterosexual marriage but, rather, about gay men who become fathers after they come out and are living openly gay lives. Though some single gay men choose to father children, the focus of this article will be on male couples becoming fathers.

The most complete resource for both clients and clinicians interested in learning about the many complexities of gay or lesbian parenting is *The Lesbian and Gay Parenting Handbook* (Martin 1993). One indicator that open lesbians and gay men are becoming parents is peer groups like "Center Kids," a program of the New York City Lesbian and Gay Community Services Center. Originally founded in 1988 by gay and lesbian parents seeking support and recreational activities for their families, the project began as an informal social network of 35 member families. It affiliated with the Center in 1989, and within the first year grew to 250 families. There are 500 active families

"Gay Men Choosing to Be Fathers" by Michael Shernoff from *Journal of Gay and Lesbian Social Services,* Vol. 4 No. 2 (1996), pp. 41–54. Copyright © 1996 by The Haworth Press, Inc. Reprinted by permission of the publisher.

who are either parents or who are considering becoming parents. Twenty-five percent of these families are headed by gay men. The mailing list now includes 1,500 lesbian- and gay-parented families (Lesbian and Gay Community Services Center 1994). Patterson (1994) reports that this kind of grassroots lesbian and gay parents group has sprung up in more than 40 locations in cities around the world. . . .

For many years, gay men have sought counseling with the expressed goal of becoming parents and have discussed wanting to father children without pretending that they were heterosexual. In conversations with both clients and other gay men, numerous people have expressed feeling angry that the traditional privileges of being a man in contemporary American society inextricably linked to being a biological parent are denied to them simply because they are openly gay. Gay men who want to be parents are uniquely different from heterosexual men wanting to father children in a number of intrapsychic and interpersonal ways. It is common for gay clients not to know how to reconcile their biological and emotional needs to parent with the reality of being homosexual. Exploring and resolving the conflict between these seemingly contradictory needs is one important task of clinical work. Most heterosexual men experience their need and desire to be fathers as normal and an inevitable part of being an adult that will be realized once they marry. It is not unusual for a gay man to doubt the normalcy and even appropriateness of these same needs and desires. In contrast to heterosexual men, many gay men do not see how their need to be a father can ever be actualized. . . .

Certain themes and issues are unique for two men who decide to become fathers, not the least of which is the absence of a woman. Not having the biological capacity to carry a child creates interesting challenges for men who wish to be biological parents, the first of which is to locate and contract with a woman to become inseminated and carry a child.

When interviewing male couples who are parents they report that it is often difficult to separate issues that are related to their sexual orientation from those that arise from the fact that they are two men raising a child or children without a woman. One male couple discussed how difficult it has always been to feel subjected to a scrutiny that wouldn't exist if they were heterosexual. They constantly felt on guard and under a microscope regarding their parenting skills. Another male couple stated that "even some lesbians involved in Center Kids express concerns related to their preconceived notion that men cannot adequately parent without a woman."

This article is based on clinical work with ten male couples seen in private practice in Manhattan over the past fifteen years, and on interviews conducted with members of fifteen other male couples who are either considering becoming fathers or have done so as openly gay men. The nonclient couples were chosen initially because of the author's social relationship with them; these couples referred me to other couples with whom they are friends. In all cases the couples were asked to describe their reasons for wanting to become fathers; their feelings about the difficulties encountered in the process be-

cause they were gay; what if anything did they feel was unique in their experience of parenting because they were gay; and how could social service
professionals have been or be more helpful to their families.

Many male couples interviewed for this article reported feeling that they
had to be better than the equivalent heterosexual couple to qualify as foster
or adoptive parents. As one man put it, "It's like being a minority executive
in a large corporation. You have to perform much better than your white colleagues simply to receive the same evaluations and promotions as them. You
feel that you're always being subjected to unfair scrutiny, and thus you strive
to become the hypervigilant, overachieving super-parent."

Gay men wish to have children for all the reasons that anyone else wants
to become a parent. Some want to share their loving relationship and affluence with a child who would not otherwise have experienced this privilege.
Recently this has taken the form of gay men adopting orphaned inner-city infants with AIDS. Some wish to give to another generation all the love and
blessings of a nurturing and devoted family that they experienced in their
own upbringing, and still others wish to provide a child with the kind of loving environment that they themselves never received. As illustrated in an example below, some wish to parent for wrong, narcissistic, or inappropriate
reasons. The skilled worker must be able to interview prospective parents in
such a way as to ascertain how realistic and prepared they are for the new responsibilities inherent in parenting. When dealing with gay men, the worker
has to be aware of any bias he or she might have about two men's capacities
to be loving and complete parents to a child of either sex.

Beginnings

Wayne and Sal had been together for twelve years when, in their capacity as
adult advisors to the peer support group, Gay and Lesbian Youth of New
York, they met Joey. Joey was a 17½-year-old with a severe hearing impedi-
ment who had been kicked out of his family home in upstate New York when
his mother found out he was gay. He had been supporting himself as a prostitute since arriving in New York City, was too old for foster care, and was
too young and irresponsible to become an emancipated minor.

Wayne and Sal offered to let Joey live with them in an informal arrangement where they would attempt to function as foster parents. Joey lived with
Wayne and Sal for approximately one and a half years, during which time
he got his high school equivalency diploma and went to trade school where he
completed a program that allowed him to qualify for the licensing exam as
a hairdresser. Once he was financially supporting himself, he moved out of
Wayne and Sal's apartment into his own place. He is still in close contact
with Wayne and Sal who he considers parental figures, but not actual parents
since his mother is still alive.

In 1986 Wayne and Sal approached a New York City funded adoption
agency in Brooklyn as a male couple wishing to adopt a child. They met and

fell in love with Hope, an interracial girl abandoned at birth. After the normal series of interviews and investigations, Hope was officially placed with them in the capacity of a legal pre-adoptive foster placement. Wayne and Sal felt that they had to be super applicants because of their openness about being a male couple. A year later Wayne and Sal approached the courts as a couple petitioning to adopt Hope. Though the judge acknowledged that in fact Hope had two fathers, he did not feel there was any legal precedent for him to be able to appoint both Wayne and Sal as parents. Sal became Hope's legal parent, and Sal has made provisions that in case anything happens to him Wayne is named Hope's legal guardian.

Wayne and Sal decided not to enroll Hope in their neighborhood elementary school when during the "Children of the Rainbow" curriculum controversy they learned that it was their community school board's policy to refer any child who wished to discuss gay- or lesbian-headed families to the guidance counselor. Thus they interviewed guidance counselors and administrators at prospective schools, explaining that they were both Hope's fathers and would be jointly involved in all decisions pertaining to her. They are very involved in the parents' association and with the community school board in the district in which Hope was enrolled, and take active roles in Hope's classroom whenever parents are invited to do so. They feel that they need to expend more energy in these areas than non-gay parents in order to both protect Hope and to prove themselves as competent and caring parents. This need to prove themselves as loving and more-than-adequate parents is a common dynamic for gay and lesbian parents. It is especially strong for male couples who are parents.

The specter of HIV and AIDS is another unique stressor facing male couples thinking about parenting. Cleve and Thomas consulted me because of the fears and feelings they were experiencing around wanting to take the HIV test. They had been a committed couple for five years at the time of the initial consultation. Their reasons for wanting to be tested centered around their desire to have children. Neither wished to raise children as a single parent, and before they took any steps toward becoming parents they wanted some assurance that both were healthy and long-term planning for children was realistic. Both men tested negative for the HIV antibodies. Cleve has since donated sperm to a single woman friend who wanted to experience having a child but had no desire to be a mother. She became pregnant and gave birth to a girl who lives with the male couple.

In contrast, Bruce and Alan, a couple for twelve years, decided to adopt a baby precisely so that there would be an important shared project that would outlive Alan, who has had full-blown AIDS for the past five years, and that would be part of his legacy. Alan is a psychiatrist and Bruce a banker. Though openly gay as a couple wishing to adopt, they have felt it necessary to keep Alan's illness a secret so as not to create any unnecessary complications. Since their son Nikoli was born in Russia and is not yet a citizen, they plan to remain circumspect about Alan's health at least until Nikoli is legally a U.S. citizen. Bruce has mused about how his being a single parent will affect his finding a new partner once he is a widower.

A major focus of the clinical work where one of the partners is HIV-positive or has AIDS has to be explicit discussions about the potential impact on the child of having the focus shift off of him or her and onto a parent who is critically ill. Similarly, helping these couples explore the impact on the child of losing a parent at an early age must be taken into consideration when they consider becoming parents.

Another male couple began treatment in the third year of their relationship with numerous problems. They were experiencing severe communication difficulties, and their anger at each other was so intense that they often became physically abusive with each other. One of the men wanted very much to have a child in the hope that it would cement their failing relationship. His partner was extremely hesitant and understandably ambivalent about the impact a child would have on their already strained relationship. Counseling helped them see the inappropriateness of having children at least at the present time, and ultimately they terminated their relationship without having a child.

Adoption

For men who wish to parent but who have not had any direct experience with children, I often suggest that they move slowly and explore some options for part-time parenting. This can take the form of becoming a big brother to a child or an adolescent. Some agencies are seeking good gay role models to function as big brothers to troubled or acting-out gay youth. The obvious advantage to this arrangement is that it introduces the prospective parents to limited doses of what it's like to have some parental responsibilities, prior to making a permanent commitment.

If this is a satisfactory experience, I then suggest that the couple consider becoming foster parents. Again this gives them the opportunity to try parenting without making a lifelong commitment. This trial run is helpful training when the foster child begins to behave in the normally difficult ways that tax any parent of a child or an adolescent. In some cases these "trial runs" evolve into long-term placements or adoptions.

Becoming foster parents or adopting a child as a male couple poses some difficulties in a number of different areas. The first is that a majority of foster care and adoption agencies have not yet confronted their heterosexist bias about gay men's abilities to be parents. Only Florida and New Hampshire statutorily prohibit gay men and lesbians from adopting. New Hampshire also prohibits placing foster children in homes with homosexuals, and Massachusetts has regulations intended to prevent gay men and lesbians from becoming foster parents (*Harvard Law Review* 1989).

No state has laws that allow two parents of the same sex to both adopt a child. As of January 1993, courts in California, Washington State, Minnesota, Vermont, Oregon, Alaska, and New York decided that it was in the best interest of specific children to have two legal parents of the same sex and granted joint adoptions by lesbian and gay couples (Curry, Clifford, and Leonard 1993).

When a same-sex couple cannot both legally adopt a child, this legal inequity has the potential to place strains upon the relationship.

One solution to the inability of a same-sex couple to jointly adopt a child has been second-parent adoptions recently approved by courts in New York, Vermont, and the District of Columbia. An adoptive co-parent becomes a legal parent of a child, but the parental rights and responsibilities of the biological parent are not extinguished (Rubenstein 1993). On June 8, 1994, a statute that blocks gays and lesbians from adopting their lovers' biological children was upheld 4-3 by the Wisconsin state supreme court (*The Advocate* 1994). This kind of legislation has serious consequences for any lesbian or gay couple considering becoming parents.

Workers at adoption agencies considering a placement with a male couple need to explore with the couple how they plan to deal with the reality that only one of the men is the legal parent. Pre-adoption counseling must address this issue in depth in order to help the men prepare for whatever strains this inequality may cause. The interpersonal issues that need discussion pertain to trust, security, and power dynamics when only one partner is the legal parent. In addition, social service professionals should urge the couple to draw up an agreement or contract that spells out custody and visitation contingencies if the legal parent dies or the couple should separate with the knowledge that these contracts may be legally contested. Even with these documents, the surviving or noncustodial father faces the real risk of having the child he has helped raise from birth taken from him by his deceased partner's parents or the child welfare authorities, or being denied access to his child. These issues represent a serious danger to the child's ongoing relationship with one of his or her parents, and social service professionals need to counsel same-sex couples to take every avenue to protect their child's emotional well-being and access to both of his or her parents.

Biological Parenting

There are a number of options for men who wish to biologically father a child. Some male couples have arranged with a woman friend to be the surrogate mother who is inseminated and carries the baby to term. Some men have paid the medical expenses of a surrogate mother who then relinquishes all involvement with the child after birth. Some male couples become co-parents with a single woman or lesbian couple, one of whom has been the biological mother to their child. This is a complicated arrangement emotionally and logistically and one that benefits from ongoing counseling in order to help navigate the many complexities. Despite the complexities of negotiating co-parenting from different households, many families have created loving co-parenting arrangements which provide a child with the richness of several devoted and responsible parents. The least desirable arrangements are informal agreements with a woman friend to carry the baby. Counselors should urge extensive pre-insemination discussion and a written contract that explicitly spells out all the specifics pertaining to medical expenses and access to the child after birth. There are currently eleven states in which surrogacy is not a crime, but the laws explicitly state that paid surrogacy contracts are not legally recognized. Five states go one step further and void unpaid contracts as well (Martin 1993).

Ron and Josh had been together five years when they began to hypothetically discuss becoming parents. The first time a lesbian couple approached them about becoming biological parents, they had not been tested for HIV and felt that they were not then ready to take the test. They had been friends with Sally and Judy, two women who live in Boston, prior to Sally and Judy becoming a couple. When the women approached Ron and Josh the men had been a couple for fifteen years, had both tested negative for HIV, and felt ready to become parents. Ron and Josh live in Philadelphia.

The two couples met about once a month for a year to discuss issues pertaining to their joint parenting including the specific contractual arrangements they would have. Before attempting to inseminate Judy, they reached impasses several times about specific issues. They felt that either mediation or counseling would be so unwieldy that they eventually resolved all their differences just in discussions among themselves specifying access to the child and ongoing shared financial responsibilities.

Ron donated sperm and their daughter Sarah was born on October 25, 1992. She lives with her mothers full time. About once a month the men go to Boston to spend a weekend with Sarah. It took Sarah about six months to become comfortable with Ron and Josh, and she now talks to both of them on the phone regularly and calls Ron "Papa" and Josh "Daddy." Though Josh is not the biological parent, the agreement drawn up by the two couples guarantees him access to Sarah and spells out that he also has responsibilities for parenting.

Sarah has four loving parents, two of whom she lives with, and the other two who take an active but long-distance role in parenting. Ron and Josh consider themselves the nonprimary caregiving parents or remote parents. As Ron put it, "In terms of parenting responsibilities and child care, our arrangement is almost identical to a family where the parents have separated or divorced and yet both have regular contact with the children." At the time this article was being written, Judy was again pregnant with a child conceived with Ron's sperm.

Providing Social Services to Gay Parents

The history of services to gay and lesbian parents is one of grassroots community organizing. An underserved population organized to meet its own needs with groups forming all around the country to run peer support groups, and to seek out sympathetic professionals for assistance when needed. The support groups each have a specific focus. Thus lesbians and gay men contemplating parenthood may choose from support groups on adoption, alternative insemination, and other options for biological parenthood. There are groups for those who are in the process of adopting a child. Ongoing groups are provided for single parents, adoptive and foster families, older children of gay parents, and families that have separated (Lesbian and Gay Community Services Center 1994).

Lesbian and gay social service agencies have responded to the growing interest in parenting by developing specific services. Among the premier examples of this are the Whitman-Walker Clinic in Washington, D.C., the Lyon-Martin Women's Health Services in San Francisco, and the Pride Foster Family Agency in Los Angeles. The Lyon-Martin Clinic sponsors a Lesbian/Gay Parenting Service which provides psychosocial supports, parenting classes, and obstetrical care for lesbian- and gay-headed families with children as well as prospective gay and lesbian parents. The support groups that are offered are led by professional health educators (Patterson 1994).

The Pride Foster Family Agency, a program of GLASS (Gay and Lesbian Adolescent Social Services), is the nation's only licensed gay and lesbian foster family agency. Begun in 1987, the Pride FFA provides foster homes to infants, toddlers, children, and adolescents, in a wide variety of settings. Currently there are nearly one hundred children in Pride FFA foster homes. Prior to certification, potential foster parents must complete thirty hours of training by GLASS social workers. Pending licensure as an adoption agency will increase the level of service available to gay men and lesbians who want to adopt.

A clinic affiliated with the University of California San Francisco Medical Center has opened to treat the children of lesbian and gay parents. The doctors who opened the Rainbow Clinic feel that pediatric care will improve when a family knows it can be open about who they are without feeling stigmatized or ostracized. The clinic provides routine and emergency pediatric services and, as it grows, intends to offer discussion groups for gay and lesbian parents, a resource library, and services for gay and lesbian adolescents (Curry et al. 1993). Whitman-Walker provides support groups, legal seminars, and parenting classes for both prospective and actual parents.

Center Kids representatives have been active advocating for gay and lesbian parenting rights at many levels of state and city government, including the New York City Child Welfare Administration, the New York State Department of Social Services, the New York City School Chancellor, and the Mayor's Office on Children and Families. Groups like Center Kids also sponsor forums and panels on topics such as legal concerns for lesbian- and gay-headed families, child development issues, choosing a pediatrician, sex roles and gender expectations in lesbian- and gay-headed families, men raising daughters and women raising sons, and empowering children to live in and cope with the wider world. In addition, dozens of smaller discussion groups are held each year covering such topics as "Divorce: What to Do When It's Over" (Lesbian and Gay Community Services Center 1994).

The variety of ways that gay men become parents create new challenges for social service and child welfare professionals who are faced with the reality of working with, and in some cases helping create, additional nontraditional families in contemporary America. Since many social service and mental health workers are resistant to the concept of homosexuals becoming parents, sympathetic professionals employed in adoption, child care, and mental health agencies need to seek out opportunities to call in outside consultants from groups like Center Kids, Whitman-Walker, Lyon-Martin, GLASS, or other local organizations to do inservice trainings about lesbian- and gay-headed families. GLASS has a full training module available for those agencies wishing to institute a specific program for gay and lesbian foster and adoptive parents.

Because two men parenting a child may encounter hostility when interacting with schools, clinics, or the parents of their child's friends, social service professionals should be prepared to educate colleagues about gay-headed families and to serve as advocates for them. Professionals doing talks to community groups about families, adoption, and foster care can include examples of gay- and lesbian-headed families to increase awareness of these families within local communities. In addition, social service professionals can seek out opportunities to educate members of the lesbian and gay communities about opportunities for and methods of creating families. Mental health and social service professionals working within the lesbian and gay community need to inquire about any feelings their gay male clients may have about becoming parents, and design specialized programs for gay men and lesbians who wish to become parents or who have already created families.

Conclusion

Much of contemporary American society has difficulty seeing men as sufficiently nurturing to parent without a woman. Gay men experience discrimination and difficulty in becoming fathers both as men and as part of an acknowledged male couple. There is an absence of support even within the gay community for men wishing to parent. Thus those gay men who have deeply felt needs to father children feel alienated from both mainstream society (which tells them that gay men aren't fit to be parents) and from gay society (that, to a large degree, has not matured enough to normalize and value its members' desires to have children). In response to the lack of existing supports, gay men have participated in peer support systems organized by them and by lesbians to meet the unique needs of the families they are creating.

Social service professionals in private practice, health care, educational, and child-care settings need to be alert to opportunities to help gay men explore and articulate any desires to become fathers. In addition, workers need to be aware of the existence of families composed of two men and their children, and should be prepared to work with them. Professionals investigating the appropriateness of placing a child with a male couple must be able to assess the strengths of the potential placement and home life without using the sexual orientation of the prospective parent as the sole determining factor in disqualifying someone. Workers should seek ways to advocate within their institutions for qualified male couples seeking to become parents. They can simultaneously offer these couples and families the opportunities to benefit from professional interventions when appropriate, without stigmatizing or pathologizing either these men or their children.

REFERENCES

The Advocate. 1994. "Around the Nation." Los Angeles, issue 660, p. 13.

Bozett, F. W. 1993. "Gay Fathers: A Review of the Literature." Pp. 437–58 in *Psychological Perspectives on Lesbian and Gay Male Experiences,* edited by L. Garnets and D. Kimmel. New York: Columbia University Press.

Curry, H., D. Clifford, and R. Leonard. 1993. *A Legal Guide for Lesbian and Gay Couples.* Berkeley, CA: Nolo Press.

Gold, M., E. Perrin, D. Futterman, and S. Friedman. 1994. "Children of Gay or Lesbian Parents." *Pediatrics in Review* 15(9):354–58.

Harvard Law Review. 1989. *Sexual Orientation and the Law.* Cambridge, MA: Harvard University Press.

Lesbian and Gay Community Services Center. 1994. *Annual Report 1994–1995.* New York, NY.

Martin, A. 1993. *The Lesbian and Gay Parenting Handbook: Creating and Raising Our Families.* New York: HarperPerennial.

Patterson, C. 1994. "Lesbian and Gay Couples Considering Parenthood: An Agenda for Research, Service, and Advocacy." *Journal of Gay & Lesbian Social Services* 1(2): 33–55.

Rubenstein, W., ed. 1993. *Lesbians, Gay Men and the Law.* New York: The New Press.

PART VII

Divorce, Remarriage, and Blended Families

In this section, we examine divorce, remarriage, and blended families. Not surprisingly, there has been more research done on divorce than on remarriage and blended families. Hopefully, this research imbalance will be corrected because we need more information on the diverse types of families formed after a divorce. Remember that in Part IV we discovered that many people are choosing to cohabit instead of remarrying after a divorce, because of their unhappiness with the institution of marriage. Other individuals are remarrying after a divorce and forming blended families. The term *blended families* is used to describe these postdivorce families reuniting via cohabitation or marriage, and it is more inclusive than the term *stepfamilies*, which usually refers only to postdivorce families that have remarried.

A marriage can be terminated in one of three ways: annulment, divorce, or widowhood. Historically, most marriages in the United States ended via widowhood. Divorce has existed in the United States since colonial times, but it was rare then, and divorce policies were inconsistent due to different colonies being settled by groups of people with differing values and beliefs. The Puritans in the northeastern colonies, for example, did allow divorce under certain conditions, whereas the southern colonies did not allow it (Riley 1991). In the northern colonies, spouses wanting to end a marriage via divorce had to prove the marriage had not fulfilled its contractual obligation, that is, the wife was barren and could not produce children or the husband had deserted the family and was not providing for them. Other traditional grounds for divorce included adultery, fraud, drunkenness, and, later, physical cruelty. However, cruelty alone usually was not sufficient grounds for a divorce because of its vagueness.

In the 1970s, many states introduced no-fault divorce laws, which were designed to eliminate fault-based grounds for divorce (Weitzman and Dixon [1980] 1994). Moreover, it was hoped that no-fault divorce would eliminate the adversarial process and lead to financial settlements that were more equitable and based on economic need. Family responsibilities postdivorce were also to be redefined as more gender neutral. No-fault divorce accomplished some of these goals, especially making it much easier to obtain a divorce because neither spouse had to be proven at fault. By eliminating blame common in fault divorces, no-fault divorces can reduce the trauma of divorce proceedings. However, divorce is still adversarial for many couples. Moreover, financial settlements are not necessarily equitable nor based on financial need as is evidenced by the numerous parents who are behind in child-support payments. Moreover, alimony or spousal support is awarded less often today, so it is more important for women to be financially independent regardless of their marital status.

Some states are working to change divorce laws because they believe the no-fault divorce laws are too lenient and make it too easy for a family to break up (Yepsen 1995). Instead of having no-fault divorces, these states want to move back to a system whereby a spouse would have to show specific grounds for divorce, and one of the spouses would be blamed for the failure of the marriage. Louisiana, for example, is pushing for covenant marriages, which would make divorce very difficult to obtain. Other scholars argue that in order to reduce the postdivorce conflicts between ex-spouses and children, we should remove divorce from our adversarial legal system and, instead, use mediation. Joyce Hauser, in her book *Good Divorces, Bad Divorces: A Case for Divorce Mediation* (1995), argues that mediation is the best method for advancing harmony and justice during and after a divorce. Unfortunately, few people know that divorce mediation exists as an option. Another innovative program, in Atlanta and Indianapolis, is a court-ordered class for divorcing parents called "Children Cope with Divorce." All divorcing parents are required to attend the four-hour course on how to lessen the impact of divorce on their children (Walker 1992).

Why is the divorce rate so high? There are many reasons, including infidelity, money and employment conflicts, differences in spousal age and education, substance abuse, and family violence. In fact, not only is family violence a precursor of divorce, it also is often a consequence as discussed by Demie Kurz in her research on violence against women (see Reading 29). Another reason divorce rates are so high is that the United States is a society which overemphasizes romantic love so that relationship expectations are too high for most couples to achieve. Moreover, the public attitude toward divorce is more favorable. There is less social stigma for divorced persons today than there was 50 years ago or even 30 years ago. It is important to note that the divorce rates vary by age, race-ethnicity, and religion. Moreover, divorce rates tend to be higher in western and southern states than in northeastern and midwestern states.

Myths about Divorce

There are many myths about divorce, including the belief that Americans are antimarriage and that divorce is an easy and casual process. Moreover, people tend to have nostalgic views about the family such as the idealized notion that marriage used to be a wonderful and stable relationship. In reality, married life has not always been blissful, and many marriages have been full of violence, substance abuse, and other problems. The difference is that, today, a person does not have to stay in an abusive situation or in an unhappy marriage. Constance R. Ahrons addresses these and other myths in her article "What Divorce Is and Is Not: Transcending the Myths." Ahrons is a professor of sociology and director of the Marriage and Family Therapy program at the University of Southern California. She began her research on divorce in 1976 when she was on the faculty at the University of Wisconsin, Madison. A single parent herself, Ahrons decided that instead of following the traditional route of looking for deviance or pathology, she would study how families reorganized themselves after divorce and that she would look for the "good divorces," divorces in which children and adults were leading healthy lives in spite of divorce. Her numerous publications, based on several major research studies and 25 years of clinical experience, have introduced new concepts in and new ways of looking at divorce. The research reported in this selection is taken from Ahrons' book *The Good Divorce: Keeping Your Family Together When Your Marriage Comes Apart* (1994). The impetus behind this excerpt came from Ahrons' public lectures on divorce. In her audiences, she often found people who had several misconceptions about divorce, including the myth that all the consequences of divorce are negative. In this reading, Ahrons first reviews six popular myths about divorce and then presents data on current trends.

Divorce Is a Gendered Experience

One reality of divorce is that the experience of divorce is very gendered. What men and women experience in going through a divorce is often different. Catherine Riessman, for example, in her 1990 book on the gendered experience of divorce, has found that many women express that divorce had many positive consequences for their lives, including feeling independent and learning to survive on their own, feeling free from subordination, and learning the competencies involved in managing a daily life, such as learning to do household repairs and controlling their own money. Moreover, many women express being challenged by needing to reenter the job market or by going back to school to finish their education. Other women express positive changes in their social relationships, where they are learning to nurture new friendships and relationships. Of course, not all the consequences of divorce are positive for women, but Riessman's research shows the variety of personal growth that occurs due to this transition in marital status.

The second article in this section, "The Social Self as Gendered: A Masculinist Discourse of Divorce," by Terry Arendell, examines the gendered experience of divorce for men. Arendell, an associate professor of sociology at Colby College, has done extensive research on gender, the sociology of the family, and divorce. She recently investigated the extent of father absence after divorce in an interview study of 75 divorced New York fathers. She found that men's perspectives on divorce and their interactions with their families postdivorce reveal similar patterns of coping and maintenance of their gender identities. Arendell concludes that these divorced men share a "masculinist discourse of divorce." This discourse involves unique understandings and definitions of the family, including a devaluation of the former wife and diverse strategies for interacting with ex-wives and children. For example, she found that many divorced fathers use father absence as a strategy to control situations of conflict and emotional tension. Other divorced fathers use fathers' rights rhetoric to argue that they have been the primary victims of divorce.

One example of concern about fathers' involvement after divorce is the increasing intervention of the state in child custody and support issues. Even though there is great scholarly debate concerning the effects of divorce on children (see Reading 20, by Paul Amato, for a complete overview), some recent research has shown that absent fathers have a negative impact on children's well-being because of the lack of parental and economic support (McLanahan and Sandefur 1994). Many states have implemented stronger sanctions against fathers who are not paying child support. These men have been labeled "deadbeat dads," because of the billions of dollars in child support that is owed to children. States are concerned that this lack of child support may be contributing to increasing numbers of women and children on welfare rolls, and they are going after fathers (and some mothers) to get it. In Massachusetts, for example, where over $18 billion is owed in child support, a father who is found to owe child support could lose his driver's license, his lottery winnings, his business license, and even his freedom. In Iowa, once a year, the *Des Moines Register* publishes a list of names of all parents (fathers and mothers) who are delinquent in child support. After this list comes out, the public shaming effectively enables the state to collect a substantial amount of unpaid support. Some states will even legally garnish a delinquent parent's wages, which means the state will take out of the paycheck the amount owed for child support, before the individual receives his or her paycheck.

Divorce and the Community

The effects of divorce on children also are addressed in the third reading in this section. In particular, another concern regarding divorce is how supportive the community will be to single parents and children after a divorce occurs. Nathalie Friedman examines this issue in her article, "Divorced Parents and the Jewish Community." Little research has been done on how divorce among Jews is affecting ties to the Jewish community. In addition to providing an overview concerning factors and problems related to divorce in Jewish families, Friedman investigates whether divorce erodes Jewish commitment and involvement. She specifically focuses on whether the family still attends synagogue, whether the children's Jewish education continues, and whether the divorced family maintains any other ties with the Jewish community. Friedman concludes that there are many obstacles to community participation after a divorce and that the Jewish community needs to recognize that divorced families need support.

Remarriage and Stepfamilies

As was argued earlier, not everything about divorce is necessarily negative. Many individuals go on to marry again and often form stepfamilies or blended families. The last article in this section, "Stepfamilies in the United States: A Reconsideration," by Andrew J. Cherlin and Frank F. Furstenberg Jr., examines remarriage and stepfamilies. Cherlin, a professor of sociology at Johns Hopkins University, first became interested in the subject of remarriage shortly after becoming an assistant professor in 1976 because of the difficulties he had noticed among stepparents who were trying to form stepfamilies. He wrote an article about these difficulties in 1978, which, to his continuing surprise, remains the most heavily cited article he has ever written. Its long life probably reflects the continuing problems that parents, stepparents, and their children and stepchildren have in forming successful new families.

Furstenberg is the Zellerbach Family Professor of Sociology and a research associate in the Population Studies Center at the University of Pennsylvania. His interest in the American family began in Columbia University where he received his Ph.D. in 1967. He has published numerous articles on teenage sexuality, pregnancy, and childbearing as well as on divorce, remarriage, and stepparenting. His current research projects focus on the family in the context of disadvantaged urban neighborhoods, adolescent sexual behavior, cross-national research on children's well-being, and urban education.

In 1994 Cherlin and Furstenberg decided to take another look at the topic of stepfamilies, and this article is the result. The selection discusses five themes related to the formation and functioning of stepfamilies, including demographic trends, new forms of kinship, the organization of stepfamilies, and the reasons remarried persons are at a higher risk of divorce than those who are in their first marriage.

REFERENCES

Ahrons, Constance R. 1994. *The Good Divorce: Keeping Your Family Together When Your Marriage Comes Apart.* New York: HarperCollins.

Hauser, Joyce. 1995. *Good Divorces, Bad Divorces: A Case for Divorce Mediation.* Lanham, MD: University Press of America.

McLanahan, Sara and Gary Sandefur. 1994. *Growing Up with a Single Parent: What Hurts, What Helps.* Cambridge, MA: Harvard University Press.

Riessman, Catherine. 1990. *Divorce Talk: Women and Men Make Sense of Personal Relationships.* New Brunswick, NJ: Rutgers University Press.

Riley, Glenda. 1991. *Divorce: An American Tradition.* New York: Oxford University Press.

Walker, Lou Ann. 1992. "To Ease Broken Hearts." *Parade Magazine,* December 6, p. 12.

Weitzman, Lenore J. and Ruth B. Dixon. [1980] 1994. "The Transformation of Legal Marriage through No-Fault Divorce." Pp. 216–29 in *Families in Transition,* 8th ed., edited by Arlene S. Skolnick and Jerome H. Skolnick. New York: HarperCollins.

Yepsen, David. 1995. "Branstad Seeks Change in Iowa's Divorce Laws." *Des Moines Register,* November 12, p. 7B.

25

WHAT DIVORCE IS AND IS NOT
Transcending the Myths

CONSTANCE R. AHRONS

Say the word *divorce* out loud. What images come to mind?

At my lectures, I hear two very different sets of responses to this question. "Pain, grief, anger, loneliness, and loss," along with "relief, freedom, strength, joy, happiness, and courage," answers one group.

"Broken homes, latchkey children, the women's movement, irresponsible fathers, the lack of family values, lack of commitment, and the 'Me Generation,'" says the other group.

Which group do you suppose includes divorced, separated, and remarried people, and which includes those who are single or married for the first time?

If you haven't lived through divorce, it's hard to think of it personally and humanly. And it's easy to dismiss the millions of people who have lived through it with the simplistic negative judgments derived from noticing only Fiery Foes.

Take the grandmother in one group I spoke to. She summed it up as follows:

"Divorce is just too easy to get nowadays. It's a sign of the breakdown of our society. People just don't take their vows as seriously as we did. They're too lazy to work on their problems. In the thirty-five years my Bernard and I have been married, we've surely had our share of problems, but we never thought of taking the easy way out! My father used to say, 'You made your bed—now lie in it.' And he was right. If everybody acted like us, the world wouldn't be in the shape it is today."

Someone says something like this at nearly every lecture I give. People with long-term marriages stand up and harangue the divorced, picturing themselves as virtuous and steadfast and the divorced as irresponsible and immature. They have stayed the course; understandably, they're proud of earned achievement. Their testimonials are usually punctuated by applause. After, the audience begins to buzz; hands fly up. "Our family values are eroding,"

I hear. "Too many women are working outside the home." "Divorce is a sign of failure," someone else may assert. "Not just personal failure," adds another, "but society's failure." Understandably, the first divorced person to speak usually is quite shy. I tell him or her to go ahead, that there are probably at least one or two other divorced people in the audience. After a few responsive chuckles, we hear quite a different kind of story.

"My parents were married for forty years. It was terrible. They fought every day, constantly." The speaker gathers courage before continuing. "We were miserable. They had three kids, and we all carry the scars. I don't agree that divorce is too easy to get. It's the hardest thing I've ever, I mean *we've* ever, done. Every day, my ex and I work hard to give our kids a sense of family. And I think we're doing okay. In fact, we're better parents now than we were when we were fighting." The speaker's voice hardens. "I'm sick and tired of this holier-than-thou attitude. And I'm sick and tired of being blamed for taking a step I think was healthy for me to take! Don't we want things to change? Don't we want our children to have it better than we did?" After another burst of applause, the debate is off and running.

The issue of divorce is so value-laden that when we even hear the word, our knee-jerk response is: "children," "family," "breakdown." We immediately overlay this chain of thoughts with social panic. "Ugh. It's a plague. Stop it quickly before it spreads!"

From the podium at my lectures, time and time again, I say the word *divorce* and watch the emotions rippling over the faces of my audience. What I then hear is the careful question, "Why is divorce so common?"

The answers people commonly give to this question reflect a fascinating range of misconceptions. From half of my audience, I hear the astounding assertions that everyone wants a divorce these days. That some people take the easy way out. And that we could solve the whole problem with just one simple, elegant solution—make divorce harder to get. Accept divorce? No way. That would be the same as accepting the total breakdown of civilization as we know it.

The other half of my audience argues back equally passionately. Such simplistic solutions, they say, penalize the innocent. The individuals who divorce are not the problem. Why not blame society? Divorce is part of a big picture, they say, not the single cause of society's demise. If we could indeed stop divorce with legislation, surely we as a society would have already done so.

The discussion could go on for hours—indeed, it often does. The conclusions are usually similar. That there's one cause for divorce is a myth. If there's a single cause, there would be a single solution. That there's a single solution is another, even more misleading myth.

If instead we view the current divorce rate as a *result* of social change rather than as a cause, a very different picture emerges. We can begin to see how complex factors—political, economic, social, and personal—work together today to make divorce a normal response. We can see how divorce is an integral part of the way families have been changing for centuries. Divorce is not a sign of individual sickness or abnormality, but a reflection of resilence. Our families are trying to survive and evolve within a rapidly changing society. ⊐

Myths of Divorce

Myth: What Keeps People Married Is Love Alone

We've had a recent rapid shift in frequency of divorce, and a more recent, less rapid shift in our attitudes toward divorce. There has been an even more dramatic shift in our attitudes toward marriage. For centuries, marriage was based on economic and social position. It is only since the beginning of this century that we shifted the foundation of marriage to love. With the coming of industrialization and urbanization in the 1920s, work was no longer centered in the home, and the family was functioning less and less as a discrete economic unit. Couples then began to expect marriage to be a source of personal satisfaction, romance, and intimacy. By the time we reached the 1950s, our romanticized notion of marriage became the cornerstone of our attitudes toward family life.

But when the emotional aspects of the partnership became primary, marriage became vulnerable. When we earn money outside the home and when we expect marriage to meet all our relationship needs, then we are far less tolerant of a marriage that doesn't fulfill us. The prevalent reasons for divorce, unlike those of our elders (alcoholism, desertion) are now loss of closeness, feelings of emotional barrenness, sexual incompatibility, boredom, and serious differences in lifestyle and values.[1]

Not only are we more likely today to leave marriages for reasons that our grandparents would have deemed frivolous, but we are also leaving more quickly than we used to. The most current figures suggest that the time of greatest risk for divorce—the modal or peak point—is around the fourth year of marriage. What used to be thought of as the "seven-year itch" is now more likely to be the "four-year itch."[2] Although the median time of about seven years—the midpoint where half of the divorces occur before this time and half occur after—has remained somewhat stable, the median duration of recent marriages is expected to be shorter.[3]

The initial romance, however strong, is a shaky foundation for long-term marriage. In the romance-driven marriages of the 1950s the initial romance often died, gender roles soon became even more stratified, motherhood was glorified into a full-time career, and the family was almost worshiped as a child-centered haven far from workaday reality. In retrospect it is easy to see how this rigid segregation of roles and functions, and the growing psychological expectations surrounding marriage and the family, led to major discontent for women as they attempted to match their inglorious reality to the glowing myth of marrying and staying married for love. Men's earning power, their presence in the work world, and thus their wider frame of political reference did nothing to dispel the popular image of the happy little woman tending the home fire, kissing cooing babies, and waiting breathlessly to hear manly footsteps on the hearth. Historian Carl Degler says it well: "The historic family has depended for its existence and character on women's subordination. The equality of women and the institution of family have long been at odds with each other."[4]

The pressures on marriage became particularly intense during the late 1960s and early 1970s, when many couples experimented with different forms of relationships. Open marriage was sometimes seen as a way to expand a spouse's autonomy by integrating infidelity into marriage. Unfortunately, many who experimented with open marriage ended up as casualties. In theory it seemed like a good idea, but in practice the partners' needs soon began to conflict, jealousy reared its ugly head, and many marriages collapsed under the pressures. Other marriages simply died through the waning of interest. Subtract romance or chemistry from marriage—as well as economics, family, and social position—and not much is left.

Myth: You're Less Likely to Get Divorced If You Cohabit First

Cohabitation also became popular at this time. This choice was often seen by the participants as at once more sensible and more romantic than marriage; it could also be perceived as a testing ground for marriage—a deterrent to divorce. It came as a big surprise when researchers found that cohabiting for a year did not solve the problems of the first year of married life. In fact, recent research reveals an even higher divorce rate for those who cohabit prior to marriage than for those who don't. Why? One hypothesis has to do with the type of people who cohabit—they tend generally to be less religious, more liberal, and less likely to be bound by societal rules than are people who don't cohabit; these individuals may be more likely to accept divorce.[5]

I feel that many cohabiting couples have the same types of problems as do many married couples: communication problems, differences in values, opposing temperaments, disparate levels of commitment. And many of these couples expect these problems simply to disappear when they marry. Add to this the problem that cohabitors are often not accepted as legitimate or serious couples by the world around them. They can use this as a bond of identity—they are rebels struggling against the outside world—and then, when they marry, they may find both their individuality and this cohabitation identity stripped from them all at once. Cohabiting for love only is just as problematic, perhaps even more so, as marrying for love only.

Myth: The Longer Your Marriage Lasts, the Better It Is

The rapid rise in the divorce rates that began in the late 1960s can be illustrated by the following calculation: Nearly 30 percent of couples who were married in 1952 were divorced by their twenty-fifth anniversary; couples married in 1956 took only twenty years; those married in 1962 took fifteen years; and couples married in 1967 took about ten years. Those 1952 marriages that reached the divorce courts did so in the late 1970s, a time when divorce hit an all-time high.[6]

Social outrage over divorce in the 1960s and 1970s by those who had married in the 1940s and 1950s does not mean that the earlier marriages were any happier or more viable; rather, that starting in the 1960s and 1970s, society awoke to a new concept of marriage. I remember the night I told my mother that my husband and I were separating. She was outraged. "But nobody in our family gets a divorce. Not even your Aunt Ina and Uncle David!" They were the miserable couple whose bedrooms—and daily lives—were as far apart from each other as possible. "But Mom," I protested, "Aunt Ina and Uncle David haven't talked to each other in ten years! They've got a horrible life!" "Maybe so," my mother responded with disdain, "but that's no reason to get divorced." To my mother, any marriage was better than being single; any divorce was shameful and sinful.

Myth: The Rise in Divorce Means We Don't Like Marriage

All this doesn't mean marriage is no longer a viable institution. Statistics for the 1990s show otherwise. The number of marriages in the United States reached an all-time high in the 1980s; in 1990, 95 percent of men and 94 percent of women between the ages of forty-five and fifty-four had been married. In fact, we like marriage so much that many of us will do it two, three, or more times. Remarriages now make up about half of all new marriages each year. Although marriage rates have fallen in some countries in recent years, generally speaking, marriage remains as popular today as it ever was.[7] While marriage rates have remained fairly stable, divorce rates have steadily increased; the number of divorces in the United States has increased 71 percent since 1970, while the number of married couples increased only 19 percent. People are postponing marriage much longer than they used to; many are choosing to forgo marriage altogether.[8]

But people now seem to be recognizing the true and tricky nature of romantic love: As powerful, generous, and creative a feeling as it may be, romance does not necessarily have one-to-one correspondence with marriage. We are also recognizing that reasons for marriage in earlier times, such as social status and economics, do not quid pro quo mean marriage either.

Interestingly, as we move into the twenty-first century, there are some indications that we are becoming less romantic and more practical about marriage again. The ancient practice of matchmaking is back in vogue. The popularity of singles groups that bring together people of similar interests, ethnicity, and education suggests renewed valuation of the importance of background and compatibility.

Our behavior suggests that, instead of viewing divorce as a sign of failure, we are moving toward placing a higher value today on forming successful marriages than did earlier generations. We are more knowledgeable about the many factors that go into marriage; as a society we are getting more flexible about accepting individual reasons for marriage. We expect more from marriage and are less willing to tolerate bad marriages. Slowly, we are moving toward accepting divorce as a solution to unbearable or unfulfilling marriages. And because most people prefer marriage to being single, even the pain of divorce and all of its accompanying social pressures do not today, and will not in the future, stop people from marrying again and again. As Samuel Johnson has said, "Remarriage is the triumph of hope over experience."

Myth: Divorce Is a Modern Affliction

History informs us that, despite our belief in the newness of divorce, our society evolved ways of dissolving marriages in tandem with ways of making marriages. Divorce is today as woven into the fabric of society as is marriage. History clearly reveals patterns that show us divorce is here to stay.

Despite the doom-and-gloom interpretations about the decaying American family that many special-interest groups place on minor fluctuations in divorce rates, as important as our personal values are, we cannot and must not cut the data to fit. History shows otherwise.

The first self-help book about divorce, *How to Get a Divorce*, was published in 1859 in New York.[9] The first recorded divorce in the United States occurred more than two centuries earlier.

In 1639, in a Puritan court in Massachusetts, James Luxford's wife asked for a divorce because her husband already had a wife. The divorce was granted. Mrs. Luxford's bigamist husband was fined, imprisoned, and then banished to England. The next recorded divorce occurred four years later, in 1643. Anne Clarke asked for a divorce because her husband had deserted her and was living with another woman. In those days, adultery was the only grounds for divorce, and only under specific conditions. A man was permitted to divorce his wife if she committed adultery (and if she had, she was shamed, banished, or put to death), but a woman needed additional grounds. In the cases of Mrs. Luxford and Mrs. Clarke, those additional grounds were bigamy and desertion.

As early as the late 1700s, Timothy Dwight, then president of Yale University, decried the high divorce rates he saw around him. He found it inconceivable that fully one in every hundred Connecticut couples had dissolved their marriages. Only fifty years later, the fact that Andrew Jackson was married to a divorced woman created a huge scandal when he ran for president, but it didn't stop him from being elected in 1828 or reelected in 1832. Social reformers, such as Robert Owen and Elizabeth Cady Stanton, pleaded with mainstream society again and again to liberalize divorce, to make it more egalitarian, and to allow people to leave bad marriages.

Myth: Strict Laws Curb Divorce

Should a couple, or shouldn't a couple, be allowed to divorce?

In Puritan America, in the 1600s, divorce was governed by the church, as were other family and social matters. Between 1600 and 1800, this responsibility shifted to the state.[10] Secularization became a cornerstone of the new

United States; it legalized religious and social freedoms and created the Constitution. In these two centuries, divorce became legal in America and in most of Western society.

The shift toward making family matters part of civil law did not come easily. Those who believed that family should continue to be governed by the church believed as passionately then, as do their counterparts today, that allowing divorce to spread would destroy the American family. Divorce must not occur, they felt and feel, except in the most extreme cases—desertion, failure to provide, bigamy, and in some cases, impotency.

Although early American divorce laws were very restrictive, as we have seen, even in early times the Scandinavian countries were more liberal. As early as 1734, incompatibility, ill treatment, drunkenness, and hatred and bitterness between spouses were all grounds for dissolution of a Swedish marriage. In 1796, Denmark allowed three years of separation to entitle one to get a divorce. Further south, in Prussia, "deadly and notorious hostility" provided grounds for divorce in 1751. In 1792, in France, if a couple could agree to petition jointly, they could obtain a divorce by mutual consent; as in today's no-fault divorces, they did not have to produce evidence. A couple did have to go through a long process in which the extended family was required to make all efforts to help the couple reconcile.

This liberalization of the divorce laws was not to last long, however. Divorce laws fluctuated with the political and religious tenor of the times. In 1816, when the French monarchy was restored, divorce was abolished. A century later, a cultural shift occurred again and divorce laws emerged in every country in Europe, with the exception of a few Catholic countries—Spain, Italy, Ireland. Today, Ireland is the one country in Western society that does not permit divorce.

In the United States the debate flourished.[11] On Independence Day 1826, Robert Owen, the social reformer (also a journalist and congressman), publicly and strongly declared that no one should be forced to remain in an unhappy marriage. Twenty-six years later, a legislative committee liberalized the laws. Lenient Indiana statutes included only a current residency statement; a resident could get a divorce even if the whereabouts of a mate were unknown. Like its current counterpart (Reno, Nevada), Indianapolis—our moral heartland—was labeled the "divorce mecca." Like Reno, Indianapolis had a good railway station, was centrally located, had good shopping and recreational facilities, and had an eager group of lawyers who courted the divorce trade.

Horace Greeley, editor of the *New York Tribune*, publicly accused Owen of causing Indiana to become "a paradise of free lovers."[12] Owen countered with the statement that free love, prostitution, and adultery flourished in New York State because of its harsh divorce laws. Does external restriction breed inner morality or its opposite? Does external liberality breed rectitude or decay? Is this a question that can be settled by legislation?

If divorce were truly a sign of moral decay, then countries and states that were more liberal about divorce might show a higher crime rate, a lower incidence of spiritual involvement, and other signs of social dissolution. The evidence does not bear this out.

The early debates about divorce, so similar in tone to the two audience members with whom I introduced this chapter, developed two major positions. One faction—the conservatives—claimed, as they do today, that divorce threatened the basic foundation of society; they called for the return of traditional sanctity to marriage. Advocating lifetime monogamous marriage, they eschewed divorce except in extreme cases. To members of this group, divorce was a social problem. The need to maintain a rigid family organization, and harmony and stability (external at least), was more important than the marital satisfaction of individual citizens.

The other faction, comprised mainly of utopian thinkers and social activists, argued passionately for divorce reform and individual rights. To them, marriage was the social problem. Individual freedom was primary. Any effort to control that freedom would erode society from within.

Today every state has some form of no-fault divorce law. Waiting periods are short, and mandatory reconciliation counseling is virtually absent. These liberalizations generally occurred during the 1970s. During the twelve years of the Ronald Reagan and George Bush administrations, a more conservative period than the one that preceded it, the liberal laws of the earlier decade once again came under fire. Now, in the 1990s, the Clinton administration seems to be focusing more on the consequences of divorce than the causes. This focus potentially could encourage legislation aimed at improving the circumstances of divorced families, such as better child-support enforcement and welfare reform, rather than discouraging people from divorcing at all.

The pattern of liberalizing divorce laws and then tightening them, seesawing from honoring the individual to honoring the society and back again, is one that we see throughout Europe and the United States over a period of two centuries. As a society we are still ambivalent about divorce, still fearful that the family is falling apart more quickly than we can patch it together. We all agree on one basic issue: The institution of family is crucial to society (although we passionately disagree on how to define family and on which family values should be paramount).

Marriage is good—and so is divorce. It all depends to whom each happens, and why, and how—and when.

Realities Affecting Divorce

How have divorce rates changed over time? And what do divorce rates really tell us?

We've seen that divorce rates have risen in the past three centuries.[13] However, in each decade there have been fluctuations. When charting these against fluctuations in politics and economics, we can see how divorce matches other trends.

Factors That Influence the Rise and Fall of Divorce Rates

Divorce rates tend to decline during hard times and to rise in times of prosperity. Divorce rates decreased during World War I, increased when the war ended, decreased after the stock market crash of 1929, and stayed low during the Great Depression and World War II. When the war ended, the rates shot up once again. They peaked around 1946, stabilized, and declined a bit during the 1950s. The decrease in the 1950s is the sole exception to the economic theory of shifting divorce rates; and the fact that most of those adults had matured during the 1930s and 1940s perhaps means that their inner reality still reflected the dynamics of those depressed times. It is interesting to note that when the children of these 1950s marriages—baby boomers—matured, they divorced in record numbers. Between 1965 and 1980—prosperous years—the divorce rates more than doubled. By the late 1980s, as the economy dipped, the divorce rate declined slightly and has leveled off at our current rate.

Politics affect divorce rates too. In times of liberalism and social experimentation, divorce rates generally rise, as they did in the late 1960s and 1970s. In more conservative times, divorce rates declined somewhat, as they did in the 1980s. From the 1960s onward there has been a rapid and dramatic increase in divorces in every country allowing the practice.[14] England's rates doubled between 1960 and 1970, then more than doubled between 1970 and the early 1980s. In France, divorce rates more than doubled between 1970 and the early 1980s. In Sweden and Germany, the rates doubled between 1960 and 1988. Today, the numbers are still highest in the United States, although it is likely that the other countries will catch up.

Each time there's a small surge in divorce rates during liberal times, conservatives respond with deep concern about the demise of the family. Many of the reforms are then repealed, only to pop up in even more lenient form the next time the cycle comes around. This does not mean that families are more content and more stable during conservative times, or even that there's a reduction in separations during those times. It just means that these already difficult times are made even harder by adding restrictive laws to economic misery.

The Probability of Divorce

The probability of divorce is associated with a number of demographic factors. Age is the strongest predictor. Those couples who are twenty years old or younger when they marry have the highest likelihood of divorce. People with less income and education tend to divorce more than those with higher education and incomes. An important exception to this principle relates to women: Well-educated women (five or more years of college) with good incomes have higher divorce rates than those who are poorer and less educated.

Geographically, there are some differences as well. People in the western part of the United States have higher divorce rates than those in the Northeast.

This may be due partly to the fact that the average age is lower in the West. Also, there is a higher concentration of Catholics in the Northeast.

There are also significant racial differences.[15] Divorce rates for the black population are two times those of whites or Hispanics. Although the explanations for the higher divorce rate among African Americans vary, socioeconomic differences seem to play a part. On the average, blacks are less educated, poorer, and more often unemployed than whites.

Religion also plays a part. Catholics and Jews have a lower divorce rate than Protestants. Since Catholicism is the religion of traditional Hispanics, part of the explanation for the racial difference in divorce rates may be attributed to religious affiliation. Although Catholics have a lower divorce rate, their rates have risen just as rapidly as the general divorce rates.

A sixfold increase in cohabitation since 1970 has also impacted divorce rates. In some European countries, a recent decline in divorce rates can be attributed to the increase in informal cohabitation arrangements. In Sweden, for example, this increase in cohabitation has decreased the marriage rate as well as the divorce rate. Breakups of these informal unions, of course, are not included in the divorce rates.

Trends and Projections

Demographic trends suggest that the current divorce rates in the United States are now fairly stable.[16] Demographers predict that 40 percent to 60 percent of all current marriages will eventually end in divorce. Those who predict the lower rates say that the divorce rate will decline as the baby boomers age; that those boomers who wish to divorce have mostly already done so, and those who haven't are past the stage of life when the odds of divorce are highest. Those who predict an increase, whether large or small, say that women's and men's roles will continue to change. That change, plus the increasing financial independence of women—historically the less satisfied party in marriage—will continue to push the rates upward.

Women's increased economic and social independence, our increased life expectancy, the continued acceptance of divorce as a fact of modern family life—and history—all lead me to believe that the rates are likely to increase slightly or stabilize at the current level, with only minor fluctuations. One major factor that must be figured into any projection is the rate of redivorce. Most divorced people remarry and over half of those who do will redivorce; some of those will remarry and redivorce again. One factor that will help balance the rates is the reduction in the marriage rates. If fewer people marry, it reduces the potential pool for divorces. Women today have more options in life, and more women may choose not to marry. Some women may choose career over marriage, may choose to cohabit instead of getting married, and may choose to parent without a husband. As we have seen, women are waiting longer to get married and in so doing also limit their chances of marriage because of the "marriage squeeze," a shortage of eligible partners due to a declining birth rate. The percentage of thirty-year-olds who have never married almost doubled between 1970 and 1990.

ENDNOTES

1. Prevalent reasons for divorce: In a recent study, 64 percent of women and 65 percent of men checked sexual intimacy problems as an important factor in their divorce, compared with 11 percent in 1967 and 4 percent in 1956. See Lynn Gigy and Joan B. Kelly, "Reasons for Divorce: Perspectives of Divorcing Women and Men," *Journal of Divorce and Remarriage* 18(1/2) (1992): 169–87.

   Using data from a large midwestern study, Gay C. Kitson with William H. Holmes (*Portrait of Divorce: Adjustment to Marital Breakdown.* [New York: Guilford Press, 1992], pp. 143–46) found that some reasons increased or decreased in importance over time and some remained consistent throughout their longitudinal study. The ones that did not change over time were alcohol, lack of communication or understanding, too young at time of marriage, problems with in-laws and relatives, and extramarital sex. Reasons that were stated at the first interview but not stated subsequently were arguing all the time, inflexible, stubborn, over-commitment to work, not enough time together, and joint conflict over roles.

2. "Four-year itch": See Helen E. Fisher, *Anatomy of Love: The Natural History of Monogamy, Adultery, and Divorce* (New York: Norton, 1992).

3. Median duration of recent marriages: Duration is calculated from all divorces in a given year. Therefore, some of the marriages used in the calculations began decades ago, under very different social conditions, and are not indicative of the likelihood of the duration for a couple marrying now. See William J. Goode, *World Changes in Divorce Patterns* (New Haven, CT: Yale University Press, 1993), p. 146.

4. "Women's subordination": Carl Degler, *At Odds: Women and the Family in America from the Revolution to the Present* (New York: Oxford University Press, 1980).

5. Cohabitation: Data from the National Survey of Families and Households show that women who cohabit have a 50 percent higher divorce rate than those who do not cohabit prior to marriage. See Larry L. Bumpass, Teresa Castro Martin, and James A. Sweet, "The Impact of Family Background and Early Marital Factors on Marital Disruption," *Journal of Family Issues* 12(1) (1991): 22–42.

6. Rise in the divorce rates: See Dennis A. Ahlburg and Carol J. DeVita, "New Realities of the American Family," *Population Bulletin* 47(2) (1992): 15.

7. Marriage remains as popular today: Although marriage rates are still high, especially in the United States, which has one of the highest rates in the world, the percentage of thirty-year-olds who have never married almost doubled between 1970 and 1990. Because the probability of getting married declines with age, this pattern of delayed age at first marriage could eventually lead to fewer people ever getting married. See Ahlburg and DeVita, "New Realities of the American Family."

8. Postponing marriage: In 1950, the average age at marriage for women was 20.3 and 22.8 for men; by 1970, it was 20.8 for women, 23.2 for men; by 1980, it was 22.0 for women, 24.7 for men; by 1991, it had increased to 24.1 for women, 26.3 for men. These U.S. patterns are similar to those of other industrialized countries.

   For blacks, the age at first marriage now exceeds that of whites by two years, and a smaller proportion of black women marry.

   See Ahlburg and DeVita, "New Realities of the American Family," for further information.

9. First self-help book: Glenda Riley, *Divorce: An American Tradition* (New York: Oxford University Press, 1991), p. 128.

10. Early American divorce laws: For an excellent and very readable history of divorce laws, see Roderick Phillips, *Untying the Knot: A Short History of Divorce* (Cambridge: Cambridge University Press, 1991).

11. The debate flourished: See Riley, *Divorce: An American Tradition*, p. 73.

12. Horace Greeley: For an interesting discussion of the progression of the divorce reform movements, see Lynne Carol Halem, *Divorce Reform: Changing Legal and Social Perspectives* (New York: Free Press, 1980), p. 25.

13. Divorce rates have risen: From the time of the first census figures, divorce rates have been rising. There was a slight downward trend during the Depression of the early 1930s and an increase in the prosperous 1970s. Rates increased after the Civil War, World War I, and World War II. For more discussion of economic trends and fluctuations in rates, see Maxine Baca Zinn and D. Stanley Eitzen, *Diversity in Families* (New York: HarperCollins, 1993), pp. 362–67.

Increasing Rate of Divorce, 1860–1990

Year	Divorce Rate per Thousand People	Percentage of Marriages Begun in Each Year Ending in Divorce
1860	.3	—
1879	.3	7%
1880	.4	8%
1890	.5	10%
1900	.7	12%
1910	.9	14%
1920	1.6	18%
1930	1.6	24%
1940	2.0	25%
1950	2.5	30%*
1960	2.2	39%*
1970	3.5	48%*
1980	5.2	49%*
1990	4.7	—

Source: Leonard Beeghley and Jeffrey W. Dwyer, "Social Structure and the Divorce Rates," *Population Today* 19(July/August 1991): 9.

*Projections.

14. Increase in divorces in every country: The following table shows the divorce rates for major industrial countries:

Country	Divorce Rate per Thousand People	Year of Data Collection
United States	4.70	1991
Russian Federation	3.96	1989
Canada	3.15	1989
Former German Dem. Republic	1.9	1990
United Kingdom	2.98	1990
Denmark	3.0	1989
Democratic Germany	3.0	1989
Sweden	2.2	1991
France	1.9	1990
Netherlands	1.9	1991
Switzerland	2.0	1990
Japan	1.3	1990
Italy	0.5	1990

The data are from *1991 Demographic Yearbook* (New York: United Nations), pp. 752–57.

15. Racial differences: The explanations for racial differences are very complex and far from conclusive. Good discussions can be found in Joseph Guttmann, *Divorce in Psychosocial Perspective: Theory and Research* (Hillsdale, NJ: Erlbaum, 1993); Ahlburg and DeVita, "New Realities of the American Family"; and Baca Zinn and Eitzen, *Diversity in Families.*

16. Demographic trends: Demographer Paul Glick ("American Families: As They Are, and Were," *Sociology and Social Research* 74 [April 1990]: 139–45) predicts the lower rate while demographer Larry Bumpass ("What's Happening to the Family? Interactions between Demographic and Institutional Change," *Demography* 27 [November 1990]: 483–98) predicts a higher rate.

26

THE SOCIAL SELF AS GENDERED
A Masculinist Discourse of Divorce

TERRY ARENDELL

D ivorce functions as a prism, making available for examination an array of issues. Pulled into question are the shape and dictates of extra-familial institutions and practices, such as the juridical and economic; and the character of family life, parenting, and domestic arrangements. Also brought into view are matters of interpersonal relations and gender identity: It is "unfamiliar situations" which call forth "taken as given identities" and present opportunities to observe the effects of identity upon behavior (Foote 1981:338). . . . Thus investigation of participants' perspectives on and responses to divorce and the postdivorce situation can illumine processes not only of interactional adjustment in the context of change but also of identity maintenance and alteration.

Family and identity transitions are located within a broader sociocultural context: The gender hierarchy and belief system and gender roles are being questioned and altered, although at broadly discrepant rates (Hochschild 1989; Pleck 1985). Specifically, the conventions of masculinity — "those sets of signs indicating that a person is a 'man', or 'not a woman' or 'not a child'" (Hearn 1987:137) and which are "the social reality for men in modern society"

Terry Arendell, "The Social Self as Gendered: A Masculinist Discourse of Divorce," *Symbolic Interaction*, Vol. 15, #2, 1992. Copyright © 1992 JAI Press. Reprinted with permission of the University of California Press.

(Clatterbaugh 1990:3) — are being challenged. Indeed, Kimmel (1987) has concluded that contemporary men, like men in other periods characterized by dramatic social and economic change, "confront a crisis in masculinity" (p. 153). Divorce both exemplifies and prompts a crisis in gender identity (Riessman 1990; Vaughan 1986).

Men's perspectives on, actions in, and adjustments to divorce have been relatively neglected in divorce research. Yet they are significant for understanding contemporary social arrangements and processes as well as for broadening understanding of men's lives: How men define their situations and act in divorce points to their positions in a gender-structured society and to their understandings of the nature of social practices, relationships, and selves. To paraphrase an argument made with regard to the study of a gendered division of labor in families, the ways in which divorced fathers "use motive talk to account for, disclaim, and/or neutralize their behavior or changes in their behavior need to be more fully explored and developed" (Pestello and Voyandoff 1991:117).

Methodology

Based on data obtained through intensive interviews examining postdivorce situations, experiences, and feelings with a sample 75 divorced fathers (Arendell 1995), this article explores the problem of the social self as gendered and specifically, the nature of the masculinist self. All participants were volunteers who responded to notices and advertisements placed in newsletters, magazines, and newspapers or to referrals from other participants. The men ranged in age from 23 to 59 years with a median age of 38.5 years. Sixty-four interviewees were white, three were black, four Hispanic, two Asian American, and two Native American. All respondents were residents of New York State, had one or more minor children, and had been divorced or legally separated for at least 18 months. The median time divorced or separated was 4.8 years. At the time they were interviewed, 18 men were remarried, 5 were living with a woman in a marital-like relationship, and the others were unmarried. Nearly half of the sample had some college education with over one-third having completed college and approximately one-sixth having earned a graduate or professional degree. Occupationally, one-third of the employed respondents worked in blue-collar and two-thirds worked in white-collar positions. Six men were unemployed at the time of the interview, three by choice.

The respondents were fathers to a total of 195 children ranging in age from 2 to 25 with a median age of 9.5 years. The number of children per father ranged from one to six; the mean number of children was 2.6 and the median was 2. Child custody arrangements varied among the men: six fathers had primary physical custody, five had co- or shared physical custody with their former wives, and 64 were noncustodial fathers. Two of those categorized as noncustodial fathers actually had split custody arrangements; each had one child living with him and another two children living with their mothers. A total of eleven fathers were "absent" fathers, meaning that they had no contact with any of their children for at least the past twelve months; another four fathers were "absent" from one or more but not all of their children.

The sample overrepresents "involved" fathers; for example, only 15 percent were "absent" compared to the national figure of about 50 percent (Furstenberg, Morgan, and Allison 1987) and 85 percent were noncustodial parents compared to a national figure of 90 percent (USBC 1989). Additionally, with only a few exceptions, the nonresidential fathers repeatedly maintained that they desired increased access to and involvement with their children; many wished for more satisfying relations with their children.

Interviews were open-ended, tended to be long, lasting between two and five hours, and were conducted primarily in 1990 with some occurring in late 1989 and early 1991. Seven respondents participated in follow-up interviews. An interview instrument, initially developed and revised on the basis of 15 earlier interviews in another state, was used as a reference to ensure that certain areas were covered during the discussions. All interviews were tape recorded and transcribed. Data were analyzed using the constant comparative method and coding paradigm developed in works on grounded theory (Glaser and Strauss 1967; Strauss 1989).

A Masculinist Discourse of Divorce

What the data in this study of divorce provide is a richly descriptive testimony of the men's perspectives on and actions in family and divorce. These divorced fathers, largely irrespective of variations in custody, visitation, marital, or socioeconomic class status, shared a set of dispositions, practices, and explanations with which they managed their identities, situations, and emotional lives. They held in common a body of *gender strategies:* plans of action "through which a person tries to solve problems at hand given the cultural notions of gender at play" and through which an individual reconciles beliefs and feelings with behaviors and circumstances (Hochschild 1989:15). In similar ways, they accounted for past and present actions and described and implied intended future lines of activity, including, significantly, the probable meanings of such movement. The participants shared a *discourse*—a particular "matrix of perceptions, appreciations, and actions" (Bourdieu 1987:83). More specifically, they shared a *masculinist discourse of divorce.* . . .

Considered specifically in this article are the interviewees' understandings and definitions of family, encompassing issues of gender differences and a *broken* family and the processes of devaluation of the former wife. Then examined is the related use of a rhetoric of *rights*. Following this is a brief discussion and analysis of the contrasting perspectives and actions of the divergent group, the postdivorce "androgynous" fathers. Lastly, several of the implications of the findings are specified.

Definition of Family

Gender Differences

The family was shown to be a threshold of masculinity in these men's accounts; it was the primary social group (Cooley 1981) that conveyed and reinforced the constructs of gender. The family of origin served as the nursery and early classroom of gender acquisition, and the family of procreation (that formed through marriage) served as a workshop where gender identity was continuously retooled. Then, as the marriage ended and the postdivorce situation entered, the family and its changes evoked a questioning of masculine identity. Made particularly evident in the divorcing process was that beneath the jointly created and shared reality of married life (Berger and Kellner 1964) were distinctive experiences and understandings, organized according to and understood in terms of gender—the "his" and "hers" of married life (Bernard 1981; Riessman 1990). Nearly all of the respondents expressed a belief that gender differences had been at play in their marriages and divorces; while some regretted the consequences of the differences and attributed marital problems to them, most nonetheless expressed confidence that, compared to their former wife's, their own experiences and perceptions had been, to use their terms, the more valid, reasonable, logical, reliable, or objective ones.

Communication patterns and conversational styles in their marriages varied along gender lines, reflecting and reinforcing gender differences. The men usually expected and reported themselves to be less expressive and self-disclosing in marriage than their former wives; they also claimed to have felt pressured during marriage to be otherwise (see also Cancian 1987; Riessman 1990; Tannen 1990). One participant, in a remark about the differences between men and women which was similar in substance to most others' comments about gender differences, noted:

> *Men compartmentalize. It's just a different pattern of doing things, it has to do with the differences between men and women. I think men are always a few months, a few steps, behind women in a relationship. And men don't talk to each other the way women do to each other so men don't know what's going on outside of the things they are already most familiar with. They are at a disadvantage, they usually don't know what's going on.*

Despite its gendered and therefore problematic character, marriage, for a large majority of these men, was essential to family; indeed, family was predicated upon the enduring "successful marriage." The "successful" and desired marriage, however, was defined in a paradoxical way as being both the traditional marriage and the companionate marriage. That is, on the one hand, most of these men wanted a marital arrangement in which they were ultimately, even if largely benignly, the dominant spouse, befitting men in relationships with women according to the conventions of masculinity. On the other hand, these men wanted a relationship in which they were equal co-partners, forging mutually a high degree of intimacy and seeking reciprocally to meet the other's needs and desires. This next person, a co-custodial parent who had opted to leave his marriage two years earlier but was now hoping for a marital reconciliation, explained his position:

> *I'm not talking about a marriage and family with a patriarchal model, but the priority of the relationship between a man and a woman as a husband and wife. I want an equal relationship, a partnership. But let me word it this way, I would like her to be able to trust me to be the leader of the family. When there are times we can't sit down at the table and make decisions cooperatively, then I will make the decisions and she will trust me. I want to be able to do that in a marriage. What I need and want is the trust from her to be able to be the leader of the family. I want her to be the first one to say: "We've talked about it and I'll let you decide." I guess I expect her to relinquish the control of the situation first.*

The improbability, even impossibility, of having simultaneously both types of marriage was largely obscured by the gender assumptions held. By conceiving of themselves as more rational, logical, and dependable than their wives, for example, assertions repeated in various ways throughout their accounts of marriage and divorce, these men were able to make claims to both types of marriage without acknowledging the contradictions or tensions between them.

The explanation for the failure to have the desired and lasting companionate marriage was the existence of fundamental differences between themselves as *men* and their former wives as *women*. In specifying these differences, the men rehearsed and reinforced the cultural stereotypes of gender and their expectations that they be the dominant partner. . . . Perceiving themselves to be fundamentally dissimilar from women had enabled these men to objectify their wives during marriage, at least as their retrospective accounts indicated, and to thereby discount or reconstruct the meanings of their communications in particular ways. . . . Accepting the conventional beliefs in gender differences and asserting the preeminence of their levels of rationality and insight served to strengthen the respondents' identities as masculine selves. For example:

> *I just mostly stayed rational and reasonable during the months we considered separation, but she just got crazier and crazier through the whole thing. I should have been prepared for that, I always knew during the marriage not to take her too seriously because she could be so illogical. I mean, you know, it's men's rationality that keeps a marriage together to begin with.*

Likewise, having dismissed or redefined a wife's expression of marital discontent was justified through claims to basic superiority. One man noted:

> *She kept saying she was unhappy, that I worked too much and was never home, and that I neither listened to or appreciated her, that I didn't help out with the kids, maybe even didn't care about them. But I insisted she was just depressed because her father had died. It just made sense but I couldn't get her to see it.*

By redefining a wife's expressed feelings of discontent with the marriage or him as a partner, an individual could rationalize and discount his own participation in the demise of the marriage. Through such disclaimers, the estranged husband reinforced his definitions of the situation and of self. . . .

A wife's sentiments about and assessments of their marriage could be discounted; entering into the wife's point of view, or attempting to "take the role of the other" — defined by Mead (1934:254) as "a uniquely human capacity which assumes the attitude of the other individual as well as calling it out in the other" — was not a constitutive element of a husband's range of activities in the conventional martial relationship. Women spoke a "different language," as one man summed up the differences between men and women which lead to divorce, a language not to be taken too seriously, or at least not as seriously as one's own *as a man*.[1] This posture toward a wife's perspectives and feelings carried over into the postdivorce situation where differences and conflicts of interest were typically highlighted and multiplied.

A "Broken Family"

Family, within the masculinist discourse of divorce, was understood to be a *broken family*, consisting essentially of two parts: the male-self and the wife-and-children or, as referred to, "'me' and 'them.'" Even men who had sought the divorce, about one-third of the group, and several of those who had primary or shared custody of children, understood and discussed the postdivorce family as being a *broken* one. Most of the noncustodial fathers perceived themselves to have been marginalized from the family, and nearly all felt stigmatized as divorced fathers. For instance:

> You're not part of the family, part of the society anymore. You really don't have a proper place, a place where you have input into what goes on in your life. You're treated as if you're just scum, that's what you are really.

One father, using the language of *broken* family explicitly, summed up the dilemma he faced, suggesting that with the fracturing of the family went a loss of power and authority:

> I guess I'm sort of at a loss in all of this; I just don't know what to do to fix a broken family. I can't say I didn't want the divorce, it was a mutual decision. But I just hadn't understood before how it would break the family into pieces. It's really become them and me and I don't know what to do. I keep thinking of the rhyme: "Humpty Dumpty sat on a wall, Humpty Dumpty had a great fall. All the king's horses and all the king's men, couldn't put Humpty together again." I ran it by my ex last week and asked her if she had any Super-Glue, but she didn't think it was funny.

The definition of the postdivorce family as a *broken* one had several sources, including the belief that family is predicated on the marriage. Other sources of the view were acceptance of the conventional definition that masculinity is the measure of mature adulthood in comparison to both femininity and childhood (Broverman et al. 1970; Phillips and Gilroy 1985),[2] meaning, therefore, that men are different in distinctive ways from women and children, and of the ideology, if not the actual practice, of a traditional gender-based family division of labor: child-rearing and caretaking are the responsibilities primarily of women, whether or not they are employed, and economic providing is the responsibility primarily of men (Cohen 1989; Hochschild 1989).[3]

Another and related factor in the view that the postdivorce family consisted of "me" and "them" was the understanding that the respective parent–child relationships differed, a perception shared by divorced mothers as well, according to other studies (Arendell 1986; Hetherington, Cox, and Cox 1976). . . . In contrast to the unique and independent mother–child unit, the father–child relationship was mediated in varying ways by the wife, consistent with her marital role as emotional worker (Hochschild 1983, 1989), and so was dependent on her actions. One father, who had read extensively about the psychological effects of divorce on children, compared the outcomes of his two divorces:

> *I would have to say that my children's primary attachment really was with their mother. I think that's typical in families, mothers are just better trained, maybe it's an instinct for parenting. Maybe fathers just don't make the effort. Anyway, even after my first divorce, I found that my ex-wife was vital to my relationship with the child of our marriage: She thought it was important that he maintain contact with me and that I be a part of his life. So she really encouraged him to do this and so it continued to be a relationship. She ran a kind of interference between us. He's 21 now and we have a good, solid relationship, but my children of this last marriage are essentially withdrawn from me. Their mother, my second wife, never really facilitated our relationship.*

The retreat by former wives from the activity of facilitating the relationship between children and their fathers after divorce was interpreted as a misuse of power, and often as an overt act of hostility or revenge. In addition to the use and misuse of their psychological power in interpersonal relations (see also Pleck 1989), former wives exercised power by interfering with visitation, denigrating them as fathers and men to their children, provoking interpersonal conflicts, being uncooperative in legal matters, and demanding additional money. . . . Nearly all of the men had an acute sense that their own power and authority in the family had been seriously eroded through divorce (Arendell 1992; Riessman 1990). This perception was central to the crisis in gender identity and was not limited to noncustodial fathers: More than half of the primary or co-custodial fathers argued that their former wives had usurped power illegitimately and at their expense. Moreover, former spouses had attained or appropriated dominance only partly through their own actions: the judiciary and legal system and the institutional and informal gender biases of both were accomplices and even instigators.

> *The legal system is such a crock, I can't believe it. The legal system is so for the woman and so against the man, it's just incredible. And the result is that all of these women get to go around screwing their ex-husbands.*

Another person explained:

> *When we went to court after the divorce was over because of disagreements*
> *over support and visitation, the court did nothing. The situation is as it is*
> *today [with the mother interfering with his visitation] because the judge did*
> *nothing except hold meeting after meeting, delay after delay. The judge even*
> *said she was an unfit mother. She violated every aspect of the agreement, she*
> *obstructed. But they let her do it.*

In support of their assertions about the unjustness of the system, numerous men cited the lack of a legal presumption in favor of joint child custody in New York State. Over half of the fathers argued (erroneously) that joint custody is not allowed in New York State (*Family Law* 1990) and nearly all of the noncustodial fathers, most of whom were granted what they called the "standard visitation arrangement" — every other weekend and one evening a week — complained bitterly about their limited access to their children.

Consistent with the categorization of "me" and "them," the perceived centrality of the former wife, and their own limited parental involvement, children most often were talked about as if they were extensions of their mothers rather than separate, unique persons. Thus, identity as a divorced father was intermixed with identity as a former spouse, adding further ambiguity and uncertainty to their place and activities in the changed family. Further, nearly all of the noncustodial and a third of the custodial fathers viewed their children as being instruments of their mothers in the postdivorce exchanges between the parents. . . . Fathers tended to merge their children with their former wives in other ways as well. In explaining their motives for or the consequences of actions, the majority of men frequently shifted from their children as the subject to their former wife. For instance,

> *I wanted the kids to have a house. So it remains as it is, with them [the kids]*
> *living in it, until the youngest is 18. But that was my biggest mistake. I*
> *should have had the house sold. Then I could have really gotten away from*
> *her [the former wife] and had no ties to her at all.*

The approach of not disaggregating the children from the former wife served varying functions. On the one hand, this approach bolstered the primacy of the former spouse in the postdivorce situation, granting her a position of centrality and augmenting the charges against her, and, on the other hand, it reduced her status by categorizing her with the children. Children's experiences and feelings could be discounted more easily than if they were respected as independent persons, thus creating more emotional distance between them. . . . Not surprisingly, then, fathers satisfied with their parent–child relations were the exception: They included the postdivorce "androgynous" fathers and eight others. The majority were discontented with and disconcerted by the nature of their interactions with, emotional connections to, and levels of involvement with their children. Most characterized their relations with their children as being strained or superficial, distrustful, and unfulfilling.

Devaluing a Wife's Family Activities

Most of the respondents specifically devalued the family activities done both during and after marriage by the former wife (Riessman 1990). Through deprecating the former partner's activities, the men were able to buttress various assertions, including that they had been the dominant spouse and had been mistreated badly by the divorce settlement. Over a third of the fathers contended that they had been exceptional men in their marriages—a "superman," as several fathers quipped, in contrast to the popularized notion of "superwoman"—carrying the major share of income-earning and participating equally or near equally in caretaking activities. These particular fathers especially generalized their critique of their former wife's activities to a broad indictment of women's family roles, thus further reinforcing their beliefs in male superiority. As one noncustodial father, whose career development had demanded exceptionally long work weeks and whose former wife had stayed home during the marriage with the children, said:

> After all, I was able to do it [work and family] all, while she did next to nothing, so I don't see what these women are complaining about.

The devaluing of a former wife's activities also helped sustain the perception that, at least in retrospect, her economic dependence during marriage had been unfair, as was any continued exchange of resources after divorce. The implicit marriage contract operative during marriage, involved a culturally defined and socially structured gender-based division of labor and exchange (Weitzman 1985), was to be terminated upon divorce. Child support was viewed as a continuation of support for the undeserving former spouse. Of the 57 fathers (three-quarters of the sample) who were paying child support consistently or fairly regularly, almost two-thirds were adamant in their assertions that men's rights are infringed upon by the child support systems.[4] One man, in a representative statement, said:

> I, a hard-working family man, got screwed, plain and simple. The court, under the direction of a totally biased judge, dictated that she and her children, our children, can relate to me simply as a money machine: "Just push the buttons and out comes the money, no strings attached." And leave me without enough money even to afford a decent place to live.

"Adding insult to injury," as one irate father put it, was the demonstrated and undeniable reality that each time money defined as child support was passed to her, the former wife gained discretionary authority over its use, being accountable to neither the former husband or any institutional authority. Resentment over the child support system and the former wife's unwarranted power over his earnings was the explanation for various actions of resistance. Such common behaviors included refusing to pay support, providing a check without funds in the bank to cover it, and neglecting to pay on time so that the former spouse was pushed into having to request the support check.

Other actions were more idiosyncratic; for example, one father of three described his strategy for protesting the payment of child support:

> *I put the check in the kids' dirty clothes bag and send it home with them after they visit. I used to put it in the clean clothes, but now I put it in the dirty clothes bag. One woman told me her husband sent back the kids' clothes with a woman's sock, then the next time a woman's bra. I won't go that far, it's too low. But I suspect even this keeps her angry and off-balance, and she can't say a word to me about it. She knows I can simply withhold it, refuse to pay it.*

The respondents defined their postdivorce situations and actions primarily in terms of the former wife, and a preoccupation with her was sustained whether or not there was continued direct interaction. Contributing were overlapping factors: lingering feelings about her, characterized generally by ambivalence, frustration and anger and remaining intense for over a third of the men (see also Wallerstein and Blakeslee 1989); the perception that she held a position of dominance in the postdivorce milieu together with the processes of devaluing her significance; and the continuing relevance of issues pertaining to their children and finances.

A Rhetoric of Rights

A rhetoric of *rights* was interspersed throughout the men's accounts: It was basic to their understanding of family and their place in it and to their postdivorce actions, perspectives, and relationships. Attitudes held toward *rights* and its use were largely independent of particular experiences. Men satisfied with their divorce and postdivorce experiences spoke of *rights* in ways analogous to those men who were intensely dissatisfied with nearly every aspect of their divorce, the general exception being the small group characterized as "androgynous" fathers.

. . .

That *rights* were to be secured in relation to another, and primarily the former wife, demystified the assertions and implications that what was at issue were matters of abstract principles of justice. Central among the various issues framed within the rhetoric of *rights* were the privileges of position of husband and father as held, or expected to be held, in the family prior to separation and divorce. As one father referring to the dominant pattern in which mothers receive custody and fathers pay child support pointedly said,

> *Divorce touches men in the two most vulnerable spots possible: rights to their money and rights to their children.*

The rhetoric of *rights* had a distinctive and complex connotation: that which was expected, desired, and believed to be deserved *as a man*. This person, for example, insisted repeatedly and explicitly throughout much of his account that his *rights* had been continuously violated. He had obtained primary custody of their children after "forcing my wife out of our home" and claiming that "she deserted us" in response to her request for a divorce:

> *The legal system abuses you as a man. You know: you have no rights. That is, you're treated as a nonperson or as a second, third, fourth or fifth class citizen. They look at us: you know, "Who is that guy with the mother?" Suddenly we're just sperm donators or something. We're a paycheck and sperm dona- tors and that's our total function in society. The legal bias for the mother is incredible. You pull your hair and spend thousands of dollars and say, "Aren't I a human being?" I mean I saw on TV: gay rights, pink rights, blue rights, everybody has rights and they're all demonstrating. I said, "Don't men have rights too? Aren't these my children? Isn't this my house? Don't they bear my name?" I mean I was the first one to hold each of them when they were first born. I was there for it all. . . . None of my rights were protected, but had I been a woman, you can bet that if I were a female, I'd have had these things automatically, without any fight at all. . . .*

This father remained locked in a power struggle with his former wife, espe- cially as he actively resisted her involvement with the children. Like many of the men in the study and even though he was a custodial parent, his relations with his children were continuously filtered through his relations and feel- ings about their mother.

. . .

The rhetoric of *rights* then was multifaceted, consisting of complex and overlapping themes pertaining to self-identity and involving issues of per- sonal efficacy, dominance, and control. It served to define, reaffirm, and re- assert a masculine self. *Rights* was a euphemism for male privilege within the family and the stratified gender system generally, and provided a means for characterizing one's place and experiences in the social order and in divorce. *Rights* then provided a framework for defining the self in relation to others, a particularly important function in a context characterized by rapid changes and ambiguity, and for explaining the changing locus of power and various actual or threatened losses.

. . .

"Androgynous" Fathers

The "androgynous" fathers, 9 out of the 75 fathers in the study, differed from the majority in broadly consistent ways. Variations in postdivorce custody status alone did not account for the differences between this small group of fathers and the others. Three of these fathers had primary custody of their children and two shared custody with their former spouses (which in their cases involved dividing equally the time spent with and caring for their chil- dren). The other four men were noncustodial fathers who were extensively involved with their children. Only one had remarried, a noncustodial father.

Eight of these men, and two of the others, marveled at how they had "learned to become a father only after divorcing." Six had found it necessary to make major alterations in their behaviors and priorities in order to become involved, nurturing fathers. For example, this postdivorce "androgynous" father assumed his role as a custodial parent of three young children suddenly when his wife left:

> *It was terrifying at first, just terrifying. I remember the night she walked out the door. And I cried at the thought of it: I said to myself, "How in the hell am I going to do this?" I was raised in a stereotypically way, stereotypically male. I did not cook. I did not particularly clean. I was working a lot so it was "come home and play with the baby." The youngest was just a year and a half, one was going towards three, and the oldest one was just about four. So it was like playtime. I didn't have any responsibility for their daily care. I'd hardly changed a diaper before. I didn't know what parenting was about, really. I mean, who teaches us how to parent? I really didn't know how to ask for help. I don't truly remember the first year. It was day by day by day. After about a year, I managed to figure out that I had my act together. But it goes deeper than all of that. I had to learn to relate to them.*

After describing in some detail his strategies for coping in the new and stressful situation, he assessed the personal changes:

> *I actually think I'm a better person, to be honest with you, and certainly a far better parent than I ever would have been had she not left. Not that it would be by choice [single parenting], but however you'd like it to be, I would rather have done what I've done. What happened by becoming single is that I was forced into all of this. Now I admit I lost the playtime when they were little, and that's my greatest regret, and all of that. And it's been very hard financially because I'm always limited in how much I can work and I felt I couldn't change jobs. But I've shared so much more with them than any other father I know, they just don't even know what I'm talking about. Now I can't imagine what life will be like when they're grown and leave home. I feel like I'll be starting all over. I thought I had this ball game all figured out.*

The postdivorce family was not characterized as a *broken* one by these fathers. Comparatively little use was made of the language of *rights* to frame experiences, relations, or feelings, although fundamental legal issues were sometimes intrinsic to their experiences also. The postdivorce family context was not characterized as a battleground on which the struggle for *rights* was actively fought and there was no talk of divorce or gender wars. Instead, family was represented in various ways as a network of relationships which, as a result of the divorce, necessitated changes in assumptions and interactions.

The areas in which these men were particularly unique were their positive assessments of their relations with their children, overall level of sustained postdivorce parental involvement, and perceptions that the postdivorce father–child relationship depended centrally on their own actions. Interactions with the former wife were aimed primarily at fostering and maintaining cooperation and open communication; the objective was to view and relate to her primarily as the other parent, the mother of the children, and not as the former wife. Thus, issues of the relationship and interpersonal tensions between them were generally subordinated to those regarding their children's well-being and their own parenting. Unlike the majority, for example, the "androgynous" fathers had little if anything to say about postdivorce father absence other than that they neither understood it nor perceived it to be an optional line of action, regardless of the extent of tensions or differences with the former wife (Arendell 1992). [Thus,] . . . with only one exception, the postdivorce "androgynous" fathers viewed their postdivorce parenting activities as being part of a team effort, done collaboratively with the former spouse. They were part of a *parenting partnership*.[5]

. . .

Issues of gender identity were present, in significant ways, however, for this subset of men also. Although they raised questions about and challenged the conventions of masculinity, its constraints and consequences, they too were agents of and participants in the masculinist discourse of divorce by virtue of their gender identity, status, and experiences in a gendered-structured society. Because the postdivorce adaptive strategies and attitudes they adopted were often inconsistent with the major themes of the gendered divorce discourse, extensive intra-gender conflict was experienced (Rosenblum 1990). Reflective about and deliberately rejecting of what they perceived to be the typical behaviors and explanations of fathers after divorce, these men "paid a price" for their divergence (see also Coltrane 1989). They were beset with doubts about their actions and motives. Seeking alternative lines of action, they too, nonetheless, used as their measure of self, the norms of masculinity. One custodial father who was struggling with questions of motive and objective said,

> I just have to keep asking myself: "Why are you doing this?" I need to constantly ask myself if I'm doing this for my child or for some other reason. Am I trying to prove something?

Self-doubt was reinforced by inexperience and a sense of isolation: They were largely unprepared for parenting in the postdivorce context and had found few, if any, adequate male role models for their situations as divorced parents. In lamenting the lack of a male role model, four of these fathers observed that their exemplar for parenting was their mother, two noted that theirs was their former wife, and another credited his sister. . . . In not conforming more fully to the conventions of masculinity, the men found themselves subject to question and even ridicule, especially from male co-workers and relatives: Certain performances of gender carry more status and power than others, and theirs were defined as deviant. As one man noted, in describing his lingering uncertainty about his decisions "to find another way,"

> Even my father and brother told me to get on with my life, to start acting "like a man" and to let this child go, that my involvement with him would just interfere with my work and future relationships with women. They told

me that other people were going to think I was a wimp, you know, unmanly,
for not standing up to my former wife.

Interpersonal and cultural pressures to conform to gender conventions were reinforced by structural practices and arrangements. The traditional gender-based division of labor, persisting not only in the domestic but also in the employment arena, hindered these fathers' attempts to act in ways generally deemed to be unconventional for men. Impediments included work schedules and demands, the gender wage gap, cultural definitions of male career success, and perceived, if not real, gender biases in the legal system as well as the culture. Individually confronting the conventions of masculinity and challenging the relevance in their situations of gender prescriptions did not alter dominant ideologies or institutionalized arrangements or constraints (see also Cohen 1989; Risman 1989).

Conclusion and Implications

The masculinist discourse of divorce, constructed and anchored in interaction and reinforced by the stratified social order, made available a set of practices and dispositions that prescribed and reaffirmed these men's gendered identities. But the template of familial relations and interpersonal interactions offered was a restricted one, often unsuited for the ambiguous and emergent character of the postdivorce circumstance. Even as the altered, and often stressful, situation called for continued interactional adjustments, negotiations, and alignment, lines of action were aimed instead primarily at repair and reassertion of self as autonomous, independent, and controlling. Those few men who sought out and engaged in some alternative behaviors also were both agents in and constrained by the gendered divorce discourse.

. . . The perspectives on and actions in family and divorce provided by the participants in this exploratory study invite further investigation into various postdivorce paternal behaviors, including, for example, noncompliance with child support orders and limited other forms of parental support, father absence after divorce, repeat child custody challenges, and the phenomenon of "serial fathering." While often counterproductive to the development and sustaining of mutually satisfying father–child relationships, these behaviors, nonetheless, may be understood by the actors as meaningful and appropriate responses given their perspectives and circumstances. The points of view, explanations, and motives underlying such behaviors warrant further investigation and analysis. So too do the findings that men typically are less satisfied with divorce than are women (Riessman 1990; Wallerstein 1989).

Clearly much more study of divorce is called for since divorce as a common event appears to be here to stay. Careful attention must be given to the voices and viewpoints of all participants in divorce—children, women, and men. A fundamental part of the research agenda needs to be consideration of the effects of gender on divorce outcomes because divorce, like marriage, is not gender neutral. But a focus on individuals' definitions of and adjustments to divorce must be coupled with investigation of the effects of institutional practices and arrangements and cultural biases. . . . Called for then, in brief, are continual assessments of what is transpiring in the lives of families; a conscious revisiting of our assumptions about family and the relations between married and former spouses, and parents and children; and a recasting of society aimed at empowering individuals to move beyond the constraints of gender roles and, most significantly, the constraints of gender identity.

ENDNOTES

Author's note: This paper is a revision of one presented at the 1991 Gregory Stone Symposium held at the University of California, San Francisco, and the research was funded in part by a PSC-CUNY grant. Appreciation is extended to Joseph P. Marino, Jr., for the many useful and provocative discussions regarding this work; Arlie R. Hochschild for her thoughtful commentary on an earlier draft; and to the anonymous reviewers for their constructive remarks on earlier drafts of the paper.

1. That most of the participants readily asserted that the superiority of their perceptions and definitions gave them the prerogative to dismiss the wife's point of view is consistent with various theoretical arguments regarding the effects of stratification and differential socialization on interactions (Chodorow 1978; Gilligan 1982; Harding 1983). Glenn (1987), for example, noted: "It can be readily observed in a variety of situations that subordinates (women, servants, racial minorities) must be more sensitive to and responsive to the point of view of superordinates (men, masters, dominant racial groups) than the other way around" (p. 356).
2. Goffman (1975), for example, early on observed that "ritually speaking, females are equivalent to subordinate males and both are equivalent to children" (p. 5) in depictions of gender in advertisements. He suggested that relations between men and women are based on the parent–child complex.
3. For a relevant analysis of gender division of labor in families which uses the meso domain or mesostructural approach, see Pestello and Voyandoff (1991). Although not utilized, the meso domain or mesostructural approach could be applied to the data obtained in this study; see, for example Maines (1979, 1982) and Hall (1987, 1991).
4. The New York State Child Support Standards Act of 1989 (referred to usually by the fathers in the study as the new Child Support Guidelines) was held almost unanimously by these fathers to be grossly unjust and biased against noncustodial parents, primarily fathers; the extensive media coverage given to the Support Guidelines had reinforced many men's sense of being victimized by divorce. Moreover, according to the men in the study, the New York State Child Support Standards Act leads fathers to conclude that they should seek sole custody in order to avoid paying the mandated levels of child support.
5. I am using the term *parenting partnership* rather than shared parenting or co-parents because it suggests a greater flexibility than do the other two terms. . . . The term is also more appropriate for the postdivorce situation than shared parenting or co-parents because the latter are commonly used in reference to parenting activities done in the context of marriage.

REFERENCES

Arendell, Terry. 1986. *Mothers and Divorce: Legal, Economic and Social Dilemmas.* Berkeley: University of California Press.

———. 1992. "After Divorce: Investigations into Father Absence." *Gender & Society* (December).

———. 1995. *Fathers and Divorce.* Newbury Park, CA: Sage.

Berger, Peter and H. Kellner. 1964. "Marriage and the Social Construction of Reality." *Diogenes* 46:1–25.

Bernard, Jessie. 1981. "The Good-Provider Role: Its Rise and Fall." *American Psychologist* 36:1–12.

Bourdieu, Pierre. 1987. *Outline of a Theory of Practice.* Cambridge: Cambridge University Press.

Broverman, I., M. Broverman, F. Clarkson, P. Rosenkrantz, and S. Vogel. 1970. "Sex-Role Stereotypes and Clinical Judgments of Mental Health." *Journal of Consulting and Clinical Psychology* 34:1–7.

Cancian, Francesca. 1987. *Love in America: Gender and Self Development.* New York: Cambridge University Press.

Chodorow, Nancy. 1978. *The Reproduction of Mothering.* Berkeley: University of California.

Clatterbaugh, Kenneth. 1990. *Contemporary Perspectives on Masculinity: Men, Women and Politics in Modern Society.* Boulder, CO: Westview Press.

Cohen, Theodore. 1989. "Becoming and Being Husbands and Fathers: Work and Family Conflict for Men." Pp. 220–34 in *Gender in Intimate Relationships: A Microstructural Approach,* edited by Barbara J. Risman and Pepper Schwartz. Belmont, CA: Wadsworth.

Coltrane, Scott. 1989. "Household Labor and the Routine Production of Gender." *Social Problems* 36:473–90.

Cooley, Charles. 1981. "Self as Sentiment and Reflection." Pp. 169–74 in *Social Psychology through Symbolic Interaction,* 2d ed., edited by Gregory Stone and Harvey Farberman. New York: Wiley.

Davis, Fred. 1985. "Foreword." Pp. ix–xi in *Signifying Acts: Structure and Meaning in Everyday Life,* by Robert Perinbanayagam. Carbondale: Southern Illinois University Press.

Emery, Robert. 1988. *Marriage, Divorce, and Children's Adjustment.* Newbury Park, CA: Sage.

Family Law of the State of New York. 1990. Flushing, NY: Looseleaf Law.

Foote, Nelson. 1981. "Identification as the Basis for a Theory of Motivation." Pp. 333–42 in *Social Psychology through Symbolic Interaction,* 2d ed., edited by Gregory Stone and Harvey Farberman. New York: Wiley.

Furstenberg, Frank, S. Philip Morgan, and Paul Allison. 1987. "Parental Participation and Children's Well-Being after Marital Dissolution." *American Sociological Review* 52:695–701.

Gilligan, Carol. 1982. *In a Different Voice: Psychological Theory and Women's Development.* Cambridge, MA: Harvard University Press.

Glaser, Barney and Anselm Strauss. 1967. *The Discovery of Grounded Theory.* New York: Aldine.

Glenn, Evelyn Nakano. 1987. "Gender and the Family." Pp. 348–80 in *Analyzing Gender,* edited by Beth Hess and Myra Marx Ferre. Beverly Hills, CA: Sage.

Goffman, Erving. 1975. *Gender Advertisements.* New York: Harper & Row.

Hall, Peter. 1987. "Interactionism and the Study of Social Organization." *The Sociological Quarterly* 28:1–22.

———. 1991. "In Search of the Meso Domain: Commentary on the Contributions of Pestello and Voydanoff." *Symbolic Interaction* 14(2):129–34.

Harding, Sandra. 1983. "Why Has the Sex/Gender System Become Visible Only Now?" Pp. 311–24 in *Discovering Reality: Feminist Perspectives on Epistemology, Metaphysics, Methodology, and Philosophy of Science,* edited by Sandra Harding and Merrill Hintikka. Dordrecht, Holland: D. Reidel.

Hearn, Jeff. 1987. *The Gender of Oppression: Men, Masculinity and the Critique of Marxism.* New York: St. Martin's Press.

Hetherington, Elizabeth, Mavis Cox, and Richard Cox. 1976. "Divorced Fathers." *The Family Coordinator* 25:417–28.

Hochschild, Arlie R. 1983. *The Managed Heart: Commercialization of Human Feeling.* Berkeley: University of California Press.

Hochschild, Arlie R., with Anne Machung. 1989. *The Second Shift.* New York: Viking Press.

Kimmel, Michael. 1987. "The Contemporary Crisis of Masculinity in Historical Perspective." Pp. 121–54 in *The Making of Masculinities: The New Men's Studies,* edited by Harry Brod. Boston: Allen & Unwin.

Maines, David. 1979. "Mesostructure and Social Process." *Contemporary Sociology* 8:524–27.

————. 1982. "In Search of Mesostructure: Studies in the Negotiated Order." *Urban Life* 11:267–79.

Marcus, P. 1989. "Locked In and Locked Out: Reflections on the History of Divorce Law Reform in New York State." *Buffalo Law Review* 37:374–95.

Mead, George H. 1934. *Mind, Self, and Society.* Chicago: University of Chicago Press.

Perinbanayagam, Robert. 1985a. "How to Do Self with Things." Pp. 315–40 in *Beyond Goffman,* edited by S. Riggins. Berlin: Mouton–de Gruyter.

————. 1985b. *Signifying Acts: Structure and Meaning in Everyday Life.* Carbondale: Southern Illinois University Press.

Pestello, Frances and Patricia Voyandoff. 1991. "In Search of Mesostructure in the Family: An Interactionist Approach to Division of Labor." *Symbolic Interaction* 14(2):105–28.

Phillips, Roger and Faith Gilroy. 1985. "Sex-Role Stereotypes and Clinical Judgments of Mental Health: The Broverman's Findings Reexamined." *Sex Roles* 12(1/2):179–93.

Pleck, Joseph. 1985. *Working Wives/Working Husbands.* Beverly Hills, CA: Sage.

————. 1989. "Men's Power with Women, Other Men, and Society: A Men's Movement Analysis." Pp. 21–29 in *Men's Lives,* edited by Michael Kimmel and Michael Messner. New York: Macmillan.

Polikoff, Nancy. 1983. "Gender and Child-Custody Determinations: Exploding the Myths." Pp. 183–202 in *Families, Politics, and Public Policy,* edited by Irene Diamond. New York: Longman.

Riessman, Catherine. 1990. *Divorce Talk: Women and Men Make Sense of Personal Relationships.* New Brunswick, NJ: Rutgers University Press.

Risman, Barbara. 1989. "Can Men 'Mother'? Life as a Single Father." Pp. 155–64 in *Gender in Intimate Relationships: A Microstructural Approach,* edited by Barbara J. Risman and Pepper Schwartz. Belmont, CA: Wadsworth.

Rosenblum, Karen. 1990. "The Conflict between and within Genders: An Appraisal of Contemporary Femininity and Masculinity." Pp. 193–202 in *Families in Transition,* edited by Arlene Skolnick and Jerome Skolnick. Glenview, IL: Scott, Foresman.

Strauss, Anselm. 1989. *Qualitative Analysis in the Social Sciences.* Cambridge: Cambridge University Press.

Tannen, Deborah. 1990. *You Just Don't Understand: Men and Women in Conversation.* New York: Ballantine Books.

United States Bureau of the Census. 1989. *Statistical Abstracts of the United States, 1988. National Data Book and Guide to Sources.* Washington, DC: U.S. Government Printing Office.

Vaughan, Diane. 1986. *Uncoupling: Turning Points in Relationships.* New York: Oxford University Press.

Wallerstein, Judith and Sandra Blakeslee. 1989. *Second Chances: Men, Women, and Children a Decade after Divorce.* New York: Ticknor & Fields.

Weitzman, Lenore. 1985. *The Divorce Revolution. The Unexpected Social and Economic Consequences for Women and Children in America.* New York: Free Press.

27

DIVORCED PARENTS AND THE JEWISH COMMUNITY

NATHALIE FRIEDMAN

According to conservative estimates, almost one of every two marriages that took place in the United States in the past 15 years will end in divorce; by 1990 half of all children under 18 will have lived for some time with a single (divorced) parent.

Some sociologists view these projections with relative equanimity as reflections of and necessary adaptations to social change. Others hear the death knell of the family as we have known it and predict increased alienation of youth, more women and children living in poverty, and the loss of the grandparent–grandchild relationship.

Most observers of the Jewish scene agree that the divorce rate among Jews is somewhat below that of the general population.[1] Projections of current rates suggest that at least one in every three or four Jewish couples married over the past 15 years will divorce, leaving an increasing number of Jewish children to grow up in the care of a single parent. The high divorce rate among Jews has triggered a good deal of unease within the Jewish community. The reasons for concern are many. A high Jewish divorce rate threatens the basic family structure, traditionally so essential to Jewish identity. It is likely to mean fewer children being born to Jewish families. And it is seen as raising a number of social, psychological, and economic problems that erode Jewish commitment, participation and involvement.

Little, however, is actually known about the impact of divorce on ties to the Jewish community. Do the social, economic, and psychological problems that often accompany divorce erode Jewish commitment and involvement? Are synagogue affiliation and attendance affected? Does the child's Jewish education continue? Do families turn to the Jewish community, and does that community serve in any way as a support system before, during, or after divorce? What about those with only minimal or no Jewish communal involvement prior to divorce—to whom do they turn, and how do they cope in the aftermath of divorce?

From Steven Bayme & Gladys Rosen, eds., *The Jewish Family and Jewish Continuity* (Hoboken, NJ: KTAV Publishing House, 1994), copyright © 1994 by the American Jewish Committee. Reprinted by permission.

This study examines these questions from the perspective of the divorced parents.

Through interviews with 40 women and 25 of their former husbands, it explores the nature of the couples' communal ties both before and after their divorces, and inquiries particularly into the impact of divorce on their religious affiliations. The study also focuses on the degree of support that Jewish communal institutions provided these couples and suggests how the institutions can become more responsive to the needs of Jewish single-parent families.

The sample selected for study spanned the religious spectrum from ultra-Orthodox to unaffiliated. The research design called for extensive interviews with 40 sets of parents: 10 Orthodox (including two ultra-Orthodox), 10 Conservative, 10 Reform, and 10 unaffiliated—all divorced or separated from one to five years and with at least one child aged 3 to 16 at the time the marriage was dissolved.

The research design presented several problems when it came to classifying the family's religious orientation. How, for example, would one classify a family where the mother said she was unaffiliated and her ex-spouse called himself Conservative? What about the family in which the mother was affiliated with a Reform temple but identified herself as Conservative? Should a family be classified by its affiliation during the marriage or after the divorce? Since one purpose of the research was to look at Jewish identity and affiliation *after* a divorce, it was decided to classify families on the basis of the temple or synagogue with which the custodial parent was affiliated, unless that parent clearly designated herself or himself otherwise. And, because the religious affiliation of a husband might differ from that of his wife, data were also collected on the current religious status of each parent, on the family during the marriage, and on each parent at the time he or she was growing up. Thus the religious odysseys of the 40 families could be traced, and Jewish affiliation after the divorce could be compared with that in the immediate and more distant past. . . .

The final sample consisted of 40 mothers and 25 fathers ranging in age between 31 and 62. All had lived in the New York City metropolitan area during their marriages. Fifteen of the fathers could not be interviewed—four were not living in the United States or their whereabouts were unknown; four were not contacted at the wife's request; and seven refused. Interviews with the mothers were conducted between the fall of 1983 and the summer of 1984, and averaged about two hours in length. Interviews with fathers were somewhat less lengthy, both because the mother had already provided the basic family information and because fathers were less likely to offer details about activities and feelings. . . .

One note of caution. This research was not designed to permit generalization to the entire population of Jewish divorced persons. Its purpose, rather, was to uncover patterns, relationships, causal links, and critical variables that might provide clues to how communal institutions can better serve that rapidly increasing phenomenon, the Jewish single-parent family. . . .

Ties to the Jewish Community During the Marriage

During the years they were married, the patterns of affiliation and observance of these 40 couples varied widely. About half were completely unaffiliated with a synagogue or temple, had minimal or no home observance, and gave their children no Jewish education. For example, only 20 of the 40 couples had actually been members of synagogues or temples in the various communities in which they had lived while married. Among the other 20 couples, four said that they had never joined but had occasionally attended services at neighborhood synagogues or temples; six said they occasionally went to their parents' or in-laws' synagogues for the High Holy Days; 10 couples stated that they had neither belonged to nor attended any house of worship.

It is difficult to attach denominational labels to the 20 couples who were affiliated while married, for some had joined synagogues of different denominations as they moved from one community to another or as their children grew ready for Sunday or Hebrew school. As one mother explained:

> First we lived in Queens, and we belonged to a Conservative synagogue there. Then we moved farther out on the Island, and when our son was ready for Sunday school we joined the Reform temple because that was where most of the Jewish families on our block belonged.

Or another:

> In Pennsylvania, where we lived the first five years of our marriage, we belonged to a Conservative synagogue — it was the only one in town. Then when we moved to Manhattan, we joined a modern Orthodox synagogue in the neighborhood.

Just prior to separation, however, eight couples were affiliated with Orthodox and five with Conservative synagogues; seven belonged to Reform temples; and 20 were unaffiliated.

Absence of synagogue affiliation or attendance generally, but not necessarily, precluded some form of Jewish education for the children. In eight instances, the divorce had occurred before the child was old enough for Sunday or Hebrew school, and in eight others, although the children were of age, they had not received any Jewish education. In 16 families children had attended a Sunday or Hebrew school, and in eight families an Orthodox day school or yeshiva. Observance in the home during the marriage ranged from "zero," as one respondent put it, to strictly Orthodox. For 12 families, observance of the Sabbath and holidays was simply not a part of their lives. As one commented:

> Home observance? None. I guess you could say we were borderline Christians because we observed Christmas, but also a little Hanukkah.

Several noted that, although they did not observe at home, they would occasionally go to their parents or in-laws for a Seder or a holiday meal. Ten families characterized their home observance as "minimal." As one explained:

We'd observe the Sabbath and holidays off and on—no regularity. Mostly in an "eating" sense, I guess. You know—a special meal.

This "culinary" theme appeared regularly as these 10 families described home observance:

Matzoh on Passover, but I guess that's about it. The family would get together for dinner on Rosh Hashanah.

A couple of times I made the Seder meal.

If there was any one holiday observed by these families, it tended to be Hanukkah:

We used to light the menorah and give the children gifts.

We thought it was important to celebrate Hanukkah because the children saw so much Christmas around them.

Several of the families said that, although they never attended services and their home observance was at best "limited," they kept their children home from school on Rosh Hashanah and Yom Kippur because "we wanted them to know they were Jewish."

In nine families home observance was fairly regular, including candles on Friday night and the celebration of such holidays as Passover, Hanukkah, Purim, and Simchat Torah with family meals, a Seder, and special foods. Respondents in this group, however, were quick to add that they did not keep kosher homes. Typical was this woman's response:

We didn't have a kosher home, but we did celebrate all the holidays— Hanukkah, Seders, Purim (I'd get hamantaschen). Friday night was always special—not in a religious sense—but we had chicken and challah, and we tried not to make other plans on Friday nights.

Finally, nine families characterized themselves as "observant," "strictly observant," or "Orthodox." Their homes ranged from "kosher" to "strictly kosher," and all the holidays as well as the Sabbath were observed, with their positive and negative commandments. . . .

In sum, the ties of these 40 couples to the Jewish community during the marriage varied widely. At the one extreme were about half the families with no synagogue or other Jewish organizational affiliation and minimal or no home observance. About one in four families described strong Jewish institutional ties, regular synagogue attendance, and strict home observance of the Sabbath, holidays, dietary laws, and other religious rituals. In between were some 10 families who were affiliated with a temple or synagogue, attended services frequently, and marked the Sabbath and/or religious holidays with some degree of regularity. Even among those with only the most tenuous institutional connections, however, Jewish education for the children was not necessarily precluded; four of these families sent their children to

Sunday or Hebrew schools and one (as long as the grandparents paid for it) to a day school.

The Divorce Experience

Factors Leading to the Divorce

The couples' reasons for ending their marriages probably reflect the experiences of most divorced couples in America. Some attributed the breakup to such unacceptable behavior on the part of their partners as violence or wife abuse (three cases), alcoholism or gambling (two cases), homosexuality (one case), and infidelity (five cases). These reasons were particularly frequent among the Orthodox couples. Although infidelity was cited as a factor in five instances, in only three was it regarded as the determining factor.

The word most frequently used by respondents as they spoke about the factors leading to the divorce was "incompatibility." This word proved to mean different things to different respondents. Some, for example, explained that they had married quite young and had grown apart over the years. In other instances, "incompatibility" referred to temperamental or personality differences. One man, for example, complained about his ex-wife's inability to communicate:

> *We weren't on the same wave length. Her tuner is way down while mine tends to be all the way up.*

A woman said of her ex-husband:

> *He's a very selfish person — totally involved with himself, egocentric. I just needed more love and affection — it was lonely living with him.*

A third kind of incompatibility was the couple's disagreement over the woman's role as wife, mother, and employed person. Often, this disagreement arose in the course of the woman's pursuit of personal growth, self-development, and career. One woman said:

> *Once I went back to work it became clear that our interests were different. He was opposed to my going back to work. His idea of my role was to bring up the children, entertain, be at home for him. But I felt that I had to develop as a person, find my own identity that was not just a part of him and the children.*

A second said that while her husband was still a student he could understand her working, but:

> *Then he graduated and got a job, and he woke up to the fact that I was busy working and not home at 4:30 when he got home. I was trying to develop my career as a teacher, but he wanted me to be a "nine-to-three" teacher. I said that if I wanted that kind of job, I would have gone to work at the post office.*

Her ex-husband confirmed that his wife's work had been a bone of contention:

She worked hard all those years supporting us while I was in graduate school. When I finished, however, and began living like a person, I kind of expected that she would go back to being the woman I had married. But she had changed—her job was very important to her. Her career was going gangbusters, and she was loving it.

Two men suggested that the women's movement played a role in their growing incompatibility with their wives. One said:

I don't know what part this played, but my wife got all wrapped up in the women's movement and with all of her divorced and divorcing friends. She stopped observing our wedding anniversary and said that the wedding ring was a symbol of slavery.

Finally, several respondents suggested that the prevailing social climate, in which divorce carried no stigma, was a factor in the breakup of their marriages. As one said:

We are probably products of our age—an age of divorce. I think that a lot of divorces that have taken place would not have taken place thirty years ago. People's expectations are higher when it comes to happiness in marriage.

The decision to divorce was generally initiated by the woman and accepted, often reluctantly, by the man. In those few instances where the divorce was initiated by the man, the cause was quite specific: He had met another woman; his wife was an "adulteress"; he couldn't make it financially and felt overwhelmed by marital and parental responsibilities. Only one of the 25 men interviewed attributed the divorce to *his* need for self-fulfillment or personal space.

The Jewish Factor

Was there a Jewish factor in the divorce decision? The answer is "yes and no." On one hand, with only a few exceptions, respondents said that religious or Jewish issues were not precipitating factors. On the other hand, as the marriage bonds weakened, dissension over these issues surfaced in 14 of the 40 couples.

In three of the five interfaith marriages, religious issues were cited by at least one of the partners. In nine other instances, while both partners were Jewish, they came from different religious backgrounds and Jewish issues surfaced. For example:

First of all, there was another woman, but that was just the straw that broke the camel's back. Basically, we were just not compatible—we had different values about almost everything. And eventually, even our differences over Judaism got to me—he ate nonkosher outside while I was strictly kosher; and he worked on Shabbos while I wanted him to go to shul with me and the boys.

A man from a Conservative background had a similar problem:

> *My wife came from a completely assimilated background, but she agreed to keep a kosher home. Then she reneged. Religion was not at all important to her, but it was to me. I felt that there should be at least a minimal observance and understanding, but she had no interest at all—not even for the High Holidays.*

In three cases where dissension over religious issues surfaced, both partners came from fairly similar backgrounds. In one instance, where both were from Conservative homes, the wife complained that her husband was too passive about Jewish observance and participation and that she was tired of having to take the lead. In another instance, although both partners had come from Orthodox homes and had attended religious day schools, the wife said:

> *He was always less religious than I, and we bickered a lot about it. I wanted to cover my head, and he thought that was silly. I didn't want to eat in a nonkosher restaurant, and he thought it was okay as long as we ate dairy. He opened up the mail and rode up in the elevator on Shabbos, and I wouldn't.*

These findings suggest that when husband and wife come from similar religious backgrounds religious issues rarely surface. When the marriage is mixed (and that term is used to denote marriages in which the Jewish backgrounds are different as well as interfaith marriages), however, religious issues often contribute to the incompatibility of the partners.

Problems Encountered Dissolving the Marriage

Ending a marriage involves more than the decision of one or both partners to go their separate ways. It also means seeing a lawyer and resolving problems over finances, child custody, visitation rights, and, in some instances, the *get,* or religious divorce decree. For 13 couples, things went relatively smoothly, both at the time of the divorce and after.

All six families who agreed upon joint custody arrangements reported relatively amicable divorces, suggesting that only when hostility between the principals is minimal can a joint custody arrangement be agreed upon and successfully implemented.

Sixteen couples reported problems in only one area—15 with finances, 1 with visitation. . . . Financial problems ranged from delayed child-support checks to the disappearance of the ex-spouse. Three mothers were receiving welfare, and several others, although employed, were dependent on their parents. Several fathers confirmed that one consequence of divorce was a reduction in their standard of living. Said one:

> *After the divorce, money absolutely disappeared. I was living in a seedy hotel with a few boxes and two jammed suitcases. That is all I owned after thirteen years of marriage. Before, it was two people working and one household, and we were still barely in the black. You can imagine what it was like stretching that money across two households. . . .*

Ten couples experienced multiple problems. In one case where finances were not an issue, custody and visitation rights were. The mother explained:

> *I really only wanted a little child support, and he sends four times more than is legally required. But custody arrangements and visitation rights were a problem, largely because of his drinking. He kept moving back and forth between California and New York and in and out of treatment programs. We couldn't draw up a custody agreement, and he couldn't visit our daughter or have her with him in any predictable fashion.*

A woman who noted that her ex-husband's lack of responsibility had left her virtually the sole support for herself and her son added that visitation rights were also an acrimonious issue:

> *I simply had to limit the visits and arrange that they always be in a supervised setting because of his total lack of responsibility.*

The multi-problem couple was usually one whose divorce had been marked by hostility and where anger and bad feelings were still very much in evidence. As a result, every issue that had to be resolved became an occasion for the release of hostility.

The Importance of the Get

Orthodox and Conservative rabbis will not marry a divorced person who has not obtained the religious divorce decree, the *get*. If a woman without a *get* marries again, any child of the remarriage will be illegitimate in Jewish law. The law imposes no such penalty on a man. Should he remarry without a *get*, a child of that marriage would be legitimate. If a wife refuses to accept the *get* from her husband, Jewish law provides alternative ways for the man to be declared free to remarry. The woman whose husband refuses to provide a *get* has no similar recourse. Thus the law places the obligation to obtain a *get* upon the woman and gives the man a unique advantage in negotiating a divorce settlement.

Ten of the 40 women in the sample had obtained a *get* at the time of, or subsequent to, their divorces. Most were either Orthodox or Conservative. One of two Reform women who had obtained a *get* said:

> *The rabbi insisted that I must have it to remarry—if ever I should. My ex paid for it.*

The other Reform woman had herself insisted on the *get*:

> *I insisted on an Orthodox get. I had been married religiously in a Conservative synagogue, and it was important to me to have the most religious divorce I could get. He [the ex] would not pay for it, but at least he went through it. His mother can't understand why I wanted it.*

One young woman from the Hasidic community in Flatbush was still trying, after almost five years, to obtain a *get*.

> *I've asked, I've tried, but he just won't do it. I've gone to some local rabbis for help but haven't gotten anywhere. Unfortunately, you need money to get them [the rabbis] to help you, and I don't have it.*

Then she added with resignation:

> *I guess it really doesn't matter because who's going to marry me anyway with my six children?*

Eight women said that they would obtain a *get* should they decide to remarry. None of them anticipated any difficulty. Fully half of the women in the sample, however, neither requested a *get* nor had any intention of doing so. Many had never heard of a *get*; it was simply "not an issue," "irrelevant," "nonsense," or "something that would never have occurred to us." From the perspective of the traditional Jewish community, should these women remarry and bear children the absence of a *get* could have serious ramifications when their children, in turn, are ready to marry.[2]

Single–Parent Families in the Jewish Community

The Affiliated

Between the time of the divorce and the time of the interview — an average of four years — changes had occurred in the pattern of Jewish affiliation of the people in the sample. Of the 20 families that had been unaffiliated during the marriage, three became affiliated with a Reform temple or school, three with a Conservative synagogue or school, and four with an Orthodox synagogue and day school.[3] In addition, two families that had been affiliated with an orthodox synagogue during the marriage identified themselves as Conservative at the time of the interview; another moved from Conservative to Reform and still another from Reform to Conservative. Two of these latter changes stemmed from geographic moves and two from dissatisfaction with a particular Sunday or Hebrew school.

More significant is the finding that, after the divorce, 10 previously unaffiliated families had joined the ranks of the affiliated, while none had moved from affiliated to unaffiliated status. This finding appears to run counter to the belief that divorce necessarily erodes Jewish affiliation and identification. Although the data offered here are too few to refute this belief, these 10 cases suggest factors that may explain the "return" of the unaffiliated. The word "return" is used advisedly because, among the 10 families that had been unaffiliated during the marriage but developed some tie afterward, there were five custodial parents who had grown up in affiliated homes. One woman, for example, who had married a non-Jew against the wishes of her parents, said:

> *When the girls got to be old enough, I decided they should have some kind of Jewish education. I guess it's a little strange, because during the marriage we*

really did nothing Jewish. But I find myself getting more and more conserva-
tive with age. Maybe it's that being the child of Holocaust parents, I feel a par-
ticular responsibility to pass on a Jewish tradition. So now the girls are in a
Reform Hebrew school, and we go to services on Friday night. They love it.

Another woman, also divorced from a non-Jew, had similar sentiments:

The minute my son was old enough, I enrolled him at the nursery school of
the Conservative synagogue here. It was highly recommended as a place where
there's real Jewish involvement. I wanted him to have this, especially after the
absence of all of this with his father. We go to shul all the time, and I'm en-
rolled in the women's Bat Mitzvah class. When I was young, I never went
to Hebrew school—only my brothers did. My son is very close to my parents
[Conservative]. We're with them on all the holidays.

And a third:

My ex was a country-club type—golf and cards. He wasn't interested in
the synagogue or the community. After the divorce, I decided I wanted my
son to have a Jewish upbringing so I enrolled him in the Conservative syna-
gogue nursery school. Now he's in the Hebrew school and will eventually be
Bar Mitzvah.

A fourth "returnee" commented:

We never belonged to anything during the marriage, although occasionally we
went to my parents' Conservative synagogue. I put the children in a Conser-
vative Hebrew school just as soon as they were old enough, and we go every
Sabbath together. I was brought up in a Conservative synagogue but never
went to Hebrew school—although my brother did. I wanted the children to
know what it was all about. In fact, at first I had put them in a religious day
school, but they had to leave it as part of the divorce settlement. It was impor-
tant to my ex that they not go, and it didn't matter that much to me.

And finally:

I joined a Reform temple after the divorce because I felt it was very important
for my son to learn about his Jewish heritage. I myself came from an observant
home but didn't have that much of a Jewish education—my brothers did, but
the girls, no!

These women had three things in common: a traditional Jewish home background; a husband who wished to have little to do with Jewish communal
life; and a child old enough for some form of religious education. It is possible, of course, that had their marriages remained intact, these women would
still have seen to it that their children received some form of Jewish education. It appears, however, that the dissolution of their marriages actually removed a barrier to their return to a more traditional Jewish life.

Four women came from completely unaffiliated homes and had been—
as one put it—"borderline Christians" while married. Three who lived in the

Bronx came under the influence of a rabbi well known for his community activism, his personal warmth and understanding, and his readiness to embrace anyone who expressed a desire to lead a traditional Jewish life. The fourth was referred by a friend to a similarly outgoing rabbi on Manhattan's West Side. All four engaged in religious study, became Sabbath observers, koshered their homes, attended synagogue regularly, and sent their children to religious day schools.

What moved these four women to take on what has been called "the yoke of Orthodoxy"? In each case the key factor was a charismatic rabbi willing to devote considerable time to the family. As one woman remarked:

> *The rabbi is one of the most extraordinary human beings I have ever met —*
> *generous, warm, giving. He is always "there," and he's willing to accept you*
> *"where you're at."*

Another commented about the same rabbi:

> *Someone had told me about this day school, and I liked the way it looked so*
> *I decided my son should go. That's how I met the rabbi. He was the one who*
> *arranged for the get. I didn't even know such a thing existed. He invited me*
> *to come to the shul, and I liked it. He explained to me about being kosher, and*
> *I did the house, little by little.*

Of the West Side rabbi, a woman said:

> *He was incredible. I was a wreck and a friend suggested him to me. I called*
> *and he said to come right over and he didn't even know me. He'll talk to you*
> *even at two o'clock in the morning. I had started getting interested in Jewish*
> *things even before the divorce. Before that it had always been a great source*
> *of pride when people would say "you don't look Jewish." The rabbi got me to*
> *take courses at the shul and to send my daughter to a day school.*

In all 10 families that moved from unaffiliated to affiliated status, it was the mother who, after the divorce, established the synagogue affiliation, enrolled the children in a religious school, and initiated observance in the home. These women did not have to deal with their ex-husbands about matters of Jewish observance and affiliation. But those fathers who still saw their children regularly did not object to the new patterns of observance and affiliation. One father commented:

> *It's true that my ex has become quite involved Jewishly because of the chil-*
> *dren. But no, it hasn't been a problem for me. I try to encourage the girls. I*
> *pick them up from Hebrew school when it's my day. I took them to shul on*
> *Purim — I even made their costumes.*

One father, whose ex-wife had become increasingly Orthodox, expressed some ambivalence over the fact that she and the children had grown so observant:

> *I have no real Jewish ties myself, but I'm very proud of my children. They have*
> *strong ties. They speak Hebrew, and they go to a yeshiva. I'm not that involved*

in their schooling because of the divorce and being an absentee father. The big problem is that I do not have a kosher home and recently their mother made their home 110 percent kosher. Now they won't eat in mine.

A father who had himself grown up in an Orthodox home noted:

When we got married, I had had my fill of religion, and I moved completely away from it—no synagogue affiliation. But since the divorce, my wife has gotten very involved, and our son is at a yeshiva. The rabbi there is very special—he believes in bringing people back in any way that he can. As a result, I find that I've slowly been moving back to religion over the past few years.

Every family that had been affiliated during the marriage retained an affiliation after the divorce. Children who had been attending Sunday or Hebrew school, day school or yeshiva, continued their Jewish educations at least until their Bar Mitzvahs or Bat Mitzvahs. Since generally it was the mother who had custody, she was the one who met with teachers and attended parent meetings, Hebrew school plays, and special Sabbath programs. In several instances, however, the father, rather than the mother, took the lead in ensuring the continued affiliation and participation of the children. For example, one father said:

During the marriage, I guess you might say we sank to the lower common denominator—hers. Whatever minimal observance there was was because of the children. Now I go to synagogue more than ever, and I'm the one that supervises the children's Jewish education. I spend a lot more time with my parents, and when I have the children on a weekend I take them to my parents' synagogue.

One mother was quite explicit about the fact that she felt that the children's Jewish education was their father's responsibility:

I occasionally go to the temple on a Sabbath with the children, but I decided that I did not want control over that whole area. As part of the divorce, I gave that responsibility—the kids' Jewish education—to him. I didn't want to have anything to do with it. I felt I had enough responsibility in other areas. I wouldn't say "don't go," but I wanted him to take control. I make my ex drive the car pools for all the kids' Jewish activities.

Her ex-husband confirmed this:

I live in the city, but I drive out to Long Island four times a week to see the children. Twice a week I pick up my son from Hebrew school at the temple and then take both kids for supper. On Saturdays I participate with them in a special parent–child religious and education program at the temple. Then on Sunday I come out again and pick up my daughter from Sunday school and take the kids for the day.

This father was clearly exerting every possible effort to keep his children identified and affiliated Jewishly. Why did he do it?

My wife doesn't give a damn about it. But I was brought up with the syn-
agogue playing a very vital role in my life. It was a central focus for my
parents — they actually founded this synagogue in Brooklyn and their lives
revolved around it. It was important to me that when I walked in, everyone
knew who I was!

Contrary to the belief that divorce is a major factor in the erosion of Jewish affiliation and identity, the sample in this study presented no case of a
family *dis*affiliating after the breakup of the marriage. It is true that a number
of men and women became synagogue or temple dropouts, particularly after
their children passed the age of Bar Mitzvah or Bat Mitzvah. But children
who had attended Hebrew or Sunday school before their parents' divorce
continued to do so after. And among the previously unaffiliated, fully half
moved to affiliated status and provided some form of religious education for
their children.

The Unaffiliated

At the time of the interviews, 10 custodial parents classified themselves as unaffiliated. None attended religious services except for an occasional visit to a
temple during the High Holy Days, and even that was rare. Nevertheless,
several of these parents maintained some institutional ties to the Jewish community. A West Side mother explained:

The children go to the community Hebrew school. It's good because no one
pounds you. Once in a while, they go to services there. I say, "Go if you want
to." My ex stuck them in this school and then wouldn't pay the tuition. I was
ready to take them out, but then they told me they'd take both boys for free. It
didn't matter to me — they'll do anything to keep those kids there.

Another unaffiliated mother said:

Our older son was 11 at the time of the divorce. I wanted to have him Bar
Mitzvah for my father's sake, but I couldn't find any place that would con-
dense the preparation time. Our son really wasn't that interested, so the end
result was no Bar Mitzvah. When it came to our younger son, he really
wanted it, so we joined a temple just until the Bar Mitzvah. There was no
pressure to continue. They were very low-key.

A third unaffiliated mother had a son attending a Hebrew school connected
with an Orthodox synagogue. She said:

I feel anger, fury, and, on the other hand, sheer delight about it. His education
is at an Orthodox synagogue. A lot of my son's friends were going there, and
he wanted to go, too. It's like a congregation of disaffected Jews. "If you want
to come, fine, if not, I wish you would, but no hard feelings." I don't really
have much to do with it. The rabbi is an ardent Zionist, and while he's totally
accepting of one's own brand of Judaism, he wants you to be a Zionist, and
that I'm not.

Several unaffiliated parents noted that they were considering Jewish education for their children. One mother commented:

> *Now that she's 10, I think I would like her to have some Jewish education. No Hebrew, and nothing religious—just cultural. The problem is that it would have to be during the week only—no weekends, because we rotate weekends, and I don't think my ex would go for that.*

And another:

> *My son, nine and a half years old, keeps telling me that he wants to go to Hebrew school. All his peers go, and he wants to "belong." I'm thinking about it. I guess it's important for my son to have a sense of belonging now with his father away and separate from him. Maybe it's particularly important for a boy—Bar Mitzvah represents a turning point in a boy's life.*

With a few exceptions, parents who identified themselves as unaffiliated spoke positively about Judaism. A woman put it this way:

> *I have a keen emotional sense of being Jewish. It's important for me to be identified as a Jew. So many thousands of years that a people has survived! I have a sympathy and empathy for my people that I want to pass on to my children.*

A man who had been married to a non-Jewish woman said:

> *Since the divorce, I feel that I've become closer to things Jewish. I've become more cognizant of the Jewish tradition and, as a single parent, I feel a responsibility to provide some of this for the kids. For example, I have them every other weekend, and I light candles with them, saying the prayer. Sometimes we do it at my parents; sometimes they each have a friend over; but often it's just the three of us—the kids and me. I also think that as I've gotten a bit older, I've been able to reflect on the traditions and they have become more valuable to me.*

Another parent mused:

> *I see a change in myself in recent years. I feel intensely, increasingly Jewish. Nothing to do with organized religion, but I tend to think more and more in terms of "is it good or bad for the Jews?"*

Thus even among those who were unaffiliated and disinterested in organized religion, there existed a sense of identification as Jews, sympathy for Jewish causes, and attachment to Jewish traditions.

Obstacles to Community Participation

Most families in the sample maintained, and some increased, existing ties to the Jewish community after the divorce. A number reported excellent experiences that illustrate how the Jewish community can reach out to single parents and their children. A majority of the respondents, however, mentioned obstacles to participation in Jewish communal life as a result of their changed marital status. Finances posed one kind of barrier. But equally, if not more, serious were lack of social support and a sense of stigmatization.

Financial Obstacles   Most of the rabbis and school personnel interviewed for *The Jewish Community and Children of Divorce* had insisted that no one was forced to drop out of synagogue or Hebrew or day school for financial reasons. While interviews with parents in this study confirmed that none had *left* because of inability to pay, several respondents — particularly mothers — explained that the synagogue's financial policy had prevented them from joining in the first place. One said:

> *I've seen Judaism lose children for financial reasons. At the temple that I first thought I would join after my divorce, I found that they charged the same amount for me as for a couple with several children, so I never joined. Frankly, I could have afforded it, but it was the principle. And there are a lot of people who are embarrassed to ask for special consideration or to say, "I can't afford that much."*

Another said that lack of money had made it impossible for her to give her son a Jewish education:

> *Jewish education for the children is always on my mind. I've asked a lot of people about it. I spoke to someone, and she said it would cost "thus and so." I spoke to a rabbi I happen to know, and he had no suggestions because I simply can't afford the money either for a temple membership or for a Jewish education. Without the money, it just doesn't seem to be possible.*

Several were grateful that after the divorce their children were able to continue in the day school on scholarships, but one noted:

> *I have a scholarship which gives me one-third off, but every chance that they get, they throw the scholarship in your face. They have bingo, and if you're on scholarship you're supposed to help out, but it's during the day, and I can't go. They said, "It's your obligation; you're on scholarship, you know." I find that very degrading. Do they think I want to be on scholarship?*

Another woman stated that after the divorce her daughter was given a scholarship at the day school she had been attending, but:

> *I find it very hard, and so does my daughter, because we're not in the same "station" as the others. The kids and the parents at the school and the shul can afford things that we just can't. It's not that anyone treats us badly — it's just knowing that we can't do the things that they can do.*

These perceptions of second-class status may or may not have been rooted in reality, but they were widely felt and frequently voiced.

Lack of Outreach   More common than financial complaints among respondents were feelings that the synagogue or temple could do far more "reaching out" to the single parent and child, both at the time of the divorce and after. All denominations were criticized in this respect. Said one woman bitterly about the neighborhood Reform temple:

> *Support from the temple at the time of the divorce? No—it never occurred to the rabbi to call me. He spoke with my husband—but, of course, my husband had been a member of the board of directors for 10 years. It certainly would have been nice, considering the fact that I had also been involved in that temple for 10 years, if they had encouraged me to stay on as a member.*

Said one woman about the suburban Reform temple that she still attended:

> *I must say that the temple did not reach out to us at all. When we "fell out," no one followed up. They never tried. I was right there kind of waving for their attention, but they never touched me. It's too bad—they put all their efforts into the strong supporters, the regulars. They should try to reach the hesitants, like us.*

Her ex-husband confirmed this:

> *I used to go regularly to classes at the temple. But after the divorce, they did not reach out in any way, shape, or form—except to ask me to pay the bills. Then when I couldn't pay—no response. Nothing! The rabbi never said a word. He made no overtures, never said, "Would you like to come in and talk?" or "How are you doing?" or "My door is open."*

Complaints about lack of outreach on the part of Orthodox institutions were expressed less frequently, but they did occur. These words from a successful woman executive echoed some of the comments above:

> *No, the shul has never reached out to me. As a matter of fact, I'll probably be dropping my membership there because a group of us are starting our own* havurah-*type service—Conservative. It's funny, though—I have so much in the way of business contacts and experience I could have contributed, but they never called on me.*

Generally, after a divorce, it is the man who leaves the household and finds housing elsewhere. Several fathers said that they would have appreciated some attempt on the part of the rabbi in the new neighborhood to draw them into the synagogue or temple. One said:

> *When I first joined the new temple—largely so that my daughter could go to Hebrew school there—I told them my situation and made arrangements about dues, mail, tuition bills, and everything. I go to services regularly, but the rabbi has never approached me.*

Another father noted:

> *I was really surprised that the rabbi did not make any effort at all to draw me in after the divorce. First of all, I hear that he has a degree in psychology so he should know better. And secondly, he himself was divorced so he should understand what it feels like to suddenly find yourself alone.*

Stigmatization   Lack of outreach efforts was usually blamed on the rabbi. Many respondents, however, spoke about their general sense of discomfort as single parents in the synagogue or school, of "feeling different," of not being welcomed by the congregation or other parents. As one woman put it:

> *I'm thinking of dropping my membership. As I see it, the temple [Reform] is regarded as the exclusive province of the family. The widowed or divorced are seen as obstacles — maybe even as threats. At times, I feel almost ostracized. Let me give you just one subtle example. I used to be a frequent reader of the Haftorah [weekly reading from the Prophets]; since my divorce almost four years ago, I have not been asked once.*

The problem is particularly critical for the Orthodox divorced woman, according to one such respondent:

> *Divorced fathers get very different treatment than divorced mothers. The whole attitude is different. You should see how respectfully the teachers at the children's yeshiva treat the fathers when they come into the school. Part of it is probably money, but that shouldn't mean that the mother should get less respect. Some of the teachers give you a look as if to say, "What more can we expect from these children since their mother is divorced?" That attitude is all wrong.*

She went on to note how difficult it is for an Orthodox woman when it comes to observance of the Sabbath and holidays:

> *The problem is that there is very little place for the Jewish woman in the Jewish community, particularly if you're Orthodox. Orthodoxy is very male-oriented. Comes Shabbos or the holidays and you're alone with your kids. It's no fun trying to make Kiddush and sing zmirot [Sabbath songs] or light the menorah by yourself — though I really try to do it. And in shul, the fathers are around with their kids. My nine-year-old son is too old to be sitting with me, but he has no one to sit with so he just runs around the shul and plays.*

A woman blamed the rabbi for the problems of single parents at her Reform temple:

> *Shortly after the divorce, a new rabbi came in. He is a jackass! He is into religion, but not into people. He has been no help at all. There happens to be a huge singles population at the temple, and several of us tried to put together a singles group, but we got no help from him. That place is for couples only. It has cliques, too. If you're not married, you can't be comfortable there.*

The fathers, too, expressed discomfort as single parents in the synagogue. As one observed:

> *There seems to be something inherent in Judaism that means a mass denial about divorce. When it happens, it's something shameful, a disgrace. People*

try to pretend that there's nothing wrong, and as a result they ignore you and the pain you're going through.

As these men and women spoke of the discomfort and aloneness they felt in the synagogue, several acknowledged that the problem was not present only there. One man said:

Sure it's hard. They're all couples at the temple, and it's a lonely feeling. But it's lonely being single in the temple, in the Jewish community, or anywhere I go. It's just lonely being single!

Positive Experiences

Although most respondents had negative feelings about the failure of the synagogue or the community to reach out to them, several had only praise and appreciation for the ways they and their children had been drawn in and made to feel comfortable. Said one about the Reform suburban temple to which she belonged:

The rabbi was extremely supportive of me and the children after the divorce. He tried to pay special attention to the children. He made a point of talking to them about things that interested them—like baseball. I was on the PTA board at the time, and he insisted that I continue. He encouraged me to remain active, to come to services Friday night, [to] work in the PTA. He made me feel that I was as good as everyone else!

Two Orthodox institutions, one in Manhattan and one in the Bronx, were warmly praised. One woman described the atmosphere:

The shul [in Manhattan] made a real effort to pull me in, as well as to pull in the boys, who were going to Hebrew school there. They have separate fees for single parents that are adjusted according to your ability to pay. They are warm, congenial. They never make you feel pitiable or like a sore thumb. . . .

About the synagogue in the Bronx, a mother said:

I love the shul. It's such a warm place. The men are wonderful to my son. For example, they make sure to put him on their shoulders and carry him around on Simchat Torah. It's little things like that, but they're important. They make him feel so welcome that he really loves going there.

Occasionally, one respondent praised and another criticized the same temple or synagogue. Perceptions vary, of course, and experiences as well. But one factor may be, as some respondents pointed out, the receptivity and behavior of the individual. The suggestion was made, for example, that the single parent has a responsibility to take some initiative. One said:

There's just so much a synagogue can do for a single parent. As difficult as it is, it's important that we make ourselves get out there and push ourselves a little so we'll get accepted, invited, and involved. I did it, and it worked.

Another suggested:

> *I think it has less to do with the synagogue than with the woman herself. You can't sit around and wait for the synagogue to come to you. If you want to be involved, you have to stop kvetching and go out and do it!*

These comments underscore the fact that the individual as well as the synagogue has an outreach responsibility. Nevertheless, the extent to which the synagogue or temple reaches out and welcomes the single-parent family probably determine whether that family will remain involved in the Jewish community.

The Bar Mitzvah and Bat Mitzvah

In *The Jewish Community and Children of Divorce*, rabbis identified a range of problems — financial, ceremonial, social, psychological — that may confront the postdivorce couple at the time of their child's Bar Mitzvah or Bat Mitzvah. In this study, the parents themselves were asked how they had coped with this event if it had occurred after their divorce. Parents with youngsters between 9 and 12 were asked if they had given any thought to the event and, if so, what their expectations and plans were.

A total of 15 families had celebrated a Bar Mitzvah or Bat Mitzvah after the parents' divorces. Five felt that things had gone very well. Recalled one mother:

> *Our son's Bar Mitzvah went beautifully, largely because of the rabbi's sensitivity. For example, normally the father and the mother sit next to each other on the pulpit, but he arranged for us to sit on opposite sides. It also helped that his father's woman friend did not come. We each invited our own friends, and our son invited the entire religious school class. So there was a head table of fourteen boys, and that made our son feel good.*

. . .

In six cases, the parent(s) reported a few problems. One father related:

> *The Bat Mitzvah took place shortly after the divorce, and I just say that although it went all right, I felt that it was a great source of acrimony in that postdivorce period. Still, we tried not to take our own problems out on our daughter.*

. . .

In four cases, the Bar Mitzvah or Bat Mitzvah provoked many problems. One mother explained:

> *The Bar Mitzvah itself didn't go too badly. We divided the* aliyahs *[blessings over the Torah], and for our son's sake we tried very hard to behave civilly. But up until the day itself, it was a difficult time. My ex absolutely didn't want a Bar Mitzvah, while my son wanted one like crazy. We had terrible fights over money since my ex thought the whole thing was unnecessary. In the end, he paid for half, but he really gave me a hard time.*

The father's side of the story was somewhat different:

> *It's not that I didn't want a Bar Mitzvah—I just didn't want one of those big, fancy affairs. I wanted to take my son to Israel instead and just have a small affair here. But his mother wouldn't let him go. So in the end, it was the big, fancy affair, and I got stuck paying for half of it.*

Eight families with children between 9 and 12 contemplated the approaching Bar Mitzvah or Bat Mitzvah with anxiety and concern. The mother of a 9-year-old said:

> *I worry about everything already. A Bar Mitzvah is usually a big function—100 to 150 people, and I don't know many people. Whom will I invite? I don't have a wide circle of friends anymore. Also, I guess my ex should be there, but I don't think I'd want that. And then, there's the cost—who is going to pay?*

In another case, both mother and father were bitter about the forthcoming Bar Mitzvah of their son. Said the mother:

> *The Bar Mitzvah is next year, and his father will not be there. I won't let him come because I've been left with all the responsibility that should have been his. I resent it terribly. All and any costs relating to a Bar Mitzvah will fall on my shoulders, so why should I let him come?*

The father said:

> *I'm afraid I won't be involved next year when my son's Bar Mitzvah takes place. She wanted me to pay for it, and she wanted it to take place at the Tavern on the Green. I said absolutely not because my whole family is kosher, and I think it would be a slap in the face to them to have it there. So I said, "Have it where you want, but pay for it yourself." I'd rather not make a fuss because it's only our son who will suffer.*

Five families anticipated the Bar Mitzvah or Bat Mitzvah with pleasure. One father said:

> *We'll make the Bat Mitzvah a very simple affair, just as our older's was, before the divorce. I'm sure it will go fine.*

A mother who looked forward to the Bar Mitzvah of her son in two years said:

> *My ex and I get along very well. We're very friendly, so I know it won't be a problem.*

Several couples reported that at the time of an older child's Bar Mitzvah or Bat Mitzvah they had already decided to separate. These parents postponed their divorces until after the ceremony so as not to mar the occasion for the child or for their respective families, underscoring the fact that many Jews—Orthodox, Conservative, Reform, and even unaffiliated—view the Bar Mitzvah or Bat Mitzvah as a significant event. . . .

Summary and Conclusions

Although the sample of 40 divorced couples was too small to permit any generalizations, the study suggests that divorce does not necessarily result in erosion of Jewish identity and community involvement but may, especially for families with young children, open the way for a restoration or strengthening of Jewish affiliation. The determining factor may well be the warmth and sensitivity with which the synagogue, temple, or other Jewish institution welcomes and involves such single-parent families.

In the conference that followed publication of *The Jewish Community and Children of Divorce*, we suggested that some rabbis, particularly among the Orthodox, are concerned that efforts to deal with the single-parent family may be seen as condoning, even encouraging, divorce. Said one rabbi at the conference:

> *A problem that emerges from giving special treatment to single parents in relation to institutional activities and fees is the loss of the couple advantage. The subtle indication of approval which emerges from such a response may shift the pro-family balance, which is part of the Jewish value system.*

While this concern is understandable, it is self-defeating. The divorce rate among Jews has risen, and even among the Orthodox divorced families have become increasingly visible. These families face all the problems associated with the breakup of marriage and, in addition, find, all too often, that the Jewish community is indifferent and unresponsive to their plight. Programs of premarital and marital counseling may help to reduce the incidence of divorce among Jews, but it will not make the problem go away. Single-parent families are a growing segment of the community. Their needs must be recognized, acknowledged, and addressed.

ENDNOTES

1. Chaim I. Waxman, *America's Jews in Transition* (Philadelphia: Temple University Press, 1983).
2. The Jewish community has taken steps to address the problem of the recalcitrant husband. A number of Orthodox rabbis are now asking couples to sign a simple prenuptial agreement stating that, in the event the marriage is dissolved civilly, both parties will agree to give or receive a *get*. The Conservative movement has incorporated a prenuptial agreement in its *ketubah* (marriage contract), and a recent case suggests that the civil courts will enforce such an agreement.

   To combat ignorance about the fact that a *get* is necessary for children of subsequent marriages to be legitimate under Jewish law, as well as to address the problem of the recalcitrant husband, an organization called GET (Getting Equitable Treatment) was formed several years ago in New York City. The organization seeks to assist men and women who are involved in battles over the *get*, as well as to forestall such problems through community education.
3. The postdivorce "family" is defined as the custodial parent and child(ren).

28

STEPFAMILIES IN THE UNITED STATES
A Reconsideration

ANDREW J. CHERLIN • FRANK F. FURSTENBERG, JR.

In the late 1970s, when rates of divorce and remarriage were at historical high points in the United States, each of us separately reviewed the surprisingly small number of studies on stepfamily life. In our reviews, we presented an agenda of ideas that guided our individual and collaborative investigations over the next one and one-half decades. Cherlin's review noted the striking absence of well-defined rules for family life among households formed by remarriage (Cherlin 1978). He hypothesized that higher rates of separation and divorce might be linked to the structural anomalies of this "incompletely institutionalized" family form. Furstenberg observed that the process of "recycling the family" replaced the nuclear family with a distinctively different family form (Furstenberg 1979; Furstenberg and Spanier 1984). He was especially concerned with the ways that remarried couples thought differently about marriage and family life after divorce and the implications of remarriage for the workings of the American kinship system. . . .

We believe that remarriage and stepfamily life constitute a strategic site for research on the family. The daily dilemmas of creating and conducting family life after divorce lead one to ask: What is a family, what are the obligations of parenthood, and how are bonds of kinship formed and maintained? There are, of course, no definitive answers to these questions; but our task as social scientists is to discover how answers are being formulated by those who experience divorce and remarriage and by those who devise policies and practices for dealing with the consequences of family change.

The Changing Demography of Divorce and Remarriage

Among developed nations, the United States has unusually high rates of divorce and remarriage. Close to a third of all Americans will marry, divorce, and remarry. But informal, cohabiting unions also are increasingly common. The substitution of cohabitation for marriage makes it more difficult to follow

---

From "Stepfamilies in the United States: A Reconsideration" by Andrew J. Cherlin and Frank F. Furstenberg, Jr. With permission from the *Annual Review of Sociology*, Volume 20, © 1994 by Annual Reviews, Inc.

remarriage trends and to describe stepfamily life. This trend toward the de-institutionalization of marriage may be partly a response to the high risks of divorce and the complexities of stepfamily life.

Until the 1960s, the remarriage rate and the divorce rate in the United States rose and fell in parallel—when the divorce rate increased, so did the rate of remarriage. It seemed that divorced people were not rejecting the idea of being married, they were just rejecting their own first marriages and trying again. Starting in the 1960s, however, the annual rate of remarriage (the number of remarriages in a given year divided by the number of previously married persons age 15 and older in the population) fell even though the divorce rate began to rise. The fall has continued ever since. At current rates, only about two thirds of separated and divorced women would ever remarry, compared to three fourths in the 1960s; the corresponding figure for men is about three fourths compared to more than four fifths in the 1960s.[1]

There are distinct variations in the propensity to remarry among subgroups of Americans. These variations reflect both choice and opportunity. For example, one study found that women who marry in their teenage years or early twenties are more likely to remarry than are women who married later; the authors speculate that women who married young may have less experience in, and less of a preference for, living independently.[2] Among women who choose to remarry, some may have more difficulty finding suitable spouses than others. Women who have three or more children, for instance, have a lower likelihood of remarrying, probably because they have a harder time finding a desirable partner willing to share the responsibilities of supporting a large family. And older women face a shrinking marriage market because of most men's preference for younger partners. Consequently, women who divorce at younger ages are more likely to remarry than are those who divorce at older ages.

In addition, remarriage is far more likely among non-Hispanic whites than among Hispanics or African Americans. According to one estimate from 1980 U.S. Census Bureau data, about half of all non-Hispanic white women will remarry within five years of their separation, compared to one third of Mexican American women and one fifth of African American women (Sweet and Bumpass 1987). These differences occur, in part, because remarriage rates are lower for the poor than for the non-poor. With few assets and little property to pass on to children, people with low incomes have less need for the legal protection marriage brings. Yet lower incomes do not account for the entire difference. The low remarriage rates for African Americans also are consistent with the lesser place of marriage in the African American family.

Cohabitation

The overall decline in remarriage, however, is deceptive. As remarriage rates have declined, cohabitation among the formerly married has increased. Figure 1 shows the change. It is based on data from the National Survey of Families and Households, conducted in 1987 and 1988. Individuals were asked

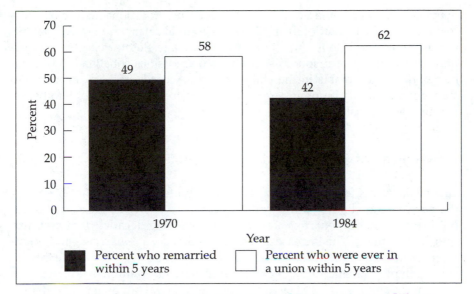

FIGURE 1 **Percentage of Maritally Separated and Divorced Persons Who Re-married within 5 Years, and Who Were Ever in a Union (Marital or Cohabiting) within 5 years, in or about 1970 and in or about 1984**

Source: Retrospective union histories provided by respondents in the National Survey of Families and Households, 1987–1988, as reported in Larry L. Bumpass, James A. Sweet, and Andrew Cherlin, "The Role of Cohabitation in Declining Rates of Marriage," *Journal of Marriage and the Family* 53 (1991): 913–27.

to recall their personal history of union formation and dissolution. The bars on the left-hand side represent the situation in approximately 1970, according to the retrospective histories given by the respondents. Forty-nine percent of persons had remarried within five years after they separated from their spouses. In addition, some had cohabited with a partner without marrying. When those who cohabited without remarrying are added to those who remarried, the sum is the number who were ever in a union—marital or cohabiting—within five years of separating. As can be seen, 58 percent had ever been in a union in 1970. By 1984, only 42 percent had remarried within five years of separating, reflecting the drop in the remarriage rate. But the percentage who had ever been in a union had increased from its 1970 level to 62 percent in 1984. In the interim, cohabitation had become so widespread among the previously married that its increase had more than compensated for the decrease in remarriage (Bumpass, Sweet, and Cherlin 1991).

Divorced persons, in other words, have not reduced their propensity to live with someone; rather, they have substituted cohabitation for remarriage. We interpret this pattern as an indication that remarriage, like first marriage, is becoming less obligatory and socially regulated. It follows that informal unions are generally less stable and secure arrangements. About one out of seven people who eventually remarry live with a different partner between marriages (Bumpass and Sweet 1989). Indeed, the provisional nature of informal unions may be part of their appeal for individuals who may be hesitant, at least temporarily, to recommit to formal marriage. So the velocity of transitions into and out of unions has surely increased since cohabitation became more widely acceptable in the United States. Accordingly, official marriage statistics are rapidly becoming unreliable indicators of patterns of family formation and reconstitution. . . .

New Forms of Kinship and Family Organization

One of the taken-for-granted aspects of family life in the West has been that the parents and children in the conjugal family will live in the same household until the children grow up. Until the last few decades, that assumption was justified. The increases, first, in divorce and remarriage and, more recently, in cohabitation and out-of-wedlock childbearing, have made this assumption problematic. Only 59 percent of American children lived with both biological parents in 1992.[3] Divorce splits the conjugal family into two households—one that typically contains a custodial parent (usually the mother) and the children and a second that contains the noncustodial parent (usually the father).

Remarriage can bring a multitude of ties across households, creating what one of us has called "the new extended family" (Furstenberg 1987). In 1992, 11.2 percent of all children were living with one biological parent and one stepparent. Consider one set of family ties studied by Anne Bernstein (1988) and diagrammed in Figure 2. This set of family ties is centered on the marriage of Carin and Josh, who reside in household 2. They have a mutual child, Alice. Josh previously was married to Peggy, with whom he had two children, Janet and Tim, who live with Peggy in household 3. Carin previously was married to Don, with whom she had two children, Scott and Bruce, who still live with her. Her former husband Don then remarried Anna and had two more children, Ethan and Ellen, who live with Anna and him in household 1. Here is how Bruce described his family:

> *Tim and Janet are my stepbrother and sister. Josh is my stepdad. Carin and Don are my real parents, who are divorced. And Don remarried Anna and together they had Ethan and Ellen, my half-sister and -brother. And Carin married Josh and had little Alice, my half-sister. (Bernstein 1988:101)*

How are we to make sense of this admixture? How many families are involved? What are their boundaries? The relationships spill over the sides of households, with children providing the links from one to the next. Let us suggest that there are two ways to define families in this context. The first is to focus on a household, even though ties extend beyond it. The advantage of this strategy is that in developed Western societies, we are accustomed to thinking of immediate families as being contained within households. We define a stepfamily household as a household that contains a parent with chil-

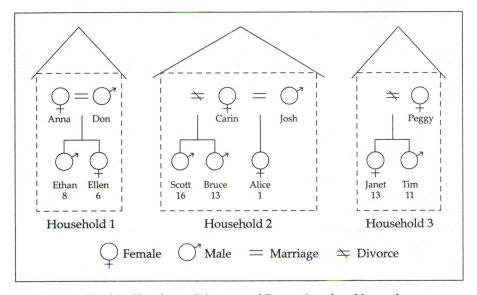

FIGURE 2   Kinship Ties due to Divorce and Remarriage in a Network
Source: Reported by Anne C. Bernstein, "Unraveling the Tangles: Children's Understanding of Stepfamily Kinship," in *Relative Strangers: Studies of Stepfamily Processes,* ed. William R. Beer (Totowa, NJ: Rowan & Littlefield, 1988), pp. 83–111.

dren from a previous union and that parent's current partner. The children from the previous union are the stepchildren, and the current partner is the stepparent. The household can be even more complex: Both partners may have children from previous unions, and they also may have a new, mutual child from the current union. But the defining criterion is that they all reside in the same household. (Although there are three households in Figure 2, only household 2 is a stepfamily household. Household 1 has no children from previous unions living there; and household 3 has children from a previous union but no current spouse or partner.) . . .

The second way to define families is to ignore household boundaries and to focus instead on the chains that extend from one household to another. The links of the chains are children from previous unions. They connect a divorced woman and her new partner with her ex-husband and his new partner. Anthropologist Paul Bohannan (1971) called these pathways "divorce chains." But it is probably more accurate to refer to them as remarriage chains, as illustrated by the complicated network of ties among the three households depicted in Figure 2. . . .

Remarriage chains can serve as support and exchange networks, when ex-spouses and new spouses give and request favors (Keshet 1988). This system depends on the quality of relations and cooperation of all involved and can easily be disrupted. In extended kin networks centered on conjugal families or on "blood" relatives (see below), people might extend favors based on goodwill and a sense of shared purpose. In remarriage chains, that sense of goodwill is limited and decisions are more likely to be made using the calculus of self-interest. It is best thought of as a system with weak rather than strong ties, a distinction between systems of support made by Granovetter (1973). Remarriage chains are more likely to provide information and referrals than direct material and emotional assistance (Furstenberg 1981; Johnson 1988; White 1993).

So we might expect to discover far more variability and instability in the kinship networks of stepfamilies than is typical in nuclear households. And it is largely unknown how these networks operate when the quasi-stepparents in cohabiting units are involved. Do family alliances become even more improvised and unpredictable when the roles of members are less clearly specified? In family systems where membership is fluid, a sense of kinship can be invoked easily; but a sense of kinship also can be withdrawn easily. We return to this point when we discuss the consequences of divorce and remarriage later in the paper.

Doing the Work of Kinship

When Americans think about kinship, they tend to think about people related through either "blood" or marriage (Schneider 1980). Mere existence of a blood tie, however, does not necessarily make two people think of each other as kin. Kinship is achieved by establishing a "relationship," seeing each other regularly, corresponding, giving or receiving help—that is, by making repeated connections. The absence of a relationship may mean that even a blood relative may not be counted as family. To be sure, almost everyone considers their parents and their children to be kin even if they have not seen them in a long time. But Americans would understand what someone meant if she said, "My father left home when I was three and I never saw him again; he's not part of my family. My stepfather is really the person I consider to be my father." And similarly a person might not regard a cousin as a relative if he never met her.

To be a relative, you must do the work of creating and maintaining kinship. Among parents and children, this happens almost automatically—so much so that we rarely think about it. But among stepparents and stepchildren it does not happen automatically. For one thing, a stepparent in a remarriage that has followed a divorce does not replace the stepchild's nonresident parent, as was the case when most remarriages followed a death. Rather, the stepparent adds to the stepchild's stock of potential kin. If both biological parents are still involved in the stepchild's life, it is not clear what role the stepparent is supposed to play. There are few guidelines, few norms. This situation is what led one of us to conclude that the role of the stepparent is incompletely institutionalized (Cherlin 1978).

In fact, there is great variability in how stepparents and stepchildren view each other. In a 1981 national survey, children ages 11 to 16 and their parents both were asked who they specifically included in their family. Although only 1 percent of parents did not mention their biological children, 15 percent of those with stepchildren in the household did not mention them. Among children, 31 percent of those in stepfamily households omitted the stepparent who was living with them; and 41 percent failed to mention a stepsibling (Furstenberg 1987).

What, then, determines how stepchildren and stepparents view each other? A key factor is how old the child was when the stepparent joined the household: The younger the child, the more likely he or she is to consider the stepparent to be a "real" parent (Marsiglio 1992). The evidence isn't precise enough to establish an age cut-off for emotional bonding. Still, we suspect that if the stepparent arrives during the preschool years (before the child is five), it is possible to establish a parent-like relationship; but if the stepparent arrives much later, strong bonds form much more rarely. Research shows that children establish strong bonds of attachment to their parents, whom they rely on for security, within their first year or two. Children's attachments become somewhat reduced after the preschool years (Parkes and Hinde 1982). A second factor is how frequently the stepchild sees his or her nonresident parent; the less frequent their interactions, the easier it is for a stepparent to take on a parent-like role (Marsiglio 1992). A third factor is the quality of the relationship between the stepparent and the biological parent in the home. The more satisfactory that relationship, the more authority the stepparent has to take on a parental role. Finally, there is probably individual variation depending on the child's temperament. Some children may be more welcoming to new parents than others. So there may be differences in the quality of relations among children in the same family.

The kinship terms used by children to designate their parents are one measure of the bonding process. There is no agreed-upon direct term of reference for a stepparent (Cherlin 1978). For example, few if any children call their stepfather "Step-Dad," and it would be equally rare for children to refer to him formally as "Mr. Jones." Instead, some will call him "Dad" but many will use the stepparent's first name. In the absence of empirical research that relates the use of terminology to bonding, we are inclined to think that the use of the first name suggests a relationship that is neither parent nor stranger, but somewhere in between. If children do not address stepparents using the parental term for the biological parent, then children may not grant stepparents the reciprocal rights and obligations ordinarily accorded to so-called "real" parents.

Residential and nonresidential biological parents often have a strong interest in the use of names (Furstenberg and Spanier 1984). A custodial mother may urge her children to call her new husband "Dad" in order to replace the role of the noncustodial father. And the latter, in turn, may contest this effort to supplant him with a surrogate. Some members of a group of inner-city African Americans interviewed by one of us (Furstenberg) made a distinction between "Fathers" and "Daddies" — the men who propagate the children and the men who care for them (Furstenberg, Sherwood, and Sullivan 1992). "Fathers" are the biological parents of the child, but "Daddies" are the men who assume responsibility for their children — who play the role of father to them. The group of African Americans hardly ever talked about having a stepfather. It may be that among African Americans, fatherhood is earned rather than accorded by birth or marriage. As we argue later on, this sort of cultural reasoning may actually be spreading more broadly in the United States as union instability increases. There is even greater variability in how more distant stepkin relate to the stepchildren. When the two of us carried out a national study of grandparents, we asked them about relationships with stepgrandchildren. Once again, the younger that children were when their parents remarried, the more that grandparents reported feeling that the children were "like biological grandchildren." One stepgrandmother, who had not acquired her stepgrandchildren until they were teenagers, was asked what they called her:

> *Harriett. I insisted on that. They started by calling me Mrs. Scott. . . .*
> *But from the beginning, you realize, these children were in their teens,*
> *and it was hard to accept somebody from an entirely different family, and*
> *they didn't know me from Adam. . . . Now if they were smaller — you*
> *know, younger — it would have made a difference (quoted in Cherlin and*
> *Furstenberg 1992:158).*

It also made a big difference where the stepgrandchildren were living: For example, it made a difference whether they resided with the grandparents' adult children (as when a son married a woman who had custody of children from a previous marriage) or were living most of the time in another household (as when a daughter married a man whose children lived with his former wife except for every other weekend and a month in the summer). Within these constraints, the closeness of the relationship depended on how much effort the stepgrandparents and their adult children put into creating the relationship. Being a steprelative depends on doing the work of kinship.

In other words, remarriage is making parenthood and kinship an achieved status rather than an ascribed status, to use the classic distinction in anthropology and sociology (Davis 1948; Eisenstadt 1966). Traditionally, being a father or a mother had been a status ascribed to individuals at the birth of their child, which generally occurred only after the couple married. To be sure, people marry and have children through their own efforts; nevertheless, one did not have to do anything else to be a parent, nor could one easily resign from the job, especially in a family system that strongly discouraged divorce. In this sort of stable family system, being a grandparent was similarly ascribed. Those rules still apply to the majority of children who are born to two married parents.

Remarriage after divorce, though, adds a number of other, potential kinship positions. Whether these positions are filled depends on the actions of the individuals involved. The most obvious positions are stepfather and stepmother. We have discussed the wide variation in the roles that stepparents play. Some are parent-like figures who are intensely involved with their stepchildren. Many others are more like friends or uncles and aunts. Others, particularly stepparents who don't live with their stepchildren every day, may be like distant cousins — available for a kinship relation but, in fact, rarely assuming an important position in the child's network. In all cases, how much like a family member a stepparent becomes depends directly on his or her efforts to develop a close relationship with stepchildren. Kinship relations in stepfamilies belong to the broader category of in-law relationships — ties created by marriage or marriage-like arrangements. Such ties are characteristically discretionary and even more so in the absence of marriage. In fact, in France, the current term for stepparent, beau-parent, also means parent-in-law.

Intergenerational ties to stepgrandparents are even more voluntary; they range from no contact to a kin-like role, depending in large part on the investment the stepgrandparents make. Our research on grandparents, in fact, reveals considerable variation in the role played by stepgrandparents in children's lives. To a large extent, remarriage restores a measure of balance between the maternal and paternal lines in the networks of kinship. However, there is reason to suspect that unless remarriage occurs early in the child's life, kinship exchanges over the long-term are strongly tilted toward the (custodial) mother's side of the family. The diminishing importance of legal marriage may accentuate this trend. It seems likely to us that cohabitation will undermine the sense of obligation to extended family that is created by matrimony. For example, the quasi-in-laws of cohabiting couples are even less likely than the in-laws created by a remarriage to form and maintain enduring bonds. But, as we noted before, research on the consequences of cohabitation is scarce.

Stepfamily "Process": Building a Stepfamily

After divorce, single parents and their children establish, often with some difficulty, agreed-upon rules and new daily schedules. They establish ways of relating to each other that may differ from the pre-disruption days. A daughter may become a special confidante to her mother. A son may take out the garbage, wash the car, and perform other tasks his father used to do. Put another way, single parents and children create a new family system. Then, into that system, with its shared history, intensive relationships, and agreed-upon roles, walks a stepparent. It can be difficult for the members of the stepfamily household to adjust to his or her presence.

Recent research suggests that the adjustment can take years to complete. One family therapist argues that the average stepfamily takes about seven years to finish the process (Papernow 1988). That is a long time, considering that more than one fourth of all remarriages disrupt within five years (Martin and Bumpass 1989). At the start, the stepparent is an outsider, almost an intruder in the system. At first, the stepparent may view himself naively as a healer who will nurse the wounded family back to health (Papernow 1988). But his initial efforts may hurt rather than help him attain his goal: A stepdaughter may resent the intimacy and support a new stepfather provides to her mother; a son may not wish to relinquish washing the car to a well-meaning stepfather who thinks he is just doing what fathers are supposed to do. As the two of us wrote, "Stepparents quickly discover that they have been issued only a limited license to parent." The wiser ones among them accept the limits of their job description and wait for their time to arrive (Furstenberg and Cherlin 1991:85).

According to recent articles, family therapists seem to agree that for a stepfamily household to be successful, the remarried couple must build a boundary around themselves and work together to solve problems. This process is made more complicated by the negative images of stepparents in the larger culture (Ganong, Coleman, and Mapes 1990) and their weak status in our legal system (Fine and Fine 1992). Their own marriage, rather than the relationship between the biological parent and the child, must become the dominant subsystem within the stepfamily household (Keshet 1988; Papernow 1988; Spanier and Furstenberg 1987). To do so, they must reserve time for each other, even if that means sometimes deferring the demands of others. The task of the remarried couple is to create a shared conception of how their family is to manage its daily business. They cannot rely on generally accepted norms, as adults in first marriages can, because few norms exist. They must draw the blueprints themselves and then construct the family. And, depending on their age, children must be brought into taking an active part in the construction of a new family (Hetherington and Jodl 1993). . . .

We do not want to leave the impression that stepfamily life in the United States is an interminable struggle. Most stepparents report that they are happy with their roles and their new families. In the 1981 survey, a large majority of parents and children in stepfamily households rated their households as "relaxed," "orderly," and "close"; and less than one third found them "tense" or "disorganized." Nevertheless, the ratings of persons in stepfamily households were slightly but consistently less positive than the ratings of persons in first-marriage households (Furstenberg 1987). Moreover, the studies suggest that there is a wide variation in the roles stepparents play (White 1993). In a 1987–1988 national survey, half of all stepfathers disagreed with the statement "A stepparent is more like a friend than a parent to stepchildren"; one third agreed; and the rest were neutral (Marsiglio 1992). Often, those stepparents who manage to integrate themselves into the stepfamily household successfully play a role somewhere between that of a parent and of a trusted friend — what Papernow (1988) calls an "intimate outsider."

Effects on Children

Fifteen years ago, the two of us thought that remarriage would improve the overall well-being of children whose parents had divorced. For one thing, when a single mother remarries, her household income usually rises dramatically because men's wages are so much higher, on average, than are women's wages. One national study found that 8 percent of children in mother–stepfather households were living below the poverty line, compared to 49 percent of children in single-mother households (Bachrach 1983). Consequently, if a divorce causes a decline in household income that hurts the well-being of children, then an increase in household income after the mother remarries should improve children's well-being. In addition, the stepparent adds a second adult to the home. He or she can provide support to the custodial parent and reinforce the custodial parent's monitoring and control of the children's behavior. A stepparent also can provide an adult role model for a child of the same gender.

Despite these advantages, many studies now show that the well-being of children in stepfamily households is no better, on average, than the well-being of children in divorced, single-parent households. Both groups of children show lower levels of well-being than do children in two-biological-parent families. For example, psychologists Mavis Hetherington, Glenn Clingempeel, and several collaborators studied about 200 white households, divided into three groups: nondivorced two-parent households; divorced, single-mother households in which the mothers had been divorced for about four years, on average; and stepfamily households that had just formed (four months average duration) and in which the wife was the biological parent and the husband was the stepparent. The sample was not selected randomly but, rather, recruited by such means as advertisements, examining marriage records, and sending notices to community organizations. All households had at least one child between nine and thirteen years old; these early adolescents were the main focus of the study. Households were evaluated using multiple methods, including personal interviews with the parents and children, standardized tests given to the children, and videotaped family problem-solving sessions. Evaluations were conducted three times: at the start of the study, again about a year later, and yet again another nine months later (Hetherington and Clingempeel 1992).

At all three evaluations, the children from both the single-mother and remarried households were not faring as well as the children in the nondivorced households. For example, all the mothers were asked which items on a list of behavior problems applied to their early-adolescent child. Scores above a certain level on this widely used behavior problems checklist are said to indicate serious difficulties that might warrant the assistance of mental health professionals. Even at the last assessment, about 25 to 30 percent of the children in the single-mother households and the stepfamily households were above this level, as opposed to 10 percent or less of the children in nondivorced households. There was little difference between the former two groups (Maccoby 1992).

A national health survey of 15,000 children in 1981 produced similar results. Children in stepfamily households and in single-parent households both received higher average scores on a checklist of behavior problems than did children in nondivorced, two-parent households. When parents were asked questions about the need for psychological help for their children, 3 percent of nondivorced parents said that their child needed help or had received help in the previous year, compared to 10 percent in single-mother households and 10 percent in mother–stepfather households. Both of the latter groups had children who were more likely to have repeated a grade in school than did children from nondivorced households. On all of these indicators, there was little difference between the children in single-parent households and in stepfamily households (Zill 1988).

There is conflicting evidence as to whether children of different ages or genders adjust differently to the arrival of a stepparent. Several studies, conducted mostly with younger children, have found that girls had a more difficult time adjusting to the presence of a stepfather than boys did adjusting to a stepmother (Bray 1988; Hetherington 1987). Some of the authors speculated that girls tend to form close bonds to their divorced mothers and that these bonds are disrupted by the arrival of a stepfather. In support of this idea, at least two studies found that daughters showed poorer adjustment when their mothers and stepfathers reported greater cohesion and bonding in their marriage; conversely, they showed better adjustment when there was less cohesion in the marriage (Brand, Clingempeel, and Bowen-Woodward 1988; Bray 1988). It is as if the daughters' sense of well-being falls at least temporarily when their mothers turn some attention and affection toward their new husbands.

However, the 1981 national health survey showed few differences by either age or gender. Neither did Hetherington and Clingempeel's recent joint study find differences between the early-adolescent girls and boys in their study, despite the expectations of the authors, each of whom had reported gender differences among preadolescent children in prior studies. Instead, Hetherington and Clingempeel now speculate that it is difficult for early adolescents of either gender to adjust to a remarriage. This period is when children must come to terms with their own burgeoning sexuality; it may be disconcerting to have an adult sexual partner of the parent move into the house—especially one for whom the traditional incest taboos do not hold.[4] Alternatively, the number of family transitions might impair the adjustment of children in stepfamilies. Having coped with a divorce, and possibly with the introduction of a live-in partner, these children must now cope with another major change in their family system. Some studies have found a relationship between the number of family transitions a child has experienced, on the one hand, and behavior problems, on the other hand (Capaldi and Patterson 1991; Wu and Martinson 1993). Finally, children and parents with unmeasured personal characteristics that impair family cohesion could be disproportionately represented in the population of divorced and remarried families. No study to our knowledge has done an adequate job of examining how much of the effect of marriage is due to selection.

Only one finding is well established concerning the long-term effects on children of having lived in a stepfamily household. Children in stepfamily households—particularly girls—leave their households at an earlier age than do children in single-parent households or in two-parent households. They leave earlier to marry; and they also leave earlier to establish independent households prior to marrying. An analysis of a large, six-year, national study of high school students showed this pattern for girls (Goldscheider and Goldscheider 1993). In a British study, 23-year-olds who had left their parental homes were asked the main reason why they left. Demographer Kathleen Kiernan (1992) reported that those who had lived in stepfamily households were substantially more likely to say that they left due to "friction at home" than were those who had not lived in stepfamily households. Again, the differences were greater for girls. An analysis of a 1987–1988 American national survey found that girls who had lived in a stepfamily household were more likely to have left home by age 19 to marry or to live independently than were girls who had lived with single parents or with two parents; the differences were much weaker for boys. If a girl also had lived with stepsiblings, her likelihood of leaving home by age 19 was even higher (Aquilino 1991).

Interviews in 1980 and 1983 with a national sample of currently married persons suggested that tensions between stepchildren and their parents and stepparents cause the early home-leaving. Those who had stepchildren in their households reported more family problems involving children. The authors hypothesize that one way these problems are resolved is by encouraging, or arranging for, the stepchildren to leave the household. During the three years between interviews, 51 percent of all the teenage stepchildren had left the households, compared to 35 percent of all the teenage biological children. Some may have chosen to live with their other parent, some may have been forced to do so, and some may have left to go to school, establish their own residence, cohabit, or marry (White and Booth 1985). If this effect is indeed more pronounced for girls, it suggests that the "friction" in the household may be due to the disruption of the mother–daughter bond or to the presence of the mother's male sexual partner, whose relationship to the daughter is ambiguous. . . .

It is important to recognize that some stepparents manage to build relations with their partner's children, though rarely so if their remarriage dissolves. Still, the odds of building durable and intimate bonds that resemble the strong ties that often occur among biological parents and children are relatively low. The discretionary quality of in-law relationships — especially relationships that have a legacy of conflict or emotional distance — often seems to dictate the kinship bonds in later life.

It strikes us that the comparison of stepchildren and biological offspring is not always the most appropriate one. Perhaps it is more reasonable to contrast the sense of obligations that stepparents and their adult children experience toward one another to obligations assumed by sons and daughters-in-law. By that standard, we may find that relations between stepchildren and their parents are not so impoverished. It would also be interesting to examine the relatively small number of stepchildren who are adopted by their parents (who become treated like "blood" relatives) with adopted children whose membership in the family was not gained through divorce and remarriage.

The structural comparisons of family types also need to be supplemented with qualitative research on the circumstances under which parents and children socially construct family bonds and how those constructions change over time. Clearly, some parents and children experience their steprelations as similar to ties with blood relatives. How do these individuals manage to ignore the signals of a culture that places strong values on blood ties? In the conclusion, we argue that such individuals may become more common in the future. The significance of blood bonds may wane to some degree if the institution of marriage continues to weaken. . . .

Implications for Research and Public Policy

From the perspective of children, these demographic changes increase the odds of experiencing substantial family flux during childhood. A near-majority of children growing up in the United States today are likely to encounter multiple parent-figures. Many must negotiate changing relations with these parent-figures as the children or their parents move in and out of their households. The children will be situated in complex and changing kinship networks that involve the loss and acquisition of relationships. On average, children in stepfamilies and quasi-stepfamilies exhibit more problems on average than do children who grow up in nuclear families. Nevertheless, many children experiencing the divorce and remarriage of their parents appear to do well.

Research on children whose family experiences include divorce and remarriage is just beginning to identify some of the family processes that make a difference for children's long-term well-being. It seems likely to us that the same processes that make for successful development of children in two-biological-parent families are likely to apply to children who grow up in stepfamilies. Some of these processes reside in the child, some in the parenting system, and some in the resources of the larger family system and community in which parent and child are embedded. The task for researchers is to map these specific sources of influence and to describe how they work in combination. This is a daunting challenge for developmentalists and family sociologists.

The family changes that we have discussed in this paper represent part of a profound cultural transformation in the American kinship system. . . .

During the past several years, Americans have witnessed on television and in the newspapers a steady stream of dramatic custody battles between biological and nonbiological parents. Not all involve conflicts resulting from divorce and remarriage, but in nearly every case the same issue recurs: Do blood ties have legal primacy over bonds created by the emotional investment of a nonbiological parent?

David Chambers, a legal scholar who has written about this issue, describes a court case that involved a boy named Danny, who was raised by his stepfather from the age of one, after his mother died. His biological father had not asked for custody initially. However, when Danny was seven, his older brother decided to live with the biological father. The father then sued for custody of Danny on the grounds that siblings should not be separated. A lower court ruled that Danny should be allowed to stay with his stepfather, who had been the primary parent for six of the seven years of Danny's life. But a higher court overruled this decision, referring to the stepparent as merely a "third party" who should not be allowed to interfere with the rightful interest of the biological parent.

Concerning the dismissive treatment of stepparents by the courts, Chambers wrote that the ruling in Danny's case almost certainly exposes "society's conflicting and unresolved attitudes about stepparents." In fact, the legal doctrine that persists can be traced back to a longstanding belief that biological parents are better equipped to care for their children. Probably, too, it reflects the idea that children are the property of their biological parents.

These legal assumptions evolved from, and helped to sustain, a family system that was culturally and socially designed to reinforce the primacy of biological ties. Or, to put it differently, these assumptions emphasize ascriptive affiliations as opposed to earned or achieved affiliations. Throughout this paper, we have argued that the justification for giving such heavy weight to ascriptive ties is being seriously undermined by new patterns of family formation. It may be time to reconsider the doctrine that family is largely determined by "blood" and to assign, rather, a higher importance to the emotional, social, and material resources that parents, biological and nonbiological, provide. In other words, perhaps we should regard parenthood both as an achieved and an ascribed status. Perhaps we should require that parents earn rights to their children by assuming responsibilities in caretaking and support. Of course, biological parents must be given an opportunity, indeed they must be expected, to assume those responsibilities. Perhaps, however, we should also accept the possibility that other parent-figures may supplant biological parents when circumstances permit or require their involvement (Woodhouse 1993).

Of course, we are aware that multiple parent-figures complicate both the legal system and the parenting system. But the idea that two parents per household is the standard and the only acceptable family form is giving way to a more diverse set of family arrangements that are not so neatly confined to a single household. The change in family forms that we have been tracing introduces a host of anomalies. We see little evidence that remarriage (formal and informal) has become more institutionalized since the two of us first began to write about this growing phenomenon. We see some troubling indications that the cultural, legal, and social anomalies associated with "recycling the family" place a considerable burden on a growing number of children — even if most children seem capable of managing that burden without serious effects.

To describe this new family system is not necessarily to endorse it. But neither can we say that the old order is invariably to be preferred. Moreover, even if we believed that the old order were preferable, we cannot imagine how it could be easily restored without considerable costs to all.

ENDNOTES

Author's note: This paper was prepared while Frank Furstenberg was a Fellow at the Center for Advanced Study in the Behavioral Sciences. He is grateful for financial support provided by the John D. and Catherine T. MacArthur Foundation, Grant No. #8900078.

1. Based on 1985 data, Larry L. Bumpass, James Sweet, and Teresa Castro Martin (1990) estimated that 72 percent of recently separated women would remarry. But remarriage rates have declined further since then. A 1992 Census Bureau report suggests that the true figure may be closer to two thirds; see U.S. Bureau of the Census (1992c). The most recent estimate for men—78 percent remarrying within 10 years—is from the 1980 Census data and is probably too high now. See James A. Sweet and Larry L. Bumpass (1987).
2. All of the findings in this paragraph are from Larry Bumpass, James Sweet, and Teresa Castro Martin (1990).
3. We calculated this figure (and the 11.2 percent figure in the next paragraph) based on information from the June 1990 Census on children living with neither parent, as reported in U.S. Bureau of the Census (1992a); information on the biological versus nonbiological status of parents of children who were living with two parents, in the June 1990 *Current Population Survey* (U.S. Bureau of the Census 1992c); and the distribution of living arrangements of all children, in the March 1992 *Current Population Survey* (U.S. Bureau of the Census 1992b).
4. In 33 of the states, it was legal in 1993 for a stepfather to divorce his wife and marry his wife's daughter. See Margaret Mahoney (1993) and Mary Ann Glendon (1989).

REFERENCES

Aquilino, W. S. 1991. "Family Structure and Home Leaving: A Further Specification of the Relationship." *Journal of Marriage and the Family* 53:999–1010.

Bachrach, C. 1983. "Children in Stepfamilies: Characteristics of Biological, Step-, and Adopted Children." *Journal of Marriage and the Family* 45:171–79.

Beer, W. R., ed. 1988. *Relative Strangers: Studies of Stepfamily Processes.* Totowa, NJ: Rowan & Littlefield.

Bernstein, A. C. 1988. "Unraveling the Tangles: Children's Understanding of Stepfamily Kinships." Pp. 83–111 in *Relative Strangers: Studies of Stepfamily Processes,* edited by W. R. Beer. Totowa, NJ: Rowan & Littlefield.

Bohannan, P. 1971. "Divorce Chains, Households of Remarriage, and Multiple Divorcers." Pp. 128–39 in *Divorce and After,* edited by P. Bohannan. Garden City, NY: Anchor.

Booth, A. and J. N. Edwards. 1992. "Starting Over: Why Remarriages Are Unstable." *Journal of Family Issues* 13:179–94.

Brand, E., W. G. Clingempeel, and K. Bowen-Woodward. 1988. "Family Relationships and the Children's Psychological Adjustment in Stepmother and Stepfather Families." Pp. 279–98 in *Impact of Divorce, Single Parenting, and Stepparenting on Children,* edited by E. M. Hetherington and J. D. Arasteh. Hillsdale, NJ: Erlbaum.

Bray, J. H. 1988. "Children's Development during Early Remarriage." Pp. 279–98 in *Impact of Divorce, Single Parenting, and Stepparenting on Children,* edited by E. M. Hetherington and J. D. Arasteh. Hillsdale, NJ: Erlbaum.

Bumpass, L. L. and J. A. Sweet. 1989. "National Estimates of Cohabitation: Cohort Levels and Union Stability." *Demography* 25:615–25.

Bumpass, L. L., J. A. Sweet, and A. J. Cherlin. 1991. "The Role of Cohabitation in Declining Rates of Marriage." *Journal of Marriage and the Family* 53:913–27.

Bumpass, L. L., J. A. Sweet, and T. C. Martin. 1990. "Changing Pattern of Remarriage." *Journal of Marriage and the Family* 52:747–56.

Capaldi, D. M. and G. R. Patterson. 1991. "Relation of Parental Transitions to Boys' Adjustment Problems: 1. A Linear Hypothesis; 2. Mothers at Risk for Transitions and Unskilled Parenting." *Developmental Psychology* 27:489–504.

Cherlin, A. J. 1978. "Remarriage as an Incomplete Institution." *American Journal of Sociology* 84:634–50.

Cherlin, A. J. and F. F. Furstenberg, Jr. 1992. *The New American Grandparent: A Place in the Family, A Life Apart.* Cambridge, MA: Harvard University Press.

Coleman, M. and L. Ganong. 1990. "Remarriage and Stepfamily Research in the 1980s: Increased Interest in an Old Family Form." *Journal of Marriage and the Family* 52:925–40.

Davis, K. 1948. *Human Society.* New York: Macmillan.

Eisenstadt, S. N. 1966. *From Generation to Generation.* New York: Free Press.

Fine, M. A. and D. R. Fine. 1992. "Recent Changes in Laws Affecting Stepfamilies: Suggestions for Legal Reform." *Family Relations* 13:334–40.

Furstenberg, F. F., Jr. 1979. "Recycling the Family: Perspectives for Researching a Neglected Family Form." *Marriage and Family Review* 2:12–22.

———. 1981. "Remarriage and Intergenerational Relations." Pp. 115–42 in *Aging: Stability and Change in the Family,* edited by R. W. Fogel, E. Hatfield, S. B. Kiesler, and E. Shanas. New York: Academic Press.

———. 1987. "The New Extended Family: The Experience of Parents and Children after Remarriage." Pp. 42–61 in *Remarriage and Stepparenting: Current Research and Theory,* edited by K. Pasley and M. Ihinger-Tallman. New York: Guilford Press.

Furstenberg, F. F., Jr. and A. J. Cherlin. 1991. *Divided Families: What Happens to Children When Parents Part?* Cambridge, MA: Harvard University Press.

Furstenberg, F. F., Jr. and C. W. Nord. 1985. "Parenting Apart: Patterns of Childrearing after Divorce." *Journal of Marriage and the Family* 47:893–904.

Furstenberg, F. F., Jr., K. E. Sherwood, and M. L. Sullivan. 1992. *Caring and Paying: What Fathers and Mothers Say about Child Support.* New York: Manpower Demonstration Resources.

Furstenberg, F. F., Jr. and G. B. Spanier. 1984. *Recycling the Family: Remarriage after Divorce.* Newbury Park, CA: Sage.

Ganong, I. H., M. Coleman, and D. Mapes. 1990. "A Meta-Analytic Review of Family Structure Stereotypes." *Journal of Marriage and the Family* 52:287–97.

Glendon, M. A. 1989. *The Transformation of Family Law: State, Law, and Family in the United States and Western Europe.* Chicago: University of Chicago Press.

Goldscheider, F. K. and C. Goldscheider. 1993. *Leaving Home before Marriage: Ethnicity, Familism, and Generational Relationships.* Madison: University of Wisconsin Press.

Granovetter, M. S. 1973. "The Strength of Weak Ties." *American Journal of Sociology* 78:1360–80.

Hetherington, E. M. 1987. "Family Relations Six Years after Divorce." Pp. 185–205 in *Remarriage and Stepparenting: Current Research and Theory,* edited by K. Pasley and M. Ihinger-Tallman. New York: Guilford Press.

Hetherington, E. M. and J. D. Arasteh, eds. 1988. *Impact of Divorce, Single Parenting, and Stepparenting on Children.* Hillsdale, NJ: Erlbaum.

Hetherington, E. M. and W. G. Clingempeel, eds. 1992. "Coping with Marital Transitions." *Monographs of the Society for Research in Child Development* 57(2/3).

Hetherington, E. M. and K. M. Jodl. 1993. "Stepfamilies as Settings for Child Development." Paper presented at the National Symposium on Stepfamilies, Pennsylvania State University, October 14–15.

Ihinger-Tallman, M. and K. Pasley. 1987. *Remarriage.* Newbury Park, CA: Sage.

Johnson, C. L. 1988. *Ex. Familia: Grandparents, Parents, and Children Adjust to Divorce.* New Brunswick, NJ: Rutgers University Press.

Keshet, K. J. 1988. "The Remarried Couple: Stresses and Successes." Pp. 29–53 in *Relative Strangers: Studies of Stepfamily Processes,* edited by W. R. Beer. Totowa, NJ: Rowan & Littlefield.

Kiernan, K. E. 1992. "The Impact of Family Disruption in Childhood on Transitions Made in Young Adult Life." *Population Studies* 46:213–34.

Maccoby, E. E. 1992. "Family Structure and Children's Adjustment: Is Quality of Parenting the Major Mediator?" Pp. 230–38 in *Coping with Marital Transitions,* edited by E. M. Hetherington and W. G. Clingempeel. *Monographs of the Society for Research in Child Development* 57(2/3).

Mahoney, M. 1993. Untitled commentary presented at the National Symposium on Stepfamilies, Pennsylvania State University, October 14–15.

Marsiglio, W. 1992. "Stepfamilies with Minor Children Living at Home: Parenting Perceptions and Relationship Quality." *Journal of Family Issues* 13:195–214.

Martin, T. C. and L. L. Bumpass. 1989. "Recent Trends in Marital Disruption." *Demography* 26:37–51.

Papernow, P. 1988. "Stepparent Role Development: From Outsider to Intimate." Pp. 54–82 in *Relative Strangers: Studies of Stepfamily Processes,* edited by W. R. Beer. Totowa, NJ: Rowan & Littlefield.

Parkes, C. M. and J. S. Hinde, eds. 1982. *The Place of Attachment in Human Behavior.* New York: Basic Books.

Pasley, K. and M. Ihinger-Tallman, eds. 1987. *Remarriage and Stepparenting: Current Research and Theory.* New York: Guilford Press.

Schneider, D. M. 1980. *American Kinship: A Cultural Account.* 2d ed. Chicago: University of Chicago Press.

Seltzer, J. A. 1991. "Relationships between Fathers and Children Who Live Apart: The Father's Role after Separation." *Journal of Marriage and the Family* 53:79–101.

Spanier, G. B. and F. F. Furstenberg, Jr. 1987. "Remarriage and Reconstituted Families." Pp. 419–34 in *Handbook of Marriage and the Family,* edited by M. B. Sussman and S. K. Steinmetz. New York: Plenum.

Sweet, J. A. and L. L. Bumpass. 1987. *American Families and Households.* New York: Russell Sage Foundation.

U.S. Bureau of the Census. 1992a. *Households, Families, and Children: A 30-Year Perspective.* Current Population Reports, Series P23-181. Washington, DC: Government Printing Office.

———. 1992b. *Marital Status and Living Arrangements: March 1992.* Current Population Reports, Series P20-468. Washington, DC: Government Printing Office.

———. 1992c. *Marriage, Divorce, and Remarriage in the 1990s.* Current Population Reports, Series P23-180. Washington, DC: Government Printing Office.

White, L. K. 1993. "Stepfamilies over the Life Course: Social Support." Paper presented at the National Symposium on Families, Pennsylvania State University, October 14–15.

White, L. K. and A. Booth. 1985. "The Quality and Stability of Remarriages: The Role of Stepchildren." *American Sociological Review* 50:689–98.

Woodhouse, B. 1993. "Hatching the Egg: A Child-Centered Perspective on Parents' Rights." *Cardozo Law Review* 14:1747–1865.

Wu, L. L. and B. C. Martinson. 1993. "Family Structure and the Risk of a Premarital Birth." *American Sociological Review* 59:210–32.

Zill, N. 1988. "Behavior, Achievement, and Health Problems among Children in Stepfamilies: Findings from a National Survey of Child Health." Pp. 325–68 in *Impact of Divorce, Single Parenting, and Stepparenting on Children,* edited by E. M. Hetherington and J. D. Arasteh. New York: Guilford Press.

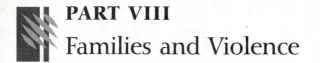

PART VIII
Families and Violence

In this section we examine domestic violence, or the violence that occurs between family members and relational intimates within and outside the household. Domestic violence takes many forms, including dating violence, spousal and partner abuse, child abuse and incest, elder abuse, and violence between same-sex couples. The four types of family violence are physical abuse, verbal abuse, sexual abuse, and neglect. The legal definitions of domestic violence vary, but most tend to focus on physical and sexual abuse, not on verbal abuse and neglect. For example, a common legal definition reads that family violence is: "any assault, battery, sexual assault, sexual battery, or criminal offense resulting in the physical injury or death of one family or household member by another who is or was residing in the same single dwelling unit" (Section 415.602, Florida Statutes). Another problem with legal definitions is that every state has its own definition of domestic violence, which means that judicial policy concerning family violence varies from state to state. Thus, one of the first issues in studying family or domestic violence is getting a clear working definition of the terms used to describe it and identifying behaviors that are consistent between states and policy makers. Moreover, the terms *domestic violence* and *family violence* themselves are seen as problematic by some researchers. These topics will be discussed further in the first reading of this section, "Old Problems and New Directions in the Study of Violence Against Women," by Demie Kurz.

Violence Against Women

In addition to studying definitions of family violence, Kurz examines how family violence research is framed and compartmentalized, which obscures its prevalence and impact. She argues that one problematic way family violence research has been framed is the argument that men and women are equally violent in their families and intimate relationships. That is, some researchers have tried to make domestic violence gender neutral—an assertion that has caused some debate concerning the gendered nature of family violence data (Gelles 1993). Most family sociologists find that domestic violence is gendered: Women are abused more frequently and in different contexts than men. Moreover, the majority of official data-gathering agencies have found women to be the main victims. For example, statistics show that domestic violence is the leading cause of injury to women between ages 15 and 44 in the United States—it injures more women than car accidents, muggings, and rapes combined (FBI Uniform Crime Reports 1991). This gendered nature of family violence has led Kurz and other scholars to conclude that family violence should be identified as violence against women. Similarly, Wardell, Gillespie, and Leffler (1983) state that "when researchers take gender into account, it becomes clear that physical violence against women should be compared, not with elder abuse, but with related types of violence against women, such as rape, marital rape, sexual harassment, and incest, all of which also result from male dominance" (p. 328).

Another important aspect of family violence is domestic violence within diverse cultural groups in the United States. Many abused immigrant and refugee women are isolated because they face access barriers to U.S. legal and social systems. These women frequently are separated from family and community networks that could help them and have difficulties with language and cultural differences between their countries of origin and the United States. Jang, Lee, and Morello-Frosch (1990) have argued that immigration laws disadvantage women. For example, new immigrants who marry can be denied U.S. citizenship if the marriage lasts less than two years. This law makes it difficult for women to leave violent relationships. Jang et al. conclude that the United States needs to provide immigrant women with cultural and language access to women's shelters, to increase the collaboration between immigrant community agencies and domestic violence projects, and to initiate legislative action to better protect battered immigrant women.

The second reading in this section, "Lifting the Veil of Secrecy: Domestic Violence Against South Asian Women in the United States," is by Satya P. Krishnan, Malahat Baig-Amin, Louisa Gilbert, Nabila El-Bassel, and Anne Waters. Krishnan et al. use focus groups to explore and discuss a variety of issues concerning domestic violence among South Asian women, some of whom are recent immigrants. The focus groups define domestic violence, and the women talk about their experiences with violence and their decisions regarding staying in or leaving an abusive relationship. Of particular importance is the number of barriers that South Asian women face in leaving a violent spouse. In addition to the legal and immigration barriers discussed by Jang et al., South Asian women face cultural barriers, such as prescribed marriage and gender roles; community and structural barriers, such as a lack of knowledge about social programs and social and material support; and individual barriers, such as fear for their safety and their children's and the lack of job and language skills. Krishnan et al. conclude that there is much work to be done in South Asian immigrant communities to help women who are experiencing violence.

Violence in Same–Sex Relationships

Another underserved population that is experiencing high rates of domestic violence is gay and lesbian couples. Part of this invisibility is due to the myth that domestic violence occurs only between men and women in family relationships. The reality is that the abuse of power and violence can occur in any human relationship, including those of same-sex couples. The third reading in this section, "Toward a Better Understanding of Lesbian Battering," by Claire M. Renzetti, examines same-sex family violence. Renzetti is a professor of sociology at St. Joseph's University in Philadelphia, and she edits the international interdisciplinary journal *Violence Against Women*. Renzetti began researching lesbian battering in 1985, after a student initially sparked her interest in the topic by giving her a copy of the *Philadelphia Gay News*, which contained an ad for a speak-out on lesbian battering. Renzetti called the contact person listed in the ad to get more information, and after several more phone conversations, she arranged for Renzetti to meet with members of a support group for battered lesbians. Together they developed the project that produced the selection excerpted here from Renzetti's book *Violent Betrayal: Partner Abuse in Lesbian Relationships* (1992). Renzetti also has had the privilege of speaking with many courageous lesbian survivors of same-sex partner abuse, who have come out about their experiences largely to help others. She continues to study, write about, and lecture on lesbian battering and is currently conducting more general research on women's use of violence in intimate relationships. Renzetti concludes her article with similar arguments to Kurz (Reading 29) and Krishnan et al. (Reading 30) that more support services need to be provided to women who are survivors of violence.

Child Abuse and Elder Abuse

The last reading in this section, "Elder Abuse and Child Abuse: A Consideration of Similarities and Differences in Intergenerational Family Violence," by Jill E. Korbin, Georgia J. Anetzberger, and J. Kevin Eckert, turns our attention to other types of domestic violence occurring within the family. This wider lens is important because we tend to think of family violence as occurring only between partners and spouses when, in fact, an abuse of power can occur in any family or intimate relationship. In this reading, Korbin et al. compare elder abuse and child abuse to discover if there are any contextual or situational variables that similarly lead to patterns of abuse. They find that the two types of abuse do share some commonalities as well as some important differences and, from this comparison, make suggestions for changes in family policy.

REFERENCES

FBI. 1991. *Uniform Crime Reports for the United States*. Washington, DC: U.S. Department of Justice.

Gelles, Richard J. 1993. "Through a Sociological Lens: Social Structure and Family Violence." Pp. 31–46 in *Current Controversies on Family Violence*, edited by Richard J. Gelles and Donileen R. Loseke. Thousand Oaks, CA: Sage.

Jang, Deeana, Debbie Lee, and Rachel Morello-Frosch. 1990. "Domestic Violence in the Immigrant and Refugee Community." *Response* 13(4), no. 77:2–6.

Renzetti, Claire M. 1992. *Violent Betrayal: Partner Abuse in Lesbian Relationships*. Thousand Oaks, CA: Sage.

Wardell, L., C. Gillespie, and A. Leffler. 1983. "Science and Violence Against Women." Pp. 69–84 in *The Dark Side of Families: Current Family Violence Research*, edited by D. Finkelhor, Richard Gelles, H. Hotaling, and Murray Straus. Beverly Hills, CA: Sage.

29

OLD PROBLEMS AND NEW DIRECTIONS IN THE STUDY OF VIOLENCE AGAINST WOMEN

DEMIE KURZ

Until recently, scholars rarely acknowledged the topic of violence against women. Fortunately, in the past two decades some researchers have focused their attention on this serious problem. These researchers have made significant progress in understanding this violence, its origins, and its consequences (Bart and Moran 1993; DeKeseredy 1995; Dobash and Dobash 1992; Kurz 1997; Stark and Flitcraft 1996; Yllö 1993). Their findings not only have contributed to our knowledge of this topic but also have been used by activists and reformers to raise awareness of this issue and to bring about changes in public policy (Dobash and Dobash 1992; Yllö 1993).

Despite this progress, however, violence against women all too often remains invisible. Two factors converge to prevent us from seeing how extensively this violence permeates our society and how it can affect all aspects of women's lives. The first is the current conceptualization of this issue in gender-neutral terms. When discussing violence against women, many social science researchers, policymakers, and those in the media use terms such as *family violence, intimate violence,* or *domestic violence* (Jones 1994; Lamb 1991). As they are currently used, these constructs convey the impression that violence is directed by all family members against all other family members, and they mask the facts of who is being violent to whom (Dobash et al. 1992; Lamb 1991, 1995). I argue in this [reading] that although a variety of types of violence occur in the family, the use of gender-neutral terms such as *family violence* can conceal the serious problem of violence against women.

The second major factor that obscures our knowledge of the prevalence of violence against women and its impact on their lives is the compartmentalization of this issue in research and social policy; that is, although more researchers and policymakers are aware of domestic violence as a general problem and refer to it in their work, they all too often fail to investigate how violence may be an important part of the particular problem they study (Kurz 1995). Thus, researchers study the family *or* violence, or work *or* violence, or divorce *or* violence, rather than understand that violence against women is an integral part of women's experiences in all of these social arenas (Kurz 1996).

In this [reading], I examine how these two practices—the framing of violence against women as a problem of family violence and the compartmentalization of this issue in current research—obscure the prevalence and impact of this important problem. It is critical that we obtain accurate data about the nature of violence against women and its impact on all areas of social life, both for research purposes and to create social policies that help women and do not put them at greater risk. This task is particularly urgent, given the prevalence of physical violence against women. It is estimated that 10 percent to 20 percent of women are beaten by a male intimate in a given year, and one quarter to one half will be beaten by a male intimate at least once in their life (Straus and Gelles 1986). Witnessing the physical abuse of their mothers can also have a negative impact on children (Jaffe, Wolfe, and Wilson 1990; "Silent Victims" 1993).

Dominant Conceptualizations of Violence Against Women

As noted, the dominant conceptualization of violence against women as a problem of family violence is widespread. Unfortunately, many social science researchers view physical violence against women as a gender-neutral problem of "family violence," with women being as violent as men (Brinkerhoff and Lupri 1988; Gelles 1993; Gelles and Cornell 1985; Gelles and Straus 1988; McNeely and Mann 1990; McNeely and Robinson-Simpson 1987; Shupe, Stacey, and Hazelwood 1987; Steinmetz and Lucca 1988; Stets 1990; Straus 1993; Straus and Gelles 1990). According to this view, the problem of violence in the family is a problem of "spousal abuse," "assaultive partners," and "violent spouses" (Arias, Samios, and O'Leary 1987), in which husbands and wives resort to physical force to solve their conflicts.

Social science data play an important role in legitimating and responding to social problems in our society. Thus, through its use of terms such as *family violence* or *domestic violence*, social science contributes to the marginalization of the problem of violence against women in our culture. Some have been critical of this terminology (Dobash et al. 1992; Jones 1994; Kurz 1997; Lamb 1991, 1995; Wardell, Gillespie, and Leffler 1983; Yllö 1993), but many social scientists continue to use it, believing that men and women are equally violent toward each other. Because a widespread knowledge of the gendered structure of power is absent in our society, few discourses provide an alternative view of the gender-based nature of violence against women.[1]

Why do social scientists continue to use gender-neutral paradigms when so much evidence indicates that it is principally women who are battered? I argue that this happens when researchers adopt models of family behavior and instruments for measuring violence that are based on misleading assumptions about the family. Family violence researchers typically interpret their data within gender-neutral frameworks such as systems theory (Gelles 1993). In this theoretical perspective, the "family system" operates to "maintain, escalate, or reduce levels of violence in families" (Gelles 1993:36). These researchers argue that all family members are part of the family system, contribute to family patterns and events, and bear responsibility for what happens in a family. Although all family members, like all individuals, are responsible for their actions, this paradigm overlooks the fact that gender norms and gendered relations of power enter into and partially constitute all social relations and activities and pervade the entire social context in which a person lives. In the case of marriage, norms promoting male dominance and males' right to use force in heterosexual relationships set the parameters for behavior in marriage.

Family violence researchers also claim that family norms are affected by norms of the wider society. They believe that a "culture of violence" in the United States and the stressful nature of modern life contribute to the creation of family violence and that violent people are also influenced by different "subcultures of violence" (Gelles 1993; Steinmetz 1987). These researchers cite evidence of a widespread cultural acceptance of violence in television programming, folklore, and fairy tales and in surveys showing widespread public acceptance of violence in U.S. culture (Straus, Gelles, and Steinmetz 1980). They believe that husbands and wives come to accept these norms, which condone violence as a means of solving conflict. The problem with this perspective, however, is that the culture of violence framework fails to explain why, overwhelmingly, women are the targets of male violence.

Finally, those who believe that stress is a critical factor in causing violence believe that violence in the contemporary U.S. family is caused by a variety of social-structural factors, including stresses from difficult working conditions, unemployment, financial insecurity, and health problems (Gelles and Cornell 1985; Gelles and Straus 1988). Once again, however, this explanation does not account for why women are the primary targets of the violence. Many women, as well as men, experience stress but do not use violence.

Researchers who use family violence frameworks base their conclusions on data produced by research instruments called the Conflict Tactics Scales (CTS; Straus 1979). Authors of surveys based on these scales conclude that "women are about as violent within the family as men" and that women as well as men are perpetrators and victims of physical violence. I argue that these scales produce misleading data. The CTS require respondents to identify those conflict resolution tactics, listed in the scales, that they have used in the previous year. These range from nonviolent tactics (calm discussion) to the most violent tactics (use of a knife or gun). Using these scales, researchers (Straus and Gelles 1986) find similar percentages of husbands and wives using violent tactics. The CTS have been used in many surveys here and abroad, and Straus' findings have been replicated in many surveys (Brinkerhoff and Lupri 1988; Nisonoff and Bitman 1979; Stets 1990), including studies of dating violence (Arias et al. 1987; DeMaris 1987; Lane and Gwartney-Gibbs 1985).

Findings from the 1985 National Family Violence Survey (Straus 1993), based on women's responses to the CTS, show that both wife and husband were violent in 48.6 percent of cases, the husband only was violent in 25.9 percent of cases, and the wife only was violent in 25.5 percent of cases. Straus (1993) concluded from these data that "regardless of whether the analysis is based on all assaults, or is focused on dangerous assaults, about as many women as men attacked a spouse who had not hit them during the one-year referent period" (p. 94). In earlier studies based on the CTS, Straus et al. (1980) found that 12.8 percent of husbands used violent tactics in conflicts with their wives and that 11.7 percent of wives directed these tactics against their husbands. Straus et al. (1980) concluded that whereas "traditionally men have been considered more aggressive and violent than women," looking at the couples in which the husband was the only one to use violence and those in which both used violence, "the most common situation was that in which both used violence" (p. 36).

Researchers who use a violence-against women framework (Berk et al. 1983; Dobash and Dobash 1979; Dobash et al. 1992; Kurz 1993; Pleck et al. 1977–1978; Saunders 1988; Stark and Flitcraft 1985; Yllö 1993) argue that the data claiming an equivalence of male–female violence, particularly data based on the CTS, are flawed and that the CTS fail to provide reliable data. They believe that the validity of the CTS is undermined for several reasons. First, the continuum of violence in the scales is so broad that it fails to discriminate among very different kinds of violence (Dobash and Dobash 1979; Dobash et al. 1992; Stark and Flitcraft 1985). Further, the scales do not ask what acts were done in self-defense, who initiated the violence, or who was injured. If these questions were asked, they believe, the picture would be clear: Overwhelmingly, men abuse women and women use violence primarily for self-defense (Breines and Gordon 1983; Brush 1990; Dobash and Dobash 1979; Dobash et al. 1992; Pleck et al. 1977–1978; Saunders 1988, 1989).

Critics of the CTS argue that data from interview studies show that when women use violence, it is typically in self-defense. Saunders (1989) found that, in the vast majority of cases, women attributed the violence to self-defense and fighting back. Emery, Lloyd, and Castleton (1989), in an interview study based on a small sample of women victims of dating violence, found that most women spoke of self-defense. They also found that women spoke of using violence in frustration and anger at being dominated by their partners and in retaliation for their partners' violent behavior. Second, there may be significant male–female differences in self-reporting. Some researchers argue that men are more likely than women to underreport the extent of their violent acts (Okun 1986).

Violence-against-women researchers also point out that the CTS focus narrowly on counting acts of violence (Dobash et al. 1992; Yllö 1993). Such a focus overlooks related patterns of abuse in relationships, including psychological abuse and sexual abuse, and does not address other means of nonviolent intimidation and domination, including verbal abuse, use of suicide threats, or use of violence against property, pets, or children or other relatives (Yllö 1993). Although it is important to focus on acts of violence, and although stopping all violent acts is a very important goal, it is important to remember that it would hardly stop abuse. Decreasing the levels of abuse would require reducing the inequality in the distribution of power and control in relationships.

Unfortunately, numbers that claim violence between men and women is "equal" and "mutual" have also been used against women to cut funding for battered women's shelters (Lewin 1992; Loseke 1992). Many fear that claims about mutual violence can be used to deny violence against women in the creation of custody and visitation agreements (Fineman 1995) and to absolve social institutions of responsibility for failing to respond to violence against women (Kurz 1993). Still others fear that the family violence perspective will reinforce the individualist bias in the field of counseling—that counselors will focus on clients' individual and personal problems without identifying the inequality between men and women, which is the context for battering (Adams 1988). They disagree with those family violence proponents who argue that violence is caused primarily by frustration, poor social skills, or inability to control anger.

By taking the family as the basis of their analysis, family violence researchers who use the frameworks and methods described here obscure the issue of violence against women. Although it is valuable for some purposes to take the family as a unit of analysis, it is misleading to assume that the family exists predominantly above and beyond the interests of its members. Men, women, and children do frequently act together as a unit in social and family activities; however, they also have different and potentially conflicting interests. The family is highly gendered. The actions of members are influenced at every point by gender norms and opportunities. When researchers take gender into account, it becomes clear that physical violence against women should be compared, not with elder abuse and child abuse, but with related types of violence against women, such as rape, marital rape, sexual harassment, and incest, all of which also result from male dominance (Wardell et al. 1983).

Compartmentalization of the Study of Violence Against Women

Another factor that prevents researchers from presenting the full extent of violence against women in social life is the compartmentalization of the study of this violence; that is, they view it and analyze it as distinct and separate from other issues. As noted earlier, researchers study women in the family, or women in the workplace, or violence against women in separate categories and fail to see the impact of violence on many aspects of women's lives. In this section, I demonstrate the impact of violence against women on two areas of social life that we do not usually associate with this issue: (a) women's experiences of divorce and (b) the lives of poor women. For women in divorce situations and for poor women, violence can seriously threaten their physical and economic well-being.

Divorce

Divorce is widespread in contemporary society and has a significant impact on family life and on social life more generally (Furstenberg and Cherlin 1991). Thus, it is particularly unfortunate that the study of divorce typically fails to consider violence in the family or violence against women (Kurz 1995). In my study (Kurz 1995), divorced mothers reported experiencing high rates of violence at the hands of their husbands during their marriages. They also stated that this violence had a significant impact on their experience of the entire divorce process. The study and the interviews focused on how women viewed the ending of their marriages, how they managed on their reduced incomes, how they negotiated for resources from ex-husbands and the state, and what custody and visitation agreements they made. For these women, violence played a role in all aspects of the divorce process.

My study of divorce is based on interviews with a random sample of 129 mothers of diverse backgrounds.[2] These women reported that they experienced high rates of violence during marriage: 50 percent of women experienced violence at least two or three times in their marriages; 16 percent experienced violence once; and 4 percent experienced violence after the separation. Of the 50 percent who experienced violence at least two or three times, 37 percent experienced serious and frequent violence (defined as more than three incidents of violence, or one very serious incident of violence).[3] These rates are higher than those found among married couples, and they are comparable with those found in other studies of divorcing women.[4] Interestingly, however, most studies of divorce do not analyze the impact of violence on the divorce process; they cite violence as another "factor" in divorce and usually not an important one (Ahrons and Rodgers 1987; Emery 1988; Price and McKenny 1988).

Women in my study cited reasons for the violence that were similar to those reported in other studies (Dobash and Dobash 1992; Yllö 1993). Women most commonly reported that violence occurred when they attempted to act independently. For example, women reported violence when they "started to change" or when their ex-husbands found that things did not go their way, when dinner was late, and when certain types of food were not available. These women also spoke of generally controlling behavior on the part of their ex-husbands, who sometimes didn't allow them to have friends, to go to work, or to go back to school. Some said they were not allowed to be in the company of other men because their husbands thought this would lead to sexual relationships. The following quote from a woman illustrates this point: "He was violent when I would go out and do things on my own. He didn't like that. For example, I went out and found myself a job. He didn't want that. He wanted me to always be home. My father gave me a car and I would take the kids places. He didn't like that."

These divorced women reported that violence affected their lives in several ways. First, they reported violence as one major reason that they left their marriages: 19 percent of women reported domestic violence as the reason for their divorce; most women reported leaving because they believed that witnessing the violence had begun to have a negative impact on the children or because they experienced a particularly serious incident of abuse. As one woman said: "All the violence was hard on my son. He saw me injured when he was 2 years old. He saw a lot. It's affected my son. He's mixed up. I left because I was afraid of what this was doing for my son." The women who left because of violence were among those who experienced the most repeated incidents of violence. Some of these women reported staying in violent relationships longer than they wanted to because they had nowhere to go; others did not leave sooner because they could not find work and feared they would not be able to support themselves and their children. Several women spoke of having stayed in relationships for extended periods of time because they wanted to try to make their marriages work.

Second, some women reported that violence played a significant role in their negotiations for child support, custody, and visitation. These women stated that their experience of violence during the marriage or separation made them fearful during divorce negotiations. In fact, 30 percent of women stated they were fearful during their negotiations for child support, and 38 percent reported fear during negotiations for custody. In both cases, these fears were related to women's experiences of violence during marriage. A statistically significant relationship was found between women's experience of violence during marriage and separation and their fear during negotiations for child support and for custody. The more serious or frequent the violence these women experienced, the more fearful they were during these negotiations.

The 38 percent of women who said they were fearful during negotiations for custody spoke of their ex-husbands' harassing behavior. Some women reported that their ex-husbands threatened to take the children. One woman said: "I was fearful the whole time [I was negotiating for child support]. He was always threatening. By this time, I had been to abuse court. He was under orders not to come near the house, the kids, or me. The teachers were notified. . . . I was terrified he would take the kids." Several other women stated that their husbands had fought for and won custody of the children even though the mothers believed that the fathers didn't really want custody. Arendell (1995) reports that substantial numbers of fathers undertake serious legal challenges to obtain custody of their children, their goal being not actually to obtain custody of their children but to try to "balance out the power of their former wives by prohibiting maternal custody, which was the prime example of men's losses and women's disproportionate authority in divorce" (p. 81). Two women reported that their husbands had kidnapped their children. Some women remained fearful of additional events of violence while they were negotiating for custody, and a few had court orders of protection mandating that their husbands stay away from the family homes. As is described below, their fears led some of these women to compromise on their demands for resources during divorce negotiations because they were afraid that if they did not give in on resources, then they could lose custody of their children.

Even for those mothers who resolved custody issues, however, this was not necessarily the end of their conflicts with their ex-husbands over children. Many of the women who faced harassment during negotiations for custody also experienced harassment during negotiations for agreements about when the fathers would visit the children. In fact, 29 percent of mothers who stated that visitation took place described conflict with their ex-husbands over visitation,[5] a rate of conflict similar to that found in other studies (Maccoby and Mnookin 1992). These mothers believed that the fathers were using visitation as a way to check up on and control them, and some were afraid that their ex-husbands would be violent again. These mothers, many of whom had experienced violence in their marriages, reported that they wanted less, not more, visitation.

In addition to problems with custody and visitation, indications are strong that their fears caused some of these women to reduce their requests for child support. A statistically significant relationship was found between women's fears during negotiations for child support and for custody and their receipt of child support. Only 34 percent of women who reported being fearful during negotiations for custody, for example, received regular child support, in contrast with 60 percent of those who did not report fear during negotiations for child support. The reports of women who received no child support because they were fearful confirm this view. They spoke of being afraid that their ex-husbands would become physically violent if they tried to get child support, and a few mentioned being afraid that their ex-husbands would kidnap the children. Others reported that, because of their fear, they compromised and accepted a child support award that was lower than what they were entitled to. Still others gave up trying to obtain increases in their child support awards at a later time, when they were entitled to additional funds because their expenses for their children had increased.

The role of violence in divorce has serious ramifications for our divorce policies (Cahn 1991). In the case of child custody after a divorce, the current recommended policy is automatic joint legal custody, which gives the non-custodial parent, typically the father, the right to participate in important decisions about his child's life, such as education and religious training, even if he does not have physical custody of the child (Fineman 1995; Maccoby and Mnookin 1992). The high level of violence toward women in marriages and the ongoing serious conflict between a significant minority of couples after marriage, however, make it imperative that guarantee of mandatory joint residential custody not be automatic. Further, the law must be ready to limit or deny access to fathers who use visitation for harassment or who engage in other threatening or dangerous behavior. Courts should consider evidence of abuse at every point in negotiations for custody and visitation. Further, because passing laws does not guarantee that judges will apply or enforce them, judges should be trained about domestic violence and its legal, sociological, and psychological implications (Arendell 1995). Similarly, because some state legislators continue to promote mandatory joint physical custody, ignoring how much harm this could inflict on women and children, they too should be trained about violence against women.

As for child support policies, to increase fathers' financial participation, states have begun to require mothers to locate and identify the fathers of their children in order to obtain child support, a procedure called *paternity establishment* (Roberts 1994). Requiring mothers to identify fathers in order to get child support is part of a general trend to try to make fathers take more financial responsibility for their children. Unfortunately, laws such as these can put an undue burden on mothers who have serious conflicts with their former partners, especially those women who have suffered physical abuse. Recent research has demonstrated that many women remain in danger of experiencing violence after a separation (Kurz 1996).

In conclusion, we see that violence against women can play an important role in the divorce process; however, as noted earlier, this fact is not addressed in most of the divorce literature. The violence literature, in contrast, does document how women leave marriages and intimate relationships with male partners because of violence. This literature has not been integrated into the literature on divorce, however, or into that of many other fields. Although the rate of male violence toward women is high, and therefore it is logical to think that we would find a high rate of violence reported by divorced women, we are accustomed to thinking of violence as a distinct issue, separate from other important areas of study. We must look for evidence of violence against women in all aspects of our research and our social policies.

Women's Poverty

In the course of my research on mothers and divorce, I found a second arena where violence had a serious impact on the lives of women but where it had not been addressed — the study of poverty. As in the case of violence and divorce, violence and poverty are not usually studied together, and thus violence is invisible in the lives of poor women. Researchers and activists have emphasized the fact that women across a range of backgrounds and income levels have experienced male violence.[6] As is described in this section, however, increasing evidence indicates that poor women experience even higher rates of violence than other women.

In my study, poorer women experienced the most violence, with the women on welfare, the poorest women in the sample, experiencing more violence than any other group: 71 percent of these women reported experiencing violence at least two or three times during their marriages or separations, in contrast with the 50 percent average for the sample. In addition to experiencing the most violence, welfare women experienced more serious violence (defined as more than three incidents of violence, or one very serious incident of violence) than women of any other group: 58 percent of these women experienced serious violence, whereas 37 percent of the sample as a whole experienced serious violence.

Large-scale survey data also show that the poorer women are, the more likely they are to experience violence at the hands of their intimate partners. According to the U.S. Department of Justice's National Crime Victimization Survey (1995), "Women with an annual family income under $10,000 were more likely to report having experienced violence by an intimate than those with an income of $10,000 or more" (p. 4). Further, rates of violence at the hands of intimates decrease with each increase in income category. Thus, the rates of "violent victimizations" per 1,000 females age 12 or older for those with an annual family income of $9,999 or less was 19.9 percent; for those with annual family incomes of $10,000 to $14,999, 13.3 percent; $15,000 to $19,999, 10.9 percent; $20,000 to $29,999, 9.5 percent; $30,000 to $49,999, 5.4 percent; and $50,000 or more, 4.5 percent. In their nationwide survey of the use of violence by married couples, Straus and Gelles (1986) found that the lower a woman's education, income, and occupational levels, the more likely she is to be battered. Other evidence on the rates of violence experienced by poor women comes from recently publicized data on the high levels of violence experienced by women who have been on Aid to Families with Dependent Children (AFDC), or welfare. Several studies have reported that roughly two thirds of women on welfare have experienced violence in their lifetime (Davis and Kraham 1995:1145; McCormack Institute & Center for Survey Research 1997; Raphael 1996). In a study of victims of violence in Massachusetts, researchers found that 20 percent of current welfare recipients had been abused by former or current boyfriends or husbands within the past 12 months (McCormack Institute & Center for Survey Research 1997).

What is the reason for the higher levels of violence reported by low-income women? Is it the case that poorer women are more forthcoming about the amount of violence they experience, or that more of them report the violence to the police because they have less access to other kinds of legal assistance? This is always a possibility, but at this point no data are available on this question. It is also possible that something about the circumstances of those living in poverty contributes to the higher rate of male violence. For example, men from lower-income groups may have a stronger belief in the legitimacy of violence than other men because they typically hold more traditional gender ideologies than other men. It is not clear, however, that lower-income men actually behave in more gendered ways than other men (Hochschild 1989).

Another explanation for the higher rates of violence reported by poorer women could be that lower-income men have fewer ways of controlling their partners than other men do. The higher men's social class, the more ability they have to control their female partners through their greater economic resources. Many women in all social classes in my sample volunteered that their husbands tried to control decisions about family life and family finances. Interviews did not specifically ask about this kind of behavior, but many women volunteered that they thought their husbands were controlling and that they did not like this. So, although according to women's volunteered statements, men of all different backgrounds were controlling, perhaps higher-income men, who control greater amounts of family income and property than poorer men do, believed that they did not need to resort to violence to control their female partners and to control family decisions.

Whatever the reason for the high rates of violence they experience, when poor women leave violent relationships, they often have few resources and experience particular hardships. Davis and Kraham (1995) point out that batterers commonly isolate their partners from financial resources. Many battered women do not have access to cash, checking accounts, or charge accounts (Lerman 1984). When poor women do leave violent relationships, they have difficulty gaining access to secure employment, the most important ticket to economic well-being. When women leave relationships and seek job training, their batterers may continue to harass and abuse them. A study conducted by the Taylor Institute in Chicago demonstrated that violence can inhibit or prevent poor women from participating in welfare-to-work programs and from obtaining employment (Raphael 1995, 1996). When women do gain employment, abusers may continue to harass them on the job (Zorza 1991). Given these problems, it is not surprising that the rate of unemployment among battered women is higher than that among other women (Strube and Barbour 1983). Homelessness is a particular problem for battered women, as evidenced by the fact that a significant portion of the homeless population is battered women (Zorza 1991).

In my sample, abused women who were poor had a particular need for resources. Some had lost their homes after the divorce because they had no money to pay for mortgages, and in a few cases their ex-husbands kept the homes and the women were forced to leave. Some women had not been allowed to work while they lived with their batterers and so had no job skills or experience. As one woman said: "I was not allowed to go out. I wasn't really allowed to talk on the phone. . . . I wasn't allowed to have a job. I wasn't allowed to have friends." Almost none of these women received child support from their batterers. For many, welfare assistance was critical as they pulled their lives back together, got more education and training, and looked for work.

The data presented here have implications for both research and policy. They demonstrate that when we study any issue related to poverty, we must look for evidence of violence against women. These data also indicate serious problems with "welfare reform" as it has been recently enacted (Fineman 1996). Elimination of the entitlement to welfare has made it much more difficult for women to live outside marriage. We must change this situation and provide all mothers, especially poor mothers, with more social welfare measures: day care, flexible working hours, health care, jobs with a decent minimum wage, health, pension and other benefits, child allowances, and basic income guarantees. We must also, of course, pass stricter enforcement measures to protect women against abusers.

The new federal welfare bill did stipulate that states may consider abused women to be exempt from some of the bill's requirements, such as the provision that women may receive assistance for only 5 years. Unfortunately, however, the federal government made this option only voluntary. Because states can exempt only 20 percent of eligible people from welfare, and because other people also deserve exemptions, many abused women will not be granted a reprieve from the requirements of the new welfare system (Vobejda 1997). This is a particularly serious situation because, as noted above, so many women who qualify for welfare have been abused by husbands and boyfriends and may be at further risk of abuse.

In concluding, I raise one note of caution about focusing attention on poor women and violence. Drawing attention to the high levels of violence that poor women experience raises the possibility that some people will use this fact to further stigmatize poor women. The consequences of violence for poor women are so great, however, that we must focus our attention on this problem while being clear that levels of violence are unacceptably high for all women.

Conclusion

The data presented in this chapter have serious implications for both research and policy. Researchers must develop new paradigms that are not based on gender-neutral concepts (e.g., family violence) but that take violence against women as their frame of reference, as well as other types of violence against women, including rape and sexual harassment. Similarly, researchers must develop new instruments and measures that specify exactly who initiated the violence in intimate relationships, how serious the acts of violence were, and what the consequences were.

Researchers must also integrate the study of violence into other areas of research. As demonstrated in this chapter, despite greater recognition of issues of violence against women, many researchers still compartmentalize this issue and still think of violence as an activity or a problem distinct from other issues that affect women. The result is that we fail to see how significant a role violence can play in women's lives. The examples given here of the role of violence in the divorce process and in the lives of poor women show how important it is to look for violence in all areas of social life. Data presented here demonstrate that male violence can deprive divorced women and poor women of resources and can make their lives even more difficult. Policymakers must understand the extent to which violence affects women in all areas of social life and develop more wide-reaching policies to reduce the incidence of this pervasive problem.

ENDNOTES

1. For further debates on the family violence perspective and the violence against women perspective, see Straus (1993) and Kurz (1993).
2. The sample included 61 percent white women, 35 percent black women, and 3 percent Hispanic women. Interviews lasted from 1½ to 3 hours and included both

open-ended and fixed-choice questions. Women were also asked questions about violence. A further discussion of the methodology is available in Kurz (1995).

3. In addition, 4 percent of women experienced violence during the separation only, and an additional 13 percent experienced violence during both the marriage and the separation. The rate of violence that women experienced during the separation was probably even higher, but one question on the survey was worded in such a way that an accurate determination of the number of these women could not be made. The levels of violence that women experienced were determined by using a modified version of the Conflict Tactics Scales (Straus 1979).

4. In a study of 362 separating husbands and wives, Ellis and Stuckless (1993) reported that over 40 percent of separating wives and 17 percent of separating husbands stated they were injured by their partners at some time during the relationship. Studies by Fields (1978) and by Parker and Schumacher (1977) found that between 50 percent and 70 percent of divorcing wives reported being assaulted by their husbands at least once during their marriages. According to Schulman (1979), two thirds of divorced women in a Harris poll reported violence in their former relationships.

5. Altogether, 25 percent of women in the sample reported conflict over visitation. The 25 percent figure includes women who reported no visitation at all. For those women who reported visitation, 29 percent reported conflict.

6. For example, some of the early and most widely read texts on battering and family violence never mention social class issues. See Dobash and Dobash (1979), Pagelow (1984), and Straus et al. (1980).

REFERENCES

Adams, D. 1988. "Treatment Models of Men Who Batter." Pp. 176–99 in *Feminist Perspectives on Wife Abuse,* edited by K. Ylló and M. Bograd. Newbury Park, CA: Sage.

Ahrons, C. and R. Rodgers. 1987. *Divorced Families: A Multidisciplinary Developmental View.* New York: Norton.

Arendell, T. 1995. *Fathers and Divorce.* Newbury Park, CA: Sage.

Arias, I., M. Samios, and K. D. O'Leary. 1987. "Prevalence and Correlates of Physical Aggression during Courtship." *Journal of Interpersonal Violence* 2:82–90.

Bart, P. and E. Moran, eds. 1993. *Violence Against Women.* Newbury Park, CA: Sage.

Berk, R., S. F. Berk, D. Loseke, and D. Rauma. 1983. "Mutual Combat and Other Family Violence Myths." Pp. 197–212 in *The Dark Side of Families: Current Family Violence Research,* edited by D. Finkelhor, R. Gelles, H. Hotaling, and M. Straus. Beverly Hills, CA: Sage.

Breines, W. and L. Gordon. 1983. "The New Scholarship on Family Violence." *Signs: Journal of Women in Culture and Society* 8:490–531.

Brinkerhoff, M. and E. Lupri. 1988. "Interspousal Violence." *Canadian Journal of Sociology* 13:407–34.

Brush, L. D. 1990. "Violent Acts and Injurious Outcomes in Married Couples: Methodological Issues in the National Survey of Families and Households." *Gender & Society* 4:56–67.

Cahn, N. 1991. "Civil Images of Battered Women: The Impact of Domestic Violence on Child Custody Decisions." *Vanderbilt Law Review* 44:1041–97.

Davis, M. F. and S. J. Kraham. 1995. "Protecting Women's Welfare in the Face of Violence." *Fordham Urban Law Journal* 22(4):1141–57.

DeKeseredy, W. K. 1995. "Enhancing the Quality of Survey Data on Woman Abuse: Examples from a Canadian Study." *Violence Against Women* 1(2):158–73.

DeMaris, A. 1987. "The Efficacy of a Spousal Abuse Model in Accounting for Courtship Violence. *Journal of Family Issues* 8:291–305.

Dobash, R. E. and R. Dobash. 1979. *Violence Against Wives.* New York: Free Press.

———. 1992. *Women, Violence, and Social Change.* London: Routledge & Kegan Paul.

Dobash, R., R. E. Dobash, M. Wilson, and M. Daly. 1992. "The Myth of Sexual Symmetry in Marital Violence." *Social Problems* 39(1):71–91.

Ellis, D. and N. Stuckless. 1993. *Hitting and Splitting: Predatory Preseparation Abuse among Separating Spouses* (Mediation Pilot Project Report #7). Submitted to the Attorney General of Ontario.

Emery, R. 1988. *Marriage, Divorce, and Children's Adjustment.* Newbury Park, CA: Sage.

Emery, R., S. Lloyd, and A. Castleton. 1989. "Why Women Hit: A Feminist Perspective." Paper presented at the Annual Conference of the National Conference on Family Relations, New Orleans, LA.

Fields, M. D. 1978. "Wife-Beating: Facts and Figures." *Victimology* 2(3–4):643–47.

Fineman, M. 1995. *The Neutered Mother, the Sexual Family, and Other 20th-Century Tragedies.* New York: Routledge.

———. 1996. "The Nature of Dependencies and Welfare 'Reform.'" *Santa Clara Law Review* 36:1401–25.

Furstenberg, E. F., Jr. and A. Cherlin. 1991. *Divided Families.* Cambridge, MA: Harvard University Press.

Gelles, R. 1993. "Through a Sociological Lens: Social Structure and Family Violence." In *Current Controversies on Family Violence,* edited by R. Gelles and D. Loseke. Newbury Park, CA: Sage.

Gelles, R. and C. Cornell. 1985. *Intimate Violence in Families.* Beverly Hills, CA: Sage.

Gelles, R. and M. Straus. 1988. *Intimate Violence.* New York: Simon & Schuster.

Hochschild, A. 1989. *The Second Shift.* New York: Viking.

Jaffe, P., D. Wolfe, and S. K. Wilson. 1990. *Children of Battered Women.* Vol. 21, *Developmental Clinical Psychology and Psychiatry.* Newbury Park, CA: Sage.

Jones, A. 1994. *Next Time, She'll Be Dead: Battering and How to Stop It.* Boston: Beacon.

Kurz, D. 1993. "Physical Assaults by Husbands: A Major Social Problem." Pp. 88–103 in *Current Controversies on Family Violence,* edited by R. Gelles and D. Loseke. Newbury Park, CA: Sage.

———. 1995. *For Richer, for Poorer: Mothers Confront Divorce.* New York: Routledge.

———. 1996. "Separation, Divorce, and Woman Abuse." *Violence against Women* 2(1): 63–81.

———. 1997. "Violence Against Women or Family Violence? Current Debates and Future Directions." In *Gender Violence: Interdisciplinary Perspectives,* edited by L. L. O'Toole and J. R. Schiffman. New York: New York University Press.

Lamb, S. 1991. "Acts without Agents: An Analysis of Linguistic Avoidance in Journal Articles on Men Who Batter Women." *American Journal of Orthopsychiatry* 61(2): 250–57.

———. 1995. "Blaming the Perpetrator: Language That Distorts Reality in Newspaper Articles on Men Battering Women." *Psychology of Women Quarterly* 19:209–20.

Lane, K. E. and P. A. Gwartney-Gibbs. 1985. "Violence in the Context of Dating and Sex. *Journal of Family Issues* 6:45–59.

Lerman, L. G. 1984. "Model State Act: Remedies for Domestic Abuse." *Harvard Journal on Legislation* 21:61, 90.

Lewin, T. 1992. "Battered Men Sounding Equal-Rights Battle Cry." *New York Times,* April 20, p. 12.

Loseke, D. 1992. *The Battered Woman and Shelters: The Social Construction of Wife Abuse.* New York: State University of New York Press.

Maccoby, E. E. and R. H. Mnookin. *Dividing the Child: Social and Legal Dilemmas of Custody.* Cambridge, MA: Harvard University Press.

McCormack Institute & Center for Survey Research. 1997. *In Harm's Way? Domestic Violence, AFDC Receipt, and Welfare Reform in Massachusetts.* Boston: University of Massachusetts.

McNeely, R. L. and C. Mann. 1990. "Domestic Violence Is a Human Issue." *Journal of Interpersonal Violence* 5:129–32.

McNeely, R. L. and G. Robinson-Simpson. 1987. "The Truth about Domestic Violence: A Falsely Framed Issue." *Social Work* 32:485–90.

Nisonoff, L. and I. Bitman. 1979. "Spousal Abuse: Incidence and Relationship to Selected Demographic Variables." *Victimology* 4:131–40.

Okun, L. 1986. *Woman Abuse.* Albany: State University of New York Press.

Pagelow, M. D. 1984. *Family Violence.* New York: Praeger.

Parker, B. and D. Schumacher. 1977. "The Battered Wife Syndrome and Violence in the Nuclear Family of Origin: A Controlled Pilot Study." *American Journal of Public Health* 67(8):760–61.

Pleck, E., J. H. Pleck, M. Grossman, and P. Bart. 1977–1978. "The Battered Data Syndrome: A Comment on Steinmetz' Article." *Victimology* 2:680–84.

Price, S. J. and P. McKenny. 1988. *Divorce.* Newbury Park, CA: Sage.

Raphael, J. 1995. *Domestic Violence: Telling the Untold Welfare-to-Work Story.* Chicago: Taylor Institute.

———. 1996. *Prisoners of Abuse: Domestic Violence and Welfare Receipt.* Chicago: Taylor Institute.

Roberts, P. G. 1994. "Child Support Orders: Problems with Enforcement." *The Future of Children: Children and Divorce* 4(1):101–20.

Saunders, D. 1988. "Wife Abuse, Husband Abuse, or Mutual Combat?" Pp. 90–113 in *Feminist Perspectives on Wife Abuse,* edited by K. Yllö and M. Bograd. Newbury Park, CA: Sage.

———. 1989. "Who Hits First, and Who Hurts Most? Evidence for the Greater Victimization of Women in Intimate Relationships." Paper presented at the American Society of Criminology, Reno.

Schulman, M. 1979. *A Survey of Spousal Violence Against Women in Kentucky* (Study #792701 for the Kentucky Commission on Women). Washington, DC: U.S. Department of Justice.

Shupe, A., W. Stacey, and R. Hazelwood. 1987. *Violent Men, Violent Couples: The Dynamics of Domestic Violence.* Lexington, MA: Lexington Books.

"Silent Victims: Children Who Witness Violence." 1993. *Journal of the American Medical Association* 269(2):262–64.

Stark, E. and A. Flitcraft. 1985. "Woman Battering, Child Abuse, and Social Heredity: What Is the Relationship?" Pp. 147–71 in *Marital Violence,* edited by N. Johnson. Boston: Routledge & Kegan Paul.

———. 1996. *Women at Risk: Domestic Violence and Women's Health.* Thousand Oaks, CA: Sage.

Steinmetz, S. 1987. "Family Violence: Past, Present, and Future." Pp. 725–65 in *Handbook of Marriage and the Family,* edited by M. Sussman and S. Steinmetz. New York: Plenum.

Steinmetz, S. and J. Lucca. 1988. "Husband Battering." Pp. 233–46 in *Handbook of Family Violence,* edited by V. Van Hasselt, R. Morrison, A. Bellack, and M. Hersen. New York: Plenum.

Stets, J. 1990. "Verbal and Physical Aggression in Marriage." *Journal of Marriage and the Family* 52:501–14.

Straus, M. 1979. "Measuring Intrafamily Conflict and Violence: The Conflict Tactics (CT) Scales." *Journal of Marriage and the Family* 41:75–88.

———. 1993. "Physical Assaults by Wives: A Major Social Problem." Pp. 67–87 in *Current Controversies on Family Violence,* edited by R. Gelles and D. Loseke. Newbury Park, CA: Sage.

Straus, M. and R. Gelles. 1986. "Societal Change and Change in Family Violence from 1975 to 1985 as Revealed by Two National Surveys." *Journal of Marriage and the Family* 48:465–79.

———. 1990. "How Violent Are American Families: Estimates for the National Family Violence Resurvey and Other Studies." Pp. 95–112 in *Physical Violence in*

American Families, edited by M. Straus and R. Gelles. New Brunswick, NJ: Transaction Press.

Straus, M., R. Gelles, and S. Steinmetz. 1980. *Behind Closed Doors: Violence in the American Family.* Garden City, NY: Doubleday.

Strube, M. J. and L. S. Barbour. 1983. "The Decision to Leave an Abusive Relationship: Economic and Psychological Commitment." *Journal of Marriage and the Family* 45: 785–93.

U.S. Department of Justice, Bureau of Justice Statistics. 1995. August. *Special Report, National Crime Victimization Survey, Violence Against Women: Estimates from the Redesigned Survey.* Washington, DC: Author.

Vobejda, B. 1997. "Welfare Waiver for Abused Women May Cost States." *Washington Post,* April 12, p. A10.

Wardell, L., C. Gillespie, and A. Leffler. 1983. "Science and Violence Against Women." Pp. 69–84 in *The Dark Side of Families: Current Family Violence Research,* edited by D. Finkelhor, R. Gelles, H. Hotaling, and M. Straus. Beverly Hills, CA: Sage.

Yllö, K. 1993. "Through a Feminist Lens: Gender, Power, and Violence." *Current Controversies on Family Violence,* edited by R. Gelles and D. Loseke. Newbury Park, CA: Sage.

Zorza, J. 1991. "Woman Battering: A Major Cause of Homelessness." *Clearinghouse Review* 25:421.

30

LIFTING THE VEIL OF SECRECY
Domestic Violence Against South Asian Women in the United States

SATYA P. KRISHNAN • MALAHAT BAIG–AMIN
LOUISA GILBERT • NABILA EL–BASSEL • ANNE WATERS

I would always be in fear. Even though I worked, I had to be home at a certain time. Even if I was five minutes late or if there was a traffic jam or something, I could not tell him that. I was in fear all the time. I was in fear that I would lose my mind if I go home late. I constantly made plans to be home on time.

— AN INTERVIEWEE'S COMMENTS

The image of a woman being abused by those who claim to love and honor her is horrifying. However, such abuse is one that many of us have heard of or, perhaps, experienced in our own lives. Domestic violence has been a part of our living landscape since the beginning of time and is still a significant component of many women's lives. Despite their abusive domestic circumstances, many women strive to work quietly, raise children, care for their families, and try to establish a "normal" existence in society.

Owing to the efforts of many dedicated community activists, the prevalence of domestic violence among South Asian women in the United States is no longer a secret. The efforts of these advocates have been crucial in bringing acknowledgment, recognition, and understanding to the issues surrounding domestic violence in South Asian immigrant communities. As the number of immigrants to the United States increases, the endeavors of these activists have begun to shed light on a neglected public health issue in a singularly underserved group, the South Asian American community.[1] Our interests in the issues of domestic violence among South Asian women stem from our research interests in immigrant women's health issues in general and our commitment to [ending] violence against women. . . .

Violence in Intimate Relationships: Issues in the Larger Society

Women often experience their greatest risk of violence not from acquaintances and strangers but from their intimate male partners.[2] Domestic violence is one of the most significant causes of injury to women, affecting about two million women in the United States every year. Today, domestic violence is being referred to as a "national epidemic" by physicians, public health experts, and politicians and is slowly becoming a part of the public consciousness in the United States.[3] Domestic violence, specifically intentional physical or nonphysical harm, or both, perpetrated by an intimate partner against a woman is pervasive and often an unrecognized cause of chronic physical and mental health problems.[4] These chronic health problems include such physical traumas as multiple contusions, fractures, bruises, bites, as well as burns on the face, head, abdomen, or genitals. In addition to direct injuries, victims may also suffer from chronic stress-related disorders such as gastric distress, lower back and pelvic pain, headaches, insomnia, and hyperventilation.[5] A variety of psychological and mental health symptoms such as anxiety disorders and panic attacks, depression, sense of helplessness and declining coping skills, self-blame, as well as lowered self-esteem may further accompany these physical impairments.[6]

Domestic Violence in South Asian Communities

The recent recognition of domestic violence in the United States and around the world as an extensive and long-existing phenomenon is largely due to the global efforts of battered women themselves. It is undeniable that the activities of community-based agencies and women's organizations have brought increasing policy, media, and research attention to intimate violence.[7] As the issues of domestic violence move from the private to the public arena in the larger community, a similar trend is reflected among South Asians in the United States.[8] Two factors appear to influence this shift: (1) the emergence and investment of South Asian women's groups and community-based organizations such as Manavi, Apna Ghar, and Sakhi for South Asian women and (2) the increased willingness of South Asian battered women to tell their stories to formal support systems.

In fact, South Asian community organizations and women's groups have played a pivotal role in bringing recognition to domestic violence within their communities. While they serve as safe havens for individual battered women, these agencies simultaneously aim to bring about social change by focusing attention on domestic violence itself. Generally, individual care comes in the form of counseling and emotional support, as well as intervention during emergencies. Social change, on the other hand, is attempted through publicizing particular issues of South Asian women in abusive relationships, training social and health-care workers, and influencing as well as improving legislation regarding domestic violence. Consequently, the visibility of women's groups and community-based organizations, and the willingness of South Asian women to talk about their experiences of violence, have begun to construct a clearer and more realistic picture of women's lives in South Asian immigrant communities.

Of the immigrants living in the United States, 2.8 percent are Asian, and the 1990 census indicates that a million are South Asians — Bangladeshi, Indian, Pakistani, Nepali, and Sri Lankan.[9] One estimate suggests that the incidence of domestic violence in these communities is about 20 to 25 percent.[10] However, this may be an underestimation because domestic violence cases in these communities often are underreported owing to underutilization of existing social and health services.[11] Issues such as immigration status, language barriers, lack of knowledge about helping services and organizations, social and cultural barriers, fear and isolation, as well as concerns of safety for themselves and their children, are often responsible for this underutilization. This constellation of issues can have a profound effect on how South Asian women respond to violence in intimate relationships. These issues, real and perceived, add to the vulnerability of battered South Asian women and influence the way they address violence in their personal lives.

Despite the prevalence of domestic violence among South Asian women living in the United States, little systematic understanding and documentation of the problem exists.[12] A lack of comprehension of the cultural and social factors that define domestic violence, difficulties in reaching out to victims, and the continued reluctance of many women to seek help all contribute to perpetuating intimate violence in our communities. However, current changing conditions within South Asian communities suggest the need for research approaches that can systematically record the scope and particularities of that violence. Such research will also provide better understanding of the factors and correlates of intimate violence, so that culturally appropriate and effective prevention and intervention strategies can be designed.

In this chapter, we hope to lift the veil of secrecy shrouding domestic violence by offering realistic views of South Asian women's experiences, concerns, needs, solutions, and hopes through the words, thoughts, ideas, and courage of the women themselves.

Domestic Violence Research and Focus Groups

In our work, we have used focus groups extensively to explore, discuss, and elaborate on a variety of issues concerning domestic violence among South Asian women living in the United States. A focus group discussion, very simply, is a qualitative method of gathering information from a group of eight to fifteen people who have at least one interest in common.[13] We chose to use focus groups over other methods because of its comfortable, safe, and sharing format. We observed that while participants told their own stories in these groups, they also heard from other women in similar circumstances and developed a sense of kinship and support for one another.

We conducted several focus groups in Chicago and in New York City, where the local South Asian women's organizations assisted us in contacting and recruiting participants for groups. Between five and ten South Asian (Indian, Pakistani, and Bangladeshi) women participated in each of the discussion groups. Some of the issues explored during the group sessions included

- Personal, family, and community definitions and perceptions of domestic violence and its consequences;
- The type, context, and circumstances in which violence occurred;
- Effects and consequences of this violence on the women themselves and their children, and on other aspects of women's lives;
- Personal, family, and community norms, attitudes, perceptions, and acceptance of domestic violence;
- The issues of social support, both formal and informal, and the types of coping strategies used;
- Factors that perpetuate domestic violence in women's lives and those that alleviate the problem;
- Barriers to care- and help-seeking behaviors and the women's suggestions for change; and
- Whether migration has affected women's domestic violence experiences.

The focus group discussions were led by two facilitators who helped to moderate the discussions among participants. For South Asian women who were still in abusive situations, these discussion sessions proved to be "safe havens" where they felt comfortable about articulating their experiences of domestic violence and discussing a variety of other related issues. Furthermore, these discussions also appeared to be "therapeutic" and "empowering," as the participants themselves indicated that they welcomed the

opportunity to talk about their lives and the violence and meet others in situations similar to theirs.

South Asian Women Define Domestic Violence

The recent interest in domestic violence has fueled a debate about what constitutes the phenomenon. Experts, politicians, activists, advocates, and academics have suggested varying definitions, including those rooted in feminist
perspectives, those from the family preservation point of view, and others
from the ecological standpoint. An important missing ingredient in this ongoing argument is the viewpoint of battered women, in this case, South Asian
women in abusive relationships. Although their definitions may differ from
those of the professionals, the South Asian women participating in our focus
groups knew intuitively what was "not right" or what was "wrong" in their
domestic lives. Meena, a young Indian woman who recently moved to the
United States, had a very simple definition of violence and declared, "Beating is domestic violence."[14]

While Meena focused on the physical aspects of domestic violence, Kismat,
a Pakistani mother of four, emphasized the psychological aspects of such
abuse. She focused on the constant lack of respect from her spouse, which
constituted domestic violence to her. This lack of respect often translated into
jealousy and suspicion and led to various types of abuse and violence, including physical beatings. She said, "[Domestic violence] is when husbands
do not give respect to their wives and are always suspicious. The persons
who live with each other must have respect for each other."

Definitions of spousal violence offered by the women participating in
the focus groups were not limited to physical or overt forms of abuse only.
Their notion of ill treatment included emotional and verbal abuse, as well as
subtle mistreatments such as standing around to overhear conversations with
friends and family members. Munni, an Indian woman living in the Chicago
area for a number of years, provided quite a comprehensive definition of
domestic violence: "Emotional abuse is domestic violence. And verbal abuse,
being suspicious, beating, and not supporting financially is domestic violence.
Sometimes men think that they should treat women like a pair of shoes."

These interpretations of domestic violence indicate that the South Asian
women in the focus groups understood intuitively that their experiences of
physical, emotional, and psychological abuse were not normative. They were
also able to distinguish among various types of domestic violence such as
physical, psychological, emotional, verbal, and sexual. This distinction affected
the consequences of abuse, as well as the demands on the women's coping
skills. Clearly, these women recognized abuse in their relationships, even when
it was perpetrated in subtle and quiet ways.

Although the women were quite willing to discuss their overall situations,
cultural as well as community influences were obvious in the emphasis they
placed on certain types of abuse and their reluctance to discuss others. For ex-

ample, many of the focus group participants felt that verbal, psychological, and emotional abuse were more pervasive and therefore critical in their lives but felt that, unlike physical abuse, these were harder to document and explain. Furthermore, all women were significantly more reticent about broaching the subject of sexual abuse.

Another culture-specific aspect was that the women did not necessarily blame themselves for the violence in their domestic relationships but considered it more a consequence of "bad fate." This ability to contextualize domestic violence in terms of bad fate gave the participants the patience, tolerance, and dignity they needed to cope with it. Sheba, an Indian mother of two grown-up children, explained: "I don't think it was my fault at all. This was my fate. I just thought that this was part of my life. You know, no one's life is perfect. There's one thing or another in everyone's life. And I just look at this [domestic violence] as something that I had to tolerate."

Obedient Daughters, Faithful Wives, and Caring Mothers: Sexual Abuse in Conjugal Relationships

All of the participating women were very reluctant to acknowledge, include, and discuss sexual abuse as an integral part of domestic violence. Sexual abuse was by far the hardest topic to introduce in the discussions, and the women even refused to elaborate on the reasons for this discomfort. One can only speculate about their rationale in terms of the women's lack of ease with issues of sex, sexuality, and self-disclosure. Although they perceived the focus groups to be "safe" and "nonjudgmental," the majority of women were conscious of the constraints of their social norms. They were socialized to be "obedient daughters," "faithful wives," and "caring mothers," and these social norms required conformity to certain behavioral standards: subservience, propriety, and putting others' needs ahead of their own. These expectations ruled out any discussion regarding sex, pleasure, and personal enjoyment. The fact that they had moved into the public arena with their stories of domestic violence was already a great departure from tradition, and to discuss sexual abuse, another taboo issue, would have further taxed their coping skills.

Decision to Stay: Insights into a Process

Recent research indicates that women's length of stay in violent relationships varies with ethnicity, assimilation to the dominant culture and acculturation levels, attitudes, and norms about family, marriage, sex roles, and domestic violence, as well as other sociodemographic characteristics. In light of these studies, we tried to examine the factors that affect South Asian women's motivations to remain in violent relationships. Thus, the women participating in the focus groups spent a substantial amount of time exploring why each stayed in their abusive situations. Their discussions indicated a decision-making process that was personal, yet complex. The following were some considerations extracted from the women's testimonies regarding the process itself:"

1. Evaluation of the pros and cons of their domestic circumstances;
2. Perceived choices and options available to them;
3. Concern for their children's safety and future;
4. Immigration status and financial stability;
5. Value placed on opinions and concerns of family members and community;
6. A sense of self-blame, guilt, and personal responsibility; and
7. Perceptions of societal norms and expectations of them.

Contrary to popular belief, the decisions these women made were neither irrational nor arbitrary. Most women based their decisions on a clear rationale. For example, Hala, a young Muslim woman, assessed her situation and found no relevant and viable solutions to her problem. In addition, she believed that she was expected to "tolerate" the violence she was experiencing. Thus, she based her decision to stay with her abusive spouse on these perceptions: "I guess that's the way its supposed to be. Women, they take it. They don't fight back, you know, like women here [American women in the United States] do. Asian women, however much educated they are, they don't fight back. That's the way I was—just be quiet, or walk out, or get out of the house, or go to the other room. Roja, another focus group participant, declared unceremoniously, "In my case, it was financial dependence."

The issue of economic dependency as a salient reason for continuing in a violent relationship was a theme that emerged often. Many of the participants were partially or totally dependent on their spouses for their finances, as well as other resources. Some perceived this dependency to be stronger than it may have been in actuality. Social isolation and lack of information about formal service provisions also contributed to exaggerating this problem of dependency. For some women in the focus groups, marriage had provided them with financial resources, a decent home, class privileges, respectability, and legitimacy in their community and families that they did not have before. In essence, the women had received respectability, a higher social class, and material comforts in exchange for private mistreatments. This exchange was a strategic choice that some participants indicated they made consciously, for themselves and for their children, for a limited length of time or for a lifetime.

For some participants, social norms, family traditions and marriage, and acceptance of men as authorities in the family were adequate reasons for maintaining their abusive relationships. Jila, a focus group participant, succinctly stated her reason for not leaving her violent husband: "Because we feel respect for our parents [and] we should try to keep good relations with our husbands—no matter what." Kamini, another woman in the groups, expressed similar sentiments: "For me, it's like everyone should be together, sit together, and there should be love amongst everyone. And it is a good impression for the children. This is what is in my faith and in my culture.

Divorce in our family is very difficult. If you have children, you have to stay together for their sake. Children need to have both mother and father."

Barriers to Leaving: A Glimpse into South Asian Women's Worlds

For most people, it is extremely difficult to comprehend why a woman continues to endure and cope with violence in her home. In our group discussions, South Asian women provided glimpses into a process of decision making that is often poorly understood and judged harshly. Despite the fear and uncertainty that most of these women face daily they seem to find a way to examine their own lives, available options, and their own capabilities in terms of complexities engendered by living in a "foreign" country. This rather calm and rational scrutiny in the midst of an otherwise chaotic life seemingly helped the group participants find reasons for continuing in their violent relationships and coming to terms with it.

Values and Norms-Related Factors

Many of the barriers to leaving that these women experienced were not individual at all. Rather, women based their decisions to stay on factors such as family and cultural values. [The values and norms that created barriers for these women include:]

1. Societal, community, and family norms;
2. Community and family expectations; and
3. Patriarchy and prescribed gender roles.

The effects of these factors are illustrated in Munni's account of the circumstances of her marriage and conjugal life: "When I got married, my father said to my husband, 'My respect and honor is in your hands. Please take care of my daughter.' From then on he was my husband. It was my job to take care of him. For my family honor, family respect, and to maintain [this] respect, we have to just put up with it [violence]. Because of the family!" This is even more clear in Nilufer's statement "My husband forced me to have more children for citizenship purposes. I am sure that what he really wanted was to have sons. He hates daughters. I couldn't even tell you how much. Back in Pakistan, it is understood that girls are no good, and you shouldn't have them." Along with the perceived relevance of patriarchy in families, Nilufer's understanding and acceptance of gender positions is evident in this statement.

Support Factors

[The focus group discussions also centered on three support factors:]

1. Lack of social support;
2. Lack of structural support and material resources; and

  3. Lack of knowledge of available formal support networks and systems.

Suman, an Indian single mother living in New York with a young daughter, discussed the lack of social support she experienced: "I have no relatives. I have nobody, just me and my daughter now. It is hard, very hard." Savitri, a mother of three children, discussed the lack of structural support and material resources in terms of the availability of affordable baby-sitting and public transportation. She felt that a scarcity of both had prevented her from developing necessary skills to become self-sufficient and independent. "I have a baby-sitting problem. The day care that is on our side is very expensive. Taking the public transport to another place itself costs five dollars," she lamented.

The lack of knowledge about available formal assistance programs can often prove to be an important reason why some South Asian women choose to continue in their violent domestic relationships. Roja, who had recently moved to Chicago from India, expressed her dilemma and her reasons for staying in her violent relationship: "And this is a new culture [the United States], language problem, no money, and with children. Where to go? And moreover, no relatives. There is nowhere to go. And there is no way to get out."

During discussions about support factors, focus group participants indicated the magnitude of their sense of isolation when they were attempting to address problems surrounding abuse in their lives. Suman declared, "It's quite difficult to make the adjustment and adapt to the new culture, and it takes quite a bit of time. There are difficulties and problems. Especially when there is no one to turn to.

Individual Factors

These individual factors emerged from the focus group discussions:

  1. Fear for safety for themselves and their children;
  2. Fear for their future and possible deportation;
  3. Inability to handle and cope with the stress of living alone in the United States;
  4. Lack of job skills, language skills, and other life skills;
  5. Desire to stay in the relationship or inability to accept and address the violence in their lives; and
  6. Fear for the children's future.

Leela, a woman living in Chicago, focused on some of the personal factors that formed barriers for her: "My English speaking isn't very good. So getting a job and working is not a possibility yet. So I cannot get the things I need without the English. In addition I do not have a green card." Roja, another woman in Chicago, indicated racism as a factor contributing to her abusive situation: "My life now is for my children. That's why I need to work and support them. I had to swallow my hopes. I have to put all my hopes in my children. There are many tensions from the outside. He [the husband] wants what he had back home [in terms of a job]. A woman accepts whatever she can get, because we want to survive and support the family. Although the men have the education, they cannot find a suitable job or sometimes they do not want to work. So there is frustration outside and inside the home for all of us."

Why Leave Now? Why South Asian Women Walk Out of Their Marriages

Despite the hopelessness and lack of support they experienced, some of the South Asian women took the "uncharacteristic" and "unlikely" step of leaving their abusive relationships for good. Many indicated that they were seriously considering this option. Others stated that they were trying hard to cope with their present, violence-filled circumstances and hoping to "make them [their marriages] work."

Those who walked away from their abusive relationships indicated that they did so not because of one defining moment, or a single violent episode, but because of the sum total of their experiences. They had reached the end of their tolerance and recognized that they could seek and receive support and assistance from formal systems. Those who had walked away from their violent relationships, however, also acknowledged that it had been excruciatingly difficult and painful to start living on their own. They indicated that the support they received from local South Asian women's organizations and culturally sensitive domestic violence shelters were crucial in their decision making and follow-through processes. Also significant in their decision making was the support they received from informal kin and friendship networks such as friends, family members, neighbors, and co-workers. For those who were continuing in their present abusive circumstances, having a job and interacting with their colleagues at work, talking to supportive siblings, family members, and friends, the support and understanding of their children, and their own unwavering religious faith had all helped them to continue to cope. These factors gave them hope for a better future and life.

Hopes for the Future: Living in Peace and Tranquillity

Despite difficult circumstances and lives filled with violence and fear, the participating South Asian women expressed hopes and expectations for a better future. Those who had left their violent lives encouraged others to consider this option and offered to help in any way possible. Madhu, an Indian woman who participated in one of the focus groups in Chicago, voiced this optimism: "My hopes are that I want to study [and] I am doing a job in the library now. It's a good position, but I want to move ahead. So that's why I want to study more. I don't want a restaurant or a store job." Kismat, a Pakistani woman and a mother of four, expressed her desires in terms of her children. She remarked, "My life is with my children. I want to see my children have a good life with a good education, have good jobs. This is my biggest wish and hope." Sheba, who had started a life on her own, had this advice for other participants: "You need to make yourself good and show that you don't have less of anything. You can raise your children without him. And better than him. And you can be happy. You need to begin to say this to yourself and foster these kinds of thoughts."

During these discussions, the participants indicated that it was important to address domestic violence through simple and tangible strategies that were empowering and meaningful to women. They suggested that these strategies need to focus first and foremost on providing life skills, job skills, and language skills so that women could slowly find the peace and tranquillity that had eluded them for so long. Their suggestions included providing the following services: English classes, transportation, baby-sitting services, advice about legal issues and immigration laws, job training such as computer classes, some seed money to start their lives again, and support groups where they can talk with others and help others.

Their focus was simple, narrow, and targeted toward themselves. They felt that with these kinds of tangible assistance and services, they could emerge from behind the veil of secrecy, talk about their lives in public, not feel responsible for the violence in their lives, and, like other people, live a life of dignity and peace. . . .

Learning from Women

Although there has been a long history of domestic violence in South Asian communities, only recently have attempts been made to document these issues systematically in these communities in the United States. Our experience is that focus group discussions are extremely effective in exploring a variety of issues regarding domestic violence in these communities. Our work with South Asian women revealed that violence experienced by South Asian women was defined by a variety of unique cultural, familial, and community factors and norms. Socioeconomic factors, immigration status, and a host of perceived barriers, including linguistic ones, further defined their experiences. Our focus group discussions revealed a complex picture of domestic violence among the participating South Asian women. Issues of patriarchy, gender roles and expectations, constricting family and community norms, attitudes and traditions about spousal violence, lack of decision-making power, and economic independence are still important in South Asian communities and have aggravated the problem of domestic violence further. Despite this bleak picture, the South Asian women who participated in our groups exhibited enviable resiliency and coping abilities. Their hopes for a peaceful and violence-free life for themselves and their children spoke volumes about their courage. With the help of South Asian women's organizations and other community-based organizations, and through their own willingness to speak out, South

Asian women have begun to challenge their communities to confront domestic violence with sensitivity and urgency. Although the process has been initiated, there is much work to be done. Part of the task is to document the nature and incidence of this atrocity systematically and implement culturally sensitive, as well as effective, interventions that address issues in South Asian contexts.

ENDNOTES

1. K. A. Huisman, "Wife Battering in Asian American Communities," *Violence Against Women* 2 (1996): 260–83.
2. M. P. Koss, L. A. Goodman, A. Browne, L. F. Fitzgerald, G. P. Keita, and N. F. Russo, *No Safe Haven: Male Violence Against Women at Home, at Work, and in the Community* (Washington, DC: American Psychological Association, 1994).
3. J. Abbott, J. McLain-Koziol, and S. Lowenstein, "Domestic Violence Against Women: Incidence and Prevalence in an Emergency Department Population," *JAMA Journal of the American Medical Association* 273 (1995): 1763–77.
4. D. Berrios and D. Grady, "Domestic Violence. Risk Factors and Outcomes," *Western Journal of Medicine* 155, no. 2 (1991): 133–35.
5. V. F. Parker, "Battered," *RN (TWP)* 58, no. 1 (1995): 26–29.
6. A. L. Kornblit, "Domestic Violence: An Emerging Health Issue," *Social Science and Medicine* 39 (1994): 1181–88.
7. S. D. Dasgupta and S. Warrier, "In the Footsteps of 'Arundhati': Asian Indian Women's Experience of Domestic Violence in the United States," *Violence Against Women* 2, no. 3 (1996): 238–59.
8. M. Abraham, "Addressing the Problem of Marital Violence among South Asians in the United States: A Sociological Study of the Role of Organizations," paper presented at the meetings of the International Sociological Association (1994); and "Transforming Marital Violence from a 'Private Problem' to a 'Public Issue': South Asian Women's Organizations and Community Empowerment," paper presented at the meetings of the American Sociological Association (1995). These papers have since been published as "Ethnicity, Gender, and Marital Violence: South Asian Women's Organizations in the United States," *Gender and Society* 9 (1995): 450–68; and "Speaking the Unspeakable: Marital Violence against South Asian Immigrant Women in the United States," *Indian Journal of Gender Studies* 5, no. 2 (June–December 1998).
9. U.S. Bureau of the Census, *1990 Census of the Population: Social and Economic Characteristics, United States* (Washington, DC: U.S. Government Printing Office, 1993).
10. Koss et al., *No Safe Haven*.
11. C. K. Ho, "An Analysis of Domestic Violence in Asian American Communities: A Multicultural Approach to Counseling," *Woman and Therapy* 9 (1990): 129–50.
12. Abraham, "Addressing the Problem" and "Transforming Marital Violence."
13. T. L. Greenbaum, *The Practical Handbook and Guide to Focus Groups Research* (Lexington, MA: Lexington, 1988).
14. Names of all participants have been changed to protect their identity.

31

TOWARD A BETTER UNDERSTANDING
OF LESBIAN BATTERING

CLAIRE M. RENZETTI

What do we now know about violence in lesbian relationships, and where do we go from here? . . .
    It appears that violence in lesbian relationships occurs at about the same frequency as violence in heterosexual relationships. The abuse may be physical and/or psychological, ranging from verbal threats and insults to stabbings and shootings. Indeed, batterers display a terrifying ingenuity in their selection of abusive tactics, frequently tailoring the abuse to the specific vulnerabilities of their partners. We have seen that there is no "typical" form of abuse, even though some types of abuse are more common than others. What emerged as significant in my research was not the forms of abuse inflicted, but, rather, the factors that appear to give rise to the abuse, and the consequences of the abuse for batterers and especially for victims.

The factor that in this study was most strongly associated with abuse was partners' relative dependency on one another. More specifically, batterers appeared to be intensely dependent on the partners whom they victimized. The abusive partner's dependency was a central element in an ongoing, dialectic struggle in these relationships. As batterers grew more dependent, their partners attempted to exercise greater independence. This, in turn, posed a threat to the batterer, who would subsequently try to tighten her hold on her partner, often by violent means. The greater the batterer's dependency, the more frequent and severe the abuse she inflicted on her partner. In most cases, the batterer eventually succeeded in cutting her partner off from friends, relatives, colleagues, and all outside interests and activities that did not include the batterer herself. Still, though she apparently had her partner all to herself in a sense, her success in controlling her partner seemed only to fuel her dependency rather than salve it.

The intense dependency of the batterer typically manifests itself as jealousy. It is not enough for the batterer to possess her partner; she must also guard her from all others who could potentially lure her away. The battering victim is subjected to lengthy interrogations about her routine activities and associations. She is repeatedly accused of infidelity, and although the accusations are almost always groundless, her denials rarely satisfy the batterer. Violence is a frequent end product of the batterer's jealous tirades. The overdependency of the batterer may also manifest itself through substance abuse, especially alcohol abuse. When under the influence of alcohol or drugs, she may feel strong, more independent, more aggressive. She may act on these perceptions by becoming violent and abusive, especially toward her partner. This is particularly likely if, along with the belief that alcohol or drugs make her powerful, she or her partner or both of them also believe that an individual under the influence of alcohol or drugs is not responsible for her actions. Thus substance abuse appears to be a facilitator rather than a cause of lesbian battering.

Another factor that emerged as a potential facilitator of lesbian partner abuse was a personal history of family violence. Although a number of researchers have found that childhood exposure to domestic violence may increase one's likelihood of being victimized in an intimate relationship as an adult, the participants in my study did not report a high incidence of exposure to domestic violence in their families of origin. Their batterers were more likely than they were to have been victimized, but there were almost as many abusive partners who grew up in nonviolent households as there were those who grew up in violent ones.

Exposure to domestic violence as a child may put one at risk of becoming abusive toward one's own partner as an adult, but the data from my study also suggest that a personal history of abuse can become, for both batterer and victim, a means to legitimate the battering. In other words, the belief that childhood exposure to domestic violence predisposes one toward violent behavior or victimization as an adult may facilitate lesbian battering much the same way substance abuse does — that is, by forming the basis of an excuse for the batterer's behavior.

One issue that remains unclear is how an imbalance of power in the relationship may contribute to partner abuse. Like other researchers who have examined the relationship between power imbalance and battering among homosexual couples, few strong associations emerged from my study. This is probably due in large part to the complexity of the concept of power. Power is multifaceted. With respect to some dimensions of power (e.g., decision making, the division of household labor), batterers could be considered the more powerful partners. However, in terms of other indicators of power (e.g., economic resources brought to the relationship), victims tended to be more powerful. It is also unclear when an imbalance of power in these terms emerges in abusive relationships; the data from my study indicate that, at least with regard to decision making, victims often ceded power to batterers in an attempt to appease them and perhaps avoid further abuse. This evidence lends support to the hypothesis that batterers are individuals who feel powerless and use violence as a means to achieve power and dominance in their intimate relationships.

The power imbalance–domestic violence link is one that obviously deserves further attention in future research. If batterers use violence as a means to overcome feelings of powerlessness, what are the sources of these feelings? Are they a further outgrowth of dependency needs? In addition, researchers need to clarify what elements compose the power construct so that the dimensions of power relevant to the etiology of lesbian partner abuse can be distinguished and addressed.[1]

It is doubtful that we will ever be able to predict with precision which relationships, be they homosexual or heterosexual, will become violent. However, findings from my research and that of others we have reviewed point to several factors that may serve as markers for identifying lesbian relationships that are particularly at risk for violence. Figure 1 presents a decision tree designed to assist lesbian partners, counselors, battered women's advocates, and others in assessing this risk. I also urge readers who feel they are at risk, or who think they may be involved in a battering relationship, to apply Figure 1 as a checklist to their own relationships.

What if one is involved in an abusive relationship? Where may one go for help? . . . As the findings of my research make clear, battered lesbians experience tremendous difficulty obtaining the help they want and need. Help sources available to battered heterosexual women (e.g., the police and the legal system, shelters, relatives) generally are not perceived by lesbian victims as viable sources of help. Or, if help is sought from these sources, lesbian victims do not typically rate it as highly effective. Even those whom lesbian victims consider to be good sources of help (i.e., counselors and friends) frequently deny the abuse or refuse to name it battering.

Based on the data gathered in my study, it is not overstating the point to say that battered lesbians are victimized not only by their partners, but also by many of those from whom they seek help. Consequently, additional research is urgently needed on ways to improve help providers' responses to battered lesbians. We will take up this issue in the sections that follow.

Providing Help to Battered Lesbians

Research has consistently documented the difficulties battered heterosexual women encounter when they seek help to address the battering. Nevertheless, battered heterosexual women appear to have considerably more success in getting effective help — or at least in eliciting positive responses from help providers — than battered lesbians do. As Pharr (1986) has pointed out:

> There is an important difference between the battered lesbian and the battered non-lesbian: the battered non-lesbian experiences violence within the context of a misogynist world; the lesbian experiences violence within the context of a world that is not only woman-hating, but is also homophobic. And that is a great difference. Therefore, an initial step in improving responses to battered lesbians is for help providers to confront and overcome their homophobia. (P. 204)

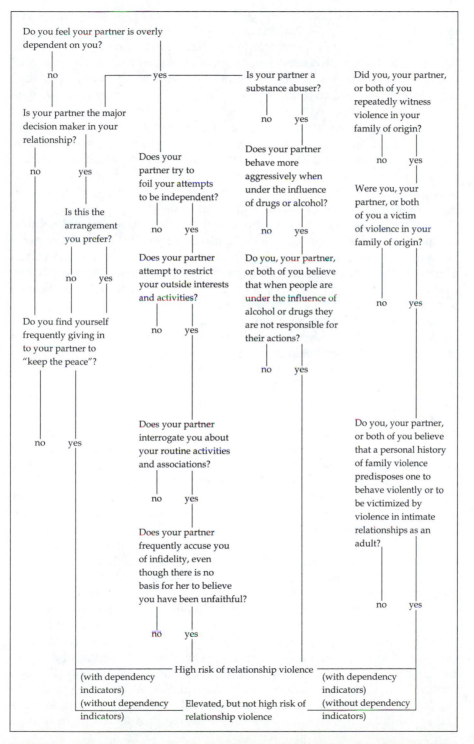

FIGURE 1   Decision Tree for Assessing Risk for Violence in Lesbian Relationships

As Elliott (1990) says, "Before you . . . can acknowledge lesbian battering, you must first acknowledge lesbian relationships" (n.p.).

While informal help providers (e.g., heterosexual friends, family members) cannot be forced to attend homophobia workshops, all official or formal help providers—that is, police personnel, shelter volunteers and paid staff, crisis hotline staffers, counselors, physicians, and emergency room personnel—should be required to participate in such workshops as part of their routine training. There are a number of excellent resources available that can be utilized for such sessions. Perhaps the best is *Confronting Homophobia*, edited by Julie Guth and Pamela Elliott of the Lesbian Advocacy Committee of the Minnesota Coalition for Battered Women. The manual includes not only training materials, but also suggestions for trainers and workshop leaders, sample training formats, and evaluation forms.

Confronting Homophobia is part of a two-volume set; the second volume, *Confronting Lesbian Battering*, is specifically designed for battered women's advocates as a resource for developing effective responses to lesbian victims. The value of *Confronting Lesbian Battering* is that it addresses the many myths that surround lesbian partner abuse and sensitively guides readers through a rethinking of our operating models of intimate violence.

In a survey of 1,505 service providers that I conducted in 1991, two thirds (66.6 percent) of the 557 service providers who responded indicated that their staff receive antihomophobia training; 56.4 percent indicated that volunteers also receive this training. However, only 47.9 percent reported that their staff received any training specifically about lesbian battering and 40.6 percent reported that volunteers receive such training. Thus, in addition to homophobia workshops, help providers also must be educated about lesbian battering, and this education must include an analysis of the many myths about partner abuse: that it is a male/female problem; that it typically involves "mutual battering"; that it is always the physically larger or "masculine" partner who batters. Education in this regard, however, should extend beyond official help providers to the communities, both lesbian and non-lesbian. This may be undertaken in the context of community speak-outs in which participants are assured safe space. It may also be done through the distribution of pamphlets or flyers and through public service advertisements. In particular, battered women's agencies should determine if their ads and literature imply (or explicitly state) that all batterers are heterosexual men and all victims of battering are heterosexual women. Often, the sex-specific pronoun "he" is used in reference to batterers, and "she" is used in reference to victims. In my survey of service providers, 96.4 percent of those who responded said they welcome battered lesbians as clients, yet just 37 percent reported that they do outreach to lesbians. Similarly, 77.7 percent said that at least some of the written materials they make available use inclusive language, but only 25.9 percent indicated that their written materials explicitly address the problem of lesbian battering and just 29.8 percent reported that they have written material specifically about lesbian battering available. Just as efforts have been made to make agency materials racially-inclusive, so too should they be inclusive of lesbians and gay men.

Strategies such as these not only educate help providers, the lesbian and gay community in general, and the heterosexual public, but may also assist lesbians involved in abusive relationships in recognizing themselves as battered, which is their first step in getting free. Still, education without action is of little use. What responses from others would lesbian victims find most helpful? This question was posed to the participants in my study of lesbian battering. Their answers have been incorporated into the following discussions.[2]

The Legal System and Alternatives

A current debate among advocates for battered lesbians is whether or not the legal system should be utilized to resolve the problem of violence in lesbian relationships. Those who support the use of the legal system maintain that bringing the force of legal authority to bear on the batterer can effectively put an end to her abuse and, at the same time, hold her accountable for her actions. From this perspective, lesbians are entitled to equal protection by the law. The difficulties are that in most states, the domestic violence statutes do not explicitly apply to homosexual couples, and in those states where they do apply, the police and the courts do not consistently or fairly enforce them in cases involving homosexual couples. Those who hold this position maintain that advocates should lobby for the revision of domestic violence statutes to include homosexual couples, and serve as watchdogs to ensure that the statutes are consistently and fairly enforced when lesbians and gay men turn to the police and courts for help.[3]

Opponents of utilizing the legal system in cases of lesbian battering point first to its well-documented mistreatment of cases involving heterosexual couples. According to Irvine (1990), "The courts deal so poorly with heterosexual abuse cases that in a case involving two lesbians they would have a 'field day'" (p. 29). Second, many see the legal system as inappropriate for resolving problems between lesbian partners. As one advocate put it: "I have a personal hatred and bias against women using the legal system and the police system in their fights with each other. I find it offensive as a feminist. Resolution of disputes between lesbians should not take place in a white male judicial court" (quoted in Irvine 1990:29).

Only two of the participants in my study indicated that they would find intervention by the police and the courts helpful. One said she would like to have legal sanctions available that are tougher than restraining orders. The second participant said that the homophobia of the police needs to be addressed. She found the police to be helpful in stopping the battering in the short-run, but reported that they were blatantly homophobic in their response to her.

If the police and the legal system should not be utilized by battered lesbians, what are their alternatives? One is mediation. The role of the mediator is to facilitate communication between partners so that they themselves can develop a mutually beneficial and impartial resolution to their conflicts (e.g., separation, a signed agreement in which the abusive partner promises to end the violence) without resorting to formal legal action (Felstiner and Williams 1978; Folberg and Taylor 1984).

The informal and private nature of mediation may make it especially appealing to lesbian victims, particularly if they prefer that most people (e.g., their families, colleagues at work, etc.) not know about their sexual orientation. However, Ellis (1988) and others (e.g., Bahr, Chappell, and Marcos 1987) warn that mediation may have limited success in ending partner abuse. Their research indicates that the more hostile the relations between partners, the less likely they are to successfully complete mediation. In addition, mediators, in their effort to be impartial, may overlook inequalities of power between partners, not only with regard to economic resources, but also in terms of fear or psychological domination. Mediation also implies co-responsibility on the part of the partners and fails to hold batterers accountable for their behavior. Weighing these findings against the potential value of mediation for lesbian victims, research should be undertaken to evaluate the effectiveness of existing mediation programs in assisting both lesbian and heterosexual clients.

Apart from the police, the courts, and mediators, battered lesbians may also turn to other formal help providers, especially shelters and counselors, for assistance. How might the responses of these professionals be improved?

Shelters and Counselors

Nineteen participants in my study stated that having a safe place to which they could go for refuge from their batterers would have been most helpful to them.[4] We have already noted that shelters can only become viable sources of help to battered lesbians when shelter staff confront and overcome their homophobia, and when lesbian partner abuse is explicitly recognized as a serious problem in public service advertisements and literature for battered women. Lesbian victims of partners abuse need to know that local battered women's shelters are open to them and that they are welcome there.

Once the battered lesbian arrives at the shelter, staff there must, of course, make good on their promise of providing her with safe space, emotional support, and other assistance that they routinely provide to battered heterosexual women. Shelter staff must not minimize the abuse experienced by the battered lesbian simply because her batterer is a woman. Lesbian battering is "real" battering, and many of the needs of battered lesbians are the same as those of battered heterosexual women.

At the same time, however, battered lesbians have several unique concerns. One of the most important is deciding to whom among shelter staff and residents one will make one's sexual orientation known. As Geraci (1986) explains:

> If a lesbian does not choose to come out this right must be respected. It
> is important to keep in mind that in the lesbian community at large, bat-

tering between women is a non-issue—it violates the idea of a safe, peaceful world of women. . . . A battered lesbian who seeks shelter is making a very courageous step which could cause her to lose the support of many of her lesbian sisters. (P. 78)

She also runs the risk of incurring hostility and ostracism from other shelter residents.[5] Among the service providers I surveyed, 92.3 percent said that their clients' sexual orientation was treated confidentially, although the majority also indicated their confidentiality policies regarding sexual orientation were not explicit.

Another serious concern of battered lesbians in shelters is the extent to which they are actually safe from their batterers. While shelter locations are well-guarded secrets from men, and both staff and residents are severely sanctioned if they disclose this information, we have already noted that the location of shelters is often well-known in the lesbian community, primarily because lesbians have been very active in the battered women's movement and because of the widely held belief that all batterers are men. Consequently it has been suggested that as an alternative to traditional residential shelters, a network of safe houses be established for battered lesbians (Irvine 1990). In Minneapolis–St. Paul, for example, a network of lesbians takes victims into their individual homes (Ojeda-Zapata 1990). Irvine (1990) points out that a drawback of this approach is that lesbian victims are not afforded the peer support that may be available at the shelters. However, a support group for battered lesbians may fill this gap (Porat 1986).

The Lesbian Battering Intervention Project of the Minnesota Coalition for Battered Women has compiled a checklist to assist shelter staff in determining if they are adequately prepared to serve battered lesbians. They have kindly permitted me to reprint it here (see Table 1). Many of the issues raised in this checklist also apply to counselors from whom lesbian victims seek help. Seventeen of the lesbian victims in my study identified specific responses from counselors that they would have found helpful. Three were cited repeatedly.

First, participants indicated that they needed professional help in regaining their self-esteem and building a strong sense of self-worth. They expressed the desire for counselors to focus therapy sessions on these goals. Importantly, however, respondents emphasized that counselors should not treat their low self-esteem as a cause of their battering but, rather, as a result of it. Lenore Walker's (1979:239) suggestions with respect to counseling battered heterosexual women are applicable here. Walker maintains that individual therapy with battered women should be more action-oriented than analytic. "The realities of present alternatives and future goal planning are explored in individual therapy. The battered woman needs to recognize concrete steps she can take to improve her situation. . . . Intervention and collaboration with other helpers are important corollaries of individual psychotherapy." These methods will help the battered woman rebuild her self-esteem and recognize and constructively experience her feelings of anger.

TABLE 1   Checklist for Shelter Programs

1. Do all written materials use inclusive language (no pronouns) and address the issue of lesbian battering?
    Mission
    Philosophy statement
    Brochures
    Arrival and departure forms
    Welcome letters, house rules, etc.
2. Is homophobia identified as an oppression and a form of violence?
    In the philosophy statement
    In the house rules
3. Are policies inclusive of lesbians?
    Does the definition of family in personal policies include lesbian families?
    Does the affirmative action statement include sexual/affectional orientation?
    Does the policy on confidentiality include confidentiality for lesbians and
        consequences for violating the policy?
4. Is the recruitment of staff, volunteers, and board members addressing homophobia?
    Are candidates questioned about homophobia and providing services to
        lesbians?
    Are position announcements distributed to reach lesbians?
    Do job qualifications include commitment to confront homophobia?
    Is homophobia training included for all new staff, volunteers, and board
        members?
    Does the program have a commitment to lesbian involvement at all levels?
5. Is the program prepared to respond to the needs of battered lesbians?
    Is information available on resources for battered lesbians?
    Does the library, video library, and/or magazine rack contain lesbian books,
        videos, periodicals, or articles?
    Is the Children's Program staff familiar with issues confronting lesbian mothers?
        (custody, coming out to children, etc.)
    Is the Women's Program familiar with issues confronting battered lesbians?
        (dangers of using the "system," closeting, etc.)
    Are all services prepared to include battered lesbians? (support group, inter-
        vention program, legal advocates, etc.)
6. Has the issue of lesbian battering been integrated into the program on an ongoing
    basis? (One or two trainings will not remove barriers or fix the problem.)

Source: Written by Lisa Vecoli for the Minnesota Coalition for Battered Women, Lesbian Battering Intervention Project; printed in Elliott 1990, pp. 73–74.

Closely related to this were the two other responses participants most would have appreciated from counselors—specifically, for counselors to identify their experiences as battering and for them not to lay blame for the abuse on those who were victimized. Like shelter staff, counselors must not minimize the abuse because it was inflicted by a woman, nor deflect attention away from the abuse and onto the abused's "other problems." Battered lesbians, like battered heterosexual women, may also benefit from group therapy and support groups, but counselors should not assume that couples counseling is more appropriate for lesbian partners involved in abusive relationships than for heterosexual couples. As Lydia Walker (1986) has pointed out, why should counselors assume that lesbian batterers are less manipulative and more likely than men to control their violence? These are false assumptions.

This is not to say that treatment for batterers should be ignored. To the contrary, a focus of future research should be on identifying the unique treatment needs of lesbian batterers and developing treatment programs specifically for them. (The vast majority of treatment programs for batterers are male-centered, and men who batter women also tend to be overtly homophobic. Thus such programs would be inappropriate and probably ineffective for lesbian batterers.) If a lesbian victim presents herself for treatment, however, the counselor must keep in mind that she alone—not her partner, nor she and her partner as a couple—is the client. Couples counseling should only be attempted at the request of the victim. The model offered by Walker (1979:245–48) may be applicable to lesbian couples, if both therapists involved are lesbians. However, even if a battered lesbian requests couples counseling, it should be attempted only if her safety can be ensured, and she should be apprised of its low probability of success in abusive relationships.

As noted [by other researchers], the couples counseling approach is based on a family systems or codependency model that sees both partners sharing responsibility for the abusive nature of their relationship. Although it has, perhaps, intuitive appeal, the codependency model is inherently victim-blaming. It may be especially damaging when the woman who has been abused fought back or defended herself against the battering. Victims who have fought back or defended themselves, we have seen, typically experience guilt or shame over their use of violence. They often question whether they are truly victims or are batterers themselves. Counselors, like others, appear to apply the label "mutually abusive" too readily and uncritically to lesbian victims who come to them for help. Thus they reinforce rather than reverse the women's low self-esteem and perpetuate the myth that the abuse is at least partially their fault.

Counselors must learn to evaluate the dialectic nature of the abusive relationship and to distinguish between battering and self-defense (or fighting back). To do this, they, along with shelter staff and other advocates, must first ask themselves some hard questions about their own acceptance of the myth of mutual battering (Walker 1986:76):

> Why are female batterers more "believable" when they blame their partner, why do workers see self-defense as "mutual battering" if the batterer is a woman, and why is it easier to believe that somehow a battered lesbian is part of the "violence problem" than to believe that a heterosexual woman is part of the "violence problem"? I challenge workers in the movement to think about how they would respond to a battered woman who says she provokes him or that she is as much to blame as him because she hits him first sometimes.

Relatives, Friends, and Community

The major barrier to relatives becoming viable sources of help for battered lesbians, as they are for battered heterosexual women, is their homophobia. However, it is probably more difficult to convince relatives to attend homophobia workshops than it is for any other group of help providers we have discussed here. Perhaps family members will be motivated by the fact that if they do confront and overcome their homophobia, they can effectively help their loved ones free themselves from abusive relationships: Recall our finding that the more helpful lesbian victims found their relatives to be, the sooner they ended the abusive relationship.

It is friends, though, especially friends in the lesbian community, from whom battered lesbians most often seek help. And it was to friends and the community that the majority of the study participants directed their suggestions for improving responses to lesbian victims.

The primary need expressed by lesbian victims is for their friends to allow them to confide in them. Thirty-two of the study participants wrote that they wanted their friends to lend emotional support, listen to them when they tried to make them aware of the problem, and reassure them that the abuse was not their fault. Twenty women said they wished their friends had named the violence "battering" instead of excusing or denying it. Fifteen women would have liked their friends to help them leave the relationship, either by offering physical assistance in moving or by verbally affirming their decision to end the relationship.

In short, friends and the community itself must recognize that battering is a problem among lesbian couples, and that its consequences are as serious as those of heterosexual battering—perhaps more serious, in fact, given that lesbians who are victimized are doubly stigmatized and have fewer sources of help available to them. Belief is essential, and like other help providers, friends and the community must not reflexively apply the label "mutual battering" simply because the partners involved are both women or because they know that the victim sometimes fought back. The words of the study participants, of course, convey these sentiments best:

> *Most helpful would have been the respect shown by believing that there actually was a problem—my friends brushed it off, didn't believe [she] was abusive, said it was a two-way street.* [Questionnaire 14]

> *To listen, believe, ask questions to gain understanding, but no "Why didn't you just do . . ." Offer practical help to get away. Encouragement to talk about it. No victim blaming. No judgmental crap about how my batterer is really my sister. Treat me as you would treat any woman who has been the victim of a violent crime.* [Questionnaire 39]

> *Support, genuine understanding. My friends knew but tried to ignore it and suggested that I overlook her "moods" because "she's just that way."*

Acknowledging that lesbian battering is a serious problem may indeed be unpleasant, even painful, for the lesbian community. But until such acknowledgment is made, until victims' needs are effectively and sensitively met, and until batterers are challenged and held accountable for their behavior, all lesbians are unsafe and the struggle for the creation of a peaceful, egalitarian community of women is violently betrayed.

ENDNOTES

1. Others (see, e.g., Island and Letellier 1991 and Coleman 1990) have hypothesized that internalized homophobia may be an underlying factor in homosexual partner abuse either by motivating a partner to be violent or by increasing one's risk of victimization. Although I did not examine internalized homophobia in my study, the issue was the focus of much discussion at my meetings with the Working Group on Lesbian Battering. Certainly the phenomenon of internalized homophobia deserves attention in future studies of homosexual partner abuse. However, the problem of developing a reliable and valid measure of internalized homophobia—a problem perhaps more difficult to resolve than that of measuring partners' relative power in a relationship—confronts researchers who wish to explore this issue further.
2. Eighty-nine participants responded to the questionnaire item, "Whether or not you sought help, please describe what response from others would have been most helpful to you." One woman wrote simply that she had gotten the help she needed. One felt that money/financial assistance would have been most helpful. And a third participant wrote, "Take my alcohol away." The majority of the women, however, responded with more than one answer.
3. According to Fagan (1989), research on heterosexual domestic violence indicates that legal sanctions appear to be most effective in deterring batterers with brief and relatively nonsevere histories of abusive behavior. At the same time, however, Fagan notes that for any legal sanctions to be effective they cannot be weak. Weak legal interventions may reinforce violence simply by not adequately penalizing it.
4. Two participants indicated that in addition to safe shelter space, they needed transportation. One suggested establishing an escort service that could be called upon at any time to transport victims to safe space. Four women also requested hotline services, and four felt that a support group for battered lesbians would be helpful.
5. Grover (1990:43) points out that children of battered lesbians who accompany their mothers to shelters must also have their privacy rights respected. "Children may be used to closeting for their mothers and themselves. They may not know who is safe to come out to and who is not. A conversation with mom about how her family typically handles this is essential."

REFERENCES

Bahr, S., C. B. Chappell, and A. Marcos. 1987. "An Evaluation of a Trial Mediation Programme." *Mediation Quarterly* (Winter):37–52.

Coleman, V. E. 1990. "Violence between Lesbian Couples: A Between Groups Comparison." Ph.D. dissertation. University Microfilms International (9109022).

Elliot, P. 1990. "Introduction." In *Confronting Lesbian Battering*, edited by P. Elliott. St. Paul: Minnesota Coalition for Battered Women.

Ellis, D. 1988. "Marital Conflict Mediation and Post-Separation Wife-Abuse." Presented at the annual meeting of the American Society of Criminology, Chicago, November.

Fagan, J. 1989. "Cessation of Family Violence: Deterrence and Discussion." Pp. 377–425 in *Family Violence*, edited by L. Ohlin and M. Tonry. Chicago: University of Chicago Press.

Felstiner, W. and L. Williams. 1978. "Mediation as an Alternative to Criminal Prosecution: Ideology and Limitations." *Law and Human Behavior* 2:221–39.

Folberg, J. and A. Taylor. 1984. *Mediation*. San Francisco: Jossey-Bass.

Geraci, L. 1986. "Making Shelters Safe for Lesbians." Pp. 77–9 in *Naming the Violence*, edited by K. Lobel. Seattle, WA: Seal.

Grover, J. 1990. "Children from Violent Lesbian Homes." Pp. 42–43 in *Confronting Lesbian Battering*, edited by P. Elliott. St. Paul: Minnesota Coalition for Battered Women.

Guth, J. and P. Elliott, eds. 1991. *Confronting Homophobia*. St. Paul: Minnesota Coalition for Battered Women.

Irvine, J. 1990. "Lesbian Battering: The Search for Shelter." Pp. 25–30 in *Confronting Lesbian Battering*, edited by P. Elliot. St. Paul: Minnesota Coalition for Battered Women.

Island, D. and P. Letellier. 1991. *Men Who Beat the Men Who Love Them*. New York: Harrington Park.

Ojeda-Zapata, J. 1990. "Battering No. 1 Lesbian Problem." *St. Paul Pioneer Press-Dispatch*, October 21. (Located in *Newsbank* [microform], Social Relations, 1990, 72:D3-5, fiche.)

Pharr, S. 1986. "Two Workshops on Homophobia." Pp. 202–22 in *Naming the Violence*, edited by K. Lobel. Seattle, WA: Seal.

Porat, N. 1986. "Support Groups for Battered Lesbians." Pp. 80–87 in *Naming the Violence*, edited by K. Lobel. Seattle, WA: Seal.

Walker, L. 1986. "Battered Women's Shelters and Work with Battered Lesbians." Pp. 73–76 in *Naming the Violence*, edited by K. Lobel. Seattle, WA: Seal.

Walker, L. E. 1979. *The Battered Woman*. New York: Harper & Row.

32

ELDER ABUSE AND CHILD ABUSE
A Consideration of Similarities and Differences in Intergenerational Family Violence

JILL E. KORBIN • GEORGIA J. ANETZBERGER
J. KEVIN ECKERT

Introduction

In the United States, awareness of and research attention to elder abuse arose after attention to child and spousal abuse. Child abuse in the 1960s and spousal violence in the 1970s emerged as significant research and policy issues. The "Graying of America" intensified concern about a range of issues

---

"Elder Abuse and Child Abuse: A Consideration of Similarities and Differences in Intergenerational Family Violence" by Jill E. Korbin, Georgia J. Anetzberger and J. Kevin Eckert from *Journal of Elder Abuse & Neglect*, Vol. 1 No. 4 (1989), pp. 1–13. Copyright © 1989 by The Haworth Press, Inc. Reprinted by permission of the publisher.

facing the elderly, and elder abuse was "discovered" in the late 1970s and early 1980s. As elder abuse became the newest form of family violence, attempts were made to fit violence against elder family members into existing frameworks developed for other forms of family violence, in particular child abuse and neglect. Postulated causal explanations of child and elder abuse are similar largely because factors implicated in the child abuse literature have been echoed in the rapidly expanding literature on elder abuse, often with little empirical justification (Block and Sinnot 1979; Legal Research and Services for the Elderly 1981; Pedrick-Cornell and Gelles 1982). As considerations of elder abuse have moved beyond the initial, and often dramatic, accounts, it is time to step back and consider what an understanding of child maltreatment can contribute to knowledge of elder abuse and vice versa.

While historical precedents and the social milieu promote tolerance of physical force directed at a recalcitrant child (Erlanger 1974; Stark and McEvoy 1970; Straus, Gelles, and Steinmetz 1980), the same attitude is not in evidence for such behaviors directed against one's parents. Admonishments dating from biblical times to "honor thy mother and thy father" are in stark contrast to "spare the rod and spoil the child." Many states continue to permit corporal punishment of children in the schools while similar treatment of elders in institutions, when it comes to public attention, arouses ire and condemnation. Acts of physical restraint or force directed at children may fall under the rubric of maintaining control and even providing instruction, while the same act directed at an adult could constitute assault, or at least a violation of rights. That both elder and child abuse constitute socially recognized problems in our society provides a critical, but as yet untapped, comparison for research on intrafamilial violence and relations among generations.

Despite obvious age and status differences, young children and elder parents exhibit similarities that make the linking of child and elder abuse compelling. Young children and oftentimes elder parents, particularly those with impairments, are in powerless positions vis-à-vis their middle-generational caretakers. They require substantial time and energy investments for caretaking. They exhibit behaviors that may be perceived as troublesome, willful, and difficult to manage. They may be a source of emotional or financial stress. However, at the same time, differences in the nature of parent-to-child and child-to-parent relationships and in the social and legal status of adulthood versus childhood argue against a too-facile linking of the two problems.

Elder Abuse and Other Forms of Family Violence

Elder abuse has been compared with both child and spousal abuse (Finkelhor 1983; Finkelhor and Pillemer 1988; Phillips 1986). While much of the literature draws the primary parallel with child abuse, Pillemer and Finkelhor (1988) found spousal abuse to be more frequent (58 percent) than abuse by offspring (24 percent). However, they also found that living circumstances were critical in that the elders were abused by those with whom they resided. Elders living with offspring were slightly more likely to experience violence than those living with spouses. In our preliminary data analysis, 86 percent of elders abused by their adult offspring also lived with that offspring. Pillemer and Finkelhor argue that dominant living arrangements mean that spousal violence among elders will be more frequent, and they suggest greater attention to spousal abuse among the elderly. While spousal violence among elders has been neglected relative to offspring abuse, the state of current knowledge demands further investigation of both of these types of elder maltreatment. Elder abuse, like other forms of intrafamilial violence, has multiple manifestations.

Neither child abuse nor elder abuse is homogeneous and cannot be studied as such. Elder abuse between spouses may have more commonalities with spousal abuse in younger couples. Elder abuse that involves self abuse or neglect must be considered separately from that involving a perpetrator. Elder abuse by filial caregivers may have important parallels with child abuse by parents. While direct parallels between child and elder abuse are clearly premature, research efforts should be directed at determining what meaningful commonalities and differences exist.

Definitions and Limitations of Official Report Data

Despite the progress that has been made in the [thirty-eight] years since the coining of the term "the battered child" (Kempe et al. 1962), problems of definitional ambiguity and unreliable incidence and prevalence statistics have hampered the formulation of adequate explanations for the occurrence of intrafamilial violence against children. The growing literature on elder abuse, borrowing liberally from experience in child abuse, is plagued by many of the same problems.

Definitional ambiguity exists in both child and elder abuse. The label "the battered child syndrome" was intentionally chosen to grasp public, professional, and legislative attention. It referred specifically to children who had been seriously injured by their caretakers, usually their parents. In [thirty-eight] years, definitions of child abuse and neglect have expanded to include a range of caretaker behaviors and child outcomes. In a sense, "child abuse and neglect" has come to be used as a singular term, encompassing almost everything deemed "bad" for children for which caretakers can be held accountable. Similarly, in the elder abuse literature, definitions cut a wide swath (Callahan 1988; Pedrick-Cornell and Gelles 1982). For example, in our research, of 545 cases reported (but not necessarily substantiated) to Cuyahoga County, Ohio Adult Protective Services over a 12 month period in 1985–86, 60.2 percent represent a designation of self-abuse. While self-abuse is a serious problem and its inclusion in elder abuse statutes allows adult protective services to provide services to the elderly, including this designation under the rubric of "elder abuse" creates substantial problems for research. The breadth of definitions of elder abuse is a problem in many states, making comparability of incidence and prevalence rates problematic (Salend et al. 1984).

Elder and child abuse share the problem that official report data are too frequently inadequate to assess the scope of the problem. Official reports are thought to underestimate actual incidence and prevalence, for both child and elder abuse. It is estimated that between one-fifth and one-sixth of actual cases of elder abuse are reported (U.S. House of Representatives 1981, 1984). Because official reports do not encompass all cases, speculation can be rampant on the bias involved. The debate continues whether the poor are over-represented in child abuse reports due to increased stress and thus increased abuse or due to increased scrutiny and bias by public service agencies (e.g., Pelton 1981). Certain types of elder abuse also may be more likely to be reported: filial more than spousal perpetrators; physical more than psychological; and severe more than mild abuse.

Differences in estimates of incidence and prevalence based on self-reported violent behavior versus official reports that depend on whether there was an injurious or potentially injurious consequence of such behavior represent a long-standing debate in the family violence literature (Straus et al. 1980). Among the limitations of official reporting statistics of both elder and child abuse that make interpretation and comparison problematic, is the heterogeneity of behaviors included (Gelles 1979; Pillemer and Wolf 1986; Rizley and Cicchetti 1981; Salend et al. 1984).

Problems may also arise from differences in the level of violence that individuals report. Parents, backed up by cultural values on discipline of children, may be unselfconscious in reporting spanking their children. However, an adult offspring might be more hesitant to admit to breaking strongly held cultural values and slapping his/her elder parent.

Commonalities and Differences: Some Suggested Dimensions

The following section considers similarities and differences between elder abuse and child abuse. The discussion will be limited to intergenerational abuse, that is, parental abuse of children and adult offspring abuse of their parents. Because the terms *elder abuse* and *child abuse* encompass a wide range of behaviors, the discussion will be limited to physical abuse. The purpose of this discussion is to suggest dimensions relevant to a comparison of these two forms of intrafamilial violence. These dimensions are amenable to research efforts, without which comparisons of forms of family violence will remain speculative; and current knowledge will continue to be limited by research and service division according to the victimized group (Finkelhor 1983; Gelles 1979; Straus et al. 1980).[1]

Culturally Approved Scripts for Modifying Behavior

Sarah sat sullenly in her chair at the kitchen table, refusing to eat. Margaret prepared Sarah's favorite cereal, hoping to tempt her to eat. After much pleading

to get Sarah to eat the cereal, Margaret asked if she would rather have eggs.
Sarah looked interested and Margaret set about preparing them. When Mar-
garet set the eggs on the table, however, Sarah flew into a rage and threw all of
the food off the table. Milk, cereal, and eggs went flying everywhere. Margaret
lost her temper, began to scream, and slapped Sarah.

How would one respond to this incident if Sarah were a two-year-old versus an eighty-year-old? If Sarah were a child, many parents would sigh with recognition, even if not necessarily approving of the use of physical discipline. But what if Sarah were one's eighty-year-old mother? While parents are expected to exert some form of discipline with their children, what are adults expected to do with respect to their elder parents?

Despite the near-continuous debate in American society about proper methods of child rearing, parents have culturally approved scripts for coping with difficult and disapproved behavior in their children. Advice on child rearing is often conflicted, and there are multiple models from which to choose. Margaret Mead once noted that the only regularity of American child rearing is that one generation is committed to doing things differently than their parents. Parents are expected, by one means or another, to mold and modify the behavior of their immatures through the process of socialization to fit the needs of society. However, there are not similar guidelines for implementing behavior changes in one's elder parents. Adult offspring caring for elder parents may have to cope with behaviors that can be difficult, but they have little recourse in demanding better. They can plead, cajole, and negotiate, but the use of force is not within the accepted cultural repertoire.

Profiles of Violence

Profiles of violence directed at children and elders may vary in frequency and severity. Children may receive more frequent, less severe violence, for example, spankings. The threshold may be different for elder parents. While children are subjected to more routine violence, when violence erupts against elder parents, it may be either more severe or perceived as such. Spanking a child may not be viewed as serious or out of the ordinary while similarly striking a parent would be (Straus and Gelles 1986). Physical discipline of children occurs with sufficient frequency in the United States that it cannot be considered unusual (Straus et al. 1980). Further, physical discipline of children is instituted early. One-fourth of those mothers visiting a health care clinic reported spanking infants younger than six months of age, and one-third spanked infants younger than one year (Korsh, Gozzi, and Carlson 1965).

It has been suggested that physical discipline of children is particularly dangerous among individuals that disapprove of it (Parke and Collmer 1975). Parents who use physical discipline as a first resort may administer it before emotions get out of hand. In contrast, if physical force is a matter of last resort, following negotiation, threats, and pleas, by the time it is actually administered emotions are frayed; and anger and frustration may be more likely to exceed acceptable boundaries. Similarly, if physical force is a culturally disapproved measure of last resort against elder parents, it may be more likely to get out of control.

This dimension squarely confronts the definitional issues facing a comparison of child and elder abuse. How is "abuse" to be operationalized? Considering the widespread acceptance of physical discipline of children, would slapping a child be equated with slapping an elder parent?

Dependency

Dependency has been raised as a contributory factor in child and elder abuse. In earlier considerations of elder abuse, it was postulated that dependent elders, like young children, put stress on their caregivers that can lead to abuse. In both child and elder abuse, this may be an oversimplification. More current research on elder abuse (e.g., Anetzberger 1987; Pillemer 1986) has indicated that it may be the perpetrator, the abusive offspring, that is the dependent one. Some proportion of abusive adult offspring are in fact dependent on their elder parents, and the frustrations of continued dependency in this direction contribute to elder abuse. Similarly, the nature of childhood leads to an easy, and usually correct, assumption that children are dependent on their parents. However, abusive parents also may be dependent on their young children. This may not be readily apparent because they are not financially or physically dependent on their children for care. Nevertheless, abusive parents may be quite dependent on their young children emotionally. The concept of role reversal has been implicated in child-abusing families, in which parents look to their young children to fulfill their emotional needs (Morris and Gould 1963; Spinetta and Rigler 1972; Steele 1980).

Caretaking Commitment and Social Isolation

Both children and dependent elder parents require a caretaking commitment of time and energy. This is necessarily so for children and becomes more likely with increasing age and the existence of physical or psychological impairment in an elder parent. Whether this is a "burden" depends importantly on the caregiver's perception. Adult offspring are more likely to abuse their elder parents when they perceive a greater burden (Steinmetz 1983). The individual's perception of stress and burden may be more closely related to abuse than seemingly more objective measures (Steinmetz 1988). Negative feelings toward elders are more related to perceived parental dependency than to actual tasks performed (Cicirelli 1983). The investment required to care for an elder parent is often perceived as detrimental to an adult offspring's own health and happiness (e.g., Koopman-Boyden and Wells 1979; O'Malley et al. 1979). Cross-culturally, the greater the mother's sole burden for caretaking and the less likely she is to receive periodic help or relief from her burdens, the more likely she is to be rejecting and harsh with her children (Minturn and Lambert 1964).

Both child- and elder-abusing families have been characterized as socially isolated (e.g., Garbarino 1977; Garbarino and Sherman 1980; Gelles 1973;

Pillemer 1986; Wolf, Godkin, and Pillemer 1984). That both types of families seem to have fewer social resources and diminished abilities to use what is available, provides an important commonality. This becomes particularly important in the face of caretaking tasks.

Role Clarity

Family roles appear to be disrupted and distorted in both child- and elder-abusing families. Role reversal, in which the parent expects the child to nurture him/her has been implicated in the etiology of child maltreatment (Morris and Gould 1963; Spinetta and Rigler 1972; Steele 1980). A comparable dynamic in families caring for elder parents, generational inversion (Steinmetz and Amsden 1983), or an unresolved filial crisis has been implicated in elder abuse.

Difficult Behaviors

Both children and elder parents may exhibit behaviors that are perceived as stressful and difficult by their caregivers. Children are at increased risk of child abuse during difficult developmental stages, particularly those dealing with issues of oppositionality. Straus et al. (1980) suggest that young children and adolescents are more likely to be abused because of noncompliant behaviors at these ages. This could apply to elders who are not accustomed to accepting the authority of their children or willing to comply with their instructions.

While child behavior is cited as an important contributor to abusive situations (Friedrich and Boriskin 1976; Friedrich and Einbender 1983; Frodi 1981; George and Main 1979; Martin 1976; Milowe and Lourie 1964), data are sparse on the precise child behaviors that precipitate maltreatment (Kadushin and Martin 1981). Child behaviors that are reported by parents as precipitating abusive incidents may be noxious and stressful or may be normal child behaviors such as crying, soiling, or refusing to eat. These "normal" behaviors are stressful in and of themselves but precipitate abuse based on the interpretation of the parent, for example, when toileting accidents are seen as defiance rather than developmentally normal. Similar behaviors are not generally expected of elders and may be stressful when they occur (Anetzberger 1987). While it is accepted that young children sometimes refuse to eat, cry inconsolably, or soil their clothing, such behavior is less anticipated in adulthood and may be equally or more problematic. Anetzberger (1987) found that elder behaviors were more bothersome to their abusive caregivers than the actual tasks of caretaking. In both child- and elder-abusing families, a single behavior or incident is rarely sufficient to precipitate abuse. Rather, continuing negative interactions escalate into abuse (Anetzberger 1987; Kadushin and Martin 1981).

Expectations of Improvement

Closely related to the above, many disturbing or troublesome behaviors in children are part and parcel of a transitory stage of normal development. In contrast, with the elderly, the same behaviors represent deterioration and de-creased capacity rather than immaturity and a stage in development. The ex-pectation is not of an upward trajectory, but of a downward one. Parents, for example, look forward to completing toilet training and relief from diapers. In contrast, one cannot wait out incontinence in an elder parent with the ex-pectation that the parent will outgrow the condition.

Cycle of Violence

While the inevitability of intergenerational transmission of family violence has been challenged (Kaufman and Sigler 1987; Widom 1989), it is the most commonly reported causal factor in the child abuse literature. That abusive parents were abused as children was reported in the cornerstone article on child abuse and neglect (Kempe et al. 1962) and has been reported as a near-constant in subsequent literature. A previous history of intrafamilial violence also has been suggested in the elder abuse literature: that abusive adult off-spring were abused as children by their now abused parents (Pillemer and Suitor 1988). Adult offspring may be retaliating for past or continued physi-cal violence from their parents (Steinmetz 1981). Pillemer (1986) cautions that an intergenerational cycle of abuse may involve different dynamics for child-abusing versus elder-abusing individuals. The child abuser does not aggress against his or her aggressor, but against a child. But for elder abuse, "the cycle becomes more direct: the formerly abused child strikes out at his or her own abuser. This involves a different psychological process—one with elements of retaliation as well as imitation" (p. 243).

Policy Implications

The policy implications involved in child and elder abuse cannot be ignored (Schene and Ward 1988). Adult protective services and related laws have been molded on experience with child abuse, assuming similarities that may or may not exist. The social and legal status of childhood versus adulthood argues against direct parallels in service provision. For example, while controversy continues concerning the degree and nature of permissible state intervention in parental rights, the state nonetheless may assume protective custody of a minor child. The child's permission is not required for protective services and intervention. In contrast, an elder, unless deemed incompetent by clearly de-fined legal procedures, must be reckoned with in decisions about out of home placement. Elders are competent adults whose custody cannot be dictated without their consent.

Concluding Remarks

In the past approximately [forty] years, multiple forms of intrafamilial vio-lence and assault have emerged from dark family secrets to matters of pub-lic and professional concern. That both child and elder abuse occur in our society despite differing cultural values demands careful research attention. This [reading] has suggested several dimensions being studied in a systematic comparison of the dynamics involved in physical violence directed at elder parents by their adult offspring and young children by their parents. It is anticipated that a better understanding of the commonalities and differences in these two populations will further knowledge about the underlying dynamics of family violence and contribute to policy decisions about how to best serve these populations.

ENDNOTE

1. Our recently completed research project has compared and contrasted intergenerational violence toward elders by their adult offspring and toward young children by their parents. The sample consists of adult offspring perpetrators of elder abuse and two comparison samples: (a) child-abusing parents and (b) non-elder-abusing offspring. Additionally, a small sample of elders who have initiated legal proceedings against their abusive offspring has been included.

REFERENCES

Anetzberger, G. J. 1987. *The Etiology of Elder Abuse by Adult Offspring.* Springfield, IL: Charles Thomas.

Block, M. R. and J. D. Sinnott, eds. 1979. *The Battered Elder Syndrome: An Exploratory Study.* College Park, MD: University of Maryland Center of Aging.

Callahan, J. J. 1988. "Elder Abuse: Some Questions for Policymakers." *The Gerontologist* 28(4):453–58.

Cicirelli, V. 1983. "Adult Children and Their Elderly Parents." Pp. 31–46 in *Family Relations in Later Life,* edited by T. Brubaker. Beverly Hills, CA: Sage Publications.

Erlanger, H. B. 1974. "Social Class and Corporal Punishment in Childrearing. A Reassessment." *American Sociological Review* 39:68–85.

Finkelhor, D. 1983. "Common Features of Family Abuse." Pp. 17–28 in *The Dark Side of Families: Current Family Violence Research,* edited by D. Finkelhor, R. J. Gelles, G. T. Hotaling, and M. A. Straus. Beverly Hills, CA: Sage Publications.

Finkelhor, D. and K. Pillemer. 1988. "Elder Abuse: Its Relationship to Other Forms of Domestic Violence." Pp. 244–54 in *Family Abuse and Its Consequences: New Directions in Research,* edited by G. Hotaling, D. Finkelhor, J. Kirkpatrick, and M. Straus. Beverly Hills, CA: Sage Publications.

Friedrich, W. and J. A. Boriskin. 1976. "The Role of the Child in Abuse. A Review of the Literature." *American Journal of Orthopsychiatry* 46(4):580–90.

Friedrich, W. and A. J. Einbender. 1983. "The Abused Child. A Psychological Review." *Journal of Clinical Child Psychology* 12(3):244–56.

Frodi, A. M. 1981. "Contributions of Infant Characteristics to Child Abuse." *American Journal of Mental Deficiency* 85:341–49.

Garbarino, J. 1977. "The Human Ecology of Child Maltreatment: A Conceptual Model for Research." *Journal of Marriage and the Family* 39:721–35.

Garbarino, J. and D. Sherman. 1980. "High-Risk Neighborhoods and High-Risk Families: The Human Ecology of Child Maltreatment." *Child Development* 51:188–98.

Gelles, R. J. 1973. "Child Abuse as Psychopathology: A Sociological Critique and Reformulation." *American Journal of Orthopsychiatry* 43(4):611–21.

———. 1979. *Family Violence.* Beverly Hills, CA: Sage Publications.

———. 1982. "Toward Better Research on Child Abuse and Neglect. A Response to Besharov." *Child Abuse and Neglect: The International Journal* 6(4):495–96.

Kadushin, A. and J. Martin. 1981. *Child Abuse: An International Event.* New York: Columbia University Press.

Kaufman, J. and E. Sigler. 1987. "Do Abused Children Become Abusive Parents?" *American Journal of Orthopsychiatry* 57(2):186–92.

Kempe, C. H., F. Silver, B. F. Steele, W. Droegmueller, and H. Silver. 1962. "The Battered Child Syndrome." *Journal of the American Medical Association* 181:17–24.

Koopman-Boyden, P. G. and F. Wells. 1979. "The Problems Arising from Supporting the Elderly at Home." *New Zealand Medical Journal* 89:265–68.

Korsh, B., J. Christian, E. Gozzi, and P. Carlson. 1965. "Infant Care and Punishment: A Pilot Study." *American Journal of Public Health* 55(12):1880–88.

Legal Research and Services for the Elderly. 1981. *Elder Abuse and Neglect: A Guide for Practitioners and Policymakers.* Boston.

Milowe, I. and R. Lourie. 1964. "The Child's Role in the Battered Child Syndrome." *Journal of Pediatrics* 65:1079–81.

Minturn, L. and W. Lambert. 1964. *Mothers of Six Cultures: Antecedents of Child Rearing.* New York: Wiley and Sons.

Morris, M. and R. Gould. 1963. "Role Reversal: A Necessary Concept in Dealing with 'The Battered Child Syndrome.'" *American Journal of Orthopsychiatry* 33:298–99.

O'Malley, H., H. Segars, R. Perez, V. Mitchell, and G. Kneupfel. *Elder Abuse in Massachusetts: A Survey of Professionals and Paraprofessionals.* Boston: Legal Research and Services for the Elderly.

Pedrick-Cornell, C. and R. J. Gelles. 1982. "Elder Abuse: The Status of Current Knowledge." *Family Relations* 3:457–65.

Pelton, L. 1981. *The Social Context of Child Abuse and Neglect.* New York: Human Sciences Press.

Phillips, L. 1986. "Theoretical Explanations of Elder Abuse." Pp. 197–217 in *Elder Abuse: Conflict in the Family,* edited by K. A. Pillemer and R. S. Wolf. Dover, MA: Auburn House.

Pillemer, K. A. 1986. "Risk Factors in Elder Abuse: Results from a Case-Control Study." Pp. 239–63 in *Elder Abuse: Conflict in the Family,* edited by K. A. Pillemer and R. S. Wolf. Dover, MA: Auburn House.

Pillemer, K. A. and D. Finkelhor. 1988. "The Prevalence of Elder Abuse: A Random Sample Survey." *The Gerontologist* 28(1):51–57.

Pillemer, K. A. and J. Suitor. 1988. "Elder Abuse." In *Handbook of Family Violence,* edited by V. Van Hasselt, R. Morrison, A. Belack, and M. Hensen. New York: Plenum Press.

Pillemer, K. A. and R. S. Wolf, eds. 1986. *Elder Abuse: Conflict in the Family.* Dover, MA: Auburn House.

Rizley, R. and D. Cicchetti, eds. 1981. *Developmental Perspectives on Child Maltreatment.* San Francisco: Jossey-Bass.

Salend, E., R. A. Kane, M. Satz, and J. Pynoos. 1984. "Elder Abuse Reporting: Limitations of Statutes." *The Gerontologist* 24(1):61–69.

Schene, P. and S. Ward. 1988. "The Relevance of the Child Protection Experience." *Public Welfare* 46(2):14–21.

Spinetta, J. and D. Rigler. 1972. "The Child-Abusing Parent: A Psychological Review." *Psychological Bulletin* 77(4):296–304.

Stark, R. and J. McEvoy. 1970. "Middle Class Violence." *Psychology Today* 4:52–65.

Steele, R. F. 1980. "Psychodynamic Factors in Child Abuse." Pp. 49–85 in *The Battered Child,* 3d ed., edited by C. H. Kempe and R. E. Helfer. Chicago: University of Chicago Press.

Steinmetz, S. 1981. "Elder Abuse." *Aging.* January–February, pp. 6–10.

————. 1983. "Dependency, Stress, and Violence between Middle-Aged Caregivers and Their Elderly Parents." Pp. 139–49 in *Abuse and Maltreatment of the Elderly: Causes and Interventions,* edited by J. Kosberg. Boston: Wright PSG.

————. 1988. *Duty Bound: Elder Abuse and Family Care.* Beverly Hills, CA: Sage Publications.

Steinmetz, S. and G. Amsden. "Dependent Elders, Family Stress, and Abuse." In *Family Relations in Later Life,* edited by T. Brubaker. Beverly Hills, CA: Sage Publications.

Straus, M. A. and R. A. Gelles. 1986. "Societal Change and Change in Family Violence from 1975 to 1985 as Revealed by Two National Surveys." *Journal of Marriage and the Family* 48:465–69.

Straus, M. A., R. A. Gelles, and S. Steinmetz. 1980. *Behind Closed Doors: Violence in the American Family.* Garden City, NY: Anchor Books.

U.S. House Select Committee on Aging. 1981. *Elder Abuse: An Examination of a Hidden Problem.* Washington, DC: U.S. Government Printing Office.

————. 1984. *Elder Abuse: A National Disgrace.* Washington, DC: U.S. Government Printing Office.

Widom, C. S. 1989. "The Cycle of Violence." *Science* 244:160–66.

Wolf, R. S., M. A. Godkin, and K. A. Pillemer. *Elder Abuse and Neglect: Final Report from Three Model Projects.* Worcester, MA: University of Massachusetts Medical Center, University Center on Aging.

PART IX

Aging and Intergenerational Relationships

In this section we explore how family relationships change over time, especially as family members get older. Issues related to the elderly and their families include prolonged intergenerational family relationships, grandparenthood, care of elderly family members, economic status and poverty, housing issues, health issues, widowhood, and elder abuse. Of particular concern in the United States is the number of elderly who are and will be retiring in the next couple of decades. Part of this concern is driven by changing demographics: As the baby-boom generation (individuals born between 1946 and 1964) ages and prepares to retire, there are fewer workers in the younger generations. Thus, an ongoing public concern is whether there will be enough funds in Social Security to cover the growing number of retired persons in the 21st century. Of course, many factors affect how well an individual will do in retirement, including two important family variables — marital status and access to dual incomes — in addition to their education, whether or not they own a home, and the amount of income and savings accrued over their lifetime. People who are single, especially women, have a greater likelihood of being impoverished in their old age than married people with dual incomes. Other issues of concern for the elderly are the costs of long-term care, mandatory retirement, and ageism in the larger society.

Who Are the Elderly?

We tend to define the elderly by using a somewhat arbitrary age of 65 years old. Supposedly, before 65 you are not old and after 65 you are old. Age 65 was first used in 1889 to define the elderly in Germany when Chancellor Otto Bismarck chose this age to set up a social service program because, at that time, living to age 65 was very rare and, therefore, a 65-year-old was definitely considered old. In the 1930s, the U.S. Social Security Administration adopted age 65 to determine when retired persons could get benefits. Since life expectancy for both men and women has greatly increased since the 1930s, the Social Security Administration has decided to raise the age of retirement to 67 years.

The reality is that "old" and "aged" are really social definitions that vary from society to society and over time. Thus, what it means to be elderly in Japan is not what it means to be elderly in the United States. The elderly are more respected within certain cultures, such as that of Japan and among Native Americans. Historically, many cultures were gerontocracies, which means that the elderly were the highest status group in the social stratification system:

They controlled the social resources and political power. What it means to be elderly also varies within societies: It varies between men and women, between different racial-ethnic groups, between people of different social classes, and also between people of different occupations. For example, what is "old" for a professional athlete? What is too "old" to become a mother? What is "old" for an academic scholar? Physical aging also varies from individual to individual based on genetic differences and life experiences, such as work, exercise, diet, supportive relationships, and socioeconomic factors.

Family scholars are less interested in the physical aspects of aging than they are in the social consequences related to aging, such as how the elderly affect intergenerational family relationships. Matilda White Riley (1983) has researched families in the aging society of the United States and has found that increasing longevity has numerous effects on individuals and on family structure. In particular, Riley argues that family relationships are never fixed but, are, instead, constantly changing, a situation that is encouraged by longer life spans. Moreover, individuals have some degree of control over their close relationships. Longevity amplifies this control: People who live longer are more likely to be able to define and choose what types of relationships they would like to have and maintain. Riley's third argument is that the lives of family members are interdependent; thus, the increasing age of one member affects all the other members. Riley's research shows that increasing life spans provide opportunities and issues for the family that have not been experienced at any other time in history. Two family issues directly affected by longevity — grandparenthood and caring for elderly parents — are the focus of the readings in this section.

Grandparenting

The first article in this section, "The Modernization of Grandparenthood," is by Andrew J. Cherlin and Frank F. Furstenberg Jr. Cherlin is a professor of sociology at Johns Hopkins University, and Furstenberg is the Zellerbach Family Professor of Sociology and a research associate in the Population Studies Center at the University of Pennsylvania. This excerpt is taken from their book, *The New American Grandparent: A Place in the Family, A Life Apart* (1987). Cherlin and Furstenberg argue that grandparenthood is a relatively recent phenomenon, developing primarily after World War II. Citing studies (both their own and those of others), statistics, and historical accounts, they propose that the current status and situation of grandparenthood, though it is assumed to be typical, is instead a construction that has developed in the last 40 to 50 years. Their research reveals the extent to which grandparenthood, and families in general, are sometimes "idealized" — that is, the reality of the situation is not necessarily reflected in the wider society's beliefs about family structure.

This idealized notion of grandparenthood can be examined by studying the normative models of grandparenting in different cultures and different racial-ethnic groups. The second reading in this section, "The Strengths of

Apache Grandmothers: Observations on Commitment, Culture, and Care-taking," by Kathleen S. Bahr, provides this cross-cultural analysis. Bahr, a professor in the Department of Family Sciences at Brigham Young University, compares the models of grandparenting common in Anglo-American culture and in Apache culture. Bahr begins by introducing these contrasting models, then provides a detailed description of contemporary grandmothering and its social context among the White Mountain Apache grandmothers living on the Fort Apache Indian Reservation. She then makes a systematic comparison between selected themes and issues in both the Anglo American and Apache ethnic contexts, including the meanings and consequences of grandparenting for community and family life. Bahr concludes her article with a summary of ways the Apache family is experiencing strain and undergoing change. Fortunately, Apache grandmothers help to buffer most of these changes in the Apache family, but not without costs. Bahr argues that Apache grandmothers face incredible physical and emotional demands taking care of children and adults in their families.

In the larger society, other families are feeling these strains and undergoing change as well. In response, grandparenting continues to change with an increasing number of grandparents living in multigenerational households or actually raising their grandchildren (estimated to be approximately 4 million families in 2000), and with more families going through divorce or moving long distances from the grandparents. Kiernan (1995), for example, argues that "the reality is that all issues affecting parents and their children — divorce, dual-career couples, social mobility and rapid cultural and technological shifts — are also altering the relationships grandparents have with their families" (p. 1T). In recent years, a grandparents' rights movement has arisen to help grandparents maintain or reestablish contact with grandchildren who have been separated from them due to divorce or family discord. Whatever the future of grandparenting, it remains a vital and important social role in American families.

Caring for Elderly Parents

The third reading in this section, "Family Care of the Frail Elderly: A New Look at 'Women in the Middle,'" is by Sandra L. Boyd and Judith Treas. In their research, Boyd and Treas build on Elaine M. Brody's classic study (1981) of "women in the middle," that is, middle-aged women who are involved in parenting children and in caring for elderly parents. Because many of these women often work outside the home, they suffer severe role strain from the competing demands of work and family (see also Brody 1985). When Treas, a professor of sociology at the University of California at Irvine, was asked why she began this research, she responded as follows:

Do I have a personal interest in "women in the middle"? You bet. My mother is an 83-year-old widow, and my children are 12 and 14. I know what it is like to juggle doctor's appointments against Little League playoffs. A lot that is written about women in the middle dwells on the downside—the stresses and burdens of caregiving responsibilities to growing children and aging parents. Let's not lose sight of the advantages. As a card-carrying member of the "sandwich generation," I have a window on youth culture as well as on the concerns of seniors. This is a terrific vantage for anyone who is thinking about growing older down the road. (Personal Interview, 1997)

The reality is that dealing with aging parents eventually affects most adults, but it is women who undertake the disproportionate amount of physical care for aging and ill parents. This labor, like other caretaking labor in the family, is gendered, and the unequal distribution of responsibility for care of an aging parent is an area of conflict, both within couples and between siblings. Moreover, an illness of an elderly parent can affect the entire family, both emotionally and financially, especially if expensive long-term care is needed.

One consequence of prolonged intergenerational family relationships, and the increasing need for parent care, is the rise in reported and unreported cases of elder abuse. Family scholars are particularly concerned because the number of elder abuse cases in the United States is growing rapidly. Unfortunately, this type of abuse is severely underreported because the elderly are often ashamed of being abused. Elder abuse takes a variety of forms, from physical and sexual abuse, to emotional abuse, to neglect, to financial abuse. Moreover, the elderly, especially elderly women, are more likely to be victims of crime, including muggings, homicide, and domestic violence, than are younger people. Elder abuse is committed by family members in the home and by some nursing aide staff in nursing homes. However, because only a small percentage of the elderly (5 to 7 percent) live in nursing homes, most of this abuse occurs in private homes where a son or daughter is caring for an elderly parent. For a more detailed discussion of elder abuse, see Reading 32 by Jill E. Korbin, Georgia J. Anetzberger, and J. Kevin Eckert.

REFERENCES

Brody, Elaine M. 1981. "'Women in the Middle' and Family Help to Older People." *The Gerontologist* 21:471–80.

Brody, Elaine M. 1985. "Parent Care as a Normative Family Stress." *The Gerontologist* 25(1):19–29.

Cherlin, Andrew J. and Frank F. Furstenberg Jr. 1987. *The New American Grandparent: A Place in the Family, A Life Apart.* New York: Basic Books.

Kiernan, Louise. 1995. "Why It's Not Easy Being a Grandparent in the 1990s." *Des Moines Register,* November, pp. 1T–2T.

Riley, Matilda White. 1983. "The Family in an Aging Society: A Matrix of Latent Relationships." *Journal of Family Issues* 4(3):439–54.

33

THE MODERNIZATION
OF GRANDPARENTHOOD

ANDREW J. CHERLIN • FRANK F. FURSTENBERG, JR.

Writing a book about grandparents may seem an exercise in nostalgia, like writing about the family farm. We tend to associate grandparents with old-fashioned families — the rural, extended, multigenerational kind much celebrated in American mythology. Many think that grandparents have become less important as the nation has become more modern. According to this view, the shift to factory and office work meant that grandparents no longer could teach their children and grandchildren the skills needed to make a living; the fall in fertility and the rise in divorce weakened family ties; and the growth of social welfare programs meant that older people and their families were less dependent on each other for support. There is some truth to this perspective, but it ignores a powerful set of historical facts that suggest that grandparenthood — as a distinct and nearly universal stage of family life — is a post–World War II phenomenon.

Consider first the effect of falling rates of death. Much of the decline in mortality from the high preindustrial levels has occurred in this century. According to calculations by demographer Peter Uhlenberg, only about 37 percent of all males and 42 percent of all females born in 1870 survived to age sixty-five; but for those born in 1930 the comparable projections are 63 percent for males and 77 percent for females.[1] The greatest declines in adult mortality have occurred in the last few decades, especially for women. The average number of years that a forty-year-old white woman could expect to live increased by four between 1900 and 1940; but between 1940 and 1980 it increased by seven. For men the increases have been smaller, though still substantial: a two-year increase for forty-year-old whites between 1900 and 1940 and a four-year increase between 1940 and 1980. (The trends for nonwhites are similar.) Consequently, both men and women can expect to live much longer lives than was the case a few decades ago, and more and more women are outliving men. In 1980 the average forty-year-old white woman could expect to live to age eighty, whereas the average forty-year-old white man could expect to live only to age seventy-four. As a result, 60 percent of all the people sixty-five and over in the United States in 1980 were women.[2]

"The Modernization of Grandparenthood" from *The New American Grandparent: A Place in the Family. A Life Apart* by Andrew J. Cherlin and Frank F. Furstenberg, Jr. Reprinted by permission of the authors.

Thus, there are many more grandparents around today than just a few decades ago simply because people are living longer — and a majority of them are grandmothers.

This decline in mortality has caused a profound change in the relationship between grandparents and grandchildren. For the first time in history, most adults live long enough to get to know most of their grandchildren, and most children have the opportunity to know most of their grandparents. A child born in 1900, according to Uhlenberg, had a better than nine-out-of-ten chance that two or more of his grandparents would be alive. But by the time the child reached age fifteen, the chances were only about one out of two that two or more of his grandparents would still be alive. Thus, some children were fortunate enough to establish relationships with grandparents, but in many other families the remaining grandparents must have died while the grandchild was quite young. Moreover, it was unusual for grandchildren at the turn of the century to know all their grandparents: Only one in four children born in 1900 had four grandparents alive, and a mere one in fifty still had four grandparents alive by the time they were fifteen. In contrast, the typical fifteen-year-old in 1976 had a nearly nine-out-of-ten chance of having two or more grandparents still alive, a better than one-out-of-two chance of having three still alive, and a one-out-of-six chance of having all four still alive.[3] Currently, then, nearly all grandchildren have an extended relationship with two or more grandparents, and substantial minorities have the opportunity for extended relationships with three or even all four.

Indeed, Americans take survival to the grandparental years pretty much for granted. The grandparents we spoke to rarely mentioned longer life when discussing the changes since they were children. *Of course* they were still alive and reasonably healthy; that went without saying. But this taken-for-grantedness is a new phenomenon; before World War II early death was a much greater threat, and far fewer people lived long enough to watch their grandchildren grow up.

Most people are in their forties or fifties when they first become grandparents. Some observers have mistakenly taken this as an indication that grandparents are younger today than in the past. According to one respected textbook:

> Grandparenting has become a phenomenon of middle age rather than old age. Earlier marriage, earlier childbirth, and longer life expectancy are producing grandparents in their forties.[4]

But since the end of the nineteenth century (the earliest period for which we have reliable statistics) there has been little change in the average age at marriage. The only exception was the 1950s, when ages at marriage and first birth did decline markedly but only temporarily.[5] With the exception of the unusual 1950s, then, it is likely that the age when people become grandparents has stayed relatively constant over the past century. What has changed is the amount of time a person spends as a grandparent: Increases in adult life expectancy mean that grandparenthood extends into old age much more often.

In our national sample of the grandparents of teenagers, six out of ten had become grandparents while in their forties. When we interviewed them, however, their average age was sixty-six. Grandparenting has been a phenomenon of middle age for at least the past one hundred years. The difference today is that it is now a phenomenon of middle age *and* old age for a greater proportion of the population. To be sure, our notions of what constitutes old age also may have changed, as one woman in our study implied when discussing her grandmother:

> *She stayed home more, you know. And I get out into everything I can. That's the difference. That is, I think I'm younger than she was at my age.*

Moreover, earlier in the century some middle-aged women may have been too busy raising the last of their own children to think of themselves as grandmothers. Nevertheless, in biological terms, the average grandparent alive today is older, not younger, than the average grandparent at the turn of the century.

Consider also the effects of falling birth rates on grandparenthood. As recently as the late 1800s, American women gave birth to more than four children, on average.[6] Many parents still were raising their younger children after their older children had left home and married. Under these conditions, being a grandparent often overlapped with being a parent. One would imagine that grandparenthood took a back seat to the day-to-day tasks of raising the children who were still at home. Today, in contrast, the birth rate is much lower; and parents are much more likely to be finished raising their children before any of their grandchildren are born. In 1900 about half of all fifty-year-old women still had children under eighteen; but by 1980 the proportion had dropped to one-fourth.[7] When a person becomes a grandparent now, there are fewer family roles competing for his or her time and attention. Grandparenthood is more of a separate stage of family life, unfettered by child-care obligations — one that carries its own distinct identification. It was not always so.

The fall of fertility and the rise of life expectancy have thus greatly increased the supply of older persons for whom grandparenthood is a primary intergenerational role. To be sure, there always have been enough grandparents alive so that everyone in American society (and nearly all other societies, for that matter) was familiar with the role. But until quite recently, an individual faced a considerable risk of dying before, or soon after, becoming a grandparent. And even if one was fortunate enough to become a grandparent, lingering parental obligations often took precedence. In past times, when birth and death rates were high, grandparents were in relatively short supply. Today, as any number of impatient older parents will attest, grandchildren are in short supply. Census data bear this out: In 1900 there were only twenty-seven persons aged fifty-five and over for every one hundred children fourteen and under; but by 1984 the ratio had risen to nearly one-to-one. In fact, the Bureau of the Census projects that by the year 2000, for the first time in our nation's history, there will be more persons aged fifty-five and over than children fourteen and under.[8]

Moreover, technological advances in travel and long-distance communication have made it easier for grandparents and grandchildren to see or talk to each other. . . . As late as the end of World War II, only half the homes in the United States had a telephone. The proportion rose quickly to two-thirds by the early 1950s and three-fourths by the late 1950s.[9] Today, more than 97 percent of all homes have telephones.[10] About one-third of the grandparents in our survey reported that they had spoken to the study child on the telephone once a week or more during the previous year.

Nor did most families own automobiles until after World War II, as several grandparents reminded us:

> *I could be wrong, but I don't feel grandparents felt as close to grandchildren during that time as they do now. . . . Really back there, let's say during the twenties, transportation was not as good, so many people did not have cars. Fortunately, I can say that as far back as I remember my father always had a car, but there were many other people who did not. They traveled by horse and buggy and some even by wagons. And going a distance, it did take quite some time. . . .*

Only about half of all families owned automobiles at the end of the war.[11] Even if a family owned an automobile, long trips still could take quite some time:

> *Well, I didn't see my grandmother that often. They just lived one hundred miles from us, but back then one hundred miles was like four hundred now, it's the truth. It just seemed like clear across the country. It'd take us five hours to get there, it's the truth. It was an all-day trip.*

But in the 1950s, the Federal government began to construct the interstate highway system, which cut distances and increased the speed of travel. The total number of miles driven by passenger vehicles increased from about 200 million miles in the mid-1930s to about 500 million miles in the mid-1950s to over a billion miles in the 1980s.[12] Not all of this increase represents trips to Grandma's house, of course; but with more cars and better highways, it became much easier to visit relatives in the next county or state.

But weren't grandparents and grandchildren more likely to be living in the same household at the turn of the century? After all, we do have a nostalgic image of the three-generation family of the past, sharing a household and solving their problems together. Surprisingly, the difference between then and now is much less than this image would lead us to believe. To be sure, there has been a drastic decline since 1900 in the proportion of older persons who live with their adult children. In 1900 the proportion was more than three out of five, according to historian Daniel Scott Smith; in 1962 it was one out of four; and by 1975 it had dropped to one in seven. What has occurred is a great increase in the proportion of older people who live alone or only with their spouses. Yet the high rates of co-residence in 1900 do not imply that most grandparents were living with their grandchildren—much less that most grandchildren were living with their grandparents. As Smith's data show, older persons who were married tended to live with unmarried children only;

children usually moved out when they married. It was mainly widows unable to maintain their own households who moved in with married children. Consequently, according to Smith's estimates, only about three in ten persons sixty-five and over in 1900 lived with a grandchild, despite the great amount of co-residence between older parents and their adult children. What is more, because of the relative shortage of grandparents, an even lower percentage of grandchildren lived with their grandparents. Smith estimates that about one in six children under age ten in 1900 lived in the same household with someone aged fifty-five or over.[13] Even this figure overestimates the number of children living with their grandparents, because some of these elderly residents were more distant kin, boarders, or servants. . . .

. . .

Grandparents also have more leisure time today, although the trend is more pronounced for men than for women. The average male can now expect to spend fifteen years of his adult life out of the labor force, most of it during retirement. (The labor force comprises all persons who are working for pay or looking for work.) The comparable expected time was ten years in 1970, seven years in 1940, and only four years in 1900.[14] Clearly, a long retirement was rare early in this century and still relatively rare just before World War II. But since the 1960s, workers have begun to leave the labor force at younger ages. In 1961, Congress lowered the age of eligibility for Social Security benefits from sixty-five to sixty-two. Now more than a half of all persons applying for Social Security benefits are under sixty-five.[15] Granted, some of the early retirees are suffering from poor health, and other retirees may have difficulty adjusting to their new status. Still, when earlier retirement is combined with a longer life span, the result is a greatly extended period during which one can, among other things, get to know and enjoy one's grandchildren.

The changes in leisure time for women are not as clear because women have always had lower levels of labor force participation than men. To be sure, women workers also are retiring earlier and, as has been noted, living much longer. And most women in their fifties and sixties are neither employed nor raising children. But young grandmothers are much more likely to be employed today than was the case a generation ago; they are also more likely to have aged parents to care for. Young working grandmothers, a growing minority, may have less time to devote to their grandchildren.

Most employed grandparents, however, work no more than forty hours per week. This, too, is a recent development. The forty-hour work week did not become the norm in the United States until after World War II. At the turn of the century, production workers in manufacturing jobs worked an average of fifty hours per week. Average hours dropped below forty during the Depression, rose above forty during the war, and then settled at forty after the war.[16] Moreover, at the turn of the century, 38 percent of the civilian labor force worked on farms, where long hours were commonplace. Even in 1940, about 17 percent of the civilian labor force worked on farms; but currently only about 3 percent work on farms.[17] So even if they are employed, grandparents have more leisure time during the work week than was the case a few decades ago.

They also have more money. Living standards have risen in general since World War II, and the rise has been sharpest for the elderly. As recently as 1960, older Americans were an economically deprived group; now they are on the verge of becoming an economically advantaged group. The reason is the Social Security system. Since the 1950s and 1960s, Congress has expanded Social Security coverage so that by 1970 nearly all nongovernment workers, except those in nonprofit organizations, were covered. And since the 1960s, Congress has increased Social Security benefits far faster than the increase in the cost of living. As a result, the average monthly benefit (in constant 1980 dollars, adjusted for changes in consumer prices) rose from $167 in 1960, to $214 in 1970, to $297 in 1980.[18] Because of the broader coverage and higher benefits, the proportion of the elderly who are poor has plummeted. In 1959, 35 percent of persons sixty-five and over had incomes below the official poverty line, compared to 22 percent of the total population. By 1982 the disparity had disappeared: 15 percent of those sixty-five and over were poor, as were 15 percent of the total population.[19] The elderly no longer are disproportionately poor, although many of them have incomes not too far above the poverty line. Grandparents, then, have benefited from the general rise in economic welfare and, as they reach retirement, from the improvement in the economic welfare of the elderly.

Because of the postwar prosperity and the rise of social welfare institutions, older parents and their adult children are less dependent on each other economically. Family life in the early decades of the century was precarious; lower wages, the absence of social welfare programs, and crises of unemployment, illness, and death forced people to rely on their kin for support to a much greater extent than is true today. There were no welfare checks, unemployment compensation, food stamps, Medicare payments, Social Security benefits, or government loans to students. Often there was only one's family. Some older people provided assistance to their kin, such as finding a job for a relative, caring for the sick, or tending to the grandchildren while the parents worked. Sometimes grandparents, their children, and their grandchildren pooled their resources into a single family fund so that all could subsist. Exactly how common these three-generational economic units were we do not know; it would be a mistake to assume that all older adults were cooperating with their children and grandchildren at all times. In fact, studies of turn-of-the-century working-class families suggest that widowed older men — past their peak earning capacity and unfamiliar with domestic tasks as they were — could be a burden to the households of their children, while older women — who could help out domestically — were a potential source of household assistance. Nevertheless, these historical accounts suggest that intensive intergenerational cooperation and assistance was more common than it is today.[20] Tamara Hareven, for example, studied the families of workers at the Amoskeag Mills in Manchester, New Hampshire, at the turn of the century. She found that the day-to-day cooperation of kin was necessary to secure a job at the mill, find housing, and accumulate enough money to get by.[21] Cooperation has declined because it is not needed as often: Social welfare programs now provide services that only the family formerly provided; declining rates of illness, death, and unemployment have reduced the frequency of family crises; and the rising standard of living — particularly of the elderly — has reduced the need for financial assistance.

The structure of the Social Security system also has lessened the feelings of obligation older parents and their adult children have toward each other. Social Security is an income transfer system in which some of the earnings of workers are transferred to the elderly. But we have constructed a fiction about Social Security, a myth that the recipients are only drawing out money that they put into the fund earlier in their lives. This myth allows both the younger contributors and the older recipients to ignore the economic dependency of the latter. The elderly are free to believe that they are just receiving that to which they are entitled by virtue of their own hard work. The tenacity of this myth — it is only now breaking down under the tremendous payment burden of our older age structure — demonstrates its importance. It allows the elderly to accept financial assistance without compromising their independence, and it allows children to support their parents without either generation openly acknowledging as much.

All of these trends taken together — changes in mortality, fertility, transportation, communications, the work day, retirement, Social Security, and standards of living — have transformed grandparenthood from its pre–World War II state. More people are living long enough to become grandparents and to enjoy a lengthy period of life as grandparents. They can keep in touch more easily with their grandchildren; they have more time to devote to them; they have more money to spend on them; and they are less likely still to be raising their own children.

The Bonds of Sentiment

Hand in hand with these changes in the structure of grandparenthood have come great changes in the emotional content of the grandparent–grandchild relationship. Here we are pressing against the limits of historical scholarship; it is more difficult to document alterations in ways of thinking than in material conditions. But on the basis of historical studies and the reports of the grandparents in our study, it seems that there has been an increasing emphasis during this century on bonds of sentiment: love, affection, and companionship.

When we asked grandparents whether grandparenthood had changed since they were grandchildren, we heard stories of their childhood that differed somewhat from the idyllic image of the three-generational family of the past. Their grandparents, we were told, were respected, admired figures who often assisted other family members. But again and again, our informants talked about the emotional distance between themselves and their grandparents:

> *The only grandmother I remember is my father's mother, and she lived with us.*
> *Interviewer:* What was it like, having your grandmother live with you?
> *Terrible [laughter]! She was old, she was strict. . . . We weren't allowed to sass her. I guess that was the whole trouble. No matter what she did to you, you had to take it. . . . She was good, though. She was real helpful. She used to do all the patching of the pants, and she was helpful. But, oh, she was strict. You weren't allowed to do anything, she'd tell on you right away.*
> *Interviewer:* So what difference do you think there is between being a grandparent when you were a grandchild and being a grandparent now?
> *It's different. My grandma never gave us any love.*
> *Interviewer:* No?
> *Nooo. My goodness, no, no. No, never took us anyplace, just sat there and yelled at you all the time.*
> *Interviewer:* Did you have a lot of respect for your grandmother?
> *Oh, we had to—whether we wanted to or not, we had to.*
> *Interviewer:* Do you think your grandchildren have as much respect for you now as you had for your grandmother?
> *I don't think so, no. Because I think if my grandchildren have something to say, they'll come up and say it. I mean, they won't hold it back. . . . Whereas before you couldn't even speak out.*

Grandma may have helped out, and she certainly was respected, even loved; but she often was an emotionally distant figure.

Gunhild Hagestad analyzed all mentions of grandparents in two volumes of *Good Housekeeping* from the 1880s. Most of the items were poems, often describing an old grandmother who might be sitting quietly by the fire. Describing the subjects of such odes as "Grandma—God Bless Her" (1887), Hagestad writes: "Seldom, if ever, was the 1880s grandmother described as dealing with the nitty-gritty aspects of everyday family life. The frail figure by the fire was not *withdrawn* from everyday living, but was *above* it. She had a place on a pedestal, and she had earned it."[22]

Many of our informants were from immigrant families. In a study of Italian immigrant families in Buffalo, New York, Virginia Yans-McLaughlin noted that the elderly were honored and revered and that grandmothers who helped with household tasks and child rearing were highly valued family members.[23] But our informants also spoke of the ways in which emotional distance could be compounded by culture and language:

> *Well, see, my grandmother was Polish, and she couldn't speak English. But she used to come every Sunday, and when she'd come, we thought the world of her. And she'd try to speak to us—it was hard. It was hard for her to speak to us, because we all spoke English and she was Polish.*
> *Interviewer:* I see. Did you ever go to church with her?

No, no.
Interviewer: Did you joke or kid at all with her?
No, we never did it.
Interviewer: You never went shopping together?
No.
Interviewer: Day trips . . .
No, no.
Interviewer: Did she ever give you money?
Oh yes, she used to treat us, she'd give us a nickel or something, and we thought it was a whole lot she gave us.
Interviewer: How about disciplining? Did she discipline you?
Well, like I said, it was hard for us to make contact with one another because she was from Poland and we were born in America.

In his well-known study of the black family, E. Franklin Frazier noted the prestige, importance, and dignity of the black grandmother, the "guardian of the generations," during and after slavery. Even during the great twentieth-century migration of blacks to northern cities, the black grandmother, he wrote, "has not ceased to watch over the destiny of the Negro families."[24] We will have more to say in later chapters about the continued authority of black grandmothers today. But here let us note that even when our black informants spoke warmly and lovingly of their grandparents, they often commented on the lack of free expression and understanding:

I grew up on a plantation. [When my grandparents] were no longer able to work in the fields, then they lived with one of their children or the other. . . . And my grandmother was a good cook. I loved that, she could make that good homemade bread. And my grandfather played with us a lot, and he would tell stories — he was a good storyteller. Then he played with us a lot and I liked that an awful lot. So they weren't grandparents that were rude or anything, they just were lovable grandparents. When they were around we just had a lot of fun.
Interviewer: Do you think you were more friendly with your grandparents than you are with Peter *[her grandchild]?*
I think I'm more friendly with Peter than I was with my grandparents. Because . . . children couldn't express themselves at that time, when I was a child, like children can now. [They could] express themselves to me; I couldn't express myself to them. They would say that was being sass or bad or whatever. . . . I think the grandparents nowadays get a better understanding of their grandchildren than the grandparents then because we couldn't talk back to them. Once in a while we could ask them if we could do something — may I do this, or something. But that was it, almost. And maybe we could talk about school or something, about our lessons or something. They did the telling, you know.

"I couldn't express myself." This inability to communicate, to gain an understanding of the other person's thoughts and feelings, to be emotionally "close," to be friends, characterized grandparent–grandchild relations two generations ago, according to the recollections of our informants.

This is not to say that affective bonds were absent from the relations between young and old. On the contrary, both affection and respect were present. For example, Jane Range and Maris Vinovskis, who analyzed the content of short fiction in a popular nineteenth-century magazine, found that 43 percent of the elderly characters received respect from the younger characters and 48 percent received affection.[25] The shift, however, has been in the balance between respect and affection, as the responses to several questions in our national survey suggest. We asked all respondents who knew at least one of their grandparents, "Are you and [the study child] more friendly, less friendly, or about the same as your grandparents were with you?" Forty-eight percent said "more friendly"; only 9 percent said "less friendly." Similarly, 55 percent said that their relationship with the study child was "closer" than their relationship with their grandparents; just 10 percent said "not as close." When we asked about respect, most grandparents thought there had been no change, although 22 percent said they were more respectful to their grandparents versus only 2 percent who said their grandchildren were more respectful toward them. On the issue of authority, the responses were mixed: 28 percent thought they had more authority over the study child than their grandparents had over them, 22 percent thought their grandparents had more authority over them, and 50 percent saw no change. Perhaps there was less agreement about changes in authority because relatively few grandparents, even at the turn of the century, had substantial authority over their grandchildren.

To be sure, it is hard to judge how accurate these recollections are of the situation two generations ago. Moreover, the extent to which people can freely express their sentiments may have increased over time. But the story that the grandparents consistently told us fits with the demographic, economic, and technological developments we have discussed. It is easier for today's grandparents to have a pleasurable, emotion-laden relationship with their grandchildren because they are more likely to live long enough to develop the relationship; because they are not still busy raising their own children; because they have more leisure time; because they can travel long distances more easily and communicate over the telephone; and because they have fewer grandchildren and more resources to devote to them.

Above all, they are more likely to be their grandchildren's companions because of the increasing economic independence of the generations. When intensive economic cooperation and assistance was more common, older people and their families were bound together by instrumental ties of the sort we recognize today mainly in the lower class. Under these circumstances, one's obligations to kin took precedence over one's feelings toward them. Michael Anderson, for example, studied the effects of Poor Law relief on the quality of intergenerational relations in the nineteenth- and early twentieth-century Britain. Poor relief, which was locally administered, varied widely from area to area. In areas where administration was strict and the burden of supporting the elderly fell more heavily on their children,

... tensions were frequently increased both by the need to contribute and by the pressures applied by the authorities, so that, while the economic functions of kinship rose in importance, affective functions frequently declined.[26]

But where relief was more generous, he argued, bonds of sentiment became more visible. He cited an observer of one such area who noted in 1909 that a "weak sense of responsibility exists side by side with much natural affection and concern for each other's health and well-being between parents and children among farm labourers."[27] From evidence such as this, Anderson reasoned that the replacement of the locally administered system with a uniform, nationwide system of income maintenance for the elderly in the mid-twentieth century "has markedly decreased the tensions and conflicts in family relationships" and allowed families to better perform "affective functions" for their members.[28]

Anderson's study suggests that with the increasing economic independence of the generations of this century, bonds of obligation have declined relative to bonds of sentiment. The responses of the grandparents in our study are consistent with this proposition. Freed of economic dependence and removed from day-to-day control over resources, today's grandparents ... strive to be their grandchildren's pals rather than their bosses. As another grandmother at the same senior citizen center said:

> *The grandchildren really do love their grandparents more today than ever. I'm positive.*
> *Interviewer:* Why?
> *You know why? The social status is almost the same. They're interested in what you're interested in.*

They share not only interests but also relative economic equality: Neither is dependent on the other. Anthropologists have described many other societies in which grandparents tend to have informal, friendly relationships with their grandchildren; this is one instance of the so-called "joking relationship" between kin.[29] Such informal relationships between grandparents and grandchildren, however, are not universal. Dorian Apple Sweetzer showed that "friendly equality" between grandparents and grandchildren is much more common in societies in which grandparents lack authority over their grown children.[30] Ours is also such a society.

Nevertheless, we do not wish to argue that the changing material conditions of grandparents in this century — demographic, technological, and economic — were the "cause" of the change in how they relate to their grandchildren in any simple sense. An increasing emphasis on sentiment in all family relations had been under way in the United States for some time. Historian Carl Degler claimed that the "modern American family" — characterized by affection and mutual respect between marriage partners, the primacy of the homemaking and child-rearing role of the wife, increasing child-centeredness, and smaller size — emerged between the American Revolution and 1830.[31] For instance, he cites research by Smith suggesting that parental control over children's choice of spouses and timing of marriage declined during that period (and, presumably, less constrained, "romantic" marriages increased).[32]

Attitudes toward children continued to evolve in the late nineteenth and early twentieth centuries. Viviana Zelizer has documented a shift in the value of children between the 1870s and 1930s from an economically useful asset to a priceless, but economically useless, object of sentiment. For example:

> In 1896, the parents of a two-year-old child sued the Southern Railroad Company of Georgia for the wrongful death of their son. Despite claims that the boy performed valuable services for his parents — $2 worth per month, "going upon errands to neighbors . . . watching and amusing . . . younger child" — no recovery was allowed, except for minimum burial expenses. The court concluded that the child was "of such tender years as to be unable to have any earning capacity, and hence the defendant could not be held liable in damages."[33]

Both the parents and the court argued solely on the basis of the child's economic worth. By the 1920s, according to Zelizer, this strict economic approach to children's worth had been replaced by a view of children as precious, priceless objects of love and affection. Judging the value of children by their potential earning power came to be seen as degrading, even immoral. Ironically, noted Zelizer, even as compulsory schooling and child labor laws reduced the economic contribution of children, awards for the wrongful death of children increased. Today, the economically useless but emotionally priceless child has great value:

> In January 1979, when three-year-old William Kennerly died from a lethal dose of fluoride at a city dental clinic, the New York State Supreme Court jury awarded $750,000 to the boy's parents.[34]

Moreover, almost every observer of historical change in the relationship between American husbands and wives has noted the increasing emphasis upon affection between the spouses. Degler claimed that this emphasis on love and affection as the basis for marriage emerged in the late eighteenth century.[35] Perhaps the best-known statement of the shift came in a widely used sociology of the family textbook written in 1945 by Ernest W. Burgess and Harvey J. Locke:

> The basic thesis of this book is that the family has been in historical times in transition from an institution with family behavior controlled by the mores, public opinion, and law to a companionship with family behavior arising from the mutual affection and consensus of its members. The companionship form of family is not to be conceived as having already been realized, but as emerging. . . . The permanence of marriage is more and more dependent upon the tenuous bonds of affection, temperamental compatibility, and mutual interests.[36]

As for the elderly, recent historical scholarship suggests shifts in public attitudes, although historians disagree about the timing of the initial changes. David Hackett Fischer contended that the status of older people began to decline between 1770 and 1820. W. Andrew Achenbaum, however, argued that attitudes about the status of the elderly began to change for the worse between the Civil War and World War I.[37] By the end of World War I, wrote Achenbaum, old age had emerged as a social problem, although political actions designed to help solve the problem did not begin until the 1920s. In fact, Achenbaum stated flatly that "the fundamental modernization of old age in America took place after 1920."[38]

Fischer linked the shift in the status of the elderly to a shift in sentiment. Prior to the American Revolution:

> Even as most (though not all) elderly people were apt to hold more power than they would possess in a later period, they were also apt to receive less affection, less love, less sympathy from those younger than themselves. The elderly were kept at an emotional distance by the young. If open hostility between the generations was not allowed, affection was not encouraged either.[39]

Conversely:

> In modern America, as the social and economic condition of the aged worsened, their psychic condition may have grown a little better, in one way at least. As elders lost their authority within the society, they gained something in return. Within the sphere of an individual family, ties of affection may have grown stronger as ties of obligation grew weak.[40]

One must be skeptical of Fischer's implicit claim that most elderly were powerful, venerated figures prior to the Revolution. Carol Haber has argued that this may have been true for older people who controlled resources or maintained powerful positions—landowners, ministers, community leaders, and the like—but for the landless, the childless, and the otherwise impoverished, "gray hair and wrinkles seemed reason for contempt instead of honor; their age alone was not deemed worthy of respect."[41] Moreover, we know that in recent decades the social and economic condition of the aged has improved, not worsened. Nevertheless, we can infer from the grandparents in our study that the increasing emphasis on affection detected by scholars such as Fischer and Anderson was still continuing during their lifetimes.

Family change in the United States, then, has been a long-term process. The still incomplete historical record (the subdiscipline of family history is only about twenty years old) suggests that change has been discontinuous, occurring in great bursts and then subsiding for a time. One great period of change, several scholars tell us, lasted from the Revolution to the 1820s. A second one occurred about fifty years later: Zelizer argued that attitudes toward children changed dramatically between the 1870s and the 1930s; and it is known that during the same period a great debate about the rising divorce rate and a corresponding shift in attitudes toward divorce occurred.[42] We would suggest that future scholars, looking back on the current era, may view the 1960s and 1970s as another great period of change.

Many of the scholars cited here have advanced cultural or ideological explanations for the change in family values: the spread of the ideas of the Enlightenment or of the French and American Revolutions, or the changing modes of thought during the Progressive Era. (Others, such as Burgess and Locke, referred to a vaguely defined change from "traditional" to "modern" societies.) Without doubt, the long-term cultural changes influenced the evolution of the grandparent–grandchild relationship. But it also seems clear that the great transformation of this relationship throughout American society could not have taken place without the profound alteration of the material circumstances of grandparents that has occurred over the past several decades. To be sure, this transformation probably was under way among middle-class families before the twentieth century began. But the demographic, technological, and economic trends that have accelerated since 1940 were a necessary, though not sufficient, condition for the nearly universal emergence of a relationship based overwhelmingly on sentiment. Although child mortality rates dropped early in the century (contributing to the change in attitudes toward children), adult mortality rates dropped fastest, as we have noted, after 1940. Although the rising wages for male workers in the early decades of the century allowed middle-class wives to concentrate on childrearing and made marriage more of an emotional refuge from the outside world, the relative economic status of the elderly improved dramatically only after 1960. The result of these developments is the spread of a style of grandparenting characterized by emotionally satisfying leisure-time activities, a lack of direct responsibility for raising the grandchildren, and irregular direct assistance. It is a style that has only spread beyond the middle class since World War II because the demographic technological, and economic changes that support it were not complete (or in some cases had hardly begun) until then. We will label it the *companionate* style of grandparenting. . . .

Grandparenting: Yesterday and Today

The grandparents in our study told us clearly what has been gained since they were grandchildren: a greater sense of understanding between the generations; more companionship, emotional warmth, and closeness; and a stronger emphasis on love. But it is not as clear what has been lost. There remains a feeling among many observers that modernization has removed something of value from the grandparent–grandchild relationship. A [1981] book by child psychiatrist Arthur Kornhaber and journalist Kenneth L. Woodward bemoaned the decline of "vital connections" between grandparents and grandchildren. When Kornhaber and Woodward asked their nonrandom sample of grandparents, "Do you have a good relationship with your grandchildren?" 75 percent responded "all of the time," 15 percent responded "most of the time," and only 10 percent responded "some of the time." Yet the authors dismissed these responses; actually, they argued, the grandparents were fooling themselves:

> The respondents did not understand that time and proximity were the basic foundations for a "good relationship." They confused spending a few pleasant moments together for a true relationship. They thought that they had a "good" relationship but upon deeper probing many expressed feelings that in reality, this relationship was not what they really wanted, that it had no relevance for them, that it wasn't enough.[43]

What is a "true relationship"? To Kornhaber and Woodward it is predicated upon grandparents living with or very near their grandchildren and spending a great deal of time with them. More important, it arises from the kind of intense commitment to family that presumably developed when family members had to cooperate economically on a daily basis to make ends meet. In fact, the authors asserted:

> These adverse economic conditions were ideal for the development of vital connections between grandparents and grandchildren. Their lives converged in the critical dimensions of time and place; survival alone demanded commitment to the intrafamily network as a community of kin.[44]

It follows from this line of reasoning that one of the costs of prosperity is the loss of instrumental intergenerational ties—the decline of grandparents as mentors, role models, and caretakers.

This argument deserves to be taken seriously, for it probably is true that regular, material contributions of grandparents have declined in importance. As the stability of family life increased between the turn of the century and the 1950s, the contributions of kin became less necessary to the family's subsistence. The more that family life is unstable and precarious, then, the greater the supportive role of grandparents and other kin. Until recently, at least, the twentieth-century trend has been toward greater stability and, hence, less intensive support by grandparents.

But the argument is overstated. First, anyone who would hark back to the extended family of a few generations ago must keep in mind the harsh reality of high rates of death. One-fourth of the grandparents in our study never knew a grandparent. Many others undoubtedly lost their grandparents before they were old enough to establish much of a relationship. Moreover, as noted previously, most grandchildren, even if they had living grandparents, did not reside with them. What would be considered small geographic distances today were at one time barriers to frequent visits. It seems safe to conclude that the three-generation economic unit, although undoubtedly more common in the past than it is today, was not part of the lives of most grandchildren for more than a short period of their childhood. To be credible, the critique of contemporary grandparenthood must be stripped of its nostalgic, romanticized view of the past.

Even so, it is fair to ask whether contemporary grandparents do anything for their grandchildren that is important. A number of observers have described the grandparental role as "empty," "ambiguous," "tenuous," or even "roleless."[45] In contrast, others have claimed that grandparents serve as stabilizing and unifying forces in their children's and grandchildren's lives. Hagestad has argued that one of the key functions of grandparents is "an elusive being here, a comforting presence which is not easily captured with the language and tools of social science."[46] The "comforting presence" provides intergenerational continuity and, should it be needed, a source of support. Lillian Troll has described grandparents as a latent source of support—the "family watchdogs," ever on the lookout for trouble and ready to provide assistance if a family crisis occurs.[47] These symbolic meanings of grandparenthood probably always have been with us. But the relative weight given to bonds of sentiment today makes them more central. For many grandparents and grandchildren today—especially those whose families are geographically dispersed, maritally intact, or relatively affluent—the function of intergenerational relationships may be defined largely in this symbolic way, by the elusive, but still deeply meaningful, being here.

But there are crosscurrents that suggest a continuing, even increasing, instrumental role for some grandparents. In low-income and minority families, for instance, parents and children sometimes rely heavily on grandparents and other kin. One study of low-income black families showed that grandmothers often provide crucial assistance to unmarried daughters who are raising children.[48] Middle-aged black men, according to a national study, were four times as likely as white men to have lived with their grandchildren for at least one year during the period 1966–1976.[49] Another study compared black and white middle-class families and found that black extended kin played a larger supportive role than white extended kin.[50] Black grandparents still are deeply involved in the rearing of their grandchildren. Even among white middle-class families, older parents often contribute to the cost of buying a house or paying college tuition. The growing affluence of the elderly may increase their importance as financial resources.

In addition, the great rise in divorce during the 1960s and 1970s has made families less stable than they were in the 1950s. Between the early 1960s and the mid-1970s, the divorce rate doubled. If current rates continue, about one out of two recent marriages will end in divorce.[51] This high level of divorce might mean that many single parents will be turning to their own parents for support. Our survey included a large number of grandparents whose children had divorced after the birth of grandchildren. One of the major themes of [our research] will be the way in which the increase in divorce has altered the roles of grandparents once again—returning to some of them the greater functional role that was more widespread a few generations ago.

Regardless of what grandparents do for their grandchildren, there is the question of whether being a grandparent has a major impact on the grandparents themselves. Every contemporary observer of grandparents has noted how important the role is in symbolic terms to the grandparents. Becoming a grandparent is a deeply meaningful event in a person's life. Seeing the birth of grandchildren can give a person a great sense of the completion of being, of immortality through the chain of generations. It is an affirmation of the value of one's life and, at the same time, a hedge against death. Grandchildren are also a great source of personal pleasure. Freed from the responsibilities of parenthood, grandparents can unabashedly enjoy their grandchildren. In our exploratory interviews, two grandparents independently recited the same aphorism: "Your children are your principal; your grandchildren are your interest."

In order to advance our understanding of the nature and importance of contemporary grandparenthood, we need to take a detailed look at the relationship between grandparents and their grandchildren. Social scientists interested in the family have not paid much attention to grandparents; perhaps this oversight is a result of the mistaken impression that grandparents belong to a bygone era. We hope this chapter has dispelled that impression. To repeat, we believe that a closer look at the changing nature of grandparenthood can help us better understand the broad, recent changes in American kinship and family life. Without a clearer picture of the strengths and limitations of intergenerational relations, our sense of the contemporary family is incomplete.

ENDNOTES

1. Peter Uhlenberg, "Demographic Change and the Problems of the Aged," in *Aging from Birth to Death*, ed. Matilda White Riley (Boulder, CO: Westview Press, 1979), 153–66; and Uhlenberg, "Death and the Family," *Journal of Family History* 5 (Fall 1980): 313–20.
2. U.S. Bureau of the Census, *Historical Statistics of the United States: Colonial Times to 1970* (Washington, DC: U.S. Government Printing Office, 1975), ser. B120 and B121; and U.S. Bureau of the Census, *Statistical Abstract of the United States: 1984* (Washington, DC: U.S. Government Printing Office, 1985), 73 and 33.
3. Uhlenberg, "Death and the Family."
4. Lillian E. Troll, Sheila J. Miller, and Robert C. Atchley, *Families in Later Life* (Belmont, CA: Wadsworth, 1979), 108; see also Nina Nahemow, "The Changing Nature of Grandparenthood," *Medical Aspects of Human Sexuality* 19 (April 1985): 185–90.
5. Andrew J. Cherlin, *Marriage, Divorce, Remarriage* (Cambridge: Harvard University Press, 1981).
6. Norman B. Ryder, "Components of Temporal Variations in American Fertility," in *Demographic Patterns in Developed Societies*, ed. Robert W. Hiorns (London: Taylor and Francis, 1980), 15–54.
7. Susan Cotts Watkins, Jane A. Menken, and John Bongaarts, "Continuities and Changes in the American Family," paper presented at the annual meeting of the Social Science History Association, Toronto, 25–28 October 1984.
8. Bureau of the Census, *Historical Statistics*, ser. A30, A31, A36, and A37; U.S. Bureau of the Census, *Current Population Reports*, ser. P-25, no. 965, "Estimates of the Population of the United States, by Age, Sex, and Race: 1980 to 1984" (Washington, DC: U.S. Government Printing Office, 1985), Table 2; and U.S. Bureau of the Census, *Current Population Reports*, ser. P-25, no. 937, "Provisional Projections of the Population of States by Age and Sex: 1980 to 2000" (Washington, DC: U.S. Government Printing Office, 1983), Table 2.
9. Bureau of the Census, *Historical Statistics*, ser. R3.

10. Bureau of the Census, *Statistical Abstract*, 558.
11. Bureau of the Census, *Historical Statistics*, ser. Q175.
12. Ibid., ser. Q202–203; and Bureau of the Census, *Statistical Abstract*, 619.
13. Daniel Scott Smith, "Historical Change in the Household Structure of the Elderly in Economically Developed Societies," in *Aging: Stability and Change in the Family*, ed. Robert W. Fogel et al. (New York: Academic Press, 1981), 91–114; and Smith, "Life Course, Norms, and the Family System of Older Americans in 1900," *Journal of Family History* (Fall 1979): 285–98.
14. U.S. Bureau of Labor Statistics, "New Worklife Estimates," bull. 2157 (Washington, DC: U.S. Government Printing Office, November 1982).
15. U.S. Social Security Administration, *Social Security Bulletin, Annual Statistical Supplement: 1983* (Washington, DC: U.S. Government Printing Office, 1983), 106.
16. Bureau of the Census, *Historical Statistics*, ser. D803.
17. Ibid., ser. D182 and D196.
18. Bureau of the Census, *Statistical Abstract*, 381 and 484.
19. U.S. Bureau of the Census, *Current Population Reports*, ser. P-60, no. 144, "Characteristics of the Population below the Poverty Level: 1982" (Washington, DC: U.S. Government Printing Office, 1984), Table 1.
20. On the differing value of elderly men and women to the household economy, see Michael Anderson, "The Impact on the Family Relationships of the Elderly of Changes since Victorian Times in Governmental Income-Maintenance Provision," in *Family, Bureaucracy, and the Elderly*, ed. Ethel Shanas and Marvin B. Sussman (Durham, NC: Duke University Press, 1977), 36–59; and Virginia Yans-McLaughlin, *Family and Community: Italian Immigrants in Buffalo, 1880–1930* (Ithaca, NY: Cornell University Press, 1977), especially 173 and 257. On intergenerational cooperation in general, see Anderson, *Family Structure in Nineteenth Century Lancashire* (Cambridge: Cambridge University Press, 1971); Tamara K. Hareven, "Historical Changes in the Timing of Family Transitions," in *Aging: Stability and Change in the Family*, ed. Fogel et al. (New York: Academic Press, 1981), 143–65; and Louise A. Tilly and Joan W. Scott, *Women, Work, and Family* (New York: Holt, Rinehart, and Winston, 1978).
21. Tamara K. Hareven, *Family Time and Industrial Time* (Cambridge: Cambridge University Press, 1982).
22. Gunhild O. Hagestad, "Continuity and Connectedness," in *Grandparenthood*, ed. Vern Bengtson and Joan Robertson (Beverly Hills, CA: Sage Publications, 1985), 31–48. Quoted at p. 33.
23. Yans-McLaughlin, *Family and Community*, 256.
24. E. Franklin Frazier, *The Negro Family in the United States*, rev. and abr. ed. (Chicago: University of Chicago Press, 1939), chap. 7.
25. Jane Range and Maris A. Vinovskis, "Images of the Elderly in Popular Magazines: A Content Analysis of *Littell's Living Age*, 1845–1882," *Social Science History* 5 (Spring 1981): 123–70.
26. Anderson, "The Impact on Family Relationships," 58.
27. Ibid., 57.
28. Ibid., 59.
29. A. R. Radcliffe-Brown, "On Joking Relationships," *Africa* 13 (1940): 195–210.
30. Dorian Apple (Sweetzer), "The Social Structure of Grandparenthood," *American Anthropologist* 58 (August 1956): 656–63.
31. Carl N. Degler, *At Odds: Women and the Family in America from the Revolution to the Present* (New York: Oxford University Press, 1980).
32. Daniel Scott Smith, "Parental Control of Marriage Patterns: An Analysis of Historical Trends in Hingham, Massachusetts," *Journal of Marriage and the Family* 35 (August 1973): 419–28.
33. Viviana A. Zelizer, *Pricing the Priceless Child* (New York: Basic Books, 1985), 139.

34. Ibid., 139.
35. Degler, *At Odds*, 14.
36. Ernest W. Burgess and Harvey J. Locke, *The Family: From Institution to Companionship* (New York: American Book Company, 1945), 26–27 and 28.
37. David Hackett Fisher, *Growing Old in America* (New York: Oxford University Press, 1978); and W. Andrew Achenbaum, *Old Age in the New Land* (Baltimore: Johns Hopkins University Press, 1978).
38. W. Andrew Achenbaum, *Shades of Gray: Old Age, American Values, and Federal Policies since 1920* (Boston: Little, Brown, 1983), 12.
39. Fischer, *Growing Old*, 72.
40. Ibid., 154.
41. Carole Haber, *Beyond Sixty-Five: The Dilemma of Old Age in America's Past* (Cambridge: Cambridge University Press, 1983), 5.
42. William L. O'Neill, *Divorce in the Progressive Era* (New York: Franklin Watts, New Viewpoints, 1973).
43. Arthur Kornhaber and Kenneth L. Woodward, *Grandparents/Grandchildren: The Vital Connection* (New York: Doubleday, Anchor Press, 1981), 240.
44. Ibid., 145.
45. See Hagestad, *Continuity and Connectedness*, for a catalog of these epithets.
46. Ibid.
47. Lillian E. Troll, "Grandparents: The Family Watchdogs," in *Family Relationships in Later Life*, ed. T. Brubaker (Beverly Hills, CA: Sage Publications, 1983), 63–74.
48. Sheppard G. Kellam, Margaret A. Ensminger, and J. T. Turner, "Family Structure and the Mental Health of Children," *Archives of General Psychiatry* 34 (1977): 1012–22.
49. Scott H. Beck and Rubye W. Beck, "The Formation of Extended Households During Middle Age," *Journal of Marriage and the Family* 46 (May 1984): 277–87.
50. William C. Hays and Charles H. Mindel, "Extended Kinship Relations in Black and White Families," *Journal of Marriage and the Family* 35 (February 1973): 51–57.
51. Cherlin, *Marriage, Divorce, Remarriage*.

34

THE STRENGTHS OF APACHE GRANDMOTHERS
Observations on Commitment, Culture, and Caretaking

KATHLEEN S. BAHR

"**M**y great grandmother is a special person to me because she did a good job of raising my mother. I am happy for what she has done and for what she is still doing for us." So begins a tribute written by Garrett Dazen, a fifth grader, published in the *Fort Apache Scout*, June 1, 1990. To persons unacquainted with Apachean families (including several Apache populations as well as the Navajo), this tribute may hint of possible failure in the family system: What happened that made it necessary for the great grandmother to raise the mother? In fact, rather than signaling family failure, the statement is testimony to one of the great strengths of Apache families, a traditional pattern of responsibility and care that continues to serve families and protect children.

This [reading] compares two normative models of grandparenting, one common in Anglo American culture and the other an Apache pattern. The introduction of these contrasting models is followed by a description of contemporary Apache grandmothering and its social context, as enacted by White Mountain Apache grandmothers living on the Fort Apache Indian Reservation. Finally, there is a systematic comparison of selected themes and issues in both ethnic contexts, and of the meanings and consequences of grandparenting for community and family life.

Ethnicity and "Normal" Family Development

Wilson (1984a), commenting on social scientific studies of black families, observed that there had been much more attention paid to their pathologies and disorganization than to their remarkable strength and resilience. So it also is with studies of Indian families. People who know very little else about Indian Americans share stereotypes about the poverty, violence, and alcoholism that

---

Kathleen S. Bahr, "The Strengths of Apache Grandmothers: Observations on Commitment, Culture and Caretaking" from *Journal of Comparative Family Studies,* Vol. 25 No. 2, Summer 1994. University of Calgary, Department of Sociology, Calgary, Alberta, T2N 1N4, Canada.

characterize their families. Yet Anglo Americans are generally unaware of the tenacity of Indian family values and the maintenance of strong kinship ties and family identity among them in the face of almost insurmountable odds.

In family matters, as in other patterns of behavior, it has been assumed by white Americans that their own cultural norms for acceptable behavior are the "right" ones, normal and morally superior to other patterns. Thus, in scholarship as well as popular stereotypes, Anglo American family patterns have been held up as optimal standards. To the degree that the families of ethnic minorities have differed, they have been defined as deficient, disorganized, or immoral (Wilson, 1984b:1333). "Help" in better adjusting and conforming to majority standards, often unsought, has been offered or imposed on Indian peoples by teachers, counselors, missionaries, social workers, politicians, and other professionals.

One of the purposes of this [reading] is to call into question the superiority of the standard "white" family pattern as it applies to grandparenting. Another is to document the continuing commitment of many Apachean grandmothers as bearers of the cultural heritage and of ultimate responsibility for the physical well-being of their families. Defined by her culture and often by circumstance as "caretaker of last resort," she devotes extraordinary effort and personal sacrifice to performing the grandmother role.

Models of Grandparenting: Anglos and Apacheans

Family scientists sometimes talk of "the" family life cycle, or "developmental stages," as if such cycles and stages were part of humanity's genetic heritage rather than social constructions. In practice, there are many ethnic and individual variations in such stages and cycles. With respect to grandparenting, many of the standard models of family life in America assume a configuration where grandparents are acknowledged as kin, but play a peripheral role in the lives of the families of their children and grandchildren. In the usual "family life cycle" model, with "stages" often presented as universals without significant ethnic qualification, American older couples "launch" their children and move into an "empty nest" stage. This is described as a stage when parents should be able to consider their parenting tasks "done," and now are free to pursue their own interests in ways heretofore impossible because of child-rearing responsibilities.

In reality many parents do not "launch" their adult children and many are directly involved in the care of grandchildren (according to the U.S. Census Bureau, 24 percent of unmarried adults aged 25 to 39 were living in the parental household, and about 5 percent of American grandchildren live in a grandparent-headed household, 1991b:9,11). However, these variations do little to weaken the strength of the norm. In fact, to vary from this norm is sometimes labeled as being "out of phase," that is, not finished with parenting at ages when most people are said to be enjoying the "freedom" associated with an "empty nest."

Being thus out of phase is reported to be associated with perceptions of high personal stress and unhappiness. The stresses are assumed to be severe if adult children and grandchildren return to live in the grandparental home. Such grandparents are said to be "developmentally disadvantaged":

> In the home with adult children, the parents' development may also suffer. As individuals, these parents are often prevented from experiencing the freedom necessary to develop further interests without the burdens of children at home. (Clemens and Axelson 1985:262)

The family structure of this three-generation household is described as "inappropriate or off-balance." It is said that "most parents do not welcome the return of these children and view their stay as a short-term arrangement," and that "older adult children and those whose sojourn [in the parental household] becomes long-term appear to both cause and experience more stress" (p. 263). In the same vein, Hagestad and Burton (1986) argue that

> the entry into grandparenthood has become a normal, expectable part of middle age, *a time when daily involvement in the demands of parenthood have ceased.* When the transition does not come in the expected life context, it may disrupt resolution of developmental tasks and hamper involvement in other roles. [Emphasis added] (P. 471)

Beyond the expectation that they will be "freed from the commitments of the child-rearing years," "the normal expectable life" of the modern Anglo grandparent also includes the assumption that they "have attained a certain level of economic security, and at a time when they are still healthy and vigorous" (Hagestad and Burton 1986:473). The combination of health and a degree of economic security means that many continue to maintain a social and economic life independent of children and grandchildren. Consider Cowgill's (1986) depiction of "Western" grandparenting:

> In Western society, despite the fact that grandparents have generally been relieved of any authoritative responsibility for the discipline and upbringing of grandchildren, the relationship is usually rather formal and distant. Grandparents are interested in and take pride in the accomplishments of grandchildren, but they are not usually intimate with them, and there is relatively little affect in the relationship. But in this case, the distance results not from any interference based on authority but from physical separation and conflicting social involvement.... Thus both grandparents and grandchildren tend to be preoccupied with interests and activities with their age peers, and all of this tends to minimize contacts, reduce interaction, and attenuate the relationship. (P. 92)

In contrast to this normative Anglo-American pattern[1] is an American Indian standard that defines the grandparent as very important in the socialization and care of children. Rather than being without responsibility or right to intervene in the rearing of the new generation, grandparents are both authorized and expected to play a major role. Among the Sioux, a new child is called "little grandmother" or "little grandfather" to help impress on her the important role of the grandparent. This custom also encourages respect for the very young and is a reminder that the grandparent generation is the model, "that you are going to grow up to be a grandparent some day and, as such, you must remember to keep these things in mind. And mutual respect and affection develop because this is a known role for the future as well as the kind one can play at when one is a child. It is a very important thing" (Attneave 1981:47).

The expectation that grandparents will play a major role in the physical care and training of their grandchildren is common among most Indian peoples. In fact, it is one of the notable similarities among the wide diversity of tribes (Ryan 1981).

Many ethnographic reports emphasize the key role Apachean grandparents have played in the rearing of their grandchildren. Shomaker (1989) notes that among the Navajo the grandparent often adopted the grandchild, and the alliance between the grandparent and grandchild was considered

> the strongest bond in Navajo culture; this was a warm association in which perpetuation of traditional teaching could be effected. The fostered child became known to others as *child of the grandparent*, changing in status from that of the biological grandchild. The biological mother withdrew from her role as parent to a more distant relationship, similar to that of an older sister. The grandchild lived with the grandparents until adulthood. [Emphasis added] (P. 3)

Historically, the Apaches were hunters, gatherers, and farmers, and Apache women played a major role in providing for their families (Stockel 1991). Their involvement as providers began when they were young girls and continued into old age for as long as they were physically able. Young Apache mothers, perhaps accompanied by an older daughter, roamed long distances to gather food and fuel. Grandmothers, less physically able, stayed close to home and cared for the children. "Older women supervised, answered questions, trained the girls, and taught them to identify various plants and how to shell, husk, and strip wild foods to obtain the edible parts" (Stockel 1991:14).

Goodwin (1942), a close observer of the Western Apache in the 1930s, described the relationship between grandmothers and grandchildren this way:

> Grandparents love to watch their grandchildren at play. It is common for a grandmother to give a small child the run of her wickiup, the child passing and repassing in front of her with a most annoying frequency, stepping over her, lolling against her, pulling at her dress, all of which she accepts with a calm inattention truly remarkable. If the child is too much in the way, the grandparent may turn about in feigned anger and dismiss it with a sharp word. The child usually obeys. Occasionally, a child will defy a grandparent. *The parents do not interfere but leave the matter to the grandparent entirely.* If the encounter ends in the child's crying, it cannot run to the parents for sympathy. *The child's attitude toward its*

grandparents is not duplicated with any other relative. The grandparent's good-naturedness and willingness to do things are taken for granted, and I have never heard a maternal grandparent mentioned with any dislike or fear. They are usually spoken of with a feeling of affection, intimacy, and respect. [Emphasis added] (P. 218)

Goodwin (1942) also writes of "a decided lack of restraint" among grown grandchildren in asking for help from grandparents. "Where a young man hesitates to use another relative's dwelling, he makes himself entirely at home with his maternal grandparents, using their belongings, lying on their beds, asking for food and money" (p. 219). To some degree, the generosity of grandparents was reciprocated by the grandchildren. At the very least, they were expected to respect the grandparents. Among the Navajo at the turn of the century, "Grandchildren served as eyes, ears, hands, and feet for their frail elderly grandparents" (Shomaker 1989:2). Adult daughters assumed the primary responsibility for the care of their elderly parents, but they were often assisted in this effort by young grandsons and granddaughters.

In a 1989 interview, an Apache medicine man told me about his relationship with his grandmother in these words:

Grandmother and I took care of each other, in her wickiup. When I was little, grandmother and I went on a donkey to get wood. My mother was with my dad, but I was with grandmother. My mother sent my sister and I to sleep with my grandmother. They [your parents] always want you to respect the older people. You never walk over them and you never talk back to them. You always listen and then they cook for you and you learn a lot of things from them.

When the Apaches lived off the land, this system of cross-generational reciprocity ensured that family members shared the necessities of life and also knowledge about life. A changing tribal economy in a changing regional and national economic system, including the modern trend toward a cash economy, has complicated but not eliminated the traditional system of reciprocal amity and responsibility.

Apache Grandmothering Today: Patterns and Contexts

As part of an exploratory study of grandparenting and family change among Navajo and Apache grandmothers, beginning in 1989 and continuing through 1991, I conducted loosely structured, in-depth interviews with 13 grandmothers, four adult daughters, a medicine man, and an Anglo elementary school teacher, all residents of the Fort Apache reservation in Arizona.[2] Potential respondents were chosen by a "snowball sampling" technique. They were members of a network that included a long-term friend and former student of mine who had been raised on the reservation.

Early in each interview, I questioned the grandmother about her children and grandchildren and sketched a genogram (Bahr 1990) of her extended family. The genogram then served as a systematic guide or "map" to her family, helping me to keep relationships straight and ask appropriate questions as the interview proceeded.

The interview data have been supplemented by published research on Apachean peoples and occasional references in the tribal newspaper to problems of parenting and grandparenting in the White Mountain Apache community. The following descriptions of contemporary Apache summarize and illustrate behaviors that I observed or that were reported by my informants or other cited sources. It is not maintained that they are statistically representative of all Apache grandmothers.

The project's initial focus was on the place of grandmothers in transmitting traditional values and teaching family work skills, that is, on grandmothers as the custodians of culture. However, I was quickly impressed by the creativity and strength shown by these grandmothers in provisioning their households. They are custodians of the culture, but many of them are also responsible for the sheer physical support of their children and grandchildren. The present discussion emphasizes their responsibilities as providers and nurturers more than their role as custodians of culture.

Role Expectations and Performance

Apache culture values the extended family and exemplifies it in many forms. In these multigenerational settings family members feel, as one respondent put it, that "there is always someone to care for the children." In many instances, the household member who seems to feel the greatest obligation to the children is the grandmother. Therefore, she tends to be the "someone" of last resort.

I was particularly interested by the acceptance of heavy obligations of child care and support by women whose counterparts in Anglo society tend to celebrate their freedom from such responsibilities. Although it is not clear precisely what percentage of Apache grandmothers assume such obligations, the pattern is well-known and quite visible in the community. Rough estimates of its frequency may be made from results of the 1990 U.S. Census. Because the Census reports list heads of household by age but not grandparent status, we cannot tell how many grandparents are caring for grandchildren. However, there are published figures for total numbers of grandchildren living in grandparent-headed households. In 1990 an Apache child was at least 3.5 times more likely to be living in the home of a grandparent than was her Anglo American counterpart.[3] Judging from what I saw and was told, the number of grandchildren living with grandparents varies considerably from day to day and week to week. Nevertheless, it is clear this is a fairly common arrangement, affecting at least one-fifth of the children on a continuing basis.[4]

The recognition of the grandmothers' ultimate responsibility is a well-established part of the Apachean culture. There is general recognition and respect in the community for these women who carry on the nurturing and caretaking functions of the "grandmother role" with energy and deep commitment until incapacitated by illness or taken by death. There are many reasons for this pattern. As indicated earlier, it is "traditional" in the sense that historically the grandmother's role was a well-defined, essential part of normal family life. For many Apache families, the need for traditional grandmothering continues and is perhaps heightened by the modern pattern of women's employment outside the home, which means that many children need supplemental care. High rates of single parenthood and of alcohol abuse put additional children at risk. There are also many grown children, marginally employed or unemployed, who continue to be supported, at least in part, by their parents or grandparents.

Many of the more economically stable members of Apache families live off the reservation, often in another state, insulated from much of the day-to-day pressure to make ends meet. When things get hard for the unemployed on the reservation, it is culturally appropriate to call upon grandparents for aid. Under such circumstances it is fairly common for adult children, with or without partners, to live with their parents, and in many cases the task of caring for and teaching their children falls almost entirely to the grandmothers.

There is also the powerful force of cultural tradition and family example. For some of these women, the memory of having been raised by a grandmother translates into the expectation that they themselves need not be a truly responsible "parent" until they reach the grandmother stage. At that point, however, they recognize that the responsibility to be "parent of last resort" is now theirs.

A related explanation for the willingness to continue nurturing behavior at an age when many women in the wider society have "graduated" to leisure and, at most, sporadic child care is that the grandmothers feel fulfilled by doing it. Caring for children and grandchildren is a source of deep satisfaction for them. In fact, the chief regret expressed by the grandmothers I interviewed was that they couldn't do more for their children and grandchildren. That sense of needing to do more was cited as the most difficult thing about being a grandmother:

> It's finding the time . . . having the chance to really talk with my teenage grandson and granddaughter. She needs to be advised about different ways of dressing and caring for herself and all these things. It seems that the time is too limited, that you can't sit down and talk without having [all of my grandchildren] pulling at me. . . . There are ways that we can deal with it, like go by yourself and get [that one] individual, but then I always feel guilty [when] the other one says, "Can I go? I want to go with you." Before I know it, I have two or three with me, without getting the chance with that one. . . . You know you are swamped by them, and then my daughter, too, still needs advice, and I need the time to spend with [her], and it is getting so that she is pushed out by these [grand]kids.

In the past few years of economic recession, Apache grandmothers enacting their traditional roles, serving as caretakers of last resort for adult children and grandchildren, have been especially hard hit. What is remarkable is that their definitions of their problems do not question the role definition that assigns them ultimate responsibility but, rather, focus on changes and other obstacles that make it harder for them to live up to the cultural expectations. A mother of five with 11 grandchildren acknowledged that the challenge of trying to feed her household kept her in a state of continual stress. Like many Apache grandmothers, the size of her household varies. At the time of the interview, two preschool aged grandchildren, two adult daughters, and an ex-son-in-law were living with her. Other adult children and grandchildren lived nearby and were frequent visitors. She was proud to have "a real close family." Her only problem was

> the feeding part of it. It is hard to feed a big family, and it is hard when just one family is not up to feeding the children, and they have to come over here and we feed them. But my grandmother, she only had a bag of beans, flour, salt and baking soda, and a bag of potatoes. But we ate good; it didn't hardly cost her anything. She fed us three times a day. But with these children [who belonged to a daughter who had recently quit work following the birth of another baby] . . . seems like we don't have anything to eat half the time. But in those days, I don't know how my grandmother managed, [but we seemed] to have plenty all of the time.

Many community members continue to recognize the grandmothers as the last line of responsibility for families in trouble. An elementary school teacher and long-term observer of the community commented,

> When you hear of a death in the family . . . you pray it's not the grand-mother, because they are the only ones there for the children in many families. I would say, in at least 15, maybe 20, percent of the students I have had, they live with their grandmother. Their mother may be around part of the time, but it is the grandmother they go home to, who comes to school to see how they are doing. . . . And they really are the only ones many times that aren't drinking. . . . And they many times are the ones who worry about getting kids their clothes and getting them into school and trying to make sure that the kids are there [attending school].

Children who do not have an able grandmother to supplement and back up the efforts of their other caretakers are disadvantaged.

What happens if the grandmother has passed away? One of the grand-mothers I talked to said that sometimes other relatives don't want to take the responsibility for the children the deceased grandmother was caring for, and then they are taken to a group home sponsored by the tribe. Usually, however, some close relative will assume responsibility. In her own case, this informant recalled, she was fortunate because she had a third "grandmother," a caring older relative in addition to her two grandmothers. "I guess [she] was my mom's aunt," she said.

> my grandmother's sister, and after my grandmother passed away she kind of took over. . . . She taught us a lot of things. By this time my other sisters were

too small to remember my real grandmother. . . . They more or less thought of her as our real grandmother.

The grandmothers I interviewed were committed to their families and devoted their lives to them. They were models of energy and industry. Such characteristics are expected of Apache grandmothers, and it was apparent that there was an accepted standard of grandmother behavior. Everyone seemed to know a grandmother or two who didn't fare too well, and some of the grandmothers I interviewed had things to say about other grandmothers—and grandchildren—who didn't measure up. For example, grandmothers whose caring behavior consisted merely of "baby-sitting" were seen as deficient, and so were some whose drinking habits made them incapable of caring for their households. Others manifested less commitment than my informants thought appropriate. I did not interview any of these "below-par" grandmothers—they were not identified to me by name—but plainly they were defined as a small and deviant minority.

Many grandmothers that outsiders might define as exploited or dominated by children and grandchildren do not see themselves as "giving in" but, rather, define their actions as the most loving, altruistic responses they know how to give, under the circumstances. They may not define being "used" by their children as exploitation. The caring grandmother is unlikely to assert herself. Rather, she gives in because "she loves her children and grandchildren," and she feels "like they are part of her." Take the grandmother who, when asked what was the most difficult thing about being a grandmother, was interrupted by her grown daughter who insisted, "Let me answer for her: Saying 'No.'" The daughter elaborated,

Like if one of my sisters comes and says, "I want to go here and I want you to take care of my children," when my Mom would want to do something else, she doesn't know how to say no. So she ends up with the kids. That's the problem.

The grandmother's reply revealed a different ethic: "I don't mind them being there. I raised a lot of my own, so having my grandkids there doesn't make too much difference." She further showed her priorities in answering a question about what was most difficult about being a grandmother: "the worry." She said she worried especially about the grandchildren who did *not* live with her and who, she felt, were not well supervised at home.

Most of these grandmothers impressed me as pragmatic and world-wise. They knew that generosity required wisdom, that gifts should not be given indiscriminately. Also, they recognized that they were personally vulnerable and were sometimes exploited. Some were openly critical of the grown children—generally not their own—who they thought took unfair advantage of parental generosity. One told of seeing a grandmother in a grocery store spending her meager Social Security checks on disposable diapers, and offered her opinion that "Grandmother shouldn't be buying those. Grandmother should buy herself good food that she likes to eat."

It was also suggested that some grandmothers might appear to be overly tolerant or generous because they were trying to make up for past mistakes. In the words of one Apache mother,

> *This one grandmother, she's trying to win their love. Try to win their love back. Somewhere she made a mistake, maybe through her drinking in her younger days, maybe the days when she was having a good time.*

There was some evidence to support her judgment. While I did not specifically ask, two grandmothers volunteered that they had been fairly heavy drinkers when their children were young, and often had left their children either to care for themselves or in the care of a grandmother. Their recollections were often poignant: "And the kids would be wondering, 'what happened to my mom?'"

Coping Strategies

Apache grandmothers, despite their limited resources, rarely turn away their own. Grandmothers too old or unskilled to participate in the conventional labor market somehow manage, as "caretakers of last resort," to support themselves and their households. Often they survive by the creative application of traditional skills.

Many are still "gatherers," combing nearby lands for anything that can be sold for cash. "Anything" includes digging for worms to sell to fishermen, retrieving quills from roadkill porcupines to use in making earrings, scavenging the countryside for aluminum cans to sell to recycling centers, and harvesting native plants to sell and to supplement the family diet. They make lunches to sell in town, sew traditional dresses, or do craftwork, making dolls, cradle boards, beadwork, and jewelry. The usual market for these products is local residents more than tourists. Often such products are sold at places of employment on paydays.

A key to the grandmother's very survival is the operation of the informal economy, whereby goods, services, and money are exchanged and transferred. The system does not always work smoothly and predictably, particularly where alcohol is involved. There also seems to be a pattern where men — sons, brothers, husbands — are more willing than daughters or sisters to take advantage of the generosity of the grandmothers. On the other hand, a daughter with an alcohol or drug problem can be as exploitive as any man.

Creative coping strategies and the workings of the informal economy are illustrated in the following brief profiles of two of the grandmothers. Grandmother A has 10 children and 17 grandchildren. When I interviewed her, two grown daughters and a preschool grandson were living with her. Three teenaged grandsons and their mother live nearby and spend a lot of time with her. When I first arrived at her home, she was mixing dough to make tortillas for another of her daughters who lives in the area.

Grandmother A receives a small income from the Veterans Administration and from Social Security, "not much, but it helps out a little." The daughter who lives nearby receives AFDC and food stamps and contributes about $10 a month to the family income, "to buy meat sometimes, or whatever." One of her sons also helps out, "off and on, not that much."

How does Grandmother A supplement this meager income? I asked if she made crafts or helped the resident grandson's other grandmother "pick worms" for sale to fishermen. "No," she said, "I have a bad heart and I have rheumatoid arthritis. What I usually do is chop wood and wash and that is about it." She is resourceful and lives simply, cooking with wood, making her own tortillas. Because of her health problems, she has not grown a garden for several years. She does, however, gather the yellow pollen from cattails and sell that to get a little extra cash.

She takes her grandchildren with her to gather the cattails, because she can't get into the water where they grow but the children can. Then she lays the cattails in the sun to dry. As they dry, she shakes out the pollen. It is a time-consuming process. It takes many cattails to get enough pollen to fill one baby-food jar. This year, she said, a jar of pollen sells for about $20, or about $5 for one tablespoon. The pollen is used in Sunrise Dance ceremonies throughout the year.

I had difficulty discovering just how much money the pollen harvest yields. When I expressed surprise that all that work would net her only about a hundred dollars, she explained, in the essential spirit of the nurturing grand-mother, that

> sometimes I just give it out free, 'cause a lot of our people are on welfare and food stamps, and it is really hard for them. . . . If they have money, they can go ahead and buy yellow powder but they can't do that with their food stamps.

Her grandsons contribute to the welfare of the household by gathering and chopping wood and cleaning house. They sweep and mop the floors and wash the dishes. She told me with satisfaction that her 3½-year-old grandson

> picks up the broom and says, "Grandma, let me sweep." He brings the wood in. And sometimes he wants to help me with the dishes, and he pulls up a chair and is standing there.

How does she see her role as grandmother? She insisted that what she does is assuredly "not baby-sitting." Instead, "They need me, and I need to be there with them to talk with them or do something with them."

Grandmother B bore 11 children, four of whom grew to adulthood. Three are still living. At present her brother lives with her. Much of the time, so do three grandsons, children of her oldest son. Her aged mother lived with her until her death a few months ago. Her mother's passing has taken away the Social Security checks that for several years were the household's only regular income. A sister who provided moral support and occasional transportation also died recently. Now the challenges of paying the rent, buying food, and making the lengthy trip to the tribal offices to apply for her monthly allotment of food stamps are much harder than before.

After her mother's death, Grandmother B went to a daughter's home in another state. On her return she discovered that her alcoholic son, father of the three grandsons who often live in her home, had claimed her food stamps. There was nothing left to enable her to buy food for the month. I asked what she thought she would do about this crisis. She looked around her home and said, "I've been thinking I could have a yard sale. I could sell a lot of this stuff."

She has only limited reading skills, and in the wake of her mother's recent death her life has been further complicated by the arrival of various official forms that must somehow be interpreted and dealt with. Even taking advantage of the transfer payments available to her ends up being a hardship. To obtain food stamps, she must apply in person each month at an office many miles away, and then, two weeks later, she must again make the trip to personally pick up the stamps. If she is unable to get a ride, she hitchhikes, and the round trip plus the waiting in line and application process may take an entire day. It can be even worse for mothers with small children in tow who have to wait in the food-stamp line in wet or freezing weather.

After the food stamps, her main source of income is "picking worms" for fishermen. Her grandsons help in this enterprise, and sometimes so do other kinfolk or temporary household members. One morning when I picked Grandmother B up to accompany me to some interviews, she told how the night before her grandsons had come to report that they had watered the grass "real good" at their maternal grandmother's house and now there were lots of worms coming up. So they had all gone over there and within about 30 minutes had picked up enough worms to make a two-inch layer in the bottom of a large can. As we drove away, we saw the boys out on the road selling worms. On a good day in summer—a weekend or holiday—Grandmother B may gross as much as $50 selling worms. Weekdays are slower: A good day's receipts may total only $10 to $15. Winters are hard. When the ground freezes worm-picking is over, and along with that loss of income comes the additional expense of having to buy wood to heat her modest home. Sometimes members of her church help out and give her wood.

As summer wanes, Grandmother B becomes a crafts worker. When she can get the materials, she makes dolls and beautiful doll clothes. When she can get silver, she makes jewelry. Her out-of-state daughter often sends fabrics and trims for the dolls. Finding an effective way to market her products is always a challenge. Grandmother B has no car and must depend on others for transportation. The small community where she lives has no stores, and the nearest commercial center is about 15 miles away. Relatives and friends passing through sometimes deliver items to distant customers or even market them for her.

There is also some direct sustenance from the land. The grandsons fish at a nearby lake. When they are successful, their catch is a significant addition to family meals. When someone kills an elk, it is butchered, cut up, and distributed to friends and relatives. Of course Grandmother B and many others like her, grandmothers whose lives exemplify the tribal ethic of sharing and who are known to be primary economic supports for children and grand-children, are included in the community distribution network.

And so the stories go. One grandmother makes and sells cradle boards, real ones for the Apache mothers who use them and miniature decorative models for the tourist trade. Another makes and sells the traditional Apache "camp dresses." Another walks along the riverbanks gathering aluminum cans to sell and occasionally is paid to teach special classes at local schools. Yet another works two jobs, as support staff in the local public schools during the school year and in a forestry camp during the summer.

Finally, as indicated above, some grandmothers also receive financial support from children and other relatives who live off-reservation. The Apache values of sharing, family commitment, and community support extend beyond the reservation boundary lines.

Summary and Discussion

In the modern Anglo milieu of "expressive individualism" (Bellah et al. 1985), older adults, and especially retired adults, are often portrayed as having reached an age of entitlement, when they deserve to be rewarded for years of work and can expect to "enjoy the good life." To those so entitled, high levels of family demand, conflict, and stress signal pathology, not maturity.

In contrast, the Apache grandmothers I talked to seemed reconciled to a "conflict" orientation to life: They accepted the reality that conflict and stress were embedded in the processes of family living. Whether they saw such experiences as growth-producing, at least they seemed to recognize that now, in the full strength of their maturity, such experiences and the responsibility to make the best of them were their lot as *grandmothers*. Resourceful, patient, even resigned, most were willing to lose themselves in the service of their families. At a life stage when many in Anglo society defined themselves as "retired" and perhaps redundant, the Apache grandmothers had arrived at the pinnacle of maturity and responsibility.

The other side of the coin is that many young Apache mothers seem to feel that now is their time to serve individualistic interests, to seek personal goals, or simply to "have a good time." Their attitudes and activities, while not always approved by the grandmothers, are defined as a normal stage of life. But if the mothers can sometimes avoid the challenging responsibilities of child care and child rearing, the grandmothers cannot. The developmental sequence has run its course, and their time has come.

It is instructive to compare some specific aspects of Apache (A) and Anglo American grandparenting (AA). In making these comparisons, I have cited some relevant descriptions of grandparenting in other tribes where they parallel my own observations of Apache grandparenting. Also, I generalize about Anglo American grandparenting according to what I perceive are central tendencies or dominant patterns reported in the literature. It is recognized that there are many other Anglo American patterns, including some that involve high commitment, frequent interaction, active economic support of grown children and grandchildren, and even formal educational efforts to improve grandparenting performance.[5]

1. Obligation and Responsibility

AA: A grandparent is a "spoiler" of grandchildren, one who may interact or give gifts but who "can have meaningful relationships with their grandchildren with minimal obligation and responsibility" (Link 1987:29).

A: For grandmothers in particular, grandparenting means heavy obligation and responsibility: "The older woman's role was that of a parent substitute within the family system" (Ryan 1981:35).

2. Gender Differences in Grandparental Role Behavior

AA: Grandmothers are more important than grandfathers in both role definition and role enactment. "Grandmothers tend to have warmer and closer relationships and serve more often as surrogate parents than grandfathers. Their close involvement in the mother role in relationships with their own children is a determining factor" (Link 1987:31).

A: Grandmothers are much more important than grandfathers. In this characteristic the Apache and Anglo patterns are similar in direction, but the role of the grandmother as provider is much enhanced among the Apache, and so is her position in the memory of Apache children (and among Indian children of other tribes as revealed in their writings as adults). In both Anglo and Apache society, the grandmothers' priority over grandfathers is partly a function of their greater longevity and partly a culturally prescribed greater affinity and responsibility for children generally.

3. Grandparents as Part of a Viable, Functioning Family Network

AA: Kinship ties are valued and maintained between parents, adult children, and grandchildren, but as economic and residential units families tend to be nuclear and two-generational (parents and children). Family households have well-defined, fairly stable boundaries. Individual households tend to be independent.

A: Kinship ties are valued and maintained, and individual households are likely to involve cross-generational and multinuclear (e.g., cousins, aunts, and uncles) members. Family households have loosely defined, rather permeable, boundaries. Individual households tend to be interdependent. Ryan (1981:28) identifies the traditional interdependent family as the key to overcoming the problems faced by many American Indians today. "The individuals I knew who were not successful were not successful because their family was not complete," he says, and the missing elements he points to are grandmothers, grandfathers, aunts and uncles.

4. Economic Security and Economic Responsibilities

AA: Elder status, retirement, and grandparenthood are typically times of fairly secure economic status. Grandparents are more likely than others to own their homes and have accumulated savings. Financial costs of rearing and educating their grandchildren are expected to be borne by the children's parents.

A: Elder status and grandparenthood are times of heavy economic demand. Adult children and grandchildren may become the economic responsibility of the grandparents, adding to the financial burdens of the older years because in the low-income reservation milieu it has been difficult to accumulate savings. Pensions, Social Security, food stamps, and other transfer payment programs do not begin to cover the Apache grandmother's expenses, and as a consequence she often works as hard as ever in her life, for as long as she is able.

Apache grandmothers are busy in good causes. Some of them are elderly, many have health problems, but they exhibit a rich variety of economic activities, in both the informal and the formal economy. Generally they not only make enough to support themselves, but also provide much and sometimes all of the support for their large, often-multigenerational households. Whether married or single, they take financial responsibility for themselves and many others.

These are strong, industrious women. Only one of more than a score of Apache and Navajo grandmothers I got to know in the course of this research was not actively working at cottage enterprises or formal employment, or both, in an effort to improve the economic status of her family. That lone exception was also the oldest grandmother I encountered. Many of these women were suffering considerable physical hardship, from handicaps, accidents, aging, and illness; several showed signs of sheer physical exhaustion; some were psychologically stretched by the responsibilities of child care along with serving as economic providers and cultural models. Most had relatively low-level job skills, in the accepted sense of formal education, human capital, and preparation for successful competition in the labor force.

Despite multiple disadvantages, these Apache grandmothers were among the most influential and active participants in community life. Occupying the respected role of grandmother, enacting a tribal role definition that includes wisdom, energy, and resourcefulness, they stand out as the effective "managers" of much of the local economy and models of independence, courage, and strength in contexts where dependence, frustration, and resignation might be seen as more realistic adjustments.

It is not merely that they are individually strong and committed. To the degree that anyone is truly responsible for the future of the Apache society and culture, I believe it is the grandmothers. More than the tribal politicians, the medicine men, the teachers, the local celebrities, or the upwardly mobile migrants to urban America, it is the local grandmothers who anchor the heritage and, very often, the physical well-being of the Apache people.

Like families in the rest of America, the Apache family is experiencing strain and undergoing change. Like families elsewhere, many Apache mothers and fathers have occupations and lifestyles that take them away from home and severely limit their time with their children. It might even be argued that the poverty and accompanying social problems that afflict the Apache people make their families particularly vulnerable to a host of problems that would have destroyed a lesser people. In the face of the problems they confront, it is fortunate that, unlike much of the rest of America, they do not set aside their older women as "retired" or irrelevant. Rather, they place them in demanding, high-status, high-intensity roles that direct their insights and energies to the benefit of the community's youngest and most helpless members. The combination of high role expectations and the sheer scale of physical and emotional need they confront seem to inspire almost superhuman efforts from them. Looking at their lives and challenges, one may conclude that Apache grandmothering is very hard on the grandmothers. On the other hand, it plainly is very good for the Apache community as a whole and for the Apache posterity.

ENDNOTES

1. In highlighting this general or "normative" pattern, I do not mean to downplay the diversity of grandparenting behavior among both Anglo and Indian populations. There is exceptional and deficient grandparenting in all societies, and millions of American grandparents are currently raising their grandchildren. Even so, I believe the literature in general, and the illustrative works cited, support a clear Anglo–Apache difference in cultural expectations about what constitutes good grandparenting and the social status accorded grandparents.
2. The Fort Apache Reservation occupies portions of Navajo, Gila, and Apache counties in east central Arizona. In 1990 the population of the Fort Apache Reservation was 10,394, of whom 9,825 were Indian Americans. There were 2,232 households (1,974 family households), with an average household size of 4.35. The Apache population is young: 45 percent are under age 18, and the median age is 20.9. Of the family households, 31 percent were headed by women ("female householder, no husband present") (U.S. Bureau of the Census 1991a:58; 1992:285).
3. According to the 1990 U.S. Census, of the 4,453 children under age 18 on the Fort Apache Reservation, 759 (17.0 percent) lived in households headed by one or both grandparents. In the entire United States, the corresponding rate was 4.9 percent (U.S. Bureau of the Census 1991b:9; 1992:285).
4. Of course this pattern is not the only pattern among the White Mountain Apache, nor the typical one. In addition to the 17 percent of all children living in households headed by a grandparent, 55 percent lived in married-couple families including at least one of their parents, 17 percent in single-parent families headed by their mothers, 4 percent in single-parent families headed by their fathers, and the remainder with other relatives or nonrelatives or in institutions (U.S. Bureau of the Census 1992:285). Plainly, the parent or parents are still the primary caretakers for the majority of children. However, even where parents are in place and functioning, Apache culture strongly encourages grandparents to participate in the socialization and nurturing of their grandchildren. Both patterns—grandparent dominant and grandparent supportive and supplemental—seem to be within the "norm."
5. As with Cowgills' statement, quoted earlier, that in the "Western" model of grandparenting, grandchild–grandparent relationships usually are "rather formal and

distant," so also the following generalizations on "minimal obligation and responsibility" need to be qualified. Not only are millions of American grandparents standing in for parents and raising their grandchildren, but substantial numbers are making a conscious effort to improve their grandparenting skills, as indicated in the emergence of formal curricula and a published literature on grandparent education (cf. Strom and Strom 1991a, 1991b, 1992).

REFERENCES

Attneave, Carolyn. 1981. "Discussion." Pp. 46–51 in *The American Indian Family: Strength and Stresses,* edited by John Red Horse, August Shattuck, and Fred Hoffman. Isleta, NM: American Indian Social Research and Development Associates.

Bahr, Kathleen. 1990. "Student Responses to Genogram and Family Chronology." *Family Relations* 39:243–49.

Bellah, Robert N., Richard Madsen, William M. Sullivan, Ann Swidler, and Steven M. Tipton. 1985. *Habits of the Heart: Individualism and Commitment in American Life.* Berkeley: University of California Press.

Clemens, Audra W. and Leland J. Axelson. 1985. "The Not-So-Empty-Nest: The Return of the Fledgling Adult." *Family Relations* 34:259–64.

Cowgill, Donald O. 1986. *Aging Around the World.* Belmont, CA: Wadsworth.

Goodwin, Grenville. 1942. *The Social Organization of the Western Apache.* Chicago, IL: University of Chicago Press.

Hagestad, Gunhild O. and Linda M. Burton. 1986. "Grandparenthood, Life Context, and Family Development." *American Behavioral Scientist* 29(4, March/April):471–84.

Link, Mary S. 1987. "The Grandparenting Role." *Lifestyles: A Journal of Changing Patterns* 8(3&4, Spring/Summer):27–45.

Ryan, Robert A. 1981. "Strengths of the American Indian Family: State of the Art." Pp. 25–43 in *The American Indian Family: Strength and Stresses,* edited by John Red Horse, August Shattuck, and Fred Hoffman. Isleta, NM: American Indian Social Research and Development Associates.

Shomaker, Dianna J. 1989. "Transfer of Children and the Importance of Grandmothers among the Navajo Indians." *Journal of Cross-Cultural Gerontology* 4:1–18.

Stockel, H. Henrietta. 1991. *Women of the Apache Nation.* Reno: University of Nevada Press.

Strom, Robert D. and Shirley K. Strom. 1991a. *Becoming a Better Grandparent: Viewpoints on Strengthening the Family.* Newbury Park, CA: Sage.

———. 1991b. *Grandparent Education: A Guide for Leaders.* Newbury Park, CA: Sage.

———. 1992. *Achieving Grandparent Potential: Viewpoints on Building Intergenerational Relationships.* Newbury Park, CA: Sage.

U.S. Bureau of the Census. 1991a. *1990 Census of Population and Housing, Summary Population and Housing Characteristics: Arizona.* Washington, DC: U.S. Government Printing Office.

———. 1991b. *Marital Status and Living Arrangements, March 1990.* Current Population Reports, Series P-20, No. 450. Washington, DC: U.S. Government Printing Office.

———. 1992. *1990 Census of Population, General Population Characteristics: Arizona.* Washington, DC: U.S. Government Printing Office.

Wilson, Melvin N. 1984a. "The Black Extended Family: An Analytical Consideration." *Developmental Psychology* 22:246–58.

———. 1984b. "Mothers' and Grandmothers' Perceptions of Parental Behavior in Three-Generational Black Families." *Child Development* 55:1333–39.

35

FAMILY CARE OF THE FRAIL ELDERLY
A New Look at "Women in the Middle"

SANDRA L. BOYD • JUDITH TREAS

Unprecedented demographic shifts in this century have profoundly affected the lives of middle-aged and older women. As the population ages, increasing numbers of women provide care to elderly relatives. The elderly population currently is the fastest growing segment of American society. By 1985, average life expectancy at birth was 71.2 years for men and 78.2 years for women.[1] Sixty percent of fifty-five-year-old women could expect to have at least one living parent in 1980, compared to just 6 percent in 1800.[2] It is estimated that 20 percent of a woman's lifetime will be spent with at least one parent over the age of sixty-five.[3]

We now know that offspring do not abandon their elderly parents[4]; family members provide roughly 80 percent of care to the elderly.[5] A vast caregiving literature shows that women in the family — primarily wives, daughters, and daughters-in-law — are most involved in caregiving.

Elaine M. Brody has coined the phrase "women in the middle" to refer to women who "are in their middle years, in the middle of older and younger generations, and in the middle of competing demands."[6] She suggests that long-term parent care has become a "normative" family stress for a growing number of middle-aged women.[7] Other researchers, however, contend that studies based on small, nonrandom samples overstate the prevalence of "women in the middle."[8] Furthermore, the gerontological literature focuses almost exclusively on the negative consequences of caregiving and competing demands; few studies have examined positive aspects.[9]

"Women in the Middle": Between Generations

Brody's definition embraces two, sometimes overlapping types of "women in the middle": (1) those who are "caught" between older and younger generations and (2) those who combine parental care and paid employment.

Although some women provide both parental care and child care simultaneously, the life cycle provides some insulation against experiencing such

TABLE 1   Women with Parents over Age 65 and Children under Age 18 in Household

Women's Ages	Percent with Parent over Age 65[a]	Percent with Children under Age 18 in Household[b]
40–44	97	17
45–49	92	8
50–54	78	4
55–59	60	2
60–64	35	1
65–74	14	less than 1

Source: Women's Studies Quarterly 1989: 1 & 2.

[a] Based on estimates applied to a synthetic cohort under 1980 conditions. Susan C. Watkins, Jane A. Menken, and John Bongaarts, "Demographic Foundations of Family Change," *American Sociological Review* 52 (3) (1987): 346–58.
[b] Children under eighteen living with one or both parents, all races, 1984. Age of parent was based on the age of the householder, defined as the homeowner or renter. Since homeowners are still more likely to be men than women, and since husbands are somewhat older on average than their wives, these percentages may slightly underestimate the number of children under eighteen living with women. Current Population Reports—Population Characteristics, Series P-20, No. 399, *Marital Status and Living Arrangements,* March 1984.

dual demands. Table 1 shows that 17 percent of women between the ages of forty and forty-four have children under the age of eighteen at home, and 97 percent have parents over the age of sixty-five. But many of these parents can be considered part of the "young-old"; they are under the age of seventy-five, enjoy relatively good health, and are married.[10] Moreover, because money, goods, and services flow down the generational ladder to a greater extent than they flow up,[11] these "young-old" parents are apt to be assets, not liabilities; rather than posing burdens to their children, they provide critical financial help and emotional support.

Sixty percent of fifty-five-year-old women have living parents; unlike the parents of younger women, these often are over the age of seventy-five, many are widowed, and a significant proportion suffer from impairments limiting their daily activities. But only a tiny fraction of women in their mid-to-late fifties still have children at home.

A constellation of factors, including postponed childbearing, "crowded nests," and increased sickness among older persons may mean that child dependency and parent care overlap more frequently in the future.

Postponed Childbearing and Childlessness

Although some well-educated women are remaining childless altogether, others in recent cohorts have delayed childbearing until their late twenties and thirties.[12] For such women, child rearing may well coincide with parent care. Moreover, responsibilities for grandchildren may impinge on some middle-aged women, especially blacks, as a result of the rise in teenage illegitimacy.[13]

"Crowded Nests"

Declining proportions of adult children over the age of eighteen are married, and increasing proportions either remain in their parental home or return there.[14] Thirty percent of eighteen- to thirty-four-year-olds lived in their parents' households in 1983, compared to 25 percent in 1970. Adult children living at home typically are single and between the ages of eighteen and twenty-two; most are in school rather than in the work force.[15] Adult children aged twenty-three to twenty-nine living in their parents' home typically either are preparing for independent living or have returned temporarily following job loss or failed marriages. The prolonged dependency of adult children may mean that middle-aged women are responsible simultaneously for their children and their parents.

Increasing Sickness of the "Young-Old"

Researchers recently have found a significant increase in the prevalence of chronic disease among the "young-old," though not among the rest of the elderly population; more people suffering from chronic illness are surviving today than in the past.[16] Some women thus may be compelled to provide parental care when their children are still relatively young.

In summary, although many middle-aged women experience competing demands, most are not "caught between older and younger generations." When middle-aged women still have dependent children, their aging parents typically have not reached an age when they are likely to be impaired and in need of assistance. Middle-aged women who do have frail elderly parents tend not to be responsible for children living at home. If future cohorts of middle-aged women care for sicker parents and have younger children or children who remain at home longer, they may be more likely to be "caught in the middle."

"Women in the Middle": Between Caregiving and Paid Employment

In addition to competing family responsibilities, "women in the middle" confront conflicting demands of care for elderly family members and paid work. Between 1947 and 1986, the number of women in the labor force grew from 29.8 to 54.7 percent[17]; the most notable increases occurred for middle-aged married women and mothers of small children. Over 60 percent of married women aged forty to fifty-four are in the labor force.[18] According to data from the National Long-Term Care Survey, 31 percent of all unpaid caregivers also hold paying jobs, including 10 percent of wives and 44 percent of daughters.[19] Some observers fear that women who simultaneously work for pay and care for parents suffer from "burnout" as a result of role strain.

Women who have competing demands from paid work and caregiving adapt in a number of ways, including leaving the labor force, making changes at work, and making changes at home.

Leaving the Labor Force

Although the three generations of women interviewed by Elaine Brody stated that women should not have to quit their jobs to provide care to elderly parents,[20] daughters are much more likely to actually do so than sons. According to a variety of studies, between 12 and 28 percent of caregiving daughters leave the work force to provide care.[21] These women often lose salary and benefits, retirement pensions, social networks, and work satisfaction. Caregiving responsibilities also may compel some women to remain unemployed.[22]

Brody found that women who quit work are older, provide more help to their mothers, and have lower-status jobs than those who remain in the work force.[23] Because their family incomes are low, such women may face financial difficulties. Some of these women, however, may prefer caregiving to unrewarding jobs and thus welcome the opportunity to depart the labor force.

Changes at Work

Women who continue to work often make changes on the job to accommodate caregiving obligations. Robyn Stone et al. (1987) reported that 20 percent of caregivers cut back their hours, 29 percent rearrange their work schedules, and 19 percent take time off without pay. The tendency to make such changes is directly related to the level of impairment of disabled parents.[24]

Patricia Archbold (1983) argues that women in higher-status positions are more able to accommodate caregiving in their work lives because they have more flexible work schedules.[25] According to Brody, however, the higher-status, career-oriented workers feel more conflicted and report more work interruptions and missed job opportunities.[26]

Changes at Home

Many working caregivers give up free time and leisure activities while maintaining rigid schedules.[27] Some also adjust their caregiving responsibilities to alleviate the strain. Although caregivers in the labor force provide the same levels of help as unpaid workers in terms of housework, financial management, and emotional support, they provide significantly less assistance with personal care and meal preparation.[28] Employed caregivers also tend to supplement their own assistance with help from other family members and paid providers.

Role Strain from Competing Demands

Most caregiving literature focuses on the negative consequences of providing care, and most studies report at least moderate stress for many caregivers. Researchers have directed considerable attention to women in the middle of paid work and informal caregiving, assuming that role conflict and overload predispose them to stress. Studies suggest that a quarter of caregivers who remain in the labor force do have conflicted feelings,[29] and many suffer from fatigue and strained personal relationships.[30] But employment does not appear to be the most important determinant of stress. The primary predictor of stress is the quality of the relationship between the caregiver and care recipient.[31] Working women providing care to older family members do not systematically exhibit more stress than their counterparts who do not work outside the home.[32] Moreover, contrary to the assumption that an increase in the number of roles is detrimental to psychological well-being,[33] there is some evidence that the ability to handle diverse roles can promote self-esteem. Multiple roles provide women with added sources of satisfaction, not simply increased burdens. Individuals also can compensate for failure in any one sphere by relying on rewards from another. Some caregivers may find that a job provides a respite from the demands, and often failures, of caregiving.

At the same time, caregiving provides a sense of usefulness, compensating for frustrations at work. Although most gerontological literature emphasized the stress of caregivers, many of the findings on caregiving stress come from small samples recruited from service agencies. Families who are most visible to community agencies are those who are experiencing more stress than they can handle and who feel that they need help. As Horowitz notes, "Most caregivers can identify at least one positive aspect of caregiving, primarily a feeling of self-satisfaction and increased self-esteem stemming from the knowledge that one is successfully fulfilling a responsibility and coping with a personal challenge."

Summary and Conclusion

Despite warnings about many women being "caught in the middle," the situation is not as grim as many observers would have us believe. The life cycle helps protect women against competing family responsibilities; only a small percentage of women care simultaneously for dependent parents and children. The addition of paid work to caregiving responsibilities may have positive as well as negative consequences. Moreover, many women cope successfully with competing demands. By focusing exclusively on the stress of caregiving, we ignore the tremendous resiliency and adaptive capabilities of many women and send young women a depressing message about their future. Although it is necessary to alert policymakers and employers to the problems of women who do find caregiving overwhelming, we should retain a sense of perspective.

It should be emphasized, however, that those women who are experiencing stress from competing responsibilities do need special assistance. A small but growing number of corporate employers offer "elder care" to assist employees with caregiving obligations. The current wave of corporate interest is encouraging, but more employers could provide programs that help working women deal with family responsibilities, whether child care or elder care. Support groups and counselors can also be a tremendous source of help to caregivers. Women who have been able to balance competing demands successfully may be an important resource to others. Finally, researchers should explore the complexities of different competing demands. Although being a "woman in the middle" may not be a "normative" experience, demographic trends suggest it may become more common in the future.

ENDNOTES

1. National Center for Health Statistics, *Vital Statistics of the United States, 1985 Life Tables,* Vol. 11, Sec. 6, Department of Health and Human Services Pub. No. (PHS) 88-1104, Public Health Service (Washington, DC: U.S. Government Printing Office, 1988).
2. Susan C. Watkins, Jane A. Menken, and John Bongaarts, "Demographic Foundations of Family Change," *American Sociological Review* 52(3) (1987): 346–58.
3. Ibid.
4. Ethel Shanas, "The Family as a Social Support System in Old Age," *The Gerontologist* 19 (1979): 169–74.
5. National Center for Health Statistics, *Vital Statistics of the United States, 1973 Life Tables* (Rockville, MD: U.S. Government Printing Office, 1975).
6. E. M. Brody, "'Women in the Middle' and Family Help to Older People," *The Gerontologist* 21 (1981): 471–80.
7. E. M. Brody, "Parent Care as a Normative Family Stress," *The Gerontologist* 25(1) (1985): 19–29.
8. Sarah H. Matthews, "The Burdens of Parent Care: A Critical Assessment of the Recent Literature" (revision of a paper presented at the Gerontological Society of America, New Orleans, 1985); Carolyn J. Rosenthal, Victor W. Marshall, and Sarah H. Matthews, "The Incidence and Prevalence of 'Women in the Middle'" (revision of a paper presented at the Gerontological Society of America, Chicago, 1986).
9. Emily K. Abel, *Love Is Not Enough: Family Care of the Frail Elderly,* APHA Public Health Policy Series (Washington, DC: American Public Health Association, 1987); Amy Horowitz, "Family Caregiving to the Frail Elderly," in *Annual Review of Gerontology and Geriatrics,* Vol. 5, ed. C. Eisdorfer (New York: Springer, 1985).
10. Rosenthal et al., "Incidence and Prevalence of 'Women in the Middle.'"
11. Vern L. Bengston et al., "Generations, Cohorts and Relations between Age Groups," in *Handbook of Aging and the Social Sciences,* 2d ed., ed. Robert H. Binstock and Ethel Shanas (New York: Van Nostrand Reinhold, 1986), pp. 304–38.
12. David E. Bloom and James Trussell, "What Are the Determinants of Delayed Childbearing and Permanent Childlessness in the United States?" *Demography* 21(4) (1984): 591–609.
13. Linda M. Burton and Vern L. Bengston, "Black Grandmothers: Issues of Timing and Continuity of Roles," in *Grandparenthood,* ed. Vern L. Bengston and Joan F. Robertson (Beverly Hills, CA: Sage, 1985).
14. David M. Heer, Robert W. Hodge, and Marcus Felson, "The Cluttered Nest: Evidence That Young Adults Are More Likely to Live at Home Now Than in the Recent Past," *Sociology and Social Research* 69 (April 1985): 437–41.
15. Jill S. Grigsby and Jill B. McGowan, "Still in the Nest: Adult Children Living with Their Parents," *Sociology and Social Research* 70 (January): 146–48.
16. Eileen M. Crimmins, "Evidence on the Compression of Morbidity," *Gerontologica Perspecta* 1 (1987): 45–49.
17. U.S. Bureau of the Census, *Statistical Abstract of the United States* (Washington, DC: U.S. Government Printing Office, 1987).
18. U.S. Bureau of Labor Statistics, *Handbook of Labor Statistics,* March 1984 Population Survey, Table 52 (Washington, DC: U.S. Government Printing Office, 1985), p. 119.
19. Robyn Stone, Gail Cafferata, and Judith Sangl, "Caregivers of the Frail Elderly: A National Profile," *The Gerontologist* 27(5) (1987): 616–26.

20. E. M. Brody et al., "Women's Changing Roles and Help to the Elderly: Attitudes of Three Generations of Women," *Journal of Gerontology* 38 (1983): 597–607.
21. Stone et al., "Caregivers of the Frail Elderly"; E. M. Brody et al., "Work Status and Parent Care: A Comparison of Four Groups of Women," *The Gerontologist* 27(2) (1987): 201–208.
22. Beth J. Soldo and Jaana Myllyluoma, "Caregivers Who Live with Dependent Elderly," *The Gerontologist* 23(6) (1983): 605–11.
23. Brody et al., "Work Status and Parent Care."
24. Robert B. Enright Jr. and Lynn Friss, *Employed Caregivers of Brain-Impaired Adults: An Assessment of the Dual Role* (San Francisco: Family Survival Project, 1987).
25. Patricia G. Archbold, "Impact of Parent-Caring on Women," *Family Relations* 32 (1983): 39–45.
26. Brody et al., "Work Status and Parent Care."
27. A. M. Lang and E. M. Brody, "Characteristics of Middle-Aged Daughters and Help to Their Elderly Mothers," *Journal of Marriage and the Family* 45 (1983): 193–202; Brody et al., "Work Status and Parent Care."
28. E. M. Brody and Clare B. Schoonover, "Patterns of Care for the Dependent Elderly When Daughters Work and When They Do Not," *The Gerontologist* 26(4) (1996): 372–81.
29. Stone et al., "Caregivers and the Frail Elderly"; Brody et al., "Work Status and Parent Care."
30. Dorothy A. Miller, "The 'Sandwich' Generation: Adult Children of the Aging," *Social Work* 26 (1981): 419–23; Andrew E. Scharlach, "Role Strain in Mother–Daughter Relationships in Later Life," *The Gerontologist* 27(5) (1987): 627–31.
31. Horowitz, "Family Caregiving."
32. Ibid.
33. W. J. Goode, "A Theory of Role Strain," *American Sociological Review* 25 (1960): 488–96.

PART X
Families and Work

In 1800, women whose work consisted largely in caring for families without pay were widely considered productive workers. By 1900, however, they had been formally relegated to the census category of "dependents" that included infants, young children, the sick, and the elderly.

Economist NANCY FOLBRE

What is adequate for the "typical" employee—a male—has to be accepted without question by females who wish to participate in the male world.

NORTON 1994:220

Early in the morning she rises,
The woman's work is never done.
And it's not because she doesn't try,
She's fighting a battle with no one on her side.

She rises up in the morning,
And she works 'til way past dusk.
The woman better slow down,
Or she's gonna come down hard.

Early in the morning she rises,
The woman's work is never done.

Woman's Work, by TRACY CHAPMAN

These three quotes reflect controversial feelings about families and work. The first quote shows how "work" is defined and redefined by governmental agencies. The redefinition may not value the work that some groups, namely women, do in society. The second quote refers to the work world as being structured for and around men and men's lives. The final quote, from song lyrics written by Tracy Chapman, illustrates that the vast amount of work women do both within the workplace and at home is compounded by women's roles and by the sex-based division of labor within the family. All three quotes suggest that there is conflict between the institution of the family and the institution of work. Moreover, they suggest that these worlds are separate gendered worlds. Students tend to affirm the ideology of "separate spheres" for family and work by believing that their work lives will be unaffected by their family lives and vice versa. In this section we challenge this ideology by showing that work and families cannot be separated and are, in fact, intimately related. Thus, we want to explore how work outside the home shapes families and how families shape work.

In addition, we examine the work done inside the home, specifically the various types of unpaid labor, such as housework, child care, kin work, food preparation, and other caretaking activities. Of particular interest to family scholars is the question "Who is doing most of this unpaid labor in the home?" As we saw in the Goldscheider and Waite article (Reading 19), some of this labor is done by children and teenagers in the form of household chores. However, the vast majority of household labor, up to 80 percent, is done by adult women; this includes preparing meals, washing dishes, cleaning the house, shopping, laundry, and paying the bills (Demo and Acock 1993). Unfortunately, most of this labor is invisible or is seen as something women do out of love for their partners and children. Thus, as apparent in the preceding data and in the above quotes, family work is very gendered. There are different expectations concerning women and men both in the workplace and in the home. The gendered nature of work is a theme throughout the four readings in this section.

Families and Paid Employment

Until recently, most of the research on families and work focused on the interaction between paid employment and families. For example, how do dual-career couples and commuter couples organize work and family life? Do workplace structures create artificial barriers between work and families? How do employed parents, in general, balance their work lives and family lives? This question is the central theme of the first reading in this section, by Arlie Russell Hochschild, titled "The Emotional Geography of Work and Family Life." Hochschild, a professor of sociology at the University of California, Berkeley, has written extensively on gender, work, and family life. In this selection, taken from *The Time Bind: When Work Becomes Home and Home Becomes Work* (1997), Hochschild discusses her research into a Fortune 500 company to see how people are balancing their work and family lives. Her goal in this study was to determine how these workers manage the work–family "speed-up" created by working mothers, inflexible jobs, and increased work hours for both men and women. She was especially interested in the difficulties of dual-earner families in dealing with child care, housework, and spending time together as a family. She found that people work too many hours, which hurts the work–family balance, yet people resist family-friendly employment policies, such as flextime, shared jobs, family leaves, and working part-time. Why? Most people reported that they do not need the pay *nor* are they worried about layoffs. Instead, Hochschild found that work and family both are emotional cultures, but many people prefer being at work to being with their family, because they receive more positive reinforcement at work.

A second question often found in the research literature is "How does father's or mother's employment affect children?" In their book *Parents' Jobs and Children's Lives* (1994), Toby L. Parcel and Elizabeth G. Menaghan consider the effects of parental working conditions on children's cognitive and social development. They also focus on how parental work affects the home environments that parents create for their children and how these home environments influence the children directly. Lois Hoffman ([1985] 1987) also studied the effects of maternal and paternal employment on children and found that parental employment shapes family values, influences the worker's psychological state, and imposes time schedules and domestic chores. Of particular importance is Hoffman's findings on the effects of maternal employment. Hoffman states that the belief that maternal employment has only negative effects on children is a myth and that there is over 50 years of research to disprove this myth. Instead, she argues that employed mothers have several positive effects on their children, including the fact that they are more likely to encourage independence in their children and are more likely to challenge the traditional sex-based division of labor in the home, thus influencing the sex-role socialization of children. Moreover, if mothers are happily employed, this has positive spillover effects on their parenting and family life.

Families and Unemployment

One of Hoffman's ([1985] 1987) conclusions is that we need more research on the effects of unemployment on children and families. Lillian B. Rubin's article, "When You Get Laid Off, It's Like You Lose a Part of Yourself," is based on her interviews with working-class husbands and wives to see how unemployment is affecting their relationships and families. Rubin, a sociologist and practicing psychotherapist in San Francisco, is also a senior research associate at the Institute for the Study of Social Change at the University of California, Berkeley. She comments:

> *My interest in working-class families began when, as a child in such a family, I saw firsthand the devastation unemployment and underemployment wrought on family life. When, as a graduate student, I listened to my professors talk about the issues of class in America, I was appalled at their abstractions and their lack of familiarity with the everyday issues working-class families face. My dissertation, therefore, was an examination of the social class issues that divided America around school busing for integration, which led to my study documenting working-class family life in a book called* Worlds of Pain *(1976).* Families on the Fault Line: America's Working Class Speaks About the Family, the Economy, Race, and Ethnicity *(1994) is a continuation of that lifelong interest and updates some of the issues I examined in that earlier work.* (Personal Interview 1997)

In the selection included here, excerpted from *Families on the Fault Line*, Rubin examines the cases of families in which the father has been laid off from his job and the mother has become the primary breadwinner. Rubin found that initially after being laid off, the husband/father is very optimistic and willing to help out around the house with housework, the children, and any other project he can think of. However, as time goes by, he becomes frustrated about his lack of employment, which often leads to depression. Rubin explains the stages a man often experiences after being laid off: (1) shock, (2) denial and then a sense of optimism, and (3) increasing distress and depression. She hypothesizes that working "earns" men "the right" to their manhood, and with the loss of employment, men must reevaluate their masculinity and their place in the family and the world. Not surprisingly, many problems often occur in a marriage as a result of the man's unemployment.

Rubin's arguments about men seeing their employment as central to their masculine identity are echoed in the work of Jessie Bernard. Bernard was a sociologist who studied gender-based family roles, especially the roles of men, including the stereotyped good provider role. In her research for "The Good Provider Role: Its Rise and Fall" ([1981] 1994), she investigated how the ideal of the good provider role came about historically and the societal pressure on men to fulfill this role. The good provider role also greatly affected the working lives of women. As Bernard argues, "The very nature of maleness and femaleness becomes embedded in the sexual division of labor. One's sex and one's work are part of one another. One's work defines one's gender" (p. 120). With this statement, Bernard is showing how the idea that a male's ability to be the breadwinner and the only paid laborer in the family, and therefore the sole "provider" for his family, has come to define his maleness as well. If his wife works outside the home, it reflects on his inability to provide for his family. As more and more women have come to work outside the home, the traditional roles of men as breadwinners have been challenged and forced to change. For recent research on the changing roles of men in families, see Reading 23, "Dilemmas of Involved Fatherhood," by Kathleen Gerson.

Housework

In addition to challenging the primary breadwinning role of men, women entering the workforce have greatly impacted the family in other ways. Specifically, women and their social roles have changed dramatically, but social structures and ideologies have not changed. Arlie Hochschild, in *The Second Shift: Working Parents and the Revolution at Home* (1989), talks about a stalled revolution for women in the home. Women have made great strides by entering the workforce and competing directly with men. At home, however, men are resisting the changes in gender roles, and women are having to take on a greater share of the work. The results are increased conflicts in marriages, women taking up the "second shift" of housework after they come home from work, and, in some cases, an increased likelihood for divorce. Hochschild finds that a critical battleground in many dual-earner households is the division of household labor. While many couples say they want gender equity in housework, the reality is that women end up doing more of the housework, enough to create a second shift of work after they complete their first shift of paid employment.

The third reading in this section, "Changing Patterns of Family Work: Chicano Men and Housework," by Scott Coltrane, investigates the gendered conflict concerning housework. Coltrane is an associate professor of sociology at the University of California, Riverside, where he does research on gender and families. In this selection, Coltrane examines the division of domestic labor and the resulting power dynamics in Chicano households. Building on the research done by Jessie Bernard on the "good provider role" and on Arlie Hochschild's concept of the "economy of gratitude," Coltrane finds that Chicano couples see the meaning of housework and individual responsibility for it as dependent on how the couple views gender roles and whether the wife works full-time outside the home. Moreover, there are both traditional families, where the wife is expected to do the housework regardless of paid employment, and full co-provider families, where housework is not automatically left for the wife to do and she does not assume that it is her responsibility.

Kin Work

As described earlier, unpaid labor in the home involves much more than cleaning the house and doing the laundry. Recently, studies of families and work have begun to examine the diverse types of labor that occur inside the household. For example, for her book *Feeding the Family: The Social Organization of Caring as Gendered Work* (1991), Marjorie DeVault studied the amount of work that goes into planning and preparing family meals. This work is invisible until you begin to examine all the steps prior to setting a cooked meal on the table. DeVault argues that food preparation is usually done by women, who spend hours planning meals, clipping food coupons, grocery shopping, preparing and cooking food. Moreover, this labor is more complex because women often are paying attention to the nutritional value of food and the personal preferences of individual family members. In addition, the meaning of food varies; in many households, for example, family meals actually help facilitate family relationships and mark special events. Thus, women are literally creating "family" by bringing family members together around the dinner table and helping to facilitate relationships. DeVault also finds that this work varies across households and income groups.

The last article in this section is "The Female World of Cards and Holidays: Women, Families, and the Work of Kinship," by Micaela di Leonardo. In this selection, di Leonardo, an anthropologist, introduces the concept of kin work and shows how it shapes family relationships among Italian Americans in northern California. Di Leonardo defines kin work as

> the conception, maintenance, and ritual celebration of cross-household kin ties, including visits, letters, telephone calls, presents, and cards to

kin; the organization of family gatherings; the creation and maintenance of quasi-kin relations; decisions to neglect or intensify particular ties; the mental work of reflection about all of these activities; and the creation and communication of altering images of family and kin vis-à-vis the images of others, both folk and mass media.

Thus, kin work involves a variety of activities that create and maintain family ties. Similar to other types of work done within the household, kin work is often invisible and undervalued. It is also work primarily done by women, and it is not until this work stops, due to illness or divorce, that the amount of labor invested in maintaining families becomes visible. In addition, di Leonardo argues that this concept of kin work can be observed cross-culturally and across social class and racial-ethnic groups.

REFERENCES

Bernard, Jessie. [1981] 1994. "The Good Provider Role: Its Rise and Fall." Pp. 117–36 in *Families in Transition*, 8th ed., edited by Arlene S. Skolnick and Jerome H. Skolnick. New York: HarperCollins. (Originally published in *American Psychologist* 36 [1981]: 1–12.)

Demo, David H. and Alan C. Acock. 1993. "Family Diversity and the Division of Domestic Labor: How Much Have Things Really Changed?" *Family Relations* 42:323–31.

DeVault, Marjorie L. 1991. *Feeding the Family: The Social Organization of Caring as Gendered Work*. Chicago: University of Chicago Press.

Hochschild, Arlie. 1997. *The Time Bind: When Work Becomes Home and Home Becomes Work*. New York: Metropolitan Books.

Hochschild, Arlie, with Anne Machung. 1989. *The Second Shift: Working Parents and the Revolution at Home*. New York: Viking Press.

Hoffman, Lois. [1985] 1987. "The Effects on Children of Maternal and Paternal Employment." Pp. 362–95 in *Families and Work*, edited by Naomi Gerstel and Harriet Engel Gross. Philadelphia: Temple University Press.

Norton, Sue M. 1994. "Pregnancy, the Family, and Work: An Historical Review and Update of Legal Regulations and Organizational Policies and Practices in the United States." *Gender, Work, and Organization* 1:217–26.

Parcel, Toby L. and Elizabeth G. Menaghan. 1994. *Parents' Jobs and Children's Lives*. New York: Aldine de Gruyter.

Rubin, Lillian B. 1976. *Worlds of Pain: Life in the Working-Class Family*. New York: Basic Books.

———. 1994. *Families on the Fault Line: America's Working-Class Speaks about the Family, the Economy, Race, and Ethnicity*. New York: HarperCollins.

36

THE EMOTIONAL GEOGRAPHY
OF WORK AND FAMILY LIFE

ARLIE RUSSELL HOCHSCHILD

Over the last two decades, American workers have increasingly divided into a majority who work too many hours and a minority with no work at all. This split hurts families at both extremes, but I focus here on the growing scarcity of time among the long-hours majority. For many of them, a speed-up at the office and factory has marginalised life at home, so that the very term "work–family balance" seems to them a bland slogan with little bearing on real life. In this chapter, I describe the speed-up and review a range of cultural responses to it, including "family-friendly reforms" such as flextime, job sharing, part-time work and parental leave. Why, I ask, do people not resist the speed-up more than they do? When offered these reforms, why don't more take advantage of them? Drawing upon my ongoing research in an American Fortune 500 company, I argue that a company's "family-friendly" policy goes only as deep as the "emotional geography" of the workplace and home, the drawn and redrawn boundaries between the sacred and the profane. I show how ways of talking about time (for example, separating "quality" from "quantity" time) become code words to describe that emotional geography. . . .

A Work–Family Speed–Up

Three factors are creating the current speed-up in work and family life in the United States. (By the term "family," I refer to committed unmarried couples, same-sex couples, single mothers, two-job couples and wage-earner–housewife couples. My focus is on all families who raise children.) First of all, increasing numbers of mothers now work outside the home. In 1950, 22 per cent of American mothers of children eighteen and under worked for pay; in 1991, 67 per cent did. Half of the mothers of children age one year and younger work for pay.

Second, they work in jobs which generally lack flexibility. The very model of "a job" and "career" has been based, for the most part, on the model of a traditional man whose wife cared for the children at home. Third, over the last 20 years, both women and men have increased their hours of work. In her book *The Overworked American,* the economist Juliet Schor argues that over the last two decades American workers have added an extra 164 hours to their year's work—an extra month of work a year (Schor 1992:26). Compared to 20 years ago, workers take fewer unpaid absences, and even fewer *paid* ones. Over the last decade, vacations have shortened by 14 per cent (Schor 1992:12–13). The number of families eating evening meals together has dropped by 10 per cent (Blyton 1985; Fuchs 1991).[1] Counting overtime and commuting time, a 1992 national sample of men averaged 48.8 hours of work, and women, 41.7 (Galinsky, Bond, and Friedman 1993:9). Among young parents, close to half now work more than 8 hours a day. Compared to the 1970s, mothers take less time off for the birth of a child and are more likely to work through the summer. They are more likely to work continuously until they retire at age 65. Thus, whether they have children or not, women increasingly fit the profile of year-round, life-long paid workers, a profile that has long characterised men. Meanwhile, male workers have not reduced their hours but, instead, expanded them.

Not all working parents with more free time will spend it at home tending children or elderly relatives. Nor, needless to say, if parents do spend time at home, will all their children find them kind, helpful and fun. But without a chance for more time at home, the issue of using it well does not arise at all.

Cool Modern, Traditional, Warm Modern Stances Toward the Speed–Up

Do the speed-up people think the speed-up is a problem? Does anybody else? If so, what cultural stances toward gender equity, family life and capitalism underly the practical solutions they favour? If we explore recent writing on the hurried life of a working parent, we can discern three stances toward it.

One is a *cool modern* stance, according to which the speed-up has become "normal," even fashionable. Decline in time at home does not "marginalise" family life, proponents say, it makes it different, even better. Like many other popular self-help books addressed to the busy working mother, *The Superwoman Syndrome,* by Majorie Schaevitz, offers busy mothers tips on how to fend off appeals for help from neighbours, relatives, friends, how to stop feeling guilty about their mothering. It instructs the mother how to frugally measure out minutes of "quality time" for her children and abandons as hopeless the project of getting men more involved at home (Schaevitz 1984). Such books call for no changes in the workplace, no changes in the culture and no change in men. *The solution to rationalisation at work is rationalisation at home.* Tacitly such books accept the corrosive effects of global capitalism on family life and on the very notion of what people need to be happy and fulfilled (Hochschild 1994).

A second stance toward the work–family speed-up is *traditional* in that it calls for women's return to the home, or *quasi-traditional* in that it acquiesces to a secondary role, a lower rank "mommy track," for women at work (Schwartz 1989). Those who take this sort of stance acknowledge the speed-up as a problem but deny the fact that most women now have to work, want to work, and embrace the concept of gender equity. They essentialise different male and female "natures," and notions of time, for men and women — "industrial" time for men, and "family" time for women (Hareven 1982).[2]

A third *warm modern* stance is both humane (the speed-up is a problem) and egalitarian (equity at home and work is a goal). Those who take this approach question the terms of employment — both through a nationwide programme of worksharing (as in Germany), a shorter working week, and through company-based family-friendly reforms.[3] What are these family-friendly reforms?

- flextime; a workday with flexible starting and quitting times, but usually 40 hours of work and the opportunity to "bank" hours at one time and reclaim them later;
- flexplace; home-based work, such as telecommuting;
- regular or permanent part-time; less than full-time work with full- or pro-rated benefits and promotional opportunities in proportion to one's skill and contribution;
- job sharing; two people voluntarily sharing one job with benefits and salary pro-rated;
- compressed working week; four 10-hour days with 3 days off, or three 12-hour days with 4 days off;
- paid parental leave;
- family obligations as a consideration in the allocation of shift work and required overtime.[4]

Together, worksharing and this range of family-friendly reforms could spread work, increase worker control over hours, and create a "warm modern" world for women to be equal within.[5] As political goals in America over the last 50 years, worksharing and a shorter working week have "died and gone to heaven" where they live on as Utopian ideals. In the 1990s, family-friendly reforms are the lesser offering on the capitalist bargaining table. But are companies in fact offering these reforms? Are working parents pressing for them?

The news is good and bad. Recent nationwide studies suggest that more and more American companies offer their workers family-friendly alternative work schedules. According to one recent study, 88 per cent of 188 companies surveyed offer part-time work, 77 per cent offer flextime of some sort, 48 per cent offer job-sharing, 35 per cent offer some form of flexplace, and 20 per cent offer a compressed working week (Galinsky, Friedman, and Hernandez 1991).[6] (But in most companies, the interested worker must seek and receive the approval of a supervisor or department head. Moreover, most policies do not apply to lower-level workers whose conditions of work are covered by union contracts.)

But even if offered, regardless of need, few workers actually take advantage of the reforms. One study of 384 companies noted that only nine companies reported even one father who took an official unpaid leave at the birth of his child (Friedman 1991:50). Few are on temporary or permanent part-time. Still fewer share a job. Of workers with children ages 12 and under, only 4 per cent of men and 13 per cent of women worked less than 40 hours a week (Galinsky et al. 1991:123).

Inside a Fortune 500 Company

Why, when the opportunity presents itself, do so few working parents take it? To find out, I set about interviewing managers, and clerical and factory workers in a large manufacturing company in the northeastern United States—which I shall call, simply, the Company. I chose to study this Company because of its reputation as an especially progressive company. Over the last 15 years, for example, the Company devoted millions of dollars to informing workers of its family-friendly policies, hiring staff to train managers to implement them, making showcase promotions of workers who take extended maternity leaves or who work part-time. If change is to occur anywhere, I reasoned, it was likely to be within this Company.

But the first thing I discovered was that even in this enlightened Company, few young parents or workers tending elderly relatives took advantage of the chance to work more flexible or shorter hours. Among the 26,000 employees, the average working week ranged from 45 to 55 hours. Managers and factory workers often worked 50 or 60 hours a week while clerical workers tended to work a more normal, 40-hour, week. Everyone agreed the Company was a "pretty workaholic place." Moreover, for the last 5 years, hours of work had increased.

Explanations That Don't Work

Perhaps workers shy away from applying for leaves or shortening their hours because they can't afford to earn less. This certainly explains why many young parents continue to work long hours. But it doesn't explain why the wealthiest workers, the managers and professionals, are among the *least* interested in additional time off. Even among the Company's factory workers, who in 1993 averaged between eleven and twelve dollars an hour, and who routinely competed for optional overtime, two 40-hour-a-week paychecks with no overtime work were quite enough to support the family. A substantial number said they could get by on one paycheck if they sold one of their cars, put in a vegetable garden, and cut down on "extras." Yet, the overwhelming majority did not want to.

Perhaps, then, employees shied away from using flexible or shorter hour schedules because they were afraid of having their names higher on the list of workers who might be laid off in a period of economic downturn. Through the 1980s, a third of America's largest companies experienced some layoffs, though this did not happen to managers or clerical workers at this company.

By union contract, production workers were assured that layoffs, should they occur, would be made according to seniority and not according to any other criteria — such as how many hours an employee had worked. Yet, the workaholism went on. Employees in the most profitable sectors of the Company showed no greater tendency to ask for shorter or more flexible hours for family reasons than employees in the least profitable sectors.

Is it, then, that workers who could afford shorter hours didn't *know* about the Company's family-friendly policies? No. All of the 130 working parents I spoke with had heard about alternative schedules and knew where they could find out more.

Perhaps the explanation lies not with the workers but with their managers. Managers responsible for implementing family-friendly policies may be openly or covertly undermining them. Even though Company policy allowed flexibility, the head of a division could, for reasons of production, openly refuse a worker permission to go part-time or to job-share, which some did. For example when asked about his views on flextime, the head of the engineering division of the Company replied flatly, "My policy on flextime is that there is no flextime." Other apparently permissive division heads had supervisors who were tough on this issue "for them." Thus, there seemed to be some truth to this explanation for why so few workers stepped forward.[7]

But even managers known to be co-operative had few employees asking for alternative schedules. Perhaps, then, workers ask for time off, but do so "off the books." To some extent, this "off the books" hypothesis did hold, especially for new fathers who may take a few days to a week of sick leave for the birth of a baby instead of filing for "parental leave," which they feared would mark them as unserious workers.

Even counting informal leaves, most women managers returned to full-time 40- to 55-hour work schedules fairly soon after their 6 weeks of paid maternity leave. Across ranks, most women secretaries returned after 6 months; most women production workers returned after 6 weeks. Most new fathers took a few days off at most. Thus, even "off the books," working parents used very little of the opportunity to spend more time at home.

Far more important than all these factors seemed to be a company "speed-up" in response to global competition. In the early years of the 1990s, workers each year spoke of working longer hours than they had the year before, a trend seen nationwide. When asked why, they explained that the Company was trying to "reduce costs," in part by asking employees to do more than they were doing before.

But the sheer existence of a company speed-up doesn't explain why employees weren't trying to actively resist it, why there wasn't much backtalk. Parents were eager to tell me how their families came first, how they were clear about that. (National polls show that next to a belief in God, Americans most strongly believe in "the family.") But, practices that might express this belief—such as sharing breakfast and dinner—were shifting in the opposite direction. In the minds of many parents of young children, warm modern intentions seemed curiously, casually, fused with cool modern ideas and practices. In some ways, those within the work–family speed-up don't seem to want to slow down. What about their experience makes this true? . . .

Work and Family as Emotional Cultures

Through its family-friendly reforms, the Company had earned a national reputation as a desirable family-friendly employer. But at the same time, it wasn't inconvenienced by having to arrange alternate schedules for very many employees. One can understand how this might benefit a company. But how about the working parents?

For the answer, we may need a better grasp of the emotional cultures, and the relative "draw" of work and family. Instead of thinking of the workplace or the family as unyielding thing-like structures, Giddens suggests that we see structures as fluid and changeable. "Structuration," Anthony Giddens tells us, is the "dynamic process whereby structures come into being" (Giddens 1976:121, 157). For structures to change, there must be changes in what people do. But in doing what they do, people unconsciously draw on resources, and depend on larger conditions to develop the skills they use to change what they do (Giddens 1976:157).

With this starting point, then, let us note that structures come with—and also "are"—emotional cultures. A change in structure requires a change in emotional culture. What we lack, so far, is a vocabulary for describing this culture, and what follows is a crude attempt to create one. An emotional culture is a set of rituals, beliefs about feelings and rules governing feeling which induce emotional focus, and even a sense of the "sacred."[8] This sense of the sacred selects and favours some social bonds over others. It selects and reselects relationships into a core or periphery of family life.

Thus, families have a more or less *sacred core* of private rituals and shared meanings. In some families what is most sacred is sexuality and marital communication (back rubs, pillow talk, sex), and in other families the "sacred" is reserved for parental bonds (bedtime cuddles with children, bathtime, meals, parental talk about children). In addition, families have secondary zones of less important daily, weekly, seasonal rituals which back up the core rituals. They also have a profane outer layer, in which members might describe themselves as "doing nothing in particular"—doing chores, watching television, sleeping. The character and boundaries of the sacred and profane aspects of family life are in the eye of the beholder. "Strong families" with "thick ties" can base their sense of the sacred on very different animating ideas and practices. Families also differ widely on how much one member's sense of the sacred matches another's and on how much it is the occasion for expressing harmony or conflict. Furthermore, families creatively adapt to new circumstances by ritualising new activities—for example, couples in commuter marriages may "ritualise" the phone call or the daily e-mail exchange. Couples with "too much time together" may de-ritualise meals, sex, or family events. Furthermore, families have different structures of sacredness. Some have thick actual cores and thin peripheries, others have a porous core and extensive peripheral time in which people just "hang out." But in each case, emotional culture shapes the experience of family life.

Emotional cultures stand back-to-back with ideas about time. In the context of the work–family speed-up, many people speak of actively "managing time, finding time, making time, guarding time, or fighting for time." Less do they speak of simply "having" or "not having" time. In their attempt to take a more active grip on their schedules, many working parents turn a telephone answering machine on at dinner, turn down work assignments and social engagements, and actively fight to defend "family time."

One's talk about time is itself a verbal practice that does or doesn't reaffirm the ritual core of family life. In the core of family life, we may speak more of living in the moment. Because a sacred activity is an end in itself, and not a means to an end, the topic of time is less likely to arise. If it does, one speaks of "enjoying time," or "devoting time." With the work–family speed-up, the term "quality time" has arisen, as in "I need more quality time with my daughter," a term referring to freedom from distraction, time spent in an attitude of intense focus. In general, we try to "make" time for core family life because we feel it matters more.

In the intermediate and peripheral zones of family life, we may speak of "having time on our hands, wasting or killing time." In the new lexicon, we speak of "quantity time."[9] In general, we feel we can give up peripheral time, because it matters less. More hotly contested is the time to participate in a child's school events, help at the school auction, buy a birthday gift for a babysitter, or call an elderly neighbour.

With a decline in this periphery, the threads of reciprocity in the community and neighbourhood grow weaker. By forcing families to cut out what is "least important," the speed-up thins out and weakens ties that bind it to society. Thus, under the press of the "speed-up," families are forced to give up their periphery ties with neighbours, distant relatives, bonds sustained by "extra time." *The speed-up privatises the family.* The "neighbourhood goes to work," where it serves the emotional interests of the workplace. Where are one's friends? At work.

Although the family in modern society is separated from the workplace, its emotional culture is ecologically linked to and drawn from it. Both the family and workplace are also linked to supportive realms. For the family, this often includes the neighbourhood, the church, the school. For the work-place, this includes the pub, the golf club, the commuter-van friendship net-work. A loss of supportive structure around the family may result in a gain for the workplace, and vice versa. Insofar as the "periphery" of family life protected its ritual core, to a certain degree for working parents these ties are not so peripheral at all.

A gender pattern is clear. Because most women now must and for the most part want to work outside the home, they are performing family rituals less. At the same time, men are not doing them very much more. Together, these two facts result in a net loss in ritual life at home.

At the same time, at some workplaces, an alternative cultural magnet is drawing on the human need for a centre, a ritual core. As family life becomes de-ritualised, in certain sectors of the economy, the engineers of corporate cultures are re-ritualising the workplace. Thus, the contraction of emotional culture at home is linked to a socially engineered expansion of emotional cul-ture at work.

Work like a Family, and Family, for Some, like Work

At a certain point, change in enough personal stories can be described as a change in culture, and I believe many families at the Company are coming to this turning-point now. Pulled toward work by one set of forces and pro-pelled from the family by another set of forces, a growing number of work-ers are unwittingly altering the twin cultures of work and family (Kanter 1977; Lasch 1977). As the cultural shield surrounding work has grown stronger, the supportive cultural shield surrounding the family has weakened. Fewer neighbourhood "consultants" talk to one when trouble arises at home, and for some, they are more to help out with problems at work.

These twin processes apply unevenly; the pull toward work is stronger at the top of the occupational ladder, and marginalisation of family life, more pronounced at the bottom. Indeed, the picture I shall draw is one in a *wide ar-ray* of work and family "structurations" resulting from various combinations of social forces.

The Model of Family as a Haven in a Heartless World

When I entered the field, I assumed that working parents would *want* more time at home. I imagined that they experienced home as a place where they could relax, feel emotionally sheltered and appreciated for who they "really are." I imagined home to feel to the weary worker like the place where he or she could take off a uniform, put on a bathrobe, have a beer, exhale—a pic-ture summed up in the image of the worker coming in the door saying, "Hi honey, I'm home!" To be sure, home life has its emergencies and strains but I imagined that home was the place people thought about when they thought about rest, safety and appreciation. Given this, they would want to maximise time at home, especially time with their children. I also assumed that these working parents would not feel particularly relaxed, safe or appreciated at work, at least not more so than at home, and especially not factory workers.

When I interviewed workers at the Company, however, a picture emerged which partly belied this model of family life. For example, one 30-year-old factory shift supervisor, a remarried mother of two, described her return home after work in this way:

> I walk in the door and the minute I turn the key in the lock my oldest daughter is there. Granted she needs somebody to talk to about her day. The baby is still up. . . . She should have been in bed two hours ago and that upsets me. The oldest comes right up to the door and complains about anything her father said or did during the evening. She talks about her job. My husband is in the other room hollering to my daughter, "Tracy, I don't ever get no time to talk to your mother because you're always monopolizing her time first before I even get a chance!" They all come at me at once.

The un-arbitrated quarrels, the dirty dishes, and the urgency of other people's demands she finds at home contrast with her account of going to work:

> I usually come to work early just to get away from the house. I go to be there at a quarter after the hour and people are there waiting. We sit. We talk. We joke. I let them know what is going on, who has to be where, what changes I have made for the shift that day. We sit there and chit-chat for five or ten minutes. There is laughing. There is joking. There is fun. They aren't putting me down for any reason. Everything is done in humour and fun from beginning to end. It can get stressful, though, when a machine malfunctions and you can't get the production out.

Another 38-year-old working mother of two, also a factory worker, had this to say:

> My husband is a great help (with caring for their son). But as far as doing housework, or even taking the baby when I'm at home, no. When I'm home, our son becomes my job. He figures he works five days a week, he's not going to come home and clean. But he doesn't stop to think that I work seven days a week. . . . Why should I have to come home and do the housework without help from anybody else? My husband and I have been through this over and over again. Even if he would pick up the kitchen table and stack the dishes for me when I'm at work, that would make a big difference. He does nothing. On his weekends off, I have to provide a sitter for the baby so he can go fishing. When I have my day off, I have the baby all day long. He'll help out if I'm not here. . . . The minute I'm here he lets me do the work.

To this working mother, her family was not a haven, a zone of relief and relaxation. It was a workplace. More than that, she could only get relief from this domestic workplace by going to the factory. As she continued:

I take a lot of overtime. The more I get out of the house, the better I am. It's a terrible thing to say, but that's the way I feel!

I assumed that work would feel to workers like a place in which one could be fired at the whim of a profit-hungry employer, while in the family, for all its hassles, one was safe. Based as it is on the impersonal mechanism of supply and demand, profit and loss, work would feel insecure, like being in "a jungle." In fact, many workers I interviewed had worked for the Company for 20 years or more. But they were on their second or third marriages. To these employed, *work* was their rock, their major source of security, while they were receiving their "pink slips" at home.

To be sure, most workers *wanted* to base their sense of stability at home, and many did. But I was also struck by the loyalty many felt toward the Company and a loyalty *they felt* coming from it, despite what might seem like evidence to the contrary—the speed-up, the restructuring. When problems arose at work, many workers felt they could go to their supervisors or to a human resources worker and resolve it. If one division of the Company was doing poorly, the Company might "de-hire" workers within that division and rehire in a more prosperous division. This happened to one female engineer, very much upsetting her, but her response to it was telling:

I have done very well in the Company for twelve years, and I thought my boss thought very highly of me. He'd said as much. So when our division went down and several of us were de-hired, we were told to look for another position within the Company or outside. I thought, "Oh my God, outside!" I was stunned! Later, in the new division it was like a remarriage. . . . I wondered if I could love again.

Work was not always "there for you," but increasingly "home," as they had known it, wasn't either. As one woman recounted, "One day my husband came home and told me, 'I've fallen in love with a woman at work. . . . I want a divorce.'"

Finally, the model of family-as-haven led me to assume that the individual would feel most known and appreciated at home and least so at work. Work might be where they felt unappreciated, "a cog in the machine"—an image brought to mind by the Charlie Chaplin classic film on factory life, *Modern Times*. But the factory is no longer the archetypical workplace and, sadly, many workers felt more appreciated for what they were doing at work than for what they were doing at home. For example, when I asked one 40-year-old technician whether he felt more appreciated at home or at work, he said:

I love my family. I put my family first . . . but I'm not sure I feel more appreciated by them (laughs). My 14-year-old son doesn't talk too much to anyone when he gets home from school. He's a brooder. I don't know how good I've been as a father. . . . We fix cars together on Saturday. My wife works opposite shifts to what I work, so we don't see each other except on weekends. We need more time together — need to get out to the lake more. I don't know . . .

This worker seemed to feel better about his skill repairing machines in the factory than his way of relating to his son. This is not as unusual as it might seem. In a large-scale study, Arthur Emlen found that 59 per cent of employees rated their family performance "good or unusually good" while 86 per cent gave a similar rating to their performance on the job (Friedman 1991:16).

This overall cultural shift may account for why many workers are going along with the work–family speed-up and not joining the resistance against it. A 1993 nationally representative study of 3400 workers conducted by The Families and Work Institute reflects two quite contradictory findings. On one hand, the study reports that 80 per cent of workers feel their jobs require "working very hard" and 42 per cent "often feel used up by the end of the work day." On the other hand, when workers are asked to compare how much time and energy they *actually* devoted to their family, their job or career and themselves, with how much time they would *like* to devote to each, there was little difference (Galinsky et al. 1993:1, 98). Workers estimate that they actually spend 43 per cent of their time and energy on family and friends, 37 per cent on job or career, and 20 per cent on themselves. But they *want* to spend just about what they *are* spending — 47 per cent on family and friends, 30 per cent on the job, and 23 per cent on themselves (Galinsky et al. 1993:98). Thus, the workers I spoke to who were "giving" in to the work–family speed-up may be typical of a wider trend.

Causal Mechanisms

Three sets of factors may exacerbate this reversal of family and work cultures; trends in the family, trends at work, and a cultural consumerism which reinforces trends in the family and work.

First, half of marriages in America end in divorce — the highest divorce rate in the world. Because of the greater complexity of family life, the emotional skills of parenting, woefully underestimated to begin with, are more important than ever before. Many workers spoke with feeling about strained relationships with stepchildren and ex-wives or husbands (White and Riesmann 1992). New in scope, too, are the numbers of working wives who work "two shifts," one at home and one at work, and face their husband's resistance to helping fully with the load at home — a strain that often leaves both spouses feeling unappreciated (Hochschild 1989).

Second, another set of factors apply at work. Many corporations have emotionally engineered for top and upper middle managers a world of friendly ritual and positive reinforcement. New corporate cultures call for "valuing the individual" and honouring the "internal customer" (so that requests made by employees within the Company are honoured as highly as those by customers outside the Company). Human relations employees give seminars on human problems at work. High-performance teams, based on co-operation between relative equals who "manage themselves," tend to foster intense relations at work. The Company frequently gives out awards for outstanding work at award ceremonies. Compliments run freely. The halls are hung with new plaques praising one or another worker on recent accomplishments. Recognition luncheons, department gatherings and informal birthday remembrances are common. Career planning sessions with one's supervisor, team meetings to talk over "modeling, work relations, and mentoring" with co-workers all verge on, even as they borrow from, psychotherapy. For all its aggravation and tensions, the workplace is where quite a few workers feel appreciated, honoured, and where they have real friends. By contrast, at home there are fewer "award ceremonies" and little helpful feedback about mistakes.

In addition, courtship and mate selection, earlier more or less confined to the home-based community, may be moving into the sphere of work. The later age for marriage, the higher proportion of unmarried people, and the high divorce rate all create an ever-replenishing courtship pool at work. The gender desegregation of the workplace and the lengthened working day also provide opportunity for people to meet and develop romantic or quasi-romantic ties. At the factory, romance may develop in the lunchroom, pub, or parking lot; and for upper management levels, at conferences, in "fantasy settings" in hotels and dimly lit restaurants (Kanter 1990:281).

In a previous era, an undetermined number of men escaped the house for the pub, the fishing hole, and often the office. A common pattern, to quote from the title of an article by Jean Duncombe and Dennis Marsden, was that of "workaholic men" and "whining women" (Duncombe and Marsden 1993). Now that women compose 45 per cent of the American labour force and come home to a "second shift" of work at home, some women are escaping into work too—and as they do so, altering the cultures of work and home.

Forces pulling workers out of family life and into the workplace are set into perpetual motion by consumerism. Consumerism acts as a mechanism which maintains the emotional reversal of work and family (Schor 1992). Exposed to advertisements, workers expand their material "needs." To buy what they now "need," they need money. To earn money, they work longer hours. Being away from home so many hours, they make up for their absence at home with gifts which cost money. They "materialise" love. And so the cycle continues.

Once work begins to become a more compelling arena of appreciation than home, a self-fulfilling prophecy takes hold. For, if workers flee into work from the tensions at home, tensions at home often grow worse. The worse the tensions at home, the firmer the grip of the workplace on the worker's human needs, and hence the escalation of the entire syndrome.

If more workers conceive of work as a haven, it is overwhelmingly in some sense *against their wishes*. Most workers in this and other studies say they value family life above all. Work is what they do. Family is why they live. So, I believe the logic I have described proceeds despite, not because of, the powerful intentions and deepest wishes of those in its grip.

Models of Family and Work in the Flight Plan of Capitalism

To sum up, for some people work may be becoming more like family, and family life more like work. Instead of the model of the *family* as haven from work, more of us fit the model of *work* as haven from home. In this model, the tired parent leaves a world of unresolved quarrels, unwashed laundry and dirty dishes for the atmosphere of engineered cheer, appreciation and harmony at work. It is at work that one drops the job of *working* on relating to a brooding adolescent, an obstreperous toddler, rivaling siblings or a retreating spouse. At last, beyond the emotional shield of work, one says not, "Hi honey, I'm home," but "Hi fellas, I'm here!" For those who fit this model, the ritual core of family life is not simply smaller, it is less of a ritual core.

How extensive is this trend? I suspect it is a slight tendency in the lives of many working parents, and the basic reality for a small but growing minority. This trend holds for some people more than others and in some parts of society more than in others. Certain trends—such as the growth of the contingency labour force—may increase the importance of the family, and tend toward reinstalling the model of family as haven and work as "heartless world." A growing rate of unemployment might be associated with yet a third "double-negative" model according to which neither home nor work are emotional bases, but rather the gang at the pub, or on the street.

But the sense of sacred that we presume to be reliably attached to home may be more vulnerable than we might wish.

Most working parents more deeply want, or want to want, a fourth, "double-positive" model of work–family balance. In the end, these four patterns are unevenly spread over the class structure—the "haven in a heartless world" more at the top, the "double-negative" more at the bottom, the "reverse-haven" emerging in the middle.

Each pattern of work and family life is to be seen somewhere in the flight plan of late capitalism. For, capitalist competition is not simply a matter of market expansion around the globe, but of local geographies of emotion at home. The challenge, as I see it, is to understand the close links between economic trends, emotional geographies, and pockets of cultural resistance. For it is in those pockets that we can look for "warm modern" answers.

ENDNOTES

1. Less time away from work means less time for children. Nationwide, half of children wish they could see their fathers more, and a third wish they could see their mothers more (Coolsen, Seligman, and Garbino 1986; Hewlett 1991:105). A growing number of commentators draw links, often carelessly, between this decline in

family time and a host of problems, including school failure and alcohol and drug abuse (Hewlett 1991).

2. In her book *When Giants Learn to Dance*, the sociologist Rosabeth Kanter suggests an alternative to mommy-tracking—company "time outs." A company requires workers to work ten weeks of 9- or 10-hour days preparing to ship a product, and then take a week-long "time out" after the product is shipped. In contrast to "mommy-tracking," these time-outs are available to men as well as women. Those who take advantage of them aren't placed on a lower track (Kanter 1990). But by design, time-outs suit the needs of the *company* more than the worker. Time-outs presume the acceptance of an industrial notion of time for men and women, and pay the worker back for this acceptance, offering periodic rest-stops in it. It does not challenge the culture of capitalism but softens the worker up, the better to accept it (Kanter 1990:359).

3. On the political agenda for the 1950s, through the 1970s, bills proposing a shorter working week were vetoed by the United States Congress, strongly opposed by business, and have since disappeared from American public discourse (Blyton 1985; McCarthy and McGaughey 1981; Owen 1989).

4. Since factory workers are normally excluded in company consideration of these reforms, this option is normally excluded from "family-friendly reforms." In addition, seniority is the unquestioned principle applied in allocating shifts (see Engelstad 1983). Unions often oppose it adamantly since it adds a principle that competes with the principle of seniority used to determine who gets to work which shift.

5. The option of shorter or more flexible schedules should not be confused with the growth of "contingency jobs" which pair flexibility with a loss of job security and benefits. As activists in and outside companies conceive of family-friendly reforms, they make "good" jobs better and don't substitute bad jobs for good ones.

6. Many studies show that family-friendly reforms pay for themselves. Those who quit their jobs for family reasons are often the most, not the least, productive workers. In addition, each trained worker who quits, costs the company money in recruiting and training a replacement.

7. The CEO's pronouncement about family-friendly reforms and the managers' non-execution of them resemble an episode in Leo Tolstoy's *War and Peace*. In the novel, the Russian Emperor Alexander dispatches an envoy, Balashev, to deliver a critical message to Napoleon, to halt this advance toward Moscow. Balashev is detained by a series of people and, when he meets Napoleon, forgets to deliver the message.

8. Taking inspiration from Emile Durkheim, Erving Goffman brilliantly applied a notion of the sacred to the individual, though Goffman does not apply this idea to the unit intermediate between society and the individual—the family.

9. The workplace speed-up has itself exacerbated a "rationalization" of family life. In the nineteenth century, Tamara Hareven argues, events were measured in "family time," according to a family timetable (births, marriages, deaths) and by family units (generations) and oriented to family needs (the need to tend newborns, the dying). Formerly resistant to rationalisation, in the last 30 years family life has become increasingly planned, and geared to the industrial clock. "Quality time" is demarcated from "quantity time," just as time at the office "working" is designated as separate from time "goofing off around the water cooler." One shouldn't, one feels, be chatting aimlessly in a "quantity" sort of way when one is having "quality" time with a child. Even life-cycle events such as marriages and births are now sometimes planned according to the needs of the office (Martin 1992).

REFERENCES

Blyton, Paul. 1985. *Changes in Working Time: An International Review.* New York: St. Martin's Press.

Coolsen, P., M. Seligson, and J. Garbino. 1986. *When School's Out and Nobody's Home.* Chicago: National Committee for the Prevention of Child Abuse.

Duncombe, Jean and Dennis Marsden. 1993. "Workaholics and Whining Women, Theorizing Intimacy and Emotion Work: The Last Frontier of Gender Inequality?" Unpublished paper, Department of Sociology, University of Essex, England.

Engelstad, Fredrik. 1993. "Family Structure and Institutional Interplay." Pp. 72–90 in *Family Sociology—Developing the Field,* edited by Annlang Leira. Oslo: Institut fur Samfunnsforskning.

Friedman, D. 1991. *Linking Work–Family Issues to the Bottom Line.* New York: Conference Board.

Fuchs, V. 1991. "Are Americans Under-Investing in Their Children?" *Society* (September/October):14–22.

Galinsky, Ellen, James Bond, and Dana Friedman. 1993. *The Changing Workforce: Highlights of the National Study.* New York: Family and Work Institute.

Galinsky, Ellen, Dana E. Friedman, and Carol A. Hernandez. 1991. *The Corporate Reference Guide to Work Family Programs.* New York: Families and Work Institute.

Giddens, Anthony. 1976. *New Rules of Sociological Method.* New York: Basic Books.

———. 1991. *Modernity and Self-Identity.* Stanford, CA: Stanford University Press.

Hewlett, Sylvia Ann. 1991. *When the Bough Breaks: The Costs of Neglecting Our Children.* New York: Basic Books.

Hochschild, Arlie. 1983. *The Managed Heart: The Commercialization of Human Feeling.* Berkeley: University of California Press.

———. 1994. "The Commercial Spirit of Intimate Life and the Abduction of Feminism: Signs from Women's Advice Books." *Theory, Culture & Society* 2 (May):1–24.

Hochschild, Arlie, with Anne Machung. 1989. *The Second Shift: Working Parents and the Revolution at Home.* New York: Viking Press.

Kanter, Rosabeth Moss. 1977. *Work and Family in the United States: A Critical Review and Agenda for Research and Policy.* New York: Russell Sage Foundation.

———. 1990. *When Giants Learn to Dance: Mastering the Challenges of Strategy, Management, and Careers in the 1990s.* S & S Trade.

Martin, Joanne. 1992. *Cultures in Organizations: Three Perspectives.* New York: Oxford University Press.

McCarthy, Eugene and William McGaughey. 1981. *Nonfinancial Economics: The Case for Shorter Hours of Work.* New York: Praeger.

Owen, John. 1989. *Reduced Working Hours: Cure for Unemployment or Economic Burden?* Baltimore: Johns Hopkins University Press.

Popenoe, David. 1989. *Disturbing the Nest: Family Change and Decline in Modern Societies.* New York: Aldine de Gruyter.

Schaevitz, Marjorie Hansen. 1984. *The Superwoman Syndrome.* New York: Warner Books.

Schor, Juliet B. 1992. *The Overworked American: The Unexpected Decline of Leisure.* New York: Basic Books.

Schwartz, Felice N. 1989. "Management Women and the New Facts of Life." *Harvard Business Review* 1 (January/February):65–76.

Skolnick, Arlene. 1991. *Embattled Paradise.* New York: Basic Books.

Tolstoy, Leo. 1966. *War and Peace.* New York: Norton.

White, Lynn K. and Agnes Riesmann. 1992. "When the Brady Bunch Grows Up: Step-, Half- and Full-Sibling Relationships in Adulthood." *Journal of Marriage and the Family* 54 (February):197–208.

37

"WHEN YOU GET LAID OFF, IT'S LIKE YOU LOSE A PART OF YOURSELF"

LILLIAN B. RUBIN

For Larry Meecham, "downsizing" is more than a trendy word on the pages of the *Wall Street Journal* or the business section of the *New York Times*. "I was with the same company for over twelve years; I had good seniority. Then all of a sudden they laid off almost half the people who worked there, closed down whole departments, including mine," he says, his troubled brown eyes fixed on some distant point as he speaks. "One day you got a job; the next day you're out of work, just like that," he concludes, shaking his head as if he still can't believe it.

Nearly 15 percent of the men in the families I interviewed were jobless when I met them.[1] Another 20 percent had suffered episodic bouts of unemployment—sometimes related to the recession of the early 1990s, sometimes simply because job security is fragile in the blue-collar world, especially among the younger, less experienced workers. With the latest recession [late 1980s to early 1990s], however, age and experience don't count for much; every man feels at risk.[2]

Tenuous as the situation is for white men, it's worse for men of color, especially African Americans. The last hired, they're likely to be the first fired. And when the axe falls, they have even fewer resources than whites to help them through the tough times. "After kicking around doing shit work for a long time, I finally got a job that paid decent," explains twenty-nine-year-old George Faucett, a black father of two who lost his factory job when the company was restructured—another word that came into vogue during the economic upheaval of the 1990s. "I worked there for two years, but I didn't have seniority, so when they started to lay guys off, I was it. We never really had a chance to catch up on all the bills before it was all over," he concludes dispiritedly.

I speak of men here partly because they're usually the biggest wage earners in intact families. Therefore, when father loses his job, it's likely to be a crushing blow to the family economy. And partly, also, it's because the issues unemployment raises are different for men and for women. For most women, identity is multifaceted, which means that the loss of a job isn't equivalent to the loss of self. No matter how invested a woman may be in her work, no matter how much her sense of self and competence are connected to it, work remains only one part of identity — a central part perhaps, especially for a professional woman, but still only a part. She's mother, wife, friend, daughter, sister — all valued facets of the self, none wholly obscuring the others. For the working-class women in this study, therefore, even those who were divorced or single mothers responsible for the support of young children, the loss of a job may have been met with pain, fear, and anxiety, but it didn't call their identity into question.

For a man, however, work is likely to be connected to the core of self. Going to work isn't just what he does, it's deeply linked to who he is. Obviously, a man is also father, husband, friend, son, brother. But these are likely to be roles he assumes, not without depth and meaning, to be sure, but not self-defining in the same way as he experiences work. Ask a man for a statement of his identity, and he'll almost always respond by telling you first what he does for a living. The same question asked of a woman brings forth a less predictable, more varied response, one that's embedded in the web of relationships that are central to her life.[3]

Some researchers studying the impact of male unemployment have observed a sequenced series of psychological responses.[4] The first, they say, is shock, followed by denial and a sense of optimism, a belief that this is temporary, a holiday, like a hiatus between jobs rather than joblessness. This period is marked by heightened activity at home, a burst of do-it-yourself projects that had been long neglected for lack of time. But soon the novelty is gone and the projects wear thin, ushering in the second phase, a time of increasing distress, when inertia trades places with activity and anxiety succeeds denial. Now a jobless man awakens every day to the reality of unemployment. And, lest he forget, the weekly trip to the unemployment office is an unpleasant reminder. In the third phase, inertia deepens into depression, fed by feelings of identity loss, inadequacy, hopelessness, a lack of self-confidence, and a general failure of self-esteem. He's tense, irritable, and feels increasingly alienated and isolated from both social and personal relationships.

This may be an apt description of what happens in normal times. But in periods of economic crisis, when losing a job isn't a singular and essentially lonely event, the predictable pattern breaks down.[5] During the years I was interviewing families for this [research], millions of jobs disappeared almost overnight. Nearly everyone I met, therefore, knew someone — a family member, a neighbor, a friend — who was out of work. "My brother's been out of a job for a long time; now my brother-in-law just got laid off. It seems like every time I turn around, somebody's losing his job. I've been lucky so far, but it makes you wonder how long it'll last."

At such times, nothing cushions the reality of losing a job. When the unbelievable becomes commonplace and the unexpected is part of the mosaic of the times, denial is difficult and optimism impossible. Instead, any layoff, even if it's defined as temporary, is experienced immediately and viscerally as a potentially devastating, cataclysmic event.

It's always a shock when a person loses a job, of course. But disbelief? Denial? Not for those who have been living under a cloud of anxiety — those who leave work each night grateful for another day of safety, who wonder as they set off the next morning whether this is the day the axe will fall on them. "I tell my wife not to worry because she gets panicked about the bills. But the truth is, I stew about it plenty. The economy's gone to hell; guys are out of work all around me. I'd be nuts if I wasn't worried."

It's true that when a working-class man finds himself without a job he'll try to keep busy with projects around the house. But these aren't undertaken in the kind of holiday spirit earlier researchers describe.[6] Rather, building a fence, cleaning the garage, painting the family room, or the dozens of other tasks that might occupy him are a way of coping with his anxiety, of distracting himself from the fears that threaten to overwhelm him, of warding off the depression that lurks just below the surface of his activity. Each thrust of the saw, each blow of the hammer helps to keep the demons at bay. "Since he lost his job, he's been out there hammering away at one thing or another like a maniac," says Janet Kovacs, a white thirty-four-year-old waitress. "First it was the fence; he built the whole thing in a few days. Then it was fixing the siding on the garage. Now he's up on the roof. He didn't even stop to watch the football game last Sunday."

Her husband, Mike, a cement finisher, explains it this way: "If I don't keep busy, I feel like I'll go nuts. It's funny," he says with caustic, ironic laugh, "before I got laid off my wife was always complaining about me watching the ball games; now she keeps nagging me to watch. What do you make of that, huh? I guess she's trying to make me feel better."

"Why didn't you watch the game last Sunday?" I ask.

"I don't know, maybe I'm kind of scared if I sit down there in front of the TV, I won't want to get up again," he replies, his shoulders hunched, his fingers raking his hair. "Besides, when I was working, I figured I had a right."

His words startled me, and I kept turning them over in my mind long after he spoke them: "When I was working, I figured I had a right." It's a sentence any of the unemployed men I met might have uttered. For it's in getting up and going to work every day that they feel they've earned the right to their manhood, to their place in the world, to the respect of their family, even the right to relax with a sporting event on TV.

It isn't that there are no gratifying moments, that getting laid off has no positive side at all. When unemployment first hits, family members usually gather around to offer support, to buoy a man's spirits and their own. Even in families where conflict is high, people tend to come together, at least at the beginning. "Considering that we weren't getting along so well before, my wife was really good about it when I got laid off," says Joe Phillips, an unemployed black truck driver. "She gave me a lot of support at first, and I appreciate it."

"You said 'at first.' Has that changed?" I ask.

"Hell, yes. It didn't last long. But maybe I can't blame it all on her. I've been no picnic to live with since I got canned."

In families with young children, there may be a period of relief—for the parents, the relief of not having to send small children off to child care every day, of knowing that one of them is there to welcome the children when they come home from school; for the children, the exhilarating novelty of having a parent, especially daddy, at home all day. "The one good thing about him not working is that there's someone home with the kids now," says twenty-five-year-old Gloria Lewis, a black hairdresser whose husband has been unemployed for just a few weeks. "That part's been a godsend. But I don't know what we'll do if he doesn't find work soon. We can't make it this way."

Teenagers, too, sometimes speak about the excitement of having father around at first. "It was great having my dad home when he first got laid off," says Kevin Sollars, a white fourteen-year-old. "We got to do things together after school sometimes. He likes to build ship models—old sailing ships. I don't know why, but he never wanted to teach me how to do it. He didn't even like it when I just wanted to watch; he'd say, 'Haven't you got something else to do?' But when he first got laid off, it was different. When I'd come home from school and he was working on a ship, he'd let me help him."

But the good times usually don't last long. "After a little while, he got really grumpy and mean, jumped on everybody over nothing," Kevin continues. "My mom used to say we had to be patient because he was so worried about money and all that. Boy, was I glad when he went back to work." . . .

Once in a while, especially for a younger man, getting laid off or fired actually opens up the possibility of a new beginning. "I figured, what the hell, if I'm here, I might as well learn how to cook," says twenty-eight-year-old Darnell Jones, a black father of two who, until he was laid off, had worked steadily but always at relatively menial, low-paying jobs in which he had little interest or satisfaction. "Turned out I liked to cook, got to be real good at it, too, better than my wife," he grins proudly. "So then we talked about it and decided there was no sense in sitting around waiting for something to happen when there were no good jobs out there, especially for a black man, and we figured I should go to cooking school and learn how to do it professionally. Now I've got this job as a cook; it's only part-time, right now, but the pay's pretty good, and I think maybe I'll go full-time soon. If I could get regular work, maybe we could even save some money and I could open my own restaurant someday. That's what I really want to do."

But this outcome is rare, made possible by the fact that Darnell's wife has a middle-management position in a large corporation that pays her $38,000 a year. His willingness to try something new was a factor, of course. But that, too, was grounded in what was possible. In most young working-class families of any color or ethnic group, debts are high, savings are nonexistent, and women don't earn nearly enough to bail the family out while the men go into a training program to learn new skills. A situation that doesn't offer much encouragement for a man to dream, let alone to believe his dream could be realized.[7]

As I have already indicated, the struggles around the division of labor shift somewhat when father loses his job. The man who's home all day while his wife goes off to work can't easily justify maintaining the traditional household gender roles. Therefore, many of the unemployed men pick up tasks that were formerly left to their wives alone. "I figure if she's working and I'm not, I ought to take up some of the slack around here. So I keep the place up, run the kids around if they need it, things like that," says twenty-nine-year-old Jim Andersen, a white unemployed electrician.

As wives feel their household burdens eased, the strains that are almost always a part of life in a two-job family are somewhat relieved. "Maybe it sounds crazy to you, but my life's so much easier since he's out of work, I wish it could stay this way," says Jim's wife, Loreen, a twenty-nine-year-old accounting clerk. "If only I could make enough money, I'd be happy for him to stay home and play Mr. Mom."

But it's only a fantasy — first because she can't make enough money; second, and equally important, because while she likes the relief from household responsibilities, she's also uneasy about such a dramatic shift in family roles. So in the next breath, Loreen says, "I worry about him, though. He doesn't feel so good about himself being unemployed and playing house."

"Is it only him you worry about? Or is there something that's hard for you, too?" I ask.

She's quiet for a moment, then acknowledges that her feelings are complicated: "I'm not sure what I think anymore. I mean, I don't think it's fair that men always have to be the support for the family; it's too hard for them sometimes. And I don't mind working; I really don't. In fact, I like it a lot better than being home with the house and the kids all the time. But I guess deep down I still have that old-fashioned idea that it's a man's job to support his family. So, yeah, then I begin to feel — I don't know how to say it — uncomfortable, right here inside me," she says, pointing to her midsection, "like maybe I won't respect him so much if he can't do that. I mean, it's okay for now," she hastens to reassure me, perhaps herself as well. "But if it goes on for a real long time like with some men, then I think I'll feel different."

Men know their wives feel this way, even when the words are never spoken, which only heightens their own anxieties about being unemployed. "Don't get me wrong; I'm glad she has her job. I don't know what we'd do if she wasn't working," says Jim. "It's just that...," he hesitates, trying to frame his thoughts clearly. "I know this is going to sound pretty male, but it's my job to take care of this family. I mean, it's great that she can help out, but the responsibility is mine, not hers. She won't say so, but I know she feels the same way, and I don't blame her."

It seems, then, that no matter what the family's initial response is, whatever the good moments may be, the economic and psychological strains that attend unemployment soon overwhelm the good intentions on all sides. "It's not just the income; you lose a lot more than that," says Marvin Reed, a forty-year-old white machinist, out of work for nearly eight months. He pauses, reflects on his words, then continues. "When you get laid off, it's like you lose a part of yourself. It's terrible; something goes out of you. Then, on top of that, by staying home and not going to work and associating with people

Not just economic hardship. Emotional too.

of your own level, you begin to lose the sharpness you developed at work. Everything gets slower; you move slower; your mind works slower. . . .

"Everything gets slower"—a sign of the depression that's so often the unwelcome companion of unemployment. As days turn into weeks and weeks into months, it gets harder and harder to believe in a future. "I've been working since I was fourteen," says Marvin, "and I was never out of work for more than a week or two before. Now I don't know; I don't know when I'll get work again. The jobs are gone. How do you find a job when there's none out there anymore?" . . .

For wives and children, it's both disturbing and frightening to watch husband and father sink ever deeper into despair. "Being out of work is real hard on him; it's hard to see him like this, so sad and jumpy all the time," laments Bill's wife, Eunice, a part-time bank teller who's anxiously looking for full-time work. "He's always been a good provider, never out of work hardly a day since we got married. Then all of a sudden this happens. It's like he lost his self-respect when he lost that job."

His self-respect and also the family's medical benefits, since Eunice doesn't qualify for benefits in her part-time job. "The scariest part about Bill being out of a job is we don't have any medical insurance anymore. My daughter got pneumonia real bad last winter and I had to borrow money from my sister for the doctor bill and her medicine. Just the medicine was almost $100. The doctor wanted to put her in the hospital, but we couldn't because we don't have any health insurance."

Her husband recalls his daughter's illness, in a voice clogged with rage and grief. "Do you know what it's like listening to your kid when she can't breathe and you can't send her to the hospital because you lost your benefits when you got laid off?"

In such circumstances, some men just sit, silent, turned inward, enveloped in the gray fog of depression from which they can't rouse themselves. "I leave to go to work in the morning and he's sitting there doing nothing, and when I come home at night, it's the same thing. It's like he didn't move the whole day," worries thirty-four-year-old Deidre Limage, the wife of a black factory worker who has been jobless for over a year.

Other men defend against feeling the pain, fear, and sadness, covering them over with a flurry of activity, with angry, defensive, often irrational outbursts at wife and children—or with some combination of the two. As the financial strain of unemployment becomes crushing, everyone's fears escalate. Wives, unable to keep silent, give voice to their concerns. Their husbands, unable to tolerate what they hear as criticism and blame—spoken or not—lash out. "It seems like the more you try to pull yourself up, the more you get pushed back down," sighs Beverly Coleride, a white twenty-five-year-old cashier with two children, whose husband has worked at a variety of odd jobs in their seven-year marriage. "No matter how hard we try, we can't seem to set everything right. I don't know what we're going to do now; we don't have next month's rent. If Kenny doesn't get something steady real quick, we could be on the street."

"We could be on the street"—a fear that clutches at the hearts and gnaws at the souls of the families in this study, not only those who are unemployed. Nothing exemplifies the change in the twenty years since I last studied working-class families than the fear of being "on the street." Then, homelessness was something that happened somewhere else, in India or some other far-off and alien land. Then, we wept when we read about the poor people who lived on the streets in those other places. *What kind of society doesn't provide this most basic of life's needs?* we asked ourselves. Now, the steadily increasing numbers of homeless in our own land have become an ever-present and frightening reminder of just how precarious life in this society can be. Now, they're in our face, on our streets, an accepted category of American social life—"the homeless." . . .

For Beverly Coleride, as for the other women and men I met, sustaining the denial has become increasingly difficult. No matter how much they want to obliterate the images of the homeless from consciousness, the specter haunts them, a frightening reminder of what's possible if they trip and fall. Perhaps it's because there's so much at stake now, because the unthinkable has become a reality, that anxieties escalate so quickly. So as Beverly contemplates the terror of being "on the street," she begins to blame her husband. "I keep telling myself it's not his fault, but it's real hard not to let it get you down. So then I think, well, maybe he's not trying hard enough, and I get on his case, and he gets mad, and, well, I guess you know the rest," she concludes with a harsh laugh that sounds more like a cry of pain.

She doesn't *want* to hurt her husband, but she can't tolerate feeling so helpless and out of control. If it's his fault rather than the workings of some impersonal force, then he can do something about it. For her husband, it's an impossible bind. "I keep trying, looking for something, but there's nothing out there, leastwise not for me. I don't know what to do anymore; I've tried everything, every place I know," he says disconsolately.

But he, too, can't live easily with such feelings of helplessness. His sense of his manhood, already under threat because he can't support his family, is eroded further by his wife's complaints. So he turns on her in anger: "It's hard enough being out of work, but then my wife gets on my case, yakking all the time about how we're going to be on the street if I don't get off my butt, like it's my fault or something that there's no work out there. When she starts up like that, I swear I want to hit her, anything just to shut her mouth," he says, his shoulders tensed, his fists clenched in an unconscious expression of his rage.

"And do you?" I ask.

The tension breaks; he laughs. "No, not yet. I don't know; I don't want to," he says, his hand brushing across his face. "But I get mad enough so I could. Jesus, doesn't she know I feel bad enough? Does she have to make it worse by getting on me like that? Maybe you could clue her, would you?"

"Maybe you could clue her"—a desperate plea for someone to intervene, to save him from his own rageful impulses. For Kenny Coleride isn't a violent man. But the stress and conflict in families where father loses his job can give rise to the kind of interaction described here, a dynamic that all too frequently ends in physical assaults against women and children.

Some kind of violence — sometimes against children only, more often against both women and children — is the admitted reality of life in about 14 percent of the families in this study.[8] I say "admitted reality" because this remains one of the most closely guarded secrets in family life. So it's reasonable to assume that the proportion of families victimized by violence could be substantially higher.

Sometimes my questions about domestic violence were met with evasion: "I don't really know anything about that."

Sometimes there was outright denial, even when I could see the evidence with my own eyes: "I was visiting my sister the other day, and I tripped and fell down the steps in front of her house."

And sometimes teenage children, anguished about what they see around them, refused to participate in the cover-up. "I bet they didn't tell you that he beats my mother up, did they? Nobody's allowed to talk about it; we're supposed to pretend like it doesn't happen. I hate him; I could kill him when he does that to her. My mom, she says he can't help it; it's because he's so upset since he got fired. But that's just her excuse now. I mean, yeah, maybe it's worse than it was before, but he did it before, too. I don't understand. Why does she let him do it to her?"

"Why does she let him do it to her?" A question the children in these families are not alone in asking, one to which there are few satisfactory answers. But one thing is clear: The depression men suffer and their struggle against it significantly increase the probability of alcohol abuse, which in turn makes these kinds of eruptions more likely to occur.[9] . . .

Many of the unemployed men admit turning to alcohol to relieve the anxiety, loneliness, and fear they experience as they wait day after day, week after week for, as one man put it, "something to happen." "You begin to feel as if you're going nuts, so you drink a few beers to take the edge off," explains thirty-seven-year-old Bill Anstett, a white unemployed construction worker.

It seems so easy. A few beers and he gets a respite from his unwanted feelings — fleeting, perhaps, but effective in affording some relief from the suffering they inflict. But a few beers often turn out to be enough to allow him to throw normal constraints to the wind. For getting drunk can be a way of absenting the conscious self so that it can't be held responsible for actions undertaken. Indeed, this may be as much his unconscious purpose as the need to rid himself of his discomfort. "I admit it, sometimes it's more than a few and I fall over the edge," Bill grants. "My wife, she tells me it's like I turn into somebody else, but I don't know about that because I never remember." . . .

One-fifth of the men in this study have a problem with alcohol, not all of them unemployed. Nor is domestic violence perfectly correlated with either alcohol abuse or unemployment. But the combination is a potentially deadly one that exponentially increases the likelihood that a man will act out his anger on the bodies of his wife and children. "My husband drinks a lot more now; I mean, he always drank some, but not like now," says Inez Reynoso, a twenty-eight-year-old Latina nurse's aide and mother of three children who is disturbed about her husband's mistreatment of their youngest child, a three-year-old boy. "I guess he tries to drink away his troubles, but it only makes more trouble. I tell him, but he doesn't listen. He has a fiery temper, always has. But since he lost his job, it's real bad, and his drinking doesn't help it none.

"I worry about it; he treats my little boy so terrible. He's always had a little trouble with the boy because he's not one of those big, strong kids. He's not like my older kids; he's a timid one, still wakes up scared and crying a lot in the night. Before he got fired, my husband just didn't pay him much attention. But now he's always picking on him; it's like he can't stand having him around. So he makes fun of him something terrible, or he punches him around." . . .

"Does he hit you, too?" I ask Inez.

She squirms in her chair; her fingers pick agitatedly at her jeans. I wait quietly, watching as she shakes her head no. But when she speaks, the words say something else. "He did a couple of times lately, but only when he had too many beers. He didn't mean it. It's just that he's so upset about being out of work, so then when he thinks I protect the boy too much he gets real mad."

When unemployment strikes, sex also becomes an increasingly difficult issue between wives and husbands. A recent study in Great Britain found that the number of couples seeking counseling for sexual problems increased in direct proportion to the rise in the unemployment rate.[10] Anxiety, fear, anger, depression—all emotions that commonly accompany unemployment—are not generators of sexual desire. Sometimes it's the woman whose ardor cools because she's frightened about the future: "I'm so scared all the time, I can't think about sex." Or because she's angry with her husband: "He's supposed to be supporting us and look where we are." More often it's the men who lose their libido along with their jobs—a double whammy for them since male identity rests so heavily in their sexual competence as well as in their work.[11]

This was the one thing the men in this study couldn't talk about. I say "couldn't" because it seemed so clearly more than just "wouldn't." Psychologically, it was nearly impossible for them to formulate the words and say them aloud. They had no trouble complaining about their wives' lack of sexual appetite. But when it was they who lost interest or who become impotent, it was another matter. Then, their tongues were stilled by overwhelming feelings of shame, by the terrible threat their impotence posed to the very foundation of their masculinity.

Their wives, knowing this, are alarmed about their flagging sex lives, trying to understand what happened, wondering what they can do to be helpful. "Sex used to be a big thing for him, but since he's been out of work, he's hardly interested anymore," Dale Meecham, a white thirty-five-year-old waitress says, her anxiety palpable in the room. "Sometimes when we try to do it, he can't, and then he acts like it's the end of the world—depressed and moody, and I can't get near him. It's scary. He won't talk about it, but I can see it's eating at him. So I worry a lot about it. But I don't know what to do, because if I try to, you know, seduce him and it doesn't work, then it only makes things worse."

The financial and emotional turmoil that engulfs families when a man loses his job all too frequently pushes marriages that were already fragile over the brink.[12] Among the families in this study, 10 percent attributed their ruptured marriages directly to the strains that accompanied unemployment. "I don't know, maybe we could have made it if he hadn't lost his job," Maryanne Wallace, a twenty-eight-year-old white welfare mother, says sadly. "I mean, we had problems before, but we were managing. Then he got laid off, and he couldn't find another job, and, I don't know, it was like he went crazy. He was drinking; he hit me; he was mean to the kids. There was no talking to him, so I left, took the kids and went home to my mom's. I thought maybe I'd just give him a scare, you know, be gone for a few days. But when I came back, he was gone, just gone. Nobody's seen him for nearly a year," she says, her voice limping to a halt as if she still can't believe her own story.

Economic issues alone aren't responsible for divorce, of course, as is evident when we look at the 1930s. Then, despite the economic devastation wrought by the Great Depression, the divorce rate didn't rise. Indeed, it was probably the economic privations of that period that helped to keep marriages intact. Since it was so difficult to maintain one household, few people could consider the possibility of having to support two.

But these economic considerations exist today as well, yet recent research shows that when family income drops 25 percent, divorce rises by more than 10 percent.[13] Culture and the institutions of our times make a difference. Then, divorce was a stigma. Now, it's part of the sociology and psychology of the age, an acceptable remedy for the disappointment of our dreams.

Then, too, one-fourth of the work force was unemployed—an economic disaster that engulfed the whole nation. In such cataclysmic moments, the events outside the family tend to overtake and supersede the discontents inside. Now, unemployment is spottier, located largely in the working class, and people feel less like they're in the middle of a social catastrophe than a personal one. Under such circumstances, it's easier to act out their anger against each other.

And finally, the social safety net that came into being after the Great Depression—social security, unemployment benefits, public aid programs targeted specifically to single-parent families—combined with the increasing numbers of women in the work force to make divorce more feasible economically.

Are there no families, then, that stick together and get through the crisis of unemployment without all this trauma? The answer? Of course there are. But they're rare. And they manage it relatively well only if the layoff is short and their resources are long.

Almost always, these are older families where the men have a long and stable work history and where there are fewer debts, some savings, perhaps a home they can refinance. But even among these relatively privileged ones, the pressures soon begin to take their toll. "We did okay for a while, but the longer it lasts, the harder it gets," says forty-six-year-old Karen Brownstone, a white hotel desk clerk whose husband, Dan, lost his welding job nearly six months ago. "After the kids were grown, we finally managed to put some money by. Dan even did some investments, and we made some money. But we're using it up very fast, and I get real scared. What are we going to do when his unemployment runs out?"[14] . . .

When I talk with Karen's husband, Dan, he leans forward in his chair and says angrily, "I can't go out and get one of those damn flunky jobs like my wife wants me to. I've been working all my life, making a decent living, too, and I got pride in what I do. I try to tell her, but she won't listen." He stops, sighs, puts his head in his hands and speaks more softly: "I'm the only one in my whole family who was doing all right; I even helped my son go to college. I was proud of that; we all were. Now what do I do? It's like I have to go back to where I started. How can you do that at my age?"

He pauses again, looks around the room with an appraising eye, and asks: "What's going to happen to us? I know my wife's scared; that's why she's on my case so much. I worry, too, but what can I do if there's no work? Even she doesn't think I should go sling hamburgers at McDonald's for some goddamn minimum wage." . . .

Eventually, men like Dan Brownstone who once held high-paying skilled jobs have no choice but to pocket their pride and take a step down to another kind of work, to one of the service jobs that usually pay a fraction of their former earnings — that is, if they're lucky enough to find one. It's never easy in our youth-oriented society for a man past forty to move to another job or another line of work. But it becomes doubly difficult in times of economic distress when the pool of younger workers is so large and so eager. "Either you're overqualified or you're over the hill," Ed Kruetsman, a forty-nine-year-old unemployed white factory worker, observes in a tired voice.

But young or old, when a man is forced into lower-paying, less skilled work, the move comes with heavy costs — both economic and psychological. Economically, it means a drastic reduction in the family's way of life. "Things were going great. We worked hard, but we finally got enough together so we could buy a house that had enough room for all of us," says thirty-six-year-old Nadine Materie, a white data processor in a bank clearing center. "Tina, my oldest girl, even had her own room; she was so happy about it. Then my husband lost his job, and the only thing he could find was one that pays a lot less, *a lot less*. On his salary now we just couldn't make the payments. We had no choice; we had to sell out and move. Now look at this place!" she commands, with a dismissive sweep of her hand. Then, as we survey the dark, cramped quarters into which this family of five is now jammed, she concludes tearfully, "I hate it, every damn inch of it; I hate it." . . .

For the children in the Materie family, the move from house to apartment took them to a new school in a distant neighborhood, far from the friends who had been at the center of their lives. "My brother and me, we hate living here," Tina says, her eyes misting over as she speaks. "Both of us hate the kids who live around here. They're different, not as nice as the kids where we used to live. They're tough, and I'm not used to it. Sometimes I think I'll quit school and get a job and go live where I want," she concludes gloomily.

Psychologically, the loss of status can be almost as difficult to bear as the financial strain. "I used to drive a long-distance rig, but the company I worked for went broke," explains Greg Northsen, a thirty-four-year-old white man whose wife is an office worker. "I was out of work for eleven and a half months. Want to know how many days that is? Maybe how many hours? I counted every damn one," he quips acidly.

"After all that time, I was ready to take whatever I could get. So now I work as an orderly in a nursing home. Instead of cargo, I'm hauling old people around. The pay's shit and it's damn dirty work. They don't treat those old people good. Everybody's always impatient with them, ordering them around, screaming at them, talking to them like they're dumb kids or something. But with three kids to feed, I've got no choice."

He stops talking, stares wordlessly at some spot on the opposite wall for a few moments, then, his eyes clouded with unshed tears, he rakes his fingers through his hair and says hoarsely, "It's goddamn hard. This is no kind of a job for a guy like me. It's not just the money; it's . . ." He hesitates, searching for the words, then, "It's like I got chopped off at the knees, like . . . aw, hell, I don't know how to say it." Finally, with a hopeless shrug, he concludes, "What's the use? It's no use talking about it. It makes no damn difference; nothing's going to make a difference. I don't understand it. What the hell's happening to this country when there's no decent jobs for men who want to work?"

Companies go bankrupt; they merge; they downsize; they restructure; they move—all reported as part of the economic indicators, the cold statistics that tell us how the economy is doing. But each such move means more loss, more suffering, more families falling victim to the despair that comes when father loses his job, more people shouting in rage and torment: "What the hell's happening to this country?"

ENDNOTES

1. It's not possible to compare the rate of unemployment in these families with those I interviewed two decades ago because the previous sample was made up of men who were employed. But comparing the unemployment rates in 1970 and 1991 is instructive. Among white men with less than four years in high school, 4.5 percent were unemployed in 1970, 10.3 percent in 1991. The figures for high-school graduates are 2.7 percent and 5.4 percent, respectively. For blacks with less than four years in high school, the 1970 unemployment rate stood at 5.2 percent, compared to 14.7 percent in 1991. For black high-school graduates, the rates are 5.2 and 9.9, respectively (*Statistical Abstract* [U.S. Bureau of the Census, 1992, Table 637, p. 400]). The number of food stamp recipients, which typically rises as the unemployment rate climbs, jumped to an all-time high in 1993, when one in ten Americans were in the food stamp program.
2. Barbara Ehrenreich, *Fear of Falling* (New York: Pantheon Books, 1989), and Katherine S. Newman, *Falling from Grace* (New York: Free Press, 1988), write compellingly about middle-class fears of what Newman calls "falling from grace." But these fears probably are more prevalent among working-class families, and with

good reason, since job security is still so much more tenuous there than in the middle class.

3. Cf. Rubin, *Worlds of Pain*, and Lillian B. Rubin, *Women of a Certain Age: The Midlife Search for Self* (New York: Harper Perennial, 1986).

4. John Hill, "The Psychological Impact of Unemployment," *New Society* 43 (1978): 118–20; and Linford W. Rees, "Medical Aspects of Unemployment," *British Medical Journal* 6307 (1981): 1630–31.

5. See Newman, *Falling from Grace*, pp. 174–201, for an excellent analysis of what happened when the Singer Sewing Machine plant in Elizabeth, New Jersey, closed and downward mobility inundated a whole community.

6. Hill, "The Psychological Impact of Unemployment"; and Rees, "Medical Aspects of Unemployment."

7. Barry Glassner, *Career Crash* (New York: Simon & Schuster, 1994), studied career crashes among baby-boomer managers and professionals and provides an interesting counterpoint to the people I'm writing about here. Unlike the men and women of the working class, Glassner found that the people he studied have a range of options and a variety of resources to help cushion the blow of unemployment.

8. A few researchers argue that, since the majority of men who batter their wives are gainfully employed, unemployment is of little value in explaining battering (H. Saville et al., "Sex Roles, Inequality and Spouse Abuse," *Australian and New Zealand Journal of Sociology* 17 [1981]: 83–88; and Martin D. Schwartz, "Work Status, Resource Equality, Injury and Wife Battery," *Creative Sociology* 18 [1990]: 57–61). But the evidence is much stronger in the direction of a relationship between unemployment and family violence; see Frances J. Fitch and Andre Papantonio, "Men Who Batter," *Journal of Nervous and Mental Disease* 171 (1983): 190–91; Richard J. Gelles and Murray A. Straus, "Violence in the American Family," *Journal of Social Issues* 35 (1979): 15–39; New York State Task Force on Domestic Violence, *Domestic Violence: Report to the Governor and Legislature: Families and Change* (New York: Praeger, 1984); and Suzanne K. Steinmetz, "Violence-Prone Families," *Annals of the New York Academy of Sciences* 347 (1980): 251–65.

9. John A. Byles, "Violence, Alcohol Problems and Other Problems in Disintegrating Families," *Journal of Studies on Alcohol* 39 (1978): 551–53; Ronald W. Fagan, Ola W. Barnett, and John B. Patton, "Reasons for Alcohol Use in Maritally Violent Men," *Journal of Drug and Alcohol Abuse* 14 (1988): 371–92; Fitch and Papantonio, "Men Who Batter"; Kenneth E. Leonard et al., "Patterns of Alcohol Use and Physically Aggressive Behavior in Men," *Journal of Studies on Alcohol* 46 (1985): 279–82; Larry R. Livingston, "Measuring Domestic Violence in an Alcoholic Population," *Journal of Sociology and Social Welfare* 13 (1986): 934–51; Albert R. Roberts, "Substance Abuse among Men Who Batter Their Mates," *Journal of Substance Abuse Treatment* 5 (1988): 83–87; J. M. Schuerger and N. Reigle, "Personality and Biographic Data That Characterize Men Who Abuse Their Wives," *Journal of Clinical Psychology* 44 (1988): 75–81; and Steinmetz, "Violence-Prone Families."

10. Reported in the *San Francisco Chronicle*, February 14, 1992. The study found that in the same year that unemployment rose from 6.5 to 9.2 percent, there was a 30 percent increase in the number of couples seeking advice from marriage counselors about their waning sex lives.

11. Ethel Spector Person, "Sexuality as the Mainstay of Identity," *Signs* 5 (1980): 605–30.

12. An article in the *San Francisco Chronicle*, October 19, 1992, surveyed several recent studies of divorce, one of which found that when income drops 25 percent, divorce rises by more than 10 percent; another predicted ten thousand divorces for every 1 percent rise in unemployment.

13. Cited in the *San Francisco Chronicle*, October 19, 1992.

14. Unemployment benefits vary from state to state. In California, a state where benefits are among the most generous, the range is $40–230 a week for a maximum of twenty-six weeks. How much a person actually collects depends upon how

long she worked and how much she earned. Even at the highest benefit level, available only to workers who have worked steadily at one of the relatively well-paid blue-collar jobs, the income loss is staggering. For workers in the lower-level jobs, for those who worked intermittently through no fault of their own, or for those who depended on the underground economy to supplement their meager wages, benefits can be so small as to be relatively meaningless.

38

CHANGING PATTERNS OF FAMILY WORK
Chicano Men and Housework

SCOTT COLTRANE

One of the most popular pejorative American slang terms to emerge in the 1980s was "macho," used to describe men prone to combative posturing, relentless sexual conquest, and other compulsive displays of masculinity. Macho men continually guard against imputations of being soft or feminine and thus tend to avoid domestic tasks and family activities that are considered "women's work." Macho comes from the Spanish *machismo,* and although the behaviors associated with it are clearly not limited to one ethnic group, Latino men are often stereotyped as especially prone toward macho displays.[1] This chapter uses in-depth interviews with twenty Chicano couples to explore how paid work and family work are divided. As in other contemporary American households, divisions of labor in these Chicano families were far from balanced or egalitarian, and husbands tended to enjoy special privileges simply because they were men. Nevertheless, many couples were allocating household chores without reference to gender, and few of the Chicano men exhibited stereotypical macho behavior.

Chicanos, or Mexican Americans, are often portrayed as living in poor farm-worker families composed of macho men, subservient women, and plentiful children. Yet these stereotypes have been changing, as diverse groups of people with Mexican and Latin American heritage are responding to the same sorts of social and economic pressures faced by families of other ethnic backgrounds. For example, most Chicano families in the United States now live in urban centers or their suburbs rather than in traditional rural farming areas, and their patterns of marital interaction appear to be about as egalitarian

Abridgement from "Stability and Change in Chicano Men's Family Lives" by Scott Coltrane. Reprinted by permission of the author.

as those of other American families. What's more, Chicanos will no longer be a numerical minority in the near future. Because of higher-than-average birthrates and continued in-migration, by the year 2015 Chicano children will outnumber Anglos in many southwest states, including California, Texas, Arizona, and New Mexico.[2]

When family researchers study white couples, they typically focus on middle-class suburban households, usually highlighting their strengths. Studies of ethnic minority families, in contrast, have tended to focus on the problems of poor or working-class households living in inner-city or rural settings. Because most research on Latino families in the United States has not controlled for social class, wife's employment status, or recency of immigration, a narrow and stereotyped view of these families as patriarchal and culturally backward has persisted. In addition, large-scale studies of "Hispanics" have failed to distinguish between divergent groups of people with Mexican, Central American, South American, Cuban, Puerto Rican, Spanish, or Portuguese ancestry. In contrast, contemporary scholars are beginning to look at some of the positive aspects of minority families and to focus on the economic and institutional factors that influence men's lives within these families.[3]

In 1990 and 1991, Elsa Valdez and I interviewed a group of twenty middle-class Chicano couples with young children living in Southern California. We were primarily interested in finding out if they were facing the same sorts of pressures experienced by other families, so we selected only families in which both the husband and the wife were employed outside the home — the most typical pattern among young parents in the United States today. We wanted to see who did what in these families and find out how they talked about the personal and financial pushes and pulls associated with raising a family. We interviewed wives and husbands separately in their homes, asking them a variety of questions about housework, child care, and their jobs. Elsewhere, we describe details of their time use and task performance, but here I analyze the couples' talk about work, family, and gender, exploring how feelings of entitlement and obligation are shaped by patterns of paid and unpaid labor.[4]

When we asked husbands and wives to sort sixty-four common household tasks according to who most often performed them, we found that wives in most families were responsible for housecleaning, clothes care, meal preparation, and clean-up, whereas husbands were primarily responsible for home maintenance and repair. Most routine child care was also performed by wives, though most husbands reported that they made substantial contributions to parenting. Wives saw the mundane daily housework as an ever-present burden that they had to shoulder themselves or delegate to someone else. While many wives did not expect the current division of labor to change, they did acknowledge that it was unbalanced. The men, although acknowledging that things weren't exactly fair, tended to minimize the asymmetry by seeing many of the short repetitive tasks associated with housekeeping as shared activities. Although there was tremendous diversity among the couples we talked to, we observed a general pattern of disagreement over how much family work the other spouse performed.

The sociologist Jessie Bernard provides us with a useful way to understand why this might be. Bernard suggested that every marital union contains two marriages—"his" and "hers."[5] We discovered from our interviews and observations that most of the husbands and wives were, indeed, living in separate marriages or separate worlds. Her world centered around keeping track of the countless details of housework and child care even though she was employed. His world centered around his work and his leisure activities so that he avoided noticing or anticipating the details of running a home. Husbands "helped out" when wives gave them tasks to do, and because they almost always complied with requests for help, most tended to assume that they were sharing the household labor. Because much of the work the women did was unseen or taken for granted by the men, they tended to underestimate their wives' contributions and escaped the full range of tensions and strains associated with family work.

Because wives remained in control of setting schedules, generating lists for domestic chores, and worrying about the children, they perceived their husbands as contributing relatively little. A frequent comment from wives was that their husbands "just didn't see" the domestic details, and that the men would not often take responsibility for anticipating and planning for what needed to be done. Although many of the men we interviewed maintained their favored position within the family by "not seeing" various aspects of domestic life and leaving the details and planning to their wives, other couples were in the process of ongoing negotiations and, as described below, were successful at redefining some household chores as shared endeavors.

Concerning their paid work, the families we interviewed reported that both husbands and wives had jobs because of financial necessity. The men made comments like "we were pretty much forced into it," or "we didn't really have any choice." Although most of the husbands and wives were employed full-time, only a few accepted the wife as an equal provider or true breadwinner. Using the type of job, employment schedule, and earnings of each spouse, along with their attitudes toward providing, I categorized the couples into main-provider families and co-provider families.[6] Main-provider couples considered the husband's job to be primary and the wife's job to be secondary. Co-provider couples in contrast, tended to accept the wife's job as permanent, and some even treated the wife's job as equally important to her husband's. Accepting the wife as an equal provider, or considering the husband to have failed as a provider, significantly shaped the couples' divisions of household labor.

Main–Provider Families

In just under half of the families we interviewed, the men earned substantially more money than their wives and were assumed to be "natural" breadwinners, whereas the women were assumed to be innately better equipped to deal with home and children. Wives in all of these main-provider families were employed, but the wife's job was often considered temporary, and her income was treated as "extra" money and earmarked for special purposes.[7] One main-provider husband said, "I would prefer that my wife did not have to work, and could stay at home with my daughter, but finances just don't permit that." Another commented that his wife made just about enough to cover the costs of child care, suggesting that the children were still her primary responsibility, and that any wages she earned should first be allocated to cover "her" tasks.

The main-provider couples included many wives who were employed part-time and some who worked in lower-status full-time jobs with wages much lower than their husband's. These women took pride in their home-maker role and readily accepted responsibility for managing the household, although they occasionally asked for help. One part-time bookkeeper married to a recent law-school graduate described their division of labor by saying, "It's a given that I take care of children and housework, but when I am real tired, he steps in willingly." Main-provider husbands typically remained in a helper role: in this case, the law clerk told his wife, "Just tell me what to do and I'll do it." He said that if he came home and she was gone, he might clean house, but that if she was home, he would "let her do it." This reflects a typical division of labor in which the wife acts as household manager and the husband occasionally serves as her helper.[8]

This lawyer-to-be talked about early negotiations between he and his wife that seemed to set the tone for current smoldering arguments about housework:

> *When we were first married, I would do something and she wouldn't like the way I did it. So I would say, "OK, then, you do it, and I won't do it again." That was like in our first few years of marriage when we were first getting used to each other, but now she doesn't discourage me so much. She knows that if she does, she's going to wind up doing it herself.*

His resistance and her reluctance to press for change reflect an unbalanced economy of gratitude.[9] When he occasionally contributed to housework or child care, she was indebted to him. She complimented him for being willing to step in when she asked for help, but privately lamented the fact that she had to negotiate for each small contribution. Firmly entrenched in the main-provider role and somewhat oblivious to the daily rituals of housework and child care, he felt justified in needing prodding and encouragement. When she did ask him for help, she was careful to thank him for dressing the children or for giving her a ten-minute break from them. While these patterns of domestic labor and inequities in the exchange of gratitude were long-standing, tension lurked just below the surface for this couple. He commented, "My wife gets uptight with me for agreeing to help out my mom, when she feels she can't even ask me to go to the store for her." . . .

In general, wives of main-providers not only performed virtually all housework and child care, but both spouses accepted this as "natural" or "normal." Main-provider husbands assumed that financial support was their "job" or their "duty." When one man was asked about how it felt to make more money than his wife, he responded by saying: "It's my job, I wouldn't feel right if I didn't make more money. . . . Any way that I look at it, I have to keep up my salary, or I'm not doing my job. If it costs $40,000 to live nowadays and I'm not in a $40,000-a-year job, then I'm not gonna be happy."

This same husband, a head mechanic who worked between 50 and 60 hours per week, also showed how main-provider husbands sometimes felt threatened when women begin asserting themselves in previously all-male occupational enclaves:

> *As long as women mind their own business, no problem with me. . . . There's nothing wrong with them being in the job, but they shouldn't try to do more than that. Like, if you get a secretary that's nosy and wants to run the company, hey, well, we tell her where to stick it. . . . When you can't do my job, don't tell me how to do it.*

The mechanic's wife, also a part-time teacher's aide, subtly resisted by "spending as little time on housework as I can get away with." Nevertheless, she still considered it her sole duty to cook, and only when her husband was away at National Guard training sessions did she feel she could "slack off" by not placing "regular meals" on the family's table each night.

The Provider Role and Failed Aspirations

Wives performed most of the household labor in main-provider couples, but if main-provider husbands had failed career aspirations, more domestic work was shared. What appeared to tip the economy of gratitude away from automatic male privilege was the wife's sense that the husband had not fulfilled his occupational potential. For example, one main-provider husband graduated from a four-year college and completed two years of post-graduate study without finishing his master's thesis. At the time of the interview, he was making about $30,000 a year as a self-employed house painter, and his wife was making less than half that amount as a full-time secretary. His comments show how her evaluation of his failed or postponed career aspirations led to more bargaining over his participation in routine housework:

> *She reminds me that I'm not doing what we both think I should be doing, and sometimes that's a discouragement. I might have worked a lot of hours, and I'll come home tired, for example, and she'll say, "You've gotta clean the house," and I'll say, "Damn I'm tired, I'd like to get a little rest in," but she says, "You're only doing this because it's been your choice." She tends to not have sympathy for me in my work because it was more my choice than hers.*

He acknowledged that he should be doing something more "worthwhile," and hoped that he would not be painting houses for more than another year. Still, as long as he stayed in his current job, considered beneath him by both of them, she would not allow him to use fatigue from employment as a way to get out of doing housework:

> *I worked about 60 hours a week the last couple of weeks. I worked yesterday [Saturday], and today—if it had been my choice—I would have drank beer and watched TV. But since she had a baby shower to go to, I babysitted my nephews. And since we had you coming, she kind of laid out the program: "You've gotta clean the floors, and wash the dishes and do the carpets. So get to it buddy!" [Laughs.]*

This main-provider husband capitulated to his wife's demands, but she still had to set tasks for him and remind him to perform them. In responding to her "program," he used the strategy of claimed incompetence that other main-provider husbands also used. While he admitted that he was proficient at the "janitorial stuff," he was careful to point out that he was incapable of dusting or doing the laundry:

> *It's amazing what you can do when you have little time and you just get in and do it. And I'm good at that. I'm good at the big cleaning, I'm good at the janitorial stuff. I can do the carpet, do the floors, do all that stuff. But I'm no good on the details. She wants all the details just right, so she handles dusting, the laundry, and stuff like that. . . . You know, like I would have everything come out one color.*

By re-categorizing some of the housework as "big cleaning," this husband rendered it accountable as men's work. He drew the line at laundry and dusting, but he had transformed some household tasks, like vacuuming and mopping, into work appropriate for men to do. He was complying, albeit reluctantly, to many of his wife's requests because they agreed that he had not fulfilled "his" job as sole provider. He still yearned to be the "real" breadwinner and shared his hope that getting a better-paying job would mean that he could ignore the housework:

> *Sharing the house stuff is usually just a necessity: If, as we would hope in the future, she didn't have to work outside the home, then I think I would be comfortable doing less of it. Then she would be the primary house-care person and I would be the primary financial-resource person. I think roles would change then, and I would be comfortable with her doing more of the dishes and more of the cleaning, and I think she would too. In that sense, I think traditional relationships—if traditional means the guy working and the woman staying home—is a good thing. I wouldn't mind getting a taste of it myself!*

. . .

Another main-provider husband held a job as a telephone lineman, and his wife ran a family day-care center out of their home, which earned her less than a third of what he made. She talked about her regrets that he didn't do something "more important" for a living, and he talked about her frequent reminders that he was "too smart for what I'm doing." Like the other failed-aspirations husbands, he made significant contributions to domestic chores, but his resentment showed when he talked about "the wife" holding a job far from home:

> What I didn't like about it was that I used to get home before the wife, because she had to commute, and I'd have to pop something to eat. Most of the time it was just whatever I happened to find in the fridge. Then I'd have to go pick up the kids immediately from the babysitter, and sometimes I had evening things to do, so what I didn't like was that I had to figure out a way to schedule baby watch or baby sitting.

Even when main-provider husbands began to assume responsibility for domestic work in response to "necessity" or "nagging," they seemed to cling to the idea that these were still "her" chores. Coincidentally, most of the secondary-provider wives reported that they received little help unless they "constantly" reminded their husbands. What generally kept secondary-provider wives from resenting their husband's resistance was their own acceptance of the homemaker role and their recognition of his superior financial contributions. When performance of the male-provider role was deemed to be lacking in some way — i.e., failed aspirations or low occupational prestige — wives' resentment appeared closer to the surface, and they were more persistent in demanding help from their husbands.

Ambivalent Co-Providers

Over half of the couples we interviewed were classified as co-providers. The husbands and wives in these families had more equal earnings and placed a higher value on the wife's employment than those in main-provider families, but there was considerable variation in terms of their willingness to accept the woman as a full and equal provider. Five of the twelve husbands in the co-provider group were ambivalent about sharing the provider role and were also reluctant to share most household tasks. Compared to their wives, ambivalent co-provider husbands usually held jobs that were roughly equivalent in terms of occupational prestige and worked about the same number of hours per week, but because of gender bias in the labor market, the men earned significantly more than their wives. Compared to main-provider husbands, they considered their wives' jobs to be relatively permanent and important, but they continued to use their own job commitments as justification for doing little at home. Ambivalent co-provider husbands' family obligations rarely intruded into their work lives, whereas their wives' family obligations frequently interfered with their paid work. Such asymmetrically permeable work/family boundaries are common in single-earner and main-provider families, but must be supported with subtle ideologies and elaborate justifications when husbands and wives hold similar occupational positions.[10]

Ambivalent co-provider husbands remained in a helper role at home, perceiving their wives to be more involved parents and assuming that housework was also primarily their wives' responsibility. The men used their jobs to justify their absence from home, but most also lamented not being able to spend more time with their families. . . .

Not surprisingly, ambivalent co-provider husbands tended to be satisfied with their current divisions of labor, even though they usually admitted that things were "not quite fair." One junior-high-school teacher married to a bilingual-education program coordinator described his reactions to their division of family labor:

> To be honest, I'm totally satisfied. When I had a first-period conference, I was a little more flexible; I'd help her more with changing 'em, you know, getting them ready for school, since I didn't have to be at school right away. Then I had to switch because they had some situation out at fifth-period conference, so that now she does it a little bit more than I do, and I don't help out with the kids as much in the morning because I have to be there an hour earlier.

This ambivalent co-provider clearly saw himself as "helping" his wife with the children, yet made light of her contributions by saying she does "a little bit more than I do." He went on to reveal how his wife did not enjoy similar special privileges due to her employment, since she had to pick up the children from day care every day, as well as taking them to school in the mornings:

> She gets out a little later than I do because she's an administrator, but I have other things outside. I also work out, I run, and that sort of gives me a time away, to do that before they all come here. I have community meetings in the evenings sometimes, too. So, I mean, it might not be totally fair—maybe 60/40—but I'm thoroughly happy with the way things are.

While he was "thoroughly happy" with the current arrangements, she thought that it was decidedly unfair. She said, "I don't like the fact that it's taken for granted that I'm available. When he goes out he just assumes I'm available, but when I go out I have to consult with him to make sure he is available." For her, child care was a given; for him, it was optional. He commented, "If I don't have something else to do, then I'll take the kids."

Ambivalent co-provider husbands also tended to talk about regretting that their family involvements limited their careers or personal activities. For instance, the school teacher discussed above lamented that he could not do what he used to before he had children:

> Having children keeps me away from thinking a lot about my work. You know, it used to be, before we had kids, I could have my mind geared to work—you know how ideas just pop in, you really get into it. But with kids it doesn't get as—you know, you can't switch. It gets more difficult, it makes it hard to get into it. I don't have that freedom of mind, you know, and it takes away

*from aspects of my work, like doing a little bit more reading or research that
I would like to do. Or my own activities, I mean, I still run, but not as much
as I used to. I used to play basketball, I used to coach, this and that . . .*

. . .

Many of these husbands talked about struggles over wanting to spend
more time on their careers, and most did not relinquish the assumption that
the home was the wife's domain. For example, some ambivalent co-provider
couples attempted to alleviate stress on the wife by hiring outside help. In
response to a question about whether their division of labor was fair, a self-
employed male attorney said, "Do you mean fair like equal? It's probably not
equal, so probably it wouldn't be fair, but that's why we have a housekeeper."
His wife, a social worker earning only ten percent less than he, said that the
household was still her responsibility, but that she now had fewer tasks to do:
"When I did not have help, I tended to do everything, but with a housekeeper, I don't have to do so much." She went on to talk about how she
wished he would do more with their five- and eight-year-old children, but
speculated that he probably would as they grew older.

Another couple paid a live-in babysitter/housekeeper to watch their three
children during the day while he worked full-time in construction and she
worked full-time as a psychiatric social worker. While she labeled the outside
help as "essential," she noted that her husband contributed more to the mess
than he did to its clean-up. He saw himself as an involved father because he
played with his children, and she acknowledged this, but she also complained that he competed with them in games as if he were a child himself.
His participation in routine household labor was considered optional, as evidenced by his comment, "I like to cook once in a while."

Co–Providers

In contrast, about a third of the couples we interviewed fully accepted the
wife's long-term employment, considered her career to be just as important
as his, and were in various stages of redefining household labor as men's
work. Like the ambivalent couples discussed above, full co-provider spouses
worked about the same number of hours as each other, but on the whole,
these couples worked more total hours than their more ambivalent counterparts, though their annual incomes were a bit lower. According to both husbands and wives, the sharing of housework and child care was substantially
greater for full co-providers than for ambivalent co-providers, and also much
more balanced than for main-providers.

Like ambivalent co-providers, husbands in full co-provider families discussed conflicts between work and family and sometimes alluded to the ways
that their occupational advancement was limited by their commitments to
their children. One husband and wife spent the same number of hours on the

job, earned approximately the same amount of money, and were employed as engineering technicians for the same employer. When we asked him how his family involvement had affected his job performance, he responded by saying, "It should, OK, because I really need to spend a lot more time learning my work, and I haven't really put in the time I need to advance in the profession. I would like to spend, I mean I *would* spend, more time if I didn't have kids. I'd like to be able to play with the computer or read books more often." Although he talked about conflicts between job and family, he also emphasized that lost work time was not really a sacrifice because he valued time with his children so highly. He did not use his job as an excuse to get out of doing child care or housework, and he seemed to value his wife's career at least as much as his own:

> *I think her job is probably more important than mine because she's been at that kind of work a lot longer than I have. And at the level she is—it's awkward the way it is, because I get paid just a little bit more than she does, I have a higher position. But she definitely knows the work a lot more, she's been doing the same type of work for about nine years already, and I've only been doing this type of engineering work for about two-and-a-half years, so she knows a lot more. We both have to work, that's for sure.*

Recognition of their roughly equivalent professional status and the need for two equal providers affected this couple's division of parenting and housework. The husband indicated that he did more child care and housework than his wife, and she gave him much credit for his efforts, but in her interview, she indicated that he still did less than half. She described her husband's relationship with their seven-year-old son as "very caring," and noted that he assists the boy with homework more than she does. She also said that her husband did most of the heavy cleaning and scrubbing, but also commented that he doesn't clean toilets and doesn't always notice when things get dirty. The husband described their allocation of housework by saying, "Maybe she does less than I do, but some of the things she does, I just will not do. I will not dust all the little things in the house. That's one of my least favorite things, but I'm more likely to do the mopping and vacuuming." This husband's comments also revealed some ongoing tension about whose housework standards should be maintained. He said, "She has high standards for cleanliness that you would have to be home to maintain. Mine tend to acknowledge that you don't always get to this stuff because you have other things to do. I think I have a better acceptance that one priority hurts something else in the background."

While this couple generally agreed about how to raise their son, standards for child care were also subject to debate. He saw himself as doing more with his son than his wife, as reflected in comments such as "I tend to think of myself as the more involved parent, and I think other people have noticed that, too." . . . Like many of the other husbands, he went on to say that he thought their division of labor was unfair. Unlike the others, however, he indicated that he thought their current arrangements favored *her* needs, not his:

> *I think I do more housework. It's probably not fair, because I do more of the dirtier tasks. . . . Also, at this point, our solution tends to favor her free time more than my free time. I think that has more to do with our personal backgrounds. She has more personal friends to do things with, so she has more outside things to do whereas I say I'm not doing anything.*

In this family, comparable occupational status and earnings, coupled with a relatively egalitarian ideology, led to substantial sharing of both child care and housework. While the husband tended to take more credit for his involvement than his wife gave him, we can see a difference between their talk and that of some of the families discussed above. Other husbands sometimes complained about their wives' high standards, but they also treated housework, and even parenting, as primarily *her* duty. They usually resented being nagged to do more around the house and failed to move out of a helper role. Rarely did such men consider it *their* duty to anticipate, schedule, and take care of family and household needs. In this co-provider household, in contrast, the gendered allocation of responsibility for child care and housework was not assumed. Because of this, negotiations over housework and parenting were more frequent than in the other families. Since they both held expectations that each would fulfill both provider and caretaker roles, resentments came from both spouses—not just from the wife.

Our interviews suggest that it might be easier for couples to share both provider and homemaker roles when, like the family above, the wife's earnings and occupational prestige equal or exceed those of her husband. For instance, in one of the couples reporting the most sharing of child care and housework, the wife earned $36,000 annually as the executive director of a nonprofit community organization and a consultant, and her husband earned $30,000 as a self-employed general contractor. This couple started off their marriage with fairly conventional gender-role expectations and an unbalanced division of labor. While the husband's ideology had changed somewhat, he still talked like most of the main-provider husbands:

> *As far as the household is concerned, I divide a house into two categories: one is the interior and the other is the exterior. For the interior, my wife pushes me to deal with that. The exterior, I'm left to it myself. So, what I'm basically saying is that generally speaking, a woman does not deal with the exterior. The woman's main concern is with the interior, although there is a lot of deviation.*

In this family, an egalitarian belief system did not precede the sharing of household labor. The wife was still responsible for setting the "interior" household agenda and had to remind her husband to help with housework and child care. When asked whether he and his wife had arguments about housework, this husband laughed and said, "All the time, doesn't everybody?"

What differentiated this couple from most others, is that she made more money than he did and had no qualms about demanding help from him. While he had not yet accepted the idea that interior chores were equally his, he reluctantly performed them. She ranked his contributions to child care to be equal to hers, and rated his contributions to housework only slightly below her own. While not eagerly rushing to do the cooking, cleaning, or laundry, he complied with occasional reminders and according to his wife, was "a better cleaner" than she was.

His sharing stemmed, in part, from her higher earnings and their mutual willingness to reduce his "outside chores" by hiring outside help. Unlike the more ambivalent co-providers who hired housekeepers to do "her" chores, this couple hired a gardener to work on the yard so they could both spend more time focusing on the children and the house. Rather than complaining about their division of labor, he talked about how he has come to appreciate his situation:

> *Ever since I've known my wife, she's made more money than I have. Initially—as a man—I resented it. I went through a lot of head trips about it. But as time developed, I appreciated it. Now I respect it. The way I figure it is, I'd rather have her sharing the money with me than sharing it with someone else. She has her full-time job and then she has her part-time job as a consultant. The gardener I'm paying $75 per week, and I'm paying someone else $25 per week to make my lunch, so I'm enjoying it! It's self-interest.*

The power dynamic in this family, coupled with their willingness to pay for outside help to reduce his chores, and the flexibility of his self-employed work schedule, led to substantial sharing of cooking, cleaning, and child care. Because she was making more money and working more hours than he was, he could not emulate other husbands in claiming priority for his provider activities. . . .

Even when wives' earnings did not exceed the husbands', some co-providers shared the homemaker role. A male college-admissions recruiter and his executive-secretary wife shared substantial housework and child care according to mutual ratings. He made $29,000 per year working a 50-hour week, while she made $22,000 working a 40-hour week. She was willing to give him more credit than he was willing to claim for child care, reflecting her sincere appreciation for his parenting efforts, which were greater than those of other fathers she knew. He placed a high value on her mothering and seemed to downplay the possibility that they should be considered equal parents. Like most of the men in this study, the college-recruiter husband was reluctant to perform housecleaning chores. Like many co-providers, however, he managed to redefine some routine household chores as a shared responsibility. For instance, when we asked him what he liked least about housework, he laughing replied, "Probably those damn toilets, man, and the showers, the bathrooms, gotta scrub 'em, argghh! I wish I didn't have to do any of that, you know the vacuuming and all that. But it's just a fact of life."

Even though he did more than most husbands, he acknowledged that he did less than his wife, and admitted that he sometimes tried to use his job to get out of doing more around the house. But whereas other wives often allowed husbands to use their jobs as excuses for doing less family work, or assumed that their husbands were incapable of performing certain chores like cooking or laundry, the pattern in this family resembled that of the failed-aspirations couples. In other words, the wife did not assume that housework was "her" job, did not accept her husband's job demands as justification for his doing less housework, and sometimes challenged his interpretation of how much his job required of him. She also got her husband to assume more responsibility by refraining from performing certain tasks. He commented:

> *Sometimes she just refuses to do something. . . . An example would be the ironing, you know, I never used to do the ironing, hated it. Now it's just something that happens. You need something ironed, you better iron it or you're not gonna have it in the morning. So, I think, you know, that kinda just evolved. I mean, she just gradually quit doing it so everybody just had to do their own. My son irons his own clothes, I iron my own clothes, my daughter irons her own clothes, the only one that doesn't iron is the baby, and next year she'll probably start.*

The sociologist Jane Hood, whose path-breaking family research highlighted the importance of provider role definition to marital power, describes this strategy as "going on strike," and suggests that it is most effective when husbands feel the specific task *must* be done.[11] Since appearing neat and well dressed was a priority for this husband, when his wife stopped ironing his clothes, he started doing it himself. Because he felt it was important for his children to be "presentable" in public, he also began to remind them to iron their own clothes before going visiting or attending church. . . .

Although sharing tasks sometimes increases conflict, when both spouses assume that household tasks are a shared responsibility, negotiation can also become less necessary or contentious. For example, a co-provider husband who worked as a mail carrier commented, "I get home early and start dinner, make sure the kids do their homework, feed the dogs, stuff like that." He and his wife, an executive secretary, agreed that they rarely talk about housework. She said, "When I went back to work we agreed that we both needed to share, and so we just do it." While she still reminded him to perform chores according to her standards or on her schedule, she summed up her appreciation by commenting, "At least he does it without complaining." Lack of complaint was a common feature of co-provider families. Whereas many main-provider husbands complained of having to do "her" chores, the co-providers rarely talked about harboring resentments. Main-provider husbands typically lamented not having the services of a stay-at-home wife, but co-provider husbands almost never made such comparisons.

Summary and Discussion

For these dual-earner Chicano couples, we found conventional masculine privilege as well as considerable sharing in several domains. First, as in previous studies of ethnic minority families, wives were employed a substantial number of hours and made significant contributions to the household income. Second, like some who have studied Chicano families, we found that couples described their decision making to be relatively fair and equal.[12] Third, fathers in these families were more involved in child rearing than their own fathers had been, and many were rated as sharing a majority of child care tasks. Finally, while no husband performed fully half of the housework, a few made substantial contributions in this area as well.

One of the power dynamics that appeared to undergird the household division of labor in these families was the relative earning power of each spouse, though this was modified by factors such as occupational prestige, provider role status, and personal preference. . . .

While relative income appeared to make a significant difference in marital power, we observed no simple or straightforward exchange of market resources for domestic services. Other factors like failed career aspirations or occupational status influenced marital dynamics and helped explain why some wives were willing to push a little harder for change in the division of household labor. In almost every case, husbands reluctantly responded to requests for help from wives. Only when wives explicitly took the initiative to shift some of the housework burden to husbands did the men begin to assume significant responsibility for the day-to-day operation of the household. Even when they began to share the housework and child care, men tended to do some of the less onerous tasks like playing with the children or washing the dinner dishes. When we compared these men to their own fathers, or their wives' fathers, however, we could see that they were sharing more domestic chores than the generation that preceded them. . . .

The economies of gratitude in these families were not equally balanced, but many exhibited divisions of household labor that contradicted cultural stereotypes of macho men and male-dominated families. Particularly salient in these families was the lack of fit between their own class position and that of their parents. Most of the parents were Mexican immigrants with little education and low occupational mobility. The couples we interviewed, in contrast, were well educated and relatively secure in middle-class occupations. The couples could have compared themselves to their parents, evaluating themselves to be egalitarian and financially successful. While some did just that, most compared themselves to their Anglo and Chicano friends and co-workers, many of whom shared as much or more than they did. Implicitly comparing their earnings, occupational commitments, and perceived aptitudes, husbands and wives negotiated new patterns of work/family boundaries and developed novel justifications for their emerging arrangements. These were not created anew, but emerged out of the popular culture in which they found themselves. Judith Stacey labels such developments the making of the "postmodern family," because they signal "the contested, ambivalent, and undecided character of contemporary gender and kinship arrangements."[13] Our findings confirm that families are an important site of new struggles over the meaning of gender and the rights and obligations of men and women in each other and over each other's labor. . . .

ENDNOTES

Author's note: This article is based on a study of dual-earner Chicano couples conducted in 1990–1992 by Scott Coltrane with research assistance from Elsa Valdez and Hilda Cortez. Partial funding was provided by the Academic Senate of the University of California, Riverside, and the UCR Minority Student Research Internship Program. Included herein are analyses of unpublished interview excerpts along with selected passages from two published sources: (1) Coltrane, *Family Man: Fatherhood, Housework, and Gender Equity* (New York: Oxford University Press, 1996); and (2) Coltrane and Valdez, "Reluctant Compliance: Work/Family Role Allocation in Dual-Earner Chicano Families," in *Men, Work, and Family,* ed. Jane C. Hood (Newbury Park, CA: Sage, 1994).

1. For a discussion of how the term *machismo* can also reflect positive attributes of respect, loyalty, responsibility and generosity, see Alfredo Mirandé, "Chicano Fathers: Traditional Perceptions and Current Realities," in *Fatherhood Today,* ed. P. Bronstein and C. Cowan (New York: Wiley, 1988), pp. 93–106.
2. For reviews of literature on Latin American families and projections on their future proportionate representation in the population, see Randall Collins and Scott Coltrane, *Sociology of Marriage and the Family* (Chicago: Nelson-Hall, 1994); William A. Vega, "Hispanic Families in the 1980s," *Journal of Marriage and the Family* 52 (1990): 1015–24; and Norma Williams, *The Mexican-American Family* (New York: General Hall, 1990).
3. Maxine Baca Zinn, "Family, Feminism, and Race in America," *Gender & Society* 4 (1990): 68–82; Mirandé, "Chicano Fathers"; Vega, "Hispanic Families"; and Williams, *The Mexican-American Family.*
4. See Coltrane, *Family Man: Fatherhood, Housework, and Gender Equity* (New York: Oxford University Press, 1994); Coltrane and Valdez, "Reluctant Compliance: Work/Family Role Allocation in Dual-Earner Chicano Families," in *Men, Work, and Family,* ed. Jane C. Hood (Newbury Park, CA: Sage, 1994); and Valdez and Coltrane, "Work, Family, and the Chicana: Power, Perception and Equity," in *Employed Mothers and the Family Context,* ed. Judith Frankel (New York: Springer, 1993). I thank Hilda Cortez, a summer research intern at the University of California, for help in transcribing some of the interviews and for providing insight into some of the issues faced by these families.
5. Jessie Bernard, *The Future of Marriage* (New York: World, 1972).
6. See Jane Hood, "The Provider Role: Its Meaning and Measurement," *Journal of Marriage and the Family* 48 (1986): 349–59.
7. Hood, "The Provider Role."
8. See Coltrane, "Household Labor and the Routine Production of Gender," *Social Problems* 36: 473–90
9. I am indebted to Arlie Hochschild, who first used this term in *The Second Shift* (New York: Viking Press, 1987). See also Karen Pyke and Scott Coltrane, "Entitlement, Obligation, and Gratitude in Remarriage: Toward a Gendered Understanding of Household Labor Allocation."
10. I am indebted to Joseph Pleck for his conceptualization of "asymmetrically permeable" work/family boundaries ("The Work-Family Role System," *Social Problems* 24: 417–27).

11. Jane C. Hood, *Becoming a Two-Job Family* (New York: Praeger, 1983), p. 131.
12. See, for example, V. Cromwell and R. Cromwell, "Perceived Dominance in Decision Making and Conflict Resolution among Anglo, Black, and Chicano Couples," *Journal of Marriage and the Family* 40 (1978): 749–60; G. Hawkes and M. Taylor, "Power Structure in Mexican and Mexican-American Farm Labor Families," *Journal of Marriage and the Family* 37 (1975): 807–81; L. Ybarra, "When Wives Work: The Impact on the Chicano Family," *Journal of Marriage and the Family* 44: 169–78.
13. Judith Stacey (1982). *Brave New Families* (New York: Basic Books, 1990), p. 17.

39

THE FEMALE WORLD
OF CARDS AND HOLIDAYS
Women, Families, and the Work of Kinship

MICAELA DI LEONARDO

Why is it that the married women of America are supposed to write all the letters and send all the cards to their husbands' families? My old man is a much better writer than I am, yet he expects me to correspond with his whole family. If I asked him to correspond with mine, he would blow a gasket.

—Letter to ANN LANDERS

Women's place in man's life cycle has been that of nurturer, caretaker, and helpmate, the weaver of those networks of relationships on which she in turn relies.

—CAROL GILLIGAN, *In a Different Voice*

Feminist scholars in the past fifteen years have made great strides in formulating new understandings of the relations among gender, kinship, and the larger economy. As a result of this pioneering research, women are newly visible and audible, no longer submerged within their families. We see households as loci of political struggle, inseparable parts of the larger society and economy, rather than as havens from the heartless world of indus-

Micaela di Leonardo, "The Female World of Cards and Holidays: Women, Families, and the Work of Kinship" from *Signs: Journal of Women in Culture & Society*, Vol. 12 No. 3 (1987), published by The University of Chicago Press. Copyright © 1987 by The University of Chicago Press. Reprinted by permission.

trial capitalism.[1] And historical and cultural variations in kinship and family forms have become clearer with the maturation of feminist historical and social-scientific scholarship.

Two theoretical trends have been key to this reinterpretation of women's work and family domain. The first is the elevation to visibility of women's nonmarket activities—housework, child care, the servicing of men, and the care of the elderly—and the definition of all these activities as *labor*, to be enumerated alongside and counted as part of overall social reproduction. The second theoretical trend is the nonpejorative focus on women's domestic or kin-centered networks. We now see them as the products of conscious strategy, as crucial to the functioning of kinship systems, as sources of women's autonomous power and possible primary sites of emotional fulfillment, and, at times, as the vehicles for actual survival and/or political resistance.[2]

Recently, however, a division has developed between feminist interpreters of the "labor" and the "network" perspectives on women's lives. Those who focus on women's work tend to envision women as sentient, goal-oriented actors, while those who concern themselves with women's ties to others tend to perceive women primarily in terms of nurturance, other-orientation—altruism. The most celebrated recent example of this division is the opposing testimony of historians Alice Kessler-Harris and Rosalind Rosenberg in the Equal Employment Opportunity Commission's sex discrimination case against Sears Roebuck and Company. Kessler-Harris argued that American women historically have actively sought higher-paying jobs and have been prevented from gaining them because of sex discrimination by employers. Rosenberg argued that American women in the nineteenth century created among themselves, through their domestic networks, a "women's culture" that emphasized the nurturance of children and others and the maintenance of family life and that discouraged women from competition over or heavy emotional investment in demanding, high-paid employment.[3]

I shall not here address this specific debate but, instead, shall consider its theoretical background and implications. I shall argue that we need to fuse, rather than to oppose, the domestic network and labor perspectives. In what follows, I introduce a new concept, the work of kinship, both to aid empirical feminist research on women, work, and family and to help advance feminist theory in this arena. I believe that the boundary-crossing nature of the concept helps to confound the self-interest/altruism dichotomy, forcing us from an either-or stance to a position that includes both perspectives. I hope in this way to contribute to a more critical feminist vision of women's lives and the meaning of family in the industrial West.

In my field research among Italian Americans in northern California, I found myself considering the relations between women's kinship and economic lives. As an anthropologist, I was concerned with people's kin lives beyond conventional American nuclear family or household boundaries. To this end, I collected individual and family life histories, asking about all kin and close friends and their activities. I was also very interested in women's labor. As I sat with women and listened to their accounts of their past and present lives, I began to realize that they were involved in three types of work: house-work and child care, work in the labor market, and the work of kinship.[4]

By kin work I refer to the conception, maintenance, and ritual celebration of cross-household kin ties, including visits, letters, telephone calls, presents, and cards to kin; the organization of holiday gatherings; the creation and maintenance of quasi-kin relations; decisions to neglect or to intensify partic-ular ties; the mental work of reflection about all these activities; and the cre-ation and communication of altering images of family and kin vis-à-vis the images of others, both folk and mass media. Kin work is a key element that has been missing in the synthesis of the "household labor" and "domestic network" perspectives. In our emphasis on individual women's responsibil-ities within households and on the job, we reflect the common picture of households as nuclear units, tied perhaps to the larger social and economic system, but not to *each other*. We miss the point of telephone and soft drink advertising, of women's magazines' holiday issues, of commentators' con-fused nostalgia for the mythical American extended family: It is kinship contact *across households*, as much as women's work within them, that fulfills our cultural expectation of satisfying social life.

Maintaining these contacts, this sense of family, takes time, intention, and skill. We tend to think of human social and kin networks as the epiphenom-ena of production and reproduction: the social traces created by our material lives. Or, in the neoclassical tradition, we see them as part of leisure activities, outside an economic purview except insofar as they involve consumption be-havior. But the creation and maintenance of kin and quasi-kin networks in ad-vanced industrial societies is *work*, and, moreover, it is largely women's work.

The kin-work lens brought into focus new perspectives on my informants' family lives. First, life histories revealed that often the very existence of kin contact and holiday celebration depended on the presence of an adult woman in the household. When couples divorced or mothers died, the work of kin-ship was left undone; when women entered into sanctioned sexual or mari-tal relationships with men in these situations, they reconstituted the men's kinship networks and organized gatherings and holiday celebrations. Middle-aged businessman Al Bertini, for example, recalled the death of his mother in his early adolescence: "I think that's probably one of the biggest losses in los-ing a family—yeah, I remember as a child when my Mom was alive . . . the holidays were treated with enthusiasm and love. . . . After she died the at-tempt was there, but it just didn't materialize." Later in life, when Al Bertini and his wife separated, his own and his son Jim's participation in extended family contact decreased rapidly. But when Jim began a relationship with Jane Bateman, she and he moved in with Al, and Jim and Jane began to in-vite his kin over for holidays. Jane single-handedly planned and cooked the holiday feasts.

Kin work, then, is like housework and child care: Men in the aggregate do not do it. It differs from these forms of labor in that it is harder for men to substitute hired labor to accomplish these tasks in the absence of kinswomen. Second, I found that women, as the workers in this arena, generally had much greater kin knowledge than did their husbands, often including more accurate and extensive knowledge of their husbands' families. This was true both of middle-aged and younger couples and surfaced as a phenomenon in my interviews in the form of humorous arguments and in wives' detailed additions to husbands' narratives. Nick Meraviglia, a middle-aged professional, discussed his Italian antecedents in the presence of his wife, Pina:

NICK: My grandfather was a very outspoken man, and it was reported he took off for the hills when he found out that Mussolini was in power.
PINA: And he was a very tall man; he used to have to bow his head to get inside doors.
NICK: No, that was my uncle.
PINA: Your grandfather too, I've heard your mother say.
NICK: My mother has a sister and a brother.
PINA: *Two* sisters!
NICK: You're right!
PINA: Maria and Angelina.

Women were also much more willing to discuss family feuds and crises and their own roles in them; men tended to repeat formulaic statements asserting family unity and respectability. (This was much less true for younger men.) Joe and Cetta Longhinotti's statements illustrate these tendencies. Joe responded to my question about kin relations: "We all get along. As a rule, relatives, you got nothing but trouble." Cetta, instead, discussed her relations with each of her grown children, their wives, her in-laws, and her own blood kin in detail. She did not hide the fact that relations were strained in several cases; she was eager to discuss the evolution of problems and to seek my opinions of her actions. Similarly, Pina Meraviglia told the following story of her fight with one of her brothers with hysterical laughter: "There was some biting and hair pulling and choking. . . . It was terrible! I shouldn't even tell you." Nick, meanwhile, was concerned about maintaining an image of family unity and respectability.

Also, men waxed fluent while women were quite inarticulate in discussing their past and present occupations. When asked about their work lives, Joe Longhinotti and Nick Meraviglia, union baker and professional, respectively, gave detailed narratives of their work careers. Cetta Longhinotti and Pina Meraviglia, clerical and former clerical, respectively, offered only short descriptions focusing on factors of ambience, such as the "lovely things" sold by Cetta's firm.

These patterns are not repeated in the younger generation, especially among young women, such as Jane Bateman, who have managed to acquire training and jobs with some prospect of mobility. These younger women, though, have *added* a professional and detailed interest in their jobs to a felt responsibility of the work of kinship.[5]

Although men rarely took on any kin-work tasks, family histories and accounts of contemporary life revealed that kinswomen often negotiated among themselves, alternating hosting, food-preparation, and gift-buying responsibilities — or sometimes ceding entire task clusters to one woman. Taking on or ceding tasks was clearly related to acquiring or divesting oneself of power within kin networks, but women varied in their interpretation of the meaning of this power. Cetta Longhinotti, for example, relied on the "family Christmas dinner" as a symbol of her central kinship role and was involved in painful negotiations with her daughter-in-law over the issue: "Last year she insisted — this is touchy. She doesn't want to spend the holiday dinner together. So last year we went there. But I still had my dinner the next day. . . . I made a big dinner on Christmas Day, regardless of who's coming — candles on the table, the whole routine. I decorate the house myself too. . . . Well, I just feel that the time will come when maybe I won't feel like cooking a big dinner — she should take advantage of the fact that I feel like doing it now." Pina Meraviglia, in contrast, was saddened by the centripetal force of the developmental cycle but was unworried about the power dynamics involved in her negotiations with daughters- and mother-in-law over holiday celebrations.

Kin work is not just a matter of power among women but also of the mediation of power represented by household units.[6] Women often choose to minimize status claims in their kin work and to include numbers of households under the rubric of family. Cetta Longhinotti's sister Anna, for example, is married to a professional man whose parents have considerable economic resources, while Joe and Cetta have low incomes and no other well-off kin. Cetta and Anna remain close, talk on the phone several times a week, and assist their adult children, divided by distance and economic status, in remaining united as cousins.

Finally, women perceived housework, child care, market labor, the care of the elderly, and the work of kinship as competing responsibilities. Kin work was a unique category, however, because it was unlabeled and because women felt they either could cede some tasks to kinswomen and/or could cut them back severely. Women variously cited the pressures of market labor, the needs of the elderly, and their own desires for freedom and job enrichment as reasons for cutting back Christmas card lists, organized holiday gatherings, multifamily dinners, letters, visits, and phone calls. They expressed guilt and defensiveness about this cutback process and, particularly, about their failures to keep families close through constant contact and about their failures to create perfect holiday celebrations. Cetta Longhinotti, during the period when she was visiting her elderly mother every weekend in addition to working a full-time job, said of her grown children, "I'd have the whole gang here once a month, but I've been so busy that I haven't done that for about six months." And Pina Meraviglia lamented her insufficient work on family Christmases, "I wish I had really made it traditional . . . like my sister-in-law has special stories."

Kin work, then, takes place in an arena characterized simultaneously by cooperation and competition, by guilt and gratification. Like housework and child care, it is women's work, with the same lack of clear-cut agreement concerning its proper components: How often should sheets be changed? When should children be toilet trained? Should an aunt send a niece a birthday present? Unlike housework and child care, however, kin work, taking place across the boundaries of normative households, is as yet unlabeled and has no retinue of experts prescribing its correct forms. Neither home economists nor child psychologists have much to say about nieces' birthday presents. Kin work is thus more easily cut back without social interference. On the other hand, the results of kin work — frequent kin contact and feelings of intimacy — are the subject of considerable cultural manipulation as indicators of family happiness. Thus, women in general are subject to the guilt my informants expressed over cutting back kin-work activities.

Although many of my informants referred to the results of women's kin work — cross-household kin contacts and attendant ritual gatherings — as particularly Italian American, I suggest that in fact this phenomenon is broadly characteristic of American kinship. We think of kin-work tasks such as the preparation of ritual feasts, responsibility for holiday card lists, and gift buying as extensions of women's domestic responsibilities for cooking, consumption, and nurturance. American men in general do not take on these tasks any more than they do housework and child care — and probably less, as these tasks have not yet been the subject of intense public debate. And my informants' gender breakdown in relative articulateness on kinship and workplace themes reflects the still-prevalent occupational segregation — most women cannot find jobs that provide enough pay, status, or promotion possibilities to make them worth focusing on — as well as women's perceived power within kinship networks. The common recognition of that power is reflected in Selma Greenberg's book on nonsexist child rearing. Greenberg calls mothers "press agents" who sponsor relations between their own children and other relatives; she advises a mother whose relatives treat her disrespectfully to deny those kin access to her children.[7]

Kin work is a salient concept in other parts of the developed world as well. Larissa Adler Lomnitz and Marisol Pérez Lizaur have found that "centralizing women" are responsible for these tasks and for communicating "family ideology" among upper-class families in Mexico City. Matthews Hamabata, in his study of upper-class families in Japan, has found that women's kin work involves key financial transactions. Sylvia Junko Yanagisako discovered that among rural Japanese migrants to the United States the maintenance of kin networks was assigned to women as the migrants adopted the American ideology of the independent nuclear family household. Maila Stivens notes that urban Australian housewives' kin ties and kin ideology "transcend women's isolation in domestic units."[8]

This is not to say that cultural conceptions of appropriate kin work do not vary, even within the United States. Carol B. Stack documents institutionalized fictive kinship and concomitant reciprocity networks among impoverished black American women. Women in populations characterized by intense feelings of ethnic identity may feel bound to emphasize particular occasions — Saint Patrick's or Columbus Day — with organized family feasts.

These constructs may be mediated by religious affiliation, as in the differing emphases on Friday or Sunday family dinners among Jews and Christians. Thus the personnel involved and the amount and kind of labor considered necessary for the satisfactory performance of particular kin-work tasks are likely to be culturally constructed.[9] But while the kin and quasi-kin universes and the ritual calendar may vary among women according to race or ethnicity, their general responsibility for maintaining kin links and ritual observances does not.

As kin work is not an ethnic or racial phenomenon, neither is it linked only to one social class. Some commentators on American family life still reflect the influence of work done in England in the 1950s and 1960s (by Elizabeth Bott and by Peter Willmott and Michael Young) in their assumption that working-class families are close and extended, while the middle class substitutes friends (or anomie) for family. Others reflect the prevalent family pessimism in their presumption that neither working- nor middle-class families have extended kin contact.[10] Insofar as kin contact depends on residential proximity, the larger economy's shifts will influence particular groups' experiences. Factory workers, close to kin or not, are likely to disperse when plants shut down or relocate. Small businesspeople or independent professionals may, however, remain resident in particular areas—and thus maintain proximity to kin—for generations, while professional employees of large firms relocate at their firms' behest. This pattern was obtained among my informants.

In any event, cross-household kin contact can be and is affected at long distance through letters, cards, phone calls, and holiday and vacation visits. The form and functions of contact, however, vary according to economic resources. Stack and Brett Williams offer rich accounts of kin networks among poor blacks and migrant Chicano farmworkers functioning to provide emotional support, labor, commodity, and cash exchange—a funeral visit, help with laundry, the gift of a dress or piece of furniture.[11] Far different in degree are exchanges such as the loan of a vacation home, a multifamily boating trip, or the provision of free professional services—examples from the kin networks of my wealthier informants. The point is that households, as labor- and income-pooling units, whatever their relative wealth, are somewhat porous in relation to others with whose members they share kin or quasi-kin ties. We do not really know how class differences operate in this realm; it is possible that they do so largely in terms of ideology. It may be, as David Schneider and Raymond T. Smith suggest, that the affluent and the very poor are more open in recognizing necessary economic ties to kin than are those who identify themselves as middle class.[12]

Recognizing that kin work is gender rather than class based allows us to see women's kin networks among all groups, not just among working-class and impoverished women in industrialized societies. This recognition in turn clarifies our understanding of the privileges and limits of women's varying access to economic resources. Affluent women can "buy out" of housework, child care—and even some kin-work responsibilities. But they, like all women, are ultimately responsible, and subject to both guilt and blame, as the administrators of home, children, and kin network. Even the wealthiest women must negotiate the timing and venue of holidays and other family rituals with their kinswomen. It may be that kin work is the core women's work category in which all women cooperate, while women's perceptions of the appropriateness of cooperation for housework, child care, and the care of the elderly varies by race, class, region, and generation.

But kin work is not necessarily an appropriate category of labor, much less gendered labor, in all societies. In many small-scale societies, kinship is the major organizing principle of all social life, and all contacts are by definition kin contacts.[13] One cannot, therefore, speak of labor that does not involve kin. In the United States, kin work as a separable category of gendered labor perhaps arose historically in concert with the ideological and material constructs of the moral mother/cult of domesticity and the privatized family during the course of industrialization in the eighteenth and nineteenth centuries. These phenomena are connected to the increase in the ubiquity of productive occupations *for men* that are not organized through kinship. This includes the demise of the family farm with the capitalization of agriculture and rural-urban migration; the decline of family recruitment in factories as firms grew, ended child labor, and began to assert bureaucratized forms of control; the decline of artisanal labor and of small entrepreneurial enterprises as large firms took greater and greater shares of the commodity market; the decline of the family firm as corporations—and their managerial workforces—grew beyond the capacities of individual families to provision them; and, finally, the rise of civil service bureaucracies and public pressure against nepotism.[14]

As men increasingly worked alongside of non-kin, and as the ideology of separate spheres was increasingly accepted, perhaps the responsibility for kin maintenance, like for child rearing, became gender-focused. Ryan points out that "built into the updated family economy . . . was a new measure of voluntarism." This voluntarism, though, "perceived as the shift from patriarchal authority to domestic affection," also signaled the rise of women's moral responsibility for family life. Just as the "idea of fatherhood itself seemed almost to wither away" so did male involvement in the responsibility for kindred lapse.[15]

With postbellum economic growth and geographic movement, women's new kin burden involved increasing amounts of time and labor. The ubiquity of lengthy visits and of frequent letter-writing among nineteenth-century women attests to this. And for visitors and for those who were residentially proximate, the continuing commonalities of women's domestic labor allowed for kinds of work sharing—nursing, childkeeping, cooking, cleaning—that men, with their increasingly differentiated and controlled activities, probably could not maintain. This is not to say that some kin-related male productive work did not continue; my own data, for instance, show kin involvement among small businessmen in the present. It is, instead, to suggest a general trend in material life and a cultural shift that influenced even those whose productive and kin lives remained commingled. Yanagisako has distinguished between the realms of domestic and public kinship in order to draw attention to anthropology's relatively "thin descriptions" of the domestic (female) domain. Using her typology, we might say that kin work as gendered labor comes into existence within the domestic domain with the relative erasure of the domain of public, male kinship.[16]

Whether or not this proposed historical model bears up under further research, the question remains: Why do women do kin work? However material factors may shape activities, they do not determine how individuals may perceive them. And in considering issues of motivation, of intention, of the cultural construction of kin work, we return to the altruism versus self-interest dichotomy in recent feminist theory. Consider the epigraphs to this article. Are women kin workers the nurturant weavers of the Gilligan quotation, or victims, like the fed-up woman who writes to complain to Ann Landers? That is, are we to see kin work as yet another example of "women's culture" that takes the care of others as its primary desideratum? Or are we to see kin work as another way in which men, the economy, and the state extract labor from women without a fair return? And how do women themselves see their kin work and its place in their lives?

As I have indicated above, I believe that it is the creation of the self-interest/altruism dichotomy that is itself the problem here. My women informants, like most American women, accepted their primary responsibility for housework and the care of dependent children. Despite two major waves of feminist activism in this century, the gendering of certain categories of unpaid labor is still largely unaltered. These work responsibilities clearly interfere with some women's labor force commitments at certain life-cycle stages; but, more important, women are simply discriminated against in the labor market and rarely are able to achieve wage and status parity with men of the same age, race, class, and educational background.[17]

Thus for women informants, as for most American women, the domestic domain is not only an arena in which much unpaid labor must be undertaken but also a realm in which one may attempt to gain human satisfactions — and power — not available in the labor market. Anthropologists Jane Collier and Louise Lamphere have written compellingly on the ways in which varying kinship and economic structures may shape women's competition or cooperation with one another in domestic domains.[18] Feminists considering Western women and families have looked at the issue of power primarily in terms of husband–wife relations or psychological relations between parents and children. If we adopt Collier and Lamphere's broader canvas, though, we see that kin work is not only women's labor from which men and children benefit but also labor that women undertake in order to create obligations in men and children and to gain power over one another. Thus Cetta Longhinotti's struggle with her daughter-in-law over the venue of Christmas dinner is not just about a competition over altruism, it is also about the creation of future obligations. And thus Cetta's and Anna's sponsorship and their children's friendship with each other is both an act of nurturance and a cooperative means of gaining power over those children.

Although this was not a clear-cut distinction, those of my informants who were more explicitly antifeminist tended to be most invested in kin work. Given the overwhelming historical shift toward greater autonomy for younger generations and the withering of children's financial and labor obligations to their parents, this investment was in most cases tragically doomed. Cetta Longhinotti, for example, had repaid her own mother's devotion with extensive home nursing during the mother's last years. Given Cetta's general failure to direct her adult children in work, marital choice, religious worship, or even frequency of visits, she is unlikely to receive such care from them when she is older.

The kin-work lens thus reveals the close relations between altruism and self-interest in women's actions. As economists Nancy Folbre and Heidi Hartmann point out, we have inherited a Western intellectual tradition that both dichotomizes the domestic and public domains and associates them on exclusive axes such that we find it difficult to see self-interest in the home and altruism in the workplace.[19] But why, in fact, have women fought for better jobs if not, in part, to support their children? These dichotomies are Procrustean beds that warp our understanding of women's lives both at home and at work. "Altruism" and "self-interest" are cultural constructions that are not necessarily mutually exclusive, and we forget this to our peril.

The concept of kin work helps to bring into focus a heretofore unacknowledged array of tasks that is culturally assigned to women in industrialized societies. At the same time, this concept, embodying notions of both love and work and crossing the boundaries of households, helps us to reflect on current feminist debates on women's work, family, and community. We newly see both the interrelations of these phenomena and women's roles in creating and maintaining those interrelations. Revealing the actual labor embodied in what we culturally conceive as love and considering the political uses of this labor helps to deconstruct the self-interest/altruism dichotomy and to connect more closely women's domestic and labor-force lives.

The true value of the concept, however, remains to be tested through further historical and contemporary research on gender, kinship, and labor. We need to assess the suggestion that gendered kin work emerges in concert with the capitalist development process; to probe the historical record for women's and men's varying and changing conceptions of it; and to research the current range of its cultural constructions and material realities. We know that household boundaries are more porous than we had thought—but they are undoubtedly differently porous, and this is what we need to specify. We need, in particular, to assess the relations of changing labor processes, residential patterns, and the use of technology to changing kin work.

Altering the values attached to this particular set of women's tasks will be as difficult as are the housework, child-care, and occupational-segregation struggles. But just as feminist research in these latter areas is complementary and cumulative, so researching kin work should help us to piece together the home, work, and public-life landscape—to see the female world of cards and holidays as it is constructed and lived within the changing political economy. How female that world is to remain, and what it would look like if it were not sex-segregated, are questions we cannot yet answer.

ENDNOTES

Acknowledgments: Many thanks to Cynthia Costello, Rayna Rapp, Roberta Spalter-Roth, John Willoughby, and Barbara Gelpi, Susan Johnson, and Sylvia Yanagisako of *Signs* for their help with this chapter. I wish in particular to acknowledge the influence of Rayna Rapp's work on my ideas. Acknowledgment and gratitude also to Caroll Smith-Rosenberg for my paraphrase of her title, "The Female World of Love and Ritual: Relations Between Women in Nineteenth-Century America," *Signs: Journal of Women in Culture and Society* 1, no. 1 (Autumn 1975): 1–29. The epigraphs are from Ann Landers letter printed in *Washington Post* (April 15, 1983); Carol Gilligan, *In a Different Voice* (Cambridge, MA: Harvard University Press, 1982), 17.

1. Heidi I. Hartmann, "The Family as the Locus of Gender, Class, and Political Struggle: The Example of Housework," *Signs* 6, no. 3 (Spring 1981): 366–94; and Christopher Lasch, *Haven in a Heartless World: The Family Besieged* (New York: Basic Books, 1977).
2. Representative examples of the first trend include Joann Vanek, "Time Spent on Housework," *Scientific American* 231 (November 1974): 116–20; Ruth Schwartz Cowan, "A Case Study of Technological and Social Change: The Washing Machine and the Working Wife," in *Clio's Consciousness Raised*, ed. Mary Hartmann and Lois Banner (New York: Harper & Row, 1974), 245–53; Ann Oakley, *Women's Work: The Housewife, Past and Present* (New York: Vintage, 1974); Hartmann; and Susan Strasser, *Never Done: A History of American Housework* (New York: Pantheon Books, 1982). Key contributions to the second trend include Louise Lamphere, "Strategies, Cooperation and Conflict Among Women in Domestic Groups," in *Women, Culture and Society*, ed. Michelle Zimbalist Rosaldo and Louise Lamphere (Stanford, CA: Stanford University Press, 1974), 97–112; Mina Davis Caulfield, "Imperialism, the Family and the Cultures of Resistance," *Socialist Revolution* 20 (October 1974): 67–85; Smith-Rosenberg; Sylvia Junko Yanagisako, "Women-Centered Kin Networks and Urban Bilateral Kinship," *American Ethnologist* 4, no. 2 (1977): 207–26; Jane Humphries, "The Working Class Family, Women's Liberation and Class Struggle: The Case of Nineteenth Century British History," *Review of Radical Political Economics* 9 (Fall 1977): 25–41; Blanche Weisen Cook, "Female Support Networks and Political Activism: Lillian Wald, Crystal Eastman, Emma Goldman," in *A Heritage of Her Own*, ed. Nancy F. Cott and Elizabeth H. Pleck (New York: Simon & Schuster, 1979); Temma Kaplan, "Female Consciousness and Collective Action: The Case of Barcelona, 1910–1918," *Signs* 7, no. 3 (Spring 1982): 545–66.
3. On this debate, see Jon Weiner, "Women's History on Trial," *Nation* 241, no. 6 (September 7, 1985): 161, 176, 178–80; Karen J. Winkler, "Two Scholars' Conflict in Sears Sex-Bias Case Sets Off War in Women's History," *Chronicle of Higher Education* (February 5, 1986), 1, 8; Rosalind Rosenberg, "What Harms Women in the Workplace," *New York Times* (February 27, 1986); Alice Kessler-Harris, "Equal Employment Opportunity Commission vs. Sears Roebuck and Company: A Personal Account," *Radical History Review* 35 (April 1986): 57–79.
4. Portions of the following analysis are reported in Micaela di Leonardo, *The Varieties of Ethnic Experience: Kinship, Class and Gender among California Italian-Americans* (Ithaca, NY: Cornell University Press, 1984), chap. 6.
5. Clearly, many women do, in fact, discuss their paid labor with willingness and clarity. The point here is that there are opposing gender tendencies in an identical

interview situation, tendencies that are explicable in terms of both the material realities and current cultural constructions of gender.

6. Papanek has rightly focused on women's unacknowledged family status produc-
tion, but what is conceived of as "family" shifts and varies (Hanna Papanek,
"Family Status Production: The 'Work' and 'Non-Work' of Women," *Signs* 4, no. 4
[Summer 1979]: 775–81).

7. Selma Greenberg, *Right from the Start: A Guide to Nonsexist Child Rearing* (Boston:
Houghton Mifflin, 1978), 147. Another example of indirect support for kin work's
gendered existence is a recent study of university math students, which found
that a major reason for women's failure to pursue careers in mathematics was the
pressure of family involvement. Compare David Maines et al., *Social Processes of
Sex Differentiation in Mathematics* (Washington, DC: National Institute of Education, 1981).

8. Larissa Adler Lomnitz and Marisol Pérez Lizaur, "The History of a Mexican Urban
Family," *Journal of Family History* 3, no. 4 (1978): 392–409, esp. 398; Sylvia Junko
Yanagisako, "Two Processes of Change in Japanese-American Kinship," *Journal of
Anthropological Research* 31 (1975): 196–224; Maila Stivens, "Women and Their Kin:
Kin, Class and Solidarity in a Middle-Class Suburb of Sydney, Australia," in *Women
United, Women Divided,* ed. Patricia Caplan and Janet M. Bujra (Bloomington: Indi-
ana University Press, 1979), 157–84.

9. Carol B. Stack, *All Our Kin: Strategies for Survival in a Black Community* (New York:
Harper & Row, 1974). These cultural constructions may, however, vary within
ethnic-racial populations as well.

10. Elizabeth Bott, *Family and Social Network,* 2d ed. (New York: Free Press, 1971);
Michael Young and Peter Willmott, *Family and Kinship in East London* (London: Rout-
ledge & Kegan Paul, 1957); and *Family and Class in a London Suburb* (London:
Routledge & Kegan Paul, 1960). Classic studies that presume this class difference are Herbert Gans, *The Urban Villagers: Group and Class in the Life of Italian-
Americans* (New York: Free Press, 1962); and Mirra Komarovsky, *Blue-Collar
Marriage* (New York: Random House, 1962). [An] example is Ilene Philipson,
"Heterosexual Antagonisms and the Politics of Mothering," *Socialist Review*
12, no. 6 (November–December 1982): 55–77. Edward Shorter, *The Making of
the Modern Family* (New York: Basic Books, 1975), epitomizes the pessimism of
the "family sentiments" school. See also Mary Lyndon Shanley, "The History
of the Family in Modern England: Review Essay," *Signs* 4, no. 4 (Summer 1979):
740–50.

11. Stack; and Brett Williams, "The Trip Takes Us: Chicano Migrants to the Prairie"
(Ph.D. diss., University of Illinois at Urbana-Champaign, 1975).

12. David Schneider and Raymond T. Smith, *Class Differences and Sex Roles in American
Kinship and Family Structure* (Englewood Cliffs, NJ: Prentice-Hall, 1973), esp. 27.

13. See Nelson Graburn, ed., *Readings in Kinship and Social Structure* (New York:
Harper & Row, 1971), esp. 3–4.

14. The moral mother/cult of domesticity is analyzed in Barbara Welter, "The Cult of
True Womanhood, 1820–1860," *American Quarterly* 18, no. 2 (Summer 1966):
151–74; Nancy Cott, *The Bonds of Womanhood: "Women's Sphere" in New England,
1780–1835* (New Haven, CT: Yale University Press, 1977); and Ruth Bloch, "American Feminine Ideals in Transition: The Rise of the Moral Mother, 1785–1815,"
Feminist Studies 4, no. 2 (June 1978): 101–26. The description of the general political-
economic shift in the United States is based on Harry Braverman, *Labor and Mo-
nopoly Capital: The Degradation of Work in the Twentieth Century* (New York: Monthly
Review Press, 1974); Peter Dobkin Hall, "Family Structure and Economic Organization: Massachusetts Merchants, 1700–1850," in *Family and Kin in Urban Communities, 1700–1950,* ed. Tamara K. Hareven (New York: New Viewpoints, 1977),
38–61; Michael Anderson, "Family, Household and the Industrial Revolution," in
The American Family in Social-Historical Perspective, ed. Michael Gordon (New York:

St. Martin's Press, 1978), 38–50; Tamara K. Hareven, *Amoskeag: Life and Work in an American Factory City* (New York: Pantheon Books, 1978); Richard Edwards, *Contested Terrain: The Transformation of the Workplace in the Twentieth Century* (New York: Basic Books, 1979); Mary Ryan, *The Cradle of the Middle Class: The Family in Oneida County, New York, 1790–1865* (Cambridge: Cambridge University Press, 1981); Alice Kessler-Harris, *Out to Work: A History of Wage-Earning Women in the United States* (New York: Oxford University Press, 1982).

15. Ryan, 231–32.
16. Sylvia Junko Yanagisako, "Family and Household: The Analysis of Domestic Groups," *Annual Review of Anthropology* 8 (1979): 161–205.
17. See Donald J. Treiman and Heidi I. Hartmann, eds., *Women, Work and Wages: Equal Pay for Jobs of Equal Value* (Washington, DC: National Academy Press, 1981).
18. Lamphere (n. 2 above); Jane Fishburne Collier, "Women in Politics," in Rosaldo and Lamphere, eds. (n. 2 above), 89–96.
19. Nancy Folbre and Heidi I. Hartmann, "The Rhetoric of Self-Interest: Selfishness, Altruism, and Gender in Economic Theory," in *The Consequences of Economic Rhetoric,* ed. Arjo Klamer, Donald McCloskey, and Robert M. Solow (New York: Cambridge University Press, 1988).

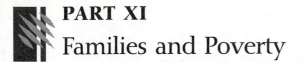

PART XI

Families and Poverty

W hy is poverty important to study in the sociology of the family? Poverty deeply affects many people's lives, with many people suffering from hunger and a lack of adequate housing. The problems of poverty are compounded when these people have families. Daniel Lichter (1997) reports that in 1994 "15.3 million or 21.8 percent of all American children lived in poor families. Although children comprised only 26.7 percent of the U.S. population, they accounted for 40.1 percent of all poor persons" (p. 123). Thus, the majority of people in poverty are mothers and their children. Low socioeconomic status greatly influences family structure and relationships, and it also affects the quality of life and resources available to the family. The articles selected for this section reflect many of the issues currently facing families in poverty.

Explanations of Poverty

There are two primary explanations of poverty used in research on families and poverty: cultural deficiency models and structural analyses. Maxine Baca Zinn (1989) argues that cultural explanations of poverty see culture as the villain. Poor people are seen to have distinctive values, aspirations, and psychological characteristics that restrict their abilities and foster behavioral deficiencies which keep families poor from generation to generation. For example, the 1965 *Moynihan Report* on poor African American families blamed their poverty on African American women who were too matriarchal and strong. Another theorist, Nicholas Lemann (1986a, 1986b) argued that African Americans raised in a southern culture of poverty had "loose" attitudes toward marriage, high illegitimacy rates, and family disintegration. According to Lemann, African Americans who migrated from southern to northern cities in the United States took this culture of poverty with them. Baca Zinn argues that the problems with culture of poverty arguments are numerous, including the fact that these theories blame the victims and their culture for being poor and ignore larger, macrostructural forces that could be keeping them poor. The culture of poverty thesis has been disproved by researchers using the University of Michigan's Panel Study of Income Dynamics (PSID). Studies that have examined family incomes over a period of years found that most families are not poor for a long enough time to create a culture of poverty. Instead, income data show that there is a high turnover in the individual families who are poor in any given year. Thus, individual motivation also cannot be used as a primary explanation of poverty.

Instead of focusing on individual and cultural explanations of poverty, Baca Zinn argues that we need to look at structural explanations of poverty, which include studying the structure of the family. William Julius Wilson

(1987), in his research on family structure and poverty, found that many family variables affect poverty rates including marital status, high divorce rates, female-headed households, the number of adults earning an income in the household, and the availability of marriageable men. Other structural variables include transformations in the economy, such as deindustrialization and the switch from manufacturing to a service economy. This change in the economy led to many jobs being deskilled or moved from urban centers, causing high rates of unemployment. Thus, the opportunity to find a decent paying blue-collar job is much harder today than it was 20 years ago. Baca Zinn argues that structural changes in urban areas also are affecting rates of poverty. More inner-city neighborhoods are isolated in deteriorating cities, with little public transportation and fewer cars to get people to jobs and resources in the suburbs.

The first reading in this section, "Hispanic Families in Poverty: Diversity, Context, and Interpretation," by Robert Aponte, builds on Baca Zinn's arguments concerning structural analyses of poverty. Aponte, a Puerto Rican–born sociologist raised in New York City, was educated at the University of Chicago. He specializes in the study of Latinos in the United States, immigration, poverty and social policy, race and ethnicity, and contemporary Cuban society. Aponte first studied the issue of families while conducting research on poverty. A hot topic related to the issue of poverty at the time was the "feminization of poverty," a term that refers to the rapid increase in representation by single-parent families, mostly headed by women, among the nation's poor over the past few decades. This phenomenon was especially prevalent among African Americans and Puerto Ricans and led to widespread stereotyping about these groups. In particular, a common belief was that the families in question were being formed primarily so that they could take advantage of supposed lucrative welfare benefits available only to single-parent families. Aponte's experience growing up in the midst of such families suggested to him that few persons would voluntarily take on such daunting responsibilities — there had to be a better explanation for the increasing numbers of families in poverty. In this selection, Aponte offers a different interpretation — one that is more consistent with his experiences and with the historical record. In particular, he argues that we must examine different Hispanic ethnic groups separately, because their immigrant and social histories vary as do their rates of poverty. His research provides valuable support for structural theories of poverty.

Women in Poverty

The second reading is "It's a Family Affair: Women, Poverty, and Welfare," by Randy Albelda and Chris Tilly. Albelda is a professor of economics at the University of Massachusetts, Boston, where she writes and teaches about women in the U.S. economy. Tilly, an economist at the University of Massachusetts at Lowell and editor of *Dollars and Sense* magazine, does research on low-wage work. Building on the arguments made by Aponte in Reading 40,

Albelda and Tilly examine why there is so much public hatred for poor women in the United States. Poor women on welfare are seen as being too dependent on welfare, too lazy to find work, and too fertile. Another erroneous belief is that many women on welfare are having more babies so that they can collect additional welfare. In fact, Republican Congressman Newt Gingrich once said that "congressional leaders argue that governmental programs 'reward dependency' and have 'had the unintended consequences of making welfare more attractive than work'" (cited in Lundgren-Gaveras 1996:136).

Albelda and Tilly challenge several of these myths regarding poor women on welfare. First, they point out that despite all the current public criticisms of the welfare system, in 1993, of the over 40 million poor people in the United States, only 14 million of them (two-thirds of them children) received welfare assistance from Aid to Families with Dependent Children (AFDC). Thus, only a small proportion of the poor in the United States actually receive welfare. Moreover, AFDC payments are minuscule compared to other social programs; AFDC accounts for less than 1 percent of the federal budget and less than 3 percent of the state budgets. In addition, Albelda and Tilly examine the economic realities of poor women in the United States and the barriers these women face in finding well-paid employment, child care, and time to do the unpaid labor of housework. They conclude their article with several policy suggestions that would bring about institutional changes to improve the lives of poor women and children.

Homeless Families

The last reading in this section on families and poverty is "Rachel and Her Children: Homeless Families in America," by Jonathan Kozol. When Kozol began his research on the homeless in the mid-1980s, he assumed that most homeless families would be urban, nonwhite, and unemployable. After interviewing homeless people in over 50 cities, he found that, during the 1980s, the fastest-growing sector of the homeless population was young children. Kozol also discovered that the adult homeless population was quite diverse and skilled; most had been hard-working individuals who had lost their farms, their jobs, their stores. Some had been plunged into poverty because of a divorce, while others had gone bankrupt due to a serious illness in the family and the resulting medical expenses. Thus, the reality of the homeless is much different from the stereotypes and myths about them in the dominant culture. Most importantly, the fastest-growing segment of the homeless population is families with young children.

The selection that appears here is taken from Kozol's book *Rachel and Her Children: Homeless Families in America* (1988). Kozol comments:

> *I am still close to some of the families portrayed in* Rachel and Her Children, *several of whom now live in the South Bronx.* Amazing Grace, *published in 1995, describes the lives they lead today. Their lives will grow considerably*

harder as the new federal welfare legislation goes into effect and as bigotry and institutionalized racism deepen in New York and in America. (Personal Interview 1997)

Kozol's writing enables the reader to intimately grasp what the lives of families and children in poverty are like. What can be done to improve the lives of homeless families? Albelda and Tilly (Reading 41) make some suggestions for social change. In addition, Rose Brewer, in her article "Race, Class, Gender and U.S. State Welfare Policy: The Nexus of Inequality for African American Families" (Reading 46), also makes suggestions for policy changes concerning poverty and welfare.

REFERENCES

Baca Zinn, Maxine. 1989. "Family, Race, and Poverty in the Eighties." *Signs: Journal of Women in Culture and Society* 14(4):856–74.

Kozol, Jonathan. 1988. *Rachel and Her Children: Homeless Families in America.* New York: Crown Publishers.

——. 1995. *Amazing Grace: The Lives of Children and the Conscience of a Nation.* New York: Crown Publishers.

Lemann, Nicholas. 1986a. "The Origins of the Underclass: Part 1." *Atlantic Monthly,* June, 31–35.

——. 1986b. "The Origins of the Underclass: Part 2." *Atlantic Monthly,* July, 54–68.

Lichter, Daniel T. 1997. "Poverty and Inequality among Children." *Annual Review of Sociology* 23:121–45.

Lundgren-Gaveras, Lena. 1996. "The Work–Family Needs of Single Parents: A Comparison of American and Swedish Policy Trends." *Journal of Sociology and Social Welfare* 23:131–47.

Moynihan, Daniel P. 1967. "The Negro Family: The Case for National Action." Pp. 39–132 in *The Moynihan Report and the Politics of Controversy,* edited by L. Rainwater and W. L. Yancy. Cambridge, MA: MIT Press.

Wilson, William Julius, with Kathryn Neckerman. 1987. "Poverty and Family Structure: The Widening Gap Between Evidence and Public Policy Issues." Pp. 63–92 in *The Truly Disadvantaged,* by William Julius Wilson. Chicago: University of Chicago Press.

40

HISPANIC FAMILIES IN POVERTY
Diversity, Context, and Interpretation

ROBERT APONTE

As we approach the 21st century, few societal changes match the significance of the coined phrase "browning of America." By midway in the coming century, "racial and ethnic groups in the U.S. will outnumber whites for the first time" (Henry 1990:28). Hispanics are a key population in this transition. Hispanics are the nation's fastest-growing minority in absolute terms. Indeed, the best available evidence indicates that Hispanics (Latinos) will almost certainly surpass African Americans in numeric strength by 2020, if not sooner.[1] Whether this growing population will obtain its fair share of the American dream is far less certain.

Like black families, Hispanic families have not fared well in recent years. The poverty rate for African American families, for example, stood at approximately 3 of every 10 families in 1991. Only one time since the late 1960s, during the recession-racked early 1980s, have black families recorded a poverty rate higher than 30 percent. Latino families have followed a similar course. Their 1991 poverty rate of 26.5 percent was substantially higher than their record low rate of 19.8 percent, recorded in 1973, and it was also more than three times higher than the 8.8 percent figure registered by whites in 1991.[2] Moreover, the poverty rates for all persons in these groups (without regard to family status) have been higher still (U.S. Bureau of the Census 1992b). Clearly associated with these indicators of deprivation, blacks and Hispanics have experienced rates of joblessness, welfare receipt, and female-headed households substantially in excess of the rates among whites (Tienda 1989; Tienda and Jensen 1988; Wacquant and Wilson 1989; Wilson and Neckerman 1986).

A large body of literature has long shown the importance of disaggregating social and economic indicators among the various Hispanic groups so that trends can be interpreted fruitfully (Aponte 1991; Bean and Tienda 1987; Portes and Truelove 1987). The significance of this is readily apparent when one considers the wide variation in family poverty rates across these groups. For example, whereas Mexican families, the largest group, registered a poverty rate of one in four in 1990 (the latest year for which group-specific data are available), Puerto Rican families, the second largest category, showed a rate of 37.5 percent, highest among all racial or ethnic groups for whom data exist. In contrast, Cuban families, the third largest group among Hispanics and the only additional group for which we have individualized data, showed a 13.8 percent poverty rate for the year (U.S. Bureau of the Census 1991).

Unfortunately, data on the various other Latino groups are difficult to obtain, primarily because of their lower aggregate numbers. However, lack of data does not mean that these groups' experiences have been trouble free. As was forcefully revealed in a report on Hispanics by a leading Washington think-tank, the minimal data available on these groups suggest that many Latinos are undergoing economic distress (Greenstein et al. 1988). Moreover, Waldinger (1989) suggests that Hispanic immigration from countries other than Cuba, Mexico, or the island of Puerto Rico has rapidly increased in recent years. Hence, in the near future, the impact of smaller Hispanic populations is likely to be more systematically gauged.

Making sense of the available data is often no small task. The variation in poverty rates noted earlier, for example, defies commonsense notions. For instance, the standard "human capital" approach, by itself, cannot explain why Mexicans, who speak less English than do Puerto Ricans and are far less educated than are Puerto Ricans (Bean and Tienda 1987; U.S. Bureau of the Census 1991), have a substantially lower poverty rate. Alternatively, a "discrimination" perspective, by itself, falls short of explaining why Puerto Ricans are poorer than blacks, even though they experience far less discrimination (Massey and Bitterman 1985). Such facts suggest that, in addition to disaggregating indicators on these groups, researchers need carefully to interpret trends.

The argument advanced here is that an informed and carefully crafted overview of the circumstances surrounding poor Hispanic families provides ample support for a structural interpretation of their problems. More specifically, lack of opportunities, low and falling wages attached to existing work opportunities, and failure of our educational institutions are the fundamental causes of poverty among Hispanic families, not popular explanations such as the lure of welfare or the dissolution of the family. Although high rates of family dissolution and welfare use among some Hispanic groups cannot be denied, a critical analysis of implicated trends provides a compelling rationale for rejecting the interpretation that such trends are causes, rather than symptoms, of the joblessness and deprivation with which they are associated.

A secondary argument presented here is that assessment of Hispanic poverty requires not only that data be disaggregated, but that indicators be assessed within the context of the groups' distinct patterns of settlement. For example, attention should be focused on items such as the locus and timing of settlement, whether groups enter legally or illegally, as political or economic migrants, and as citizens or noncitizens. Such information is important because the rate and types of economic activities that have prevailed in the United States have varied considerably over time and across regions and urban areas, thereby providing differing opportunities for arriving groups. In addition, incoming groups may vary on such characteristics as their average human, social, or material capital stock, which could easily affect their subsequent levels of well-being.[3]

The following sections present an overview of the settlement patterns of the major Hispanic groups in poverty as well as selected indicators of their poverty-related problems. Such background material underscores the importance of disaggregating the trends and contextualizing the preliminary interpretations. In addition, some key competing explanations for the implicated poverty-related problems are examined and policy directions are offered.

Diversity and Context

To speak of Hispanic poverty in the United States is to speak of the two largest groups — Mexicans and Puerto Ricans — who together account for roughly 75 percent of all Hispanics in the United States. These groups also have the highest rates of poverty. Together they accounted for nearly 80 percent of all Hispanic poor in 1990, whereas Cubans, the next largest group, accounted for only approximately 3 percent of the Hispanic poor that year and approximately 7 percent of all Hispanic families (U.S. Bureau of the Census 1991). In turn, the remaining groups taken together account for only approximately 17 percent of poor Hispanics. Thus, this article focuses primarily on poverty among Mexicans and Puerto Ricans.

Before dismissing the Cubans, however, it is worth emphasizing how their situation underscores the utility of the approach presented here. The circumstances surrounding their entry into the United States relate strongly to their relatively superior levels of living in subsequent years. Indeed, the favorable background characteristics of their initial and major migratory waves, along with the positive reception accorded their arrival, provided Cubans with a far more advantageous base for advancement than that afforded other Latino groups. More specifically, the initial migrations of Cubans were composed almost entirely of well-to-do political refugees fleeing Fidel Castro's revolution. These Cubans were welcomed by the federal government. Their upper- and middle-class backgrounds provided the human-capital potential for success, and their favorable reception by the U.S. government (including nearly $1 billion in expenditures on the "Cuban Refugee Fund") supported and facilitated their upward mobility (Pedraza-Bailey 1985). These unique circumstances have not been shared by most other incoming Latino groups, particularly Mexicans and Puerto Ricans.

The settlement processes of Mexicans and Puerto Ricans have various common features as well as important differences. Shared characteristics include language, economic or labor-migrant status, and relatively low levels of skill, command of English, and formal education. Moreover, these groups generally did not receive special government assistance.

Whereas the settlement of Puerto Ricans on the mainland occurred rapidly, was highly concentrated in a major northern city, and began largely after World War II, the settlement process for Mexicans spanned the entire century, was far less concentrated, and was limited largely to the Southwest. Indeed, Mexicans and Puerto Ricans maintain substantial co-residence in only a few midwestern cities. In addition, Puerto Ricans entered as citizens and were thereby entitled to certain rights that were available to only some Mexicans, in that many Mexicans entered the United States illegally. Finally, the Mexican group far outnumbers the Puerto Rican group.

The number of Puerto Ricans in the mainland United States increased from less than 100,000 at the end of World War II to more than 1 million by 1970 and nearly 2 million by 1980. Most reside in large metropolitan cities of the Northeast, particularly New York, a pattern maintained throughout the past four decades (Bean and Tienda 1987; Moore and Pachon 1985). In contrast, the highly urbanized character of Mexicans today represents the culmination of a shift that began in 1930, a time when Mexicans in the United States were at least half rural and were already approximately 1 million strong (Bean and Tienda 1987). Moreover, whereas roughly 75 percent of all mainland Puerto Ricans resided in central cities in 1987 (latest available data), slightly less than 50 percent of Mexicans resided in central cities (U.S. Bureau of the Census 1989). Finally, whereas rapid immigration by Puerto Ricans has long ceased, Mexican immigration continues at a rapid pace. Therefore, the numeric dominance of Mexicans over Puerto Ricans is likely to increase in the foreseeable future. Indeed, in 1990, approximately 14 million Mexicans lived in the United States (approximately 63 percent of all Hispanics), compared with approximately 2.4 million Puerto Ricans (U.S. Bureau of the Census 1991).

Thus, Puerto Ricans live predominantly in northern areas of the United States, continue to be more highly concentrated in central cities, and currently are augmented by few migrants. Mexicans, on the other hand, are less tied to central cities, tend to live in the Sunbelt, and continue to receive new immigrants, many of whom lack citizenship.

These settlement differences can affect social mobility in several ways. First, the economic well-being of Puerto Ricans hinges on economic conditions in the major northeastern cities, especially New York, and is particularly dependent on the opportunities for unskilled workers in those areas. Work conditions and opportunities have not been favorable in recent decades due to the widely documented decline in manufacturing, trade, and other forms of low-skilled employment in northern inner cities (Kasarda 1983, 1985, 1990; Wacquant and Wilson 1989). Moreover, such jobs have not returned to northern cities (e.g., New York, Boston) whose economies have sharply rebounded. The newer jobs in these areas tend to require more skills or credentials (Kasarda 1983, 1990).

In contrast, the economic fate of Mexicans rests upon the opportunities available in a large array of southwestern cities and their suburbs. These areas have better job prospects for workers with fewer skills than do northern cities. These areas have generally experienced employment growth in low-skilled jobs throughout the entire postwar period (Kasarda 1985, 1990; Wacquant and Wilson 1989).

Social welfare provisions are a second major difference between these areas of settlement. Specifically, Puerto Ricans have settled in the relatively more "generous" states in the North, whereas Mexicans have settled in a band of states that traditionally offer low levels of public assistance. A notable exception to this is California—the state with the largest number of Mexicans. However, many Mexicans in California are ineligible for public assistance because they lack citizenship, and others may not apply because they fear discovery of undocumented persons who live with their families or households. Thus, as a whole, Puerto Ricans receive more public assistance than do Mexicans.

Organization of labor is a third potentially relevant difference between the two areas of settlement. Puerto Ricans entered the more highly protected and unionized labor markets that prevailed in the North. Hence, wages and conditions were generally more favorable (even in nonunion jobs) than in the less organized southwestern states where Mexicans tended to settle. The resulting deficits in compensation endured by employed Mexicans were further compounded by the high number of noncitizens among them. Low wages accepted by illegal aliens tend to exert downward pressure on the wages of other Mexicans as well.

Given these differences in settlement patterns, the following results are likely. Mexicans might be expected to work more steadily but to earn less and be represented by the working poor as opposed to the dependent poor. Puerto Ricans might be expected to earn more but work less and to rely more upon public assistance, though perhaps at the cost of higher rates of family dissolution. In addition, they might be expected to sustain more poverty and to be more represented by the dependent poor as opposed to the working poor.

Statistical indicators on these groups are consistent with such expectations. For example, among men aged 20 years and older, Puerto Ricans had a labor-force participation rate (74.4 percent) more than 10 percentage points lower than that of Mexican men (85 percent) in 1992. In addition, the Mexican men's rate is substantially higher than that of either white (77.8 percent) or black (73.1 percent) men, whereas the Puerto Rican men's rate is lower than the rate of whites and only marginally higher than that of blacks (U.S. Bureau of Labor Statistics 1993). Moreover, the 1992 gap separating the two Hispanic groups is 5 percent greater than the 1977 gap (Newman 1978). Consistent with the indicators on participation, the Mexican men's 1992 unemployment rate (10.4 percent) was four percentage points lower than that of Puerto Rican men (14.4 percent). In addition, Mexican women have higher employment participation (53.6 percent) and lower unemployment (10.4 percent) than do Puerto Rican women (49.0 percent and 11.1 percent, respectively), although both groups show relatively low participation rates when compared with black or white women (U.S. Bureau of Labor Statistics 1993).

Data on other indicators also conform to expectations. Puerto Ricans are substantially poorer than Mexicans. Likewise, the proportion of families headed by women among Puerto Ricans is much greater than that of Mexicans. Data reveal that approximately 43 percent of Puerto Rican families were headed by women without a spouse present in 1991, whereas only 19 percent of Mexican families were so structured. The comparable figure for blacks in 1991 was 46 percent, which parallels the high rate of Puerto Ricans. The 14 percent rate for whites is even lower than that of Mexicans (U.S. Bureau of the Census 1991, 1992b).[4]

Data from the 1988 survey also reveal that poor Mexican families have more members in the work force than do poor Puerto Rican families, whereas a substantially higher proportion of Puerto Rican families receive government assistance. For example, in 1987, approximately 72 percent of all Mexican-origin families in poverty had at least one member in the work force, compared with approximately 24 percent of Puerto Rican families. In contrast, approximately 61 percent of poor white families and 51 percent of poor black families had at least one worker in the family. In addition, 1979 data from the 1980 decennial census (Bean and Tienda 1987) and 1988 data from the 1989 Current Population Survey (Cresce 1992) reveal that, as expected, Puerto Ricans employed full-year and full-time earn, on average, significantly more than do comparably employed Mexicans.

Whereas 72 percent of Puerto Rican families in poverty in 1988 received all of their income from some form of assistance or transfer, only approximately 25 percent of Mexican-origin families received such assistance (U.S. Bureau of the Census 1989). Clearly, impoverished Mexicans epitomize the image of the "working poor," whereas Puerto Ricans in poverty appear to receive a disproportionate amount of welfare assistance. Despite the high levels of "assistance," however, not a single family was lifted over the poverty line and many were left with incomes well below the poverty line (Jencks and Edin 1990; National Social Science and Law Center 1987; U.S. Bureau of the Census 1989).

To summarize, the settlement contexts of the major Latino groups provide important insights for interpreting these groups' varying rankings on indicators of economic well-being. In addition, various preliminary assessments have been outlined. In the following section, hypotheses regarding family poverty of Puerto Ricans and Mexicans are examined in an effort to determine the relative merits of explanations of poverty that emphasizes three distinct factors: changes in family structure, the availability of welfare benefits, and deficiencies in the opportunity structure.

Interpretations

Family poverty, especially poverty among minority families, is often blamed on welfare. A second and related explanation for poverty is that family dissolution and the rise of the single-female-headed family is a major cause of poverty today. These two explanations are highly interrelated, in that many believe that welfare supports family breakups or out-of-wedlock childbearing (in order to qualify for benefits) and thereby indirectly causes poverty. However, such explanations have almost no relevance to the poverty of Mexican families in that relatively few Mexican families are headed by women or receive assistance. Mexicans account for fully 60 percent of all poor Hispanic families; thus, the welfare-as-cause and feminization-of-poverty arguments are weakened when applied to Hispanic families. However, many Puerto Rican families receive welfare and are headed by females. Thus, such arguments may apply to them.

Murray (1984) offers the most systematic elaboration of these views. In *Losing Ground,* Murray argued that the liberalization of welfare during the late 1960s and the hike in AFDC benefit levels at the same time were the fundamental causes of family poverty. Changes in the "rules of the game" made work less beneficial than welfare and encouraged low-income people to avoid both work and marriage in order to reap the benefits of welfare. According to Murray, these factors supported increases in female-headed households, joblessness, and poverty.

Murray's arguments rest on the fact that poverty began to increase, after a long decline, at roughly the same time that social spending (particularly benefit levels) began to increase, the proportion of female-headed households began to rise, and joblessness among blacks shot upward (for Murray, African Americans served as proxies for the poor). In essence, Murray believes that welfare benefits have risen to the point where the disposable income provided by AFDC significantly outweighs that of low-wage work. Consistent with the "rational actor" model of behavior, whereby behavior is determined in large part by costs–benefits calculations on the part of the "actor," lucrative provisions induced low-income parents to forgo or dissolve marriages and to avoid employment so they could collect benefits. Marriage was avoided to ensure eligibility, and work was avoided to maximize gains.

This theory, however, begs the question of why, if welfare payments were so lucrative, did the poor, who jammed the case loads, fail to escape poverty. Murray does not address this issue. Nevertheless, the strength of his argument is that it simultaneously explains rising joblessness, female-headed families, increased use of welfare, and, indirectly, poverty itself.

Numerous studies on the effects of welfare availability or generosity on family structure, however, have failed to support this theory. For example, the incidence of female-headed households across states has not been found to correlate with the corresponding state variations in benefit levels. Indeed, states with benefits set at the lowest levels often produced the highest number of children in female-headed families (Ellwood 1988). Moreover, as the incidence of female-headed families soared during the 1970s and early 1980s, the number of children in the case loads actually decreased, a damning result for the welfare-based theory (Ellwood 1988; Greenstein 1985).

The overall consensus in the literature is that the effects of welfare on family dissolution are relatively weak (U.S. General Accounting Office 1987;

Wilson and Neckerman 1986). Recent work on this issue indicates that welfare's major impact on family structure is in facilitating the formation of independent households by single mothers, who, in lower-benefit areas, tend to live within other households (Ellwood and Bane 1985). Furthermore, it has been noted repeatedly that real welfare benefits (as opposed to government spending) plummeted across the board after the early 1970s, yet joblessness and the formation of female-headed households among blacks continued to rise sharply, contrary to the implications of Murray's arguments (Danziger and Gottschalk 1985; Greenstein 1985; Wilson 1987).

In 1969 and 1970, when AFDC benefits were roughly at their peak levels in real dollars and the basic benefit provided approximately 97 percent of the poverty-line income in New York (where Puerto Ricans are heavily concentrated), less than a quarter of Puerto Rican families were headed by females. By 1987, when the average benefit level had declined approximately 38 percent (nearly 40 percent in New York), the proportion of Puerto Rican female-headed families had increased to 44 percent and both joblessness and poverty had increased (National Social Science and Law Center 1987; Tobier 1984; U.S. Bureau of the Census 1989). Clearly, something other than lucrative welfare benefits must underlie increases in female-headed families among Puerto Ricans.

Although the welfare system may not fuel Puerto Ricans' changing family structure, it underlies much of the group's relative deprivation. In fact, it may be viewed as a major cause of Latino poverty in general, insofar as so many legally entitled and impoverished Hispanic families are left destitute by miserly benefit levels and other equally needy families are denied benefits altogether.

A *structural* explanation provides a more comprehensive view of the poverty problem. This view holds that the fundamental cause of poverty is the economy's inability to generate enough jobs at high-enough wages. Once again, there is little need to make a case for Mexicans. It has already been shown that Mexicans are vastly overrepresented among the working poor. One might ask, however, why Puerto Ricans are underrepresented in the work force. A tentative yet viable explanation is offered by the so-called *mismatch hypothesis*. This hypothesis (Kasarda 1983, 1985, 1990) applies to large, northern cities where Puerto Ricans are concentrated, suggesting that urban poverty is rooted in the movement of manufacturing and other blue-collar employment away from large cities in the Snowbelt. As blue-collar industry moved out of the cities, central-city job growth occurred primarily in white-collar jobs, for which the less-educated minority residents often did not qualify. For example, Kasarda (1990) shows that from 1953 to 1986, New York, Boston, Baltimore, and Philadelphia lost 1.35 million jobs in manufacturing and wholesale/retail trades. Over that same period, the southern and western cities of Atlanta, Houston, Denver, and San Francisco gained nearly 420,000 such jobs. Moreover, in the northern cities, total employment declined after 1970, except in Boston, whereas Sunbelt cities continued to gain jobs, although manufacturing declined slightly in Atlanta, Denver, and San Francisco after 1970.

Although this explanation has received mixed reviews in the abundant literature it has spawned (see Holzer 1991), the well-documented declines in central-city manufacturing and other blue-collar jobs are not at issue. Nor are the correspondingly high rates of joblessness among central-city black workers (virtually the sole focus of these studies up to now). Rather, the arguments against *mismatch,* broadly put, tend to be based on analyses that produce insufficient evidence to link joblessness among African Americans with employment mobility. Generally, these studies suggest that discrimination is a more important cause of joblessness among blacks. However, whereas studies based on data for 1970 or earlier have generally tended to disconfirm the hypothesis, analysis based on more recent periods has tended to support the hypothesis (Holzer 1991). The appropriateness of applying this hypothesis to Puerto Ricans is supported by the fact that Puerto Ricans are more tied to northern cities than are blacks, experience virtually the same high levels of joblessness, and experience an even higher poverty rate despite experiencing less discrimination.[5]

The increase in female-headed households among Puerto Ricans is perhaps not so easily explained. However, the rise in female-headed families is hardly a trend limited to minorities or the poor. For various reasons, but particularly increases in female earnings and changing gender roles, marriages are less stable throughout society (Ellwood 1988; Weitzman 1985). Hence, the question that must be asked is not why such families are forming among Puerto Ricans, but why so many Puerto Rican families (and black families) are at peril in relation to others (e.g., white and Mexican families).

A viable hypothesis, which follows directly from the structural arguments noted above, may be termed the "male marriageable pool index" (MMPI) explanation. Developed by Wilson and Neckerman (1986), this hypothesis suggests that the phenomenal increase in female-headed black families (nearly 50 percent) has been caused by the dramatic increases in joblessness among black men. The joblessness factor, in concert with high rates of incarceration and premature mortality among black men, has depleted the supply of marriageable (i.e., employed) men, thereby fueling the growth in female-headed families. In fact, data indicate that the increase in female-headed families among blacks parallels employment decreases among black men.

Jencks (1988) argued that the highly aggregated MMPI figures exaggerate the relationship between female-headed households and decreasing employment opportunities, because such data work best at younger ages (e.g., younger than 24 years), when men are not likely to marry, whether employed or not. However, a recent analysis examining the argument in the context of specific urban areas found strong support for the hypothesis, even though it focused on black and white women at least 20 years of age (Lichter, LeClare, and McLaughlin 1991). Furthermore, the hypothesis received additional support from a large, multigroup sample. Testa, Astone, Krogh, and Neckerman

(1989) showed that black, white, Mexican, and Puerto Rican men in the poverty areas of Chicago were more likely to marry the mother of their first child if they were employed at the time of conception. These findings are especially important because they show that the hypothesized relationship between marriage and employment holds for groups other than blacks.

Application of this hypothesis to Puerto Ricans, therefore, seems amply justified. Puerto Rican families' high rates of poverty and female-headed households closely parallel the rates among black families. In addition, joblessness among male Puerto Ricans registered at virtually the same rate as among black males in 1992, and both groups have experienced correspondingly long-term declines in employment during the past two decades (Tienda 1989; U.S. Bureau of Labor Statistics 1993; Wilson and Neckerman 1986). Therefore, the unemployment–marriage stability relationship should be considered a viable hypothesis for explaining the prevalence of female-headed households among Puerto Rican families.

Once formed, such families are extremely vulnerable to poverty for obvious reasons. Unless the single parent has an exceptionally high earnings potential, it is virtually impossible to fulfill adequately the dual roles of provider and caretaker, given the high costs of living and child care and the paucity of benefits attached to low-wage work (Ellwood 1988; Jencks and Edin 1990). This is one reason that the most frequent route out of AFDC appears to be marriage or remarriage rather than increased earnings. In turn, the fact that welfare termination is connected to marital status might also explain why minority single mothers are more prevalent than are white single mothers and why minority single mothers tend to remain on welfare longer: After these women become the head of the family (or begin to rely on welfare), their marriage prospects are likely to be lower than those of white women (Ellwood 1988).

A final issue concerns human-capital attainment. Although human-capital credentials do not always provide access to secure employment, their importance should not be undervalued. Not only have unemployment rates been higher for the less educated than for the more educated, but the gap has widened considerably in recent years (Jencks 1991; Kasarda 1990). Of equal importance, the work that is available for unskilled workers is characterized increasingly by low wages. For example, a government report found that since 1979 the number of full-time, full-year workers earning poverty-level wages has been increasing steadily (U.S. Bureau of the Census 1992a).

Accordingly, approximately 23 percent of the heads of poor Hispanic families worked full-time full-year in 1991 (disaggregated data not available). The proportion might have been higher if the recession had not occurred; the economic downturn may have pushed other low-wage heads of households into unemployment. Moreover, the 23 percent figure represents a sharp increase from the group's 1979 figure of 17 percent (U.S. Bureau of the Census 1981, 1992b). Thus, a key factor linking Hispanic families to poverty, whether through unemployment or wage insufficiencies, is the human-capital handicaps of their workers.[6]

But the basis for these deficiencies should not be pinned on the shoulders of poor Hispanics alone. The failure of public policy loom large on this score. The *mis*education of Hispanics (and blacks) is the direct result of such features of the nation's schools as the high levels of segregation by race and class that result in warehousing poor minority students in districts with abysmally low per-capita spending, high dropout rates, chronic shortages in materials, less-qualified teachers, low achievement test scores, and so forth (Breslin and Stier 1987; Griffin and Bagnato 1987; Hess 1986; Spratling and Christoff 1988). In short, the systems' iron-clad jurisdiction boundaries, in combination with school districts' heavy dependence on locally raised revenues, ensure that those with the most needs receive the fewest resources, and vice versa. Small wonder that noted education specialist Jonathan Kozol titled his 1991 book on this topic *Savage Inequalities*.

Implications

The data and interpretations presented here, although far from providing a definitive analysis of Hispanic poverty, nevertheless support various generalizations about the problems and potential solutions. Decreased employment opportunities for the less skilled or educated, severely depressed wages among the employed, restrictive and scanty social benefits, and inequalities in public education are the key proximate causes of poverty among Hispanics. Expanding employment, increasing wages, providing adequate support for those unable to work, and promoting higher levels of human capital attainment for all are major public policy imperatives.

Massive investments are sorely needed in at least three areas. First, employment and wage strategies are needed to ensure an adequate living for all persons who are willing and able to work. This goal can be achieved by hikes in the minimum wage, wage subsidies (e.g., increasing the earned income tax credit), and public employment. Given the decay of much of the nation's infrastructure (West 1990), public employment projects need not amount to meaningless "make-work" endeavors. Second, real educational reform must be implemented. The gross inequities of the nation's educational system must be confronted. Either the poorer schools must be integrated with more elite schools, massive investments made in poor schools, or some combination of both strategies should be pursued. Finally, those persons who are unable to provide for themselves or their families need public support. The widely held beliefs about lucrative welfare benefits and their dependency-producing powers are patently false. Moreover, the miserly levels at which benefits are actually allotted have been shown to be extremely detrimental to recipients (Jencks and Edin 1990).

Helping poor children achieve at school requires more than improving the school systems. Rather, school achievement demands that children be well fed, provided with ample space and materials, and provided with encouragement to work and to succeed. This, in turn, requires that parents have the basic supports that will allow them to nourish and encourage their children. However, the minimal standard of living necessary to ensure such support is exactly what the current mix of programs *deny*!

Child-care provision and adult education and vocational training must be expanded. Among poor and nonpoor alike, family structures are changing, and single-parent families are a reality. These families need both direct and indirect support. Most important, tax policies must be overhauled, the progressive tax structure of the pre-Reagan years restored, and loopholes and other subsidies to the wealthy curtailed (McIntyre 1991; Phillips 1991) so that social investments can be financed without further burdening the working and middle classes. Indeed, as history demonstrates, the vagaries of the market will inevitably provide more for some and less for others. Without adequate compensatory mechanisms in place, poverty will persist and worsen into the 21st century and beyond.

ENDNOTES

1. Typical examples of such projections are provided by Davis, Haub, and Willette (1983) and U.S. Bureau of the Census (1986). The population projections of Hispanics indicate that Hispanics will outnumber blacks by 2020. In 1990, the Hispanic population reached 22.4 million. Moreover, the broader population base in place in 1990 ensures continued rapid growth, even if immigration falters. However, most observers predict accelerated growth throughout the 1990s and beyond (Portes 1992).
2. Data on individual groups that make up the Hispanic population have been published in the *Current Population Reports* series since 1971. However, the quality of the data was not very good before the 1975 report. Even in 1975, data were reported only for Puerto Ricans, Mexicans, and Cubans, and no historical data from the series are available. However, data for these groups are available from the public-use samples for the censuses of 1960, 1970, and 1980. Bean and Tienda (1987) provide a wealth of information on these groups covering these periods.
3. Portes and Borocz (1989) present an elaborate paradigm, called "mode of incorporation," for taking these kinds of factors into account.
4. Several caveats are in order here. First, it must be noted that the reported proportions refer to all families. If consideration is limited to families with children younger than 18, the proportion of families headed by women rises for all groups. Likewise, if consideration is limited to poor families, the corresponding proportions also rise. However, the relative rankings remain unchanged in all these cases. A second caveat concerns the relatively low rate of female-headed families among whites. Those numbers can be misleading because a disproportionate number of intact white families (with children) are actually "reconstituted" families (Ellwood 1988). Whites tend to form more single-parent families than indicated by cross-sectional tabulations. However, many of the single parents marry or remarry and thus are dropped from tabulations.
5. The employment–population ratio for Puerto Rican men aged 20 years and older in 1992 was 63.7 percent, virtually identical to the 63.3 percent figure registered by comparably aged black men that year. The corresponding figures among whites and Mexicans (72.9 percent and 76.1 percent, respectively) were substantially higher.
6. The data on the educational attainment of Hispanics were published in 1991. Data are disaggregated by groups but not by sex. Data show that among Mexicans aged 25 or older, nearly 44 percent had high school diplomas, whereas the comparable

figure for Puerto Ricans was 58 percent (U.S. Bureau of the Census 1992b). Comparable data for blacks and whites in 1992 show much higher educational attainment; approximately 81 percent of whites and 68 percent of blacks held high school diplomas at that time (U.S. Bureau of the Census 1991).

REFERENCES

Aponte, R. 1991. "Urban Hispanic Poverty: Disaggregations and Explanations." *Social Problems* 38:516–28.

Bean, D. and M. Tienda. 1987. *The Hispanic Population of the United States.* New York: Russell Sage Foundation.

Breslin, S. and E. Stier. 1987. *Promoting Poverty: The Shift of Resources Away from Low-Income New York School Districts.* New York: Community Service Society.

Cresce, A. R. 1992. "Hispanic Work Force Characteristics." In *Hispanics in the Workplace,* edited by S. B. Knouse, P. Rosenfeld, and A. L. Culbertson. Newbury Park, CA: Sage.

Danziger, S. and P. Gottschalk. 1985. "The Poverty of *Losing Ground.*" *Challenge* 28(2): 32–38.

Davis, G., C. Haub, and J. Willette. 1983. "U.S. Hispanics: Changing the Face of America." *Population Bulletin* 38(3):1–43.

Ellwood, D. T. 1988. *Poor Support: Poverty in the American Family.* New York: Basic Books.

Ellwood, D. T. and M. J. Bane. 1985. "The Impact of AFDC on Family Structure and Living Arrangements." *Research in Labor Economics* 7:137–207.

Greenstein, R. 1985. "Losing Faith in *Losing Ground.*" *New Republic* 192(12):12–17.

Greenstein, R., K. Porter, I. Shapiro, P. Leonard, and S. Barancik. 1988. *Shortchanged: Recent Developments in Hispanic Poverty, Income, and Employment.* Washington, DC: Center on Budget and Policy Priorities.

Griffin, J. L. and A. Bagnato. 1987. "Poor Getting Poorer in School-Aid System." *Chicago Tribune* (June 14).

Henry, W., III. 1990. "Beyond the Melting Pot." *Time,* April 9, pp. 28–31.

Hess, F. 1986. *Race and Academic Segregation: Relationships with the Dropout Rate.* National School Desegregation Project. Working Paper No. 2. Chicago: University of Chicago.

Holzer, H. J. 1991. "The Spatial Mismatch Hypothesis: What Has the Evidence Shown?" *Urban Studies* 28(1):105–22.

Jencks, C. 1988. "Deadly Neighborhoods." *New Republic* 198(24):23–32.

————. 1991. "Is the American Underclass Growing?" In *The Urban Underclass,* edited by C. Jencks and P. E. Peterson. Washington, DC: Brookings Institution.

Jencks, C. and K. Edin. 1990. "The Real Welfare Problem." *The American Prospect* 1(1):31–50.

Kasarda, J. D. 1983. "Caught in the Web of Change." *Society* 21(1):41–47.

————. 1985. "Urban Change and Minority Opportunities." In *The New Urban Reality,* edited by P. E. Peterson. Washington, DC: Brookings Institution.

————. 1990. "Structural Factors Affecting the Location and Timing of Underclass Growth." *Urban Geography* 11:234–64.

Kozol, J. 1991. *Savage Inequalities.* New York: Crown.

Lichter, D. T., F. B. LeClare, and D. K. McLaughlin. 1991. "Local Marriage Markets and the Marital Behavior of Black and White Women." *American Journal of Sociology* 96:843–67.

McIntyre, R. S. 1991. "How Should We Tax?" *Social Policy* 22(2):2–6.

Massey, D. S. and B. Bitterman. 1985. "Explaining the Paradox of Puerto Rican Segregation." *Social Forces* 64:306–31.

Moore, J. and H. Pachon. 1985. *Hispanics in the United States.* Englewood Cliffs, NJ: Prentice-Hall.

Murray, C. 1984. *Losing Ground: American Social Policy 1950–1980.* New York: Basic Books.

National Social Science and Law Center. 1987. "Adequacy of Current AFDC Need and Payment Standards." *Clearinghouse Review* 21:141–49.

Newman, M. J. 1978. "A Profile of Hispanics in the U.S. Workforce." *Monthly Labor Review* 101(12):3–14.

Pedraza-Bailey, S. 1985. *Political and Economic Migrants in America: Cubans and Mexicans.* Austin: University of Texas Press.

Phillips, K. 1991. *The Politics of Rich and Poor: Wealth and the American Electorate in the Reagan Aftermath.* New York: Random House.

Portes, A. 1992. "Immigration and the Reshaping of America." *Baltimore Sun,* May 13.

Portes, A. and J. Borocz. 1989. "Contemporary Immigration: Theoretical Perspectives on Its Determinants and Modes of Incorporation." *International Migration Review* 23:606–30.

Portes, A. and C. Truelove. 1987. "Making Sense of Diversity: Recent Research on Hispanic Minorities." *Annual Review of Sociology* 13:359–85.

Spratling, C. and C. Christoff. 1988. "Unequal Opportunity." *Detroit Free Press,* March 6.

Testa, M., N. M. Astone, M. Krogh, and K. M. Neckerman. 1989. "Employment and Marriage among Inner City Fathers." *Annals* 501:79–91.

Tienda, M. 1989. "Puerto Ricans and the Underclass Debate." *Annals* 501:105–19.

Tienda, M. and L. Jensen. 1988. "Poverty and Minorities: A Quarter-Century Profile of Color and Socioeconomic Disadvantage." In *Divided Opportunities: Minorities, Poverty, and Social Policy,* edited by G. D. Sandefur and M. Tienda. New York: Plenum Press.

Tobier, E. 1984. *The Changing Face of Poverty: Trends in New York City's Population in Poverty: 1960–1990.* New York: Community Service Society.

U.S. Bureau of Labor Statistics. 1993. *Employment and Earnings* 40(1).

U.S. Bureau of the Census. 1973. *1970 Census of Population.* Vol. 2, Subject Reports: Puerto Ricans in the United States. PC70-2-1E. Washington, DC: Government Printing Office.

————. 1981. *Characteristics of the Population below the Poverty Level: 1979.* Current Population Reports, Series P-60, No. 130. Washington, DC: Government Printing Office.

————. 1986. *Projections of the Hispanic Population: 1983 to 2080.* Current Population Reports, Series P-25, No. 995. Washington, DC: Government Printing Office.

————. 1989. *Poverty in the United States: 1987.* Current Population Reports, Series P-60, No. 163. Washington, DC: Government Printing Office.

————. 1991. *The Hispanic Population in the United States: March 1991.* Current Population Reports, Series P-20, No. 455. Washington, DC: Government Printing Office.

————. 1992a. *Workers with Low Earnings: 1964 to 1990.* Current Population Reports, Series P-60, No. 178. Washington, DC: Government Printing Office.

————. 1992b. *Poverty in the United States: 1991.* Current Population Reports, Series P-60, No. 181. Washington, DC: Government Printing Office.

U.S. General Accounting Office. 1987. *Welfare: Income and Relative Poverty Studies of AFDC Families.* Publication No. HRD 88-9. Washington, DC: Government Printing Office.

Wacquant, L. J. D. and W. J. Wilson. 1989. "Poverty, Joblessness, and the Social Transformation of the Inner City." In *Welfare Policy for the 1990s,* edited by P. H. Cottingham and D. T. Ellwood. Cambridge, MA: Harvard University Press.

Waldinger, R. 1989. "Immigration and Urban Change." *Annual Review of Sociology* 15:359–85.

Weitzman, L. J. 1985. *The Divorce Revolution.* New York: Free Press.

West, J. 1990. *Legacy of Neglect: America's Decaying Roads and Bridges.* Washington, DC: AFL-CIO.

Wilson, W. J. 1987. *The Truly Disadvantaged: The Inner City, the Underclass, and Public Policy.* Chicago: University of Chicago Press.

Wilson, W. J. and K. M. Neckerman. 1986. "Poverty and the Family Structure: The Widening Gap between Evidence and Public Policy Issues." In *Fighting Poverty: What Works and What Doesn't,* edited by S. H. Danziger and D. H. Weinberg. Cambridge, MA: Harvard University Press.

41

IT'S A FAMILY AFFAIR
Women, Poverty, and Welfare

RANDY ALBELDA • CHRIS TILLY

Hating poor women for being poor is all the rage—literally. Radio talk show hosts, conservative think tanks, and many elected officials bash poor single mothers for being too "lazy," too "dependent," and too fertile. Poor mothers are blamed for almost every imaginable economic and social ill under the sun. Largely based on anecdotal information, mythical characterizations, and a recognition that the welfare system just isn't alleviating poverty, legislatures across the land and the federal government are proposing and passing draconian welfare "reform" measures.

It is true that current welfare policies do not work well—but not for the reasons usually presented. Welfare "reform" refuses to address the real issues facing single-mother families and is heavily permeated by myths.

Aid to Families with Dependent Children (AFDC), the government income transfer program for poor non-elder families in the United States, serves only about 5 percent of the population at any given time, with over 90 percent of those receiving AFDC benefits being single mothers and their children. In 1993, 14 million people (two-thirds of them children) in the United States received AFDC. That same year, just under 40 million people were poor. Despite garnering a lion's share of political discussion, AFDC receives a minuscule amount of funding: It accounts for less than 1 percent of the federal budget and less than 3 percent of the state budgets.

Single mothers work. Not only do they do the unpaid work of raising children, they also average the same number of hours in the paid labor force as other mothers do—about 1,000 hours a year (a full-time, year-round job is about 2,000 hours a year).[1] And while close to 80 percent of all AFDC recipients are off in two years, over half of those return at some later point—usually because their wages in the jobs that got them off welfare just didn't match the cost of health care and child care needed so they could keep the jobs. In fact, most AFDC recipients "cycle" between relying on families, work, and AFDC benefits to get or keep their families afloat.[2] That means that, for many single mothers, AFDC serves the same function as unemployment insurance does for higher-paid, full-time workers.

And, contrary to a highly volatile stereotype, welfare mothers, on average, have fewer kids than other mothers. And once on AFDC, they are less likely to have another child.

Poverty and the "Triple Whammy"

Poverty is a persistent problem in the United States. People without access to income are poor. In the United States, most people get access to income by living in a family with one or more wage earners (either themselves or others). Income from ownership (rent, dividends, interest, and profits) provides only a few families with a large source of income. Government assistance is limited — with elders getting the bulk of it. So wages account for about 80 percent of all income generated in the United States. Not surprisingly, people whose labor market activity is limited, or who face discrimination, are the people most at risk for poverty. Children, people of color, and single mothers are most likely to be poor (see Boxes).

In 1993, 46 percent of single-mother families in the United States were living in poverty, but only 9 percent of two-adult families with children were poor.[3]

Why are so many single-mother families poor? Are they lazy, do they lack initiative, or are they just unlucky? The answer to all of these is a resounding "No." Single-mother families have a very hard time generating enough income to keep themselves above the poverty line for a remarkably straightforward reason: One female adult supports the family — and one female adult usually does not earn enough to provide both child-care expenses and adequate earnings.

To spell it out, single mothers face a "triple whammy." First, like all women, when they do paid work they often face low wages — far lower than men with comparable education and experience. In 1992, the median income (the midpoint) for all women who worked full-time was $13,677. That means that about 40 percent of all working women (regardless of their marital status) would not have made enough to support a family of three above the poverty line. Even when women work year-round full-time, they make 70 percent of what men do.

Second, like all mothers, single mothers must juggle paid and unpaid work. Taking care of healthy and, sometimes, sick children, and knowing where they are when at work, requires time and flexibility that few full-time jobs afford. All mothers are more likely to earn less and work less than other women workers because of it.

Finally, *unlike* married mothers, many single mothers must juggle earning income and taking care of children without the help of another adult. Single-mother families have only one adult to send into the labor market. And that same adult must also make sure children get through their day.

The deck is stacked — but not just for single mothers. All women with children face a job market which has little sympathy for their caregiving responsibilities and at the same time places no economic value on their time spent at home. The economic activity of raising children is one that no soci-

BOX 1
Who's Poor in the United States?

In 1993, one person in six was living below the official poverty line. The poverty line is an income threshold determined annually by the Department of Commerce's Census Bureau. The dollar amount is based on the price-adjusted determination of the 1960s cash value of a minimum adequate diet for families of different sizes multiplied by three (at the time, budget studies indicated that low-income families spent one-third of their incomes on food). In 1993, the poverty threshold for a family of four is about $11,631.

While 10 percent of all men are poor, 16 percent of women and 25 percent—a full quarter—of all children in the United States are poor. Further, 36 percent of all black persons and 34 percent of Latinos are poor, versus 17 percent of Asians and 13 percent of white persons. Does education help stave off poverty? Yes—but not very evenly. Consider the table in Box 2. Those with low levels of education are much more likely to be poor—but gender matters. For men, getting a high school diploma cuts the chances of being poor by half—20 percent versus 10 percent. For women, poverty rates are more than halved by getting that degree, but the rates are still high—15 percent. For women to lower their likelihood of poverty to that of men with high school diplomas means getting some college education.

**Percent Poor Persons in the United States
(All Ages) by Selected Characteristics, 1993**

	All	Men	Women	Children
All	**16.4%**	**10.2%**	**16.1%**	**25.2%**
By race				
White	13.2%	8.6%	13.2%	19.8%
Black	35.9%	20.6%	34.5%	50.8%
Asian	17.0%	14.3%	17.4%	20.0%
By ethnicity				
Non-Latino	14.5%	8.9%	14.5%	22.0%
Latino	33.7%	22.2%	32.5%	45.2%
By residence				
City	24.1%	14.4%	22.6%	38.8%
Suburb	11.4%	7.1%	11.2%	17.4%
Rural	18.1%	11.8%	18.4%	25.9%

Source: U.S. Census Bureau, Current Population Survey, 1994.

ety can do without. In our society, we do not recognize it as work worth paying mothers for. For a married mother, this contradiction is the "double day." For a single mother, the contradiction frequently results in poverty for her and her children.

BOX 2
Poverty Rates for Adults in the United States by Educational Attainment, 1993

Years of Education	All Adults	Men	Women
8 or less	31.6%	26.4%	36.7%
9–11	27.5%	19.9%	34.3%
12	13.1%	10.0%	15.6%
13–15	9.0%	6.8%	10.9%
16	4.3%	3.8%	4.8%
17+	2.9%	2.8%	3.1%

Source: U.S. Census Bureau, Current Population Survey, 1994.

Denying the Real Problems

The lack of affordable childcare, the large number of jobs that fail to pay living wages, and the lack of job flexibility are the real problems that face all mothers (and increasingly everyone). For single mothers, these problems compound into crisis.

But instead of tackling these problems head-on, politicians and pundits attack AFDC. Why? One reason is that non-AFDC families themselves are becoming more desperate and resent the limited assistance that welfare provides to the worst-off. With men's wages falling over the last 30 years, fewer and fewer families can get by with only one wage earner. The government is not providing help for many low-income families who are struggling but are still above the AFDC eligibility threshold. This family "speed-up" has helped contribute to the idea that if both parents in a two-parent household can work (in order to be poor), then all AFDC recipients should have to work too.

Instead of facing the real problems, debates about welfare reform are dominated by three dead ends. First, politicians argue that single mothers must be made to work in the paid labor market. But most single mothers already work as much as they can. Studies confirm that AFDC recipients already do cycle in and out of the labor force. Further, as surveys indicate, mothers receiving AFDC would like to work. The issue is not whether or not to work, but whether paid work is available, how much it pays, and how to balance work and child care.

Second, there is a notion of replacing the social responsibilities of government assistance with individual "family" responsibilities: Make men pay child support, demand behavioral changes of AFDC recipients, or even pressure single women to get married. While child support can help, for most single mothers it offers a poor substitute for reliable government assistance. Penalizing women and their children for ascribed behaviors (such as having more children to collect welfare) that are supported by anecdotes but not facts is at best mean-spirited.

Third, there is an expectation that people only need support for a limited amount of time—many states and some versions of federal welfare reform limit families to 24 months of aid over some period of time (from a lifetime to five years). Yet limiting the amount of time women receive AFDC will not reduce or limit the need for support. Children do not grow up in 24 months, nor will many women with few skills and little education necessarily become job ready. But more important, many women who do leave AFDC for the workplace will not make enough to pay for child care or the health insurance they need to go to work.

In short, welfare "reform" that means less spending and no labor market supports will do little beyond making poor women's lives more miserable.

Beyond Welfare Reform

What could be done instead? Welfare reform in a vacuum can solve only a small part of the problem. To deal with poverty among single-mother families, to break the connection between gender and poverty, requires changing the world of work, socializing the costs of raising children, and providing low-wage supports.

If we as a nation are serious about reducing the poverty of women and children, we need to invest in seven kinds of institutional changes:

- *Create an income-maintenance system that recognizes the need for full-time child care.* Policies that affect families must acknowledge the reality of children's needs. To truly value families means to financially support those (women or men) who must provide full-time child care at home or to provide dependable, affordable, and caring alternative sources of child care for those who work outside the home.
- *Provide support for low-wage workers.* If leaving welfare and taking a job means giving up health benefits and child-care subsidies, the loss to poor families can be devastating. Although high-salary workers receive (or can afford) these benefits, low-wage workers often don't. Government should provide these supports; universal health care and higher earned income tax credits (EITC) are a first step in the right direction.
- *Close the gender pay gap.* One way to achieve pay equity is to require employers to reevaluate the ways that they compensate comparable skills. Poor women need pay equity the most, but all women need it. Another way to close the pay gap is to increase the minimum wage. Most minimum-wage workers are women. An increase from the current $4.25 an hour to $5.50 would bring the minimum wage to 50 percent of the average wage.
- *Create jobs.* Create the opportunity to work, for poor women and poor men as well. Full employment is an old idea that still makes sense.

- *Create jobs that don't assume you have a "wife" at home to perform limitless unpaid work.* It's not just the welfare system that has to come to terms with family needs; it's employers as well. With women making up 46 percent of the workforce—and men taking on more child-care responsibilities as well—a change in work styles is overdue.
- *Make education and training affordable and available for all.* In an economy where the premium on skills and education is increasing, education and training are necessary for young people and adults, women and men.
- *Fix the tax structure.* Many of these proposals require government spending consistent with the ways our industrial counterparts spend money. Taxes must be raised to pay for these programs: The alternative—not funding child allowances, health care, and training—will prove more costly to society in the long run. But it is critically important to make the programs universal and to fund them with a *fairer* tax system. Federal, state, and local governments have taxed middle- and low-income families for too long without assuring them basic benefits. Taxes paid by the wealthiest families as a percentage of their income have fallen dramatically over the last 15 years, while the burden on the bottom 80 percent has risen; it's time to reverse these trends.

The changes proposed are sweeping, but no less so than those proposed by the Republican Contract with America. With one out of every four children in this nation living in poverty, all our futures are at stake.

ENDNOTES

1. These data, and others throughout the paper, were calculated by the authors using current population survey tapes.
2. Five recent studies have looked at welfare dynamics and come to these conclusions. LaDonna Pavetti, "The Dynamics of Welfare and Work: Exploring the Process by Which Young Women Work Their Way Off Welfare," paper presented at the APPAM Annual Research Conference, 1992; Kathleen Harris, "Work and Welfare Among Single Mothers in Poverty," *American Journal of Sociology* 99, no. 2 (September 1993): 317–52; Roberta Spalter-Roth, Beverly Burr, Heidi Hartmann, and Lois Shaw, "Welfare That Works: The Working Lives of AFDC Recipients," Institute for Women's Policy Research, 1995; Rebecca Blank and Patricia Ruggles, "Short-Term Recidivism Among Public Assistance Recipients," *American Economic Review*, 84, no. 2 (May 1994): 49–53; and Peter David Brandon, "Vulnerability to Future Dependence Among Former AFDC Mothers," Institute for Research on Poverty discussion paper DP1005-95, University of Wisconsin, Madison, Wis., 1995.
3. U.S. Department of Commerce, Census Bureau, "Income, Poverty and Valuation of Noncash Benefits," *Current Population Reports*, 1995, pp. 60–188, p. D-22.

42

RACHEL AND HER CHILDREN
Homeless Families in America

JONATHAN KOZOL

He was a carpenter. She was a woman many people nowadays would call old-fashioned. She kept house and cared for their five children while he did construction work in New York City housing projects. Their home was an apartment in a row of neat brick buildings. She was very pretty then, and even now, worn down by months of suffering, she has a lovely, wistful look. She wears blue jeans, a yellow jersey, and a bright red ribbon in her hair—"for luck," she says. But luck has not been with this family for some time.

They were a happy and chaotic family then. He was proud of his acquired skills. "I did carpentry. I painted. I could do wallpapering. I earned a living. We spent Sundays walking with our children at the beach." They lived near Coney Island. That is where this story will begin.

"We were at the boardwalk. We were up some. We had been at Nathan's. We were eating hot dogs."

He's cheerful when he recollects that afternoon. The children have long, unruly hair. They range in age from two to ten. They crawl all over him— exuberant and wild.

Peter says that they were wearing summer clothes: "Shorts and sneakers. Everybody was in shorts."

When they were told about the fire, they grabbed the children and ran home. Everything they owned had been destroyed.

"My grandmother's china," she says. "Everything." She adds: "I had that book of gourmet cooking . . ."

What did the children lose?

"My doggy," says one child. Her kitten, born three days before, had also died.

Peter has not had a real job since. "Not since the fire. I had tools. I can't replace those tools. It took me years of work." He explains he had accumulated tools for different jobs, one tool at a time. Each job would enable him to add another tool to his collection. "Everything I had was in that fire."

They had never turned to welfare in the twelve years since they'd met and married. A social worker helped to place them in a homeless shelter called the Martinique Hotel. When we meet, Peter is thirty. Megan is twenty-eight. They have been in this hotel two years.

She explains why they cannot get out: "Welfare tells you how much you can spend for an apartment. The limit for our family is $366. You're from Boston. Try to find a place for seven people for $366 in New York City. You can't do it. I've been looking for two years."

The city pays $3,000 monthly for the two connected rooms in which they live. She shows me the bathroom. Crumbling walls. Broken tiles. The toilet doesn't work. There is a pan to catch something that's dripping from the plaster. The smell is overpowering.

"I don't see any way out," he says. "I want to go home. Where can I go?"

A year later I'm in New York. In front of a Park Avenue hotel I'm facing two panhandlers. It takes a moment before I can recall their names.

They look quite different now. The panic I saw in them a year ago is gone. All five children have been taken from them. Having nothing left to lose has drained them of their desperation.

The children have been scattered—placed in various foster homes. "White children," Peter says, "are in demand by the adoption agencies."

Standing here before a beautiful hotel as evening settles in over New York, I'm reminded of the time before the fire when they had their children and she had her cookbooks and their children had a dog and cat. I remember the words that Peter used: "We were up some. We had been at Nathan's." Although I am not a New Yorker, I know by now what Nathan's is: a glorified hot-dog stand. The other phrase has never left my mind.

Peter laughs. "Up some?"

The laughter stops. Beneath his streetwise manner he is not a hardened man at all. "It means," he says, "that we were happy."

By the time these words are printed there will be almost 500,000 homeless children in America. If all of them were gathered in one city, they would represent a larger population than that of Atlanta, Denver, or St. Louis. Because they are scattered in a thousand cities, they are easily unseen. And because so many die in infancy or lose the strength to struggle and prevail in early years, some will never live to tell their stories.

Not all homeless children will be lost to early death or taken from their parents by the state. Some of their parents will do better than Peter and Megan. Some will be able to keep their children, their stability, their sense of worth. Some will get back their vanished dreams. A few will find jobs again, and some may even find a home they can afford. Many will not.

Why are so many people homeless in our nation? What has driven them to the streets? What hope have they to reconstruct their former lives?

The answers will be told in their own words.

Mr. Allesandro is too shaken to attempt to hide his frailties from me. He tells me: "When you're running scared you do some things you'd rather not . . ." He does not regard himself as saint or martyr. There are virtues, feelings and commitments he has forfeited during this long ordeal. Love is not one of them. His desperation for his son and daughters and his adoration of his mother are as solid and authentic as the marble pillars of the Martinique Hotel. The authenticity of love deserves some mention in discussion of the homeless.

Houses can be built without a number of ingredients that other ages viewed as indispensable. Acrylics, plastics and aluminum may substitute for every substance known to nature. Parental love cannot be synthesized. Even the most earnest and methodical foster care demonstrates the limits of synthetic tenderness and surrogate emotion. So it seems of keen importance to consider any ways, and *every* way, by which a family, splintered, jolted and imperiled though it be by loss of home and subsequent detention in a building like the Martinique, may nonetheless be given every possible incentive to remain together.

The inclination to judge harshly the behavior of a parent under formidable stress seems to be much stronger than the willingness to castigate the policies that undermine the competence and ingenuity of many of these people in the first place.

"Men can be unequal in their needs, in their honor, in their possessions," writes historian Michael Ignatieff, "but also in their rights to judge others." The king's ultimate inequality, he says, "is that he is never judged." An entire industry of scholarship and public policy exists to judge the failing or defective parent; if we listen to some of these parents carefully we may be no less concerned by their impaired abilities, but we may be less judgmental or, if we remain compelled to judge, we may redirect our energies in more appropriate directions.

New Year's Eve.

She stalks into the room. Her eyes are reddened and her clothes in disarray. She wears a wrinkled and translucent nightgown. On her feet: red woolen stockings. At her throat: a crucifix. Over her shoulders is a dark and heavy robe. Nothing I have learned in the past week prepared me for this apparition.

She cries. She weeps. She paces left and right and back and forth. Pivoting and turning suddenly to face me. Glaring straight into my eyes. A sudden halt. She looks up toward the cracked and yellowish ceiling of the room. Her children stand around her in a circle. Two little girls. A frightened boy. They stare at her, as I do, as her arms reach out—for what? They snap like snakes and coil back. Her hair is gray—a stiff and brushlike Afro.

Angelina is twelve years old, Stephen is eleven, Erica is nine. The youngest child, eleven months, is sitting on the floor. A neighbor's child, six years old, sits in my lap and leans her head against my chest; she holds her arms around my neck. Her name or nickname (I do not know which) is Raisin. When she likes she puts her fingers on my mouth and interrupts the conversation with a tremolo of rapid words. There are two rooms. Rachel disappears into the second room, then returns and stands, uneasy, by the door.

Angie: "Ever since August we been livin' here. The room is either very hot or freezin' cold. When it be hot outside it's hot in here. When it be cold outside we have no heat. We used to live with my aunt but then it got too crowded there so we moved out. We went to welfare and they sent us to the shelter. Then they shipped us to Manhattan. I'm scared of the elevators. 'Fraid they be stuck. I take the stairs."

Raisin: "Elevator might fall down and you would die."

Rachel: "It's unfair for them to be here in this room. They be yellin'. Lots of times I'm goin' to walk out. Walk out on the street and give it up. No, I don't do it. BCW [Bureau of Child Welfare] come to take the children. So I make them stay inside. Once they walk outside that door they are in danger."

Angie: "I had a friend Yoki. They was tryin' to beat her. I said: 'Leave her.' They began to chase me. We was runnin' to the door. So we was runnin'. I get to the door. The door was stuck. I hit my eye and it began to bleed. So I came home and washed the blood. Me and my friends sat up all night and prayed. Prayin' for me. 'Dear Lord, can you please help me with my eye? If you do I promise to behave.' I was askin' God why did this happen. I wish someone in New York could help us. Put all of the money that we have together and we buy a building. Two or three rooms for every family. Everybody have a kitchen. Way it is, you frightened all the time. I think this world is coming to the end."

Stephen: "This city is rich."

Angie: "Surely is!"

Erica: "City and welfare, they got something goin'. Pay $3,000 every month to stay in these here rooms . . ."

Rachel: "I believe the City Hall got something goin' here. Gettin' a cut. They got to be. My children, they be treated like chess pieces. Send all of that money off to Africa? You hear that song? They're not thinking about people starvin' here in the United States. I was thinkin': Get my kids and all the other children here to sing, 'We are the world. We live here too.' How come do you care so much for people you can't see? Ain't we the world? Ain't we a piece of it? We are so close they be afraid to see. Give us a shot at something. We are something! Ain't we *something*? I'm depressed. But we are *something*! People in America don't want to see."

Angie: "Christmas is sad for everyone. We have our toys. That's
           not the reason why. They givin' you toys and that do help.
           I would rather that we have a place to be."

Erica: "I wrote a letter to Santa Claus. Santa say that he don't have
           the change."

Raisin: "I saw Santa on the street. Then I saw Santa on another
           street. I pulled his beard and he said something nasty."

Angie: "There's one thing I ask: a home to be in with my mother.
           That was my only wish for Christmas. But it could not be."

Raisin: "I saw Mr. Water Bug under my mother's bed. Mr. Rat be
           livin' with us too."

Angie: "It's so cold right now you got to use the hot plate. Plug it
           in so you be warm. You need to have a hot plate. Are you
           goin' to live on cold bologna all your life?"

Raisin: "Mr. Rat came in my baby sister's crib and bit her. Nobody
           felt sorry for my sister. Then I couldn't go to sleep. I started
           crying. All of a sudden I pray and went to sleep and then I
           woke up in the mornin', make my bed, and took a bath, and
           ate, and went to school. So I came back and did my home-
           work. And all of a sudden there was something *irritatin'* at
           my hand. I looked out the window and the moon was goin'
           up. And then—I had a dream. I went to sleep and I was
           dreamin' and I dreamed about a witch that bit me. I felt *dead.*
           When I woke back up I had a headache."

Angie: "School is bad for me. I feel ashamed. They know we're not
           the same. My teacher do not treat us all the same. They know
           which children live in the hotel."

Erica: "My teacher isn't like that. She treats all of us the same. We
           all get smacked. We all get punished the same way."

Stephen: "I'm in sixth grade. When I am a grown-up I be a computer."

Erica: "You're in the fifth. You lie."

Raisin: "When I grow up I want to be multiplication and subtraction
           and division."

Angie: "Last week a drug addict tried to stab me. With an ice pick.
           Tried to stab my mother too. Older girls was botherin' us.
           They try to make us fight. We don't fight. We don't start fires.
           They just pickin' on us. We ran home and got our mother.
           They ran home and got their mother."

Raisin: "Those girls upstairs on the ninth floor, they be bad. They
           sellin' crack."

Erica: "Upstairs, ninth floor, nine-o-five, they sellin' crack."

Raisin: "A man was selling something on the street. He had some
           reefers on him and the po-lice caught him and they took him
           to the jail. You know where the junkies put the crack? Put
           the crack inside the pipe. Smoke it like that. They take a

torch and burn the pipe and put it in their mouth. They go like this." [Puffs.]

I ask: "Why do they do it?"

Erica: "Feel good! Hey! Make you feel fine!"

Angie: "This girl I know lives in a room where they sell drugs. One day she asks us do we want a puff. So we said: 'No. My mother doesn't let us do it.' One day I was walkin' in the hall. This man asked me do I want some stuff. He said: 'Do you want some?' I said no and I ran home."

Raisin: "One day my brother found these two big plastic bags inside his teddy bear. Po-lice came up to my room and took that teddy bear." [She's interrupted.] "I ain't finished! And they took it. One day we was by my uncle's car and this man came and he said: 'Do you want some?' We said no. We told my uncle and he went and found the man and he ran to the bar and went into the women's bathroom in the bar. And so we left."

Angie: "I think this world is ending. Yes. Ending. Everybody in this city killin' on each other. Countries killin' on each other. Why can't people learn to stick together? It's no use to fightin'. Fightin' over nothin'. What they fightin' for? A flag! I don't know what we are fightin' for. President Reagan wants to put the rockets on the moon. What's he doin' messin' with the moon? If God wanted man and woman on the moon He would of put us there. They should send a camera to the moon and feed the people here on earth. Don't go messin' there with human beings. Use that money to build houses. Grow food! Buy seeds! Weave cloth! Give it to the people in America!"

Erica: "When we hungry and don't have no food we borrow from each other. Her mother [Raisin's] give us food. Or else we go to Crisis. In the mornin' when we wake up we have a banana or a cookie. If the bus ain't late we have our breakfast in the school. What I say to President Reagan: Give someone a chance! I believe he be a selfish man. Can't imagine how long he been president."

Raisin: "Be too long."

Angie: "Teacher tell us this be a democracy. I don't know. I doubt it. Rich people, couldn't they at least give us a refund?"

Raisin: "This man say his son be gettin' on his nerves. He beat his little son 'bout two years old. A wooden bat. He beat him half to death. They took him to the hospital and at five-thirty he was dead. A little boy. [Interrupted.] Let me talk!"

Erica: "The little boy. He locked himself into the bathroom. He was scared. After he died police came and his father went to jail. His mother, she went to the store."

Raisin, in a tiny voice: "People fight in here and I don't like it. Why
          do they do it? 'Cause they're sad. They fight over the world.
          I ain't finished!"
   Erica: "One time they was two cops in the hall. One cop pulled his
          gun and he was goin' shoot me. He said did I live there? I said
          no. So I came home."
   Raisin: "I was in this lady room. She be cryin' because her baby died.
          He had [mispronounced] pneumonia. He was unconscious
          and he died." [Soft voice:] "Tomorrow is my birthday."

The children are tended by a friend. In the other bedroom, Rachel, who
is quieter now, paces about and finally sits down.

"Do you know why there's no carpet in the hall? If there was a carpet it
would be on fire. Desperate people don't have no control. You have to sleep
with one eye open. Tell the truth, I do not sleep at night.

"Before we lived here we were at the Forbell shelter [barracks shelter on
Forbell Street in Brooklyn]. People sleep together in one room. You sleep
across. You have to dress in front of everybody. Men and women. When you
wake, some man lookin' at you puttin' on your clothes. Lookin' at your children too. Angelina, she be only twelve years old . . .

"There's one thing. My children still are pure. They have a concept of life.
Respect for life. But if you don't get 'em out of here they won't have anything
for long. If you get 'em out right now. But if you don't . . . My girls are innocent still. They are unspoiled. Will they be that way for long? Try to keep 'em
in the room. But you can't lock 'em up for long.

"When we moved here I was forced to sign a paper. Everybody has to do
it. It's a promise that you will not cook inside your room. So we lived on cold
bologna. Can you feed a child on that? God forgive me but nobody shouldn't
have to live like this. I can't even go downstairs and get back on the elevator.
Half the time it doesn't work. Since I came into this place my kids begun to
get away from me."

There's a crucifix on the wall. I ask her: "Do you pray?"

"I don't pray! Pray for what? I been prayin' all my life and I'm still here.
When I came to this hotel I still believed in God. I said: 'Maybe God can help
us to survive.' I lost my faith. My hopes. And everything. Ain't nobody—no
God, no Jesus—gonna help us in no way.

"God forgive me. I'm emotional. I'm black. I'm in a blackness. Blackness
is around me. In the night I'm scared to sleep. In the mornin' I'm worn out.
I don't eat no breakfast. I don't drink no coffee. If I eat, I eat one meal a day.
My stomach won't allow me. I have ulcers. I stay in this room. I hide. This
room is safe to me. I am afraid to go outside.

"If I go out, what do I do? People drink. Why do they drink? A person
gets worn out. They usin' drugs. Why they use drugs? They say: 'Well, I won't
think about it now.' Why not? You ain't got nothin' else to do, no place to go.
'Where I'm gonna be tomorrow or the next day?' They don't know. All they

know is that they don't have nothin'. So they drink. And some of them would rather not wake up. Rather be dead. That's right.

"Most of us are black. Some Puerto Rican. Some be white. They suffer too. Can you get the government to know that we exist? I know that my children have potential. They're intelligent. They are smart. They need a chance. There's nothin' wrong with them for now. But not for long. My daughter watches junkies usin' needles. People smokin' crack in front a them. Screwin' in front a them. They see it all. They see it everywhere. What is a man and woman gonna do when they are all in the same room?

"I met a girl the other day. She's twelve years old. Lives on the fourteenth floor. She got a baby the same age as mine. Her mother got five children of her own. I don't want my daughter havin' any baby. She's a child. Innocent. Innocent. No violence. She isn't bitter. But she's scared. You understand? This is America. These children growin' up too fast. We have no hope. And you know why? Because we all feel just the same way deep down in our hearts. Nowhere to go . . . I'm not a killer. My kids ain't no killers. But if they don't learn to kill they know they're goin' to die.

"They didn't go to school last week. They didn't have clean clothes. Why? Because the welfare messed my check. It's supposed to come a week ago. It didn't come. I get my check today. I want my kids to go to school. They shouldn't miss a day. How they gonna go to school if they don't got some clothes? I couldn't wash. I didn't have the money to buy food.

"Twice the welfare closed my case. When they do it you are s'posed to go for a fair hearing. Take some papers, birth certificates. So I went out there in the snow. Welfare worker wasn't there. They told me to come back. Mister, it ain't easy to be beggin'. I went to the Crisis. And I asked her, I said, 'Give me somethin' for the kids to eat. Give me *somethin'*! Don't turn me away when I am sittin' here in front of you and askin' for your help!' She said she had nothin'. So my kids went out into the street. That's right! Whole night long they was in Herald Square panhandlin'. Made five dollars. So we bought bologna. My kids is good to me. We had bread and bologna.

"Welfare, they are not polite. They're personal. 'Did you do this? Did you do that? Where your husband at?' Understand me? 'Cause they sittin' on the other side of this here desk, they think we're stupid and we do not understand when we're insulted. 'Oh, you had another baby?' Yeah! I had another baby! What about it? Are you goin' to kill that baby? I don't say it, but that's what I feel like sayin'. You learn to be humble.

"I'm here five miserable months. So I wonder: Where I'm goin'? Can't the mayor give us a house? A part-time job? I am capable of doin' *somethin'*.

"You go in the store with food stamps. You need Pampers. You're not s'posed to use the stamps for Pampers. Stores will accept them. They don't care about the law. What they do is make you pay a little extra. They know you don't have no choice. So they let you buy the Pampers for two dollars extra.

"Plenty of children livin' here on nothin' but bread and bologna. Peanut butter. Jelly. Drinkin' water. You buy milk. I bought one gallon yesterday. Got *this* much left. They drink it fast. Orange juice, they drink it fast. End up drinkin' Kool Aid.

"Children that are poor are used like cattle. Cattle or horses. They are owned by welfare. They know they are bein' used—for what? Don't *use* them! Give 'em somethin'!

"In this bedroom I'm not sleepin' on a bed. They won't give me one. You can see I'm sleepin' on a box spring. I said to the manager: "I need a bed instead of sleepin' on a spring.' Maid give me some blankets. Try to make it softer."

The Bible by her bed is opened to the Twenty-third Psalm.

"I do believe. God forgive me. I believe. He's there. But when He sees us like this, I am wonderin' where is He? I am askin': Where the hell He gone?

"Before they shipped us here we lived for five years in a basement. Five years in a basement with no bathroom. One small room. You had to go upstairs two floors to use the toilet. No kitchen. It was fifteen people in five rooms. Sewer kept backing up into the place we slept. Every time it flooded I would have to pay one hundred dollars just to get the thing unstuck. There were all my children sleepin' in the sewage. So you try to get them out and try to get them somethin' better. But it didn't get no better. I came from one bad place into another. But the difference is this is a place where I cannot get out.

"If I can't get out of here I'll give them up. I have asked them: 'Do you want to go away?' I love my kids and, if I did that, they would feel betrayed. They love me. They don't want to go. If I did it, I would only do it to protect them. They'll live anywhere with me. They're innocent. Their minds are clean. They ain't corrupt. They have a heart. All my kids love people. They love life. If they got a dime, a piece of bread, they'll share it. Letting them panhandle made me cry. I had been to welfare, told the lady that my baby ain't got Pampers, ain't got nothin' left to eat. I got rude and noisy and it's not my style to do that but you learn that patience and politeness get you nowhere.

"When they went out on the street I cried. I said: 'I'm scared. What's gonna happen to them?' But if they're hungry they are goin' to do *something*. They are gonna find their food from somewhere. Where I came from I was fightin' for my children. In this place here I am fightin' for my children. I am tired of fightin'. I don't want to fight. I want my kids to live in peace.

"I was thinkin' about this. If there was a place where you could sell part of your body, where they buy an arm or somethin' for a thousand dollars, I would do it. I would do it for my children. I would give my life if I could get a thousand dollars. What would I lose? I lived my life. I want to see my children grow up to live theirs.

"A lot of women do not want to sell their bodies. This is something that good women do not want to do. I will sell mine. I *will*. I will solicit. I will prostitute if it will feed them."

I ask: "Would you do it?"

"Ain't no 'would I?' I would do it." Long pause . . . "Yes. I *did*.

"I had to do it when the check ain't come. Wasn't no one gonna buy my arm for any thousand dollars. But they's plenty gonna pay me twenty dollars for my body. What was my choice? Leave them out there on the street, a child like Angelina, to panhandle? I would take my life if someone found her dead somewhere. I would go crazy. After she did it that one time I was ashamed. I cried that night. All night I cried and cried. So I decided I had one thing left. In the mornin' I got up out of this bed. I told them I was goin' out. Out in the street. Stand by the curb. It was a cold day. Freezin'! And my chest is bad. I'm thirty-eight years old. Cop come by. He see me there. I'm standin' out there cryin'. Tells me I should go inside. Gives me three dollars. 'It's too cold to be outside.' Ain't many cops like that. Not many people either . . .

"After he's gone a man come by. Get in his car. Go with him where he want. Takin' a chance he crazy and he kill me. Wishin' somehow that he would.

"So he stop his car. And I get in. I say a price. That's it. Go to a room. It's some hotel. He had a lot of money so he rented a deluxe. Asked me would I stay with him all night. I tell him no I can't 'cause I have kids. So, after he done . . . whatever he did . . . I told him that I had to leave. Took out a knife at me and held it at my face. He made me stay. When I woke up next day I was depressed. Feel so guilty what I did. I feel real scared. I can understand why prostitutes shoot drugs. They take the drugs so they don't be afraid.

"When he put that knife up to my throat, I'm thinkin' this: What is there left to lose? I'm not goin' to do any better in this life. If I be dead at least my kids won't ever have to say that I betrayed them. I don't like to think like that. But when things pile up on you, you do. 'I'm better if I'm dead.'

"So I got me twenty dollars and I go and buy the Pampers for the baby and three dollars of bologna and a loaf of bread and everyone is fed.

"That cross of Jesus on the wall I had for seven years. I don't know if I believe or not. Bible say that Jesus was God's son. He died for us to live here on this earth. See, I believe—Jesus was innocent. But, when He died, what was it for? He died for nothin'. Died in vain. He should a let us die like we be doin'—we be dyin' all the time. We dyin' every day.

"God forgive me. I don't mean the things I say. God had one son and He gave His son. He gave him up. I couldn't do it. I got four. I could not give any one of them. I couldn't do it. God could do it. Is it wrong to say it? I don't know if Jesus died in vain."

She holds the Bible in her hands. Crying softly. Sitting on the box spring in her tangled robe.

"They laid him in a manger. Right? Listen to me. I didn't say that God forsaken us. I am confused about religion. I'm just sayin' evil overrules the good. So many bad things goin' on. Lot of bad things right here in this buildin'. It's not easy to believe. I don't read the Bible no more 'cause I don't find no more hope in it. I don't believe. But yet and still . . . I know these words." She reads aloud: "'Lie down in green pastures . . . leadeth me beside still waters . . . restores my soul . . . I shall not want.'

"All that I want is somethin' that's my own. I got four kids. I need four plates, four glasses, and four spoons. Is that a lot? I know I'm poor. Don't have no bank account, no money, or no job. Don't have no nothin'. No foundation. Then and yet my children have a shot in life. They're innocent. They're pure. They have a chance." She reads: "'I shall not fear . . .' I fear! A long, long time ago I didn't fear. Didn't fear for nothin'. I said God's protectin' me and would protect my children. Did He do it?

"Yeah. I'm walkin'. I am walkin' in the wilderness. That's what it is. I'm walkin'. Did I tell you that I am an ex-drug addict? Yeah. My children know it. They know and they understand. I'm walkin'. Yeah!"

The room is like a chilled cathedral in which people who do not believe in God ask God's forgiveness. "How I picture God is like an old man who speaks different languages. His beard is white and He has angels and the instruments they play are white and everything around is white and there is no more sickness, no more hunger for nobody. No panhandlin'. No prostitutes. No drugs. I had a dream like that.

"There's no beauty in my life except two things. My children and"—she hesitates—"I write these poems. How come, when I write it down, it don't come out my pencil like I feel? I don't know. I got no dictionary. Every time I read it over I am finding these mistakes.

> Deep down in my heart
> I do not mean these things I said.
> Forgive me. Try to understand me.
> I love all of you the same.
> Help me to be a better mother.

"When I cry I let 'em know. I tell 'em I was a drug addict. They know and they try to help me to hold on. They helpin' me. My children is what's holdin' me together. I'm not makin' it. I'm reachin'. And they see me reachin' out. Angelina take my hand. They come around. They ask me what is wrong. I do let them know when I am scared. But certain things I keep inside. I try to solve it. If it's my department, I don't want them to be sad. If it be too bad, if I be scared of gettin' back on drugs, I'll go to the clinic. They have sessions every other night.

"Hardest time for me is night. Nightmares. Somethin's grabbin' at me. Like a hand. Some spirit's after me. It's somethin' that I don't forget. I wake up in a sweat. I'm wonderin' why I dream these dreams. So I get up, turn on the light. I don't go back to sleep until the day is breakin'. I look up an' I be sayin': 'Sun is up. Now I can go to sleep.'

"After the kids are up and they are dressed and go to school, then I lay down. I go to sleep. But I can't sleep at night. After the sun go down makes me depressed. I want to turn the light on, move around.

"Know that song—'Those Monday Blues'? I had that album once."

I say the title: "'Monday Blues'?"

"I got 'em every day. Lots of times, when I'm in pain, I think I'm goin' to die. That's why I take a drink sometimes. I'm 'fraid to die. I'm wonderin': Am I dying?"

PART XII

Family Policy and Social Change

We consider ourselves a nation that cares about children and their families. Yet, this notion is something of a romantic or self-serving idealization: policies and practices at every level in our society reveal subtle biases against children and their families.

GARBARINO, GABOURY, AND PLANTZ, 1995

This last section of the book focuses on social policies that affect families and the potential for social change within the institution of the family in the United States. Family life is defined and altered by community, employer, and government policies. If we want to improve or change conditions within the family, such as reduce the amount of poverty, or eliminate domestic violence, or provide higher-quality, accessible child care, we need to understand how social policy can affect social change. As reflected in the quote above, many current social policies actually harm children and families. Garbarino et al. (1995) argue that many social policies which affect families were put into place without considering the impact they would have:

> We do not believe that our country, governments, courts, business, industries, and human service agencies have instituted policies deliberately to undermine family unity and effectiveness. The policies and practices of these institutions certainly were not intended to have family-threatening effects. Their purpose was to address specific problems (sometimes problems that seem to be quite unrelated to families) with effective and cost-efficient solutions. In most cases, in fact, the potential family impact was not even considered when the policy decisions were enacted. And therein lies the problem. In most instances, the potential impact of proposed actions or policies on families was not even considered. (P. 274)

Thus, we need to more closely examine current social policies as well as proposed future policies for the impact they will have on families and children.

We actually have been reading about social policy and families throughout this book. For example, Glenn (Reading 8) discussed immigration policies and how they affected Chinese American family strategies. Stacey (Reading 14) examined social policies concerning same-sex marriage. Sugarman (Reading 18) discussed historical and contemporary social policies that affect single-parent families. And Amato's article (Reading 20) on children and divorce concluded with a section on policy suggestions that could improve the lives of children and parents going through a divorce. Similarly, Friedman's article (Reading 27) on divorced parents provides policy suggestions to improve postdivorce family situations within the Jewish community. Korbin et al. (Reading 32) discuss the need to change policies regarding child abuse and elder abuse. In addition, Hochschild (Reading 36) examines family policies in a Fortune 500 company to see how individuals are balancing the demands of work and family. Both Aponte (Reading 40) and Albelda and Tilly (Reading 41) address problems and myths concerning welfare policy.

Building on these earlier readings, in this section we examine four diverse areas of family social policy: policies concerning domestic partnerships, teen pregnancy, transracial adoption, and the U.S. welfare system. All four of these areas are among the most controversial and debated topics concerning the institution of the family in recent years. Part of the reason for much debate in these areas is that some people see these issues as evidence for the demise of the American family. They believe domestic partnerships threaten traditional, heterosexual marriage, teen pregnancy is a consequence of the breakdown in moral and family values, and transracial adoption is racist and damaging to the racial-ethnic heritage of children. And they see welfare problems as being caused by people who are having too many children and are too lazy to work. As the following articles will demonstrate, the family research literature shows all of these notions to be false.

Domestic Partnerships

The first reading in this section, "Domestic Partnerships: A Concept Paper and Policy Discussion," is by Steven K. Wisensale and Kathlyn E. Heckart. Wisensale is an associate professor of public policy at the School of Family Studies, University of Connecticut. Heckart is a policy analyst with an M.A. in social work; as an undergraduate, she wrote her senior honors thesis on domestic partnerships, and Wisensale was her thesis adviser. For the selection that appears here, Wisensale and Heckart investigated 23 organizations (including local governments, corporations, and other organizations) to determine the extent to which domestic partnership policies have been adopted. This article provides an overview of domestic partnership policies commonly enacted in the United States. About this research, Wisensale comments:

> Although my initial research focused on aging policy and general equity issues, I became more interested in family legal issues as I developed new courses on family policy and family law. I began to see the family change in structure and watched with much interest as the courts and legislatures tried to keep pace with these changes. As the debate over family values heated up in the early 1990s, I began to explore the growth in domestic partnerships, particularly at the local level and, surprisingly, even in very conservative corporations. I was intrigued by the sharp contrast between the national debate over family values on one level and the move to completely redefine the family in local communities and businesses that are far removed from Washington on another level. (Personal Interview 1997)

Domestic partnerships are an excellent example of social change occurring within the family that is due in large part to innovative policies in the private sector and in local governments. This corporate and community response is needed because federal and state governments have been slow in granting nonmarried couples legal and economic rights.

Teen Pregnancy

The second reading in this section is "Dubious Conceptions: The Controversy over Teen Pregnancy," by Kristin Luker, a professor of sociology and law at the University of California, Berkeley. In this selection, taken from her book *Dubious Conceptions: The Politics of Teen Pregnancy* (1996), Luker argues that the United States is *not* experiencing an epidemic of teenage pregnancy as is widely stated in the press. Instead, U.S. teenage pregnancy rates have always been high; what is different now is that fewer teenagers are married when they give birth to children. Luker also challenges a welfare myth about teen pregnancy by arguing that there is *not* a causal relationship between age of first pregnancy and socioeconomic standing. Instead, the public hysteria over teen pregnancy is deeply rooted in the U.S. political culture and its conflicting attitudes about sexuality, birth control, and poverty. In particular, Luker finds that even though many teenagers knew about contraceptives and reproductive issues before getting pregnant, most of their pregnancies were unplanned and unintended. Therefore, the solutions are not as clear as they may appear, that is, simply telling teenagers to wait to have children. She concludes by stating that the nation needs to rethink its understanding of teen pregnancy to advocate better public policy.

Transracial Adoption

The third reading is "Adoption and the Race Factor: How Important Is It?" by Rita J. Simon. Simon, a professor at American University, has been a primary investigator of the short-term and long-term effects of transracial adoption and has published numerous studies, including a book, *The Case for Transracial Adoption* (1994), coauthored with Howard Alstein and Marygold Melli. Transracial adoption has been at the center of debate and social policies regarding cross-racial parenting and families. Since the 1970s, several groups have opposed transracial adoption, including the National Association of Black Social Workers (NABSW) and several councils of Native Americans These groups believe that children of color should *not* be placed with white families because they will lose their racial-ethnic heritage. On the other hand, there are not enough families of color available to adopt these children, so they wait longer in orphanages and foster care for permanent homes. In this selection, Simon reports the major research findings of the past 25 years that pertain to transracial adoptions. The findings show that transracial adoptions serve the children's best interest and are consistent with the 1996 federal law that prohibits a state from delaying or denying adoption on the basis of race, color, or national origin.

U.S. Welfare Policy

The final reading in this section, "Race, Class, Gender and U.S. State Welfare Policy: The Nexus of Inequality for African Americans," returns our attention to public policies concerning poverty and welfare. The author, Rose Brewer, is an associate professor of Afro-American and African Studies at the University of Minnesota. In this selection, Brewer argues that the economic inequality among African American families is due to the complex interplay between race, social class, and gender. Building on arguments made by Robert Aponte (Reading 40), and Randy Albelda and Chris Tilly (Reading 41), Brewer states that in order to understand poverty, we need to look beyond the current U.S. welfare system and focus on global capitalism and the new international division of labor based on race and gender. Thus, the lives of poor families in the United States are inextricably linked to international economic and political policies. Brewer argues that national policies must address the influences global capitalism has on U.S. poverty and welfare. She concludes her article with four specific policy suggestions for social change.

REFERENCES

Garbarino, James, Mario T. Gaboury, and Margaret C. Plantz. 1995. "Social Policy, Children, and Their Families." Pp. 271–97 in *Children and Their Families in the Social Environment,* edited by James Garbarino. New York: Aldine de Gruyter.

Luker, Kristin. 1996. *Dubious Conceptions: The Politics of Teen Pregnancy.* Cambridge, MA: Harvard University Press.

Simon, Rita J., Howard Alstein, and Marygold Melli. 1994. *The Case for Transracial Adoption.* Washington, DC: The American University Press.

43

DOMESTIC PARTNERSHIPS
A Concept Paper and Policy Discussion

STEVEN K. WISENSALE • KATHLYN E. HECKART

L ike many institutions, the American family has been subjected to numerous social and economic pressures that not only have had an impact on its basic structure but also have called into question its general definition. Today, single parents, gay couples with adopted children, surrogate mothers, grandparent-headed families, and stepfamilies challenge the traditional definition of the family. Works by Blankenhorn, Bayme, and Elshtain (1991); Cherlin (1988); Duff and Truitt (1992); Levitan, Belous, and Gallo (1988); Levy and Michel (1991); Popenoe (1988); and Rubin (1986) have all concluded that most families do not consist of the traditional family (a mother and father living with their children under 18 or stepparents and stepchildren). Independent surveys have reached similar conclusions.

In 1990 the Massachusetts Mutual Life Insurance Company asked 1,200 randomly selected adults to define the word *family*. Only 22 percent chose the legalistic definition: "A group of people related by blood, marriage or adoption" (Massachusetts Mutual Life Insurance Company 1990:2). Almost 75 percent chose a much broader definition: "A group of people who love and care for each other" (Massachusetts Mutual Life Insurance Company 1990:2). More focused studies documented a steady rise in nonmarital cohabitation. Glick (1990), for example, reported an increase in cohabiting couples from .5 million in 1970 to 2.6 million in 1988. Bumpass and Sweet (1989) and Bumpass, Sweet, and Cherlin (1989) concluded that nearly half of those individuals entering first marriages in the late 1980s cohabited prior to marriage, over half of those persons who remarry live with a partner between their marriages, and nearly a quarter of all American adults have cohabited at some point in their lives. "It is clear that what has been normatively proscribed in the recent past has now become the modal behavior pattern" (Sweet and Bumpass 1992:143).

In an effort to keep pace with these changing demographics, particularly with respect to living arrangements, the United States Bureau of the Census revised its survey questionnaire in 1990. For the first time in American history, the Bureau permitted couples of the same or opposite sex to distinguish themselves from those who are not intimately involved. That is, unmarried partners were given the opportunity to classify themselves separately from housemates-roommates (United States Bureau of the Census 1990). It is estimated that there are 2.6 million unmarried couples of the opposite sex and 1.6 million couples of the same sex who are cohabiting (Isaacson 1989). But regardless of how current the research may be on living arrangements or how adaptable the U.S. Bureau of the Census may be to shifting demographics, judicial bodies and legislative chambers are engaged in a continuing struggle to define, redefine, and clarify the concept of family.

Faced with this new challenge, policymakers, researchers, and family life educators in particular will be called upon to pose relevant questions, offer realistic solutions, and impart important and credible information. How these professionals respond to changing demographics, particularly with respect to the legal aspects associated with various living arrangements, may ultimately determine the condition of the family [in the early] 21st century.

Defining the Family in Legal Terms

Historically, the American legal system has discouraged two people from entering into their own form of marriage. Courts and legislatures established policies that were designed to promote so-called traditional families. Any alternative form was viewed as a threat to not only the family but also to the state (Krause 1990). Therefore, traditional families have always had more rights than nontraditional families. These include the right to live in a neighborhood zoned for single families; to have access to health insurance, sick, and bereavement leave; to inherit without a will; to sue for loss of consortium, workers' compensation, or unemployment compensation; to obtain visitation rights in hospitals or jails; and to authorize emergency medical treatment (Krause 1990). Still, today almost one-third of the states recognize informal or common-law marriages. These include Alabama, Colorado, Georgia, Idaho, Iowa, Kansas, Montana, New Hampshire, Ohio, Oklahoma, Pennsylvania, Rhode Island, South Carolina, Texas, Utah and the District of Columbia (Duff and Truitt 1992).

With a rise in cohabitation as a lifestyle, along with a greater acceptance of it by society as a whole, it is not surprising that the rights of so-called spousal equivalents have had to be clarified more frequently before the courts. Over the last two decades there have been at least four important court cases which attempted to define the family by clarifying the rights of individuals involved in cohabiting relationships. The four cases are Marvin, Renshaw, Watts, and Braschi.

In *Marvin v. Marvin* (1976), the California Supreme Court recognized the right of unmarried couples to contract between themselves and emphasized that courts have the power to determine the division of property of spousal equivalents according to "reasonable expectations" (Krause 1990:135). In *Renshaw v. Heckler* (1986), the U.S. Court of Appeals ruled that a woman who cohabited with a man for 20 years should be granted access to his Social Security benefits after his death. In *Watts v. Watts* (1987), the Wisconsin Supreme Court ruled that a woman who supported her live-in companion through medical school was entitled to fair compensation when their relationship ended. The settlement included both alimony and child support.

In addition to cohabitation, the courts have also taken a closer look at same-sex relationships. Though homosexual marriages were clearly denounced in *Baker v. Nelson* (1971) and in *Jones v. Hallahan* (1973), the picture changed significantly nearly 20 years later. In *Braschi v. Stahl Associates Co.* (1989), the New York Court of Appeals ruled that a gay couple's relationship went well beyond that of roommates and, therefore, the couple could be considered a family under New York City's rent-control regulations. Thus, the court ruled that a rent-controlled apartment could be held by the survivor after his partner died of Acquired Immune Deficiency Syndrome. The definition of a family, stated the court, "should not rest on fictitious legal distinctions or genetic history, but instead should find its foundation in the reality of family life" (Krause 1990:160). Although the ruling was narrowly focused on rent-control laws, it raised other significant issues, such as partners' access to medical coverage, inheritances, spousal support after a breakup, ownership of property, power of attorney, and even child custody in some cases.

Clearly, as indicated in the various court actions identified above, the legal definition of the family is undergoing significant change. Another example can be found in the growth of domestic partnership laws throughout the nation. Adopted by more than a dozen local governments and several private corporations and nonprofit organizations in the last three years, such laws allow unmarried couples access to joint medical, health, and dental coverage among other benefits. To date, however, neither the federal government nor the state legislatures have enacted similar laws.

Because very little research has been conducted on domestic partnership laws to date, and because this concept may become a policy trend of the future, an exploratory research project was undertaken to examine the issue in greater detail. The purpose of this article, therefore, is threefold: first, to identify those communities, corporations, and organizations which have adopted domestic partnership laws; second, to explore the various similarities and differences among those policies which have been adopted; and third, to raise appropriate questions for future research and policy development.

Methodology

In the spring of 1992 a study was conducted to identify the extent to which domestic partnership policies were adopted to local governments, corporations, and organizations. The research process consisted of four steps. First, a list of those communities, corporations, and organizations that adopted domestic partnership policies was generated. Hewitt Associates (1991) and Lambda Legal Defense and Education Fund (1992), both of which maintain files on domestic partnerships, provided lists of those communities, corporations, and organizations with domestic partnership policies. This process produced a list of 12 communities, 4 corporations, and 3 organizations.

Second, those subjects identified in step one were contacted by telephone and asked to submit copies of their policies and other related material related to this subject. They were also asked to identify other communities,

TABLE 1   Domestic Partners Policies for City Employees in 14 United States Cities—1992*

Municipality (year policy instituted)	Enactment Process	
	Ordinance	Executive Order
Berkeley, CA (1985)	X	
West Hollywood, CA (1985)	X	
Santa Cruz, CA (1986)	X	
Los Angeles, CA (1988)	X	
Takoma Park, MD (1988)	X	
Madison, WI (1988)	X	
New York, NY (1989)		X
Seattle, WA (1990)	X	
San Francisco, CA (1990)	X	
Laguna Beach, CA (1990)	X	
Ithaca, NY (1990)	X	
Ann Arbor, MI (1991)	X	
Minneapolis, MN (1991)	X	
West Palm Beach, FL (1992)	X	

*X = Enactment vehicle, registration required, benefit available.

corporations, and organizations that they knew had adopted such policies but were not included on the original list. This process produced two additional communities, one corporation, and one organization. These too were surveyed, bringing the total of participants in the study to 23. It should be emphasized that despite a very painstaking effort, this list is by no means exhaustive.

Third, the policies were then analyzed and categorized according to the adoption process, qualification requirements, registration procedures, and benefit coverage.

Finally, a follow-up telephone call was made to each of the survey participants to both verify and clarify the written documents that were submitted previously. The results are presented below.

Results

Fourteen cities with domestic partnership laws were surveyed. The results, presented in Table 1, can be discussed under three major categories: (a) the enactment process, (b) registration, and (c) health benefits and personal leave policies. Each category is discussed below.

The Enactment Process

With respect to the enactment process, 13 of the 14 communities passed city ordinances that recognized domestic partnerships. Although most passed unan-

TABLE 1 *(continued)*

		Benefit/Leave Policies		
Require Registration	Medical/Health/Dental	Eye Care	Sick Leave	Bereavement Leave
X	X		X	X
X	X	X	X	X
X	X	X	X	X
			X	X
			X	X
			X	X
				X
X	X		X	X
X				
X	X		X	X
			X	X
				X
X			X	X
				X

imously, some city council actions, such as in Seattle, were prompted by the threat of law suits based on various civil rights codes. New York's policy is the only one that was created through an executive order, which was signed by then-mayor Edward Koch.

The Registration Procedure

Seven of the 14 communities (as indicated in Table 1) require that domestic partners publicly register. That is, in order to be eligible for benefits, participants must complete an affidavit of domestic partnership which usually consists of three important components: (a) a statement that the partners are not related by blood or marriage; (b) a commitment of mutual support, caring, and responsibility for each other's welfare; and (c) an agreement to notify the city within a specified time of any changes in the contract and an understanding that another affidavit of domestic partnership cannot be filed until 6 (sometimes 3) months after a statement of termination has been filed. Examples of Santa Cruz's Affidavit of Domestic Partnership and its Termination Statement are presented in Figures 1 and 2 respectively.

Health Benefits and Personal Leave Policies

Five of the 14 communities include medical benefits. For example, the City of Berkeley offers its 1,500 employees three different health insurance plans, including two health maintenance organizations. Similar programs exist in West Hollywood, Santa Cruz, Seattle, and Laguna Beach.

CONFIDENTIAL

CITY OF SANTA CRUZ
AFFIDAVIT OF DOMESTIC PARTNERSHIP

I, _____ , certify that:
          Name of Employee (Print)

1. I,_____ , and _____
          Employee (Print)   Domestic Partner

reside together as a non-married cohabitating couple and intend to do so indefinitely at:
(Address) _____
_____

and share the common necessities of life.

2. We affirm that the effective date of this domestic partnership is _____. (Date)

3. We are not married to anyone.

4. We are at least eighteen (18) years of age or older.

5. We are not related by blood closer than would bar marriage in the State of California and are mentally competent to consent to contract.

6. We are each other's sole domestic partner and intend to remain so indefinitely and are responsible for our common welfare.

7. We agree to notify the City if there is any change of circumstances attested to in this Affidavit within thirty (30) days of the change by filing a statement of Termination of Domestic Partnership. Such termination statement shall be on a form provided by the City and shall affirm under penalty of perjury that the partnership is terminated and that a copy of the termination statement has been mailed to the other partner.

8. After such termination I, _____ ,
                                        (Employee)

understand that another Affidavit of Domestic Partnership cannot be filed until six (6) months after a statement of termination of the previous partnership has been filed with the Personnel Department.

9. We understand that any persons/employers/company who suffer loss because of a false statement contained in an Affidavit of Domestic Partnership may bring a civil action against us to recover their losses including reasonable attorney's fees.

10. We provide the information in this Affidavit to be used by the City for the sole purpose of determining our eligibility for domestic partnership.

TERMINATION OF DOMESTIC PARTNERSHIP COVERAGE

I, _____ , request removal of my domestic partner, _____ from my insurance coverage effective _____ .

I understand that I will not be able to apply for another domestic partner coverage until six months has passed.

_____
Print Name

_____
Signature

_____
Date

Domestic Partner:

Name: _____

Address: _____

_____

FIGURES 1 AND 2 "Affidavit of Domestic Partnership" and "Termination of Domestic Partnership Coverage" for the City of Santa Cruz. Reprinted by permission of the City of Santa Cruz Personnel Department.

TABLE 2   Domestic Partners Benefits Available from Nine Corporations and Organizations in the United States — 1992*

Corporation/Organization	Benefits Available			
	Medical/Health/Dental	Eye Care	Sick Leave	Bereavement Leave
American Friends Service Committee, PA (1987)	X			
University Students Cooperative Association, CA (1988)	X		X	X
American Civil Liberties Union, CA (1988)	X			
Lambda Legal Defense and Education Fund (1988)	X		X	X
Ben and Jerry's Ice Cream, VT (1989)	X			X
Montefiore Medical Center, NY (1989)	X	X		X
Village Voice, NY (1989)	X			X
Gardener's Supply Company, VT (1990)	X			X
Lotus, MA (1991)	X	X		X

*X = Benefit available.

In addition to health care benefits, 2 communities (West Hollywood and Santa Cruz) include eye care for their employees, 10 of the 14 communities offer unpaid sick leave, and 13 of 14 allow for bereavement leave.

Policies in the Private and Nonprofit Sectors

A similar pattern of domestic partnership policies has emerged in the private sector. By the spring of 1992, 14 corporations or nonprofit organizations were identified as offering domestic partnership benefits to their employees. Of these, nine participated in the survey. The results are presented in Table 2.

As is usually the policy in the public sector, employees of private firms and nonprofit organizations are required to register with their employer by filing a signed affidavit that documents the partnership and also by agreeing to submit a statement of termination if and when the relationship ends. Also similar to the public sector is the extent of benefit coverage. As presented in Table 2, all nine participants in the study offer medical and health care coverage to their employees' partners. In addition, Montefiore Medical Center and Lotus offer eye care, the University Students Cooperative Association and Lambda offer sick leave, and seven of the nine participants include bereavement leave in their benefit package.

Not included in Table 2 are two large national organizations and one major corporation that also offer domestic partner benefits but were not participants in the survey. These include the American Psychological Association, the National Organization for Women, and Levi Strauss and Company. Although they provided descriptive information about their programs, they chose not to respond directly to the survey questionnaire. Levi Strauss's policy, which became effective on June 1, 1992, makes it the largest private company in the United States to extend health benefits to the partners of its unmarried employees. To be eligible for benefit coverage, the employee and partner must identify themselves in writing as life partners, reside at the same address, be financially interdependent, and have joint responsibility for each other's welfare.

Beyond actions by local governments, private corporations, and non-profit organizations, at least two states have introduced domestic partnership bills in their legislatures. In 1990 Illinois introduced such a bill that was originally drafted by that state's Gay and Lesbian Task Force. One year later, New York saw a similar bill introduced in both houses of its legislature. In neither case did the proposed bill move beyond a committee hearing.

At the national level, domestic partnership proposals are virtually nonexistent. This is in sharp contrast to Denmark, where, in 1989, the Parliament created what is referred to as the *registered partnership*. Under the statute, only couples of the same sex, regardless if they are living together or not, may assume a state comparable to marriage and thus become eligible for various health care and social welfare benefits under Danish law (Nielsen 1990). However, it should be emphasized that the law does not apply to couples of the opposite sex who are cohabiting. This of course could open a major chasm between Denmark's heterosexual and homosexual communities (Nielsen 1990). On the other hand, existing policies in the United States apply to cohabiting couples regardless of their sexual preference.

Discussion

It has been reported in this article that the American family has experienced major changes, that one of these changes has been a marked increase in cohabitation, and that some local governments, private corporations, and non-profit organizations have responded to this particular change by establishing domestic partnership policies. Also presented here is the fact that the states and federal government have not enacted such policies so far.

Because it is likely that more communities — perhaps even state legislatures — will be debating and considering this policy option in the near future, it may be necessary for researchers, policymakers, and family professionals to become familiar with some of the major issues usually associated with domestic partnerships. What follows is a discussion of those issues.

The Issues

At least five issues, converted to key questions, can be identified in relation to domestic partnerships. How should domestic partnerships be defined?

How extensive should the benefit coverage be? What are the anticipated costs of domestic partnership policies? How should the tax structure respond to domestic partnerships? Should there be a national domestic partnership law? Each is discussed in some detail below.

How should domestic partnerships be defined? Before a policy can be debated, enacted, and implemented, it is important that the terms of the debate be clearly defined. This becomes particularly troublesome when new policies such as domestic partnerships, begin to emerge. If demographers are correct in their prediction that cohabitation will soon become the majority experience, then policymakers will be required to respond accordingly (Duff and Truitt 1992). For example, should domestic partners be viewed in the same light as spousal equivalents, common-law spouses, or significant others? Can a domestic partner be a sister, mother, another relative, or a roommate? Must partners reside together? Should they be the same sex or opposite-sex partners, or does it matter? How do two individuals prove that they have formed a domestic partnership? What should be the determining factor when it is declared that a domestic partnership no longer exists?

To date, established policies tend to recognize both homosexual and heterosexual partners, require proof of commitment such as a joint address, bank account, insurance policy, and pension program, and require the filing of both registration and termination forms with appropriate authorities. Further, almost all policies require that between 3 and 6 months elapse before another domestic partnership can be created and officially registered.

How extensive should the benefit coverage be? Under existing policy, married men and women are granted various privileges that normally are not available to cohabiting couples. These include employment-based health insurance and family leave; visiting privileges in hospitals; and access to special family rates offered by airlines, car insurance companies, health clubs, recreation programs, amusement parks, and museums.

Most domestic partnership policies include some form of family leave, either for personal illness or for bereavement. Only about half of public sector employers, but almost all of private sector employers with domestic partnership policies, offer some sort of health coverage. But should coverage be more extensive?

According to Lambda (1992), an ideal benefit package made available to married couples should include nine important components: sick leave, bereavement leave, parenting leave, health insurance, dental insurance, disability benefits, accidental death and dismemberment insurance, retirement and death benefits, and family access to a credit union. This raises an important policy question: Should domestic partners be granted the same level of benefits as married couples? Equally important, while the domestic partnership is a move toward privilege on one hand, it is unlikely that its evolution will go smoothly without a serious discussion of responsibility on the other hand. This issue becomes especially acute when children are involved.

What are the anticipated costs of domestic partnership policies? One of the concerns raised, particularly in a tight economic climate, is the potential cost of expanding benefits for employees. These concerns can become particularly acute and controversial with respect to domestic partnerships. As a result, the questions can become very complicated. For example, can the insurer's policy on providing coverage to domestic partners differ from its policy on married couples? Will expanding dependent medical or life insurance coverage to domestic partners significantly raise benefit costs for others covered under the same plan? In the end, who will pay the cost of domestic partnership coverage? Will the cost be borne by the employer, employee, or both?

Surprisingly, and despite the growing anxiety over exploding health care costs, very little research has been conducted in this area of domestic partnerships. However, studies completed in Berkeley, California; Seattle, Washington; and Madison, Wisconsin indicate that the expansion of health benefits does result in increased costs (Lambda 1992). In Berkeley, for example, health insurers raised premiums by 2 percent, which eventually converted into a cost increase of $2 per month per employee. In Seattle, the increased costs rose by about 2 percent for health services but remained unchanged for dental care. And, in Madison, the increased cost in health care coverage ranged from 1 percent to 3 percent during the first year that domestic partnerships were recognized and covered. It should be emphasized, however, that any number of reasons could be used to explain the rise of health care costs in these communities. But the fact that these cost increases occurred almost immediately after the adoption of domestic partnership policies may be more than coincidence. More research is needed in this area.

How should the tax structure respond to domestic partnerships? How the Internal Revenue Service (IRS) views employer contributions to domestic partner health coverage is a concern to most private businesses. According to the federal tax code, employee health coverage is tax deductible for employers if the insured is married or he or she can prove that there are dependents. Therefore, the IRS has recognized domestic partnerships as being tax deductible by the employer. For employees who cover their domestic partners, however, the picture is less clear. According to Hewitt Associates (1991), the IRS has concluded that for federal tax purposes, the determination of marital status (legal spouse) is based on state law. Dependent status, on the other hand, depends partially on state and local law. For example, most Seattle employees who receive benefits for their domestic partners will also have to pay taxes on those benefits unless the partner otherwise qualifies as a dependent under the federal tax code. Therefore, whether or not domestic partners can claim certain deductions may depend solely on where they live. Employers tend not to be subjected to such uncertainty.

Recognizing that such policies create different tax treatments in different states, the IRS argues that its position "illustrates the deference Congress has demonstrated for state laws in this area and its attempt to insure that, in the application of federal tax law, taxpayers will be treated in their intimate and personal relationships as the state in which they reside treats them" (Hewitt Associates 1990:10). Still, in light of the changing structure of the American family as manifested in the rapid growth of domestic partnership policies, should the United States tax code be adjusted accordingly in an effort to standardize tax policies on a national scale? If a national standard exists for corporations, should individuals be accorded equal treatment? This is a policy question that deserves closer scrutiny.

Should there be a national domestic partnership law? For the United States to enact a national domestic partnership law at this time is highly unlikely. Such an initiative has not been introduced at the federal level to date, nor is one expected to be proposed in the near future. Furthermore, during the 1992 presidential campaign, both candidates agreed that benefits guaranteed to married couples should not be extended to unmarried cohabiting partners. While such a national policy was adopted in Denmark in 1989 and is currently under consideration in Sweden, no other nation, including the United States, has chosen to move in this direction (Nielsen 1990).

To complicate matters even more, the concept of domestic partnerships is apparently not even attractive at the state level where, historically, most family policy initiatives have originated. The states are where marriage and divorce laws are created and enacted, where child custody and child support statutes are usually designed and implemented, and where major reforms in family law are initiated. Yet, as of 1992, only two states (Illinois and New York) have even considered debating the concept of domestic partnerships (Hewitt Associates 1991).

How ironic it must seem to some that during the past twelve years of conservative politics [1980–1992]—a period that witnessed a deliberate attempt by the Reagan and Bush administrations to shift power away from Washington and toward state and local governments—that the very definition of the family would be challenged and even rewritten at the grassroots level and in communities that are far removed from Washington's beltway politics.

But despite what some may consider to be a rapid growth in domestic partnership policies throughout the country, their pattern of development has neither been smooth nor consistent. For as new policies emerge, new questions arise and, as a result, the potential for an increase in legal disputes is enhanced. Once again the courts become overburdened and the taxpayers are forced to foot the bill. Although it may be unrealistic to expect Congress to enact a national domestic partnership law at this time, or even expect states to do so for that matter, it is realistic to believe that the creation of a nonbinding uniform code on domestic partnership laws would help to both focus and diffuse the debate simultaneously.

Modeled after similar concepts such as the Uniform Marriage and Divorce Act or the National Advisory Panel on Child Support Guidelines, both of which are nonbinding, a national Uniform Code on Domestic Partnerships would serve as a guide to those communities, corporations, or organizations that choose to discuss or even adopt such policies (Krause 1990). Such an approach would be expected to appeal to those who recognize domestic partnerships as well as to those who continue to argue for a decentralization of political power. Through some form of consensus-building activity, such as reaching an agreement on a nonbinding uniform code for domestic partners, it may be possible to avoid costly legal battles that are otherwise inevitable within the current political environment.

Implications

The debate over domestic partnerships strikes at the very heart of what may become one of the most important public policy issues of this decade. That is, what constitutes a family? How shall its needs be met? Who, in the end, is responsible for addressing those needs?

For policymakers concerned with family issues in general and domestic partnerships in particular, there are at least three questions that demand attention. First, should policies on domestic partnerships be limited to municipalities, corporations, and organizations, or should an effort be made to create greater uniformity through the passage of state and federal laws? What are the advantages and disadvantages of each approach? Second, should domestic partnership policies be keyed to gender? That is, should they be confined solely to cohabiting homosexuals or should they apply to unmarried cohabiting heterosexual partners as well? What are the moral and legal ramifications associated with one choice over the other? And third, what role should cost play in deciding whether or not to adopt domestic partnership laws? That is, in the midst of a sluggish economy and rising health care costs, should existing benefit packages be expanded to include those who would not have been considered family less than 10 years ago? What are the political and economic consequences of such choices?

With respect to researchers, there are numerous questions concerning domestic partnerships that demand exploration. For example, in terms of age, sex, economic status, race, and other categories, who tends to register as domestic partners? How long do such relationships last, on average, in comparison to marriage? In either the private or public sector, what impact does a domestic partnership policy have on recruitment, retention, and overall productivity of employees? What are the similarities and differences among communities, corporations, and organizations that adopt domestic partnership policies? What conclusions can be reached about those who oppose or choose to reject such policies? Are there particular models of domestic partnerships, based on the registration process, available benefits, and termination procedures, that tend to be more appealing to potential participants than other models?

Finally, for family life educators, the debate over domestic partnerships can be employed as a vehicle for discussing the definition and meaning of the concept of family. What do we mean by *family*, and how should our definition be converted into legal terms? Domestic partnerships can also be referred to as examples of social change and help illustrate the growing diversity in living arrangements and family types. Further, domestic partnerships can serve as teaching tools in at least two other respects. One, they can serve as springboards for discussions concerning benefits and entitlements and how access to them is usually anchored to the definition of family. And two, they serve as an example of how the family can easily become a political football. Why, for example, are most state and federal legislative bodies unwilling to consider domestic partnerships, while certain municipalities, corporations, and organizations adopt such policies? How family professionals respond to the policy issues, frame the research questions, and educate the general public about domestic partnerships may well determine the next version of America's family portrait.

ENDNOTE

Author's note: The authors would like to thank Carrie Lapp for her assistance throughout this research project.

REFERENCES

Baker v. Nelson. 1971. Supreme Court of Minnesota, 291 Minn. 310, 191 N.W. 2d 185, appeal dismissed 409 U.S. 810, 93 S. Ct. 37, 34 L. Ed. 2d 65.

Blankenhorn, D., S. Bayme, and J. Elshtain. 1991. *Rebuilding the Nest: A New Commitment to the American Family.* Milwaukee: Family Service America.

Braschi v. Stahl Associates Co. 1989. New York Court of Appeals, W.L. 73109.

Bumpass, L. and J. Sweet. 1989. "National Estimates of Cohabitation: Cohort Levels and Union Stability." *Demography* 26:615–25.

Bumpass, L., J. Sweet, and A. Cherlin. 1989. "The Role of Cohabitation in Declining Rates of Marriage." NSFH Working Paper No. 5, National Survey of Families and Households, University of Wisconsin, Madison.

Cherlin, A. 1988. *The Changing American Family and Public Policy.* Washington, DC: Urban Institute Press.

Duff, J. and G. Truitt. 1992. *The Spousal Equivalent Handbook.* New York: Penguin Books.

Glick, P. 1990. "Marriage and Family Trends." Pp. 2–3 in *2001: Preparing Families for the Future.* Minneapolis: National Council on Family Relations.

Hewitt Associates. 1991. *Domestic Partners and Employee Benefits.* Lincolnshire, IL: Author.

Isaacson, W. 1989. "Should Gays Have Marriage Rights?" *Time,* November 20, pp. 101–102.

Jones v. Hallahan. 1973. Kentucky Court of Appeals, 73 KY.

Krause, H. 1990. *Family Law: Cases, Comments, and Questions.* Minneapolis: West.

Lambda Legal Defense and Education Fund. 1992. *Domestic Partnership: Issues and Legislation.* New York: Author.

Levitan, S., R. Belous, and F. Gallo. 1988. *What's Happening to the American Family?* Baltimore: Johns Hopkins University Press.

Levy, F. and R. Michel. 1991. *The Economic Future of American Families.* Washington, DC: Urban Institute Press.

Marvin v. Marvin. 1976. Supreme Court of California, 18 Cal 3d 660, 134 Cal Reptr. 815, 557 P.2d 106.

Massachusetts Mutual Insurance Company. 1990. *The Changing American Family.* Springfield, MA: Author.

Nielsen, L. 1990. "Family Rights and the Registered Partnership in Denmark." *International Journal of Law and the Family* 4:297–307.

Popenoe, D. 1988. *Disturbing the Nest: Family Change and Decline in Modern Societies.* New York: Aldine de Gruyter.

Renshaw v. Heckler. 1986. United States Court of Appeals, Second Circuit, 787 F. 2d 50.

Rubin, E. 1986. *The Supreme Court and the American Family.* New York: Greenwood Press.

Sweet J. and L. Bumpass. 1992. "Young Adults' Views of Marriage, Cohabitation, and Family." Pp. 143–70 in *The Changing American Family: Sociological and Demographic Perspectives,* edited by S. South and S. Tolnay. Boulder, CO: Westview Press.

United States Bureau of the Census. 1990. *Statistical Abstract of the United States, 1989.* 110th ed. Washington, DC: U.S. Government Printing Office.

Watts v. Watts. 1987. Supreme Court of Wisconsin, 137 Wis. 2d 506, 405 N.W. 2d 303.

44

DUBIOUS CONCEPTIONS
The Controversy over Teen Pregnancy

KRISTIN LUKER

The conventional wisdom has it that an epidemic of teen pregnancy is today ruining the lives of young women and their children and perpetuating poverty in America. In polite circles, people speak regretfully of "babies having babies." Other Americans are more blunt. "I don't mind paying to help people in need," one angry radio talk show host told Michael Katz, a historian of poverty, "but I don't want my tax dollars to pay for the sexual pleasure of adolescents who won't use birth control."

By framing the issue in these terms, Americans have imagined that the persistence of poverty and other social problems can be traced to youngsters who are too impulsive or too ignorant to postpone sexual activity, to use contraception, to seek an abortion, or failing all that, especially if they are white, to give their babies up for adoption to "better" parents. Defining the problem this way, many Americans, including those in a position to influence public policy, have come to believe that one attractive avenue to reducing poverty and other social ills is to reduce teen birth rates. Their remedy is to persuade teenagers to postpone childbearing, either by convincing them of the virtues of chastity (a strategy conservatives prefer) or by making abortion, sex education, and contraceptives more freely available (the strategy liberals prefer).

Reducing teen pregnancy would almost certainly be a good thing. After all, the rate of teen childbearing in the United States is more similar to the rates prevailing in the poor countries of the world than in the modern, industrial nations we think of as our peers. However, neither the problem of teen pregnancy nor the remedies for it are as simple as people think.

In particular, the link between poverty and teen pregnancy is a complicated one. We do know that teen mothers are poorer than women who wait past their twentieth birthday to have a child. But stereotypes to the contrary, it is not clear whether early motherhood causes poverty or the reverse. Worse yet, even if teen pregnancy does have some independent force in making teen parents poorer than they would otherwise be, it remains to be seen whether any policies in effect or under discussion can do much to reduce teen birthrates.

These uncertainties raise questions about our political culture as well as our public choices. How did Americans become convinced that teen pregnancy is a major cause of poverty and that reducing one would reduce the other? The answer is a tale of good intentions, rising cultural anxieties about teen sex and family breakdown, and the uses — and misuses — of social science.

How Teen Pregnancy Became an Issue

Prior to the mid-1970s, few people talked about "teen pregnancy." Pregnancy was defined as a social problem primarily when a woman was unmarried; no one thought anything amiss when an eighteen- or nineteen-year-old got married and had children. And concern about pregnancies among unmarried women certainly did not stop when the woman turned twenty.

But in 1975, when Congress held the first of many hearings on the issue of adolescent fertility, expert witnesses began to speak of an "epidemic" of a "million pregnant teenagers" a year. Most of these witnesses were drawing on statistics supplied by the Alan Guttmacher Institute, which a year later published the data in an influential booklet, *Eleven Million Teenagers*. Data from that document were later cited — often down to the decimal point — in most discussions of the teenage pregnancy "epidemic."

Many people hearing these statistics must have assumed that the "million pregnant teenagers" a year were all unmarried. The Guttmacher Institute's figures, however, included married nineteen-year-olds along with younger, unmarried teenage girls. In fact, almost two-thirds of the "million pregnant teenagers" were eighteen- and nineteen-year-olds; about 40 percent of them were married, and about two-thirds of the married women were married prior to the pregnancy.

Moreover, despite the language of epidemic, pregnancy rates among teenagers were not dramatically increasing. From the turn of the century until the end of World War II, birth rates among teenagers were reasonably stable at approximately 50 to 60 births per thousand women. Teen birth rates, like all American birth rates, increased dramatically in the period after World War II, doubling in the baby-boom years to a peak of about 97 births per thousand teenaged women in 1957. Subsequently, teen birth rates declined, and by 1975 they had gone back down to their traditional levels, where, for the most part, they have stayed (see figure).

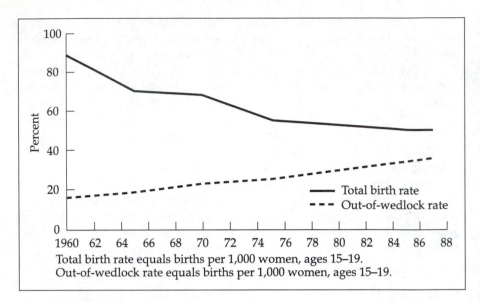

Trends in Teen Birth Rates

Sources: National Center for Health Statistics, *Annual Vital Statistics,* and *Monthly Vital Statistics Reports;* U.S. DHEW, Vital and Health Statistics, "Trends in Illegitimacy, U.S. 1940–1965."

Were teen births declining in recent decades only because of higher rates of abortion? Here, too, trends are different from what many people suppose. The legalization of abortion in January 1973 made it possible for the first time to get reliable statistics on abortions for women, teenagers and older. The rate among teenagers rose from about 27.0 to 42.9 abortions per 1,000 women between 1974 and 1980. Since 1980 teen abortion rates have stabilized and may even have declined somewhat. Moreover, teenagers account for a declining proportion of all abortions: In the years just after *Roe v. Wade,* teenagers obtained almost a third of all abortions in the country; now they obtain about a quarter. A stable teen birth rate and a stabilizing teen abortion rate mean that pregnancy rates, which rose modestly in the 1970s, have in recent years leveled off.

What has been increasing—and increasing dramatically—is the percentage of teen births that are out-of-wedlock (see figure). In 1970 babies born out of wedlock represented about a third of all babies born to teen mothers. By 1980 out-of-wedlock births were about half, and by 1986 almost two-thirds. Beneath these overall figures lie important racial variations. Between 1955 and 1988 the out-of-wedlock rate rose from 6 to 24.8 per thousand unmarried, teenage, white women, while for unmarried, nonwhite teenagers the rate rose from 77.6 to 98.3 per thousand. In other words, while the out-of-wedlock birth rate was rising 25 percent among nonwhite teens, it was actually quadrupling among white teens.

The immediate source for this rise in out-of-wedlock teen pregnancy might seem to be obvious. Since 1970 young women have increasingly postponed marriage without rediscovering the virtues of chastity. Only about 6 percent of teenagers were married in 1984, compared to 12 percent in 1970. And although estimates vary, sexual activity among single teenagers has increased sharply, probably doubling. By 1984 almost half of all American teenage women were both unmarried and sexually active, up from only one in four in 1970.

Yet the growth of out-of-wedlock births has not occurred only among teens; in fact, the increase has been more rapid among older women. In 1970 teens made up almost half of all out-of-wedlock births in America; at present they account for a little less than a third. On the other hand, out-of-wedlock births represent a much larger percentage of births to teens than of births to older women. Perhaps for that reason, teenagers have become the symbol of a problem that, to many Americans, is "out of control."

Whatever misunderstandings may have been encouraged by reports of a "million pregnant teenagers" a year, the new concept of "teen pregnancy" had a remarkable impact. By the mid-1980s, Congress had created a new federal office on adolescent pregnancy and parenting; 23 states had set up task forces; the media had published over 200 articles, including cover stories in both *Time* and *Newsweek;* American philanthropy had moved teen pregnancy into a high-priority funding item; and a 1985 Harris poll showed that 80 percent of Americans thought teen pregnancy was a "serious problem" facing the nation, a concern shared across racial, geographic, and economic boundaries.

But while this public consensus has been taking shape, a debate has emerged about many of its premises. A growing number of social scientists have come to question whether teen pregnancy causes the social problems linked to it. Yet these criticisms have at times been interpreted as either an ivory-tower indifference to the fate of teen parents and their babies or a Panglossian optimism that teen childbearing is just one more alternate lifestyle. As a result, clarity on these issues has gotten lost in clouds of ideological mistrust. To straighten out these matters, we need to understand what is known, and not known, about the relation of teen pregnancy to poverty and other social problems.

Distinguishing Causes from Correlations

As the Guttmacher Institute's report made clear, numerous studies have documented an association between births to teenagers and a host of bad medical and social outcomes. Compared to women who have babies later in life, teen mothers are in poorer health, have more medically treacherous pregnancies, more stillbirths and newborn deaths, and more low-birthweight and medically compromised babies.

Later in life, women who have babies as teenagers are also worse off than other women. By their late twenties, women who gave birth as teenagers are less likely to have finished high school and thus not to have received any subsequent higher education. They are more likely to have routine, unsatisfactory, and dead-end jobs, to be on welfare, and to be single parents because either they were never married or their marriage ended in divorce. In short, they often lead what the writer Mike Rose has called "lives on the boundary."

Yet an interesting thing has happened over the last twenty years. A description of the lives of teenage mothers and their children was transmuted into a causal sequence, and the often-blighted lives of young mothers were assumed to flow from their early childbearing. Indeed, this is what the data would show, if the women who gave birth as teenagers were the same in every way as women who give birth later. But they are not.

Although there is little published data on the social origins of teen parents, studies have documented the effects of social disadvantage at every step along the path to teenage motherhood. First, since poor and minority youth tend to become sexually active at an earlier age than more advantaged youngsters, they are "at risk" for a longer period of time, including years when they are less cognitively mature. Young teens are also less likely to use contraceptives than older teenagers. Second, the use of contraception is more common among teens who are white, come from more affluent homes, have higher educational aspirations, and who are doing well in school. And, finally, among youngsters who become pregnant, abortions are more common if they are affluent, white, urban, of higher socioeconomic status, get good grades, come from two-parent families, and aspire to higher education. Thus, more advantaged youth get filtered out of the pool of young women at risk of teen parenthood.

Two kinds of background factors influence which teens are likely to become pregnant and give birth outside of marriage. First is inherited disadvantage. Young women from families that are poor, or rural, or from a disadvantaged minority, or headed by a single parent are more likely to be teen mothers than are their counterparts from more privileged backgrounds. Yet young mothers are not just disadvantaged; they are also discouraged. Studies suggest that a young woman who has other troubles — who is not doing well in school, has lower "measured ability," and lacks high aspirations for herself — is also at risk of becoming a teenaged mother.

Race plays an independent part in the route to teen motherhood. Within each racial group, according to Linda Waite and her colleagues at the Rand Corporation, teen birth rates are highest for those who have the greatest economic disadvantage and lowest academic ability. The effects of disadvantage, however, vary depending on the group. The Rand study found that among young high-ability, affluent black women from homes with two parents, only about one in a hundred become single, teenage mothers. For comparable whites, the risk was one in a thousand. By contrast, a poor, black teenager from a female-headed household who scores low on standardized tests has an astonishing one in four chance of becoming an unwed mother in her teens. Her white counterpart has one chance in twelve. Unwed motherhood thus reflects the intersecting influences of race, class, and gender; race and class each has a distinct impact on the life histories of young women.

Since many, if not most, teenage unwed mothers are already both disadvantaged and discouraged before they get pregnant, the poor outcomes of their pregnancies as well as their later difficulties in life are not surprising. Consider the health issues. As the demographer Jane Menken pointed out some time ago (and as many other studies have corroborated), the medical complications associated with teen pregnancy are largely due not to age but to the poverty of young mothers. As poor people, they suffer not from some biological risk due to youth, but from restricted access to medical care, particularly to prenatal care. (To be fair, some research suggests that there may be special biological risks for the very youngest mothers, those under age fifteen when they give birth, who constitute about 2 percent of all teen mothers.)

Or, to take a more complicated example, consider whether bearing a child blocks teenagers from getting an education. In the aggregate, teen mothers do get less education than women who do not have babies at an early age. But teen mothers are different from their childless peers along exactly those dimensions we would expect independently to contribute to reduced schooling. More of them are poor, come from single-parent households, and have lower aspirations for themselves, lower measured ability, and more problems with school absenteeism and discipline. Given the nature of the available data, it is difficult to sort out the effects of a teen birth apart from the personal and social factors that predispose young women to both teen motherhood and less education. Few would argue that having a baby as a teenager enhances educational opportunities, but the exact effect of teen birth is a matter of debate.

Educational differences between teen mothers and other women may also be declining, at least in terms of graduating from high school. Legislation that took effect in 1975 forbade schools to expel pregnant teens. Contrary to current skepticism about federal intervention, this regulation seems to have worked. According to a study by Dawn Upchurch and James McCarthy, only 18.6 percent of teenagers who had a baby in 1958 subsequently graduated from high school. Graduation rates among teen mothers reached 29.2 percent in 1975; by 1986 they climbed to 55 percent. Teen mothers were still not graduating at a rate equal to other women (as of 1985, about 87 percent of women ages 25 to 29 had a high school diploma or its equivalent). But over the decade prior to 1986, graduation rates had increased more quickly for teen mothers than for other women, suggesting that federal policies tailored to their special circumstances may have made a difference.

Since education is so closely tied to later status, teasing out the relationship between teen pregnancy and schooling is critical. The matter is complicated, however, because young people do many things simultaneously, and sorting out the order is no easy task. In 1984 Peter Morrison of the Rand team reported that between a half and a third of teen mothers in high school and beyond dropped out before they got pregnant. Upchurch and McCarthy, using a different and more recent sample, found that the majority of female dropouts in their study left school before they got pregnant and that teens who got pregnant while still in school were not particularly likely to drop out. On the other hand, those teens who first drop out and then get pregnant are significantly less likely to return to school than other dropouts who do not get pregnant. Thus the conventional causal view that teens get pregnant, drop out of school, and as a result end up educationally and occupationally disadvantaged simply does not match the order of events in many people's lives.

The Sexual Roots of Public Anxiety

Teen pregnancy probably would not have "taken off" as a public issue quite so dramatically, were it not for the fact it intersects with other recent social changes in America, particularly the emergence of widespread, anxiety-producing shifts in teen sex. Academics debate whether there has been a genuine "sexual revolution" among adults, but there is no doubt in regard to teenagers. Today, by the time American teenagers reach age twenty, an estimated 70 percent of the girls and 80 percent of the boys have had sexual experiences outside of marriage. Virtually all studies confirm that this is a dramatic historical change, particularly for young women. (As usual, much less is known about the historical experiences of young men.) For example, Sandra Hofferth and her colleagues, using nationally representative data from the 1982 National Survey of Family Growth, found that women navigating adolescence in the late 1950s had a 38.9 percent chance of being sexually active before marriage during their teenage years. Women who reached their twentieth birthday between 1979 and 1981, in contrast, had a 68.3 percent likelihood.

Yet even the statistics do not capture how profoundly different this teen sexuality is from that of earlier eras. As sources such as the Kinsey Report (1953) suggest, premarital sex for many American women before the 1960s was "engagement" sex. The woman's involvement, at least, was exclusive, and she generally went on to marry her partner in a relatively short period of time. Almost half of the women in the Kinsey data who had premarital sex had it only with their fiances.

But as the age of first marriage has risen and the age at first intercourse has dropped, teen sexuality has changed. Not surprisingly, what scattered data we have about numbers of partners suggest that as the period of sexual activity before marriage has increased, so has the number of partners. In 1971, for example, almost two-thirds of sexually active teenaged women in metropolitan areas had had only one sexual partner; by 1979 fewer than half did. Data from the 1988 National Survey of Family Growth confirm this pattern for the nation as a whole, where about 60 percent of teens have had two or more partners. Similarly, for metropolitan teens, only a small fraction (about 10 percent) were engaged at the time of their first sexual experience, although about half described themselves as "going steady."

Profound changes in other aspects of American life have complicated the problem. Recent figures suggest that the average age at first marriage has increased to almost 24 years for women and over 25 years for men, the oldest since reliable data have been collected. Moreover, the age of sexual maturity over the last century has decreased by little under six months each decade owing to nutritional and other changes. Today the average American girl has her first menstrual period at age twelve and a half, although there are wide individual variations. (There is less research on the sexual maturity of young men.) On average, consequently, American girls and their boyfriends face over a decade of their lives when they are sexually mature and single.

As teenagers pass through this reproductive minefield, the instructions they receive on how to conduct themselves sexually are at best mixed. At least according to public opinion polls, most Americans have come, however reluctantly, to accept premarital sex. Yet one suspects that what they approve is something closer to Kinsey-era sex: sexual relations en route to a marriage. Present-day teenage sex, however, starts for many young people not when they move out of the family and into the orbit of what will be a new family or couple, but while they are still defined primarily as children.

When young people, particularly young women, are still living at home (or even at school) under the control, however nominal, of parents, sexual activity raises profound questions for adults. Many Americans feel troubled about "casual" sex, that is, sex which is not intimately tied to the process by which people form couples and settle down. Yet many teenagers are almost by definition disqualified as too young to "get serious." Thus the kinds of sexuality for which they are socially eligible — sex based in pleasure, not procreation, and in short-term relationships rather than as a prelude to marriage — challenge fundamental values about sexuality held by many adults. These ambiguities and uncertainties have given rise to broad anxieties about teen sexuality that have found expression in the recent alarm about teen pregnancy.

Raising Children without Fathers

While Americans have had to confront the meaning and purpose of sexuality in the lives of teenagers, a second revolution is forcing them to think about the role — and boundaries — of marriage and family. Increasingly for Americans, childbearing and, more dramatically, childrearing have been severed from marriage. The demographer Larry Bumpass and his colleagues have estimated that under present trends, half or more of all American children will spend at least part of their childhood in a single-parent (mainly mother-only) family, due to the fact that an estimated 60 percent of recent marriages will end in divorce.

At the same time, as I indicated earlier, out-of-wedlock births are on the rise. At present, 26 percent of all births are to single women. If present trends continue, Bumpass and others estimate, almost one out of every six white women and seven out of ten black women will give birth to a child without being married. In short, single childbearing is becoming a common pattern of family formation for all American women, teenagers and older.

This reality intersects with still another fact of American life. The real value of inflation-adjusted wages, which grew 2.5 to 3.0 percent a year from the end of World War II to at least 1973, has now begun to stagnate and for certain groups decline; some recent studies point to greater polarization of economic well-being. Americans increasingly worry about their own standard of living and their taxes, and much of that worry has focused on the "underclass." Along with the elderly and the disabled, single women and their children have been the traditional recipients of public aid in America. In recent years, however, they have become especially visible among the dependent poor for at least two reasons. First, the incomes of the elderly have improved, leaving behind single mothers as a higher percentage of the poor; and second, the number of female-headed households has increased sharply. Between 1960 and 1984, households headed by women went from 9.0 percent to 12.0 percent of all white households, and from 22.0 percent to 43 percent of all black households. The incomes of about half of all families headed by women, as of 1984, fell below federal poverty levels.

Raising children as a single mother presents economic problems for women of all ages, but the problem is especially severe for teenagers with limited education and job experience. Partly for that reason, teenagers become a focus of public concern about the impact of illegitimacy and single parenthood on welfare costs. Data published in the 1970s and replicated in the 1980s suggested that about half of all families supported by Aid to Families with Dependent Children (AFDC) were started while the mother was still a teenager. One estimate calculated that in 1975 the costs for these families on public assistance alone (not including Medicaid or food stamps) amounted to $5 billion; by 1985, that figure increased to $8.3 billion.

Yet other findings—and caveats—have been ignored. For example, while about half of all AFDC cases may be families begun while the woman was still a teenager, teens represent only about 7 percent of the caseload at any one time. Moreover, the studies assessing the welfare costs of families started by teens counted any welfare family as being the result of a teen birth if the woman first had a child when under age twenty. But, of course, that same woman—given her prior circumstances—might have been no less likely to draw welfare assistance if, let us say, she had a baby at age twenty instead of nineteen. Richard Wertheimer and Kristin Moore, the source of much of what we know about this area, have been careful to note that the relevant costs are the marginal costs—namely, how much less in welfare costs society would pay if teen mothers postponed their first births, rather than foregoing them entirely.

It turns out, not surprisingly, that calculated this way, the savings are modest. Wertheimer and Moore have estimated that if by some miracle we could cut the teen birth rate in half, welfare costs would be reduced by 20 percent, rather than 50 percent, because many of these young women would still need welfare for children born to them when they were no longer teens.

Still other research suggests that most young women spend a transitional period on welfare, while finishing school and entering the job market. Other data also suggest that teen mothers may both enter and leave the welfare ranks earlier than poor women who postpone childbearing. Thus teen births by themselves may have more of an effect on the timing of welfare in the chain of life events than on the extent of welfare dependency. In a study of 300 teen mothers and their children originally interviewed in the mid-1960s, Frank Furstenberg and his colleagues found seventeen years later that two-thirds of those followed up had received no welfare in the previous five years, although some 70 percent of them had received public assistance at some point after the birth of their child. A quarter had achieved middle-class incomes, despite their poverty at the time of the child's birth.

None of this is to deny that teen mothers have a higher probability of being on welfare in the first place than women who begin their families at a later age, or that teen mothers may be disproportionately represented among those who find themselves chronically dependent on welfare. Given the disproportionate number of teen mothers who come from socially disadvantaged origins (and who are less motivated and perhaps less able students), it would be surprising if they were not overrepresented among those needing public assistance, whenever they had children. Only if we are to argue that these kinds of women should never have children—which is the implicit alternative at the heart of much public debate—could we be confident that they would never enter the AFDC rolls.

Rethinking Teen Pregnancy

The original formulation of the teen pregnancy crisis seductively glossed over some of these hard realities. Teen motherhood is largely the province of those youngsters who are already disadvantaged by their position in our society. The major institutions of American life—families, schools, job markets, the medical system—are not working for them. But by framing the issue as teenage pregnancy, Americans could turn this reality around and ascribe the persistence of poverty and other social ills to the failure of individual teenagers to control their sexual impulses.

Framing the problem as teen pregnancy, curiously enough, also made it appear universal. Everyone is a teenager once. In fact, the rhetoric has sometimes claimed that the risk of teen pregnancy is universal, respecting no boundaries of class or race. But clearly, while teenage pregnancies do occur in virtually all walks of life, they do not occur with equal frequency. The concept of "teen pregnancy" has the advantage, therefore, of appearing neutral and universal while, in fact, being directed at people disadvantaged by class, race, and gender.

If focusing on teen pregnancy cast the problem as deceptively universal, it also cast the solution as deceptively simple. Teens just have to wait. In fact, the tacit subtext of at least some of the debate on teen pregnancy is not that young women should wait until they are past their teens, but until they are "ready." Yet in the terms that many Americans have in mind, large numbers of these youngsters will never be "ready." They have already dropped out of school and will face a marginal future in the labor market whether or not they have a baby. And as William J. Wilson has noted, many young black women in inner-city communities will not have the option of marrying because of the dearth of eligible men their age as a result of high rates of unemployment, underemployment, imprisonment, and early death.

Not long ago, Arline Geronimous, an assistant professor of public health at the University of Michigan, caused a stir when she argued that teens, especially black teens, had little to gain (and perhaps something to lose) in postponing pregnancy. The longer teenagers wait, she noted, the more they risk ill health and infertility, and the less likely their mothers are to be alive and able to help rear a child of theirs. Some observers quickly took Geronimous to mean that teen mothers are "rational," affirmatively choosing their pregnancies.

Yet, as Geronimous herself has emphasized, what sort of choices do these young women have? While teen mothers typically report knowing about contraception (which they often say they have used) and knowing about abortion, they tell researchers that their pregnancies were unplanned. In the 1988 National Survey of Family Growth, for example, a little over 70 percent of the pregnancies to teens were reported as unplanned; the teenagers described the bulk of these pregnancies as wanted, just arriving sooner than they had planned.

Researchers typically layer their own views on these data. Those who see teens as victims point to the data indicating most teen pregnancies are unplanned. Those who see teens as acting rationally look at their decisions not to use contraceptives or seek an abortion. According to Frank Furstenberg, however, the very indecisiveness of these young people is the critical finding. Youngsters often drift into pregnancy and then into parenthood, not because they affirmatively choose pregnancy as a first choice among many options but, rather, because they see so few satisfying alternatives. As Laurie Zabin, a Johns Hopkins researcher on teen pregnancy, puts it, "As long as people don't have a vision of the future which having a baby at a very early age will jeopardize, they won't go to all the lengths necessary to prevent pregnancy."

Many people talk about teen pregnancy as if there were an implicit social contract in America. They seem to suggest that if poor women would just postpone having babies until they were past their teens, they could have better lives for themselves and their children. But for teenagers already at the margins of American life, this is a contract that American society may be hard put to honor. What if, in fact, they are acting reasonably? What can public policy do about teen pregnancy if many teenagers drift into childbearing as the only vaguely promising option in a life whose options are already constrained by gender, poverty, race, and failure?

The trouble is that there is little reason to think any of the "quick fixes" currently being proposed will resolve the fundamental issues involved. Liberals, for example, argue that the answer is more access to contraception, more readily available abortion, and more sex education. Some combination of these strategies probably has had some effect on teen births, particularly in keeping the teen pregnancy rate from soaring as the number of sexually active teens increased. But the inner logic of this approach is that teens and adults have the same goal: keeping teens from pregnancies they do not want. Some teens, however, do want their pregnancies, while others drift into pregnancy and parenthood without ever actively deciding what they want.

Consequently, increased access to contraceptives, sex education, and abortion services are unlikely to have a big impact in reducing their pregnancies.

Conservatives, on the other hand, often long for what they imagine was the traditional nuclear family, where people had children only in marriage, married only when they could prudently afford children, and then continued to provide support for their children if the marriage ended. Although no one fully understands the complex of social, economic, and cultural factors that brought us to the present situation, it is probably safe to predict that we shall not turn the clock back to that vision, which in any event is highly colored by nostalgia.

This is not to say that there is nothing public policy can do. Increased job opportunities for both young men and young women; meaningful job training programs (which do not slot young women into traditional low-paying women's jobs); and child support programs (see Theda Skocpol, "Sustainable Social Policy, Fighting Poverty without Poverty Programs," *TAP*, Summer 1990) would all serve either to make marriage more feasible for those who wish to marry or to support children whose parents are not married. But older ages at first marriage, high rates of sex outside of marriage, a significant portion of all births out of wedlock, and problems with absent fathers tend to be common patterns in Western, industrialized nations.

In their attempts to undo these patterns, many conservatives propose punitive policies to sanction unmarried parents, especially unmarried mothers, by changing the "incentive structure" young people face. The welfare reform bill of 1988, for example, made it more difficult for teens to set up their own households, at least in part because legislators were worried about the effects of welfare on the willingness to have a child out of wedlock. Other, more draconian writers have called for the children of unwed teen parents to be forcibly removed and placed into foster care, or for the reduction of welfare benefits for women who have more than one child out of wedlock.

Leave aside, for the moment, that these policies would single out only the most vulnerable in this population. The more troublesome issue is such policies often fall most heavily on the children. Americans, as the legal historian Michael Grossberg has shown, have traditionally and justifiably been leery of policies that regulate adult behavior at children's expense.

The things that public policy could do for these young people are unfortunately neither easy to implement nor inexpensive. However, if teens become parents because they lack options, public policy toward teen pregnancy and teenage childbearing will have to focus on enlarging the array of perceived options these young people face. And these must be changes in their real alternatives. Programs that seek to teach teens "future planning," while doing nothing about the futures they can expect, are probably doomed to failure.

We live in a society that continues to idealize marriage and family as expected lifetime roles for women, even as it adds on the expectation that women will also work and be self-supporting. Planning for the trade-offs entailed in a lifetime of paid employment in the labor market and raising a family taxes the skills of our most advantaged young women. We should not be surprised that women who face discrimination by race and class in addition to that of gender are often even less adept at coping with these large and contradictory demands.

Those who worry about teenagers should probably worry about three different dangers as Americans debate policies on teen pregnancy. First, we should worry that things will continue as they have and that public policy will continue to see teens as unwitting victims, albeit victims who themselves cause a whole host of social ills. The working assumption here will be that teens genuinely do not want the children that they are having, and that the task of public policy is to meet the needs of both society and the women involved by helping them not to have babies. What is good for society, therefore, is good for the individual woman.

This vision, for all the reasons already considered, distorts current reality and, as such, is unlikely to lower the teen birth rate significantly, though it may be effective in keeping the teen birth rate from further increasing. To the extent that it is ineffective, it sets the stage for another risk.

This second risk is that the ineffectiveness of programs to lower teen pregnancy dramatically may inadvertently give legitimacy to those who want more punitive control over teenagers, particularly minority and poor teens. If incentives and persuasion do not lead teenagers to conduct their sexual and reproductive lives in ways that adults would prefer, more coercive remedies may be advocated. The youth of teen mothers may make intrusive social control seem more acceptable than it would for older women.

Finally, the most subtle danger is that the new work on teen pregnancy will be used to argue that because teen pregnancy is not the linchpin that holds together myriad other social ills, it is not a problem at all. Concern about teen pregnancy has at least directed attention and resources to young, poor, and minority women; it has awakened many Americans to their diminished life chances. If measures aimed at reducing teen pregnancy are not the quick fix for much of what ails American society, there is the powerful temptation to forget these young women altogether and allow them to slip back to their traditional invisible place in American public debate.

Teen pregnancy is less about young women and their sex lives than it is about restricted horizons and the boundaries of hope. It is about race and class and how those realities limit opportunities for young people. Most centrally, however, it is typically about being young, female, poor, and nonwhite and about how having a child seems to be one of the few avenues of satisfaction, fulfillment, and self-esteem. It would be a tragedy to stop worrying about these young women—and their partners—because their behavior is the measure rather than the cause of their blighted hopes.

45

ADOPTION AND THE RACE FACTOR
How Important Is It?

RITA J. SIMON

Introduction

On August 20, 1996, President Clinton signed into law a provision that prohibits "a state or other entity that receives federal assistance from denying any person the opportunity to become an adoptive or a foster parent solely on the basis of the race, color, or national origin of the persons or of the child involved (Small Business Job Protection Act [SBJPA] of 1996). The provision also prohibits a state from denying or delaying the placement of a child for adoption or foster care solely on the basis of race, color, or national origin of the adoptive or foster parent of the child involved (SBJPA). States which violate these provisions will have their quarterly funds reduced by 2 percent for the first violation, by 5 percent for the second violation, and by 10 percent for the third or subsequent violation (pp. 1903–1904).

Passage of these provisions represents the culmination of more than thirty years of national debate about whether transracial adoptions serve the best interests of the child. The federal statute which went into effect on January 1, 1997 should expedite the placement of tens of thousands of children currently in institutions and foster care into permanent loving homes. According to the GAO and to William Pierce of the National Council For Adoption (NCFA), there are some 500,000 children currently in foster care. About 50 percent are Black and some 40 to 50,000 are available for adoption.[1] Even though Black families have always adopted at a higher rate than White families, given the percentage of minority children, most of whom are Black, those children tend to remain in institutions and foster care two and three years longer than White children. But whether the enactment of the federal statute will, in fact, end the debate, which at times has been very bitter, remains to be seen.

At this point, what is especially gratifying is that the newly adopted federal standard is consistent with the empirical work that has been done on transracial adoption for more than 25 years and which shows that transracial adoption serves the children's best interests. The following paragraphs summarize the major findings of those studies going back to the early 1970s.

Rita J. Simon, "Adoption and the Race Factor: How Important Is It?" in *Sociological Inquiry*, Vol. 68, No. 2 (1998), pp. 274–279. Copyright © 1998 by the University of Texas Press. Reprinted with permission from the publisher.

Empirical Studies

The case for transracial adoption rests primarily on the results of empirical research. The studies show that transracial adoptees grow up emotionally and socially adjusted, and aware of and comfortable with their racial identity. They perceive themselves as integral parts of their adopted families, and they expect to retain strong ties to their parents and siblings in the future. The data show that transracial adoptions clearly satisfy the "best interest of the child" standard.

Indeed, when given the opportunity to express their views on transracial adoption, most people—Black and White—support it. For example, in January 1991, "CBS This Morning" reported the results of a poll it conducted that asked 975 adults, "Should race be a factor in adoption?" Seventy percent of White Americans and 71 percent of African Americans said "No." These percentages are the same as those reported by Gallup in 1971 when it asked a national sample the same question.

Published in 1974, *Black Children, White Parents* by Lucille Grow and Deborah Shapiro of the Child Welfare League, represents one of the earliest studies of transracial adoption. Its major purpose was to assess how successful the adoption by White parents of Black children had been (Grow and Shapiro 1974). Their respondents consisted of 125 families. Grow and Shapiro concluded that the children in their study made about as successful an adjustment in their adoptive homes as same-race-adopted white children had in prior studies. They claimed that 77 percent of their children had adjusted successfully and that this percentage was similar to that reported in other studies.

In 1977, Joyce Ladner conducted in-depth interviews with 136 parents in Georgia, Missouri, Washington, D.C., Maryland, Virginia, Connecticut, and Minnesota (Ladner 1977). Before reporting her findings, she introduced a personal note:

> This research brought with it many self-discoveries. My initial feelings were mixed. I felt some trepidation about studying White people, a new undertaking for me. Intellectual curiosity notwithstanding, I had the gnawing sensation that I shouldn't delve too deeply because the findings might be too controversial. I wondered too if the couples I intended to interview would tell me the truth. Would some lie in order to cover up their mistakes and disappointments with the adoption? How much would they leave unsaid? Would some refuse to be interviewed because of their preconceived notions about my motives? Would they stereotype me as a hostile Black sociologist who wanted to "prove" that these adoptions would produce mentally unhealthy children? (Pp. xii–xiii)

By the end of the study, Ladner was convinced that "there are Whites who are capable of rearing emotionally healthy Black children." Such parents, Ladner continued, "must be idealistic about the future but also realistic about the society in which they now live" (p. 254).

Using a mail survey in 1981, William Feigelman and Arnold Silverman compared the adjustment of 56 Black children adopted by White families against 97 White children adopted by White families (Feigelman and Silverman 1983). The parents were asked to assess their child's overall adjustment and to indicate the frequency with which their child demonstrated emotional and physical problems. Silverman and Feigelman concluded that the child's age—not the transracial adoption—had the most significant impact on development and adjustment. The older the child, the greater the problems. They found no relationship between adjustment and racial identity.

W. M. Womack and W. Fulton's study of transracial adoptees and non-adopted Black preschool children found no significant differences in racial attitudes between the two groups of children (Womack and Fulton 1981).

In 1981, Ruth McRoy and Louis Zurcher reported the findings of their study of 30 Black adolescents who had been transracially adopted and 30 Black adolescents who had been adopted by Black parents (McRoy and Zurcher 1983). In the concluding chapter of their book, McRoy and Zurcher wrote,

> The transracial and inracial adoptees in the authors' study were physically healthy and exhibited typical adolescent relationships with their parents, siblings, teachers, and peers. Similarly, regardless of the race of their adoptive parents, they reflected positive feelings of self-regard.

Throughout the book, the authors emphasized that the quality of parenting was more important than whether the Black child had been inracially or transracially adopted: "Most certainly, transracial adoptive parents experience some challenges different from inracial adoptive parents, but in this study, all of the parents successfully met the challenges" (p. 130).

In 1993, Christopher Bagley compared a group of 27 transracial adoptees with a group of 25 inracially adopted Whites (Bagley 1993). Both sets of adoptees were approximately 19 years old and were on average about two years old when adopted. Bagley concluded his study with the following statement:

> The findings of the present study underscore those from previous American research on transracial adoption. Transracial adoption . . . does appear to meet the psychosocial and developmental needs of the large majority of the children involved, and can be just as successful as inracial adoption. (P. 294)

The Simon–Altstein Twenty–Year Longitudinal Study
(Simon and Altstein 1992; Simon, Altstein, and Melli 1994)

In 1971–72, Simon contacted 206 families living in the five cities in the Midwest who were members of the Open Door Society and the Council on Adoptable Children (COAS) and asked whether she could interview them about their decision to adopt nonwhite children. All of the families but two (which declined for reasons unrelated to adoption) agreed to participate in the study. The parents allowed a two-person team composed of one male and one female graduate student to interview them in their homes for 60 to 90 minutes at the same time that each of their children, who were between four and seven years old, was being interviewed for about 30 minutes. In total, 204 parents and 366 children were interviewed.

All of the children (adopted and birth) had been given a series of projective tests including the Kenneth Clark doll tests, puzzles, pictures, etc., that sought to assess racial awareness, attitudes and identity. Unlike all other previous doll studies, our respondents did not favor the White doll. It was not considered smarter, prettier, nicer, etc., than the Black doll either by White or Black children. Neither did any of the other tests reveal preferences for White or negative reactions to Black. Yet the Black and White children in our study accurately identified themselves as White or Black on those same tests. Indeed, the most important finding that emerged from our first encounter with the families in 1971–72 was the absence of a White racial preference or bias on the part of White birth children and the nonwhite adopted children.

Over the years, we continued to ask about and measure racial attitudes, racial awareness, and racial identity among the adopted and birth children. We also questioned the parents during the first three phases of the study about the activities, if any, in which they, as a family engaged to enhance their transracial adoptee's racial awareness and racial identity. We heard about dinnertime conversations involving race issues, watching the TV series "Roots," joining Black churches, seeking Black godparents, preparing Korean food, traveling to Native American festivals, and related initiatives. As the years progressed, especially during adolescence, it was the children, rather than the parents, who were more likely to want to call a halt to some of these activities. "Not every dinner conversation has to be a lesson in Black history," or "We are more interested in the next basketball or football game than in ceremonial dances" were comments we heard frequently from transracial adoptees as they were growing up.

In the 1991 phase of the study, the transracial adoptees, who, by this time were young adults, were asked how they felt about the practice of placing nonwhite—especially Black—children in White homes, what recommendations they might have about adoption practices, and what advice they might offer White parents who are considering transracial adoption. We also asked the respondents to evaluate their own experiences with transracial adoption.

We opened the topic by stating, "You have probably heard of the position taken by the National Association of Black Social Workers (NABSW) and several councils of Native Americans strongly opposing transracial adoption. Do you agree or disagree with their position?" All of the respondents were aware of NABSW's position. Eighty percent of the adoptees and 70 percent of the birth children disagreed with the NABSW position. Among the latter, 17 percent agreed and 13 percent were not sure. Only 5 percent of the transracial adoptees agreed with NABSW's position. The others were not sure how they felt about the issue. The reasons most often given for why they disagreed were that "racial differences are not crucial," "TRA is the best practical alternative," and "having a loving, secure, relationship in a family setting is all-important."

One Black male adoptee said, "My parents have never been racist. They took shit for adopting two Black kids. I'm proud of them for it. The Black Social Workers' Association promotes a separatist ideology."

Another Black female commented, "It's a crock—it's just ridiculous. They [the NABSW] should be happy to get families for these children—period. My parents made sure we grew up in a racially diverse neighborhood. Now I am fully comfortable with who I am."

Another commented, "I feel lucky to have been adopted when I was very young [24 days]. I was brought up to be self-confident—to be the best I can. I was raised in an honest environment."

Concluding Remarks

After more than two and a half decades, in which numerous studies were conducted on the impact of transracial adoption on minority children, the data show unequivocally that transracial adoptions serve the children's best interest. The children emerge as highly intact Black adults, aware of and sensitive to their identity and community. The families live with the knowledge they have nurtured a productive member of society, at ease in both Black and White worlds. No empirical work has been reported that contradicts these generalizations.

Concerning my own work, I began the study with no social or political agenda, and I exit with none. I was interested in assessing how persons of different races could live together in so intimate an environment as a family at a time in American society, the late 1960s, when relations between Blacks and Whites were tense and strained.

The passage of the 1996 Federal Statute is consistent with and supportive of the results reported in the more than 20 years of empirical research. Let us hope that it accomplishes its two-fold goal: prohibits race to be used as a factor to delay or deny adoption; and expedites the placement of thousands of minority children into permanent, caring homes.

ENDNOTE

1. These figures have been cited various times in the *National Adoption Reports* published by the National Council For Adoption.

REFERENCES

Bagley, Christopher. June 1993. "Transracial Adoption in Britain: A Follow-up Study." *Child Welfare* LXXII:3.

Feigelman, William and Arnold Silverman. 1983. *Chosen Child: New Patterns of Adoptive Relationships.* New York: Praeger.

Grow, Lucille and Deborah Shapiro. 1974. *Black Children, White Parents: A Study of Transracial Adoption.* New York: Child Welfare League of America.

Ladner, Joyce. 1977. *Mixed Families.* New York: Archer Press, Doubleday.

McRoy, Ruth and Louis A. Zurcher. 1983. *Transracial and Inracial Adoptees.* Springfield, IL: Charles C. Thomas.

Shireman, Joan and Penny Johnson. 1988. *Growing Up Adopted.* Chicago: Chicago Child Care Society.

Simon, Rita J. and Howard Altstein. 1992. *Adoption, Race and Identity.* New York: Praeger.

———. 1977. *Transracial Adoption.* Wiley-Interscience.

———. 1981. *Transracial Adoption: A Follow-Up.* Lexington Books.

———. 1987. *Transracial Adoption: A Study of Their Identity and Commitment.* New York: Praeger.

Simon, Rita J., Howard Altstein, and Marygold Melli. 1994. *The Case for Transracial Adoption.* Maryland: The American University Press.

Small Business Job Protection Act of 1996, Pub. L. No. 104-88, 1808, 110 Stat. 1755, 1903.

Womack, W. M. and W. Fulton. 1981. "Transracial Adoption and the Black Preschool Child." *Journal of the American Academy of Child Psychiatry* 20:712–24.

Zastrow, Charles H. 1977. *Outcome of Black Children–White Parents Transracial Adoptions.* San Francisco: R&E Research Associates.

46

RACE, CLASS, GENDER AND U.S. STATE WELFARE POLICY
The Nexus of Inequality for African American Families

ROSE BREWER

This article is about the United States welfare state and African American family inequality. It is a sociological analysis of the welfare state, race, class, gender, and the family which is both critical and historical in perspective. Although the growing literature on the state and public policy in sociology indicates its sociological significance (Dickinson and Russell 1986; Wilson 1980, 1987; Zaretsky 1976), little of the existing work on state form and state practice tackles the welfare state in the context of the multiple inequalities which shape American society with a specific focus on African American families. A major gap in the literature is the small amount of theorizing about state formation and change in the context of the interaction of race, class and gender.

Although racial, gender, and class inequalities have been examined from the perspectives of social roles, organizational structure, and social attitudes, few if any analyses have looked at these inequalities in the context of state theory, political economy, and the welfare state simultaneously. Even the new scholarship by Black feminists (see Barkley-Brown 1989; Collins 1986, 1990) is developed largely on the basis of the everyday. The intersection of everyday life with structural phenomena is undertheorized. Thus there is a crucial need to interrogate these levels of social reality.

Indeed, in examining race, class and gender simultaneously, it is evident that they are pointedly expressed in the social positioning of Black Americans. Blacks "have not made it," as it is aptly put by Lieberson (1980). By any indicator — occupational, educational, political — African Americans are still heavily marginalized and excluded from equal participation and equal rewards in American society. Racism in its advanced form is alive and well (Baron 1985). Class differences do exist, and they suggest that a segment of the Black population is somewhat well articulated into the labor market (Wilson 1980). Nonetheless the working-class poor and very poor have increased. Moreover, poverty is increasingly concentrated in female-headed households (Brewer 1988). These structural realities have profound consequences for African American family formation and change. Most critically, family formation is increasingly around women and children. Nearly 60 percent of all African American children are born to single women (Brewer 1988). Unfortunately, most of these families are poor. They illustrate the convergence of Black women's and men's disadvantage under late capitalism. Marriage is difficult to forge under these conditions. Thus families are often built around consanguineal kin networks.

Although family inequality can be demographically delineated, the *why* of persistent inequality remains. Why the persistent poverty of Black women, men, and children — families — in the United States? I would say the answer cannot be given in a single term. A robust explanation involves teasing out the confluence of a number of social forces. The crux of my argument is that African American family inequality is not due singularly to race or class or gender but to their complex interplay. These complexities must be much better understood in order to create social policy and social change that will make a difference in the lives of African Americans.

Where to Begin?

I believe Grubb and Lazerson (1982) depict an essential truth in the following assessment of family policy:

> Because the issues of race are so stark, they make clear the essential challenge of family policy: The most appropriate approach to racial issues within family policy is to ignore issues of the family altogether and to

concentrate instead on the most obvious and pernicious forms of discrimination—in employment, in education, in housing, and in access to
political power. (Pp. 262–63)

They alert us to the idea that in a society in which resources are so starkly distributed along racial lines, policy makers are in trouble if they do not place
systemic discrimination at the center of their analyses. I believe this admonition is especially important for analysts who are trying to make sense out of
the changing African American family. Moreover, I would take the Grubb and
Lazerson analysis a step further. Under conditions of advanced capitalism,
crucial to policy analysis is an explication of the intersection of race, class,
and gender. The separate literatures and research practices which characterize race, class and gender studies are partial perspectives. But these deeply
rooted inequalities are also highly embedded in one another. Racial inequality shapes and takes form through class and gender relations. A thorough understanding of African American families requires comprehension of those
social relations internal to it and the social structure in which it is embedded.
This point is central to the current discussion.

Indeed, the policy debate on Black families has been too much dominated
by conservatives who lay the burden of family crisis on the Black community.
They see declining median family incomes, teen pregnancy, and poor female
heads of households as examples of the so-called internal pathology of African
American families. Thus conservatives in the United States have traditionally
resisted the idea that the state has a role to play in the family—for example,
to promote a social wage. They have resisted state minimum-income policies,
public-sector jobs, and a liberal social safety net. Conservatives do not, however, pass up the opportunity to use the state for moral purposes and to constrain sexual expression. The moral agenda of the Far Right has been infused
into a broader discussion of sexuality and "family values." This has been transferred to those families which don't conform to the "nuclear family" model
by characterizing them as culturally defective and morally lax.

Unfortunately, structural critiques of inequality have not dominated or
been at all prominent in the recent public-policy debates or public-policy initiatives on families. Take as an example the "Family Policy Act," a conservative policy proposal. Critics showed, in a close examination, that this act was
rooted in a narrow and unrealistic conception of American family life (Currie and Skolnick 1988). The proposed legislation based its policy recommendations on a family form which is found less and less in the United States
today: a full-time homemaker with a husband in the workplace. A structural
analysis would be more inclined to explain the fact of impoverished, female-
headed, single-parent households as a growing family form by acknowledging the truncated participation in the labor force of African American men
and the race/gender wage and occupational inequality of African American
women (Amott and Matthaei 1991). Thus a structural analysis of Black family changes is related to broader political-economic and cultural changes.
The deindustrialization of the economy has left little or no work for African

American men and women. Traditional nuclear family formation under such profound economic disjuncture is very difficult.

Baron (1985) makes the crucial observation that progressives must come to terms with the state in advanced capitalist orders. The welfare state is an especially awkward proposition given the tendency of some radicals to view welfare simply as an example of regulating the poor. Yet we must come to grips with race, state, and economy in interplay if we are to understand the African American family experience today. Given this, my starting points are two. First, I assert that discussions of African American families are cast too narrowly. In academic and social-policy debate, the Black family is treated as a unit separate and apart from broader social dynamics. It is viewed as a personal sphere in which interpersonal dynamics determine its form and structure. Although Zaretsky (1976) challenged the notion of the personal in isolation from the political economy, many analysts still continue to use the personal pathology notion of the Black family twenty-five years after the Moynihan report. Thus the racial, class, and gender dynamics of the broader American social structure are overlooked. We need to understand these dynamics in the context of economic and state restructuring.

We also need to understand the interplay between interpersonal dynamics and the broader social structure. Black family resistance and cultural creation are key here. Although a fully elaborated discussion of interpersonal dynamics and cultural creation is not possible in this essay, it is important to keep these issues in mind. Structural inequality is not simply imposed. Resistance and response reshape structural realities in cultural context. My point here is that a structural analysis alone is not enough. However, it is a good starting point for conceptualizing African American families and the state and it will be the focus of this discussion.

Second, I argue that the intersection of racial, class and gender inequality is the crux of African American families' crises. The challenge is to center our analyses in multiple articulations of social structure: gender, class, and race. Yet, explicating the interaction of class, race, and gender, even among Marxist feminists, is in its infancy (Glenn 1985; Matthaei 1988; Sacks 1989). No doubt, especially in the context of advanced capitalist society, class and gender inequality powerfully intersect with race to create a complex dynamic of social inequality. This has monumental implications for Black families and Black family policy.

Like class, racism remains a powerful social force for families. Historically, and under current conditions of advanced racism (Baron 1985), the forging of family bonds has been difficult for African people in the United States. Today, racial formation, the re-creation of race as a central organizing principle of American society (Omi and Winant 1987), takes the sophisticated form of institutionalization and cultural hegemony. The social reproduction of racial inequality persists even as formal racial divisions collapse. For example, Black families remain exceedingly wealth- and income-poor in this social order. Inherited family wealth and property advantages whites. A good deal of this "white" wealth has come from the persistent disadvantaging of

African Americans. Thus, the fusion of class and race inequality is a key marker of neo-racism.

Consequently, more complicated racial/class interactions appear to be at play. Wilson (1980, 1987) makes a powerful argument that within the African American community there is a significant split between a middle class living outside impoverished inner cities and a poor and working poor population marginalized within them. The inner-city population, thus, is left more vulnerable under conditions of advanced capitalism. These class and race issues are complicated by gender/race realities. The configuration of gender relations—the social construction of maleness and femaleness—means African American women and men are socially located somewhat differently under conditions of advanced racism and capitalism. For example, the significant representation of African American women in service work today means that these women contribute to social reproduction through public tending and caring. Jobs such as nurses' aides, cafeteria workers, and others in geriatric and mental hospitals are disproportionately occupied by poor Black women (Simms and Malveaux 1986). Such jobs cannot provide a family wage but represent highly exploitable labor arrangements.

This contrasts with the experience of poor African American men whose labor-force participation has stood at 46 percent for some years (Model 1990). Unemployed or opting out of low-waged work, men enter the irregular economy. This work is often intermittent or risky. Family formation is complicated by this economic marginalization of Black men. Welfare becomes the state structural backdrop to the political economy of Black men's irregular labor. Marriage is less desirable for both women and men under these systemic realities. The inequality in which Black families are situated is a complex interplay of race, class, and gender forces. Accordingly, we need to understand more about the social constitution of Black family life under conditions of advanced capitalism.

Economic Transformation, Advanced Capitalism, and the Restructuring of the State: The Context for the Social Construction of Black Families

The key problems for African Americans in an advanced capitalist order such as the United States are clear-cut: too few jobs, too much poverty, too many Black children suffering. Let me now turn more directly to the issue of economic restructuring, for it is there that I anchor the changing social-structural realities of Black families in the United States.

The emergence of capitalism and the emergence of racism coincided quite closely. These systems of oppression, in turn, are mutually reinforcing and deeply embedded within one another. (See Baron 1985; Omi and Winant 1987; Shulman and Darity 1989; Wilson 1980, 1987 for accounts of this relationship.) What is happening today? I say that the current economic, political, and social crises affecting large numbers of people in the Black community should be understood in the light of continued racial discrimination in the labor market—segmentation of American labor markets—and the restructuring of the current economy—the global division of labor in an international labor force and the new international division of labor by gender. In the latter case, capital mobility strikes at the heart of economic decline in urban areas through the process of deindustrialization and the division of labor internationally (Bluestone and Harrison 1982).

Moreover, reindustrialization, when it has occurred, has not led to the demise of particularistic tendencies within new growth regions. Growth remains heavily uneven within the United States. This means that race plays a key role in new growth regions (Brewer 1988). At the same time, there is a new social structure of accumulation in the making. As World War II expansion came to an end, fueled by the oil crisis of the early 1970s, it was imperative for the system to generate new ways of ensuring corporate profit. Thus, the new structure of accumulation was reflected initially in dramatic cutbacks in the—largely male—industrial working class. More specifically, the shaping of a minimalist welfare state is a key part of this general crisis of accumulation in post–World War II capitalism (see Gordon, Edwards, and Reich 1982 for support for this view).

The economic role for government and the maintenance of a hegemonic military posture to protect American corporations' opportunities to invest abroad had all begun to decay as the post–World War II accord came to an end. The post–World War II wave of global capital accumulation was exhausted in the seventies, and American and British structural weaknesses became more severe. The contradictions inherent in the Keynesian welfare state have meant that its development has always been political. This dynamic became more marked in the seventies. The current crisis stems from the deterioration of a social structure of accumulation (Gordon et al. 1982). Moreover, the channeling of class and racial conflict into contestation over governmental policy has produced a dramatic increase in the role and cost of the state. The restructuring of the welfare state in the United States occurred in this political-economic context.

State practices during the decade of the 1980s supported high levels of military spending and a minimalist role for government social spending—shifting this onto individual states. But it proved to be a contradictory state restructuring. Social spending was gutted, but corporate support, primarily through military spending, remained at record levels (Currie and Skolnick 1984). Although not overtly implicated in social spending, the infrastructure of the social welfare state remained constant through perks for the upper middle classes and continued tax support and supplements for the rich. Along with tax breaks and Social Security, guaranteed mortgages and highways are instances of middle-class and upper-class welfare subsidization by the state.

While the American social welfare state may not have been dismantled, it was being changed. Blacks figured poorly in this equation because they are disproportionately represented in those sectors of state spending which were being cut back or eliminated; they possess little wealth and are heavily marginalized from the private sector (Beverly and Stanback 1986).There is a blurring of lines between social and economic markets. And the preference for private enterprise over public intervention has reasserted itself. Blacks in declining cities and deindustrialized areas, confronting massive unemployment, are the first and most vulnerable point of attack on the social wage (Beverly and Stanback 1986).

Indeed, there are two welfare states. One supports the income of households, and the other supports the profitability of firms. These might be called social wage and state capital, respectively. Each is composed of some combination of government contracting, subsidies, transfer payments, and public production net of taxes. It is the welfare state for business which has received less attention, and this dimension of state intervention in the private market has received relatively little scholarly analysis. Nonetheless, it is quite significant. Reich (1983) estimated that government support for private firms in the United States, including subsidies, tax expenditures, loan guarantees, and low-interest financing, amounted to almost 14 percent of GNP in 1980.

The conservative strategy for the stimulation of growth focuses on dismantling the welfare state for households. The argument is that higher levels of public spending for transfer payments to households depress economic growth. Research suggests that this is not the case, however. Block (1987) shows how transfer payments to support household income stimulate economic growth over several years, while transfers to sustain firm profitability do not. Contrary to the conventional wisdom of the conservatives, transfers to households do appear to stimulate growth, whether due to increased household spending or labor adaptation to technological change. Cuts in this form of government support for household income are unlikely to stimulate economic growth. They simply "place the costs of public policy failures to achieve growth on the least powerful victims of economic downturn" (Friedland and Sanders 1985:421).

Of central importance to the process is state legitimization. O'Connor (1973) argued that the state must try to maintain or create the conditions in which profitable capital accumulation is possible. However, the state must also try to maintain or create the conditions for social harmony. A capitalist state which openly uses its coercive forces to help one class accumulate capital at the expense of other classes loses its legitimacy and hence undermines the basis of its loyalty and support. But a state which ignores the necessity of assisting the process of capital accumulation risks drying up the source of its own power—the economy's surplus production capacity and the taxes drawn from this surplus (and other forms of capital). The state must involve itself in the accumulation process. But either it must mystify its policies by calling them something they are not, or it must try to conceal them, according to O'Connor. If the welfare state is implicated in capital accumulation, why has so much emphasis been placed on social welfare spending, especially on Black AFDC recipients? This question is central. It brings together issues of economy, polity, and ideology in an analysis of the Black poor. In order to answer it, the emphasis must shift somewhat, from accumulation to legitimization.

Legitimization refers to the maintenance of an atmosphere of consent and support. Ideology involves beliefs as well as practices that help solidify a new social structure of accumulation. As an assault on the social wage occurs across race, class, and gender, one way to maintain legitimization is to step up the level of rhetoric on the so-called undeserving poor. This has been the key strategy of neo-conservatives and neo-liberals. The other strategy is to mystify the support given to corporations and upper-income groups. Both strategies are key to the creation of the minimalist social welfare state. Thus, rhetoric is high regarding the imperative of work for the poorest sectors of the social order, while the state camouflages subsidies to corporate coffers.

Increasingly, so-called "feminist" ideology cross-cuts economic and state issues: Poor women are expected to work, even if they have small children. Fox-Genovese (1994) asks us to look hard at the universalizing and essentializing tendencies of feminist public policy. What young African American women contribute to social reproduction is done under horrendous conditions. But the fact remains that their work at trying to survive is intensified through the expectation of forced (public) wage work. African American women's labor in the form of household labor and social reproduction is unrecognized in much of the liberal-feminist policy agenda.

This omission represents the contradictory and flawed legacy of liberal feminism. This ideology overlooks the privileged position of two-earner families compared with single-parent households. Poor Black women must do everything, but their work at making a home and rearing children is devalued. Despite the fact that they accomplish such domestic work under trying circumstances—substandard housing, few of the amenities enjoyed by the upper middle class, and highly strained resources—Black women's reproductive labor is viewed as inessential to society's sustenance and to social reproduction.

Neo-liberal and conservative policy makers have conveniently appropriated an element of liberal feminist thinking—women's access to paid labor—and use it to the detriment of women who are living on the edge. Yet, abstracting women's work from a broader critique of patriarchy and capitalism illustrates the co-optability and the contradictions of a liberal feminism that is rooted in an unreflective notion of women's work and other public policies more generally (see Fox-Genovese 1994). Clearly the contradictions of race and class in the context of gender must be figured into feminist thinking on women's work and public policy.

In sum, the issues discussed around public policy, welfare reform, and Black poor families are rooted in processes of economic transformation and restructuring. And the ideology of the welfare state is embedded in issues of state legitimation and capital accumulation.

Restructuring Family Policy in the Interest of African American Families

An explication of the intersection of gender, race, and class should be the cornerstone of an emancipatory perspective for forging new Black family policy. Progressive social policy must be predicated on the notion that class and gender inequality are highly implicated in the dilemmas confronting African American families. For example, initiatives in social policy, such as workfare, are targeted at the Black female poor. Workfare serves the two-fold purpose of retracting the social welfare state as well as creating a class of highly exploitable labor. If there is work for young Black women to be coerced into, it is work at the bottom. These women take on the least desirable, lowest-paid jobs of the service economy. A move away from a policy analysis based solely on young Black women's so-called "cultural predilection to have children" (see Klaus 1986; Mead 1986; and Murray 1984) to one which emphasizes the interplay of structure and culture is crucial to the forging of progressive social policy.

Given the economic assault on Black families (the median income of which was 56 percent of that of white families in 1989 and is currently falling), public policies must express economic democracy and sensitivity to the race and gender structure of the labor market. Social policy must be viewed in the context of economic reorganization (Wilson 1987). Data show that business and corporate decisions can be highly damaging to communities, especially inner-city minority communities (Brewer 1983). Decisions to move plants to suburbs or out of the country altogether gut areas of economic development and growth possibilities. This has been the African American economic legacy of the past twenty-five years. The availability of low-paid service work has not resolved the economic dilemma.

Indeed, understanding gender, race, and class in intersection illustrates that these multiple inequalities are the linchpin of Black women's poverty specifically, and African American family poverty more generally. As Black *women*, we are likely to be in a narrow range of female jobs, thus sharing a fate with women across racial-ethnic and class lines. As Black *women*, we are likely to be the last hired, first fired, and performing the least desirable work in women's jobs: dirty, dangerous, temporary (Simms and Malveaux 1986). Ending *race/gender* discrimination on the job should be an essential feminist/progressive policy issue.

African American Family Policy and the State

The idea that the state should develop strategies which affect the lives of families is the crux of the family policy issue. Nonetheless, there has been widespread resistance to visible public action on families, which means that families are *inadvertently* shaped politically (Zinn and Eitzen 1987). The resistance exists largely because families in the United States have been viewed as part of the private sphere, autonomous and exempt from governmental tinkering. The resistance also occurs because families are racially typed. In fact, economic, political, and social forces have always impinged upon families. Zaretsky (1976) has argued forcefully that there would not have been an American family without state intervention. Yet we still mystify the role of the state in shaping family dynamics.

Nonetheless, as has been pointed out in this article, the years since World War II have been absolutely essential in framing the family/state interplay, and the last twenty-five years have been especially strategic because they coincide with state response to racial crisis in this country (Piven and Cloward 1971). Although explicit family policy is mystified, it is evident that the state has "some kind of family policy" (Grubb and Lazerson 1982). In this context, what I refer to as the restructuring of the American economy and state undergirds the need for a structural analysis of African American families and changed theoretical lenses for scholars who are studying Black families in the United States. The assumptions of an earlier historical moment have to be refined and reinterpreted in the light of current realities. In short, we need holistic analyses of Black families. More specifically, I mean spelling out the full range of relations within the Black community: embedding economic and political discussions in the context of gender with the various ideologies and social constructions which constrain people of color in U.S. society. I fully believe we must ground analysis of contemporary Black families in the United States in critical perspectives of economy and state, not simply culture.

Although family compositional changes are the subject of much current policy debate on African Americans, the response, the "what's to be done," varies according to ideological position. I believe renewed political struggle, new alliances, and revitalized coalitions are crucial to what eventually becomes possible: cutbacks, workfare, or economic transformation. Indeed, at minimum, progressive family policy for African Americans involves the following:

1. *Economic transformation: economic democracy and equity policy* Corporate decisions marginalize various groups from economic participation and gut communities of economic viability. Since many African American families are in trouble or are suffering because of corporate and multinational-level decision making, national- and state-level planning should be undertaken to ensure economic justice for all groups. The deindustrialization policy which is the center of the post–World War II economic crisis in the United States must be addressed head-on. Is there going to be corporate responsibility toward issues of race, class, and gender inequality? Democratic planning in the interests of the masses of American people is key to this recommendation.

2. *A full-employment economy in the nation and the state* Clearly, from a progressive perspective, the issue is not simply one of finding low-paid work for the welfare population, as presented in the Family Security Act and welfare reform, but one of addressing the employment needs of a broader group of unemployed and working poor people — many of whom are underemployed at extremely low wages. Full employment cuts across racial-ethnic lines and

would include the majority of families in the nation. Who stands to benefit from economic democracy embodied in a full-employment agenda? There is still too little work with too little pay, and this has an adverse effect on all families.

3. *Racial/gender pay equity, solidary wage policy, and the strong enforcement of affirmative action and antidiscrimination laws in the workplace* Black women suffer from race, gender, and class inequality. However, poverty is present nationally among fully employed women whether Black, Native American, Asian, Chicana/Latina, or white. And poverty is especially present among female-headed households. Indeed, the concerns of female-headed families which are impoverished are crucial to forging progressive family policy. Real education and retraining come as a key part of employment initiatives, and a solidary wage policy which will raise the wages of all low-paid work should be introduced into the public debate on wage equity.

Because a near majority of Black families with children under the age of eighteen are headed by women who are generally the sole wage earners, large numbers of Black families suffer because of occupational segregation and the resulting low wages of the mothers/sisters/aunts/grandmothers who head them. Since Black women participate in the labor force in great numbers, disproportionately concentrated in low-paying female jobs and too often unemployed, decent jobs and employment for all are essential.

4. *Local community development and cooperative enterprises* An imperative in creating economic democracy involves using the strengths of the communities to buttress families (Simms and Malveaux 1986). Thus, beyond national and state policies for economic democracy, cooperative economic development emanating out of Black communities is in order. Buying apartment buildings, credit unions, food co-ops, etc., are essential initiatives which go considerably beyond the idea of "Black (Asian, Native American, or Hispanic) capitalism." It means support of collective work and responsibility on the part of ethnic groups. It also means that new politics and forms of political struggle are in order.

When one turns to the question of the achievement of these policy changes, new grounds for political struggle are called for. Historical alliances which are organized exclusively on issues of class or race or gender must be superseded by alliances that focus on the simultaneity and relational nature of these inequalities. Emancipatory strategies which center on alliances reflecting the multiple social locations of women, racial-ethnic groups, and working people must be created for generating shared agendas across differences. As Fox-Genovese points out (1994), the model of autonomous individualism is proving incapable of meeting women's needs. Such an organized political struggle goes beyond existing Democratic and Republican party politics. Localized struggles which center on issues of health, jobs, and schools must be embedded in an awareness of gender, race, and class and their complex interrelationship. Struggle should proceed from this recognition. Spawning a broadbased economic and political democracy is central to policies which will make a difference for African American families and countless others. This is the struggle for the socially just society.

Clearly, with a Democratic administration in office, potential exists for placing on the current centrist platform the complexities around race, class and gender raised in this essay. This means that Clinton and the Democrats will have to be more nuanced in the attention they give to the complexities of economic, racial, and gender inequality.

Conclusions

I have argued here that at the center of the current turmoil engulfing broad sectors of the Black population and African American families is the operation of the economy, the state (particularly in its "welfare" form), advanced racism, and the distinctive situating of African American men and women in the context of gender inequality. A key part of economic restructuring has been state restructuring. The squeeze for Blacks under current reprivatization is profound due largely to their extremely vulnerable position in the private sector. The operation of the economy and the state are implicated in the structuring of racial divisions and the imposition of occupational inequality which characterize contemporary Black life in the United States. Blacks can be marginalized or excluded from the economy and other institutions as long as capitalism generates a surplus population and there is a segment of white labor which protects its interests. Indeed, many Blacks will be "out" as long as race and the racialization of gender and class can channel the brunt of the costs of economic and state restructuring to African Americans.

America's social welfare state is conservative, some say nonexistent. The tremendous cutback of transfers to the working poor, who make up the lower level of the service economy, presents a case in point. Clearly, other strategies are needed. Indeed, the cultural strengths and innovations of African Americans must be part of new emancipatory strategies. Taking seriously and buttressing the strengths of Black communities is vital, and this will involve African American women's organizations (see Dickerson 1994). The challenge for feminists/progressives is to forge a social-justice agenda into the twenty-first century.

REFERENCES

Amott, Teresa and Julie Matthaei. 1991. *Race, Gender and Work*. Boston: South End Press.

Barkley-Brown, Elsa. 1989. "African American Women's Quilting." *Signs* 14(4):921–29.

Baron, Harold. 1985. "Racism Transformed: The Implications of the 1960s." *Review of Radical Political Economics* 17(3):10–33.

Beverly, Creigs C. and Howard J. Stanback. 1986. "The Black Underclass: Theory and Reality." *The Black Scholar* 17:24–32.

Block, Fred. 1987. "Rethinking the Political Economy of the Welfare State." Pp. 109–60 in *The Mean Season*, edited by Fred Block, Richard A. Cloward, Barbara Ehrenreich, and Frances Fox Piven. New York: Random House.

Bluestone, Barry and Bennett Harrison. 1982. *The Deindustrialization of America: Plant Closings, Community Abandonment, and the Dismantling of Industry*. New York: Basic Books.

Brewer, Rose M. 1983. "Black Workers and Corporate Flight." *Third World Socialists* 1 (Fall):9–13.

———. 1988. "Black Women in Poverty: Some Comments on Female-Headed Families." *Signs* 13:331–39.

Collins, Patricia Hill. 1986. "Learning from the Outsider Within." *Social Problems* 33: 514–32.

———. 1990. *Black Feminist Thought*. New York: Unwin Hyman.

Currie, Elliott and Jerome Skolnick. 1988. *America's Problems*. Boston: Little, Brown.

Dickerson, Bette J. 1994. "Ethnic Identity and Feminism: Views from Leaders of African American Women's Associations." Pp. 97–114 in *Color, Class, and Country: Experiences of Gender*, edited by Gay Young and Bette J. Dickerson. London: ZED Books.

Dickinson, James and Bob Russell. 1986. *Family, Economy & State*. Toronto: Garamond Press.

Fox-Genovese, Elizabeth. 1994. "Difference, Diversity, and Divisions in an Agenda for the Women's Movement." Pp. 232–48 in *Color, Class, and Country: Experiences of Gender*, edited by Gay Young and Bette J. Dickerson. London: ZED Books.

Friedland, Robert and Jimmy Sanders. 1985. "The Public Economy and Economic Growth in Western Market Economies." *American Sociological Review* 50(4):421–37.

Glenn, Evelyn Nakano. 1985. "Racial Ethnic Women's Labor: The Intersection of Race, Gender and Class Oppression." *Review of Radical Political Economics* 17(3):86–108.

Gordon, David, Richard Edwards, and Michael Reich. 1982. *Segmented Work, Divided Workers*. Cambridge: Cambridge University Press.

Grubb, W. Norton and Marvin Lazerson. 1982. *Broken Promises*. New York: Basic Books.

King, Deborah. 1988. "Multiple Jeopardy, Multiple Consciousness: The Context of a Black Feminist Ideology." *Signs* 14(1):42–72.

Klaus, Mickey. 1986. "The Work Ethic State." *The New Republic* 195 (July):22–33.

Lieberson, Stanley. 1980. *A Piece of the Pie: Black and White Immigrants since 1880*. Berkeley: University of California Press.

Matthaei, Julie. 1988. "Political Economy and Family Policy." Pp. 141–48 in *The Imperiled Economy: Through the Safety Net*, edited by Robert Cherry. New York: Union for Radical Political Economics.

Mead, Lawrence. 1986. *Beyond Entitlement*. New York: Free Press.

Model, Suzanne W. 1990. "Work and Family." Pp. 130–59 in *Immigration Reconsidered*, edited by Virginia Yans-McLaughlin. New York: Oxford University Press.

Murray, Charles. 1984. *Losing Ground*. New York: Basic Books.

O'Connor, James. 1973. *The Fiscal Crisis of the State*. New York: St. Martin's Press.

Omi, Michael and Howard Winant. 1987. *Racial Formation in the United States*. New York: Routledge & Kegan Paul.

Piven, Frances Fox and Richard Cloward. 1971. *Regulating the Poor*. New York: Vintage Books.

Reich, Michael. 1983. *Racial Inequality in the U.S.* Berkeley: University of California Press.

Sacks, Karen. 1989. "Toward a Unified Theory of Class, Race, and Gender." *American Ethnologist* 16:534–50.

Shulman, Steven and William Darity Jr., eds. 1989. *The Question of Discrimination*. Middletown: University of Connecticut Press.

Simms, Margaret C. and Julianne M. Malveaux, eds. 1986. *Slipping through the Cracks: The Status of Black Women*. New Brunswick, NJ: Transaction.

Wilson, William J. 1980. *The Declining Significance of Race*. Chicago: University of Chicago Press.

———. 1987. *The Truly Disadvantaged*. Chicago: University of Chicago Press.

Zaretsky, Eli. 1976. *Capitalism, the Family, and Personal Life*. New York: Harper & Row.

Zinn, Maxine Baca and D. Stanley Eitzen. 1987. *Diversity of American Families*. New York: Harper & Row.